After the Reich

After the Reich

The Brutal History of the Allied Occupation

GILES MacDONOGH

BASIC
BOOKS

A Member of the Perseus Books Group
New York

© 2007 by Giles MacDonogh
Published by Basic Books,
A member of the Perseus Books Group

For information, address Basic Books,
387 Park Avenue South, New York, NY 10016–8810.

First published in Great Britain in 2007
by John Murray (Publishers)
A division of Hodder Headline

A CIP catalog record for this book is
available from the Library of Congress.

ISBN-13: 978-0-465-00337-2
ISBN-10: 0-465-00337-0

Typeset in Bembo by M Rules

1 2 3 4 5 6 7 8 9 10

For Joseph Maximilian Cornelius MacDonogh
born 8 December 2002

Absumet heres Caecuba dignior
servata centum clavibus et mero
tinget pavimentum superbo,
pontificum potiore cenis.

Contents

CONTENTS

PART IV: The Road to Freedom

Illustrations

27. Marshal Koniev and General Sir Dick McCreery award the cups at a race meeting at the Freudenau in Vienna
28. British Pilot Officer W. K. Sewell crashes his aircraft
29. Hitler's 'Kraft-durch-Freude' car – the 'Beetle'
30. A drunken American officer sleeps through a striptease in his Darmstadt mess, April 1948

The author and publishers would like to thank the following for permission to reproduce illustrations: Plates 1, 2, 8, 21, 22 and 29, Herder-Institut Marburg, Bildarchiv; 3, 4, 5, 6, 7 and 15, Sudetendeutsches Archiv; 11, 12, 13 and 14, Oberhausmuseum, Passau; 19, Sebastian Cody; 23, 24 and 26, Private Collection; 25, Provost and Fellows of Eton College; 27, Bob McCreery; 28, Dennis Sewell; 29, Volkswagen AG; 30, akg-images/Tony Vaccaro. Plates 9 and 10 are from the author's collection; plates 16, 17 and 18 are taken from Josef Schöner, *Wiener Tagebuch 1944/1945*, edited by Eva-Marie Csáky, Franz Matscher and Gerald Stourzh, and reproduced with permission. Every effort has been made to clear permissions. If permission has not been granted please contact the publisher who will include a credit in subsequent printings and editions.

Preface

This book is about the experience of the Germans in defeat. It is about the occupation imposed on them following the criminal campaigns of Adolf Hitler. To some extent it is a study in resignation, their acceptance of any form of indignity in the knowledge of the great wrongs perpetrated by the National Socialist state. Not all of these Germans were involved in these crimes, by any means, but with few exceptions they recognised that their suffering was an inevitable result of them. I make no excuses for the crimes the Nazis committed, nor do I doubt for one moment the terrible desire for revenge that they aroused.

I have tried as much as possible to use individual accounts to give the flavour of the time. Many of these are by women. There is an obvious reason for this: there were not many men left. Those who survived did so in a variety of places, from internment camps to Soviet mines. The subject is so vast that I have had to use a broad brush. Some elements are immensely well covered, such as the American Zone and the beginnings of the Cold War. It was the start of the American century and the end of isolation, after all. Other parts of the story are hardly told: the French occupation, for example. Because I wished to give the tenor of everyday life at the time, I have divided the book into four parts: the first looks at the chaos that followed the end of the war within the lands that were then Germany, and the punitive stance of the Allies; the second looks at the day-to-day existence of the Germans and Austrians; the third examines crime and punishment; and the fourth introduces the chronology and records the major political developments from Potsdam to the foundation of the two German republics. The Austrian State Treaty lies outside the scope of this book, as it did not occur until 1955.

My 'Germans' are the German-speaking peoples as they are massed in central Europe. I have therefore included Austria, which called itself 'German Austria' until it was annexed in 1938, and subsequently became part of the Greater German Reich. I mention the South Tyrol in Italy, because Austrians saw that as part of their lands, as well as other satellites in Yugoslavia, for instance. I have also examined the plight of the so-called 'ethnic' Germans who were expelled, mostly from Czechoslovakia, but also from Hungary and Romania. Elsewhere 'Germany' is defined by its 1937 borders, and I have referred to towns and villages by the names Germans would have known. Where possible I have included the Polish or Czech names too.

Although it was my first intention to study the German-speaking peoples as they suffered their chastisements on the ground, I soon realised that it was impossible to make any sense of what was happening without reference to what was taking place on Mount Olympus: the Allied command HQs and the political forces behind them. I had to travel *de haut en bas* and vice versa – to examine the effect of the occupation on the Germans, but also to look upstairs at what the Olympians were doing, and see what they had in store. On the other hand I have always tried to focus on Germans, not on the Allies.

The book is the fruit of my long acquaintance with both Germany and Austria. My interest began during a short stay in Cologne in my mid-teens and a meeting with one of the two modern German novelists whose writings have most coloured this book. I was a guest of the Böll family and one afternoon the later Nobel Prize winner Heinrich Böll came to tea. He introduced me to Underberg, the viciously powerful bitters, and I can still feel the wave of fire travelling up from my stomach to my cheeks. We argued about Irish Republicanism, which he favoured. It wasn't until much later that I began to respect his books, and admire the picture of the returned soldier in those early stories and novels.

I met Ernst Jünger many years later, through my friend the eccentric hotelier Andreas Kleber, who was then still in possession of his family hotel, the Kleber Post in Saulgau in Württemberg (incidentally one of the first venues for the writers' group Gruppe 47). One night I had dinner with Jünger there and the two of us spoke to ZDF television about the meaning of Prussia. Jünger was a writer from the generation before Böll, but outlived the younger man by decades. He was a mere ninety-seven when I met him and had another six years to live. Again conversation turned to drink: the bottle of Pommard he consumed with his wife every night (he had two-thirds of it, he confessed), and his real love – Châteauneuf-du-Pape.

He became more serious when he complained that he could not wear his Pour le Mérite medal, which he had won in the Great War, when he had been left for dead on the field of battle. He was, I think, the last surviving *military* holder of the medal. The Allies had swiftly banned the wearing of decorations, and the Federal Republic has followed suit. War could not be officially celebrated, and that went for acts of heroism too. I recalled the First World War memorial in the little park in Berlin-Friedenau where I had stayed with friends. The inscription had been chipped off: in Germany such things were taboo, while in Britain war memorials were still placed at the focal point of any town or hamlet. In Germany there were no more heroes. The Germans had lost the right to them.

Friends of mine, even published historians, have often told me that the Germans 'deserved what they got' in 1945: it was a just punishment for their behaviour in occupied lands and for the treatment of the Jews at home. This book is not intended to excuse the Germans, but it does not hesitate to expose the victorious Allies in their treatment of the enemy at the peace, for in most cases it was not the criminals who were raped, starved, tortured or bludgeoned to death but women, children and old men. What I record and sometimes call into question here is the way that many people were allowed to exact that revenge by military commanders, even by government ministers; and that when they did so they often killed the innocent, not the guilty. The real murderers all too often died in their beds.

It is true that some of the old men and a lot of the women had voted for Hitler, but it should be recalled once again that he never achieved more than 37.4 per cent of the vote in a free election, and in the last one he was down to 33.1 per cent.[1] That meant that, even at his most popular, 62.6 per cent of the German electorate were unmoved by his programme. Of course, at that point it did not propose the slaughter of the European Jews (he never made any public statement on this subject other than dark allusions that have become easier to read in retrospect); nor did it mention his desire to confront Soviet Russia and enslave the Slavs; nor did it hint that he would eventually bring the roof down on the German house and kill a large number of its inmates. It is possible that he might have secured more votes that way, but I think not. To make all Germans responsible for the relatively docile Hitler of 1933 is to apply the Allied weapon of collective guilt. Collective guilt makes them all responsible: women, old men and children, even newborn babies – they were German and they could also be slaughtered or starved to death. Indeed, the Soviet propagandist Ilya Ehrenburg exhorted the Red Army not to save 'the child in its mother's womb'.[2]

There were many Russians, Poles and Czechs who were not ashamed to feel that way in the heady days of liberation. Some of them were as young as fifteen at the time they joined *ad hoc* police squads and they may still be alive today and healthy; but I think few of them would now own up to the acts of terrible violence they committed.

If children are included in collective guilt, this could be accepted on the basis that they were going to grow up to be Germans and therefore possibly Nazis. Then, of course, we need to determine at what age a child becomes a German, and can be blamed for the crimes of his country. It is clearly not twenty-one (when many are already in the army), or eighteen (when they were likely to have been called up, and were often among the bravest and most ruthless fighters), or sixteen (when they had already been drafted into anti-aircraft units or, like Günter Grass, about to be forced into the SS), or indeed younger (Hitler Youth boys as young as twelve distinguished themselves in the Battle of Berlin). Maybe in an indoctrinated society a cut-off point for guilt needs to be imposed at seven, and, if so, a date needs to be fixed when the child had attained that age. Was it 1933 or 1945 (twelve years after the last free election)?

Of course the real reason why the Allies imposed the idea of collective guilt was that it was a useful way of depriving the Germans of rights and national sovereignty. Once their guilt was assumed, they could be punished. They were to be at the mercy of the Allies until their conquerors had decided what to do with them, and in the meantime they could not protest about their treatment.

Then there is the issue of tit-for-tat. The Anglo-Americans wisely fought shy of exacting reparations because they realised that they would then have to pay to feed the Germans; and that if they left the Germans an industrial base they might be able to feed themselves. The tit-for-tat school of retribution and revenge goes back a long, long way. Historically minded Germans might blame the French for the Thirty Years War (which caused bloodshed on a similar scale to the Great War) or for the territorial ambitions of Louis XIV. More might recall the Napoleonic invasion of Germany and the occupation of Prussia. Bismarck was famously intractable in 1871 when the French demanded mercy, saying there was not a tree in his country that did not bear the scars of the French years. Then the jackboot was on the other foot. On each occasion there were territorial cessions and crippling reparations to pay. Someone needed to cry halt. But the business surfaced again at Versailles in 1919, and there was the same punitive peace. After the Second World War most wise men understood that a peace treaty would have been a farce. It was left to what Churchill called 'our consciences to civilisation' to determine how the enemy was to be treated.

Post-war Germany is a problem that has taxed me for years and it is hard to know now who has helped me with this particular book. Some, perhaps many of them, are already dead. Some names stand out in my mind, others were often nameless people I met on my travels, and who unburdened themselves over a late-night drink, or a second glass at lunchtime.

In London my friends Karl-Heinz and Angela Bohrer have been constant in their encouragement over the years. Karl-Heinz was kind enough to give me an extensive interview on his childhood in post-war Germany. Angela long ago gave me a copy of her mother Charlotte von der Schulenburg's privately printed memoirs. I also learned much from the writings of her aunt, Tisa von der Schulenburg, and from my meetings with her. My neighbour in Kentish Town Nick Jacobs, owner of the German-specialist publisher Libris, was kind enough to lend books and copy interesting articles. In Oxford I thank Sudhir Hazareesingh; Robert Gildea for providing me with some suggestions for reading on the French occupation of Germany; and Blair Worden for explaining the role of Hugh Trevor-Roper.

Germany provides me with many memories and much assistance, from my friend Ursula Heinzelmann in Berlin; Gertrud Loewe; Eva Raps in Wiesbaden; and in the wine country growers told me of their experiences of the immediate post-war years. The late Prince Franz von Sayn-Wittgenstein in Munich sent me his privately printed memoirs; Daria Fürstin von Thurn und Taxis the unpublished memoirs of her uncle Willy; and Christiane von Maasburg gave me permission to quote from the *Magisterarbeit* she wrote on Nikolaus von Maasburg. A kind lady in Hildesheim recounted harrowing details of the trek she undertook from Pomerania as a child of six; the retired border guard Captain Schmidt in Coburg told me no less moving stories of his childhood in Silesia; an anonymous man in Malbork, Poland, briefly informed me of how he evaded the Polish authorities after the war; an ethnic German woman in Opolne offered to pray for me, if I gave her ten marks; a former Danzig policeman I met in Titisee-Neustadt told me about his time in an American camp in Passau, surrounded by members of the French Division Charlemagne.

In Vienna, enormous thanks are due above all to my friends Christopher Wentworth-Stanley and Sebastian Cody. Christopher found me literature on post-war Austria and read a part of the manuscript, as did Ambassador Erwin Matsch. Sebastian was kind enough to read and comment on a number of chapters. Johannes Popper von Podhragy sent me articles from his late father's archive. Dr Wolfgang Mueller provided me with much help and a useful book list. On Lake Bled, Janez Fajfar showed me the wonderful mural in the hotel he has run for decades in the palace where Tito and Stalin fell out in 1947. In Prague I was counselled by Dr Anna Bryson and in Sofia by my old friend Professor Evgeni Dainov.

I am also grateful to all those who helped locate or donated pictures: John Aycoth in Washington, Sebastian Cody and Christopher Wentworth-Stanley in Vienna, Lady Antonia Fraser, Livia Gollancz and Dennis Sewell in London, Manfred Pranghofer and Rudi Müller of the Oberhaus Museum in Passau, Bob McCreery, Klaus Mohr of the Sudetendeutsches Archiv in Munich, Bengt von zur Mühlen of Chronos Films in Berlin, Eva Reinhold-Weisz of Böhlau Verlag in Vienna, Elisabeth Ruge of the Berlin Verlag in Berlin, Thomas Urban of the Herder Institut in Marburg, Mrs C. Skinner at Eton College, Manfred Grieger and Ulrike Gutzmann at Volkswagen in Vienna.

My thanks are due to the staffs of the British Library and the German Historical Institute. At John Murray I am grateful to my editor Roland Philipps, to Caro Westmore and Rowan Yapp, to Douglas Matthews, for making me yet another exemplary index; and to Peter James, whose demanding questions sent me back to my books over and over again.

I would also like to thank my family for their patience, especially in the last days when my body was over-charged with adrenalin and I was able to think and talk of little else.

Giles MacDonogh
London, October 2006

Chronology

February 1945	Yalta Conference
30 March 1945	Danzig falls
8 April 1945	The Red Army enters Vienna
9 April 1945	Königsberg falls
13 April 1945	Vienna capitulates
2 May 1945	Berlin falls
6 May 1945	Breslau capitulates
7 May 1945	Germany surrenders
23 May 1945	The Dönitz government is arrested
5 June 1945	Germany is divided into zones
9 July 1945	Austrian zones finalised
17 July–2 August 1945	Potsdam Conference
22 July 1945	Western Allies move into Vienna
30 July 1945	First meeting of the Allied Control Council
15 August 1945	The end of the Second World War
September 1945	London CFM (Conference of Foreign Ministers)
25 November 1945	Austrian general election
December 1945	Moscow CFM
5 March 1946	Churchill's Iron Curtain speech
July 1946	Paris CFM
September 1946	Paris Peace Conference
6 September 1946	Byrnes's Stuttgart speech
22 October 1946	Berlin elections
12 December 1946	New York CFM
16 January 1947	London CFM
25 February 1947	Prussia abolished by Control Council Law 46
March 1947	Moscow CFM
June 1947	Robert Schuman president of the council in France. Paris CFM. Marshall's Harvard speech

November 1947	London CFM
6–7 December 1947	People's Congress for Unity in East Berlin
17 March 1948	Brussels Pact and Prague Coup
17–18 March 1948	Second People's Congress for Unity in East Berlin
20 March 1948	Russians leave the Control Council
31 March–2 April 1948	Little Berlin Blockade
April to June 1948	London CFM
7 June 1948	London Agreement
17 June 1948	The Russians quit the Kommandatura
24 June 1948	Motorway blocked to Berlin
25 June 1948	Introduction of the D-mark
1 July 1948	Berlin cut off from the West
27 July 1948	London CFM agrees to create a West German state
9 September 1948	Reichstag demonstration in Berlin
11–12 May 1949	Traffic resumed to Berlin

CENTRAL EUROPE IN 1945

Baltic Sea

Memel
Kurisches Haff
Tilsit
Rauschen
Pillau
Königsberg
Gumbinnen
Hela Peninsula
Trisches Haff
R. Pregel
Köslin
Stolp
Danzig
Insterburg
ANIA
Elbing
EAST PRUSSIA
Allenstein
enberg
e
JRG
DER)
PRE-1937 GERMAN BORDER
Kulm
R. Vistula
Warsaw
rg.
POLAND
gau
gnitz
Breslau
Hirschberg
Oppela
nberg
Neisse
R. Oder
Riesengebirge Mts
Glatz
R. Glatzer Neisse
Auschwitz
Freiwaldau
Pless
andskron
ECHOSLOVAKIA
n
Brno
Nikolsburg
BURGEN LANDEN
Vienna
Odenburg
R. Danube
Budapest
A
HUNGARY
GOSLAVIA

BERLIN

FRENCH SECTOR
BRITISH SECTOR
AMERICAN SECTOR
SOVIET SECTOR

MILITARY ZONES

British
American
Soviet
French
South Tyrol

German-speaking areas of Czechoslovakia

VIENNA

AMERICAN SECTOR
FRENCH SECTOR
SOVIET SECTOR
BRITISH SECTORS

Introduction

In the years 1945 to 1946 Germany was a collection of denouncers, black-marketeers, prisoners, refugees from justice and tireless whingers. The Allies announced that the Germans needed to be handled with a rod of iron. It was pure nonsense.

Franz Prinz zu Sayn-Wittgenstein, *Streifzüge durch die Landschaften meines Lebens*, privately printed, Munich 2000, 166

The war had been the bloodiest yet, particularly for civilians. Laying aside some three million dead German soldiers, by 7 May 1945 at least 1.8 million German civilians had perished and 3.6 million homes had been destroyed (20 per cent of the total), leaving 7.5 million homeless; and the bloodshed was going to continue for a lot longer. As many as 16.5 million Germans were to be driven from their homes. Of these some two and a quarter million would die during the expulsions from the south and east.[1]*

It was called *die Stunde null* (Zero Hour), though it was nothing of the kind. Germany was wrecked from top to bottom, but memories were still acute, the country had a past, and a large body of people who had supported the *ancien régime* needed to be assessed and rendered harmless. As it was, like Weimar, many of them were carried over into the new post-Nazi world.[2] There were simply too many of them, and most had lost their faith in Hitler when his armies were defeated at Stalingrad.

In May 1945 National Socialism was as good as dead. Apart from a few desperate ideologists, as anxious to save their skins as defend their creed, the vast majority of Germans had already come to the conclusion that it had been founded on a terrible fallacy. Defeat was one thing, but, as the

---

* Gerhard Ziemer gives the figure of 2,280,000, Alfred de Zayas 2,211,000.

dramatist Carl Zuckmayer pointed out a few years after the end of the conflict, Germans – even those in the Hitler Youth and the Waffen-SS – were already conscious of the country's 'moral bankruptcy'. The defeated Germans surprised their conquerors by their docility. They offered next to no resistance to them. They did what they were told. Of the promised Werewolves – Nazi guerrillas trained to fight in occupied territory – there was virtually no sign.

To some extent Germans believed the Allied propaganda: the Russians, the Americans, the British and the French had come to 'liberate' them. The Allies may have freed the Germans of their National Socialist shackles, but they did a lot of other things to them first. The novelist and psychiatrist Alfred Döblin records a conversation he had with a well-brought-up girl in the Black Forest. 'We received the Allies with so much joy', she told Döblin, 'as liberators. And in the first week everything made us happy. The Allies were so lucky with us. Then they started requisitioning rooms, hotels, flats; we could take nothing with us. That took the wind out of our sails.' Döblin told her that the war wasn't over yet. She asked him when it would be concluded. He said: 'When the ruins are knocked down and the rubble cleared away, and when new houses have been built where everyone can have a home and they can come out of their shelters and sheds. When the economy has taken off once more, when politics are stable again. Fräulein E., you are young. You will live to see the peace. Later, when you look back on the present time, you will be astonished that you were young enough to believe that it was peace.'[3]

For some Germans defeat was what they were waiting for: it fulfilled their most eager hopes. In his dark first novel, *Kreuz ohne Liebe*, written in the years immediately following German defeat, Heinrich Böll explores the feelings of an anti-Nazi who has been fighting in the army from day one. Christoph Bachem's brother has been shot. He is a Nazi who repents in the end and saves Christoph's life. Christoph's best friend has spent the war in a concentration camp, a victim of the same brother. Christoph enjoys a brief sojourn with his wife, Cornelia, before losing her for good after deserting and fleeing to the west. He indulges his feelings of utter nihilism. 'No,' he said tiredly, 'I want no more. It is horrible to have been a soldier in a war for six years and always to have had to wish that it would be lost; to see the collapse, and at the same time to know that whatever power succeeds it, and kicks the daylights out of the corpse of this state, will quite probably be equally diabolic; the devil possesses all the power in this world, and a change of power is only a change of rank among devils, that I believe for certain.'* Bachem has no faith in the Allies either. As he tells Cornelia,

> Do you believe, then, that these people who are about to conquer us with their rubber soles and tins of Spam, will ever understand what we have suffered? Do you believe they will understand what it feels like to be showered with their bombs and shells and at the same time to be sullied by this diabolic state; what it means to be crushed between these two millstones? They simply cannot have suffered as much as us, and since Christ's death there has been a hierarchy of suffering in which we will remain the victors, without the world ever learning or understanding what it was we felt.[4]

The Allies may have chosen to style themselves as 'liberators' but they came in hate. In the cases of the Russians, French, Poles and Czechs, this was understandable. To be occupied is to be violated, even when it is not coupled with regular atrocities. The atrocities committed by the SS and the Wehrmacht in Poland and Russia were horrendous, and they were not lacking in France and Czechoslovakia either. It is hardly surprising that there were acts of revenge. Any SS man found in the east was liable to be subjected to the most fabulous torture and death. Such things we may understand, but surely never condone.

As the Soviets chose to introduce their own brand of ideology along the way, controlled 'revolutions' were carried out too, by the 'Lublin' Poles (those patronised by Moscow rather than the West) and the Czechs. The middle and upper classes were ruthlessly dispossessed. Their homes were sequestered, while they themselves were imprisoned, tortured and in many cases killed. In the Prussian east the old, Junker squirearchy was wiped out without mercy.

The French worked the hatred out of their systems in a few acts of grisly violence. Demonstrations of gross brutality were comparatively rare in the British army. For a few years Germany became another colony, dealing with the Germans a burden placed on the Christian white man. It was like India all over again. The Americans, however, saw it differently: although both the British and the Americans used films and photographs of the camps to encourage their soldiers to be hard-hearted and to chastise Germans, it seems to have had more effect on American GIs, who took their brief that much more seriously – that is, until the politicians decided

---

* To some extent he based the book on his own family. As a teenager the author was privileged to meet his two brothers. One had literally shot himself in the foot to avoid fighting Hitler's war.

the German people were to be wooed. There was a PR war to win now, against the new enemy, the Soviet Union.

With the exception of the death camps in Poland, which had already been closed and blown up by the Germans, all the most infamous concentration camps together with work camps were put back to use by the Allies: Auschwitz-Birkenau,[5] Sachsenhausen and Buchenwald for the Russians; Dachau for the Americans and Bergen-Belsen for the British, not to mention the grisly Ebensee in the Salzkammergut, where the Americans kept 44,000 SS men. This strikes us as disgusting now, but there were obvious logistical reasons for using them, together with an understandable temptation to 'rub the Germans' noses in their own mess'. Central Europe was teeming with homeless DPs (displaced persons) who were in the process of resettlement after ethnic cleansing. Millions of POWs were also held in camps. In the east they were earmarked for work details and they needed to be housed. Some were to be allotted a more sinister fate. They too needed to be put in a secure place until their destiny was decided.

While the fate of the Jews shocked the British and the Americans and – particularly in the case of the Americans – sharpened their attitudes towards the conquered nation, the Soviet authorities made little of it. The anonymous author of *A Woman in Berlin*, for example, was surprised: 'no Russian has so far reproached me for the German persecution of the Jews'.[6]

When the Allies invaded Germany in the first half of 1945, they came bearing war aims and plans. They had gone to war because they had been provoked by the Axis powers. Now the desire was to crush Germany and its allies. 'Their effort to emerge victorious included neither an aim to destroy any segment of the German population nor a plan to save any part of Germany's victims,' one historian has written. 'The post-war punishment of perpetrators was largely a consequence of afterthoughts. The liberation of the survivors was almost entirely a by-product of victory. The Allies could harmonise with their war effort all sorts of denunciations of the Germans, but there was no disposition to deviate from military goals for the deliverance of the Jews. In that sense the destruction of the Jews presented itself as a problem with which the Allies could not effectively deal.'[7]

The Allies needed to win first, before they could even think about how they would clear up the mess. The first war aim was to establish security, which the Treaty of Versailles of 1919 had singularly failed to do.

At first there were only the British. When Churchill came to power in 1940 'appeasement' was already a dirty word. 'Vansittartism', which saw the Germans as a tribe of incorrigible louts from the time of Tacitus to the present day, had become the dominant thinking in governing circles. It was developed by the diplomat Lord Vansittart, who spent part of the war giving radio broadcasts which examined different Germans in turn, pointing out how nasty they all were. Vansittartism inspired historians to search archives for further evidence of the deep-seated evilness of the Germans. To some extent it is still alive today.[8]

The first Vansittartite directive to emerge from Whitehall was 'absolute silence'. Officially, at least, Her Majesty's Government would not talk to Germans. With time 'absolute silence' gave way to 'unconditional surrender'. There was to be no negotiated peace this time. The opposite school was that of the historian E. H. Carr, who thought that a civilised Germany was merely a question of finding the right man. In Britain's first studies for a post-war Germany there was discussion of reparations: Germany would thereby be deprived of the means to make war. From the summer of 1943 the task of planning the occupation was handed over to Clement Attlee, who would become one of the 'Big Three' at the Potsdam Conference[9] when the Conservatives lost the July 1945 election.

The Western Allies tended to agree with Robert Vansittart that the Second War had been largely caused by the perpetrators of the First, and that meant Prussia. It was a long time before they came to terms with the idea of Nazism as a non-Prussian movement. The Atlantic Charter of 14 April 1941 had a little flavour of Woodrow Wilson's Fourteen Points twenty-three years before. An expression of the principles on which the peace was to be based, it was drawn up by Churchill and amended by Roosevelt. The American president added the passages condemning aggressive war and calling for German disarmament.[10] It was followed by the Declaration of the United Nations signed by twenty-six governments on 1 January 1942, an agreement to uphold the Atlantic Charter.

The first meeting between Churchill and Roosevelt to discuss war aims was held in Newfoundland in August 1941. Churchill was more pragmatic than Roosevelt; the American leader was much more hostile to the Germans. He had been partially educated in Germany and he had come home with strongly held anti-German views. He had no desire to meet a member of the German resistance who came to see him at the beginning of the war.[11] The two leaders decided that there would be no annexations after the successful campaign, and no territorial changes would be effected that did not accord with the freely expressed wishes of the peoples concerned. The high-minded principles expressed at that time formed the basis for the Atlantic Charter – *Pax Americana*. Future wars would be prevented by stopping Germany from disturbing the peace. Germany was to be demilitarised, denazified and made to restore the land it had poached from its neighbours.[12]

German and Austrian émigrés played an important role in shaping American thinking after 1941. Many of them worked in the Research and Analysis Branch (R & A) of Military Intelligence (OSS). Prominent were the historians Hajo Holborn and Felix Gilbert, the politicologues Otto Kirchheimer, John Herz and Franz Leopold Neumann and the philosopher Herbert Marcuse. The most important of them was Franz Neumann, the author of *Behemoth: The Structure and Practise of National Socialism*. Neumann argued for a radical reconstruction of Germany to avoid repeats of Hitler's coming to power. One key plank to his doctrine was the establishment of some sort of European Union. The traditional Germany was to be removed by a social revolution.[13] There was only a brief window when the Western Allies tried to woo the Jews. This corresponded to the time of the first Nuremberg trials. When East and West fell out for good, the Allies – the West in particular – were prepared to sweep a good deal under the carpet in order to groom their new German ally and relieve themselves of the unpleasant business of censuring its people for their past conduct.

The Allies had nonetheless been influenced in their designs by a sizeable body of literature penned by exiles. Books by Hermann Rauschning and Konrad Heiden, and Sebastian Haffner's *Germany – Jekyll & Hyde*, instructed the Allies on how to deal with a post-Nazi Germany. The bacillus (to borrow a word from the Nazis themselves) had to be wiped out completely. Haffner wanted to see Germany broken up into small states, a much more extreme solution than the eventual Federal Republic, which created autonomous regions. For the British the Prussians were still the enemy. Churchill, for one, wished to see the south Germans more mildly treated than the 'Prussians' in the north: Nazy tyranny and Prussian militarism 'must be absolutely destroyed'.[14]

By 1943 the Allies knew they were going to win. Stalingrad and the subsequent collapse of Hitler's Russian offensive made that abundantly clear. The Allies could now sit down and decide what they were going to do with Germany. The military plan was enshrined in Operation Eclipse. In the winter of 1943 the European Advisory Commission or EAC met to work out how Germany would be administered. It met again on 18 February 1944, and by this time the cake had been properly portioned out: Soviet Russia was to receive 40 per cent of Germany's land mass, 36 per cent of its population and 33 per cent of its productive capacity.* Britain and America took the remainder. Likewise Berlin was to be divided in three.

Stalingrad engendered a new mood among the Allies. Both the Americans and the British were smitten with Stalin and the great progress he was making. The Americans now saw themselves carving up the world with the Soviet Union and were worried that the Russians would not approve of their close relations with the British and their ideologically unacceptable empire. Churchill was worried – and continued to be worried even after victory – that the Americans would not stay in Europe and would leave him to face the Russians across the ideological divide.[15] At the Casablanca Conference in January 1943 the Allies decided that Germany was to surrender 'unconditionally'. What that meant Churchill explained to the House of Commons on 22 February 1944. The Allies would not stain their 'victorious army by inhumanity': 'unconditional surrender means the victors have a free hand . . . If we are bound, we are bound by our own consciences to civilisation.'[16] What else that meant was not really clear to anyone, but it gave Churchill room for manoeuvre.

The American who was urging the greatest retribution against the Germans was Roosevelt's treasury secretary, Henry Morgenthau – although the text of his plan was largely written by his assistant Harry Dexter White.† Morgenthau was 'touched by atrocities against the Jewish race'.[17] His idea was a 'peace of punishment' which involved splitting the country into four states that would be almost entirely agrarian. Austria was to be cut in two. The secretary of war, Henry L. Stimson, thought this idea of 'pastoralisation' unnecessarily harsh, but 'the President's vindictiveness kept the Treasury proposal alive'. At that time Roosevelt was still keen to see the United States and Soviet Russia rule the world together.[18]

Germany was to be reformed by the 'four Ds': decentralisation, demilitarisation, denazification and democracy. The US War Department's Civil Affairs Division (CAD) was responsible for post-war planning. The army also liked the Morgenthau Plan as it promoted the sort of chaos that suited their strategic aims: it was therefore at the heart of the crucial US Joint Chiefs of Staff document JCS 1067. Both Roosevelt and Churchill had their moments of flirtation with the draconian plan. In August 1944 Roosevelt for one had lost patience with the Germans. 'The German

---

* At this stage the Soviet share included eastern Germany within its 1937 borders. Much of this was later hived off and awarded to Poland.

† This is disputed. Michael Balfour says Morgenthau wrote the first draft: Michael Balfour and John Mair, *Four Power Control in Germany and Austria 1945–1946*, Oxford 1956, 20 n3.

people should be taught their responsibility for the war and for a long time they should have only soup for breakfast, soup for lunch and soup for dinner.' His then secretary for mobilisation, James Byrnes, added: 'It did not sound like President Roosevelt. He was very angry.'[19]

In these moments Churchill played along. Roosevelt's Morgenthau mood reached its height at the Quebec Conference in August 1943, when he expressed his approval for an eliminatory 'Carthaginian Peace'. At the time he pretended that he only wanted to shore up Britain; to 'keep Britain from going into complete bankruptcy at the end of the war'. The Ruhr was going to give Britain the means to survive.[20]

At Teheran (28 November to 1 December 1943) Britain agreed to a change in Poland's eastern borders. Later Churchill would make a great play of the fact that he had tried his best for Poland, but he gave himself away in the House of Commons on 27 February 1945 when he offered British citizenship to any Poles who did not wish to return to their country. He knew that they were not to regain their liberty, or even all their territory. Roosevelt was more cautious about accepting Stalin's demands for a ratification of the treaty signed with Hitler: there were elections coming up and there were lots of Polish Americans who might object. He didn't like the idea of Stalin annexing the Baltic States either.[21]

Roosevelt began to backtrack about the Morgenthau Plan after the meeting in Quebec. It was not Morgenthau but the cooler Byrnes who accompanied him to the Yalta Conference from 5 to 11 February 1945. By that time the idea of splitting Germany up into autonomous regions was no longer so popular. The US was for a federal system. At the Teheran Conference the call had been for five pieces; by the time the leaders met in Moscow, they were down to two. Roosevelt's vice-president and successor Harry Truman was not at all keen on the Morgenthau Plan, which he branded 'an act of revenge'. 'My aim is a unified Germany with a centralised government in Berlin.' Morgenthau himself was rather miffed.[22]

Stalin was also a supporter of the Morgenthau Plan, but the noises he put out to the West altered several times: at Teheran he was in favour of a divided Germany; at Yalta he wanted unity, but Allied zones of occupation; at Potsdam he argued for a single economic unit. He feared that the German beast would rise again and seek revenge if it were not well and truly slain. He was also keen to satisfy Russian public opinion by granting a 'day of judgment', when the Germans would feel the full weight of their conquerors' fury. The West was afraid that he meant ultimately to extend communism to the Rhine, or even the Atlantic, but if he was to export it to central and western Europe he would need support on the ground: the punishment of the Germans could not go on for too long, as he needed to have them on his side.[23] Stalin also feared the West. He believed that Britain and America were planning to make a separate peace with the Germans and would use the German army to attack him. It was only when the Americans fought the bloody campaign in the Ardennes, which ended in January 1945, that he was satisfied that the West would not sign a separate peace.[24]

France had yet to join the top table and for the time being French goals were subtly different. When the EAC met in February, France was still occupied by the Germans. The French nonetheless drew up a list of war aims: German surrender, withdrawal from occupied territory, the destruction of the Wehrmacht, Allied occupation of Germany, punishment of war criminals and large-scale reparations, particularly in German coal and coke.[25] There was not much new from Clemenceau at Versailles. This changed a little at the liberation. Now France's chief concern was its recognition as a great power. It was quick to field an army to that effect. Its wartime leader in exile, Charles de Gaulle, wanted to grab what he could while the going was good.

The Soviets' aims have been the subject of prolonged discussion, as their apparent desire to inflict communism on the whole of mainland Europe was the reason for the Cold War. What documentary evidence there is has been examined since the end of that war by – among others – Vojtech Mastny. We know, for example, that the plans were drawn up by a team composed of Maisky, Litvinov and Voroshilov. Assistant foreign minister Maisky was responsible for Germany and reparations, while Litvinov handled peace treaties and Voroshilov was in charge of military planning. According to Mastny, Stalin was flexible and pragmatic, 'lest he ask for too much, or too little'.[26] Though there was no master-plan, there were minimum war aims: Stalin wanted to retain Russia's western borders as established by the Hitler–Stalin Pact of 1939. That meant hanging on to Poland east of the Bug, as well as the Baltic States; he wanted no repetition of the small power blocs that had dominated eastern central European politics in the 1930s. The Soviet Union was to be the sole military great power in mainland Europe – this included France and Italy – a policy that caused friction with Tito, who aspired to that position.

Stalin also wanted to see the establishment of strong communist parties in all the lands occupied by his armies and was keen for these parties to play important roles and to be active. On the other hand they were not to bring about revolutions and they were not to follow the Soviet model. He told Maurice Thorez, the French communist leader, that he was to find friends.

So far as Germany was concerned, Stalin was open on all issues but the Polish one: he wanted to compensate the Poles with German land. He also sought to avoid recreating a German 'pressure-cooker' by hemming the country in with antipathetic neighbours. However, he was anxious not to breed a lasting desire for revenge. He wanted reparations. He told Maisky to take as much out of Germany as he could without starving its people.[27] It was obviously also to be deprived of its military might, but Stalin was indifferent to the form of regime: multi-party democracy or communist party.

In his relations with the Western Allies, Stalin sought a co-operative *Realpolitik* to allow for Germany's reconstruction. Europe was to be carved into two interest blocs controlled by the Soviet Union and Britain. Russia would extend its sphere to include Sweden and Turkey, whereas Britain would take in all of western Europe to the Rhine as well as Greece. At the centre would lie a neutral zone made up of Germany, Austria, Italy, Denmark and Norway. Stalin told German exiles in Moscow that he had opposed the repackaging of Germany in small states. Even so, he wanted to exploit central Europe for his arms programme. The Cold War was definitely not desired by the Soviet leader, although his distrustful and antagonistic nature may have contributed to worsening relations. The Soviet consolidation of eastern Europe was in response to the Marshall Plan, America's programme of economic aid launched in 1947.[28]

The reduction of Germany to a number of states was another project that failed to come to fruition after the First World War. Splitting Germany up into manageable units had been advocated by Haffner, as already noted. The French were keen to wrest away the western regions. On 12 August 1944 de Gaulle proposed an indefinite occupation of 'Rhenania', expressing a policy that had been at the heart of French ambitions in central Europe since the Thirty Years War. He reiterated his determination in January 1946: 'we hold on to the Rhine'.[29] There should be no return to a centralised Reich. The Russians were less keen on breaking up Germany, and were unimpressed by de Gaulle's projects for 'Rhenania', despite the French pandering to them by advocating the cession of German regions east of the Oder to the Poles and the Russians.[30] In October 1944 de Gaulle pushed for a separate zone of occupation for France. He would achieve 'Rhenania' by hook or by crook. He demanded the Rhineland north of Alsace, the Saar and the west bank of the Rhine as far as Cologne, as well as the Palatinate, Baden and all the Hesses. The British pledged him part of their zone.[31]

De Gaulle rejected Morgenthau's proposal to 'pastoralise' Germany.

He felt it would create an economic crisis, and besides France needed the produce of German industry. He also had to reckon with a French desire for revenge. A poll taken early in 1945 showed that 76 per cent of the French wanted Germany split up; 59 per cent wanted a proportion of all Germans deported; 80 per cent supported General Leclerc's proposal to shoot five Germans for any attack on French army personnel; two-thirds were in favour of annexing the Saar; 87 per cent thought the Soviets would be able to punish the Germans properly; while only 9 per cent had any confidence in the Americans.[32] De Gaulle was still wrestling with proposals for massive changes to the shape of Germany and, if needs be, shifting huge numbers of Germans. Silesia was to be given to the Poles, while the Rhineland and Westphalia would be administered by the Allies. Originally he thought that the fifteen million Germans living in the latter could be moved out, but then decided that the project would be 'too grandiose'.[33]

There was a an element of *bella figura* too. As Georges Bidault, the head of the resistance organisation, put it, the French had to play a major role in the war after the liberation, otherwise 'the Germans will not look on them as conquerors'.[34] Unfortunately the Americans, Roosevelt in particular, were unwilling to equip the French army to play that major role. At the end of 1944, de Gaulle tried his hand in Moscow. Stalin managed to get de Gaulle to recognise his 'Lublin' Poles over the London government in exile as the price for a Franco-Soviet treaty.

The Allied zones were ratified at Yalta in February 1945. France was once again excluded. Russia was making strides towards winning the war. Its troops were poised to cross the Oder while the Western Allies had yet to cross the Rhine. Churchill argued for including the French among the victorious powers. Stalin reluctantly agreed. He did not think the French had pulled their weight and in 1940 they had let the Germans in. France might have a zone, 'but only as a kindness and not because she is entitled to it'.[35] Roosevelt sent Harry Hopkins to Paris to sugar the pill:[36] the French were to have a small zone in the west, carved out of the British and American portions. An Allied Control Council was to be set up to deal with questions affecting all four zones. It would meet in Berlin.

In April 1945 the Western Allies had second thoughts. The Americans had pushed far into Saxony, which had been allotted to the Soviets; and the British had taken a sizeable chunk of Mecklenburg. Some people were hoping that the Western Allies would push on, take Berlin and turn on Soviet Russia. Chief among these was Hitler himself, and his propaganda minister, Goebbels. As it was, the British and Americans did not turn on their Russian ally – possibly *because* Hitler, Himmler and Goebbels were so anxious for them to do so; but they did hang on to their booty for a while, and Churchill for one was anxious to use it as a counter for Soviet assurances about their territorial acquisitions. The new US president – Roosevelt died that April – Harry Truman would not listen, however, and the Russians moved into Mecklenburg and Saxony without providing satisfactory assurances about Germany's borders or the status of Berlin. Stalin prevaricated for as long as he could so that he might strip Berlin bare and install his toadies in all the worthwhile positions of power.

The French were still worrying about their own status as their troops marched into Germany with the Anglo-Americans. A total of 165,000 troops under arms meant a lack of labour at home. Germans would have to be sent to France to carry out the work in the same way as the French had been obliged to toil in Germany. De Gaulle spoke of needing two million Germans, although he never managed that. He was still keen to annex the Rhineland. As Maurice Couve de Murville, a member of the French provisional government, put it pathetically, 'If we do not achieve this we have lost the war.'[37] France's attitude led to friction, particularly with the Americans. When French troops occupied Stuttgart – which was meant to form part of the American Zone as the capital of Württemberg – the Americans ordered them to leave. De Gaulle refused, saying he would stay put until the zones were finalised. The French were causing problems in the Levant too, and in an act of bravura against the Italians (who had taken back Haute Savoie and Nice during the war) they occupied the French-speaking Val d'Aosta. The American solution was to offer them some bits of Baden and Württemberg while keeping the lion's share for themselves.[38] In Berlin on 5 June the Western Allies formally came into the zones and sectors, but it was not until 26 July, while the Big Three were deliberating at Potsdam, that the Soviets finally recognised the French Sector of Berlin. The French were still clamouring for more of Baden and Württemberg. They had been given a curious territory along Germany's western borders with two big lumps sticking out to the east. It was mocked as 'the brassière'.*

There were other nations which expected to be in the running for something at the peace, principally the Poles and the Czechs. They placed their hopes on the tit-for-tat cessions and annexations that had become a feature of the twentieth century. The process had started with the

---

* This was an Anglo-American brassière: the French word applies to a baby garment, and has no lumps.

population transfers between the Bulgarians and the Turks in 1913. In that instance 50,000 people had voluntarily switched lands. In 1923 the exchange of Greeks and Turks was more acrimonious, and the figures more disturbing: 400,000 Turks went east, and 1,300,000 Greeks took their place in what was to become a mono-racial homeland. In the spring of 1943 Roosevelt told Anthony Eden, the British foreign secretary, that the transfer of Germans from East Prussia would be similar to the business with the Turks and Greeks. In 1945 Stalin wanted revision of the Treaty of Riga of 1921, which had created three Baltic states out of Russia's old Baltic territories. The expulsion of the Germans from the lands east of the Oder and Neisse rivers came down to that, and the fact that Roosevelt had always been prepared to give Stalin what he wanted: Russo-American co-operation was to become 'the cornerstone of the new world order'. Britain tagged along in the hope of hanging on to its great-power status.[39]

Stalin was not going to relinquish Poland east of the Bug. With a blank cheque from the Russians as far as their western borders were concerned, the Poles were keen to recoup as much as they could by acquiring German territory. The idea of advancing to the Oder – and beyond – went back to the neo-Piast thinkers, Roman Dmowski and Jan-Ludwig Popławski.[40] As Germany walked into Poland again, the idea became more and more attractive. Hitler was seen as Prussia, and Prussia needed to be docked. Berlin was mentioned as a fitting 'showplace for Prussia's death'.[41] In London Władysław Pałucki began clamouring for the Oder–Neisse line as early as 1942. It can have been no surprise when Stalin adopted this view too, at Yalta.

Poland's eastern borders, with the Soviet Union, presented a trickier problem. At Yalta Churchill and Roosevelt were slightly at variance over the Curzon Line, first proposed by the British foreign secretary Lord Curzon in 1920. Roosevelt held out for Lvov, a city that was chiefly Polish. Churchill was prepared to abandon Lvov to the Russians. As regards the western borders, Stalin made his feelings abundantly clear. When the Anglo-Americans expressed their doubts about the size of the German population to be evicted, he stood up and in an impassioned voice declared: 'I prefer the war should continue a little longer although it costs us blood and to give Poland compensation in the west at the expense of the Germans . . . I will maintain and I will ask all friends to support me in this [that] . . . I am in favour of extending the Polish western frontier to the Neisse river.' It was at this point that Churchill uttered his line about stuffing the Polish goose so full that it died of indigestion. The figure of six million Germans was conjured up as the number who would be required to move. In private Churchill told Byrnes that it was more like nine mil-lion.[42] Poles would have to be resettled too, from Lvov and the lands east of the Bug, but the population was mixed, with the Poles in the towns and owning the big estates, which was hardly the case in East Prussia, Pomerania or Lower Silesia.

Edvard Beneš, head of the Czechoslovak government in exile, had taken a long time to recover from the humiliation of Munich. He had spent seven years in exile. It was his plan from the beginning to reduce the size of the minorities in the young republic: Hungarians and Germans in Bohemia and Moravia. The Germans made up some 23 per cent of the Czechoslovak population. Other lessons he had learned from the rape of his country were the need to co-operate with the Poles (who had grabbed the region of Teschen while the Czechs were prostrate and defenceless), and to secure the patronage of the Soviet Union. The Poles could be accommodated in Freistadt (Fryštát) and he would expel two-thirds of the Hungarians in Slovakia. As for the Germans, his '5th Plan' provided for the cession of certain border regions with an overwhelmingly German popu-lation. That would relieve him of a third of his Germans; a third more would be expelled. He would keep the Jews, democrats and socialists.[43]

Later the plans were adapted. The three cantons he was prepared to cede to Germany – Jägerndorf, Reichenberg and Karlsbad – grew smaller. The border adjustment would still leave him with 800,000 Germans. He decided that some of these would flee, some would be expelled and the rest 'organised for transfer'. When the peace came he quite forgot about the idea of losing territory and actually claimed land from Germany, but the Allies did not respond.[44] For much of the war Beneš had clung to the idea of a reduction in the number of his German subjects. He had the backing of the British. On 6 July 1942 the war cabinet ruled that the Munich Accords were invalid and agreed in principle to the idea of a transfer of the German populations of central and south-east Europe to the German fatherland in cases where it seemed 'necessary and desirable'. Ten months later Roosevelt also came round to this view, although American military planners thought it could be done more humanely by transferring six small territories to Germany. Stalin too agreed to the transfer on 12 December 1943 after the Czech ministers Jan Masaryk and Hubert Ripka spoke to the Soviet ambassador to the exile regimes, Bogomolov.[45]

Austria

Hitler's armies went into Austria on 12 March 1938. Very soon the Germans made the place intolerable for certain groups of people. The Jews were an obvious target, and the Nazis introduced a regimen that was far more extreme than that current in Germany – at least until November that year, when Berlin turned up the heat with the 'Reichskristallnacht', when mobs throughout Germany smashed Jewish properties. Adolf Eichmann was placed in charge of antisemitic activities in Austria and went about his business with all the diligence that Himmler expected of him. But it was not just Jews: in two great trainloads the 'Prominenten' were also shipped out to Dachau. These were the members of the governing elite who had banned the NSDAP or Nazi Party and thrown its members into Austria's own concentration camp at Wöllersdorf in Lower Austria. They had executed a few of these Nazis for their part in the murder of Chancellor Dollfuss four years before. It was time for Nazi revenge. The fates of the Austrian elite are in part recounted in Bruno Heilig's book *Men Crucified*: ministers, civil servants and magistrates, most of them of an age when they were no longer capable of hard labour, were physically broken and beaten to death. Some of them went on to Buchenwald, others to Mauthausen. Those who survived returned as martyrs. No one begrudged them that title.

Despite the treatment of their leading politicians, many on the right and left in Austria might have been prepared to back Hitler. Perhaps 10 per cent of the country's adult citizens joined the NSDAP, but a certain Teutonic heavy-handedness failed to win them all the friends they might. Austrian industry was appropriated by Göring's Four Year Plan and increasing numbers of Germans swanned about their newly acquired territory all the while, treating Austrians with a disdain they have yet to forget. Worse, Austrians tended to be despatched to the toughest theatres of war. For the Allies, however, Austria was now part of Greater Germany and they were at war. Exiles tried to guide their hands, and plead that the Austrian case was different. Many Allied leaders found that hard to take, but for political reasons they evolved the idea of Austria as a victim. Although no one had seriously considered granting it a government in exile, the Allies had to entertain the idea that Austria had an exile community that wished to meet and discuss the country's future, and there might be added benefits if their discussions caused problems for the German administration.

There were five possible solutions for a post-war Austria. The first was a simple reversion to the independent state it had been between 1918 and 1938. The second proposed leaving Austria in bed with Germany. A third involved making some sort of Danube Confederation based loosely on the most positive side of the Austro-Hungarian Empire; and a fourth was that favoured by the Morgenthau plan: a separation of Austria's provinces with perhaps the Vorarlberg going to Switzerland, the Tyrol and Salzburg to Bavaria* (which would then be detached from Germany) and the eastern parts attached to a federation of Danubian lands. A fifth possibility was simply to roll up Austria and Bavaria together to make a Catholic south-German state.[46]

The Allies probably felt that a little confusion would do some good – it did not pay to let the Austrians feel they were completely off the hook. They would have to labour to show their love before they could receive the prize of renewed independence. This ambivalence was enshrined in the Moscow Declaration of 30 October 1943: 'Austria, which was the first victim of Nazi aggression, must be liberated from German domination.'[47] The Anschluss, the annexation of 15 March 1938, was declared null and void: 'Austria is nonetheless reminded that it bears a responsibility from which it may not escape, for having participated in the war on the side of Hitler's Germany and that, in the final reckoning, the role that it plays in its own liberation will inevitably be taken into account.'[48] The Austrians were not so much to be exonerated from the roles they had played in the 'Movement' and war as encouraged to *rebel* against the Germans.

The pretender to the Austro-Hungarian throne, Otto von Habsburg, blamed the Russians for the mealy-mouthed nature of the Declaration, but it is likely that Edvard Beneš had a hand in it too.[49] The Declaration also rejected the idea of a Danubian Federation and put paid to the hopes of a Habsburg restoration. This was Stalin's work. Otto himself had left for America in 1940, leaving his brother Robert in London to campaign for the cause there. Otto's name figured on a Nazi hit-list. He went first to New York and then to Quebec. Naturally he was hoping that the Allies would look favourably on a Habsburg restoration, but there was little chance of that. He found certain figures remarkably unsympathetic in their attitude to Austria. One of these was Churchill's foreign secretary Eden, who had apparently defined the country as 'five Habsburgs and a hundred Jews'. Otto wanted to change Roosevelt's mind. It will be recalled that the president was smitten with the Morgenthau Plan at Quebec. Otto claims that he was able to bring both Churchill and Roosevelt round.[50]

---

* Once again Bavaria was seen as the harmless part of Germany. The monster was always Prussia.

On 25 October 1944 the Soviets asked for an acceleration of the Austrian solution. They wanted to stipulate their future zone. At that point the French were neither particularly interested in Austria nor included in the handing out of the spoils. It was only later, when they located some of their own industrial base in Austria, that they started to clamour for reparations along with the Russians.[51] As far as territory was concerned, the Soviets plumped for Burgenland and the eastern half of Lower Austria. They also wanted to keep the eastern half of Styria together with Graz, where the main industries were located – many of them out-housed from Germany at a safe distance from Anglo-American bombers. The British would have to be satisfied with the western half and Carinthia; the Americans would have the rest. The Viennese *Sachertorte* would be cut in three, but Russia would take the inner-city 1st Bezirk or district, the 3rd Bezirk and the northern parts that abutted the Danube. Even then they intended to control traffic on the river. The other slices would go to the Anglo-Americans.[52]

Meanwhile Austrian exile groups met to discuss the future. In Britain there were as many as 30,000, of whom 90 per cent were Jews.[53] The Austrian Centre was based in Westbourne Terrace in Paddington and had its own restaurant, library and reading room, as well as a newspaper, *Zeitspiegel*. Before the full horror was known and even as late as April 1945, there was an active campaign among exiles to make the Jews return. That month appeared the pamphlet *Vom Ghetto zur Freiheit. Die Zukunft der Juden im befreiten Österreich* (From the Ghetto to Freedom: The Future of the Jews in a Liberated Austria). It called for the punishment of those who had committed crimes against the Jews and the restitution of their property.[54]

Austrian exile groups began to plan for a non-Nazi, independent Austria even before the war started. In June 1939 a discussion group had called itself 'Das kommende Österreich' (The Coming Austria). It was not just among the British exiles that such discussions took place. One of the most influential figures was Ernst Fischer, who led the Austrian Communist Group in Moscow. In 1944 he published *The Rebirth of my Country* in which he advocated the complete economic divorce of Austria and Germany after the war and suggested alliances with Czechoslovakia and Yugoslavia.[55] With the establishment of the provisional government in the autumn of 1945 he was made minister of education.[56]

F. C. West, president of the Austrian Centre, brought up the question that loomed largest in the minds of most exiles with his lecture 'Zurück oder nicht zurück – das ist keine Frage' (To return or not to return, that is not the question). Most Jews had reservations, and these were positively encouraged by Zionist groups. Willi Scholz (who was not a Jew) was at pains to reassure Jews that not only would the new Austria welcome them, they were needed there – 'Österreichische Juden, geht nach Österreich zurück!' (Austrian Jews, go back to Austria!).[57] In 1941 the Free Austrian Movement (FAM – it became the FAWM, or Free Austrian World Movement, in March 1944) was founded as the political voice of the Centre. It was dominated by the communists, and very soon the monarchists and even the social democrats withdrew their support.[58]

Young Austria with its slogan 'Jugend voran' (youth forward) was a dynamic movement for those under twenty-five. At its height it had a thousand members, and a hundred of these fought in the British armed forces.[59] Jews, social democrats and communists signed up. The communists had been declared illegal by Dollfuss in February 1934 and had been driven into exile even before the Jews. Austria's biggest party before the Anschluss was the Christlichsozialen or Christian Socialists, but these were as good as unrepresented in the exile colony. They were often antisemites, and would have been put off by the heavy Jewish presence. Monarchists, supporting the candidature of Otto von Habsburg, were not without influence, but this bore fruit with the Gentiles, not with the Jews.[60]

Otto von Habsburg had tried to raise an Austrian battalion in America in 1942, and the recreation of a post-war independent Austria gave monarchists leave to hope.[61] Legitimists such as Baron Leopold Popper von Podhragy were pushing for a National Committee and an Austrian fighting force. The legitimists were often noblemen (nobles figured largely in the early Austrian resistance groups) and were among the first to fall out with the Nazis, who treated them with disdain, and vice versa. The British Foreign Office was lukewarm about the creation of an Austrian force. Eden's response was merely to stress that German influence was to be removed; besides he did not think that he had the proper cadre among the 30,000 Austrians in London.[62] A year later the Foreign Office was able to invoke bad experiences in America as a reason for not raising such a battalion. A document dated 15 March 1943 shows how divided Austrians in London were.[63]

The leaders of Austrian Social Democracy, Viktor Adler and Otto Bauer, had also fled from Paris to New York. At first the Molotov–Ribbentrop Pact had thrown a predictable spanner into the works, but the position altered after Hitler's invasion of the Soviet Union and the Russo-British Alliance, and it was once again respectable to be left-wing. The Social Democrats had traditionally taken the line that Austria was not capable of a wholly independent existence and had tarred their image by supporting union with Germany. Initially Young Austria stood for the liberation of 'Germany': 'Ohne ein freies demokratisches Deutschland – kein unabhängiges Österreich' (Without a free, democratic Germany, no independent Austria). They encouraged a worldwide levée-en-masse to overthrow the Nazis with violence. The most important thing was to make the British authorities recognise their right to fight – their right to possess, like the Poles and the Czechs, their own fighting units.[65] Communists were powerful behind the scenes in almost all the British-based organisations. Their plan was that Soviet Russia would form the basis of a system of security that would prevent further warfare and protect the smaller states of south-eastern Europe from German aggression.[66] Towards the end of the war there were sheaves of publications describing the political form of the new Austria, though in order not to frighten the monarchists – who had been liable to Nazi persecution from 1942 – the word 'republic' was avoided.[67] They had no desire to fall out until Hitler was beaten.

The communist journalist Alfred Klahr was a leading theorist of a new Austria divorced from Germany. Klahr advocated a rewriting of recent Austrian history to emphasise unity and resistance to Hitler. It was necessary to tread gently when it came to the Ständesstaat or Corporate State, which replaced democratic government in Austria in 1934, to limit the traitors to a mere handful of high-ranking collaborators. Germany could not sell itself as a victim – it did not possess this card.[68] One of the tactics used was to describe Austria as a culturally separate entity to Germany, which meant concentrating on writers who were anti-German, like Grillparzer. Music was also big: Austria could claim to be more international, that musicians from all over the world had lived in Vienna; that the Beethoven of the Ninth Symphony and the setting of the Ode to Joy was a Viennese incarnation. The nationalistic, antisemitic Wagner was billed as a purely German phenomenon.

On 19 February 1942 Churchill promised to free Austria from the 'Prussian yoke'. He had actually overstepped the mark, and his speech was disowned by the Foreign Office, but it had an encouraging effect in exile circles. Finally, the independence of Austria did become a war aim, as recognised by the colonial secretary Lord Cranborne in the Lords in May 1942 and Eden in the Commons in September. This line of argument was eagerly lapped up by the Austrian exiles, who were more anxious than ever to put the blame on the 'Piefkes', 'Preussen' or 'Nazipreussen'. The Austrians who occupied positions of power, they argued, were denatured opportunists: true Austrians had nothing to do with the regime.[69] Any small act of resistance or non-cooperation was held up in triumph. When they returned to Austria after the war, they had to admit that they had been living in cloud-cuckoo land.[70]

In their hearts and minds, Foreign Office officials remained unconvinced by the exiles. In November 1942 Roger Makins spoke in his master's voice and cast doubt on the importance of a group principally composed of Jews and royalists, while others pointed to the communist influence and were sceptical as to whether Austrians would accept its decisions. The presence of so many Jews on the committee could only damage its credibility.[71] On the other hand some progress was made through their champions in Britain like Sir Geoffrey Mander, and there were voices raised in Parliament for the creation of Austrian fighting units in the Allied armies.[72]

Austrian exiles had the French example before their eyes after June 1944. The French were rapidly accorded the right to organise their country behind the lines and escape from the threat of military occupation and government. The exiles were deluding themselves in making this comparison, but this did not prevent their dreaming.

The non-political Jews, who made up the bulk of the exiles, were less likely to be convinced of Austria's lamb-like innocence, because many of them had witnessed the barbarity of the Austrian Gentile population in 1938. They were also unconvinced by attempts to 'relativise' the atrocities perpetrated against the Jews by including them in a host of other brutalities as a way of focusing on the general monstrosity of the Germans. They were also doubtful of the Austrian Centre's picture of the Jews as loyal Austrians. Their ideal would have been a popular uprising against the Nazis. At the very end they were successful and there was a small-scale mutiny when the Russians loomed at the border. Hitler sent the Austrian-born Ernst Kaltenbrunner, head of the SD, or Sicherheitsdienst, the Security Service of the SS, to put it down, and three officers were publicly hanged in Floridsdorf.[73]

Soviet Russia clung to the idea of an independent Austria within its 1938 borders, but the power in east central Europe was to be Czechoslovakia. Austria was to be 'neutralised' and also to be refused any form of confederation with its neighbours, as the Russians feared a revival of a Catholic or Austro-Hungarian empire. Nor were there to be any concealed unions, of the NATO or EU sort; in return Austria was not to be brought into the communist camp. The zones were also mapped out: the Soviets wanted the industry (particularly the arms industry) in the east. The east also had the railway hubs for their planned satellites in Hungary, Czechoslovakia and Yugoslavia.[74]

The Allies connived at the 'myth' of Austria's victimhood,[75] but this was largely dictated by their own convenience. For the Jews the 'liberation' was the moment of truth. The Marxists had failed to come to terms with the genocide because such things had nothing to do with class struggle. When they were faced with the facts, they were speechless. The Anschluss and the war nonetheless strengthened the Austrian sense of independence. In the 1930s this had been at best half formed. Now all Austrians accepted the idea of the independent state, and rejected the notion of Grossdeutschland. It is an attitude which colours Austrian minds to this day, to the degree that the flirtation with Germany that started with the pan-German antisemites like Schönerer and Lueger and reached its height between the wars is all but forgotten. It was being put away in the recesses of the Austrian collective memory as the Red Army mustered at the gates of Vienna.

PART I

Chaos

I

The Fall of Vienna

14 April 1945
A shocking view from the Graben: the marvellous high-pitched roof of the cathedral with its eagle-motif has disappeared and the left-hand incomplete tower has been burned out. The finials and gables appear miserable and black against the heavens. Only the tower is still standing, the symbol of my beloved city.

Josef Schöner, *Wiener Tagebuch 1944/1945*, Vienna, Cologne and Weimar 1992, 160

As the Russians approached the former Habsburg capital the Austrian Centre and the BBC together tried to dispel the fears of the population. The Austrian Centre even went so far as to stress the Red Army's reputation for good behaviour. Marching from the Hungarian town of Koszeg the 3rd Ukrainian Front under Marshal Tolbukhin crossed the frontier on Maundy Thursday, 29 March 1945, at Klostermarienberg in South Burgenland, and moved towards Rechnitz. Graz lay at the end of the Raab Valley, but the Red Army predictably wheeled right towards Vienna. On 1 April the battle for Wiener Neustadt began. After a fight lasting a week, the capital ceded and the Red Army entered Hitler's 'Fortress Vienna' on 8 April. The Austrian Centre was jubilant: *Zeitspiegel* described the brotherly greeting given to the conquerors, with both the Red flag and the red, white and red flag of Austria on prominent display. Once more they were out of touch with reality.

The women of Vienna were not so enthusiastic, to say the least. Joseph Goebbels had made it abundantly clear what would happen to them. Some people dismissed his warnings as 'terror propaganda', but it was sadly true that the Red Army raped wherever they went. They even raped Russians and Ukrainians. The worst and most aggravated rapes were perpetrated against the women of the enemy – first the Hungarians, then the Germans. Bulgarian women, however, were spared some of the worst excesses,

25

possibly because Russians and Bulgarians generally feel empathy for one another. The Red Army raped Yugoslav women too, although they were on the same side. It was not likely that they would spare the Viennese just because the Moscow Declaration had made them 'victims of fascism'.

There has been much discussion of why the Russians raped and murdered so many women on their march to the River Elbe. They were certainly egged on by Ehrenburg and other Soviet propagandists who saw rape as an expression of hatred, and therefore good for morale. Soviet soldiers had also been shown pictures of the Nazi victims of Majdenek, where the dead had simply been identified as 'Soviet citizens'. The Germans had been in Russia; they had burned their towns and villages and posed as a *Herrenvolk* – a nation of lords.* The Slavs were racially inferior, no better than helots.† In the circumstances rape must have seemed an irresistible form of vengeance against these 'superior' women and the best way to humiliate them and their menfolk. The worst offenders, it seems, were soldiers from Belorussia and the Ukraine – areas invaded by the Germans. The older soldiers and those having higher education were the least likely to rape. The higher the standard of living the Russian soldiers encountered, the more they raped. They were disgusted by the plenty, the comfortable houses and the well-stocked larders they found, which stood in such contrast to the poverty they knew from home.[1] The manor house or castle was particularly prone.

Commanders generally turned a blind eye to the rapes. When the Ukrainian Jewish intellectual Lev Kopelev tried to intervene to save a German woman from a group of rampaging soldiers, he was accused of 'bourgeois humanism' and imprisoned for nine years.[2] It was only much later that any punishment was handed out. The reason why Russian generals accepted such appalling lack of discipline was that rape was condoned at the very top. Stalin told the Yugoslav communist leader Milovan Djilas, 'Can't he understand it if a soldier who has crossed thousands of kilometres through blood and fire and death has fun with a woman or takes some trifle?'[3] Added to the semi-official sanction, the Red Army was sex-starved. Its soldiers had been fighting for four years, and in most cases they had not

---

* The assistant Soviet commander in Germany, Sokolovsky, specifically mentioned the *Herrenvolk* to justify the rapes. (See Norman M. Naimark, *The Russians in Germany – A History of the Soviet Zone of Occupation, 1945–1949*, Cambridge, Mass. and London 1995, 79.)
† In February 1943 Hitler drove past a group of Russian slave-labourers working on the road outside Zaporozhe. Filled with loathing he remarked, 'It is quite right to make Slavs do this, these robots! Otherwise they would have no right to their share of the sun!' Henrik Eberle and Matthias Uhl, eds, *The Hitler Book*, translated by Giles MacDonogh, London 2005, 102.

received compassionate leave. The raping became worse again after 23 June 1945, when many female soldiers were sent back to Russia. It became a part of everyday life in the remote villages of Burgenland and Lower Austria where it continued until the end of 1946 or the beginning of 1947.[4]

The Germans had been pulling out from the 6 April 1945, and they took most of the police with them. They had been made up of elderly soldiers anyhow, mostly unfit for service at the front. The real Viennese police had been incorporated into the SS and sent to Russia. The departure of the ersatz police exposed the city to even greater dangers when the looting started. Later an auxiliary squad was formed by the Russians and issued with armbands, but by then the damage had been done. It was not only the police who had vanished: the prudent Nazis had also quit the city, leaving their homes at the mercy of the plunderers.[5]

The Red Army appeared in the wake of the retreating Germans. The Viennese were in the dark. The wireless had ceased to function and the last newspapers appeared on 7 April – some were printed on the 8th, but they were not distributed. There was then a total news breakdown until communications were restored with the issue of the communist-backed *Neues Österreich* on the 15th. All that remained was Mundfunk – a play on *Rundfunk* or radio station, but meaning word of mouth, or gossip.[6] 'On the 7th the Red Army occupied the giant Anker bakery in Favoriten, cutting off the city from its main source of bread. For the next ten days the Viennese were reduced to 250 grams of bread each daily. It got worse: citizens had to make do with 500 grams to a kilo of bread a week: 'A slice of bread was a considerate present.'[7]

On 8 April there was a rumour that the Russians had reached the Zentralfriedhof or main cemetery. On that day the economist Eugen Margarétha was still living off his well-stocked larder: he had a slap-up Sunday lunch of 'wonderful' potato soup with vegetables and meat, a plain pork schnitzel, which was a little too salty, and *risipisi*,* which his wife had not salted, to compensate for the pork. There was a cream dessert and Turkish coffee. After that he smoked a Swiss cheroot.[8] Margarétha lived in the Bossigasse in St Veit in the plush suburb of Hietzing. There were still SS units operating in the centre. The next day he noted a Russian scratching at the door opposite. Then he heard the sound of rifle butts hammering on his own door. The Czech-speaking housekeeper Franek was sent to

---

* A variant on a Venetian dish, *risibisi* (rice and peas), and popular in Vienna. The author came across it as a child, at a rare surviving Jewish home in the 2nd Bezirk.

deal with them. A whole troop of Russians came in carrying their heavy machine guns. They disappeared into the cellar and then went upstairs, where they took up positions, firing at the SS from the windows.

Margarétha noted in his diary that they were 'nice chaps'. A Russian NCO gave Franek six cigars after he had assured him the householders were not 'Germanski' but Czechs. One of the soldiers took a fancy to Franek's watch. The housekeeper pleaded that he was a poor man and had but one watch. Another soldier told his comrade to give it back. Most of the shooting came from the Russians. There was just a little desultory gun-fire from the SS. When the Russians departed, Margarétha went upstairs to find they had broken around twenty window panes. They had helped themselves to food and cigarettes. They had also wrecked Margarétha's precious typewriter, and broken the wireless set and the bathroom scales. In one bedroom the mirror on the dressing table had been smashed with a bayonet. They had cut the wires on the telephone and smashed it. It hadn't functioned for six weeks. They had taken two bicycles. 'All in all the soldiers were not wild but disciplined . . . Really many worse things might have occurred.' Later he was able to replace some of the broken panes with the glass from his picture collection, and his 'remembrance certificate' from the Great War.[9] Elsewhere the first wave of Red Army troops considerately warned Austrian civilians about the occupation troops that followed. They advised them to bury their valuables.[10]

The Viennese received the Red Army with a degree of innocence. It was to be their first experience of occupation since Napoleon's time. In the Josefstadt the Russians were 'joyfully and amicably' greeted 'by women and girls who sometimes kissed or embraced them, a warm-heartedness that was often misunderstood'.[11] Josef Schöner had been a member of Austria's diplomatic corps before March 1939, but his distaste for the Nazis led to his retirement. The new broom retained very few of the Austrian elite: in the Foreign Office only 10 per cent of the officials continued to serve under the Nazis. Schöner survived by working for his parents, who had a number of restaurants and cafés in the city. They had made the mistake of applying for Nazi Party membership. Schöner did not. After the war he was ambassador to Bonn and finally London.

On 10 April Schöner noticed a brace of Russians wearing fur hats in the Siebensterngasse in the 7th Bezirk. The German army was withdrawing from the centre. He watched the behaviour of the locals. They tried to speak to the new arrivals using any Slavic language they knew, generally Czech, and offered them cigarettes, which the Russians refused. 'The longing for peace is so widespread that no one believes there will be prolonged resistance in Vienna.'[12] Schöner was struck by the appearance of the Russians. Many of them carried swords, but none seemed to possess a scabbard. The Viennese were remarkably at ease: 'everywhere gay, warm faces, there is not a hint of fear or mourning'. The Russians asked if the houses in the street concealed any soldiers or Germans. The Viennese replied with the pride of the liberated: no, just Austrians.[13]

As soon as it became clear that the German army had abandoned an area, looting would begin. Margarétha thought it had started in Penzing, in the 14th Bezirk, but it spread to neighbouring Hietzing where the 'mob' emptied the grocer Meinl and the fashion shops Wallace and Oser. A neighbour, the engineer Kienast, complained they had also stolen his gold watch, and given him an inferior one in return.[14] There were relatively few Austrian men about: those aged between twenty and fifty were generally away and there were huge numbers of foreign workers in the city who had been drafted in by Hitler's labour organisation to allow all good Germans to go to war. They were suspected of playing a major role in the looting. In Favoriten or Floridsdorf, on the north bank of the Danube, you were more likely to hear French or Greek than German. After 9 April the foreign workers were armed, and sometimes identifiable by armbands. The communist Franz Honner estimated there were as many as 700,000 of these in Vienna in April 1945 and that the bulk of the looting had been carried out by them, but he did not discount the Viennese population. Together with Austrian natives the foreigners formed the 'mob' that performed 'various acts of violence'. Sometimes they would strip the premises clean, at other times they were more selective. A building used by the Hitler Youth was denuded even of its decorations. The veteran socialist politician Adolf Schärf* was anxious to point out that the looters were often men of good standing, 'even people who prided themselves on their titles of nobility in their everyday life'.[15]

Schöner noticed it first at the department store Herzmansky in the Mariahilferstrasse. He thought the Viennese more reprehensible. A few foreign workers joined in. They had already been active in sacking the outlying suburbs.[16] Schöner watched sick at heart as bales of cloth, suits and women's dresses came flying out of the building. One man was not in the slightest embarrassed to try on a stolen suit in a doorway. The day before the same mob had attacked the food shops on the Gürtel, the 'belt' road surrounding the inner boroughs or Bezirke. 'So it wasn't the Russians, but

---

* Schärf had suffered at the hands of Dollfuss's Corporate State when he had been put in the concentration camp at Wöllersdorf, and again under the Nazis when he had spent a few months in captivity after the Anschluss.

the dear Viennese themselves.'[17] A boon to the Russians and the looters were the big wine houses in Döbling and Heiligenstadt. The Russians emptied the great tun in Klosterneuburg and then sprayed it with machine-gun fire when it would provide them with no more solace.[18] People were seen carrying off wine from Heiligenstadt in large vessels.[19]

Schärf had been in hospital when the city fell. The patients had been transferred to the hospital cellars. He noted the mendaciousness of his fellow citizens during those days. One of his fellows was a butcher from Ottakring, who later put it about that he had been a leading member of the resistance and had shot at the SS from under a car. The truth was that he had been lying on his back at the time, like Schärf. There was a gentle 'revolution' in the hospital: pictures of Hitler were taken off the walls and the hospital's administration was arrested. The military personnel had discarded their uniforms and fled. On 10 April a Russian soldier appeared in the courtyard. The war was over.[20]

Schärf made his way home on his daughter's arm. All the jewellers' shops in the Alserstrasse had been looted. A curfew had been imposed, starting at 8 p.m. No one was clear as to whether Vienna had fallen. In the morning of the 9th the Russians had advanced to the Gürtel. By the evening German soldiers had abandoned the city centre. This gave the Austrian resistance movements their cue and they proudly emerged from the woodwork wearing red, white and red armbands. The most active of these had been the small group headed by Major Carl Szokoll, three of whose members had beenf hanged shortly before the Red Army occupied the city. Szokoll takes the credit for saving Vienna from Hitler's 'Nero Order', which required the city's destruction, but in reality the German army was in no position to carry out the order. Sepp Dietrich joked that his Sixth Tank Army was so named because he had but six tanks. Most soldiers had no more than a few rounds of ammunition.[21]

The resistance made the Palais Auersperg their headquarters. The red–white–red Austrian flag flew from the roofless Rathaus. In the Schöner household they 'ate in a very light-hearted mood at midday and drank a toast to our beloved Austria'. That afternoon the main body of Red Army troops followed the advance guard into the city. Again it was a remarkable sight. They came in every form of transport, horse-drawn coaches and dogcarts. They held harmonicas and waved to the people as they passed. The Viennese waved their handkerchiefs and doffed their hats. The Russians shouted and blew kisses at the women.[22]

Schöner and the other Viennese were prepared to give the Russians the benefit of the doubt: 'The fear of rape repeatedly promised by the propaganda seems to be not so great in the case of the Viennese.' Schöner tried to make it into the centre of the city – the 1st Bezirk – but, at the sight of the inner Ring at the bottom of the Burggasse littered with the detritus of war, he decided not to attempt it. Russians were already stealing bicycles. He was stopped by some Red Army men outside the Exhibition Centre (the former royal stables and riding school) and was forced with others to dig a grave for one of their dead comrades. They had found a German corporal in the complex of buildings and shot him. One of his fellow gravediggers complained that the soldiers had stolen his gold watch and leather coat.[23] Work details of this sort had become a hazard. Johann Böhm was appointed state secretary for social administration in the heady days after the Russian arrival. Detained in the street by a soldier, he showed him a paper attesting to his new dignity. 'Papier nix gut!' said the Russian (Your papers are worthless). He was then set to work. The wiser citizens found means of deterring the Russians. Some put their arms in slings, while others went to the extremes of having a plaster cast put on a good arm.[24]

Nazism had become a solely German commodity and Nazis were therefore Germans, or honorary ones. Threatened with plunder, the Viennese had directed the soldiers to the homes of the Pgs.* It was open season on the Nazis, and many of them who remained in the city tried to cast out the evidence as best they could. Large numbers committed suicide, like the coal merchant whose business was in the same building as Margarétha's aunt, or the banker Josef Joham's friends, the Böhm-Bawerks. The husband had fled. His wife, sister and daughter all took their own lives. The Russians shot a neighbour, Christoph Bauer, son of a well-known architect, presumably because they believed him to be a Nazi. His mother had to bury him in the garden. The Soviet secret police or GPU flushed out another called Hackmüller from the house next door. He was alleged to have been the Gauleiter Baldur von Schirach's secretary.[25] Schöner prudently left his watch at home and went out in a curious combination of clothes that was meant to remove any suspicion of bourgeoisie: skiing trousers, hobnail mountain boots and a Styrian hat. Later he added an old coat made in the 1920s and was careful to leave his tie at home. Wearing spectacles was also risky. The Russians saw all men in glasses as fascists or 'burschuj', and picked on them.[26]

The Styrian hat was an informal symbol of resistance among the Austrians, or rather an emblem of resurgent national pride. When Schöner

* From *Parteigenosse*: Party comrade of member of the Nazi Party (NSDAP).

went to the Palais Auersperg he found that many if not most of the men present were wearing such hats. The Palais Auersperg was owned by Princess Agathe Croy, and it was thronged with members of the old nobility. The resistance leader Willy Prince Thurn und Taxis was a cousin, and Nikolaus von Maasburg was related to the Croys by marriage. There were many *G'schaftlhuber* and *Adabeis* in the building which served as a refuge for well-heeled women during the wild days of the liberation.[*] It was also the HQ of O5,[†] which had become the most important resistance group. There was an air of unreality about the place. O5's chief Raoul Bumballa was handing out ministerial portfolios to various noblemen and receiving the Russians as if he were already head of state.[27]

The real aristocracy of the resistance in the palace were the 'Dachauer', members of the pre-1938 governing elite who had been shipped out to Dachau *en masse*. Many of them were still there, if they had not died as a result of their treatment. Schöner met Major Stillfried at the Auersperg. He had been the camp commandant at Wöllersdorf. His job had been to punish both leftwingers and Nazis, and for this last reason he was despatched to Dachau as well, the gamekeeper had become a poacher.[28] He must also have been uncomfortable to see the many communists and socialists who were coming out of the woodwork. A Russian officer was incredulous at the sight of the princes and barons of the resistance: 'I had imagined the anti-fascists somewhat differently.' Later the men acknowledged their mistake: they should have chosen more plausible leaders. Maasburg was subsequently arrested when he tried to make contact with some mild Nazis. He managed to escape to the West.[29]

If middle-class Austrians wore curious clothing, that was nothing to the garb the Russians were wearing. The rare officer possessing operatic epaulettes reminded Schöner of the Serbians in the First War. Many were sporting trophies too, such as SA or SS daggers. The rest could not be described as wearing uniform. 'Handsome human material,' wrote Schöner, 'many tall and blond ("Teutonic"!), and among them lots of Mongolian faces.' Margarétha also noted their blondness and blue eyes. They were powerful people, aged between eighteen and twenty, with a number of fourteen- to fifteen-year-old boys in their train. He, on the other hand, estimated the Mongol element to be a mere 2 per cent.[30]

The Viennese were still enjoying a honeymoon with the Red Army. Schöner's father gave a soldier a bottle of wine from the restaurant's cellars.

[*] *G'schaftlhuber*, a busybody; *Adabei*, from *auch dabei*, meaning also present: someone who doesn't want to miss the party.
[†] O + the fifth letter of the alphabet = Oe, or Ö (Austria).

The soldier offered to pay. That night Schöner went to bed full of optimism: 'God give us a peaceful night and a better future.' The night passed comfortably, but Schöner's father had made a fatal mistake in giving the soldier drink. Now his comrades came back for more. In Hietzing some female neighbours of Eugen Margarétha expressed concern about what might happen to their 'innocence' should the soldiers drink wine.[31] Adolf Schärf had the same thought: 'The great provision of wine and schnapps in Vienna, above all in the vineyard areas, possibly provided a foundation for the raping of the women when it took place.' It is true that some of the most aggravated instances were in the great cellars of Döbling, where Austrian sparkling wine or *Sekt* is made, and the wine 'village' of Grinzing.[32]

At midday the Schöners sat down to a lunch of goulash, potatoes and red cabbage, and Josef tried to console his mother. In the Mariahilferstrasse the Hotel Windsor was burning. There was no water to put out the flames. Schöner made another attempt to reach the centre. On the Ring he saw that the dealer Kasimir (who had robbed the Jews of their art collections in 1938) had been looted himself. Schöner's objective was the cavernous Hotel Astoria on the Kärntner Strasse, where the restaurant was franchised to his sixty-seven-year-old aunt. In the foyer a Russian offered him wine: 'Austria karascho!' (Austria will be all right).[33] The hotel was still functioning, although a shell had hit the third floor. His aunt seemed in control. She was feeding the Russians, while the officers practised old-world manners. So far they had left the chambermaids in peace, but Aunt Mili had been propositioned by a first lieutenant who had asked her up to his room.[34]

The fighting continued in the areas of the city that bordered the Danube. The Russians were across the canal in the Leopoldstadt – the 2nd Bezirk – which explained the terrible damage done to the quay as the two sides continued the shelling. On the 10th the Russians moved into the Prater Park and occupied the race-track at the Freudenau without a fight. The Germans were only cleared from the Leopoldstadt on the 13th. A day later they were flushed out of Brigittenau, and the city was finally at peace.[35] Schöner was free, however, to wander on towards the cathedral. On the corner of the Stock-im-Eisen Platz the Haas Haus was burning. No one attempted to put out the flames. Soldiers stood around watching. It was not known who had started the fire: German shells or Viennese looters. A third possibility was the Russians.* At the time it was common

---

* This was Willy Prinz von Thurn und Taxis's view ('Memoiren', unpublished MS, 25).

to blame Werewolves: the wicked Nazis were destroying the Austrian capital from motives of revenge. Later Schöner thought it might have been plunderers with candles. The looters had broken into the premises of the up-market grocer Wild on the Neue Markt. Margarétha heard that a Russian general had threatened to shoot anyone caught looting, but that seemed not to deter them. Schöner was offered schnapps by a soldier on the Marco-d'Aviano-Gasse. The soldier told him that Stalin had ordered that 'Austria should not be treated as an enemy but as a liberated land. It will be much better for us than for the Hungarians or the Germans, no one is going to be shot.' When Schöner returned to his house he found a cart outside. Russian soldiers were emptying the restaurant cellars of schnapps and *Sekt*. Two Viennese stood by, watching with 'malicious pleasure'.[36]

It was the time to settle scores. In the factory where Margarétha had been working, the foreign workers were demanding the head of the boss, who had prudently disappeared. One of the Schöner cooks had returned from suburban Oberlaa. He reported that the women there had been repeatedly raped. 'The rape chapter that we had previously – and even at the beginning of the occupation – lightly placed on the German propaganda ledger, had become stark reality.' The victims were now reporting to the doctors. Neither age nor social status provided any protection. The Russians are reported to have raped women as old as eighty. Schöner heard a story from Ober St Veit that one woman had complained to the Russian commandant, who had laughed in her face. In general officers excused their men on the grounds of 'long abstinence'. Even the 'first victims' were not immune: the Austrians were not going to enjoy the taste of liberation.[37]

The Russians had located the rich stocks of alcohol in the Schöner cellars and the banging on their door never ceased. They thanked their God for the massive door on their old Viennese house. The women were naturally terrified. 'Sleep was out of the question.' On 12 April, Schöner found that the Russians had plundered their Café Fenstergucker, opposite the famous Hotel Sacher. Before setting it alight they had removed all the wine and schnapps. There were reports of plunder and rape on all sides, so much so that they were forced to admit that Goebbels had ill prepared them for the truth. The most awful revelation, however, was even harder to swallow: in almost every case of rape or plunder, the Russians had been guided to their quarry by foreign workers or by the Viennese themselves. The chosen victims were the middle classes. There were the predictable consequences too: women committed suicide after the event; many contracted venereal diseases; others became pregnant and had to seek abortions. Doctors who had refused to terminate pregnancies in the past were now prepared to waive their moral objections. The only women who would not hear of it were the nuns, who stolidly awaited their fate in a Viennese hospital. Women responded to the danger by dressing down: 'all the women are inelegant; most forgo hats or stockings. It is a lot safer on the streets than it is in the houses at night . . .'[38]

Vienna's famous gawping *Adabeis* had assembled before the Schöners' house in the Siebensterngasse to watch the spectacle. 'The scene of our looting attracts hundreds of spectators, who are constantly trying to push their way into the house to lend a hand.' They were hoping to receive a few scraps from the Russians' table. 'In the hall lie the fragments of a few dozen bottles of Veuve Cliquot and Lanson.' One Croat tried to steal Josef's watch, but he was so drunk he could not stand up and had to support himself by clasping Schöner round the neck. The Russians were accompanied by some women, who guided them towards the older vintages. Their advice was rewarded with some bars of 'couverture' or cooking chocolate. The raiders found 200 more bottles. 'Another group is sitting around a table in the courtyard knocking back our old bordeaux from coffee cups.' Josef's parents complained to a first lieutenant, who responded by distributing some of the bottles to the waiting crowd. The Schöners joined the queue and were rewarded with a few bottles of their own wine. To add insult to injury, a member of the resistance came to see Schöner's father and accused him of making the Russians drunk, thereby placing the city's women in jeopardy.[39]

The Margaréthas in Hietzing were luckier. The gourmand economist was trading 'liberation wine' for endive salads. They hung up a sign in German and 'Cyrillic' saying 'Unarmed civilians'. Russians came up the garden path to demand drink. Margarétha's wife gave them water. Later Franek set up a buffet to distribute water to any Russian with a thirst, although that was certainly not what he wanted. They camped in the garden and when it was time to eat they supped from their helmets, which doubled as mess tins. The helmets were unlined, and the soldiers wore woollen or fur hats underneath. They cut their meat up with their bayonets. Margarétha still found them friendly, even if they tended to keep their distance from the Austrians.[40]

He was plundered for all that, if not badly. He returned from doing his deal with the gardener to find the door wide open. Franek had been put up against a wall. All three of the servant's watches were gone. The Russians had been upstairs where they had created a wild disorder. They had filched a bottle of German brandy, but left the Dreher-cognac from

Hungary. They had nabbed his wife's wedding ring, two cameras (one was then rejected – he found it in the neighbour's garden) and a brooch, which they had subsequently returned. More Russians came for his car, but he was able to tell them that it had been requisitioned by the Wehrmacht a year before. 'You are powerless in the face of such attacks,' he reflected. A notice had appeared outside the Café Gröpl in Hietzing telling all Germans aged between sixteen and sixty to report to the Russians.[41]

The Germans and the Russians were still fighting on the outskirts, in the industrial areas along the Danube. Marshal Tolbukhin issued a proclamation on 12 April: the Russians were not fighting the Austrian people; they had come to restore the country as it had been before 1938. Simple Nazis, it said, would not be prosecuted; private property would be respected![42] Meanwhile the city was putting together a form of government. Schöner heard a rumour that Schärf had been named mayor. Two men wearing red–white–red armbands had indeed been to see Schärf and told him he was needed urgently at the Palais Auersperg. He found the place filled with 'feverish activity'. The man in charge was Raoul Bumballa, head of the resistance group O5. The Russians found the Austrian resistance hard to quantify: they dissolved O5 and packed a number of military opponents of Hitler off to the Soviet Union.

It was decided that Tolbukhin could not restore the Austria of 1938 without bringing back the 'Austro-fascists'. The men in the Palais Auersperg wanted a return to 1933. Schärf was not offered the mayor's job – that eventually went to the Russian-speaking socialist General Körner. He was offered instead the subaltern position of mayor of Josefstadt, which he declined.[43] Körner learned who the real bosses were when he tried to take possession of the Rathaus on 18 April. He found his path blocked: the Russians were searching the vast building for weapons. He was obliged to sit on a park bench until they had finished.[44]

The Muscovites had also checked in: Ernst Fischer, Johann Koplenig, Franz Honner and Friedl Fuernberg. For the past few years they had been living in Moscow's Hotel Lux with the privileged German communists. Honner was an ex-intern of Wöllersdorf. He had left early to raise two 'freedom' battalions to form the Green Division of some 2,000 men, which had campaigned alongside Tito's partisans in Yugoslavia. He was a former miner and shoemaker from Grünbach who had fought in the Spanish Civil War. Fischer was the intellectual and poet – the Austrian equivalent of the later cultural commissar of the Russian Zone in Germany, Johannes R. Becher – and was the son of a colonel and a staunch patriot. Fischer was expecting Stalin to allow him and his fellow communists to play a major role. He was apparently furious when he heard that the Russians had sought out the former chancellor Karl Renner and were going to allow other parties, like the hated socialists,* to coexist with them.[45] The Western Allies were also eagerly awaited: there were rumours that they would be in Vienna as early as 22 April. Schöner had heard that the Americans were already in nearby Mauer and had flown into Baden-bei-Wien.[46]

On 13 April the Russians had reached Linz: 'the city that had nurtured the Führer was evacuated without a fight'. The Schöners had managed to bury a small part of their cellar in the garden. Locking the door no longer kept the Russians out – they blew in the windows. The first wave came with a Viennese gunwoman who directed them down to the cellar where they found more wine, breaking some two-litre *Doppler* bottles in the process. The next wave came through another window accompanied by cries of 'Wino!' The Russians had been to the banks and forced the clerks to open the safes. One of the Russians gave Schöner a RM1,000 note for a roll-up. When the family at last ran out of wine the Russians took eggs, bread and butter.[47]

They were still heady times. On one of his walks around the city Schöner was struck by the sight of a female Red Army soldier directing traffic in the Wiedner Hauptstrasse dressed in a very short skirt. Margarétha had admired these women too, particularly the blondes. The traffic in question was Russian carts loaded with booty. These lined the Rennweg. Cows and foals were tethered behind and the vehicles were piled high with suitcases, balalaikas, sewing machines, radios and gramophones: 'it was the picture of a gypsy train'. The Russians had even stolen the tyres and engines of the cars. As Schöner walked on he witnessed a horse being skinned on the Wollzeile. The Stephansplatz was all burned out from the Haas Haus to the Rotenturmstrasse. The Hotel Bristol near the Opera had been gutted by fire. There were no fire engines to extinguish the flames. When the Viennese found a pump it was so weak that the water hardly made it to the first floor.[48] Cardinal Innitzer's palace had been pillaged, and the primate had fled. Schöner doffed his cap at the sight of the cathedral, denuded of its roof. It had been set alight after the departure of the Germans. 'It is a sight that grabs everyone by the heart.'[49]

The Palais Auersperg had become the place to jockey for power in the provisional government. Not all the solicitors were respectable. Schöner noted that Vinzenz Schumy had swum with the tide after the Anschluss, and was more or less compromised. Yet he too was looking for a ministerial portfolio. Schöner thought the palace was full of Nazi spies. Former Pgs

---

* The socialist had supported the Anschluss with Germany. The communists had not.

were looking for victims of the Nazis in the hope that they would give them a good reference once the witch-hunt started. Margarétha had been dismissed from his job, and his son had married a Mautner-Markov, a member of a prominent, ennobled, originally Jewish family. Schöner went back to his old job at the Foreign Office. The building had been badly damaged in the bombing, but it was still functioning. They put him in charge of the grandfather clocks. There were more and more signs that life was returning to normal.[50]

Margarétha was obliged to join a work detail. Along with the rest of the men he had to clear streets of obstacles and repair bridges. The first stint was not so bad. He worked all day and found it no more tiring than doing four hours in the garden. He came to the conclusion that the Russians were kinder to civilian workers than the Nazis had ever been. It got tougher. While he was working near his house his wife brought him a snack of a couple of sandwiches. The bread was already two weeks old, and he had to drink a lot of black coffee to swallow it. The detail worked for twenty-four hours this time. When they let him go he slept for ten hours.[51]

With the hostilities at an end and the Nazis gone, Margarétha and his wife joined the resistance. This presumably meant no more than that they could prove themselves to have been consistently anti-Nazi during the Third Reich. Once they had signed the register they were issued with red–white–red armbands. There was a political opening for Eugen in the fledgling, Christian democrat Austrian People's Party or ÖVP. This was being formed from a wide base: the white- and blue-collar workers were under Leopold Kunschak and Lois Weinberger, the peasants' league was being led by Leopold Figl and Schumy, and the middle class by Julius Raab. For the time being it was respectable to be on the left. The 'Liberation Movement' was made up of 50 per cent socialists, 40 per cent communists and just 10 per cent 'bourgeois' parties.[52] Schärf was one of the men behind the recreation of the Austrian socialists. At their session on the 14 April they rejected the idea of calling it the Social Democratic Party and plumped for the Austrian Socialist Party, or SPÖ instead. That way it was hoped people would forget that it had condoned the Anschluss. It very quickly fended off Soviet-backed moves to amalgamate with the communists. Fischer had returned from Moscow with instructions to eschew Marxism–Leninism for the time being. The stress was to be on Austria: 'The glorious Austrian past must be given its true worth . . . The Radetzky March must become a national song, sung in schools.'[53]

The economist Margarétha noticed that most of the shops in the 1st

Bezirk were boarded up, with 'Empty' written on the shutters. Foreign workers were free-wheeling their carts piled high with loot. Both the Parliament building and the Ministry of Justice were partly burned out.[54] Schöner too resumed his walks. On the 18th he stopped to admire a fresh Russian grave on the Heldenplatz which was festooned with flowers. Drunken Russians in the Burggasse were pummelling on doors, but the Viennese knew their game by now, and no one opened up. There were long queues outside the butchers and bakers: meat had virtually disappeared and bread was a rarity. A day or two later the Austrians' mouths began to water when they saw a hundred or so Hungarian cows with strange horns driven through the centre of the city by Red Army soldiers.

The Viennese were making trips out to the woods with prams and wheelbarrows to gather wood and to look for wild mushrooms or crayfish. The Café Fenstergucker had been plundered again, but the raiders had not taken the schnapps. Schöner concluded that they had been robbed by the Viennese: the Russians would not have left the alcohol, and some precious tea had gone. It was generally easy to tell who robbed you for that reason. The Russians wanted drink, gold or watches. If anything else went, the authors were civilians. At the Hotel Astoria, Aunt Mili was driven to distraction by the nightly hunts for chambermaids. The Astoria was more fortunate than the Hotel Metropol, which burned down on the 19th. It had ceased to be a hotel in 1938, when it became Gestapo Headquarters.[55] No one regretted its passing.

On 20 April, Hitler's birthday, the eighty-three-year-old Graf Albert Mensdorff came into the Foreign Office to offer his services. He had been Austro-Hungarian ambassador to the Court of St James's in 1914. Schöner recalled the count expressing very Nazi views in the Jockey Club two years before.* He died of starvation on 15 June 1945. The Austrian Foreign Office was ready for action, although it was touch and go whether the Russians would allow its officials to do anything. Schöner had been given a pass by the city council, but another diplomat who had presented his to the Red Army sentry had seen it rudely tossed into the canal.[56]

The following day Schöner learned that the Americans had reached Pilsen in Czechoslovakia. Everyone was looking forward to the arrival of the Western Allies. They had all had enough of the Russians, who were certain to install Karl Renner as chancellor. Everyone chose to remember the open letter in which he had pledged his support for the Anschluss in 1938. On 23 April news of the arrest of the former German ambassador to

---

* This now seems unlikely.

Austria, Franz von Papen, was a cause of jubilation. He had been in Vienna in 1938: 'he deserved something for Austria's sake', wrote Schöner.[57]

The refurbishment of Renner was Stalin's idea. As Austria was being discussed one day he asked, 'Where is that social democrat Renner now, the one who was a disciple of Kautsky? For years he was one of the leaders of Austrian social democracy and was, if I recall, president of the last Austrian Parliament.'[58] No one knew the answer at the time, but as soon as the dust had settled the Russians had gone looking for the vintage socialist who had brought in the First Republic. They considered him the sort of soft ideologist who would allow their men to move safely behind the scenes. They didn't trust him, and were aware that he had voiced his support for the Anschluss. They found him on 3 April when, as luck would have it, he protested about the behaviour of Soviet troops to the Russian commander in the Lower Austrian village of Gloggnitz. Gloggnitz was close to Wiener Neustadt, where the Red Army met heavy resistance for the first time. The Russians scooped him up with his family and installed him in the nearby Schloss Eichbüchl.[59] Renner proceeded to heap praise on the Soviet system, and claim that 'liberation' by the Russians was all they – and he – had ever dreamed of. The Social Democrats, together with the Communist Party, of course, would now be in a position to provide the necessary political security.[60] His puppet-status inspired distrust in the West, and he played innocent when the Americans asked him later how big a role the Russians had had in his appointment. He insisted that the Russians did not interfere with his decisions, but the American agent who saw him in August 1945 was all too aware of the Russian captain who sat in on their interview.[61]

There was a meeting at Renner's Viennese home in the Wenzgasse in Hietzing on 23 April. The idea was raised of freely distributing the undersecretaries of state among the three interested parties: socialists, communists and conservatives. Renner made his first stab at a cabinet on the 24th. A controversial choice was the Muscovite Honner for minister of the interior and chief of police. It was, however, standard Stalinist practice to place a communist in this role. Joham at finance was controversial in a different way: he had been friendly with the Nazis during his time at the Credit Anstalt. Dr Gerö was nominated minister of justice. Schöner noted that he was a 'Mischling' – he had Jewish blood. That other Muscovite, Ernst Fischer, was also to be given a job.[62]

Schöner was not so unhappy about Honner. It was a 'thankless and difficult post' and with any luck he would prove unpopular. The Russians were pushing for the reopening of the theatres and cinemas. Because of the war damage, most of Vienna's great cultural institutions had to make do with what space they could find. The Burgtheater performed in the Ronacher.* The Opera had been bombed out. Klemens Krauss was appointed chief conductor amid widespread disappointment. Krauss had blotted his copybook in 1934 when he had emigrated to Germany at the time of Dollfuss's assassination by the Nazis, and his scandalous behaviour had not been forgotten. The first post-Nazi newspaper came out, but that was a disappointment too, as it looked too much like Goebbels's *Völkische Beobachter* – short on news and big on propaganda. It was no surprise that the editor was the communist Fischer.[63]

News reached Schöner on the 24th of a new Andreas Hofer[†] fighting the Nazis in the Tyrol. The man gave his name as Plattner. He seems to have been a flash in the pan, although it was true that the Tyroleans were pushing the Nazis out before the arrival of the Americans. With Austria the 'victim' and Italy a former Axis power, 'everyone was waiting for the return of the South Tyrol' to Austria. There was a rumour that reached the ears of both Schöner and Margarétha that the former chancellor Kurt von Schuschnigg had been poisoned in Sachsenhausen concentration camp. As it was he was on the way to the South Tyrol himself.[‡] On 26 April, an interim government was formed under Karl Renner.

It was an attempt to balance the interests of the Christian socialists, the socialists and the communists, albeit dominated by moderate socialists like Renner and his vice-chancellor, Adolf Schärf. Of the communists, Fischer was given the important portfolio of 'popular enlightenment, education and culture' and Honner was made minister of the interior. The Christian Democrat minister Kunschak was a notorious antisemite, which made the Jews who formed the bulk of the Austrian Centre reluctant to go home.[64] Margarétha heard about it when a girl gave him a copy of the Soviet-sponsored *Neues Österreich* which contained the details of Renner's cabinet and the proclamation. He thought the latter 'excellent, a real masterpiece'. It declared that Austria would return to the constitution of 1920. The Anschluss, said the proclamation, had been involuntary; it had been imposed on Austria and was therefore null and void. Margarétha then repaired to the Naschmarkt, where he was able to purchase some precious root vegetables.[65]

On Friday 27 April the representatives of the permitted political parties

* The equivalent of the Royal National Theatre performing in a music hall.
† The Tyrolean innkeeper Andreas Hofer had fought Napoleon, and was shot by the French in 1810.
‡ See below pp. 82–4.

signed a declaration of independence from Germany. The Soviets recognised Renner's regime, but only as far as the Danube, because Tolbukhin's troops were still fighting in the Weinviertel. The Second Republic was born under the aegis of the Red Army. That afternoon Schöner abandoned his old coat and skiing trousers for a silk shirt and a dark suit. The Vienna Philharmonic was going to play its first concert since the liberation. At 4 p.m. there was a private performance at the Large Concert Hall, as the Musikverein building had been damaged. The hall was only three-quarters full, but a substantial number of *Adabeis* had gathered to watch the arrival of civil servants, communists and Russian army officers. The orchestra was heartily applauded, Krauss audibly less so. Some people even hissed. The programme was Schubert's Unfinished, Beethoven's *Leonore 3* and Tchaikovsky's Fifth Symphony: 'A tribute to the immortal spirit of Vienna and the great, classic time of Viennese music and to the musical genius of Russia.' The Philharmonic played the Schubert 'without soul'; they were better at the Beethoven. The Tchaikovsky was 'brilliantly played'.

In the interval the assistant mayor, the communist Steinhardt, made a speech in which he thanked the Red Army for liberating them from the 'brown plague'. There was loud cheering. He then announced a full programme of cultural events: there was to be a performance by the Burgtheater company of *Sappho* on the 30 April and the State Opera company would do *The Marriage of Figaro* at the Volksoper. At the Akademie Theater they would have Nestroy's *Mäd aus der Vorstadt*. The stress was clearly on 'Austrian culture' for the time being. The Raimund and Josefstadt* theatres were to reopen together with nine cinemas. In reality this meant showing a lot of Soviet films without subtitles.[66]

It was only at the end of April that the Western Allies appeared at the Austrian border. The Americans took Innsbruck, Salzburg and Linz; the British came up through Italy on the 28th and marched into Carinthia and Styria before meeting up with Soviet forces. That same day the Nazi fellow traveller Joham was rejected as a member of the provisional government. Loudspeakers played 'O Du mein Österreich'. The Russians stood by and tacitly blessed the regime they had ushered in. The British, however, had had their worst fears confirmed, and promptly refused to recognise Renner's government. The Americans followed suit. Renner responded by hailing Stalin as the 'greatest military commander of all time'. Later Schöner met a friend who had just returned from suburban Weidling. There had been persistent raping at his country house. A

---

* The Josefstadt is where Anna Schmidt is engaged as a soubrette in *The Third Man*.

seventeen-year-old girl who had tried to defend herself had been shot. 'On the periphery it is much worse than it is in the inner city.'[67]

On the 29th five tramlines began to work again. Renner appeared in the company of two Russian officers at the Foreign Office dressed in a stiff collar, a tie with pearl pin, grey spats and an old brown hat. He had a white goatee beard stained with nicotine from his diet of cigars[68] and boasted a small pot belly. He was ready for his detractors. He did not deny that he had been in favour of the Anschluss, only that he had wanted union with the Nazis. He was keen to do down the Austro-fascists of the Corporate State. He told the diplomats that Dollfuss people were as unwelcome in the new Austria as Nazis. He let it be known that he wanted the Austro-fascists excluded from the suffrage for ten years. As it was, it proved easy to restock the ministries with untainted civil servants: all they had to do was reappoint those prematurely retired in the time of the Corporate State.[69] Naturally, most of them were socialists, and Wöllersdorf old-boys.

It was May Day, and a big parade was laid on for the Russians. Austrian flags had been made out of old swastikas, and the women had fashioned headscarves out of the same material. The people wore red carnations and greeted one another with the word 'Freiheit' or 'freedom', rather than the usual 'Grüss Gott!' The Russians made the city a present of tons of provisions. The Viennese said it was all food they had plundered from them in the first place.[70] The gift was supposed to last for a month. It meant a daily ration of 1,620 calories for heavy workers, 970 for white-collar staff and 833 for children.[71] The French arrived in Bregenz on Lake Constance that same day. On 6 May they had established themselves in a small part of their zone, the Upper Tyrol. By the time of the German capitulation on 8 May, the whole of Austria was occupied. Just in case anyone was to forget, the French put up signposts for their own troops: 'Ici Autriche, pays ami' (This is Austria, these are our friends).[72]

The Western Allies were still a long way off. There were rumours that the Americans were making difficulties for Austria because of Stalin's sponsorship of the Lublin Poles. On 3 May a story did the rounds about the partition of Vienna. The British, it seemed, were going to receive the 1st Bezirk. It was the first time the Viennese had heard that the French too were to have their slice of the cake. Schöner was later told that the French were to receive central Vienna, and also the 7th Bezirk where he lived. The new communist police president, Hautmann, decreed that all foreigners and forced labourers had to leave Vienna. They were to assemble in Wiener Neustadt until transport could be arranged for them. The Schöners lost their two Ukrainian servant girls and an Italian cook.[73]

The Führer had committed suicide on 30 April, but the Wehrmacht and the SS were still fighting. Schöner was appalled to see that the Austrians were among the most dogged. 'In the end it is once again apparent that the Austrians, providing they are really Nazis, are also the most unremitting partisans of Hitler. German generals from the Reich are capitulating; the Löhrs and Rendulics* in the south and the north are fighting on.'[74]

The British and the Yugoslavs had finally come to blows over Trieste, which the former were keen to award to the Italians. Meanwhile the Russians had begun to deport 500 Austrians from Floridsdorf in the suburbs. Field Marshal Alexander was thought to be in Vienna, staying at the Hotel Imperial, and between Stockerau, Tulln and Korneuburg in Lower Austria the Wehrmacht and the SS were still holding out on 6 May. Vlasov's army was leaving its positions in Prague and heading south to Lower Austria, and it looked as if fighting could flare up again. Vlasov and his Cossacks had been fighting alongside the SS, and he did not wish to be captured by the Red Army who would have executed him immediately as a traitor. His departure coincided with the Soviet-inspired uprising in Prague. On the 7th Schöner heard a distorted rumour that Hitler's successor Admiral Dönitz had surrendered unconditionally in Copenhagen. Eisenhower had said the war was over, but there was still gunfire to be heard. Margarétha concluded that it was Vlasov's army fighting a path to the Western Allies.[75] The truce was pronounced at 2 p.m. that day, but there was no more champagne to celebrate with. They made good with meatballs, and in the evening 'goulash, like in peacetime!'[76]

---

* Romanian-born Colonel General Alexander Löhr was handed over to the Yugoslavs by the British, and later executed for ordering the bombardment of Belgrade. Colonel General Lothar Rendulic, born in Wiener Neustadt, was sentenced to twenty-five years for war crimes. He was released in 1951.

2

Wild Times: A Picture of Liberated
Central Europe in 1945

On 8 May Germany had surrendered unconditionally and was occupied by the victorious powers. Everyone was freed from National
Socialist tyranny. Those whose lives were in danger from the regime
were finally spared. But for many others, however, the misery and risk
of death had not disappeared. For countless people the suffering only
began with the end of the war.

Richard von Weizsäcker, *Vier Zeiten: Erinnerungen*, Berlin 1997, 95

Liberation from the East

What was true of Vienna applied, to a lesser or greater extent, to every
town and city in Germany and Austria: if they had not been
knocked flat, they had been at least partially destroyed. Many insignificant
market towns and villages had been reduced to piles of rubble as well, victims of the Allied advance, and the process continued until the Allies
believed they had wholly subdued the enemy. Besides the terrible loss of
human life, much treasure was gone for good, and cities that had been the
glory of central Europe were no more.

There were the *Residenzen*, the former court capitals: Dresden had been
smashed to smithereens as a Valentine's Day present to the Red Army; in
Munich the destruction of so many cultural monuments prompted Richard
Strauss's most moving composition, *Die Metamorphosen*; and the baroque
gem of Würzburg, Dresden's equivalent in the west, had been reduced to
rubble by the USAAF in the last days of the war. The Welf capitals of
Hanover and Brunswick had suffered the loss of their palaces;[*] Bayreuth
was the victim of its Wagner-cult; two-thirds of Weimar was flattened on
account of Goethe and Schiller. Cassel was so badly damaged that the

---

[*] Brunswick's palace was pulled down and replaced by a shopping centre.

ruins were bulldozed. The lack of any remaining infrastructure obliged the American army to plant its HQ in the spa town of Wiesbaden, which had come out of the war only slightly mauled, because bad weather had caused the air force to drop the bulk of its payload on the outlying woods.

Not all Germany's gems had been homes to small courts. There was Hildesheim, where the wooden houses burned for a fortnight before the flames could be extinguished, and where the two largest Carolingian churches went up in smoke. Hamburg had been the testing ground for Britain's and America's weapons of mass destruction in 1943: in two days of bombing, 50,000 had died. The ancient centre of Frankfurt-am-Main was gone; a few façades on the latter's Römerberg recalled the glories of what had been before. Little remained of the centres of the former Roman cities of Cologne and Trier, or of Charlemagne's capital, Aachen, where the baptistery lay open to the skies; the Bavarian cities of Augsburg and Regensburg had been pulverised. Leipzig, the capital of the German book trade, was badly bruised; Breslau smouldered long after the end of the war as the Russians lit fires in the ruins. The medieval cores of Stettin and Danzig had been levelled by Soviet artillery. The list is endless.

The inhabitants of urban Germany were dead or scattered. The survivors generally headed west, hoping to reach the Western Allies who – they believed – would treat them more fairly than the Red Army. Only a few brave souls ventured east. One of these was Ursula von Kardorff, who undertook a mission to Berlin in September 1945 and listed the shattered cities as she went: 'Darmstadt, Mannheim, Hanau – a landscape of craters provoking extreme sadness. Add to this the prison camps surrounded by barbed wire and their watchtowers, the ruins, the detonated bridges and autobahn viaducts. Scorched earth, just as Hitler dreamed up for his people.'[1]

East Prussia

East Prussia was the first German region visited by the Red Army, and to some extent the worst treated. The first incursion, at Nemmersdorf on 21 October 1944, was to be a foretaste. In the course of a single night the Red Army killed seventy-two women and one man. Most of the women had been raped, of whom the oldest was eighty-four. Some of the victims had been crucified. Gauleiter Koch refused to allow the population to flee. Hitler wanted East Prussia to prove the resilience of the German people. That autumn the East Prussians watched the departure of the birds: 'Yes, you are now flying away! And us? What is to become of us and our land?'[2]

Then in January 1945 the Soviet offensive began. The Russians broke through the German lines on the 17th. Insterburg was the first to fall, followed by Tilsit and Gumbinnen. Koch, who had been named commissar for the defence of the Reich, finally gave permission for the civilian population to leave. Almost simultaneously, however, the Red Army reached Elbing on the Baltic, thereby cutting East Prussia off from the Reich. The East Prussians resorted to every conceivable means of leaving the beleaguered territory and reaching what was believed to be the safety of the west bank of the Vistula. Trains, however, ran head on into the Russian advance and were stopped in their tracks. Passengers froze in the icy temperatures, and the dead were thrown from the windows.[3]

Ships fared no better. They were sunk as they left the harbour of Pillau outside Königsberg. Hundreds of thousands of refugees trekked across the ice that covered the inland seas of the Frisches and Kurisches Haff in heavily laden carts and proceeded towards Danzig. The Russians warned them they would fire at the ice from their warships on 15 February. The shells hit men and horses. Where the ice was smashed, the trekkers put up temporary bridges and persevered. The night was pitch black. All they could hear was 'Shooting, screaming and screeching'. When dawn broke they realised the full horror: body upon body, man and horse; and every now and then the chassis of a cart sticking out of the ice. Those who succeeded in making it to the thin strip of land that borders Haff and Nehrung had a choice of heading north to the ships at Pillau or south-west towards Danzig.[4]

One family that left an account of the crossing headed south to Stutthof, the home of the infamous concentration camp to the east of Danzig. The road to Danzig was barred; one of the horses went into labour; and the Russians continued the bombardment of the refugees from the sea. The family was lucky enough to reach Hela Point. From there they were shipped to Jutland. They did not see Germany again until they were repatriated from Denmark in November 1948.[5] The noose tightened around Königsberg on 26 January 1945. Very soon the road to the sea and Pillau was cut off. The city held out until 9 April. The first the surgeon Hans Lehndorff knew of the fall of Königsberg was when Russians soldiers broke into his hospital and robbed his patients of their watches, beating up anyone who stood in their way. Fountain pens were the next craving. The sick and injured were tipped out of their beds, bandages ripped from their wounds, and papers burned to create more light to steal by. All the hospital's provision in food was consumed or squandered in a matter of hours.[6] One of the attackers, 'a really young fellow, suddenly burst into tears because he had yet to find a watch. He struck three fingers in the air. He was going to shoot three people if he did not get one at once.' They found him a watch.[7]

General Lasch* capitulated the next day and swarms of soldiers attacked the population as they ventured out of the warrens they had inhabited during the long siege. They were beaten, robbed, stripped and, if female, raped. The women's screams could be heard everywhere: 'Schieß doch!' they shouted. 'Go on, shoot!' The sisters in the hospital were raped by 'blood-crazed children', sixteen years old at the most. The pious Lehndorff could feel the women's souls dying. 'Is not every word an accusation against me? Is there no opportunity to throw oneself between them and through it to find an honourable death?'[8] Some of the women were laughing hysterically. One of the conquerors was Alexander Solzhenitsyn. He wrote of the rapes in a poem called 'Prussian Nights':

> The little daughter's on the mattress,
> Dead. How many have been on it
> A platoon, a company perhaps?
> A girl's been turned into a woman.
> A woman turned into a corpse.[9]

Bunkers and shelters were simply torched with flame-throwers. A very large number of Königsberger took their own lives to escape the indignity of Soviet revenge. That night the surgeon looked out into the hospital courtyard to see it filled with horses and caravans. It could have been deepest Asia.[10]

Lehndorff was touched by the help he had from the French forced labourers. They too were robbed by the Red Army. 'Adieu, docteur!' one of them cried out as Lehndorff successfully ran away from a Russian soldier with a submachine gun who was angry that the surgeon had pushed him out of the way, making him fall on his back. Lehndorff removed his white coat, and the soldier did not recognise him again. Episodes of this sort did not make the business of treating the sick and wounded any easier. The instruments were pilfered off the operating table. One glimmer of light came when they were visited by a Russian major who wanted a wart removed. After the hospital staff cut it out, he gave them temporary protection.[11]

Worse was to come when the Russians found alcohol. On 11 April they located the Menthal distillery. They now set fire to the undamaged parts of the city. The bad mood of the Red Army was made more acute

* Lasch was sentenced to death *in absentia* and his family arrested. Koch escaped from Pillau after telling the population to stand firm.

by syphilis and gonorrhoea. The soldiers ran back to the hospitals and demanded treatment at gunpoint. In their wilder orgies, however, they had smashed the dispensary to smithereens. Even Lehndorff could not resist a moment of *Schadenfreude*.[12] It did not last long. His soulmate – designated simply by the name 'Doktora' – was dragged from the operating table and raped. Lehndorff had not been there at the time, and at first he did not notice the change in her. She stood at the table, binding wounds in the same way: 'but these eyes! A barb stuck into the remains of my soul.' A little while later she came to him in her torn tracksuit. She asked for her Bible. She had put pills aside for when she needed them. The horror had yet to abate, and she fought off three more attacks. Finally when she burst into tears Lehndorff was relieved: 'I am happy that she has finally given in.'[13]

The city was burning. Once the fun was over the remaining citizens were assembled for forced marches to camps. Anyone who was too old or too ill was shot there and then, either in their beds or in the gutters. On 12 April Lehndorff was one of those rounded up and marched out of the city. As he walked out, the Russians cheered, shouting, 'Gitlair Kapoot!' (Hitler's had it!). He marched for twenty-five kilometres. With the help of Polish auxiliaries the women were dragged away from the column with cries of 'Davai, suda!' (Come, woman!). Before he left the hospital Lehndorff had found a female patient with a head wound who had been raped countless times without ever being aware of it.[14]

They were marched to camps, some of which were in Königsberg itself, like the one in the garage of the Rothenstein Barracks. On the promise of better treatment, some Germans acted as kapos – prisoners who had wormed their way into positions of trust – dealing out blows for their Soviet masters. A number of these were allegedly communists, who believed their day had come.[15] Had they expected to become masters of the city now that the Nazis had been deposed, they were deluding themselves. Königsberg had been awarded to the Soviet Union and it was now administered as a Soviet city. The German population would be at best deported, at worst exterminated. The remaining buildings that had escaped the British raid in August 1944, or which had not been filled with Soviet political bureaux – like the Kommandatura, or military command, in the Ziethenstrasse and the old Gestapo Headquarters – were rased to the ground. A Soviet city would be built on the site of the old capital of the Teutonic Knights.

The Russians were expecting to find the Amber Room from Tsarskoe Selo in the shattered Royal Schloss. The invading Germans had packaged it up and sent it back to a secret location in Germany.* Later it was put on display in the Schloss, where Marianne Günther visited it on 15 March 1943. The Russians appear to have accidentally incinerated the room themselves in their zeal to put the city to the torch; they then accused the Germans of hiding it to cover up its wanton destruction by their own men.[16]

It is estimated that there were as many as 110,000 Germans left in Königsberg on 9 April. When the Soviets conducted a head count in June, 73,000 remained. Graf Plettenberg maintained that the Russians had actually tied Hitler Youths to horses and torn them limb from limb, but in the absence of any other reports of this taking place in Königsberg, it has to be discounted.[17] Nonetheless, as one Königsberger maintained, 'a man was worth less than the watch he wore'.[18]

Valiant efforts were made to preserve life against all odds. Professor Wilhelm Starlinger ran a hospital for Germans in the Ziegelstrasse until he was deported to Siberia. It handled 13,200 patients until it was closed in 1947. Of these around 15 per cent died, chiefly of typhus and malaria. Others were treated at the Barmherzigkeit, or Sisters of Mercy, a bombed-out building administered by Professor Arthur Böttner. He was assisted by Lehndorff and the hygienist Hans Schubert. Both left records of their experiences in Königsberg. Lehndorff's are possibly the most moving account of human suffering written anywhere and at any time.

Those who lived in the villages of East Prussia fared no better than the townsfolk. A witness who made it to the west talked of a poor village girl who was raped by an entire tank squadron from eight in the evening to nine in the morning. One man was shot and fed to the pigs.[19] Another woman tried to take the last train from Mohringen, but it was derailed and the passengers proceeded on foot, only to run into the Russians. She describes these soldiers breaking into a farmhouse and finding an Iron Cross, Second Class. The owner of the decoration and his wife were taken out and shot in the back of the head. The narrator herself was raped around twenty times the night she was captured, but there was worse in store. She was carried off by two officers and seven men, whom she suspected were deserters, or temporarily estranged from their unit. They lodged her and eight other females, including a fourteen-year-old girl, in a house in the forest, where they raped them for a week. Their ordeal came to an end only when the GPU, the secret police, found the house. The

---

* The irony was that the room had been made for the Royal Schloss in Berlin – another victim of the war – and Prussia's first king, the spendthrift Frederick I. His austere son, Frederick William, gave the room to Peter the Great in exchange for a squad of tall soldiers, a commodity he valued more highly than amber.

woman was then taken to Insterburg and shipped beyond Stalingrad to the north-eastern Urals. She was in a carriage with fifty women for three weeks. During that time she had only two hot meals. The guards gave them salted herrings. They were so thirsty that they licked the condensation off the window panes. Five of the women had died by the time they reached their destination. They were suffering from typhus, dysentery and facial erysipelas. In August 1945 she was sent back to Germany.[20]

Christel Beckmann reached Mecklenburg, whence she sent the teacher Marianne Günther news of the tiny village of Gertlauken at the end of 1945:

> Hildegard Schustereit was dragged off with the other girls and died in the Urals. In the village practically all the old people are dead. My cousin Ingrid Iwahn is also dead, so are Aunt and Uncle Matschull, my classmate Lotte Jakobeit and her mother, Lies Wallat and Eva Gronwald. Siegfried Schwarm has also died, his mother buried him in the gutter. Herr von Kohs was killed, Frau von Kohs came back to the village and died of typhus. Their children have been shared out: little Franka has gone to Frau Kather, one of the boys is with Frau Schwarm, the other with Frau Fröse. My dear cousin Herta was frequently raped, the other women too. The Russians behaved badly in Mecklenburg, but it was nothing to what they did at home. The farms lie dormant. The land is overgrown with thistles and thorns. They all have to work in Deimehöh, Gertrud Beckmann and my cousin Herta too. As regards animals they have only dogs, cats, mice and rats; there is not a cow, a pig or a hen. They have all lost their things: the last bed, clothing, shoes, everything; they have just the rags on their bodies.[21]

Pomerania

The war had ended much earlier for the Krockows at Glowitz in eastern Pomerania. The Russians came in March, announcing their arrival by setting fire to the manor house. At the time no one could understand why they should destroy a useful building. They attributed the Russian wrath to a portrait of an ancestor, resplendent in his uniform as a colonel of the hussars, that had made the invaders think of Hermann Göring. It was more likely, however, that the manor excited a class-hatred among the Russians and accounted for their cheering from the elegant parterres as this symbol of hated *Junkertum* went up in flames. The Junkers fared no better on the whole. Even an implacable opponent of the Nazis, like Eberhard von Braunschweig, was hauled out with his family and shot.[22]

The refugees and the Russians had arrived with plagues of disease, venereal and other (dysentery, typhoid and spotted fever). Not even the animals were spared: the cows caught foot and mouth disease, the pigs erysipelas and the horses equinia. Not that it mattered much. The Russian arrival had been the cue for hecatombs in every farmyard. The beasts were butchered and salted away. No one knew when food would be available again. The farms and houses were stripped of everything. There was even an order issued that all musical instruments be delivered to the railway stations. There they lay, braving the elements, until children began to take them back, anything that was still workable.

To protect themselves against the Russians the women covered themselves with ashes to make themselves look old, hobbled around on crutches or painted on red spots to feign disease. In a village near Greifenberg, in the western part of East Pomerania, the squire's wife Käthe von Normann took the precaution of removing her false front tooth to make herself look older, and dressed herself in peasant costume. The other women adopted the same attire. It rarely worked – the Russians were none too choosy anyhow, and the victims ranged in age from tiny children to great-grandmothers. Others kept their children by them at all times. Libussa von Krockow had recently given birth, and the baby at her breast proved a disincentive to Russian attacks. The Russians were often very taken with the German children, hugging and kissing them and giving them things to eat.

Käthe von Normann saw her first Russians on 5 March. An officer asked for her gold watch, telling her that his own had been destroyed when his hand was wounded. Frau von Normann tried to ascertain whether this was true or not, but he hid his hand. The next thing he needed was a race-horse. Her horse was led out and she began to cry. 'Why woman cry?' the officer asked in fractured German. 'About an animal, it is war, and about people.' A short while later the horse returned by itself, having thrown its Russian rider.[23]

The next visitors were a couple of grimy soldiers demanding shoes. Philipp von Normann was obliged to hand over his own. When they noticed his wife one of the men uttered the terrible words, 'Frau, komm!' Käthe von Normann did not know what he wanted and ran behind her husband, sobbing. The man shouted to her again to come, but his companion began to yell at him, and both left. Herr von Normann had to explain to his wife what was at stake: 'It might happen now that I will have to protect you, and then I shall be shot.' They assembled the family in one room and prepared for the siege.[24]

The Russians moved into the house, together with an interpreter, who counselled them to lock themselves in at night. That night they were helpless to prevent the Russians from stealing the silver, making off with it over the sleeping children. Next they found the schnapps. Frau von

Normann's mother was obliged to try each bottle first, lest it be poisoned. She replied with a few lines of broken Polish that had no effect on the Russians. They drank three of the four bottles, then fell asleep, and the Normanns were relieved to hear their snores. Käthe's mother had indeed prepared poison, but for them. Philipp von Normann refused to countenance suicide: 'It is still a sin, and even if we can justify it for ourselves, the three children have a right to live. We cannot justify it to God.'[25] Dawn was an age coming. While Herr von Normann went out into the farmyard, his wife went to the kitchen where she found Russian women soldiers with unruly hair, washing themselves. The boarders had run through a stock of some 3,000 eggs that had been destined for the military hospital; the lavatories were a sight to behold.

The Russians were becoming ever bolder in their demands. Philipp lost his watch, his wedding ring and his signet ring. Then he was interrogated. Although he had not been a member of the Party (the Polish estate workers confirmed this), his military ID was enough to condemn him. He was taken away. He hugged his wife and children: 'God protect you!' He died of dysentery in a Russian camp in Schwiebus in May.[26]

It was Käthe von Normann's turn next. She was told to go with the soldiers. She sent for a worker who could translate: she would go only with her children, otherwise they should shoot all four of them straight away. The Russians reconsidered: she and her family had five minutes to pack and get out of the house. Soon afterwards she saw the Russian general arrive.

As the women of the estate left *en masse* to find a refuge, the Russians kept coming back to search for arms and watches. Then they caught sight of a Frau Westphal and tried to drag her away. She was defended by her ten-year-old son with an axe, until the Russians finally desisted and merely robbed her of a pot of lard. The women made for comparative shelter in the woods, although the weather was bitterly cold and there were frequent snowfalls. Eventually they found quarters in one of the many farmhouses abandoned by Germans fleeing across the Oder. The usual news came in from the neighbouring villages: a woman raped twenty times, and she was not the only one. Frau von Normann looked at her son. 'He doesn't cry, but the sight of indescribable misery in the eyes of my ten year old I shall never forget so long as I live.'[27]

On 12 March rumours reached Käthe von Normann that Polish units had occupied some of the local villages. She drew the wrong conclusions – she thought they would want to see the farms working again under their industrious German owners. She had no inkling, any more than anyone else, that her land had already been promised to the Poles.

It was on 30 March that General Berling's First Polish Army raised their flag on Danzig town hall. The fighting had come to an end, and the people were gradually emerging from the cellars where they had lived through the Russian shelling. The Western Allies were informed that a *Wojewoda* or provincial governor had been appointed. Only later did the Americans realise that this was all part of the *fait accompli*, and that Danzig was going to be incorporated into a Polish state shifted westwards, to allow the Soviets to hang on to the territory they had negotiated over with Ribbentrop in 1939.[28]

The Soviets estimated that 39,000 dead bodies lay in the city. They had captured 10,000 German soldiers. Others held out on the tip of the Hela Peninsula where General von Sauken was performing a remarkable job in transporting citizens and troops to Schleswig-Holstein. Some 1,200,000 escaped the Red Army in this way before Sauken capitulated on 9 May. Not all of them survived the crossing. Two out of four barges containing prisoners from the Stutthof concentration camp at the mouth of the Vistula failed to make it: one was scuttled by the SS, the other was bombed by the RAF. The two that reached Neustadt, north of Lübeck, were fired on by SS men and naval personnel.[29] The Russians did not actually bother to enter Stutthof until 9 May, more than a month after the fall of Danzig. Stutthof was just one of 2,000 camps, great and small, liberated by the Allies between the autumn of 1944 and the late spring of 1945. Most of the prisoners at Stutthof were women, and most of the women Jews. About 3,000 had been shot or thrown into the icy waters of the Bight in January.[30]

Germany's prisons were also evacuated. Once again it seemed that the Nazis did not want the world to know what they had been perpetrating. In November prisons had been emptied on the left bank of the Rhine. A month later they emptied the gaols of Königsberg. The inmates were transferred to penal institutions in central Germany. Prisoners were divided into three groups: those who could be released; those who could be despatched to army formations; and those who were under no circumstance to be liberated. This last group was largely made up of racial types that were anathema to the Nazis: Jews and 'half-Jews' above all, but gypsies, Poles and Czechs as well. Also in this category were the worst criminals – murderers and psychopaths. These could be shot if necessary.[31]

The marches took place in a fiercely cold winter, and many died. Nonetheless the death rate was not as high as on the similar treks that took place on the closing of the extermination and concentration camps. It has been estimated there were fifty-two of these 'death marches' involving 69,000 people, of whom 59 per cent perished.[32] Women prisoners proved frailer, and many were raped by retreating German soldiers, or captured and killed by the Red Army. The prison warders who accompanied the treks were not as brutal as concentration camp guards, and up to a third of the convicts managed to escape. More closely watched were the 'NN' or *Nacht und Nebel* (night and fog) prisoners, who had simply been abducted and never formally tried. At best they were to be transferred to a concentration camp; at worst shot.[33]

In Danzig it was open season for the Russian soldiers once again. They raped, murdered and pillaged. Women between the ages of twelve and seventy-five were raped; boys who sought to rescue their mothers were pitilessly shot. The Russians defiled the ancient Cathedral of Oliva and raped the Sisters of Mercy. Later they put the building to the torch. In the hospitals both nurses and female doctors were subjected to the same outrages after the soldiers drank surgical spirit. Nurses were raped over the bodies of unconscious patients in the operating theatres together with the women in the maternity ward. Doctors who tried to stop this were simply gunned down. The Poles behaved as badly as the Russians. Many Danzigers took their own lives.[34] The men were rounded up, beaten and thrown into the concentration camp at Matzkau. From there 800 to 1,000 were despatched to Russia twice daily.

The scene is familiar from Günter Grass's novel *The Tin Drum* of 1959. Grass was a Danziger, and, although he was serving with the Waffen-SS when Danzig fell, he speaks with authority. When the Russians break into his 'presumed' father's grocers shop they rape the widow Greff while playing with little Kurt. Rapists and child-lovers – two clichés of the invasion. Not all Red Army soldiers spared children by any means, and not all of them were rapists either. The protagonist Oskar Matzerath's father famously swallows his Nazi Party badge to conceal it, choking to death in the process: a powerful metaphor for Germany in its hour of defeat.[35] In his 2002 novella *Im Krebsgang* about the sinking of the *Wilhelm Gustloff* at the end of January 1945 Grass has returned to the theme. The ship was being used as part of the efforts to evacuate the German population. Anything up to 9,000 people died in the icy waters, many of them children. It was the worst maritime tragedy of all time.[36]

Silesia

As the Red Army approached German Silesia it liberated the camps at Auschwitz. The sight that confronted its soldiers doubtless sharpened their resolve when it came to the Germans. The Russians arrived on the heels of the retreating SS, which had been busy destroying the evidence of what had gone on there. Twenty-nine out of thirty-five storerooms had also been destroyed, but in the six that remained there was more than enough evidence to condemn them: 368,280 men's suits, 836,255 women's coats and dresses and 5,525 pairs of women's shoes. In the tannery they found seven tons of human hair. Seven thousand inmates survived to greet them. Their places were taken by German POWs and Silesian civilians.

The rest of the victims of Nazi terror had been hurriedly marched towards the Reich to the more political camps that were in German and Austrian territory. Mauthausen, which had not been a Jewish camp before, suddenly became one; Sachsenhausen, Ravensbrück and Buchenwald were similarly transformed. Belsen was crammed to bursting point with Jewish prisoners, many of them already suffering from typhus. Other camps that were restocked in this way were Dora Mittelbau, Gross Rosen and Flossenbürg. Thousands died *en route*.[37]

The Russians reached the old Silesian frontier as early as 19 January 1945. The Gauleiter had proclaimed, 'They will not cross the Silesian border.' The next day he authorised the departure of 700,000 Breslauer, most of them women and children who marched off to Germany in temperatures of twenty degrees below zero.[38] Some arrived in Dresden and were camping in the streets when the Anglo-Americans destroyed the city. Others went to Berlin, where they were burned to death in the great February raids. The capital of Lower Silesia, Breslau was surrounded on 16 February; it finally surrendered on 6 May. The day before, Hitler's last favourite, Field Marshal Ferdinand Schörner, marched his troops away leaving the commander of the garrison, General Niehoff, to go to the Villa Colonia to sign the capitulation. Niehoff's soldiers were led off to captivity in the east. The city had been one of Hitler's *Kesseln*: fortresses to be defended to the last drop of German blood. It had suffered horribly, and so had its people. Now they hung white flags from their windows and prepared for the ordeal.

Those who escaped from Breslau crossed the Neisse river at Görlitz. Conditions were so bad there that it has been described as 'the worst city in Germany' at the time. In one appalling incident thirty women were driven into a barn and raped. When one refused she was shot. The local Soviet commander heard about the atrocity and went to the barn and shot four of his own men. In another incident eight Russian soldiers died after drinking methylated spirits. Forty more were struck blind.[39]

Apart from hunting down women to rape, the Russians were anxious to weed out the major Nazis of Breslau. On 7 May the Red Army deliberately started fires in the ruins. What was left of the city was looted. On 10 May the library of the university or Leopoldina for which Brahms had written his famous Academic Festival Overture went up in flames; on the 15th it was the turn of the city museum. On the same day the twin towers of one of the city's great *Backsteingotik* churches – St Mary Magdalene – were blown up. Rival units fought over the remaining food left by the Germans. 'The idea that Breslau had been completely destroyed by the siege was a post-war fiction.'[40]

The occupation followed the usual pattern of three waves: first came the bombardment and the armies; these were replaced by the second force that took possession of the land, and anything else for that matter, including the women; and finally the Poles came in their wake. The last chunk of Silesia to be taken was the county of Glatz and the Riesengebirge mountains, which fell to the Red Army only after the ceasefire, so that at least the quaint villages and the town of Glatz were spared destruction.[41] After the initial rage and lust abated, the Soviet armies turned their hands to de-montage. On 1 June they dismantled the power station at Kraftborn. The major factories went next, followed by street lights, overhead cables and freight trains. The *soldateska* continued to steal watches, window frames, wheelbarrows and bicycles. They also took every piano they could find.

In the Upper Silesian town of Steinau one mother of two small children frankly described her ordeal at the hands of the Red Army: 'A young Russian with a pistol in his hand came to fetch me. I have to admit that I was so frightened (and not just of the pistol) that I could not hold my blad-der. That didn't disturb him in the least. You got used to it soon enough and realised there was no point in putting up a fight.'[42] Later she went with her heavily pregnant sister to see a Russian doctor, believing that he would be a civilised man. They were both raped by the medic and a lieutenant, even though she herself was menstruating. That was no disincentive either.[43]

The soldiers raped every female they found; one twelve-year-old girl complained of the terrible tearing they had caused her. On another occa-sion when all the surviving Steinauer were taking refuge in a cellar and the women were once again threatened with gang rape, this same mother gave her children coffee that had been laced with poison. But the dose was not strong enough to do them any harm. She thought she was doing the right thing then: 'I can only assure people that a mother never believes her-self more holy than at that moment.' When she was subjected to what she feared would be rape by an entire platoon, she remembered a Russian word for 'child'. The rapist got up and escorted her from the room, before the eyes of the others waiting their turn. The Steinau woman repeated the story – often told – that the Russians treated children with kindness. She had seen a tank come up to a child in the middle of a road and the driver climb out and pick up the boy and place him on the pavement.[44]

Peace came to Europe two days after the Russians took Breslau. The Breslauer scarcely noticed. The remaining German citizens were well behind the lines. Their fate was mostly decided: unless the Western Allies were capable of pulling a rabbit out of a hat at the Peace Conference, Prussia's second city would fall to Poland and they would be driven west.

Brandenburg

The Red Army encountered death in all its forms on the road to the German capital. At the Sonnenburg Prison – 'die Sonne' as it had been known to its inmates – they found that 800 chiefly foreign prisoners had been slaughtered as recently as 30 January 1945, and it had not been deemed worth while to repatriate them across the Oder.[45] The last batch of prisoners to be executed at Brandenburg-Görden were killed on 20 April, Hitler's birthday. The Russians liberated the prison a week later. The Russians, accompanied by Polish soldiers, chanced upon Sachsenhausen concentration camp as they moved to invest Berlin. The camp was in Oranienburg, and the fall of that former royal borough brought it home to Hitler that his days were numbered.

There were just 5,000 prisoners left in Sachsenhausen of a population that had reached 50,000. The rest had been taken on 'death marches'.[46] As in most concentration camps, a number of Sachsenhausen's prisoners had been out-housed, in this case in smaller camps in Lieberose and Schwarzheide in the Mark Brandenburg. This had been the fate of many of the Jews brought to Sachsenhausen from Slovakia and Auschwitz. As the Russians closed in on the Mark, the prisoners were marched out of the camps towards the coast. Many were beaten to death or shot on the way. The camp administrators, including the notorious Obersturmbannführer Höss, also fled from their HQ in Ravensbrück. They ran to the comparative safety of Flensburg to seek out their master Himmler. The latter advised Höss to save his skin by crossing into Denmark. Höss received false papers as Able Seaman Franz Lang, but was caught and hanged for all that.[47]

In the middle of May, the writer and journalist Margret Boveri finally made it to her country cottage in Teupitz in the Spreewald. She and a Frau Becker undertook a hair-raising journey on bicycles, dodging – successfully and not so successfully – the Soviet troops who wanted to appropriate their valuable vehicles. They found it sinister that the place names had been crossed out and rewritten in Cyrillic script, which they took for a sign that eastern Germany was to be incorporated into the Soviet Empire.

> The place seemed to have died, even if most of the houses seemed undamaged from the outside [in the square a few corpses in uniform were lying around, stiff like giant puppets]; the house was completely wrecked behind which we moor the boat on our trips into the little town, the next-door property likewise. On Kohlgarten (our peninsula), I spoke to one man only. He said, 'My child is dead, my wife in the hospital.' In my house I found the usual picture of destruction: everything was shattered, smashed and plundered, and the three boats were gone. The clothes had all been taken, just like the food, down to the last grain of salt; the last naturally snatched by our dear compatriots. My archive portfolios were strewn about the place. The oil paint for painting the house had been emptied out and everything was stuck to it. In the flower beds cows and horses had grazed and for the first time we found some proper manure.[48]

The Schloss had taken the brunt of the destruction: the lords had fled, presumed dead, and the Russians had turned the building into a hospital; despite that they spent the night bawling and brawling and playing gramophone records. The two women made their way back to Berlin. The normally resilient Frau Becker was reduced to tears by the sight of German civilians being marched into captivity. Those who straggled or stumbled were beaten with whips.[49] Ruth Friedrich and her doctor friend Frank went on a journey into Brandenburg in pursuit of food. They stopped at a country inn. Eventually a woman came out with a headscarf pulled down over her brow: the usual device to conceal her age from the rapists. Here and there they could see some soiled straw, but nothing else. They asked the peasant woman if she had food. She told them it had all been stolen. 'Russians or Germans?' Frank asked. 'Thieves,' the woman replied impassively. The pair ran into a trek on the road. These unfortunates were aged between twelve and thirty. One of the children told her, 'We are all going to die . . . Why not? Death is not the worst thing.'[50]

Liberation from the West

The Rhineland

The Rhineland was the first part of Germany to be liberated from the west, and the first city was Aachen. The place of Charlemagne's coronation had been pitilessly pummelled by Anglo-American bombers so that there was little left of it. Of the 15,000 homes in the city only a fifth were vaguely intact. The American-installed administration estimated that they could make the damaged properties habitable within a year, but to rebuild the city would take twenty.[51]

One of the first Americans into Aachen was Saul Padover, who was then working for the Psychological Warfare Division. He followed behind the troops, interviewing Germans to compile a dossier on their affiliation to Nazism. His memoirs of the campaign provide a variety of snapshots, but many of them are coloured by the anti-German propaganda he was cooking up as he went. In Jülich he found two Flemings who had been living the life of Riley in an air-raid shelter. They believed themselves the only civilians left in the bombed-out town, and had a huge stock of champagne and cognac, tins of food, eggs and chicken. In their 'drowsy moments' they read travel books or romantic novels.[52]

Padover was keen to record the moral loucheness of the German survivors. Wiesbaden 'was packed with German civilians, many of whom were gaily attired. There were lots of pretty girls, and they smiled at us broadly and invitingly.'* The Americans had entered the spa town on 28 March 1945 and the defenders had prudently tossed their weapons into whatever expanse of water they could find. The Americans fenced off the centre of town with barbed wire and moved into the Hotel Rose. Denazification began on 10 April, when all Pgs and SA men were asked to report to the American authorities.[53]

Missie Vassiltchikov managed to get herself attached as a nurse to a convoy of children from Bremen who were returning home. They had been sent to Austria after the destruction of the city by bombing. For the Russian-born Missie it was the first time she had seen her country of adoption for a year. The train passed though Munich in the middle of the night. All that remained of the station was 'a huge iron skeleton'. She caught a glimpse of Nuremberg, Bamberg and Würzburg. They looked much the same – ruins. She jumped train at Fulda and eventually made it to Hanau, Frankfurt and Geisenheim by hitching lifts from engine drivers. She was trying to reach the Metternichs at their bombed-out home among the vines of Schloss Johannisberg in the Rheingau. Her sister Tatiana was

---

* The sexual attraction of conquerors to the women of the defeated should have appealed to the 'psychologist'. The straitlaced Helmuth James von Moltke had been shocked when he visited Paris in August 1940 to find the women 'positively queuing up to get a German soldier into bed' (*Letters to Freya*, London 1991, 97).

married to Prince Paul von Metternich. 'It took me quite some time to reach the ruined castle. It, too, was a sorry sight. Only one of the gate-houses still stands.'[54]

The Americans had moved into the Mumm property next door. They were behaving badly – throwing furniture and china out of the windows and giving away the clothes from the wardrobes to the 'Fräuleins'. Brat von Mumm had just been released from a POW camp near Rheims. He had been arrested at the champagne house that he had taken over in 1940 in the wake of the German advance. It had been seized by the French state in 1914 as a 'bien d'ennemi'. He was living elsewhere as his house had been declared off-limits. There was not much to eat, but the wine was a consolation. The majordomo served Missie exquisite things, muttering each separate vintage in her ear.[55]

Elena Skrjabina was another Russian, if not quite as grand as Missie, a relative of the composer. She had been pressed into labour service by the Nazis in Russia and put to work in a factory in Bendorf on the outskirts of Koblenz where she seems to have been well treated. When the Americans arrived in April the Russian girls all feared the worst. Drunken GIs hammered on the door. When that failed they tried to lure the women away from their friends and plundered their meagre possessions. As with the Russians on the other side of the country, alcohol tended to amplify the dangers: 'The Americans found large supplies of Rhine wine which had been kept for years in the cellars . . . they were dreadfully drunk.' Later Elena confirmed that the Americans had 'emptied all the cellars' as they passed through.[56]

Before they left, a friendly American doctor brought the Russian women 'cotton-like' bread that proved – to their evident surprise – 'completely edible'.[57] Koblenz and its environs were picked over by a number of nations before the area settled down to being French. First the Russians came up from the local camp and tried to throttle the factory manager. They then smashed anything they could find. In June the area was occupied by Belgian troops. On 2 July worried Germans declared 'with horror that we would be occupied by the French'.[58]

Carl Zuckmayer was a Rhinelander by birth. He had fled Germany after the Nazis burned his books and became an American citizen in 1939. The sight of the burned-out shell* of his parents' house in the cathedral city of Mainz brought home the scale of the destruction and made him aware of the enormity of the task ahead. Germany was still full of contrasts: 'From

---

* Mainz was bombed early on in the war, and grass was already growing on the ruins.

the vision of the destroyed Badger-house* to the completely unchanged farmhouse parlour in the Weismühl, from Heidelberg to the German Theatre, from the town park in Schöneberg to the Riemergasse, from the first night in Zurich to the morning celebrations in Vienna, from the out- rages and obscenities with our "Intelligence" and so forth – how can a heart bear it.'[59] Zuckmayer listened to the German soul among the ruins that winter. He went to Frankfurt-am-Main and gazed at the remains of the Römerberg, the medieval core of the city. A woman caught him gaping in astonishment at the extent of the damage and said in a dialect he had known from childhood: 'Yes, that's what we wanted all right, and that's what we got.'[60]

Karl-Heinz Bohrer was ten when the Americans arrived in the village where he was living in his grandparents' holiday home near Remagen Bridge. The Wehrmacht had famously failed to blow up the bridge, and the Americans were able to form an impressive bridgehead on the eastern bank of the Rhine before the structure collapsed. Young German boys had been taught that the Americans were cowards, who fought wars by dropping bombs. Karl-Heinz had seen the disembowelled body of a black airman in the snow. The Americans took him prisoner briefly, because he was wearing a steel helmet to take some milk over a dangerous meadow. The village was searched for arms. Meanwhile the old men and young boys were lined up against a wall with their hands up. Karl-Heinz did not find the experience frightening, but rather exhilarating. The first indica- tion that peace had come was the silence. The war had gone elsewhere, across the Rhine, towards the centre of Germany. Where he was, it was over.

Bavaria

The East Prussian writer Ernst Wiechert had been waiting for this moment. He had suffered at the hands of the Nazis, who had thrown him into Buchenwald. Now he could muster a brief moment of happiness: 'The patient had been stronger than the strong.' American forces passed through the village. One moment they were there, the next they were gone, but 'with the dust behind their vehicles an era sank; one of evil, darkness and bloody violence and we didn't have to think of the past, but of what was to come . . .'[61] Wiechert was refreshed by the thought that the guillotine would cease its bloody business, that the gallows would rot, that

* Zuckmayer called his parents 'the Badgers'.

death would cease its nightly visits to women and children in cellars. His wish was not to be granted at once.

Once Wiechert explained to the Americans who he was, they treated him with kindness. The CO sent up a couple of men to keep watch over his house and one of them killed a deer for him – 'so that you don't go hungry', he said. It was a world of humanity Germans had forgotten over the past dozen years. But not all the Allies proved such perfect gentle knights. When the French came four days later they surprised the house while the guards were off duty, locked the Wiecherts in the kitchen and stole everything of value: silver, jewellery, watches and typewriters.[62]

Wiechert was a celebrity and now he received visits from the literary world in uniform: 'Captain' Auden, one of Thomas Mann's sons-in-law, Mann's son Golo, and Pastor Niemöller (another German who had suffered under the Nazis) and his wife, together with numerous journalists. Wiechert was not happy with his own people, however. His outspoken attitude to Nazism and the privileged treatment accorded to him by the Americans aroused the envy of the locals. His writings were deplored and the man who had preferred inner emigration, and criticised those who had actually left, was forced to flee to Switzerland, at a time when other exiles were drifting home.

The Jew Victor Klemperer had made a miraculous escape from the ashes of Dresden. He had kept his head down in a small Bavarian village until the war ended. On 11 May he also expressed his shock at the German attitude to the very recent past.

> The people are absolutely without history, in every respect. In the evening a young woman came . . . young, not unintelligent. She seemed to be originally from Munich, and had been by bicycle to Munich for a day . . . I asked the woman if she had heard anything of Hitler and the other big names of the NSDAP: *no*, she had not had time to ask about that, in other words: this did not interest her any more. The Third Reich is already as good as forgotten, everyone had been opposed to it, had 'always' been opposed.[63]

Klemperer naturally saw things from his perspective. Like many other Germans, the Munich woman had evidently lost faith in Nazism some time before; with the terror apparatus halted, she could now breathe freely.

Jewish prisoners in an outside dependency of Dachau could not believe their eyes when they saw American tanks flying white flags. They wondered if they were imagining things. They thought at first it might be a German trick. Once they had conquered their apprehensions they went down to the streets where the Americans were waiting. They tidied up their prison uniforms on the way.[64]

The French reached Jettingen on 26 April. It was a pretty old town filled with half-timbered houses. Ursula von Kardorff, a former journalist from an old Prussian noble family who had been in contact with many members of the opposition to Hitler, had taken refuge there since fleeing Berlin in February. Her decision to head for Jettingen had been influenced by the fact that it was the home town of Claus Schenk von Stauffenberg, the man who had placed the bomb at the Wolfsschanze in the July Plot against Hitler of 1944. Suddenly the main street was filled with men in khaki uniforms. The next day they politely requisitioned her room at the Hotel Adler and evicted her friends from the Schloss, although the officer in charge said that the valuables could be locked up in the dining room, and they could take the key away with them.

The gloves were off the next day when 'two nasty characters' came round to her digs in pursuit of eggs and 'snaps'. Ursula von Kardorff was firm with them. 'Wir die besten Soldaten of the world!' they shouted at her. 'I don't believe it,' she replied. Later she had a furious argument with a Gaullist officer, who offered her coffee for all that. He told her that the Berliners would suffer the same fate as the Russians under German occupation: 'I became angry. I told him that the fate of the Germans would not be so easy to deal with. I had not risked life and limb for twelve years fighting against the Nazis in order to be held to account for all the crimes committed by the SS. Both my brothers fought in Russia and one died there, and they would never have behaved as the French are doing now at the Klingenburg [Schloss in Jettingen].'[65] The French captain was impressed. The plunder ceased, and Ursula von Kardorff was able to indulge a few long-cherished ambitions, such as throwing a collection of Party badges into the River Mindel. "We are now free from the Nazis, there is no Gestapo now to summons, disturb, arrest, torture or persecute us. We cannot praise our good fortune enough for this; but even now we are not free, we must still obey and comply with the curfew, and follow the orders as they are posted.'[66]

The other occupying army (the Americans had arrived in the wake of the French) presented few problems at first. Ursula von Kardorff was concealing the identity of her friend Wilhelm Bürklin, who was a colonel of the General Staff. In the eyes of the Western Allies a General Staff officer was an even more pungent commodity than a high-ranking Nazi. Bürklin had learned to keep his mouth shut when the Americans were present. They brought the women chocolate and spoke to them about politics in 'fabulously bad English'. Her friend Erna Bähr washed a uniform jacket for one of them, and received packets of tea and soap. Later they also received buckets filled with slops from the mess. These were granted to a stylish Berlin woman of their acquaintance, to feed her wolfhound. What the dog didn't want was given to them. Once they had volunteered to wash and iron the Americans' uniform blouses the women received unheard-of treats: real coffee, meat, salad and chocolate pudding, such as they had not eaten for years.[67]

Unlike some, Ursula von Kardorff lived those first moments of occupation in relative calm. She had found peace after the struggle and its aftermath that had seen so many of her friends strung up in Plötzensee Prison after the July Bomb Plot. The Allies were courteous towards this member of the old governing class, at least, and she had wine as a consolation in her 'small, warm island in the chaos'.[68]

Not everyone had been so lucky. When the women visited a Stauffenberg castle that had apparently been set on fire, the tenant took them over the plundered, windowless property and stopped to show them the bed where his daughter had been raped by American soldiers and the bullet holes in the wall. 'In a way I am not so unhappy about the plundering, it shows that soldiers will always be soldiers and that the others are therefore also not necessarily better than us.'[69]

One of Ursula von Kardorff's friends was Gräfin Alexandrine von Üxküll-Gyllenbrand, who was the sister of the Stauffenberg brothers' mother. The children of Claus and Berthold had been taken away by the SS after their fathers' arrest, and given new names and identities. A French POW had tipped off Ursula and Bärchen that the children were in Bad Sachsa. The two women set off on bicycles to obtain a pass for Gräfin von Üxküll so that she could go and fetch the children. They rode as far as Günzburg to see the local American commander, Captain Herrell. While they waited, two Americans made indecent propositions. Herrell had not heard of Graf von Stauffenberg, but examined the women to find out if they were 'good Germans'. They passed muster, and the Stauffenberg children were recovered in June.

On the night of 1 May, Ursula von Kardorff and her friends listened to their wireless set in secret. Hitler was dead.

> This is the moment that I have so hotly awaited these last years, and that for which I have prayed and implored. And now? As the National Anthem was played just now I stiffened as I have not done for years. Is that just sentimentality? Jürgen's death, the deportation of the Jews, our defiled land . . . Fritzi Schulenburg, Halem, Hassell, Leber, Haeften, Stauffenberg . . .

Mutius, Mandelsloh, Wolf Schulenburg, Raschke, three Schweinitz brothers, three Lehndorff brothers, Veltheim – all of them who have lost their lives
either here or out there, but for Germany?*

But we will manage. We will work, be happy with our lot, modest – and
trust in God. Maybe one day there will be a new, admirable Germany again.
The death of so many by the bullet or the rope – was it in vain? Or was
there a deeper purpose?[70]

The Americans liberated the terrible camp at Flossenbürg on 26 April.
Just 2,000 half-starved prisoners remained to welcome them. Another
15,000 had been marched off, many of them shot along the way.[71] It was
not until the 29th that the Americans reached Dachau. They were appalled
by what they saw. Dachau was the original concentration camp – a vast
place and the centre of 240 subsidiaries, some of which had operated for
barely a month, others for years.

Buchenwald had been built around Goethe's oak, Dachau had been set
up in a former artists' colony complete with Schloss, the Bavarian
Barbizon – famous for the misty light that rose off the marshy plain.
Dachau boasted the full range of prisoners, apart from the Jews, who had
been sent east when 'facilities' were created for them there. At the end of
the war they had returned and made up around a third of the inmates.[†] In
essence there were two camps at Dachau: a work camp with comparatively
healthy prisoners, and another, more sinister division, a 'Little Camp',
housing the bedraggled transfers.

Dachau was liberated by the 157th Infantry Regiment of the 45th US
Division, as well as by the 222nd of the 42nd, which converged on the

* Jürgen von Kardorff had died in action in Russia in 1943; Graf Fritz-Dietlof von der
Schulenburg together with Nikolaus von Halem, Ulrich von Hassell, Julius Leber, Werner
von Haeften, and Claus von Stauffenberg had all died as a result of their roles in 20 July 1944;
Bernhard von Mutius, Dietrich von Mandelsloh, Graf Wolf Werner von der Schulenburg,
Martin Raschke, Josias and Werner von Veltheim had all died as soldiers in the war. The
Lehndorffs and the Schweinitzes were noble Prussian families. For Graf Heinrich von
Lehndorff-Steinort see below p. 164; the others, presumably, died in Hitler's war.

† The inmates were recognisable by the coloured triangles they wore. The original concentration camp prisoners were political: they wore red; anti-social groups such as drunks,
beggars and the 'work-shy' wore black; the professional criminal, green; Jehovah's Witnesses,
lilac; returned emigrants, blue; homosexuals, pink. It should be recalled that homosexual-
ity was also illegal in Britain until the 1960s. The Jews wore two triangles stitched together
to make a Star of David, one yellow and one with the colour of the crime that had given
the pretext to incarcerate them. See Bruno Heilig, *Men Crucified*, London 1941, 73–4. The
lion's share at Dachau was made up of 44,401 'reds'. There were 22,100 Jews, 1,066 'blacks',
759 'greens', 126 Wehrmacht men, 110 'pinks' including one who had been readmitted after
discharge, 85 'lilacs' and 16 'blues'.

town to take a bridge that would bring them to their prize – Munich. They wanted to rescue the *Prominenten*, who had been housed in the 'Special Building', but they were already gone.* Various plans had been aired to kill the prisoners by bombing the camp or by poisoning their soup, but fortunately these had proved unfeasible in the chaos of the time.[72] There was a little resistance from the SS units guarding the place, but that was soon wound up, then the Americans found freight trains filled with as many as 2,000 corpses from the 'Little Camp'. There were the usual scenes of revulsion and physical sickness brought on by the sight and stench of the living and the dead. The Americans described the neat stacks of bodies as looking 'like cordwood'.

It was said that an SS man briefly turned his submachine gun on the prisoners who left their huts to watch the arrival of the Americans. This led to fury on the part of the conquerors, who shot anyone they found defending the complex and flushed the guards out of the watchtowers and killed them. They were left with an initial bag of 122 prisoners. One American shot the lot with his machine gun. Just as he was killing the last three who were standing – two with their hands up, the other defiant with his arms crossed[†] – an officer arrived and kicked him in the head. 'The violence of Dachau had a way of implicating all, even the liberators.'[73]

At first the prisoners indulged in an innocent game of making the guards dance to their tune. They shouted 'Mützen ab!' And the SS men had to doff their caps. Then the Americans aided and abetted the prisoners in their revenge. One soldier lent an inmate a bayonet to behead a guard. A kapo was found lying naked with cuts all over his body and a gunshot wound to his head. They had rubbed salt into his wounds. Another was beaten to death with spades. Other guards were shot in the legs to immobilise them. Later reports drew a veil over what happened then, although it is clear that some of the Germans were ripped limb from limb. It seems that around forty more guards and kapos died this way.[74]

Once enough blood had been let to satisfy occupants and occupiers, the Americans were shown over the camp. The crematoria and the gas chamber were an important part of the tour, although it was never clear whether the latter had been put to use. The normal method of execution was the *Genickschuss* – a shot in the back of the head – and there was a special part of the camp where the killing took place.[75] To gas the Dachauer, the usual

* See below pp. 82–4.
† There is a photograph of this.

method was to transfer them to Hartheim, across the border in Austria. Over 3,000 died in this way.[76]

The prisoners were moved into the SS barracks, but they continued to die in droves. In May alone, 2,266 perished.[77] Later the Americans intercepted a party of 3,000 prisoners from Straubing Prison that had been sent to Dachau but had been forced to turn back when the warders learned that Dachau had been liberated.[78]

In the bombed-out towns and cities a humanitarian disaster loomed. In Bayreuth, for example, the water was contaminated, the sewers fractured. Typhus and diphtheria swept through the town. There was no medicine left to deal with the epidemic.[79]

Holstein and Hanover

Germany capitulated unconditionally on 8 May 1945, but it wasn't quite true that the Allies were the only power in the land. For the time being Hitler's chosen successor Admiral Dönitz still dressed himself with the trappings of authority in Flensburg on the Schleswig-Holstein coast, albeit surrounded by British troops under Field Marshal Montgomery. The arrangement of his ministerial portfolios had been bequeathed by Hitler in his political testament, but Dönitz tore up the list and appointed his own government of technocrats. Speer was one of only two survivors from the old elite, the others had been at most junior ministers: Stuckart, Backe, Seldte and Dorpmüller. Dönitz sought to divorce his regime from the Party. He chose Hitler's finance minister Graf Lutz Schwerin von Krosigk to be his foreign minister and chancellor, a man with strong anti-Bolshevik views like his master. Dönitz liked the idea of a return to the political thinking of 1933–4 when President von Hindenburg was still alive. He would have an active chancellor, and in himself a president who applied the brakes.[80] Schwerin von Krosigk refused to be chancellor, however – he didn't like the name. He became 'leading minister' instead.[81]

Everywhere Germans were laying down their arms. In Italy Kesselring surrendered on the 2 May. Dönitz was in Plön at the time, with the British army rapidly advancing on him. His government decided to move to the Baltic coast and Flensburg. Dönitz and Schwerin von Krosigk spurned the worst Nazis when they came looking for work. Alfred Rosenberg, the Party ideologist, was one of these. He consoled himself with drink, and was seen about Dönitz's HQ, as drunk as a lord.[82] Himmler visited on the 3rd, 4th and 6th, but Dönitz considered him to be a political liability, and he was shown the road.[83] When Admiral von Friedeburg returned from

Rheims he brought back some of the pictures of German atrocities that had circulated during the signing of the peace.[84]

Churchill tolerated the Dönitz government for a while until the Soviets began to clamour for its elimination. He was of the view that the Germans could look after themselves to some degree. A campaign organised by Stalin appeared in *Pravda*. The Russians demanded an end to the 'militarist-fascist clique' around Dönitz.[85] Radio Moscow even suggested that Dönitz was trying to blackmail the West. That was on 18 May, when the Allies started to get tough with the admiral. Two days later *Pravda*, *Izvestia* and *Krasnaya Zvezda* demanded that Dönitz be deposed at once. Dönitz had been pleading with the West to launch a joint crusade against the Bolsheviks, and the Soviets naturally got wind of it. They also knew that the British had simply placed German arms at a distance from the captured men. Churchill must have been considering his options. If the Russians did not convince him, Eisenhower did, when he ordered Dönitz's arrest.[86] The Americans were not prepared to work with the relics of Hitler's regime, and there was JCS 1067 – the Joint Chiefs of Staff document laying down that no Nazis were allowed to continue in office.[87]

The Times postulated that the new German government consisted of nothing more than Dönitz, Schwerin von Krosigk and a microphone, and that the microphone had been the most important member.[88] Admiral Dönitz was not popular with Germans – Margret Boveri called him an *Obertrottel*, a supreme idiot – but many could see some good in Schwerin von Krosigk, who had entered the Cabinet under Franz von Papen in 1932 and seemed for the time and circumstances not only moderate but intelligent. This cut no ice with SHAEF, the Supreme Headquarters Allied Expeditionary Force. If Dönitz and the Flensburg government had any role it was only to disarm, disband and feed the Wehrmacht.

The Dönitz government must have been feeling over-confident of British love when on 11 May Field Marshal Busch gave a broadcast on Radio Flensburg to announce that he was in charge in Schleswig-Holstein, 'with the agreement of the British'.[89] The Allies had been using various high-ranking military officials to help them shut down the Wehrmacht and its organs,[90] but JCS 1067 made it clear that no Nazis were to remain in authority. Busch's broadcast aroused fury among the other Allies who suspected that Montgomery had recognised the Dönitz government.[91]

Not just the other Allies – the *Daily Mail* was outraged by this 'mysterious station'. Busch had let the cat out of the bag and Dönitz had sealed his fate.[92] Dönitz was giving himself airs and graces as well. British soldiers had to salute high-ranking German officers, which angered many.[93] The next day Churchill sent his 'Iron Curtain' telegram to Truman. He was worried, he told the American president, about what would happen when America transferred its forces to the Pacific and he was left alone with the French to face the Russians. The inference is clear: he might need German help.[94] There were a million German soldiers chewing the cud in Schleswig-Holstein; their weapons had been taken from them, but they were not far away.

Sir Bernard Montgomery had just returned from the Russian lines at Wismar. He gave orders that German weapons should not be destroyed, 'in case they might be needed for any reason'.[95] It may be that the sight of the Russians at close quarters had confirmed his worst fears. The Russians, on the other hand, were not pleased to learn that 'the Flensburg criminals', Hitler's designated successor and his ministers, were walking freely about the streets of the little port.[96] On 13 May the Allied Control Commission came to collect the chief of the German Armed Forces High Command (the OKW) Field Marshal Keitel and bear him off to captivity. Dönitz thought it prudent to remove a bust of Hitler from his office. He also ordered the end of the Hitler salute, but he drew the line at the Allied request that the Germans should cease wearing their medals. Admiral von Friedeburg was apprehensive about what the Allies would do, but Dönitz assured him that they would observe the Geneva Convention.[97]

On 17 May a Soviet officer joined the Allied team on the SHAEF passenger ship *Patria* and Dönitz was invited to appear before them in Flensburg harbour. He was received with pomp and had an interview with Bob Murphy, political adviser to SHAEF. Dönitz turned to his favourite theme: the Bolshevisation of Europe, and how the Germans were needed to prevent it. The Allies were also worried, but they didn't like it coming from him, any more than they had from Himmler. Albert Speer had decided to jump ship. He resigned from Dönitz's government and retired to his family in the doubtless palatial surroundings of Schloss Glücksburg.[98]

A day later – on the 18th – the Allies returned the visit to the seat of the Dönitz regime in the barracks at Mürwik. Their delegation was led by the British brigadier E. J. Foord and the American major-general Lowell Rooks. On 22 May Dönitz was summoned aboard the *Patria* for 9.45 the following morning. The Allied generals had received their instructions from Eisenhower. If Dönitz felt he had any claim to immunity as a head of state, he was rapidly disillusioned. He was told to consider himself a prisoner. General Lucius Clay of the Allied Control Commission had said that Dönitz was on the list of war criminals and would be treated as a POW.

The Allies sent the Germans away: 'Pack your bags!' they said.[99] Clay made it clear that all war criminals would pay for their acts with 'their lives, freedom, sweat and blood'.[100]

Three battalions of British troops commanded by Brigadier Churcher surrounded the government's HQ in the Mürwik Barracks and finally stormed it brandishing sten guns and grenades. The leading minister's cabinet meeting had just begun. 'Hände hoch! Ausziehen!' (Hands up! Strip!) The participants and their secretaries were put against a wall and strip-searched: Dönitz, Jodl and the rest. Schwerin von Krosigk allegedly found a Tommy tugging at his trousers saying, 'Bitte – please?', although it is hard to believe that they had any problem communicating with the former Rhodes Scholar.[101]

The leading minister tells the story differently: 'as nothing went unexamined, the blood went to my head. General von Trotha, who was standing next to me, noticed that I was on the point of turning round and lashing out with my fist. He whispered to me: "Keep smiling."' Schwerin von Krosigk felt Trotha had saved his life.[102] Some sources claim that the men were forced to strip naked, as well as the female secretaries the British had found in the other offices. Others suggest that their examination was confined to the areas below the waist.[103]

A British sergeant equipped with a surgical glove searched anuses and other orifices of ministers, officials and secretaries. Speer had been fetched from Schloss Glücksburg and was subjected to the same indignity. He thought it was because Himmler had slipped though the British net (by biting on a cyanide capsule) and they were determined it would not happen again, but Himmler died only later that day.[104] The idea of humiliating the prisoners could not have been far from their minds either. Admiral von Friedeburg poisoned himself in a lavatory to escape the defilement, as did Dönitz's secretary. Squaddies plundered Friedeburg's body.[105]

The only other person to be let off was the deputy chief of operations at the OKW, whose boots were so tight the Tommies couldn't get them off. The captain commanding the operation was so angry he ripped the German officer's *Ritterkreuz* from his neck and stamped on it.[106] Watches and rings vanished into the British soldiers' pockets. Dönitz's baggage was rifled and his bejewelled admiral's baton stolen. Schwerin von Krosigk also complained of theft. For three-quarters of an hour photographs and newsreel films were taken of the Germans while they stood in the courtyard with Tommies peering at them over the sights of their weapons. The pictures appeared in the British papers showing some of the men and women *en déshabille*. The headlines suggested that the *Herrenvolk* had been caught napping. The truth was they had not been given time to cover up after their examinations.[107] When Churchill heard the story, he was scandalised and wrote Montgomery a letter of protest. The Flensburg government had lasted three weeks.[108]

Charlotte von der Schulenburg knew the war was over when she saw a British jeep in Testorf, where she had taken refuge after her flight from Mecklenburg. East Holstein was to be turned into a huge detention camp for captured German soldiers. Chaos reigned until September when the post was restored and she was able to make contact with others in her situation. She learned that her mother and sister were still alive in the Russian Zone and hiked to Bremen to see Mausi Lehndorff, a member of the noble East Prussian clan, whose husband had been another of Hitler's victims following the abortive plot. The worry was how she and her children were to survive. She had lost everything in the east. Then she received a letter from one of her late husband's cousins. Jonny von der Schulenburg lived in the original family Schloss at Hehlen on the Weser. He invited her to stay and to bring her children with her. She was not altogether convinced: she had heard that the Hehlener Schulenburgs 'hätten nicht alle Tassen im Schrank' (an idiomatic translation would be 'A sandwich short of a picnic'.) She went to inspect the house with Marion Gräfin Dönhoff – later editor of *Die Zeit*.

They set off for the ruins of Hamburg. A bus took them to Hanover, where they were able to pick up a train to Hameln. The bridges over the Weser were all down and there were no trains leaving in that direction. Then she saw two men, one in a military leather coat, waiting on a low cart on rubber wheels drawn by a chestnut. This was Mathias von der Schulenburg and his cousin, the owner of Schloss Hehlen, Jonny. The house was filled with former German POWs that Jonny had invited back to live with him and drink up the contents of the cellar.

The house resembled so many that had been occupied by soldiers. In places the electric wiring had been pulled out; windows had been smashed; the books in the library lay scattered on the floor; there were empty bottles everywhere. Jonny gave Charlotte a lift back to Hanover the next day in a Fiat Topolino without doors in which he sat on a wobbly milking-stool. The servants often had to push it to get it started. Sometimes it needed a horse. That autumn she moved into Hehlen with her six children and the few belongings she had been able to take from the family Schloss at Trebbow in Mecklenburg. Their journey to the Schloss was an adventure in itself.

In Hamburg they were arrested for breaking the curfew and spent some days in a barracks with more POWs, who shared their meagre rations with the children. The latter were delighted with English white bread and ersatz honey. Antediluvian figures speaking an unintelligible language jumped on the bus seeking a lift to Bremen and were finally shaken off near Bergen-Belsen. In Celle they found quarters in a Red Cross camp that had been set up in a gym. In the ruins of Hanover they met Jonny – an apparition in a white linen suit.

Charlotte and her children were allotted a tower and a kitchen in the servants' quarters, so that they could maintain their independence from the wilder shores of the castle. A gemstone proved enough to procure a stove on the black market. With Jonny's permission, they collected furniture from other parts of the house. When Charlotte had finished, her tower room was so lovely that visitors compared it to the Marschallin's bedroom in Act One of *Der Rosenkavalier*.

In 1946 the entire population of an evacuated Upper Silesian village was accommodated in a back wing of the Schloss. The men were found work in the village and oven pipes protruded from the windows as they installed kitchens in their rooms. The bridge and courtyard buzzed with women and children dressed in traditional headscarves. That Christmas Charlotte organised a nativity play at the Schloss in which her children and the Silesians performed the roles. It was the village's first taste of post-war ecumenicalism, as the Silesians were all Catholics and the Hanoverians were Lutheran to a man. British soldiers came to hunt at the Schloss and paid for their pleasure in cigarettes and alcohol – much to Jonny's delight. The parties at the castle were as mad as ever as he drove his motorbike round the knights' hall and hurled bottles at the portraits of his ancestors.[109]

In the chaos that was Germany in 1945, it was hard to know if the writer Ernst Jünger had survived. Many of his friends and admirers had perished on Hitler's gibbets. Others had fallen victim to bombs and bullets – both soldiers and civilians. Jünger, however, was at home in his house in Kirchhorst near Celle in Hanover. He watched the American advance in a detached way. It literally passed him by. The black soldiers in the American army were the subject of much gossip. A little boy of nine told Jünger, 'I am frightened of him.' He meant a black GI. The Negroes were accused of perpetrating several rapes, in one instance of a fourteen-year-old girl in the village of Altwarmbuch.[110]

Americans and Poles searched Jünger's house, but he had wisely hidden incriminating objects such as his weapons (in the pond) and his hunting rifle (buried) and stashed away his collection of burgundy where he thought no one would find it: 'It would be a criminal offence to let nectar like this fall into the hands of the Kentucky men.'[111] Sadly for him, some GIs were billeted on him. The usual bands of DPs were stealing and murdering – coming for spirits, meat and bicycles – but Jünger had the Americans on the ground floor to protect him: 'downstairs is Wallenstein's Camp:* loudspeakers announce news of victory, patrols bring in prisoners whom they have tracked down in the bog'. Jünger read his way slowly through the Bible, turning to the poet Rückert and others when he wanted a break. He was relieved to hear that the Americans were not allowed to talk to the Germans.

All around him order was breaking down, and the Allies were doing little to restore it while they advanced on Berlin. On 28 April the owner of the neighbouring estate was killed by DPs looking for benzene. He had been tortured first. Another local had been tied to a car and dragged along the road. The villages were full of drunken American blacks with women on their arms, looking for beds. DPs would visit the men-less houses and 'feast like the suitors of Penelope'. Mussolini's and Hitler's deaths prompted more classical references: 'We are living now in the time of the fall of Galba, Otho and Vitellius, repeating events in every detail . . .'[112]

Some things could not be found in the lives of the later Augustan emperors. On 4 May he had two prisoners from nearby Belsen to breakfast, and was fascinated by their yellow faces and parchment-like skin. One of them had had one of the best positions in the camp: he was the kitchen-kapo, and if there were any food, he had first pick. On 6 May Jünger was visited by six Jews from the camp. The youngest was a boy of eleven. He watched the child devour a picture with his eyes. It was not just food they craved. And then the child was in raptures when he saw the Jüngers' cat.[113]

The novelist Jünger was calmly jotting down the stories brought to him by refugees. A woman from the east told him how prosperous Prussians had committed suicide *en masse*. During their trek they would look in at the windows of large houses and see a 'party of corpses sitting around a table covered with a cloth'.[114] Two American journalists came to see him; the day before they had visited a 'concentration camp on the outskirts of Weimar'. Jünger had not heard of Buchenwald. They told him about the crematorium and the sign that read 'Wash your hands. In this room cleanliness is a duty.' The job of the journalists was to 'put together a sort of spiritual stock-taking in our field of rubble'. He had seen no journalists for six years: it was the 'first thread in a new weave'. When they left they gave him some of their food.

* An allusion to Schiller's play of that name.

The war ended for the Kaiser's only daughter, Victoria Louise, on Hitler's Birthday, 20 April. She was living with her husband the Duke of Brunswick in Blanckenburg in the Harz Mountains when the Americans arrived. Soon after the Americans had paid a visit to the Schloss, the British came by. They were interested in some cases that had been lodged in the cellar. After the British left, Americans arrived to carry off the cases. They were unconcerned when they were told that the British had already claimed them. One of the Americans who came for them had been brought up in Potsdam, where he had played golf with the crown prince, William, and had been present at the arrest of her Nazi brother, Auwi, in Frankfurt.

Victoria Louise was much struck by the arrival of blacks – 'niggers', as she called them. They were, in her report, friendly and cheerful. To the princess's staff they shouted, 'We are slaves, now you are slaves!' The Americans behaved well in general, but the British who relieved them left a bad impression. The colonel ordered the duke and duchess to report to him; failed to get up when they entered the room; and threatened to shoot them because they had concealed weapons. Victoria Louise observed that it was not à propos to shoot a prince of the Hanoverian royal house, which was Britain's own! The guns in question had been locked up by the Americans in a wing of the house and the keys removed to the command post.[115]

Princess Victoria Louise opened the door one day to find her brother Oscar standing before her. He had left his house in Potsdam on foot and walked to safety. He was 'at the end of his strength. He had battled through the advancing American forces, through fields and thicket, from hiding place to hiding place, in constant fear of being taken prisoner'. Prince Oscar had begun the war as a regimental commander, and there had even been a suggestion that he should receive a division, until Hitler slapped it down. He wanted no heroes among the princes. Oscar's eldest son had been the first of the Hohenzollerns to die in action, in 1939. When there was a massive demonstration of royalist sympathy in Potsdam at the burial of the crown prince's eldest son, William, the following year, Hitler resolved to dismiss the princes from the armed forces.[116]

The British had their first experience of a Nazi death camp near Celle as they advanced towards the Elbe in the second week of April 1945. The 11th Armoured Division was pushing towards its military objectives when its forward troops were met by a Mercedes staff car containing two Wehrmacht colonels. They had come to offer them Bergen-Belsen camp, where, they said, the inmates were dying of typhus. It was three days before the British entered the camp, and they were naturally horrified by what they saw.[117]

Belsen was not an extermination camp like Auschwitz, Treblinka or Majdanek. It had been set up as recently as 1943 to house 'exchange Jews'. These were Jews with non-German passports who Himmler believed could be bartered for money or for German nationals in Allied captivity. The idea of selling Jews to the West went back to the abortive Evian Conference of 1938. Conditions at Belsen had been as good as any until the end of the war, when the SS began driving the inmates of the camps west, in order to prevent them falling into the hands of the advancing Red Army. As much as possible, evidence of the Final Solution was to be destroyed. Hitler was furious with Himmler when he learned on 13 or 14 April that the Americans had liberated Buchenwald and found 20,000 prisoners the SS had failed to evacuate or shoot. Hitler had barked into the telephone at the SS chief: '. . . make sure that your people don't become sentimental!'[118]

Large numbers of former prisoners from eastern camps were shipped into Belsen. They were not only Jews. Estimates for the number of Jews in Belsen at the time of the liberation vary, but at most they were not much more than half. There were prisoners from all over Europe as well as the usual concentration camp inmates: political prisoners, 'anti-social elements' and criminals – including homosexuals – who had contravened Article 175 of the Prussian Legal Code. Not only were the food and medical supplies inadequate to deal with them, but they brought typhus. Lack of food had resulted in outbreaks of cannibalism. By the time the British had made up their minds to go in, the plague had reached epidemic proportions. Over the next few weeks a quarter of the 60,000 inhabitants would die. Most of these were deemed to have been beyond medical care, but some died because the British were at a loss to know how to treat and feed them.[119] In hindsight it is easy to accuse them of negligence, but they still had military objectives. There was a war to be won, and a pressing need to prevent the Red Army from absorbing the whole of Germany. Himmler knew that many Britons wanted to push on and fight the Russians, and while he bartered Jews with the Swedish count Bernadotte, he hoped that he himself might be retained in the fight against Bolshevism.

The living skeletons of Belsen wrought their revenge on the hated kapos, throwing some 150 of them out of first-floor windows under the eyes of the British soldiers.[120]

Baden and Württemberg

The Badenese university town of Heidelberg was liberated by the Americans on 30 March. The philosopher Karl Jaspers recorded the event in his diary. He had been put out to grass because he refused to divorce his Jewish wife Gertrud – or Trudlein – and they had lived through recent years in mortal fear that she would be deported to the east.

> No electricity, no water, no gas. We are trying to equip ourselves. A spirit stove will do for a short time. Water can be fetched from the spring at the Klingentor. The young people are in the best mood. It is magnificent fun for them to live like Indians . . .
>
> . . . this morning the Americans arrived on the Neuenheimerlandstrasse, they found all the bridges destroyed and stood in front of them with tanks. They discovered the boathouse near the new bridge, took the paddleboats and paddled across the river, landing at the grammar school where they are stationed. They must have arrived upstream by the Neckar.
>
> Frau von Jaffe came to congratulate us that at last our Trudlein is free: a moment without words. It is a miracle that we are still alive.[121]

Jaspers clearly enjoyed the spectacle of the limp German resistance. It was not long before the Americans sought him out as a representative of the 'other Germany' and gave him responsibility for the university. Jaspers had none of the misgivings about the liberators that Germans felt elsewhere; when he delivered the principal speech on the reopening of parts of the university on 15 August, he dwelt on the experience of liberation. Most likely his attitude towards the Americans was one of heartfelt gratitude.[122]

The end of the war found the future mayor of Berlin and president of the Federal Republic Richard von Weizsäcker at a family chicken farm near Lindau on Lake Constance crammed full of family members, almost exclusively women. There was his sister, a refugee from East Prussia, whose husband had been missing since 1944 and was never to return; his aunt Olympia from Breslau, with her two daughters – both sons had been killed and her husband interned like his brother, the physicist Carl Friedrich. In the summer another pair joined them – his sister's parents-in-law, the eighty-year-old Siegfried Eulenburg (who had commanded the First Foot in the Great War) and his wife. They had come from their estates in East Prussia in an old landau driven by three horses.[123]

The town of Pforzheim had suffered horribly in the bombing. With great interest Alfred Döblin, novelist and psychiatrist, watched people climbing on top of heaps of rubble: 'What was their business there? Did they want to dig something out? They carried flowers in their hands. On the heap they set up crosses and signs. These were graves. They put down the flowers, knelt and said their prayers.'[124] Another writer, Ernst Jünger, witnessed the scenes in Pforzheim that year. He too saw the walls of rubble, the white crosses and the flowers for those who had been buried alive.[125]

Baden was also an objective of French forces, and it was in the Black Forest that their behaviour got out of hand. The French were officially supposed to follow behind the Americans, but, with the backing of de Gaulle, the commander de Lattre de Tassigny disobeyed orders. De Gaulle had told him, 'You must cross the Rhine even if the Americans are not agreeable . . . Karlsruhe and Stuttgart await you.'[126] The French II Army Corps had taken Speyer before advancing to Karlsruhe. On 12 April they reached Baden-Baden before entering the Black Forest and heading for Freudenstadt. A further French army was to join them there after liberating Strasbourg. Whether the French commander was in some way influenced by the name of the town is not easy to say now, but Freudenstadt (it means 'town of joy'), the so-called 'pearl of the Black Forest', was subjected to three days of killing, plunder, arson and rape.

There had been reports of a band of Werewolves under a Hans Zöberlein, who had recently killed German civilians he considered had lost some of their National Socialist zeal. The town, however, was undefended, and filled with hospitals, but it may be that the French were unaware of that; or it may be that the very absence of soldiers gave them the idea of getting their revenge for countless barbaric acts committed by the Germans during their occupation of France.[127] One of the French officers is supposed to have said, 'We are the avengers, the SS of the French Army.'[128]

On 17 April they shelled the small town, completely destroying the centre. The units that entered Freudenstadt were made up of French soldiers from the 5th Armoured Division, Foreign Legionaries and Moroccan and Algerian troops from the 2nd Moroccan and the 3rd Algerian Infantry Divisions. It is reported that local Polish workers joined in. From the first the French made it clear that the people were going to be properly punished. There would be three days of plunder. A sergeant said that the troops would be released from discipline, and a quartermaster added, 'In the next few nights no woman will go untouched.'[129]

The patients were robbed of their watches in the hospitals, and a Frenchman they found there was gunned down in his bed. The surviving houses were systematically destroyed with benzene: 649 were burned down in this way. It was now open season for any women aged between sixteen and eighty. It is generally said that the Moroccans behaved worst.[130] Anyone who tried to stand in the way was simply shot. One of the victims was a stout lady lorry-driver called Sofie Hengher who tried to stop the soldiers assaulting her children. After the French passed on, some 600 women reported to the local hospital. Ten per cent of those examined were pregnant. Seventy people had been killed. Freudenstadt was certainly the most prominent example of a breakdown of discipline in the French army, but there were others, and the French were not above threatening Königsfeld and the university town of Tübingen with similar treatment.

French soldiers' behaviour in Stuttgart, where perhaps 3,000 women and eight men were raped, was thought to have added to American fury at their overstepping their lines.* A further 500 women were raped in Vaihingen, where the French army found a large number of dead and dying in a satellite concentration camp. The villagers in nearby Neuenbürg were cleared out to make way for the sick and the French garrison.[131] In all these instances the Moroccans were blamed.[132] The American general Devers wrote to complain to de Lattre. Freudenstadt had not added to the reputation of the French army.[133] Later the Germans wanted to know who had allowed the troops to run riot in this way. The commander in Freudenstadt appeared to have been a swarthy southern type called Major Deleuze; but a Captain de l'Estrange was also mentioned, as well as a Major Chapigneulles and his adjutant, Poncet from Lorraine, who was a famous beater. Tortures were carried out by one Guyot and an alleged former Jesuit called Pinson. The British press blamed the atrocities on a Major de Castries, a scion of one of France's oldest families.

The French dug in at Stuttgart and refused to budge. On 13 May they held a provocative Joan of Arc Festival.[134] It was just a leap and a bound to the old university town of Tübingen. The 5th Tank Division arrived on 19 April. Tübingen had been saved by declaring itself a hospital town, but there was rape and pillage before the French calmed down. One of the first men to beard the French in the town hall was the professor of law, Carlo Schmid. His mother was a Catalan from near Perpignan and his perfect French must have made the invaders feel at home. He probably spoke less about his time in the administration of Lille during the war. On the 23rd he was denounced as a Werewolf, however, and locked up in a lavatory for two days. The French searched his house and found the texts of his Baudelaire translations.[135]

---

* R. F. Keeling (*Gruesome Harvest*, Chicago 1947, 56–7) gives the official figure as 1,198, but the Germans thought it more like 5,000.

On 9 November that year a Frenchman came home to Germany. It was the anniversary of both the Beer-Hall Putsch and Reichskristallnacht. Alfred Döblin had left Germany on 3 March 1933 and, after a harrowing escape, spent the war years in Hollywood. His ship docked in Le Havre. From the deck he watched 'a body of men, all dressed the same, disappearing into the belly of the vessel; they reappeared dragging casks and cases . . . They were Germans, prisoners of war. That is how I saw them again.'[136]

He had become a French citizen after leaving Germany. One of his sons had died fighting in the Vosges. After he had seen his friends he crossed the Rhine at Strasbourg. In the waters of the river 'there lay a felled elephant: the shattered railway bridge'. He was now in Germany. 'You see the fields, well laid out in an orderly land. They had cleaned up the meadows and swept the paths. The much lauded German woods: the trees were bare, a few still wearing the colourful autumn foliage . . . But now it became more clear: heaps of rubble, holes, grenade or bomb craters, the remaining backs of houses, then fruit trees again, bare with supports. A saw mill intact, but the houses next to it in ruins.' His train passed though the Black Forest: 'Then I see your misery and I see that you have not yet learned from what you have learned. It isn't easy. I'd like to help.'[137]

Upper Austria

As the Americans crossed into Austria they were able to paint a bigger picture of the Nazi death camps. In the last months of the war Jews had also been shipped from Auschwitz and Gross Rosen to Mauthausen in Upper Austria. A large number of them died or were put to death on the way. Up to now Mauthausen had been a criminal and political camp,* and many Austrian opponents of Nazism had been sent there from Dachau. Apart from Stutthof, which the Russians allowed to fester until 9 May, Mauthausen was the last big camp to be liberated, when the Americans went in on 5 May.[138] The most appalling sight in Mauthausen was the deadly quarry, where many prisoners lost their lives. It was called the 'Wiener Graben' after the thoroughfare in Vienna, because from here the stone was excavated for the streets of the capital.[139]

* In 1939 there were nearly 3,000 prisoners. Just under a thousand of these were 'greens' or criminals, and 688 were political prisoners. There were 930 'anti-socials', 143 Jehovah's Witnesses and 51 homosexuals. (Robert H. Abzug, *Inside the Vicious Heart*, New York and Oxford 1985, 106.)

The Americans found a fully formed committee waiting for them composed of Hans von Becker of the Fatherland Front, the communists Ludwig Soswinski and Heinz Duermayer – who had fought in Spain and was later chief of police in Vienna – Hans Maršálek of the Vienna Czechs, Bruno Schmitz, the son of the mayor of Vienna, and the former minister of justice Baron Hammerstein-Equord. Once again the concentration camp had formed a cadre for later Austrian political life.[140]

The Americans also liberated the camp at Gusen on the 5th. Gusen was part of the wider Mauthausen complex, which had around fifty satellites including Ebensee. There were between eight and ten thousand inmates including some 1,200 Jews housed in a separate compound. Roughly 3,000 of the prisoners were made up of the 'work-shy'. The Americans found evidence that inmates had been killed with gas: Russian typhus victims had been sealed up in their huts and gas canisters had been thrown in.[141]

The third big shock for American forces was Hartheim, which had been used principally for the extermination of the mentally ill. Some of the victims were housed in Niedernhart near Linz, but they were taken to Hartheim to be killed. The Americans compiled a report on the activities in Hartheim, and found evidence that the mental patients often fought their warders after their arrival in the Schloss, and that the Nazis suffered minor injuries at their hands.[142]

Tyrol

One dramatic discovery made by the Allies was the location of a clutch of *Prominenten* at Schloss Itter near Kitzbühel. This had been the prison for the French presidents Reynaud and Daladier and the generals Weygand and Gamelin, as well as trade-union leader Léon Jouhaux, Michel Clemenceau, the son of the statesman, the tennis star Jean Borotra, the politician and *résistant* Colonel de La Rocque and Madame Alfred Cailliau, sister of Charles de Gaulle. The Luftwaffe picket guarding the French had run away at the approach of the Americans, but it was feared that some local SS would harm the prisoners or seek to use them as bargaining tools to ensure a safe passage out of Austria. On 5 May the Schloss was indeed attacked by an SS unit that blew up an American tank. The prisoners helped defend the building. An Austrian, Major Gangl, was killed in the attack.[143]

One of the most bizarre liberations that April took place in the South Tyrol, Italian since 1919, but whose population was still largely German speaking. On 24 April a lorry – one of several – left Dachau concentration camp for Munich. It contained the former Abwehr officer and Munich lawyer Josef 'Ochsensepp'* Müller. Müller looked at the others squashed on to the benches in the back of the lorry: there were Hungarians like the former prime minister Miklós Kállay, his interior minister Peter Baron von Schell, the Dutch minister Dr van Dyck, the Greek field marshal Pagagos and his staff officer, the German generals Halder and Thomas, the former president of the Reichsbank Schacht, Stalin's nephew Kokorin, General Pjotr Privalov and eight RAF officers.

The lorries went south after Munich, crossing the old Austrian border near Kufstein before proceeding to Innsbruck and the concentration camp at Rosenheim. There the prisoners were taken out. In all, the lorries contained 136 people from seventeen nations. There were fourteen Britons, including a captain bearing the name of Churchill, although no relation, and a 'Wadim Greenewich' from the Passport Control Office – that is, MI6 – as well as his colleagues from the 1939 Venlo Incident, Stevens and Payne Best; there were five Russians; the French included the former prime minister Léon Blum and his wife, Gabriel Piquet, Bishop of Clermont-Ferrand, Prince Xavier of Bourbon-Parma and the writer Joseph Joos; the Poles included a Zamoyski; there were four Czechs; the Greeks sported their field marshal and no fewer than four major-generals; there was the Dutch minister and six Danes, a Norwegian, a Swede, a Swiss, a Latvian and four Italians, including the partisan Garibaldi – a descendant of the Risorgimento leader – and his chief of staff Ferrero; in the Hungarian team there was not only the prime minister but Admiral Horthy's son and his secretary; the Austrians numbered the former chancellor Schuschnigg and his wife and the pre-Anschluss mayor of Vienna, Schmitz, as well as the writer Konrad Praxmarer. The biggest delegation was naturally from Germany: State Secretary Pünder, Prince Philip of Hesse, Halder and his wife, the former military governor of Belgium General von Falkenhausen, the pastor Martin Niemöller, Prince Frederick Leopold of Prussia, Fabian von Schlabrendorff and Fritz Thyssen. Another group was made up of *Sippen*, that is relatives of the 20 July plotters: various Goerdelers, Stauffenbergs, Hammersteins, Lüttwitzes, Plettenbergs and one Gisevius (Hans Bernd had managed to escape), together with relatives of Jakob Kaiser, Isa Vermehren and Fey Pirzio-Biroli, the daughter of the hanged former ambassador to Rome, Ulrich von Hassell.[144]

The men and women were hostages of the SS: so-called *Prominenten* to be killed or bartered for freedom as the Allies tightened their grip on

---

* Literally 'Oxen Joe'. As a boy, Müller had looked after the cows on his parents' Bavarian farm.

Germany. At Rosenheim the Austrian *Prominenten* in particular were hor-rified to see Austrian SS guards mercilessly beating members of the Tyrolean freedom movement. The Austrians had themselves been in cap-tivity since March 1938. For Schuschnigg it was 'difficult to keep one's self-control', but there was the pleasure of seeing Schmitz again and meet-ing the two 'saints' on the transport: Niemöller and Piquet.[145]

After three days at Rosenheim the prisoners were reloaded on to buses and driven to the Brenner Pass. Their guards amounted to thirty more or less docile SS men under the command of Obersturmführer Stiller, and another twenty or so heavily armed 'sinister types' led by Untersturm-führer Bader. Bader had instructions to liquidate the prisoners. Müller had been singled out as one to die. The SS showed Schuschnigg the list, with the names of himself and his wife neatly inscribed.[146] The buses entered Italian territory in driving rain, passing Bruneck and the Pustertal before coming to a halt before the village of Niederdorf. Stiller allowed some of the prisoners to go into the village with him where Müller soon ran into a Wehrmacht general in full uniform. This led the prisoners to hope that the SS might respond to a superior officer, so they went back to fetch Falkenhausen: he was another general, after all. Meanwhile Müller was shouting, 'Schuschnigg is behind me! Schuschnigg is behind me!', know-ing that the South Tyroleans had an affection for the former Austrian leader.[147]

The general had few soldiers with him, but a 'prisoner of honour' Colonel Bogislaw von Bonin was able to put through a call to General Heinrich von Vietinghoff in Bolzano. When he informed the commander of the presence of the *Prominenten*, Vietinghoff despatched troops to pro-tect them. They were not due before dawn, however, and Bader's men were still eager for blood. The prisoners went to a hotel on the market square where Frau Heiss, manager of the Hotel Elefant in Brixen, regaled them with *Kaiserschmarrn** – a great treat after the food they had eaten in their various concentration camps. Bader, however, had not given up: 'Müller raus!' (Come out, Müller!). Colonel von Bonin, however, had been allowed to go into captivity with his pistol. He drew it and aimed it at the SS man: 'Ich zähle bis drei, bei zwei sind sie eine Leiche!' (I'll count to three. On two you are a dead man). Bader's men took the hint.[148]

Meanwhile Sante Garibaldi had established contact with the local par-tisans. They wanted to hang Stiller from a window in the hotel, but Müller

---

* An atomised sweet omelette filled with raisins and a favourite of the Emperor Franz Joseph – hence the name.

talked them out of it. Instead Müller was made a member of the Tridentine Division of the partisans. This involved eating a piece of raw eagle's flesh, decidedly less palatable than the *Kaiserschmarrn*. On Sunday 30 April the prisoners were finally rescued by the Wehrmacht under the command of a Captain von Alvensleben. On 4 May they were liberated by the Americans, who took them to HQ in Caserta, and thence to Capri.

Disputed Areas

Thuringia

Yalta had decreed it otherwise, but Thuringia was liberated by the Americans. It was here and not in Bavaria that the Americans came face to face with the horrors of the Third Reich. It was not quite the first time they had been exposed to evidence of Nazi barbarity. During their advance through Alsace they had come across Natzwiller camp, but the Nazis had evacuated the buildings. When the French liberated it in November 1944, it had been empty for two months. American reporters had also flown to Lublin in Poland in September 1944 where they were told of a warehouse containing 800,000 shoes, but it did not prepare them for what they were going to see in sleepy Thuringia.[149] They first came across its Jewish victims in Nordhausen-Dora, working on the V2 rocket. The camp was one of many dependencies of Buchenwald. Among the liberators was an American Jew who was repelled by the sight of his fellows. 'These people are something else,' he wrote. 'I am not one of them.'[150] Some 12,000 people were living in tunnels, with forty to seventy-five dying daily. The Americans found 3,000 corpses as well as 700 people who were clinging to life by a thread. Many of the Americans were sick. In the town Germans were evicted from their flats* to make room for clinics, and 2,000 locals were rounded up to bury the dead in long trenches.[151]

But Nordhausen was child's play compared to Ohrdruf. The village near Gotha was the location of another branch of the more famous Buchenwald camp. It was a labour camp, containing around 10,000 slaves. One of the liberators was the Jewish American war reporter Mayer Levin. The first indication that they had chanced on a camp was when they spotted some skeletal figures coming towards them along the road. They said they were Poles, and told the soldiers to enter the town and rescue the

---

* There can have been very little left of the town. The Allies had bombed it relentlessly. Only a thin strip of old houses remained when the author visited it in the early 1990s.

camp inmates. They spoke of deep caves and death squads. The Americans feared an attack and waited until daylight. When they finally reached the camp they found heaps of bodies in striped uniforms. Each one had a hole in its skull: a sign that they had been executed by a single *Genicksschuss*. In another place was a stash of naked prisoners, their corpses flat and yellow like planks.[152]

Many hardened soldiers vomited at the scenes that confronted them, above all on encountering the nauseous smell. The survivors could hardly be classed as humans. They behaved like animals – showing no inkling of goodness or friendship, they merely grabbed at the food they were offered, ran off with it into the corners and lashed out at anyone who approached them. The Nazis had robbed them of their most precious possession, dignity.[153] On 12 April the camp was visited by the big three of American army command: Eisenhower, Patton and Bradley. The latter recalled, 'The smell of death overwhelmed us before we passed through the stockade.' They were shown the corpses of 3,200 naked, emaciated men. Patton was physically sick.[154] It was a bad omen: it was the day President Roosevelt died. Patton turned to an aide: 'Still have trouble hating them?' Eisenhower ordered all units not in the front line to visit Ohrdruf: 'We are told the US soldier doesn't know what he's fighting for. Now, at least, he will know who he is fighting *against*.'[155]

Ohrdruf established a policy and a gloves-off treatment for all Germans. The most famous city in the hilly region, Weimar, was taken on the 12th. Buchenwald was so close to Weimar that its ancient trees had been the object of Goethe's daily walks, and yet the Weimarer insisted that they had not known what was happening behind the barbed wire. To some extent this was true, but prisoners were used for menial tasks around the town and had been involved in the often mortal work building the new Adolf-Hitler-Platz between the old town and the railway station. Even if they had been unclear about the extent of the brutality, they knew full well that the prisoners were abused and maltreated. Buchenwald had its soft days in the early 1940s. The Jews were sent east, and the inmates – particularly the 'greens' or criminals – tended to look after themselves. The commandant, Koch, was proved to be corrupt, and was executed by the Nazis. His wife was the infamous Ilse: 'the Beast of Buchenwald'. Saul Padover was shown the famous collection, supposedly assembled for Ilse Koch, of lampshades and trophies made from human skin and organs. He also saw a card index in which the causes of death were dutifully recorded: the victims all died of two ailments, heart or pneumonia.[156]

The place was used as a distribution centre for labour, and a lot of

French and Belgian prisoners were brought in. The saddest cases were confined to the Little Camp where they were left to die in their own filth. In the last ten months the camp had filled up with 20,000 or so inmates from the east, bringing numbers up to 45,000–50,000. Another 20,000 were transferred to other camps – Flossenbürg, Theresienstadt and Dachau. Meanwhile communist prisoners conspired to take over the camp. Shortly before the Americans arrived the order had been given to kill the prisoners, but Himmler had failed to carry them out. He was still hoping to use the Jews to save his own skin. Hitler appears to have ordered Himmler to kill all the prisoners in Germany. There was plenty of evidence around to show that some of his men took these instructions seriously.[157]

The prisoners Himmler had failed to kill broke out of the camp after the liberation and began to plunder Weimar. Hitler was furious when he heard this, and renewed the orders to kill the concentration camp inmates. It was the beginning of the end of Hitler's relations with his SS chief.[158] Some of the leaders of this small-scale revolt were roving around when the Americans arrived on 11 April. Padover treated the German communists with disdain. They weren't real prisoners, being the aristocracy of the camp, and they looked down on the others. 'Being Germans, they had been made trusties by the SS.' Some prisoners had pinned guards to the ground with stakes. About eighty of the guards were massacred, 'sometimes with the aid and encouragement of the Americans'. It was reported that the Americans looked on while a prisoner beat a German soldier to death with a four-foot log.[159]

The Allies were slow to liberate the Little Camp. The stench was appalling. They found a number of children there when they finally braved it, including a three-year-old boy. The inmates died in large numbers even after the Americans began to feed them. The liberators learned that they could function only by repressing all emotion. On 16 April George Patton decided that the inhabitants of Weimar should know what had been happening on the Ettersberg. His men made a thousand or so inhabitants line up in the Paulinenstrasse and marched them off to the camp a kilometre away. Among them were some of the Nazi bigwigs of the city. American cameramen were on hand to film their reactions. The Americans wanted the full propaganda effect, and news of the site-inspection spread as far as Vienna.[160] On the way to the camp there was much amused talk, particularly from the women and girls dressed for the occasion in their last finery. They showed no sign of knowing what to expect.

Their cheerful mood vanished when they saw the heaps of bodies covered with quick-lime. Women began to weep and faint. The men covered their faces and turned their heads away. Many of them huddled together for comfort. One of the inmates who had been spared Hitler's order to murder the last inhabitants of the camp was Imre Kertész, the Hungarian writer, then aged fifteen. He remembered the scene: the Americans had given him some chewing gum, which he belaboured with his jaw while he gazed lazily from the typhus isolation huts to the mass graves in the distance. Suddenly he was aware of the:

> society of ladies and gentlemen. Coats were flapping in the wind. There were flamboyant ladies' hats and dark suits. Behind the society were a few American uniforms. They reached the mass-grave and fell silent, assembling slowly around the ditch. The gentlemen's hats came off one after another. Handkerchiefs were pulled out. There were one, two minutes of mute stillness, then life came back to the stunned group portrait. The heads turned to the American officers. Arms lifted and spread out at shoulder height, then fell again to the upper thigh before coming up again. The heads shook in denial . . . they knew nothing about it. No one knew anything about it.[161]

That the Weimarer knew nothing was the message delivered in Superintendent Kuda's homily in church that Sunday, the church where the enlightened philosopher Herder once officiated, and where Goethe and Schiller had once been parishioners. 'In Buchenwald events have come to light about which we knew absolutely nothing before now . . . so we must confess to God that we played no part whatsoever in this atrocity.'[162] On 1 May the Americans appointed Fritz Behr, a Buchenwald man, as mayor.

Saxony

As the Americans advanced they found more and more evidence of lawless bands of DPs who were terrorising the countryside in the absence of Nazi law. In Brunswick there were more alluring women waiting to tempt Padover up to their lairs. 'I live all by myself, would you like to come up and see me?'[163] Lower Saxony was, like Mecklenburg, originally taken by the Western Allies. It was the Americans who crossed the Harz Mountains and seized the ruins of Halberstadt and Magdeburg, which the Anglo-American air forces had only recently reduced to heaps of ashes.

Padover and his men had a comic exchange with a ten-year-old boy on a scooter in Magdeburg. He explained that his mother was a schoolmistress and that his father had fallen in Russia. Padover began his usual interrogation-banter, but was possibly surprised by the reply to the question 'What did he think of the Führer?' The boy said: 'Der Führer kann mir den Arsch lecken' (He can lick my arse). They supposed he was unaware that it had been the Anglo-Americans who had levelled his home town, but the boy was ready for them: 'The Führer made you do it . . . and he is prolonging the war when everybody knows it's hopeless.' The boy told them he wanted to go to America and join the 'American Luftwaffe'. Then he would come back and bomb Germany. They asked him why he wanted to bomb his fatherland: 'Oh . . . the Russians will be here then.'[164]

In Gernrode the people had some weeks to study the Americans at close range. When the Russians arrived in July they compared the Red Army to the American Negroes. The latter were 'less like victors and more like fellow sufferers of aggression and humiliation'.[165] The American armies discovered yet more evidence of Hitler's last-minute orders to exterminate concentration camp inmates and slave labourers. In Gardelegen they had driven the men into a barn and set it alight. At Wolfsburg, where the big Volkswagen factory was located, the prisoners had been able to free themselves at the last moment, and had seized weapons from their guards. Some had died from eating raw flour in desperation; others had raided a vermouth factory and made themselves hopelessly drunk. They were so light and weak that when they tried to fire their weapons they fell over backwards. They nonetheless managed to kill a number of German civilians, including a mayor.[166]

There had been another bloodbath in Thekla, a suburb of Leipzig. It had been a labour camp staffed with political prisoners. When the SS left they had shot and set fire to the men, some of whom had been burned alive. There was the usual rage directed at the locals, but at Thekla the Germans proved helpful and showed how appalled they were by the massacre. As one of the Americans put it, 'ninety-nine out of a hundred Germans seem to eat and breathe as we do, seem to react to the same emotions, seem to be perfectly human and responsive.'[167]

Marianne Günther was a schoolmistress in Penig near Chemnitz, close to the Czech border, when the small town was taken by the Americans on 15 April. The US troops found a camp there too, filled with starving Hungarian Jewesses. They immediately imposed a curfew. Polish and Russian forced labourers ran wild in the streets. A month later Marianne Günther was able to continue her diary – her illusions had been shattered: 'The monstrosities that we have heard about the concentration camps – I didn't want to believe it. The atrocities are far worse than I imagined. Who could have planned such devilishness? . . . And now the ghastly stories from Bohemia! When the war ended on 8 May the horrors began. A whole nation [has been] driven homicidal mad, [they are] murdering innocent women, murdering children. You can see the terror on the faces of the refugees.'[168]

Before coming to Saxony she had been at the school in Gertlauken, an exceptionally quiet village in East Prussia. She got out before the Russian breakthrough. Gradually she learned the fate of her pupils and colleagues as rare letters broke through. Fifteen-year-old Christel Beckmann had made it across the frozen Nehrung to Danzig, and then walked through Pomerania to Mecklenburg, where she and her family believed they had found comparative safety. Then on 3 May, the Russians arrived. The girl wrote: 'For four weeks we found a place in the hayloft and stayed put. We looked dreadful. Herta's face was covered with scales. In the night we heard the screaming and wailing of the village women. No man could protect his wife, he would have been beaten half dead had he tried, and the women were threatened with guns, they had to obey. We were almost crazy . . .'[169]

Mecklenburg

Fritz-Dietlof von der Schulenburg's sister Tisa was also liberated by the Americans. She was living in the large manor of her first husband in Mecklenburg together with 120 refugees. The German army wanted the house too, to billet soldiers retreating from the Russian advance. For days it was touch and go whether their liberators would be American or Russian. Then six American jeeps appeared: 'we were free'.[170] Free, but not without worries. 'Waves of liberated P.O.W. and Polish workers swept over the countryside. They broke into farms and country houses, looted, beat the proprietors and chased them away.'[171] The Russian Zone began only five miles away. 'Sometimes they paid us short visits, robbing and plundering on the way.'[172] If the Poles and Russians were not enough, Tisa was threatened by the Germans who remained on the estate, who found her fraternising with former French forced labourers disgraceful.[173]

Americans ran across the transit camp at Woebbelin near the grand-ducal palace of Ludwigslust. Jews, Poles, Hungarians, Russians and western Europeans had all ended up there after being moved out of their original camps. No one had fed them and there were cases of cannibalism. The soldiers can hardly have helped them much by giving them sweets, but the thought was there. The American commander pursued the usual policy of making the townsfolk responsible. All inhabitants of Ludwigslust over ten had to come and view the dead. Photographs show trenches filled with corpses stretching far and wide before the gates of the Schloss.[174]

The Americans made way for the British. Very soon Tisa began to hear rumours that the zones were to be adjusted, and that the Russians would be taking over her part of Mecklenburg. Once she heard confirmation of the story she hitched up a caravan – a former army signals wagon – and prepared to flee. One day she had a visit from a Polish officer who arrived brandishing roses. He wanted to thank her for the way she had treated Poles and other prisoners. 'But get out! The Russians are coming here.'[175] She needed no more prompting. As soon as she had received the appropriate papers, she drove her caravan to Lübeck in the British Zone.

Eastern Mecklenburg had been captured by the Russians. In Carwitz and Feldberg, where the family of the writer Rudolf Ditzen (Hans Fallada) were living, the *Honoratioren* – the town's elite – committed suicide. The chemist killed his children first. There were rapes, and Ditzen's estranged wife Suse was not exempted.[176] In September Ursula von Kardorff finally traced her mother Ina, who had last been heard of on her estate at Böhlendorf in Mecklenburg. She arrived in Berlin, with the usual tale to tell. She and her husband, the painter Konrad von Kardorff, were old, and were not prepared to run from the Russian advance. Konrad expired in March, and was saved from the bitter experience of the rest of his family. They had lived modestly, slaughtered few animals and drunk little from the collection of wine in the cellar, and despised all those who cut and ran.

Even when Stettin fell, the Kardorffs stayed put. They hoped that it would be the English that conquered them: 'gentlemanly types, and sort of cousins'. Long lines of refugees from East Prussia and Pomerania passed the gates and, despite the implorings of relations, they would not budge. Then one May morning the Cossacks appeared on the horizon: 'they came en masse, with tanks, on motorbikes, on foot, on horseback, even on sleighs drawn by teams of four dogs'. They fell on the wine cellar, so prudently preserved; then the destruction began, of furniture and pictures. Aunt May and Uncle Willi committed suicide. As May put it to Ina, 'The Kardorffs have been at home here for five hundred years, what could we do elsewhere? I think God will have mercy on us.' Ursula's uncle Egon, former commander of a cavalry regiment, saw the bodies in the wood and went to Ina: 'Now I will have to leave you alone. I can't bear a life like this, and I have no fear of death.' He went to his parents' grave in the wood, where Ursula's father was also buried, and took poison.

Ursula's mother was now on her own. She packed some things in a rucksack and walked. In the local villages the same scene repeated itself: drunken soldiers, dead nobles. A woman had shot fifteen members of her family single-handed then drowned herself. Ina von Kardorff was robbed of her watch and her last possessions. In a small town she was given lodging by some artisans and a pastor's wife until she was ordered to leave again.

She arrived in Güstrow, and found an attic room with a baker's wife. She painted pictures and gave drawing lessons, sewed and embroidered. She even helped a painter do a portrait of Stalin. All around her were the sick and dying, and disease. At night houses were searched and she heard the screams of women, followed by shots. In the church on Sundays the pastor announced long lists of the dead. She spoke to Ursula of Russians, too, some of whom were good and generous, and gave things to the people. Some even went to church.[177]

Werewolves

Underground resistance to the occupation either petered out quickly or failed to materialise at all. The Werewolves, who had been formed in October 1944 to make life impossible for the Allies, committed the odd dastardly deed such as the murder of the American-appointed mayor of Aachen, Franz Oppenhoff, carried out by two men dressed as paratroopers in March 1945. After that, they fizzled out. The killing of Oppenhof remains controversial: Goebbels was naturally pleased, and described the men as partisans, but his lack of prior knowledge would suggest that the mayor was not killed by direct orders from Berlin. Others have stated that he was killed as a *rendement de compte* of mere local significance.[178] It might instead have been the work of an SS hit-squad rather than Werewolves. In Austria, Franz Fehrer had been given the job of training Werewolves in Wiener Neustadt, but as foreign troops crossed Austria's borders the Gauleiter, Eigruber, gave orders to discontinue the training and not to attack the American forces. The American OSS came to the conclusion that there were no more active cells of Werewolves in Austria in July 1945.[179] Carl Zuckmayer claimed that the spirit of the Werewolves collapsed at the same time as Germany, and not a trace remained. Certainly Lucius Clay could find no trace of anyone trying to form a 'Nazi underground' in early July 1945.[180]

There were, however, some very isolated incidents. In Glowitz in Pomerania a forester called Drambusch, a fanatical Nazi, withdrew to the forest where he built himself a bothy and planned to recruit others in his fight against the conquerors. No one listened and later the Russians tracked him down and shot him. He died of his wounds soon after in Stolp.[181] Goebbels had made a loud noise about German resistance and there was still a jittery feeling about Werewolves in May, which the Russians used as an excuse to slaughter any young men they found. The Czechs were even less kind than the Russians. Dr E. Siegel heard about the arrival in the Little Fortress of Theresienstadt (now Terezin in the Czech Republic) of twenty-one men branded Werewolves. They were stood against the wall. During the night the doctor heard the usual screams and cracking of whips. Later he heard that prisoners had cleared the gatehouse of blood, brains, teeth and hair and had to scatter fresh sand. The men were officially listed as 'dead on arrival'.[182]

Accusing someone of being a Werewolf could seal his or her fate, and there must have been many cases where individuals sought revenge in this way. In Dalliendorf in Mecklenburg in the SBZ (the Soviet Zone, or Sowjetische Besatzungszone), twenty-six-year-old Paul Schröder had emerged from concentration camp wearing the green triangle of a criminal, but he quickly converted his record to make out that he was a former member of the Communist Party. He told the authorities that a Frau Westphal, the owner of an estate in the village, together with two men called Holst and Redicke, were Werewolves. All three were shot on 2 July 1945. When it transpired that Schröder had been lying, he too was shot.[183]

There was a little bravado at the beginning when battle-hardened soldiers observed the punier members of the Allied armies and imagined how easy it might be to overpower them.[184] In general, however, the Allied soldiers were more a danger to themselves, as the writer James Stern, an Englishman in an American uniform, discovered when he chanced on an American cemetery on the way home from Bamberg to Nuremberg in the summer of 1945. The war had been over for two months, but the caretaker told him that bodies came in at an average of thirteen a day. Stern was incredulous, but it seemed that drunken and reckless driving was the chief cause, together with suicide.[185]

Illustrious Bones

The arrival of the Allies, the Red Army in particular, had initiated a series of bizarre journeys – bones were shifted from ancient vaults to escape desecration. The first to go were of comparatively recent date: those of Hindenburg and his wife, who had been laid to rest in the Tannenberg Monument in 1934.[*] The retreating German army exhumed Hindenburg's

---

[*] The monument had been built in 1927 to commemorate the German victory over the Russians in 1914 – which had actually been achieved elsewhere. The battle was deemed to have been won in Tannenberg to compensate for the resounding defeat inflicted on the Teutonic Knights by the Poles in 1410.

corpse in January 1945 and blew up the monument before they left. The corpses were conveyed across the Baltic on the cruiser *Emden*.

Once landed, the Hindenburgs' remains were driven to Potsdam, and stored in Luftwaffe HQ Kurfürst in Wildpark near by. They joined the royal refugees that had been extracted from the vault under the Garrison Church: Frederick the Great and his austere father, Frederick William I, who had been taken from the crypt by candlelight one night in February. At the same time Wehrmacht officers had removed all the captured standards. The Garrison Church was destroyed on 14 April 1945, and the bodies escaped the bombing and subsequent firestorm as a result.[186]

By the time of the Allied raid, the Hindenburgs, Frederick William and Frederick had already left Potsdam.* On Sunday 11 March Hauptmann Wilfried Seegebarth received orders to take them to a salt mine in Thuringia along with the standards and other precious objects associated with Prussia's most famous son: musical instruments, tapestries and Frederick the Great's library. In the late afternoon of the 13th, the transport had reached Bernterode in Thuringia. The coffins were lodged in the mine and concealed behind blocks of salt. All those involved were sworn to secrecy.

American soldiers reached the mine on 27 April and found the coffins. When they left Thuringia in keeping with the decisions taken at Yalta and in preparation for the meeting at Potsdam, they carried the dead bodies off with them. They took them to the university city of Marburg where they were initially housed in the cellar of the Schloss, before being brought to the basement of the city archive.

On 21 August 1946 the royal bodies were secretly reburied in the St Elisabeth's Church in the city. A few days later they were joined by the Hindenburgs. The pastor agreed to lodge the bodies under pressure from the Americans and Oskar von Hindenburg, the president's son, who had commanded POW camps during the war and had been arraigned as a war criminal. He was let off with a fine.[187] The royal bodies were finally walled up in the church on the 21st, in the presence of Prince Louis Ferdinand of Prussia – the crown prince's eldest surviving son – and his wife, Princess Kira.† Somewhere along the way an act of petty larceny had been carried

---

* Hindenburg and his wife for good; Frederick William and his son returned after much controversy in 1991. The remains of the Garrison Church having been dynamited in the 1960s, Frederick William was reburied in the Friedenskirche. Frederick the Great finally achieved his original wish and was interred on the terrace at Sanssouci, next to his dogs.
† The two kings were moved again in 1952, when they were sent to Burg Hohenzollern near Hechingen in Württemberg. It was here that Frederick the Great's coffin collapsed, and a new one had to be made.

out against the person of Frederick the Great: his Order of the Black Eagle had been pilfered, probably by an American soldier. You could still see where it had been by the star-shaped patch of pure Prussian blue on his otherwise faded uniform tunic.*

* Information from Prince Friedrich Wilhelm von Hohenzollern-Sigmaringen, 14 May 1996. The prince told the author he had noticed the theft when the coffin was changed in 1952.

3

Berlin

When I rode through the area around the Tiergarten yesterday, I thought to myself: one day they will talk of May 1945 in the same way as they describe the Sack of Rome. Naturally, it was different to 1527, because Berlin was already half finished, but had it not been for the lunacy of the defence it would not have been so much of a battlefield. It was only when we now see what the Russians are taking away that we can see how fundamentally rich we were.

Margret Boveri, *Tage des Überlebens*, Frankfurt/Main 1996, 140–1

There was no shortage of bones in Berlin on 2 May 1945 when General Weidling signed the ceasefire in that city. The Russians had finished the business a day late: they had hoped to have defeated the Germans by – if not on – May Day;[1] but still, the enemy was soundly thrashed. Of the 150,000 homes in the centre of the city, only 18,000 were undamaged, and 32,000 were completely destroyed. After Goebbels had incited Berliners to fight to the last, his deputy Fritzsche told them to stop: 134,000 soldiers laid down their arms.[2] Ruth Friedrich, who had been a member of a low-key resistance group, thought the Third Reich had vanished like a ghost. She exulted in the deaths of Hitler and Goebbels: 'Go to hell, Führer and Reich Chancellor! *Tempi passati!* You don't interest us any more.'[3]

At least, Berliners might have imagined it was over, but they knew what to expect. The only thing Goebbels had not mooted were the occasional acts of kindness. Charlottenburg, where the journalist Margret Boveri lived, was an affluent area, and one of the last to surrender. She became aware of the change in the situation when she ventured out on to the streets to obtain her last quarter-pound of butter. She found Russians already sniffing at the queues. Most of the Berliners had thought it prudent to don white armbands. They openly complained of the Party for the first time. When she got home she found that German soldiers had broken into a neighbour's cellar to steal civilian clothes. They intended to make a break for the west: no one wanted to be caught by the Russians.*

The Russians picked over the city, exploring their new prize. The impotent and ruinous Reichstag building became the symbol of Russian victory. It had ceased to function as a democratic assembly soon after Hitler came to power. Marshal Zhukov added his signature to the others on the stonework of the interior.[4]† The journalist Konstantin Simonov wandered around the Tiergarten. He looked in at the Zoo to see the dead and emaciated animals lying beside the bodies of SS men. He went to the huge Anti-Aircraft Tower that had fought to the last. Inside there had been drunken orgies as the last act had been played out. There were the bodies of suicides everywhere. In one cubicle he found a dead SS general, his uniform tunic unbuttoned and a bottle of champagne between his legs. He had committed suicide with his mistress, who lay beside him in a pretty white blouse and skirt. He went on to the Reich Chancellery where agents of Soviet Military Intelligence, or Smersh, had already identified the bodies of Goebbels and his wife and children. Hitler and Eva Braun eluded them for the time being.[5] Schwerin von Krosigk spoke on the airwaves: 'The world can only be pacified if the Bolshevik wave can be prevented from overwhelming it.'[6]

The Russians were drunk, and not just with victory. 'Woina kaputt!' (The war's over!) and 'Gitler durak!' (Hitler's a blockhead!). The terror began quietly in Margret Boveri's Charlottenburg. 'Ich Pistol!' announced the soldiers. 'Du Papier!' That meant that they had guns, and no amount of paperwork was going to do you any good if you wanted to hang on to property or virtue. 'There is nothing in this city that isn't theirs for the taking,' reported another woman who lived near Neukölln in the south.[7] At first the Russian soldiers came for watches. With a cry of 'Uhri! Uhri!'‡ they snatched, sometimes discarding the previous acquisition, which had simply stopped and needed to be rewound. This anonymous 'Woman' saw many Red Army soldiers with whole rows of watches on their arms 'which they continuously kept winding, comparing and correcting – with childish, thievish pleasure'.[8] For the Russians, Berlin – even in its ruinous state – was the picture of sophistication. They thought that the light was

---

* This had been going on for days, despite the draconian methods the Party used to deter soldiers and civilians from leaving.
† When the British architect Lord Foster adapted the building for use by the Bundestag, the more decorous graffiti were retained; the obscenities, however, were scratched out. (Author's visits to the Reichstag building, see *Financial Times*, 9 August 2002 and 2 September 2004.)
‡ From the German word *Uhr*, meaning watch.

captured in lightbulbs and unscrewed them to send them home. They were fascinated by lavatories with flushes – and allegedly used them to wash their potatoes in. Little things, like cigarette lighters, were not only new, but utterly enchanting to them.[9]

Some Berliners came out well from the experience. One Charlottenburger was seized and stripped of his elegant leather jacket. The Russian assailant tossed him his windcheater in return. His initial despondency at the exchange soon turned to jubilation: in the pockets of the soldier's garment he found two watches and two pieces of jewellery, including a valuable ring. Ruth Friedrich watched a Mongol soldier, who had befriended them, empty his pockets of wristwatches, lighters, golden rings and silver necklaces, 'like a child, calling them "trophies"'.[10] Margret Boveri remarked that the men of the Red Army:

> were like children in their glee over the new watches. One of them gazed alternately at his wristwatch and then pulled a pocket watch out and held it to his ear; we watchless ones, on the other hand, could only guess at the time. They sang and danced and played mouth organ and harmonica . . . and then they played ancient German records on a stolen German gramophone. The scene in the courtyard was reminiscent of the description of the Cossacks in *Memories of an Old Man** . . .[11]

The Woman saw her liberators discard a collection of classical 78s, including *Lohengrin* and Beethoven's Ninth, in favour of a record playing an advertising jingle from C&A in the Spittalmarkt.[12]

Nicolas Nabokov had a clear memory of Berlin at this time: 'In front of the Adlon [hotel] stand two trucks. The first one contains a mountain of brass: tubas, trumpets and trombones covered by heavy Bokhara rugs. On top of the rugs sit three sullen-looking Mongoloid soldiers. Their uniforms are tattered. They are eating bread. The second truck stands half-cocked on three wheels, blocking the traffic. It contains thousands of naked typewriters, and standing in their midst a cow moos . . .'[13]

Gramophones were the Russians' special delight. They played them non-stop until they were broken and then they had to purloin another. The Russian inability to master anything technical was 'an inexhaustible chapter'.[14] They stole all the bicycles they could find. The Woman saw them take them up to a street near the Hasenheide where they practised riding them. They sat 'stiff on the saddles like chimpanzees in the zoo'.[15] They frequently fell off before they mastered the use of the two-wheeled beast. Many bicycles were broken in the process and the wreckage strewn

---

* Almost certainly a reference to Tolstoy's *The Cossacks*.

over the street. Ruth Friedrich's friends collected up the bits and assembled new vehicles from them.[16] The Russians were in the main 'as good-natured as children. Some of them were sadists for all that.'[17]

Later they came looking for all stocks of food the Berliners had so carefully amassed. They liberated any alcohol they could lay their hands on. Drunk, they were even less easy to control. Then they amused themselves by setting fire to buildings. Anything they did not steal they destroyed: valuable antiques and musical instruments, elegant clothes and works of art. Flats were requisitioned for the use of officers, the occupants chased away with knives and pistols. But on that first day the Charlottenburger were more frightened of what the Americans would do; it was thought they were even more bent on revenge than the Russians.[18]

Then the rape and slaughter began in earnest. Conservative estimates place the number of Berlin women raped at 20,000.[19] It began in Neukölln at 6 p.m. on 27 April. In the Woman's cellar they went for the distiller's wife first, as she appeared to promise two pleasures; after that it was the baker's wife. The Woman thought the fattest were most in danger, because fat, for a Russian, represented good health. The rapists left the scrawnier, half-starved Berlin women until last.[20] Anxious parents hid their still virginal daughters in lofts, in cupboards or under sofas. The Woman described the dislocated experience of rape. The feeling was more of paralysis than disgust. She felt an utter coldness, 'the spine seems to be frozen, icy dizziness encircles the back of the head . . . It's like sinking through the floor.' When her attacker left he tossed her a packet of cigarettes.[21]

Margret Boveri first came face to face with it when she visited some friends in plush Dahlem in the south-west of the city. They had been 'liberated' several days before. The worst cases involved very young children or elderly ladies, and the victims were often killed afterwards. Sometimes they took their own lives. In one instance soldiers raped the sisters who worked as nurses in the military hospital, infecting them with syphilis at the same time.[22] It was rumoured that the severity of the rapine was caused by the fact the Russians had sent in units made up of criminals – such as the Nazis had used at the time of the Warsaw Uprising – but this was later revealed to have been untrue. Rapists were threatened with gruesome punishments, but the prospect of satisfying their lust proved stronger than the fear of chastisement.

That the Russians had received some sort of order was made clear to the Woman, who spoke a rudimentary Russian and could understand some of the exchanges between the conquerors. One officer reprimanded a soldier with the words 'ukas Stalina' (Stalin's orders), but the man answered back, saying the Germans had raped his sister. While the Woman was raped later by two Russians, a female soldier interrupted her comrades. When she saw what they were doing she merely laughed. The Woman promptly complained to another officer, but he dismissed her. They had not done her any harm, and all his men were healthy, he said.[23]

Ruth Friedrich was spared, largely because her lover, the conductor Leo Borchard, spoke fluent Russian. She visited a friend who had been raped by seven soldiers, 'one after the other, like beasts'. 'We need to commit suicide . . . we certainly can't live like this,' the friend said.[24] Ruth's friend Frank addressed the Russian need for women: the euphoria of victory manifested itself in the flesh of Berlin's womenfolk; the Russians took bodily possession of German soil, bit by bit; and bodily they consumed German flesh, night by night.[25]

The preferred form of suicide was poison, and there was much discussion of the best and most painless way to quit life. The discussions had started before the Russians arrived. It had been a favourite topic of conversation between Hitler and his secretaries at their nocturnal teas.[26] Berlin women, it seems, were short of food, but well provided with poison. There were instances of mass-suicide by poison. The actor Paul Bildt and some twenty others despatched themselves thus, only he woke again and lived for another dozen years. His daughter was among the dead. Attesting once more to the incidence of suicide among the nobles, especially those who lived on isolated estates in the Mark Brandenburg, the writer cites a number of cases showing how far the old families would go to protect the dignity of their daughters: death was preferable to dishonour.

Elsewhere the rapes soon became routine and when it was not accompanied by violence it could eventually be laughed off. A kind of gallows humour grew up that was encapsulated in the expression 'Besser ein Iwan auf dem Bauch als ein Ami auf dem Kopf!' (Better a Russki on the belly than a Yank on the head!), meaning that rape was preferable to being blown up by a bomb. The Woman's friend, a widow, was over fifty when she was raped by an unbearded boy. He later paid her a compliment, saying she was considerably tighter than the women of the Ukraine. She was proud of the remark and repeated it to other women.[27] One journalist of Margret Boveri's acquaintance, for example, was able to make light of her rape, even if she had cried at the time – 'in retrospect the story sounded very funny: the hanging water bottle and all the other bits of equipment getting in the way, the inexperience of the young man and the speed at which it was consummated'.[28] Margret commented: 'Middle-class people have never spoken so frankly about sex before. Are they really sympathising with the victims, or is it more erotic titillation? There is a good deal of longing for love in our city, deprived of men, and there are many unconscious ways to compensate.'[29] Her friend Elsbeth, herself a victim of a savage rapist who had not only cracked her skull but knocked out most of her teeth, lost her middleclass prudishness with the experience. Such matters were discussed openly for the first time: 'naturally there is lots to laugh about'.[30]

In a frightful twist in the gallows humour of the time, Berlin children used to play the 'Frau komm mit!' game, with the boys taking the part of the soldiers and the girls their victims. In normal times the children had mimicked 'Zurücktreten, Zug fährt ab!' (Stand back! The train is leaving!), a line they heard every time they took the U- or S-Bahn, Berlin's metro system. During the war it had been 'Achtung! Achtung! Schwacher Kampfverband über Perleberg in Richtung auf die Reichshauptstadt' (Warning! Warning! A light enemy squadron is over Perleberg, flying in the direction of the Imperial Capital).[31]*

Very few escaped the rapine, although the Swiss Max Schnetzer reported areas that were spared 'like a hailstorm that only destroys part of the harvest'.[32] One acquaintance of Margret Boveri's who refused was shot. Another, who was left miraculously alone, explained this by telling the writer that the Russians didn't like women who wore spectacles. The presence of very small children cooled off the lusty Russians on occasion. As we have seen, Russian sentiment about children was well known. Also pregnant women were avoided. The Russians were 'horribly normal' and the Woman could think of no instance of 'Man come!' There was a lesbian living in her block who dressed as a man, and who was never molested.[33]

Men didn't help much. In some instances they told the women to go quietly so as not to put their own lives in jeopardy. Some gallantly but bootlessly tried to come between the rapists and their women, like an Aryan man who had protected his Jewish wife throughout the war, and who bled to death while his wife was raped.[34] There was a trade in stars of David, which sold for up to RM500, but in the end the Russians couldn't care less if the woman was Jewish or the house they plundered had a Jewish owner. They had not gone to war to protect the Jews after all.[35]

Sometimes the presence of a husband was a deterrent, but it was a risky business, particularly if the soldier was drunk.[36] The Russian-speaking Leo

---

* James Stern found an echo of this in bombed-out Nuremberg. He observed two boys playing in the sand. They had built a castle. Suddenly one of the boys began to make a wailing noise like a siren: 'Ich bin ein Amerikaner!' The other jumped up with a tin can filled with sand: 'Ich bin ein Engländer!' They flapped their arms and cried, 'Boom! Boom! Boom!' and launched their sand at the castle.

Borchard was able to save one girl by saying she was his daughter. He sat up drinking schnapps with the Russians and, by doing so, was able to protect the female members of his gang, while down in the cellars the 'victims squealed like stuck piglets'.[37] Men receive a bad press in contemporary accounts, but it must have been an emasculating experience for a man to see or hear his loved one violently raped and be unable to stop it. One man, who had witnessed his wife laughing and drinking and sleeping with the Russians, killed her before shooting himself. Others tortured themselves with reproaches about their passivity at the crucial time. The women complained that their men spurned them after the experience, but conversely many women became frigid after being raped and rejected their husbands and lovers. The fact that the victims discussed their experiences with other women within their husbands' earshot cannot have made it easier.[38]

Canny Berlin women learned quickly that it was wisest to give in and receive the Russians one at a time than to have to put up with terrifying gang rapes. The wisest found an officer and stuck with him: a 'wolf' to protect you from wolves, and as high-ranking as possible. In return for sexual favours he was able to prevent any attacks by the routine *soldateska*. This was true for an eighteen-year-old in Klein Machnow who had been raped sixty times. She found a captain and they left her in peace.[39] The Woman in Berlin did likewise. After a few tussles with soldiers she found a sympathetic lieutenant, and finally a major, who wanted more companionship than sex. She described the blissful sensation of lying fearless at his side. When she was later asked the standard question about how many times it had happened to her she could not say with certainty: 'No idea. I had to work my way up through the ranks as far as a major.'[40]

Even those who laughed about the rapes in retrospect found their nerves ground down by the nightly attacks. Most of the rapists in Charlottenburg, Margret Boveri discovered, were simple soldiers sleeping rough in the park. Those who had been properly billeted behaved better. She resorted to sleeping pills to get though the night, and didn't wake when the Russians knocked at her door. Only in the morning did she hear the grim news from the neighbours.

The rapes continued throughout the time the Russians had Berlin to themselves, but they slackened off markedly after 4 May. Their initial lust sated, some Russians, at least, looked for greater refinements. Margret Boveri's pretty journalist friend Frau Zetterberg was confined to a hospital for some time after a two-hour session with a drunken chauffeur. Another acquaintance suffered a particularly disgusting attack. Margret spares us the details, but reminds us of the line of the Empress Theodora, who had regretted that God had given her just four ways to satisfy her lust.[41]*

Even when Berlin women were not driven so far as to take their own lives, the rapes had inevitable consequences in the form of disease and babies. On 18 August Ruth Friedrich noted that there would be an epidemic of babies in six months' time 'who don't know who their fathers are, are the products of violence; conceived in fear; and delivered in horror. Should they be allowed to live?' Some of these unwanted babies were placed in a home in Wilmersdorf. In 1946 it was estimated that one in six of the children born out of wedlock had been fathered by Russians.[42] Coping with syphilis and gonorrhoea without antibiotics was part of a woman's life at the time. Ten per cent of those raped were infected, and antibiotics cost the equivalent of two pounds of coffee.[43] Eventually the Russians decided to treat the local population themselves. Most of the unwanted Russian children were aborted, although there was the usual rumour that Stalin had forbidden the women to dispose of their children because he wanted to see an alteration in the racial mix. Abortion was a crude business, normally carried out without anaesthetic and costing about RM1,000. Many women performed the act on themselves, with inevitable consequences. Despite the massive incidence of abortion, it is estimated that between 150,000 and 200,000 'Russian babies' survived to see the light of day.[44]

Despite the terror and the rape, sometimes there were sympathetic moments between the conquerors and the largely unprotected Berlin women in those first days. Margret Boveri recounts the story of an impromptu dinner party when Russian soldiers, whom she and her friends had fed on turnips, returned the favour and arrived bearing wine, still and sparkling, bread and other edibles and gave the women news of the probable division of the country into zones of occupation. Such largesse was a common experience. As the Woman put it, 'they love to play Father Christmas'.[45]

The daily threat of rape petered out only when the Western Allies arrived in July, and when the Soviet authorities realised that it was damaging their chances of political success among the civilian population. When the first free elections were held it became clear that the Red Army had

---

* Procopius, *The Secret History*, trans. G. A. Williamson, London 1990, 41, has just three ways: 'And though she brought three openings into service, she often found fault with nature, grumbling because nature had not made the openings in her nipples wider than is normal, so that she could devise another variety of intercourse in that region.'

not won over 'hearts and minds' and that Berliners, like the Viennese, wanted anything but a Moscow-inspired communist regime.[46]

By the time Ursula von Kardorff returned in September, she called Berlin a 'city without Eros'. 'Women over thirty look old, frustrated and sad. Make-up covers up so little. "Frau komm", the cry that rang through the city as the victor called for his rights to rape, plunder and shoot, rings still in every ear.' She heard her fair share of rape stories: of a girl of her class who was raped by five Russians and abandoned by her noble fiancé; and of a friend in Zehlendorf who hid behind a coal dump from the Russians but was given away by another women who sought to protect her own daughter. She was raped by twenty-three soldiers and had to be sewn up afterwards. She could not imagine having sex with a man ever again. Ursula heard another story, of a girl who had found a lover in an English soldier. One day she had pointed to a German soldier in rags, called him a 'prolonger of war' and slapped him. The English soldier gave the man cigarettes and abandoned the girl on the spot.[47]

The Soviets in the Saddle

Officially peace came to Berlin on 8 May. Despite the terror of the past two weeks, Ruth Friedrich was still positive: 'free from bombs, free from blackouts, free from the Gestapo and free from Nazis! . . . *pax nobiscum!*'[48] It had taken a while to bring in the other Allies to sign the surrender document: the Briton Tedder, the American Spaatz and the Frenchman de Lattre de Tassigny.* They came with a band of accredited journalists. Zhukov represented the Red Army. The German side was represented by Field Marshal Keitel, Admiral von Friedeburg and air force General Stumpff. It was Keitel's last public engagement before Nuremberg.

The location was the Soviet HQ in an old military engineering school in Karlshorst in the east of the city. At 10 p.m. – midnight Russian time – the German delegation was ushered in. Looking like 'Boris Karloff', Keitel handed over a document signed by Dönitz confirming the unconditional surrender arranged in Rheims the day before. Keitel allegedly trembled as he signed the Allied paper, and his monocle fell out. The Germans were bundled out again before a dinner was thrown for the Allied plenipotentiaries. It was now 1 a.m. Russian time. The party and dancing went on

---

* Eisenhower's mistress, Kay Summersby, was there and took a dim view of the Russian women soldiers in their knee-length skirts: 'No British, American or French girl would been caught dead in their uniforms' (*Eisenhower was my Boss*, Watford 1949, 224).

until the morning. The generals danced, Zhukov performing a *Russkaya*. There were four full hours of toasts and many of the soldiers were literally under the table.[49] When the festivities came to an end there was a massive cannonade, which some Berliners misinterpreted, imagining the war had started up all over again.[50] The Soviets had known where to find the wine: 65,000 bottles of claret had been located to this end, and others beside. They had taken it from a walled-up section of the cellars of Berlin's best hotel, the Adlon. The fate of the hotel was sealed by the discovery of the wine cellar. Russian lorries came to take away the contents, and very soon a fire broke out that was to destroy one of the few buildings in the street that had survived the conflict.[51]

The 'Muscovites' came home in three waves: first the Ulbricht Group, who arrived behind the 1st Belorussian Front on 27 April; secondly the Ackermann Group, which followed on the heels of the 2nd Belorussian Front on 1 May; and thirdly Gustav Sobottka's men, who landed in Mecklenburg on 6 May. The Ulbricht Group was the cream of the Muscovites. They had been housed in Moscow's Hotel Lux. Ten of them were flown back to Germany as the Russians moved in for the kill. They landed at Bruchmühle, thirty kilometres east of Berlin. On the beautiful spring morning of May 1, as the Red Army concluded its operations in the capital, a German woman told them of the widespread rape that had accompanied the Soviet advance. The Muscovites dismissed her claims as fantasy.[52] Later Walter Ulbricht conceded that such things might have happened, but he was not prepared to discuss the matter: 'Any concession to these emotions is, for us, quite simply out of the question.'[53] Whether that meant these matters were trivial in the long term or that he did not have enough power to take it up with the Soviet authorities is not made clear.

Ulbricht emphasised to his colleagues what the task ahead would be. They were to create cells – 'our task will be the building of German agencies for self-government in Berlin'. The group made its way into Berlin. It was 'a picture of hell'. They noticed the women around the pumps with their white and red armbands, confirmed both their peaceful natures and their friendliness to the Soviet Union. No one was ever in any doubt that the red had been taken from redundant swastika flags.[54] The Muscovites had been given the task of finding a means of supplying food to the survivors: there was a propaganda role as there were hearts and minds to be won. The rations for Germans were to be similar to those in the USSR: 300–600 grams of bread daily.[55] Not only did they want to know where food and water were to be procured, but Ulbricht was anxious for news of the comrades who had gone into hiding in the city.[56]

Before 1933 the communists had jockeyed for supremacy in Germany. In the last free elections of Weimar Germany in November 1932, they had won 100 seats to the Nazis' 196. Some had subsequently gone over to the NSDAP, becoming 'beefsteak Nazis' – brown on the outside, red in the middle. Some had merely observed the forms. Others had gone underground and many went into concentration camps. For Ulbricht these men would provide the material he needed to set up his administration. Some of the communists were distinctly primitive rebels. They wanted to change the day of rest to Friday and replace the greeting 'Guten Tag!' with 'Rote Front'. The Muscovites were generally more urbane. Some had been in the Russian capital for years and had taken out Soviet citizenship. Some, like the later spymaster Markus Wolf, had been brought up in Moscow. Hans Klering, the actor appointed to run the DEFA film studios, had been in Russia for fourteen years and had a Soviet wife. The Russian colonel Alexander Dymshitz said 'He is really a Soviet actor.'[57]

Muscovites were strategically placed in every administration. At the head they installed a 'harmless idiot' who could be guaranteed to rubber-stamp the decisions taken by the Russian commandant. So the man installed as mayor of Berlin was the sixty-eight-year-old architect Dr Arthur Werner, 'who, coughing and slurping, is hardly capable of delivering his Goethe-quotation-filled speech during the five-minute council-meeting'. Because the Russians had controlled the city since May, the Allies were not party to the appointments and had to put up with a Soviet *fait accompli*. Communists occupied 100 council seats of the 230 in Berlin.[58] It was the same pattern as Vienna, only a little more so.

The Muscovites' policy was revealed after the defection of the youngest of their number, Wolfgang Leonhard. In his book *Child of the Revolution* he gave the flavour of Ulbricht's style of government. Ulbricht determined matters. As Berlin could not be openly communist, it was decided against placing communists in charge. They could get away with it, perhaps, in Wedding or Friedrichshain, because both areas had always been 'red'. 'In working-class areas mayors as a rule should be social democrats and in middle-class precincts – Zehlendorf, Wilmersdorf, Charlottenburg, etc – we need men of bourgeois background, former members of the Zentrum [Catholic party], the Democratic or the German People's Party. Best, those who have a doctorate and anti-fascist past and are prepared to co-operate with us . . .' Attention was also paid to the mayors' comrades: 'The first deputy mayor, the head of personnel and administration and the man who's in charge of education must be our chaps. And you've also got to find one comrade who's totally trustworthy. He's the one who takes over the police . . . it's got to look democratic, but all that really matters must be in our hands.'[59]

Ulbricht had been behind the selection of Dr Werner. When he had first aired the name his fellow Muscovites, Maron, Gyptner and Winzer, had been less than enthusiastic. Werner was too old, and it was suspected that he was 'not quite right in the head'. 'What's the matter?' retorted Ulbricht. 'The deputy will be our man.' So it was that the pliant Werner became the first post-war Oberbürgermeister of Berlin, and Karl Maron became his deputy, albeit with extreme reluctance on Maron's part. He wanted to be top dog.[60]

As the Russians consolidated their power in Berlin prior to the arrival of the Western Allies, Zhukov on 12 June authorised the formation of bourgeois anti-fascist parties like the conservative CDU and the liberal LPD. Politically the British and the Americans lagged hopelessly behind. The British first flexed their muscles when on 17 August they acted to curtail the political power of the block and street wardens – communists who had inherited the job from the Nazis. Four days later the Americans scrapped the posts altogether, which had really only been about spying and denunciation.

The Muscovites set out to eliminate the hated socialists who had dominated Berlin for most of the Weimar Republic. Fusion was the answer: the SED or Socialist Unity Party was formed with the compliance of the leader of the SPD – socialist party – in the SBZ, Otto Grotewohl. Grotewohl was increasingly compromised: he had run off with a new woman. She had been in the Bund Deutscher Mädel (BdM – the female version of the Hitler Youth) and a Pg, and the Russians knew it. Local elections were held in the first half of September 1945. Heavily monitored by the Soviet authorities, they must have resembled Hitler's last cynical stab at democracy in the spring of 1933.

The bourgeois parties were permitted to field candidates only in certain constituencies. The CDU ran less than 20 per cent of those presented by the SED, and the LPD a little over 10 per cent. The results came as no surprise to any one: the SED won with an aggregate score of 57.1 per cent, having received more than half the votes in Brandenburg and Mecklenburg – once the bastion of reaction.[61] Kurt Schumacher, who led the Socialist Party in the Western zones of Germany, was incensed by the Soviet emasculation of the SPD; nor were the socialists won over in Berlin's Western sectors. In March 1946 the call to join the SED was rejected by 82.2 per cent of socialists. In the east they were not consulted. The German Social Democrats had rejected a system intended for all

Germany, and made the first move towards creating a separate state out-side the SBZ.[62]

With virtually all men of an appropriate age dead, missing or interned, the Allies created a gerontocracy, using politicians who had been tried and tested in the Weimar Republic and who had been impotent during Nazi times. The heads of the CDU in Berlin, for example, were Messrs Schiffer and Külz. Külz was an ambitious seventy-year-old, while Schiffer was more than ten years older and a contemporary of Friedrich Naumann. Andreas Hermes, who created the CDU in the Soviet Zone, was a sprightly sixty-seven, but he had been a minister as far back as 1920. After 20 July 1944 he had been arrested, but then released.

Wolfgang Leonhard had been given his instructions. He provides a good example in his appointment of a mayor to the middle-class borough of Wilmersdorf in Berlin. He met a man in the street who had been put in a concentration camp after 20 July. Leonhard wanted to appoint him mayor, but the man refused the job. The man in the street knew of another man, a Dr Willenbucher, who completely fitted the description Ulbricht gave to his lieutenants. Willenbucher was the usual wrecked figure who had crawled out of a hole after 2 May, but when he was summoned to meet Ulbricht and have his appointment ratified, he appeared in a black suit, and stood upright: 'he was no longer bent, and there was a new dignity in his walk'. Ulbricht broke open the vodka to celebrate his appointment.[63] In Berlin-Zehlendorf, the first post-Nazi mayor was a Werner Witgenstein; a man with vision who wanted to turn the borough into a centre for the arts and culture. Cultural policy was in the hands of a Herr Rühmann, an actor of a very average abil-ity who naturally put the weight on cinema and theatre. A Herr Glum (a former general director of the Kaiser-Wilhelms-Gesellschaft) sought to start a university – a difficult undertaking when books were being systematically impounded and taken to Russia.

The authorities in the SBZ were better when it came to marshalling the talents of prominent pre-war Berliners to help in specific sectors. Thus the former minister for the food supply, Dr Hermes, was responsible for food; the great surgeon Sauerbruch was given the health portfolio; and the archi-tect Hans Scharoun was assigned building. In the first weeks of June a fresh delivery of Muscovites included the prudish Wilhelm Pieck, Fred Oelssner, Paul Wandel, the expressionist poet Johannes R. Becher, Edwin Hörnle and Marthe Arendsee. The former exiles lived a communal life at 80 Prinzenallee, which fairly buzzed with activity.[64] Their final destination was 76–79 Wallstrasse. Their arrival was the cue to refound the KPD or Communist Party, except it was now to be 'antifa' or anti-fascist, and not

Marxist. Of the sixteen founder members at the meeting on 12 June, thirteen were Muscovites.[65]

The Berliners were largely without news. Snippets of gossip were exchanged around the pretty Wilhelmine pumps that stood in all parts of the city as the people went to fetch water to wash and cook. The Soviets remained in sole custody of Berlin for a couple more months, however, claiming that the texts did not make it clear how the Western Allies were to have land access to their sectors of the city from the Western zones, even if the air routes had been mapped out – a detail that was to prove advantageous to the West during the airlift of 1948–9.[66]*

The Soviets divided their conquered world into Nazis and non-Nazis. Suddenly the number of people prepared to admit to having been among Hitler's nine million began to drop. In Wannsee, for example, the first postwar headcount established just eighty members. By July that figure had risen to a thousand, largely as a result of denunciations.[67] The Pgs were at a disadvantage in what was already a desperate situation: they received no rations, and had to spend their days in *Schippen*, the process of clearing away the debris and dismantling industry to be shipped back to Russia. The politically suspect had to assemble at the labour exchanges at 7 a.m. Details were sent off to clear rubble, bury corpses, clean streets, clear drains and prepare bricks for rebuilding.[68] There was a rumour that the so-called *Alte Kämpfer* – the people who joined the Party even before Hitler achieved power – were treated the worst, and had to carry out the most backbreaking work in exchange for bread and water.

They worked hard. Margret Boveri reported that ten days after the fall of Berlin the piles of rubble left by four years of bombing had been cleared from the streets. Once again the women bore the brunt. 'Rubble-women' formed chains with buckets which they filled with broken bricks and mortar. The few men that were involved in the clearances only worked when the Russian supervisor looked on. The Russians were quick to create an infrastructure in Berlin. Financial and cultural institutions were set up. Sporting fixtures were arranged.[69] The time became Moscow time, and it was light at midnight as a result. By 13 May a bus route was working again and on the 14th the first U-Bahn set out since the fall. The airfields were patched up and put back to work.[70] The Soviet authorities treated with consideration petitioners who came to them wanting to set up essential businesses. Bakers were encouraged to go back to work, and flour was promised to help them make bread. On 16 May the anonymous Woman

* See below Chapter 20.

diarist was attached to a Russian officer who had been sent to get the banking system working again. He suddenly began to speak to her in French, and she realised he was a *Biwsche* – a survival from the pre-1917 *ancien régime*.[71]

The Soviet authorities were severe when it came to Pgs. Before the Western Allies arrived, they closed 1,400 shops owned by Party members and sacked nearly 12,000 functionaries. *Nacht und Nebel* kidnappings also removed nearly 5,500 Berliners, many of them members of the press and the police. A number of former resisters headed east into captivity as well, such as Alexander Werth, who had been incarcerated by the Nazis and worked with Adam von Trott in the Information Department of the German Foreign Office; and Horst von Einsiedel, a member of the Kreisau Circle around Helmuth James von Moltke who was to die in a Soviet prison camp in 1947. Another was an unnamed Baltic baron who had been in Admiral Canaris's Abwehr or military intelligence and who was kidnapped in the British Sector. Sometimes the Soviets arrested their own men, as was the case with Makar Ivanov, a culture-boffin who had contacts with the British through Leo Borchard.[72] The police in the SBZ were run by Paul Markgraf, a former Wehrmacht colonel who had been captured at Stalingrad and who converted to communism during his imprisonment by the Russians.[73] There were exaggerated rumours: the actor Heinrich George had been shot and his colleague Gustaf Gründgens arrested. George had been the *Intendant* of the Schiller Theatre and, as such, a fellow traveller. He didn't die for another eighteen months, when he succumbed to the treatment he received at the liberated Sachsenhausen concentration camp. The killing had continued under new masters.

Gründgens had been taken in, but he fared better than George. He had run the State Theatre during the Third Reich, but used his position to protect a number of people who had fallen foul of the regime. The Russians released him soon after. The danger was denunciation. The Russians encouraged people to denounce others in order to save their own skins. The Soviets were especially anxious to discover the whereabouts of the top officials of the Nazi Propaganda Ministry. Pleading innocence did not help. If you could not provide an answer you were led away and never heard of again. Goebbels's Propaganda Ministry ('ProMi') had been responsible for seemingly harmless organisations such as the Foreign Press Club, but as far as the Russians were concerned anyone tarred with its brush was liable to arbitrary arrest. Working for the Press Club had had advantages, as had the Press Department of the Foreign Office, which was Ribbentrop's rival organisation to the official Information Department – journalists received bigger rations. It did not necessarily follow that the people who performed the relatively menial roles within these organisations were members of the Party, though many were.

A small number of Jews had gone through the war unscathed – they were the so-called *U-Booten* or submarines. One man, whom Margret Boveri encountered on her bicycle, turned out to be a rabbi, who had lived in comparative peace under an assumed name. Another case she unearthed was a certain Frau Nerwig, a pure Jewess whose Aryan husband had died in 1939, but who had married an English Mr Lind *pro forma* and had therefore survived the war. As a *Mischling*, her son Klaus was exempted from army service and obliged to go to the Todt construction organisation, where he would have surely died had he not fled at the right moment. The boy was powerful and blond, and the Russians refused to believe that he was not an SS man in disguise. The mother responded by pulling the commanding officer on to the sofa with her. Klaus thereby survived.

A Viennese Jew in British army uniform, George Clare found another Jewess who had survived the war because her Aryan husband had refused to divorce her. He had been the headmaster of a Berlin Gymnasium or grammar school. The Nazis forced him out of his job and he had to work as a commercial traveller. Then the Russians came and he refused to hand over his bicycle, so they shot him.[74] Later the Russians were keen to use what Jews they could find to fill important roles in the city. The machinist Walter Besser was put in charge of a hospital. The last Berlin Jews were all lodged in the Jewish Hospital in the Iranische Strasse. They included twenty or so informers who had been protected by the Gestapo, as well as a further 800 'privileged Jews' married to Gentiles. As early as 6 May a religious service was performed in the hospital by the Rabbi Kahane and five days later the Sabbath was celebrated at the Jewish Cemetery in Weissensee.[75] On 21 June there was a Jewish cultural evening at the Levetzower Strasse synagogue. That month the Soviet authorities appointed the dentist Moritz Blum as the first head of the Jewish Governing Board based in the ruins of the old synagogue on the Oranienburger Strasse.

Subsistence

Food was an obsession for all Berliners. Ruth Friedrich and her friends had been thrown out of the billet where they had spent the last weeks of the war. They moved into a deserted house hoping to find food. Onions was all there was. Later they located a cache of sherbet powder, sweet chews and stock cubes. Their Mongol friend was not impressed when he came to call. With Russian help, however, they killed a cow. As they hacked the beast into manageable pieces they were astonished to see people creep out of holes in the ground with buckets in their hands and beg for a slice of bloody meat. 'Give me the liver . . . Give me the tongue!' they cried.[76]

The Russians provided some food from the beginning. There were fixed and mobile canteens serving hot soup. In three months they delivered 188,000 tons of food to Berlin. Baking began again on 9 May. It was black and wet, but it was bread of sorts. Ration cards were introduced on the 17th. The cards were graded I–V. Later a card VI was printed. The largest rations went to the workers who were eligible for card I: 600 grams of bread, 30 of fat and 100 of meat; Nazis and housewives received the 'Hunger Card' – number V: that meant 300 grams of bread, 7 of fat and 20 of meat. Ruth Friedrich knew a woman who had card V. Her husband had been a Pg, and she had five children. As they received the food, she lay in bed, because she was too hungry to stand. She weighed just forty kilos.[77]

Margret Boveri lists the contents of her larder and the occasional feasts she ate during those meagre days. A surprise visit from Elvira von Zitzewitz was used as a pretext to bring out some of the best things she had: soup made from a stock prepared from the lung of a horse slaughtered in the street below, in the last moments of the war; then potatoes boiled in their skins; the remains of some *pasta e piselli*; and, to finish, a dessert made from 'pudding powder' and some cherry compôte that had begun to ferment: 'a meal for the gods!'[78] Many Berliners grew potatoes among the ruins. Others had window boxes filled with chervil and borage.[79] The Charlottenburger seem to have had the pick of the horses. When Ruth Friedrich walked down the Chaussee (now Strasse des 17 Juni) on 17 May the street stank of rotting horse carcasses. The bones were picked quite clean.[80]

It could only get worse. Shortage of milk drove mothers in Neukölln to the local Russian command, or Kommandatura. They said their children would die without milk. The Soviets replied that it made no difference if they died now or in a year's time. At the end of June the Russians rounded up the ninety cows in the model farm in Dahlem. Their milk had been largely reserved for them anyhow, but it was bad for morale to see them leave for Russia. The animals were suffering from foot and mouth disease, and it was questionable whether they would make it alive.[81] That being said, the Russians stressed from the beginning that they intended to feed the Berliners; they created a political structure and encouraged cultural activity. They did not treat the Germans as the Germans had vowed to deal with them. The Germans were not to be exterminated.

Those who acquiesced when it came to marauding Russian soldiers could do considerably better. After a visit by the usual posse of Russians, the Woman counted her blessings. She had bread, herrings (they had been cut up on the mahogany table), tinned meat and the remains of a flitch of bacon, all brought by her visitors. When the Russians left, they took only the alcohol away with them: 'I have not eaten so well in years,' she concluded. Later a Russian arrived with a couple of small turbot. Even more astonishing was a later visit when one of her admirers brought her a bottle of tokay.[82]

By mid-June the prices of food on the 'free' market were astronomical: strawberries (then in season) were 7.50 Reichsmarks a pound; a kohlrabi, 50 Pfennigs, but you had to queue for four hours to get one and the chances were that the shop would be sold out. On the black market a pound of meat fetched 100 Reichsmarks, and by July the price of a kilo tin of dripping had risen to RM500. Watches and jewellery could be exchanged for food from the Russians in the Keithstrasse.[83] The wartime staple had been potatoes. Margret Boveri's last delivery had been in October 1944, which she eked out until mid-July, by which time they were quite blue inside. Every now and again she and her friends alighted on a windfall crop in a park or garden. On 18 July she made a list of what she had been able to obtain so far that month: two kohlrabis, a small lettuce, 250 grams of blackcurrants, 600 grams of sugar, 'and for 500 gm worth of coupons, 300 gm of meat. There are no potatoes and no fat. There is neither salt nor vinegar. Now, however, I can queue up for bread.' By the end of the month there had been much promised, but little received: no fat, meat, fruit, vegetables, vinegar, ersatz coffee or salt all month; just a part of the potatoes, bread, 620 grams of sugar, 600 grams of flour and seven stock cubes.[84]

Berliners felt totally cut off from the outside world. There was no transport (all bicycles and cars were liable to requisition) and there was no telephone. Meanwhile the Russians were pulling up one set of railway lines on every track and taking these away with them. Anyone who had illegally retained their wireless set had to reckon with highly irregular power. The effect in the long term was to alter the nature of Berlin, from being the industrial powerhouse that it had been since the nineteenth century to being a city devoid of industry in the late twentieth.

Two things were important for the dignity of the new helots, particularly the women: hairstyling and flowers. Margret Boveri took pride in the flower arrangements she created in her bombed-out house. During the Berlin Blitz, there had been hairdressers on hand in the flak towers ready to groom the women until the all-clear sounded. Fuel was another problem. With time the Berlin parks – the Tiergarten and the massive Grunewald – would be shorn of their flora. Even in the summer of 1945 the Grunewald was being cleared of fallen branches, while others looked for blackened beams in the burned-out buildings.[85] Electricity was restored on 25 July, however, and on 5 August a limited postal service began to function. Berlin was no longer isolated from the rest of Germany. But the agony was not over. After the blights of murder, rape and starvation came disease: by mid-June a hundred Berliners a day were dying of typhus and paratyphus carried by human lice, and Berliners were forbidden from entering premises commandeered by the Western Allies.[86]

The Arrival of the Western Allies

Everyone waited for the Western Allies in the hope that their arrival would improve matters. Stalin, however, was playing for time so that he might remove anything valuable from the city, and sink trusty communists deep into any positions of power. Had he been able to renege on the deal to allow the Anglo-Americans in, he would have done so. Soviet permission to proceed to Berlin hung on the Western Allies retreating to the demarcation lines drawn up at Yalta. The Anglo-Americans were to fall back behind the Elbe.[87]

On 2 June Lieutenant-General Lucius Clay, who was to head the American mission in Berlin, had yet to receive instructions. The Americans' first attempt to reach Berlin failed utterly. On 17 June Colonel Frank Howley left with a reconnaissance party of 500 men in a hundred vehicles. He was well prepared. Behind him he had left a pool of 2,000 college-educated Berlin women who were to be his secretariat in the city and he had acquired a Horsch Roadmaster – Germany's best car – and draped it with the Stars and Stripes. As he crossed the Elbe at Dessau in his Horsch the Soviet authorities insisted he reduce his train and continue with just thirty-seven officers in fifty vehicles. The convoy, Howley later wrote, reached 'Babelsburg [sic] . . . a sort of German Hollywood' near Potsdam under Soviet escort where it was forced to stop and eventually return to the west. Howley was allowed to go up and look at the future American airfield at Tempelhof. No one else had been permitted to leave their cars.[88]

Howley went back to a Schloss near Halle and sulked. 'Gentlemen,' he told his officers, 'we are never going to Berlin.'[89] On 29 June Clay and his British counterpart General Sir Ronald Weeks and the civilian advisers Robert Murphy and Sir William Strang landed in Berlin to discuss arrangements with Marshal Georgii Konstantinovich Zhukov. At that meeting the frail land lines were established that were to become the Allied routes to the city until 1989. Howley made another attempt to reach Berlin on 1 July with 85 officers and 136 men. This time he got through – although the Russians made him less than welcome when he started putting up the Stars and Stripes in the American Sector.

Howley says the Americans celebrated their arrival with a fist-fight with the Russians in a restaurant: a Polish American major apparently floored six of his Russian allies.[90] Attitudes were clearly beginning to change: the Germans did not seem such a bad lot after all, and the Russians were not exactly the sort of people you wanted to have as allies. Summing up his initial feelings about them in 1945, Howley was to recall that he had thought of them as 'big, jolly, balalaika-playing fellows, who drank prodigious quantities of vodka and liked to wrestle in the drawing room'.[91]

The British too made a move on 1 July, only to be told that Magdeburg Bridge was closed. They found another bridge and slipped into Berlin, but a full entry was still delayed until the 4th. Officers later recalled the shock of seeing the lakes in the prosperous west filled with the corpses of women who had committed suicide after being raped. It was weeks before the Anglo-Americans achieved a real military presence, even if Ruth Friedrich reported seeing an American in the Schlossstrasse in Steglitz on 3 July.[92]

The main force of the Anglo-Americans arrived on Friday 6 July after withdrawing their troops from the disputed parts of Saxony, Thuringia and Mecklenburg – much to the chagrin of their inhabitants. The Control Council had been created in November 1944, and its seat was to be a 'jointly occupied' Berlin. As yet no one knew how that was to be managed. Would there be checkpoints between the sectors? Were Berliners to be issued with passports?[93] It was agreed that the presidency of the Kommandatura would be rotated. Zhukov allegedly informed the Americans that he would not guarantee food for the Berliners, but visitors to the Allied conferences were well looked after. The Soviet marshal claimed that twice as many officers attended the Russian-hosted meetings because of the quantities of caviar and vodka that were laid out. This feast was apparently known euphemistically as 'tea'.[94]

Howley relates that the Americans were much taken up with the abuse of Berlin women by the Russians, conveniently forgetting the widespread incidence of rape by American soldiers. A Russian general excused his countrymen, admitting that the rapes had done his country's reputation no good, but it was nothing to what the Germans had done in his country. As the Russians had had Berlin to themselves for two months, they had haunts in the American Sector they were loath to give up. On one of these expeditions a girl was killed by some Russian sailors. The Americans complained, but the Russian commander told them there were no Russian sailors in Berlin: they had to be bad Germans in stolen Russian uniforms. The atmosphere grew tense. The Americans self-righteously decided that they were allowed to shoot to kill when women were involved. Changing their tune, the Russians excused their conduct by suggesting the men had been drunk or that they were deserters. In an exchange of fire in a railway station, some Russians were killed. At this the Russians launched a complaint. They cited a British sergeant who had knocked a Russian's teeth out and dumped him across the border. That was an appropriate chastisement; it was wrong to shoot. Howley claimed the shooting ceased with the end of Russian rape and looting.[95]

In Berlin the Russians received the more populous working-class areas to the east, while the Western Allies carved up the richer districts to the west. There were enclaves and exclaves: the radio station was in the British Sector, but remained in Soviet hands; and the village of Steinstücken was included in Berlin. There were other anomalies that persisted until 1989: the Soviets had to be able to tend their war memorial in the Tiergarten, and each army had the right to monitor the others, which meant issuing passes to one or two privileged intelligence men who had the right to roam in a Western or Eastern sector or zone.

The Americans proved a disappointment. The Berliners had the feeling that they did not know why they were there. Margret Boveri, who had worked as a journalist in the United States and had been interned there at the beginning of the war, discovered that many of them spoke less English than she did. It was better to speak Spanish. Sometimes a little French helped. Other women were initially relieved that they could sleep in peace – unbothered by Russian interlopers; but, if that was true in the main, there were exceptions on both sides. Margret Boveri recounts the case of an estate-owning family on the edge of Berlin who were out walking when the Russians arrived and so ran back to the house petrified with fear as to what the soldiers would do to their daughters and their friends. They found to their surprise that the Russians had touched nothing and had been exceptionally polite. When the Americans arrived, however, one of the girls was so brutally raped that it took her years to recover from the shock. In general, however, Margret Boveri thought that whatever occupying army controlled your sector was the worst in the eyes of the Berliners. Every inhabitant envied the soldiers of their neighbours. The Americans were particularly naive. Dr Hussels, medical chief for Zehlendorf, was asked to provide 2,500 beds. She asked where they thought she could find them. The officer replied, in the hospitals. She had to inform him that the Russians had already taken them.[96]

The chief excitement was what could be gleaned from American dustbins. Margret Boveri was working for the publishers Ullstein, where she came across a review of an American book that said the average American threw away more than the consumption of a Russian civilian. It was American policy that nothing should be given away and everything should be thrown away. So those German women who worked for the Americans were fantastically well fed, but could take nothing for their families or children. A woman who had put some cheese-parings on a windowsill to take home received a tremendous dressing down, and even the unfinished coffee was poured down the sink at the end of the day. The Americans were outraged that the starving Berliners should dare to help themselves to their food. Colonel Frank Howley had arrived in Berlin with a couple of tame wild boars the army had adopted on their drive east. When a German tried to eat one of the boars he was brutally knocked to the ground. Howley's fellow officers, however, impressed on him that the boars were more trouble than they were worth, and the Americans ate both.[97]

Margret Boveri's friend Elsbeth together with her sausage-dog Batzi came across a real treasure trove discarded in Grunewald. Bread of a whiteness Berliners had not seen for years, wrappers from butter and margarine packets, firm onions; but the Americans found out that someone had raided their refuse and were more careful after that. There were still finds to be made, however, and Elsbeth managed to live for five days on a rice pudding that she had filched out of an incinerator. That pudding had the makings of an epic. Margret Boveri was still singing its praises days later. Then she also received some chicken bones, and had the pleasure of making a soup with a little more body than the vegetable broth she more habitually used. The supreme delight, however, came when Fräulein Roscies found a half-eaten sponge cake and a dish of a sort of 'tapioca-white-bread pudding' that contained half a squeezed lemon: 'a proper, grown-on-a-tree lemon'. The eating of this plunder runs to a long paragraph in her account.[98]

Despite the largesse to be found in rubbish bins, there was still a considerable shortage in the third week of July. So far they had had no meat that month; it was the sixth week without fat and probably the twenty-fifth without milk or eggs. Margret Boveri consoled herself by picking some magnificent flowers and setting them up in her airy if smashed-up room. In 1950, Howley nonetheless claimed that the Americans were spending their time worrying about the subsistence of the Berliners. He criticised the Russian rye loaf, which required 100 lb of flour to make 145 lb of bread. It was too wet, he said, and rotted.* It is somehow unconvincing, in the light of later events at least, when Howley reports a conversation with the French colonel Dalade in which he asks whether food can be political. The Frenchman replies, 'Of course!' Howley and the Americans were already fully immersed in the war for hearts and minds, and started teaching Berlin children baseball and basketball.[99]

The refusal to look kindly on the starving Berliners was part of the same policy that forbade 'frat' or socialising with the enemy. Initially frat was punishable by six months' imprisonment. Soldiers were forbidden to shake German hands or give presents and were to treat them as a conquered race. Very soon the Americans in particular were out in pursuit of 'Fräuleins', and there were a few curiosities to see. The wife of a former foreign minister, Frau Solf, for example, who had been condemned to death by the Nazis for having operated an oppositional salon and spent over a year in Ravensbrück, began to receive visits from the British and the Americans; but, although she was no more than skin and bone, they brought her nothing to eat.[100] The Anglo-American policy on frat stood in sharp contrast with the Russian one, whereby contact with the civilian population was informally permitted as a reward for the one and a punishment for the other. Some Berliners believed that the Russian policy was kinder than the ostracism decreed by the Anglo-Americans. Some even went so far as to say that the Berlin women had been relieved by their attentions – they had been so long deprived of their own menfolk.

Treating the Berliners like a conquered people engendered sympathy for the former Nazis. No distinction was to be made between good Germans and bad Germans, so the good Germans began to muck in with the bad. In some cases only the names had changed. The *Blockwart*, the resident sneak, of Nazi times had briefly reappeared as the *Hausobmann*. Margret Boveri's emerged with the denazification questionnaire, the *Fragebogen*, in his hand, crippled with anxiety at the thought that the authorities would discover he had been a Pg. Ruth Friedrich was stormed by ex-Nazis asking for testimonials that they had helped Jews.[101] When the people had

---

*Howley must be confused: in our more prosperous times a kilo of rye flour would require 700 ml of water for a 1.6 kg German rye *Landbrot*: it is therefore more than a third water and may be happily kept for a week.

joined the Party as a matter of routine, of officious lip-service, even anti-Nazis were prepared to help them.

Worse than the ban on frat was the requisitioning of houses in the smarter western suburbs such as Zehlendorf and Dahlem. This was the American Sector, and the area where there were the most comfortable villas. The US authorities even briefly requisitioned the Titania Palast as an officers' club until Leo Borchard succeeded in getting it back. The Muscovites took over big houses in a largely unscathed Pankow, while the top Soviet brass settled in Karlshorst. In total some 3,000 flats and houses had to be made available. 'Whether anti-Nazi or pro-Nazi, whether rich or poor, whoever had to get out, had to go,' wrote Ruth Friedrich.[102]

By the autumn of 1945 the Berliner's living space was reduced to less than ten square metres.[103] The French had finally pitched up after they were allotted a morsel of the British Sector in Reinickendorf and Wedding on 23 July, and found themselves a few nice villas in Frohnau, Wittenau and Tegel. The British came out of it the worst, as there were fewer palatial residences in Wilmersdorf or Spandau. Wherever, the grabbing of houses by the Allies led to acute misery on the part of the stricken population. Not even Jews who had returned from the camps were immune and were thrown out at pistol-point. The victims were given a few hours to pack up their things. The result was that they had to find some space in a friend's flat until that too was grabbed by another officer of the garrison. Meanwhile, women who had once led a privileged life in Germany struggled to find a place as a servant or cleaner to the invaders. One Berliner who had been kicked out of his house commented bitterly that first the women had been raped by the Russians, now they had to wait on the Americans' whores.[104] Despite their superior airs the Americans wanted to be greeted as liberators and resented the fact that they were not. Their cold-blooded approach contrasted strongly with that of the Russians.

Preaching in Dahlem in July the anti-Nazi theologian Otto Dibelius drew attention to the mortality figures for Berlin. In normal times, the daily rate was around 200; in the war it had risen to nearer 250 as a result of the bombing; now the figure was around 1,000, and this in a far smaller city. The famine was becoming acute. People, chiefly men, were falling like flies. The final killing spree and the high mortality rate after the cessation of hostilities meant that there were lots of dead to bury. There was nowhere to put them and no coffins, and the Allies would not help. Families had interred their loved ones in the ruins or laid them out in mortuary chapels. Berliners resorted to using large wooden cupboards or simply wrapping the body in a horse blanket tied up with cord. Ruth Friedrich records seeing an instance of this: a bundle with a pair of yellow, wooden-seeming feet protruding from the end.[105] All over the city there were *ad hoc* graveyards. In front of the cinema opposite the Woman there was a collection of crosses. The first to be buried there was a girl who had leaped from a third-storey window to avoid being raped. Fresh crosses began to appear soon after.[106] Questioned, the Russian general Gorbatov said the famine was the result of the Nazis, who had sabotaged supplies.[107]

The Honeymoon is Over

At the beginning there was some feeling of community among the victorious Allies. Frank Howley, who liked to think he had understood the Russians' bad faith from the first, cites his superior officer Clay saying naively, 'I like Sokolovsky [the Soviet assistant commander], he wouldn't lie to me.'[108] It didn't take long for the Allies to fall out, not only causing friction between the soldiers, but also creating a danger for Germans who showed too much sympathy for one or other of their conquerors. A German who worked for the Russians was likely to be harried or imprisoned by the Americans. Germans who threw in their lot with the Americans needed to be careful when they entered the Russian Sector.

A tragedy occurred on 23 August that highlighted the fickle relations between the Allies and the difficulty in bringing culture back to the shattered city. Leo Borchard, the first post-war conductor of the Berlin Philharmonic, was shot by an over-zealous American sentry. The orchestra's chief conductor, Wilhelm Furtwängler, had fled to Switzerland at the end of the war, and the Western powers had banned him from the stage. His crime was to have performed before Hitler, both in Berlin and at Bayreuth, despite his early resistance to the cultural policies of the Third Reich. During the war Borchard been a part of an underground resistance group called Onkel Emil. He had managed to charm the Soviet authorities by speaking their language (he was born in St Petersburg). Having obtained the Russians' trust, on 12 May he cycled across Berlin with his friends to have a look at the Philharmonie Concert Hall. He was going to steal a march on Furtwängler and take advantage of his Swiss exile to conduct the Berlin Philharmonic. Ruth Friedrich wondered if Furtwängler had ever pitched up at the concert hall like this. 'A gruesome still life revealed itself among the shattered arcades' – where Bruno Walter (and more recently Furtwängler) had once directed the orchestra, there lay a dead horse.[109]

Borchard knew how to deal with the Soviets. He obtained larger rations for the Philharmonic's musicians: 'you can't blow a trumpet with a rumbling stomach'.[110] By 26 May he was performing Mozart, Tchaikovsky's Fourth and Mendelssohn's incidental music to *A Midsummer Night's Dream* in the Titania Palast to an audience of starving, ragged Berliners.[111] He conducted the orchestra twenty-two times before his death. That fateful Thursday he and his mistress, Ruth Friedrich, had been invited to dinner with a music-loving British colonel. It had been a real treat: sandwiches made from white bread filled with proper meat, and whisky. They talked passionately about Bach, so much so that they missed the curfew which came into force at 11 p.m. The colonel decided to drive them home himself. The night before there had been shots exchanged between Russian and American soldiers, and the Americans had issued orders to stop all cars heading towards the Eastern Sector. The sentry failed to notice that the vehicle was British because the headlights were too bright and signalled the colonel to stop as he drove under the S-Bahn bridge towards the Bundesplatz. He had meant to aim at the tyres, but managed to shoot Borchard through the head. He was killed instantly.[112]

Autumn 1945

Berliners had got used to conditions in their city by September, but it came as a shock to others, especially those who had enjoyed relative prosperity in the south-west. Ursula von Kardorff finally made it back to Berlin at the beginning of the autumn, having left in February. Food was very scarce, and the people shared the same, half-mad look as a result of their experiences since the Russian conquest. She stayed with her friend Bärchen on the Savigny Platz, in a room without an outside wall. Berliners called such buildings *Sperlings-Lust*, or 'Sparrows' Delight', because at any moment you might take off into thin air. She went out on the Kurfürstendamm. The ban on frat was not being closely observed: she noticed elegantly dressed German girls milling around the American, British and French soldiers. There was jazz playing in establishments offering hot drinks but no solid food.

Ursula von Kardorff borrowed a bicycle to look at the city centre. The Wilhelmstrasse had vanished, the Foreign Office was just a ruin. Only the ProMi was still undamaged. On the Pariser Platz the Adlon Hotel was a burned-out shell. Her own house had collapsed. On the square there was a huge statue of Stalin.

The two guardhouses flanking the Brandenburg Gate were piles of rubble. Soldiers from the four powers walked around adding a living aspect to the landscape of ruin. Around the Reichstag building a black market had grown up. There were Russian graves on the Ranke Platz and abandoned tanks on the pavements. The latter served as kiosks, announcing dance schools, new theatres and newspapers and toys for urchins reminiscent of the pictures by Heinrich Zille. The Franziskus Hospital was the only undamaged building, and the nuns looked timeless in their habits, as if they had emerged from somewhere on the Castilian *Meseta*. Near by, the Tiergarten was a blackened shambles, looking more like a battlefield than a landscaped garden.

Fräulein von Kardorff ran into a former colleague from the *DAZ* (*Deutsche Allgemeine Zeitung*) newspaper, Ludwig Fiedler, who told her a typical story. At the end of the war he had been drafted into the Volkssturm, or home guard, like any other man between fifteen and sixty. This last remaining human material was charged with defending Germany in a *guerre à l'outrance*. In the ruins of the pub Gruban und Souchay, he had come up against a Russian officer who was about to shoot him. Fiedler had produced some 'disgustingly sweet' schnapps and the Russian and he had sat down in the middle of the battle and got drunk. The Russian was so befuddled that he began to kiss his German enemy, then he wanted to kill him again, then he was so drunk that he forgot all about it.[113]

One day Ursula von Kardorff went to see her aunt Kathinka, the wife of the politician Siegfried von Kardorff-Oheimb. She lived in an elegant villa near the Tiergarten that had miraculously retained some of its contents even if it too had lost part of the outer wall. They went to the Hotel Esplanade near by, the only grand hotel to have partially survived the war. Only one reception room survived. They had to pay a deposit of 80 marks for the knives and forks, because so many had been stolen. The potato soup they ate cost as much as an entire meal in the past.

After lunch they went to the Russian Sector as Aunt Kathinka wanted to visit her friend Friedrich Ebert, the corpulent, alcoholic son of the first Weimar president, and 'a sort of Gauleiter of Brandenburg' for the Russians. He looked shabby and hungry. He said he was envious of Ursula von Kardorff because she was going to return to Jettingen, 'but I love this city so much that I want to help it'.[114]

Everyone was tense in Berlin. People you hardly knew fell upon you with delight on seeing that you were still alive. Everyone was *Du* where in the past a strictly formal style of address was maintained in circles like Ursula von Kardorff's. The theme of every conversation was who had survived. Someone had killed himself, but no, he had been arrested by the

Gestapo or the GPU, or perhaps he made it to the British Zone. Another was shot by the SS because he had hoisted the white flag ten minutes too early. A third had been polished off by a drunken Russian because he could not provide him with alcohol. A fourth had spent several days with the GPU and had then been released. She heard stories that made her blood run cold; of Gerhard Starke, who was the liaison between her newspaper and the SD, and a man who had kept the authorities off their backs. He had been arrested by the Russians and condemned to die from a bullet in the head. His captors made him kneel, get up, kneel again, get up until finally they brought him to a door and opened it. He could scarper, while he still had the chance.

Old Graf Hardenberg, who had shot himself in the stomach after 20 July 1944, had found his way out of the concentration camp in Oranienburg where he was being held. Despite his terrible wounds he had fled and hidden in the woods, while the guards killed out of sheer spite anyone who might have contributed a positive element to a new Germany. It had been a miracle – the whole family had survived, even the son who had been punished by being sent to Courland where, as a result of Hitler's pig-headedness, many divisions sat idly by until they were herded together by the Red Army and led into captivity. He had also chosen his moment to run.[115]

At another time Ursula von Kardorff's attempts to write were disturbed by the arrival of one of Bärchen's cousins, with four little girls. She had arrived from Poland. The little boy had died on the way: 'He looked like a little angel, a little angel,' she repeated mechanically. The woman's head was shaved, and she looked drawn and starving. The surviving children were covered in pus and lice. Bärchen washed, brushed, deloused and bandaged them one by one.

Renée Bédarida was a former *résistante* who had been sent to work in the administration of the French Sector. On 15 October she communicated some of her first impressions of the city to a friend in France. The Berliners were 'dirty, badly dressed, and always carried a bag of potatoes or a bundle of kindling . . .' The canal that runs along the Charlottenburg Chaussee 'stank to high heaven of corpses', and yet she thought the Germans were getting more meat than the French, even if she was shocked to see children begging for bread and chewing gum.[116]

She made visits to the black markets in the Tiergarten and on the Alexanderplatz.* Five cigarettes procured a film for a camera or an iron

---

* At Advent a ramshackle Christmas market appeared by the ruins of the Schloss. It was a refreshing symbol of the return of normality.

cross. One of the opera houses was still standing and she went to see *Rigoletto*. She was amazed to find the Berlin women all dressed up in their finery: 'how could these women dare to walk through Berlin dressed this way?' With another French administrator she watched German POWs arrive at the Stettiner Bahnhof: 'We felt disarmed, the temptation to despise them or hate them became impossible at the sight of these miserable people, they were also victims of Hitler's madness.'[117]

Renée lived in Frohnau in the French Sector. It had come through the war more or less unscathed, but the requisitioning of houses and rooms had created bad blood. The French were an odd and suspicious collection: there were old resistance hands, civil servants on secondment, 'Vichy men hoping that France would forget about them who had come to wipe the slate clean on the other side of the Rhine, adventurers and profiteers'. The French perpetrated a few acts of childish spite: they mutilated a few inscriptions on the Siegessäule – or Victory Column – in the Tiergarten, which commemorated German triumph in the Franco-German War, and festooned it with French tricolours. In Schwanenwerder they found a fragment of the Tuileries Palace which had been burned down by the Paris Communards in 1871, and removed a high-minded panel that talked of the fate of nations.[118] The Germans themselves did not waste much time on the French – they realised they were second-division conquerors.[119]

Libussa von Krockow arrived from Pomerania in February 1946. It had been two years since she had lived there, monitoring BBC broadcasts for Ribbentrop's research bureau. She recognised the troglodyte dwellings of the Berliners by the stove pipes protruding from the ground. She was so dishevelled that the maid of one of her mother's friends offered her a 50 Pfennig piece and slammed the door in her face. Her body finally gave way after her ordeal: she was ill for a week.[120]

Spring 1946

The military train delivered George Clare to Berlin in the spring of 1946. It had been a perishing winter with poor shelter. As it got progressively colder the lack of amenities had begun to pinch. Berliners collected wood from the ruins and bought candles on the black market. They scavenged for coal. Infant mortality stood at 80 to 90 per cent. As there was no glass in the windows, the cold wind came howling through the damaged buildings. Berliners still went in droves to see *Macbeth* when it was below zero in the auditorium. Lady Macbeth shivered with cold on the stage. At Christmas, there was no warmth, no presents and no tree.[121]

When the spring came a semblance of normality reappeared: there were excursions to the cherry orchards of Werder. A Russian stripped off and leaped into the waters of the Havel, excusing himself this time – it was 'very hot'.[122] Attitudes to the conquerors appeared to have changed. Clare, in British uniform, says the British were liked most. The 'Tommies' still exuded a feeling of fair play. The Americans – *die Amis* – came second. They were tougher and rougher and their Military Police was particularly feared. The French continued to be treated as something of a joke: conquerors who had played no part in the conquest. *Iwan* – the Russian soldier – was by now universally despised.[123]

It was not just fresh troops who arrived to restock the Allied garrisons, exiles gradually returned to look at the city they had once loved. Even more than a year after the cessation of hostilities, the post-war condition of Berlin had the power to shock Carl Zuckmayer. Writing to his wife Alice on 24 November 1946, Zuckmayer said the city was 'unrecreatable and *almost* indescribable'.[124] Some very different exiles flew in on 19 July 1947 when seven old Nazis returned to Berlin: the war criminals who had escaped the noose at Nuremberg were being flown to Spandau. Speer stared excitedly out of the window of the Dakota as it came in to land. He was able to discern the remains of his own contributions to the city: 'the East–West Axis, which I had completed for Hitler's fiftieth birthday. Then I saw the Olympic stadium, with its obviously well-tended green lawns, and finally the Chancellery I had designed. It was still there. Although damaged by several direct hits. The trees of the Tiergarten had all been felled, so that at first I thought it was an airfield. The Grunewald and the Havel Lakes were untouched and beautiful as ever.'[125] It would be twenty years before he was allowed a second look.

4

Expulsions from Czechoslovakia, Hungary and Yugoslavia

On 4 May complete calm reigned. Even the three days of public mourning for the death of Hitler decreed by Secretary of State Frank passed everywhere without incident. You could never have supposed or expected that the Czechs, who had in the course of the war never dared offer even the slightest open resistance to the German armed forces, would descend into an unprecedented orgy of horror against defenceless people after the surrender, that spared neither helpless, wounded soldiers, women or children.
'H.K.', 21 June 1947. Quoted in Wilhelm Turnwald, ed., *Dokumente zur Austreibung der Sudetendeutschen*, Munich 1951, 18

The so-called Sudetenland and its German population had been one of the causes of the war. Hitler had taken up the complaints of the Sudetenländer: Bohemians and Moravians under the leadership of Konrad Henlein. Their mistreatment had prompted the Munich Agreement of September 1938, which ceded much of the border area to Germany, leaving the rest of the country defenceless. In the spring of 1939, German tanks rolled into Prague.

It is true that the Sudetenländer had their grievances. Former subjects of the Austrian Crown, their towns and villages formed a deep ring around the Czech lands. They also made up a large percentage of the populations of Prague and Brno (Brünn), Iglau and Zwittau. In Slovakia there were *Insel und Streudeutsche* (Island and Straw Germans); there were German communities in the Carpathian Mountains and a colony amounting to just under a third of the city of Pressburg or Bratislava. In Troppau they were wholly intermingled with the Slavs and spoke their own patois called *Slonzakische*, but in most areas they maintained a fierce division. They felt they had been duped at Saint-Germain-en-Laye in October 1919 when the Allies finally refused them a right to 'self-determination' as promised by President Woodrow Wilson's Fourteen Points.[1] Beneš, representing

Czechoslovakia, had proclaimed that his state would be the 'new Switzerland' with minority rights ensured by a system of cantons. This never happened.[2] All German-speakers (including German-speaking Jews) were affected by the new state which cut them off from *their* capital, Vienna – from their businesses, government, friends and relations.[3]

The West had granted the Czechs' leader the historic Czech territory of Bohemia and Moravia, together with Slovakia. Over the centuries, however, huge numbers of Germans had settled in the Czech lands and Hungarians in the Slovak east. The Czechs became the political lords and masters of the new state, though they amounted to just 51 per cent of the population.[*] The Germans formed nearly a quarter, but the Slavic Slovaks could not be expected to side with them, so it would always be two against one. Conflict was 'pre-programmed'.[4] There were even attempts to break up the German lands by planting Czech colonies.[5†]

As grieving Germans were quick to point out, their numbers in Bohemia and Moravia were greater than the entire Norwegian people and almost the same as the Danes or the Finns. They had their political organisations: Henlein's SdP, or Sudetenland Party, represented 68 per cent of the Germans, and was the biggest party in the Czechoslovak state. There was also the Sudetenland Socialist Party, which co-operated with the Czechs. If the Germans could never achieve any political clout, until recently, they still had topped the bill socially and financially – though many Germans had been hard hit by the Depression. The Czechs were employed in their businesses, on their farms. The nobility and captains of industry were German-speaking as were many lawyers and doctors. In 1945 there were many instances of farmworkers appropriating German farms, the junior doctors snatching the German practice, and the junior managers taking over German businesses – to some extent repeating the process that had taken place in 1938 when the Germans became top dogs again. There were cases of pure opportunism: Czechs, who had up till then moved in German circles,

---

* In the Czech lands in the west, the Germans made up just over a third of the population in the 1930 census, with roughly two-thirds of these in Bohemia and the rest in Moravia. In Czechoslovakia as a whole, Germans were 22.53 per cent of the population, with Czechs and Slovakians making up 66.24 per cent together. There was a significant Magyar minority in Slovakia. Of these 3,318,445 people, 3,231,688 had Czech nationality. (Theodor Schieder, ed., *Tschechoslowakei*, Berlin 1957, 7.)

† The German population was declining. In 1920 it had been 23.64 per cent. In the German core, towns had seen the Czech communities grow: in Aussig they had advanced from 10 per cent in 1910 to a third in 1930; in Brüx from 20 per cent to a third; in Reichenberg the Germans had declined by 10 per cent; in Troppau the Czechs had been 10 per cent, now they were a third, and so on. (Schieder, ed., *Tschechoslowakei*, 10.)

had German wives or German-speaking children, suddenly became the apostles of Czech nationalism and hunted down former friends. When the communists took over in 1948, those who had profited from the Revolution launched in May 1945 lost most of what they had gained.

The events of September 1938 and the occupation of the rest of Czechoslovakia had made the Czechs more than bitter towards the German minority. The German-speaking area became part of the Reich, and the people Germans – this change of nationality was to prove fatal in 1945. The previously grieving regions were attributed to the nearest German landmass: a Reichsgau Sudetenland encompassed the core towns of Troppau, Aussig, Eger and Reichenberg; the region around Hultschin was attached to Oppeln in Upper Silesia; northern Bohemia to Lower Bavaria; southern Bohemia to the new Austrian Reichsgau Upper Danube; southern Moravia to the newly forged Reichsgau Lower Danube; and Teschen to the recaptured Polish parts of Upper Silesia centred around Kattowitz.[6] In the remaining areas of the 'Protectorate' citizenship was awarded on racial grounds: ethnic Germans were attached to the Reich. For many German-speakers the change was tantamount to signing their death warrants.[7]

It was enough for a lawyer to have practised German law to receive a death sentence.[8] The Czechs had not welcomed Hitler as the Austrians had and even some members of the German-speaking population had been more than apprehensive: socialists, Jews and the large number of Germans from the Reich who had sought refuge in Prague. When the tide turned in the war the Czechs looked forward to the moment when they could deal with the 'German problem' once and for all.

When he felt that victory was certain, Beneš had left London for Moscow. Before he went he told the British ambassador to the Czech government in exile, Philip Nicols, that he would need to effect the transfer of the German population and deprive them of their citizenship, otherwise 'riots, fights, massacres of Germans would take place'. Molotov assured him that the expulsions would be but a 'trifle'. Beneš received the necessary assurances from Stalin: 'This time we shall destroy the Germans so that they can never again attack the Slavs.' He also assured the Czechs in Moscow that he would not meddle in the domestic affairs of a Slav nation, which, in retrospect, gives a rather clearer idea of how much his word could be relied upon.[9]

Beneš's Return

Beneš left Moscow on the last day of March 1945. On 1 April he was in the Ukraine. His goal was Košice in Slovakia where he remained for thirty-three days while the Russians and Americans carved up the country and the Czechs rose up in their wake. Patton's American troops moved up rapidly behind Field Marshal Schörner's 800,000-man army. On 4 May they crossed the mountain passes from Germany to assume their preordained positions along the line Carlsbad–Pilsen–Budweis. The American general had been told that Prague was out of bounds. He stopped in Beraun. The Czechs wanted to grab the credit for the liberation of the capital. On the night of 8 May the Red Army formed a protective shield around the city allowing the uprising to take its course.[10]

On 6 May the Red Army reached Brno. The day before Beneš heard that Prague had risen against the Germans. He moved on to Bratislava. The progress of the Russians was the signal for most of Vlasov's divisions to head south into Austria;* the Cossacks were in two minds about being captured by the Red Army, although some did go into Prague, and effectively liberated it before the regular Russian forces.[11] In Prague the resistance formed the ČNR (Česka národni rada, or Czech National Council). The first Red Army tanks entered the city on the 9th and military operations ended two days later when Schörner retreated. Beneš did not make his triumphal entry until the 16th. His excuse for coming so slowly had been his own safety – there were German snipers about.[12]

Beneš showed his hand first in his Košice Statutes† of 5 April 1945: 'Woe, woe, woe, thrice woe to the Germans, we will liquidate you!' he intoned on the wireless. There followed his famous decrees. Number five, for example, declared all Germans and Hungarians to be politically unreliable and their possessions were therefore to fall to the Czech state. The Košice Programme unleashed a 'storm of retribution, revenge and hatred . . . Wherever the troops of the Czech General Svoboda's army – which was fighting alongside the Russians – and the Revolutionary Guards (Narodni vybor) emerged, they did not ask who was guilty and who was innocent, they were looking for Germans.'[13]

On 12 May Beneš repeated his threats in Brno: 'We have decided . . . that we have to liquidate the German problem in our republic once and for all.'[14] On 19 June came the first of the 'Retribution Decrees': 'Nazi

* See above p. 44.
† *Kaschauer* in German, from the German name of the town, Kaschau.

criminals, traitors and their supporters' were to be tried before 'Extraordinary People's Courts'. These were primitive tribunals. It took all of ten minutes to try a man and send him down for fifteen years. There were 475 'official' capital sentences. Thirty death sentences were handed out for those involved in the Lidice Massacre.[15] A national court would examine war crimes. On 21 June came the next decree: all persons of German or Hungarian nationality, traitors or Quislings were to lose their land. Germany would pay reparations. There was to be no compensation for loss of citizenship or property. The last measure was the so-called 'Little Decree' of 27 October which laid down the punishment for those who had offended against national honour.[16] On 6 August Beneš had spoken at Prague University, a discourse that had particular resonance for Germans, not least because it was considered Germany's oldest seat of learning. He had hardened his heart against all pleas for humanity: 'We know that liberal society is in theory and practice an anachronism.'[17] Already 800,000 Germans had been chased out of the country.

To implement Beneš's various decrees there were 'judicial volunteers' and a Central Committee of Investigation (Ústřední vyšetřující vybor). There were a fair number of KZler, or former concentration-camp inmates, among them, graduates of Dachau and Buchenwald. Many of their acolytes were mere 'half-grown' boys.[18] Those who suffered agreed that the sixteen to twenty-five-year-olds were the worst.[19] By September they had around 100,000 prisoners: 89,263 German-speakers, 10,006 Czechs and 328 others. They had released 1,094 Czechs and 613 anti-fascist Germans. The most pernicious decree was the 'Little' one, employed for 'settling various personal accounts', although the process had started long before. Beneš himself was not immune, and wrought his revenge on various Czechs. His apologists admit a popular desire for retribution;[20] it was the 'duty of the government to turn the turbulent mood', however.

Instead, many politicians, including Beneš himself, exploited it. As another historian puts it, the atrocities 'were not driven from above, but without the toleration of the authorities in Prague they would hardly have been able to persist into the summer months'.[21] In the end even the British (who had encouraged the purge) protested to Beneš about 'excesses' and there was a distinct turning down of the heat while the Big Three met in Potsdam.[22] Expelling the Germans was a vote catcher, but not a measure likely to make friends – except possibly with the Poles. In retrospect it has been hard to find mitigating circumstances to excuse Beneš, apart from the fact that he was old and ill and thought he might defeat the communists by unleashing the terror himself.[23]

Revenge

For seven years the Czechs and Slovaks had suffered humiliation at the hands of the Germans. In the extreme Nazi view *all* Slavs were *Untermenschen* and the German regime treated them as second-class citizens. As in other Slavic lands there were plans to 'Germanise' parts of the country, no doubt partly in response to the cold wind that had greeted the Germans after 1919, which had – for example – seen the decline of the German population in the city of Brno from 60 to 20 per cent. In Znaim the number of Germans had also dwindled after 1918, but had increased sharply after 1938. A Bohemian and Moravian Land Company had been formed to find areas for settlement by Germans. The company ran a model farm. During the Protectorate 16,000 agrarian holdings were confiscated, totalling 550,000 hectares. Some 70,000 Czechs lost their homes. At the beginning of April 1945 treks were organised to evacuate the German colonists and take them back to the Sudetenland.[24] The numbers of Germans had been further expanded by evacuations and the advance of the Red Army. There were around 600,000 of the former and 100,000 Slovakian Germans together with 1.6 million Silesians taking refuge in the region.[25] Some of the Slovakian Germans had already gone to Lower Austria.[26]

The resistance had been wiped out as early as the autumn of 1941, and was unable to re-form until 1943 and 1944, when there was an uprising in Slovakia. Nazi brutality was measured: apart from the massacre at Lidice – provoked by the British-masterminded assassination of the deputy protector Reinhard Heydrich – there were no startling atrocities.[27] The country was hardly touched by the aerial bombardment that struck terror into the rest of Europe.[28] The French bore far worse, and behaved better towards the defeated Germans; but then again, the French were not considered to be racially inferior.

The clue to the severity of the post-war response is the Revolution. This was to be revenge for everything that had happened since the Battle of the White Mountain in 1620 when Imperial troops wiped out the native Bohemian nobility. Germans were still the masters, the Czechs the servants; the nobility was all German- or Hungarian-speaking and gravitated towards Vienna or Budapest. Prague's old university was German once again, and there were German Gymnasiums and Realschulen. The Czechs resented these institutions as many of their own had been closed during the 'Protectorate'. It is significant that these were turned into 'wild' or unofficial concentration camps in May. Brno too had its Technische Hochschule, German institutions, shops and pubs. With the backing of the Red Army, and a clear idea that the Western Allies would turn a blind eye to all that happened, the Czechs would seize their moment for some spectacular ethnic cleansing.

Measures were introduced consciously aping those taken by the Germans against the Jews: they could go out only at certain times of day; they were obliged to wear white armbands, sometimes emblazoned with an 'N' for *Němec* or German;[29] they were forbidden from using public transport or walking on the pavement; they could not send letters or go to the cinema, theatre or pub; they had restricted times for buying food; and they could not own jewellery, gold, silver, precious stones, wireless sets or cameras. They were issued with ration cards, but were not allowed meat, eggs, milk, cheese or fruit. The Germans also had to be ready to work as slaves on farms, in industry or in the mines.

There were two waves of atrocities: Russian liberators, who raped and pillaged, and the Czech partisans who arrived in their wake. As elsewhere, the Russians had been given *carte-blanche*. The Czechs were less prone to sexual crimes, but were often accused of acting as talent spotters for their Soviet friends. There are several reported instances, however, of the Russians putting a stop to the worst excesses of the Czechs.[30] The Czech atrocities committed in the following weeks and months were led by the RG (Revoluční Garda) and the special police or SNB (Sbor Národní Bezpečnosti) who wore German military trousers and SA shirts, together with the army, or with civilian mobs bent on plunder and sadistic violence. The reports read like some of the most gruesome moments of the French Revolutionary Terror.

For prosperous Germans a striking aspect was blatant theft. The Czech partisans took anything that appealed to them and piled it up on a waiting lorry which then disappeared into the Protectorate. Sometimes they simply moved into the house, adopting the former owner's possessions and putting on the banished Germans' clothes. The train from Prague to the north was called the 'Alaska Express', alluding to the gold rush, and those who took it were *zlatokopci* or 'gold-diggers'.[31] Once the wilder days were over, the new Czech Republic moved to regulate the plunder so that the booty came to the state. In 1947 the expellees assessed the value of the stolen effects at 19.44 milliard dollars.[32]

Prague

At the end of the war Prague contained around 42,000 Germans native to the city, together with a further 200,000 or so 'Reich' Germans working for the various staffs and ministries, as well as refugees.[33] The streets of Prague were quite used to hearing the German language spoken – many of Prague's Jews communicated in German. As soon as the battle for Prague ended, Czech partisan units began to imprison German civilians and intern them at various points around the city. The morning of 5 May 1945 was quite calm. Germans still walked the streets in uniform. The mood changed at 11.00 a.m. Suddenly there was a great cry and people began to wave Czech flags. Arms were being handed out at Buben railway station. Some units of the Vlasov Army appeared. A hospital train was shot up. The insurgents captured the radio station and began broadcasting the slogan 'Smrt Němcům! Smrt všem Němcům! Smrt všem Okkupanten!' (Death to the Germans! Death to all Germans! Death to all occupiers!). There was to be no mercy for old men, women or children – even for German dogs: Margarete Schell's was stoned by Czech children and had to be shot. It was the first day of the Revolution.[34]

It was the day Margarete Schell was taken into custody by a 'nasty butcher' of her acquaintance. The RG were attended by people who knew the Germans and could show them where they lived. Margarete was well known – a voice on Prague Radio and an actress. She was incarcerated in a cellar and then transferred to Hagibor Camp. It was March 1946 before she was taken in a goods wagon to freedom in Germany. As a born Praguer, she did not know how to answer the 'Gretchen Question':[*] 'Why do you admit to being a German?' She was a *Prague* German. Doubtless there were Prague Germans who thought it wiser not to say; and some of these would have escaped denunciation. Another ruse was to make out you were an Austrian. The Austrian ambassador appeared in their temporary prison to reclaim Austrian subjects, but his intercession did little for the 40,000 Austrians who were living in terror outside the capital.[35]

Many of the city's most notable Germans were put to death during this bloodletting. Professor Albrecht, the last rector of the German university, was arrested at the Institute for Neurology and Psychiatry. He was beaten up and hanged outside the lunatic asylum. The director of the Institute for

---

[*] From Part One of Goethe's *Faust*. Gretchen asks Faust the question he most dreads: whether he believes in God.

Dermatology suffered a similar fate. Hans Wagner, a Prague-born German physician attached to the German army, last saw his former colleague, the dean of the German Medical Faculty, Professor Maximilian Watzka, in Pankrác Prison. The German-speaking nobles were also targeted: Alexander Thurn und Taxis was thrown into a wild concentration camp with his family. He and his two sons had to watch while his wife, her mother and the governess were repeatedly raped. When the sport was over he was marched off to a Russo-Polish run Auschwitz.[36]

A truce was declared at midday on the 8 May when the German army began to leave the city. No adequate arrangements had been made between the Czech National Council and the Wehrmacht for the transport of sick and injured soldiers and some 50,000 soldiers were left behind. On the 9th the Red Army finally appeared in Prague and Germans were told to bow when they saw a Soviet car.[37] The physics graduate 'K.F.', who had been imprisoned on the 5th, was taken out and forced to clear the barricades which had been built by the Czechs as they rose up against the garrison and which were preventing the Russians from getthing their tanks down the streets.[38] Germans were beaten bloody with iron bars and lead pipes by a civilian mob and made to remove their shoes and run over broken glass. The biggest barricades were 2.5 to 3 metres high, and made up of paving stones, iron bars and barbed wire. They had to dismantle the obstacles and repave the streets.

Women too were forced to clear the barricades. Helene Bugner was first beaten by the porter of her block of flats, then a Professor Zelenka drove her and twenty other women off to clear the streets. 'Here, I have brought you some German sows!' said the professor. Their hair was cut with bayonets and they were stripped of shoes and stockings. Both men and women died from the beatings. A large crowd of Czechs stood by and cheered whenever a woman was struck or fell. At the end of their work they had to tread on a large picture of Hitler and spit on it. Margarete Schell saw people being forced to eat pieces of such pictures as she too was put to work on the barricades.[39] As they were driven off, one woman heard a Czech tell another, 'Don't hit them on the head, they might die at once. They must suffer longer and a lot more.' When Helene Bugner returned that evening she was unrecognisable to her children.

Marianne Klaus saw her husband alive for the last time on the 9th. She received his body the next day – the sixty-six-year-old had been beaten to death by the police. On the same day she saw two SS men suffer a similar fate, kicked in the stomach until blood spurted out; a woman Wehrmacht auxiliary stoned and hanged; and another SS man hung up by his feet from a lamppost and set alight.[40] Many witnesses attested to the stringing up and burning of Germans as 'living torches', not just soldiers but also young boys and girls. Most were SS men, but as the Czechs were not always too scrupulous about looking at the uniforms, a number of Wehrmacht soldiers perished in this way too. In part this savagery was a response to a rumour that the Germans had been killing hostages. There was reportedly a repeat performance on the day when Beneš finally arrived in Prague: Germans were torched in rows on lampposts.[41]

The Ministry of Education, the Military Prison, the Riding School, the Sports Stadium and the Labour Exchange were set aside for German prisoners. The Scharnhorst School was the scene of a massacre on the night of the 5th. Groups of ten Germans were led down to the courtyard and shot: men, women and children – even babies. The others had to strip the corpses and bury them. Alfred Gebauer saw female SS employees forced to roll naked in a pool of water before they were beaten senseless with rifle butts. There were as many as 10,000–15,000 Germans in the football stadium in Strahov. Here the Czechs organised a game where 5,000 prisoners had to run for their lives as guards fired on them with machine guns. Some were shot in the latrines. The bodies were not cleared away and those who used the latrines later had to defecate on their dead countrymen. As a rule all SS men were killed, generally by a shot in the back of the head or the stomach. Even after 16 May when order was meant to be restored, twelve to twenty people died daily and were taken away from the stadium on a dung wagon. Most had been tortured first. Many were buried in mass graves at Pankrác Prison where a detachment of sixty prisoners was on hand to inter the corpses. Another impromptu prison was in a hotel up in the hills. This had been the Wehrmacht's brothel. A number of Germans were locked up in the cellar, and the whores and their pimps indulged in a new orgy of sadism and perversity. German men and women had to strip naked for their treatment. One of them was Professor Walter Dick, head of a department at the Bulovka Hospital. He was driven insane by his torturers and hanged himself on a chain.

One witness who was too ill to work was sent to the hospital camp at Motol, where there was an SS 'cellar'. This contained eighty to a hundred men who were brought out every day for beatings. A local speciality was to get the men to beat one another. In this case they had to slap one another round the face. They were often stripped naked prior to the torture and then literally booted down the steps to their cell once the guards had tired of their fun. The SS cellar contained a number of Hitler Youth boys of fourteen. Whenever it was deemed to be too full, guards fired at random though the bars to create more space. Gebauer swore that Czech collaborators were also badly treated, particularly women who had had German lovers. Thousands of dead Germans were buried in the cemetery in Wokowitz.[42]

Some German Bohemians eluded arrest by helping the Russians and Czech authorities. Hans Wagner indicated a Dr Rein from Postelberg, a prison doctor who was especially cruel. The Russians wanted the pick of the women. In the cellar where Margarete Schell was imprisoned, a plump doctor – possibly a Jew – came to take some of the women to safety before the Russians made their tour. A woman wanted to bring her children: 'Kinder hier lassen, Kindern tun sie nichts,' he said (Leave the children here, they won't do anything to the children). When they returned the Russians had taken four girls who returned exhausted in the morning.[43] Acts of kindness by Czechs were numerous. Some risked their lives to protect friends and acquaintances. 'Hansi' Thurn und Taxis reached safety in Austria through the intercession of a Czech general. He was assisted at the beginning by a Russian forced labourer on his estate.[44]

One wounded German officer had been in the Oko cinema since the 6 May. After helping tear down the barricades that day he was taken back to his temporary prison. There was no peace that night: the Russians and Czechs came for the women. Men who tried to protect them were beaten up, children who would not let go of their mothers' skirts were dragged out with them and forced to watch. Several women tried to commit suicide. The officer remained in the cinema until Whitsun. That day the cries of tortured Germans coming from the Riding School mingled with the voices of churchgoers next door, 'praying for mercy and neighbourly love'.[45]

After Whitsun the officer was taken to the Scharnhorst School. There was an ominous sign over the door reading 'Koncentrační Tabor'. 'There they tried to surpass in everything all that they had learned of concentration camps.' Cinemas were popular sites for 'concentration camps'. The Slavia in Řipská ulice was also used for around 500–700 prisoners.[46] The physics graduate 'K.F.' was taken there too and tortured. On the 10th he was taken off to Wenceslaus Square and driven towards three naked bodies hanging by their feet from a billboard. They had been covered with petrol and set alight, their faces punched in and the teeth knocked out – their mouths were just bloody holes. With others he was then obliged to drag the corpses back to the school.

Once they had laid down the bodies, one of the Czechs told the graduate: 'To jsou přece vaší bratrí, ted' je políbejte!' (They are your brothers, go on . . . kiss them!). Scarcely had he wiped the blood from his mouth than he was taken to the 'death cellar' to be beaten to death. They despatched the young Germans one by one. The graduate was the fourth in line. After the second killing a door opened and a Czech man came in. The graduate learned later that this was the nephew of the minister Stránský. He asked them who they were, and led out the graduate and a seventeen-year-old Hitler Youth, because they were the two that spoke Czech. In general, knowledge of Czech helped, but no one was immune: former officials, police officers and German-speaking Jews were subjected to imprisonment – even if they had just emerged from Nazi concentration camps. The minister's son told them with a grin on his face that they were the only ones who had ever emerged from the cellar alive.[47]

Anna Seidel was a sixty-seven-year-old engineer's widow living in Prague-Smichow. On the 9th she was rounded up with three other ladies, two of them of her age. They were robbed and beaten black and blue; their hair was shorn, their foreheads daubed with swastikas; they were then paraded through the streets on a lorry, shouting 'My jsme Hitler-kurvy!' (We are Hitler-whores!). If they did not shout loudly enough they were beaten again. After four weeks in Pankrác they were taken to Theresienstadt, where they remained for a year. Helene Bugner was taken away to Hagibor, which was seen as one of the better camps. From there she went to Kolin where the younger women were raped by Russians, some of them as many as forty-five times in a night. A Czech woman working for the Red Cross had set herself up as the talent-spotter. The women returned from these nightly sessions badly bitten by their paramours. Helene Bugner was released from agricultural work after three and a half months following complaints by the British: she had been a secretary in the legation for twelve years.[48]

Hans Wagner went to the Russian commander to beg for more beds for the sick and wounded. He took the precaution of going with a Czech colleague, Dr Dobbek. The Russian general Gordow was not in the slightest bit interested: 'If you have no room for your wounded, throw them in the Vltava, there is plenty of room for them there!'[49] Wagner went for a walk on the afternoon of the 14th. Hanging from the sign to the famous restaurant U svatého Havla were the half-carbonised remains of a German soldier who had been strung up by his heels. His right arm was missing from the shoulder. Wagner concluded that he was an amputee. Everywhere he noted the signs that the communists had taken over, under the shadow of the liberating Red Army. After popping into the Elekra, the family coffee house, he went towards the railway station. A blonde woman was being attacked by a mob. She was shouting in perfect Czech, but in a moment she was surrounded and stripped of her clothes. A dray wagon came by, and each of her limbs was attached to one of the horses. The beasts were driven off in opposite directions.

With the re-establishment of government, the wild concentration camps in Prague's cinemas and schools were wound up and the prisoners despatched to proper camps. One woman who had been in the Slavia cinema and claimed to have been spared from lynching by a semi-miraculous thunderstorm was taken to the main station on a sort of death march, which saw many German Bohemians beaten to death to the applause of the local mob. They were pushed into coal trucks where they were robbed one last time and then taken away. Others endured the death march to Theresienstadt. It is estimated that only 10 per cent of those who set out from Prague survived.[50] Modřany was another infamous Czech camp, mostly populated by Prague Germans; another was Bystřice, where Margarete Schell went on 28 July. The prisoners were welcomed by a demonstration of brutality. Anyone with professional titles was singled out for extra beating. She was whipped. She began to despair: 'We will never get out of here, this is the last stop.'[51]

The fate of the Prague Germans slowly became known to the outside world. The Austrians were busy trying to show the Allies that they had never had any affection for Germany and the Nazis, and they had their own problems. In Vienna the former diplomat Josef Schöner was visited by a Prague Czech on 18 May who gave him a misleading report that all the Germans had been interned or were working on rebuilding. The German-speakers were finished; they had defended themselves fiercely during the uprising, particularly the women, while the Russians had plundered the city like Vienna. They had also looted freely in Bratislava, and there had been a high incidence of rape, 'so that the first elation at liberation had much abated'.[52]

Many Germans spent a prolonged period in Pankrác Prison. Wagner claimed that a special treat for visiting Russian bigwigs was to be taken over the prison and witness a German being beaten to death. Another was to toss a prisoner from a second-floor parapet and shoot at him while he plummeted to the ground. Some boys from Reichenberg were accused of being Werewolves. They had to fight one another until they were bloody and then lick up the blood. When that resulted in vomiting, that too had to be licked up. When they had cleaned up the mess they were stripped and beaten with whips until the skin hung from their bodies. Then they were tossed into a cellar. Those who did not die from their wounds were later hanged.[53]

Caught up in the massacres were not just Prague Germans but refugees from eastern Bohemia and Moravia. Wagner saw a miserable troop of old men, women and children from Ohlau. He tried to give them milk but the RG dashed the bottles out of his hands and threatened to shoot the children who were prepared to lick it up from the pavement. International condemnation had little effect. In the 'revolutionary' days, the International Red Cross was too frightened of the Russians to act. In Prosecnice camp there was an IRC inspection in April 1946. As soon as the visit was over, the treatment of prisoners became worse.[54]

Landskron

The massacres were by no means confined to the capital. As soon as the Russians had liberated a town or village, partisans arrived to administer revolutionary justice. The primary targets were members of the Nazi or Sudetenland Party (SdP), or members of those organisations Beneš decreed had aided the Nazis in their tyranny. Partisans also listened to denunciations from local Czechs before they struck. The rich were particularly vulnerable. Also susceptible were doctors, grocers, butchers and publicans, and anyone who might have denied credit, or schnapps. In many places all Germans were considered guilty. In other places the action was coloured by some German outrage. In Littau near Iglau, the German-speaking pocket south of Prague, the Waffen-SS had torched the Czech village of Javoricka in March 1945. The partisans responded by driving the Germans into a forester's house and the Schloss and murdering them.[55]

In Landskron the fighting stopped on the 9 May. The Russian liberators were chiefly interested in the townswomen, whom they pursued into the night. There were few Czechs to speak of, and they were mainly concerned to protect their own property from plunder. This idyll changed when on the 17th some lorry-loads of armed Czech partisans arrived. All the male German inhabitants were hunted into the main square. By the early afternoon there were as many as a thousand. The Czechs amused themselves by drilling them, forcing them to lie down and get up, all the while walking among them, spitting and kicking them in the groin and shins. Those who fell during this humiliation were taken to a water tank and drowned. Any who bobbed up were shot. Meanwhile a 'People's Court' had been established with a jury composed of local Czechs. The Germans had to crawl to the bench. Most of the men then had to run a 50–60 metre gauntlet. Many fell and were beaten to pulp. The next day the survivors were reassembled. One man was strung up from a lamppost. The court adjourned only when a horrified woman set fire to her house which threw the crowd into a panic. Twenty-four Germans had been killed. An even greater number committed suicide.

Brno Death March

Brno was another German enclave. Before the Great War it was considered to be a 'suburb of Vienna'.[56] Even with the post-war migration it contained 60,000 Germans, and there were many more between Brno and the border. The Russians reached the city on 25 April. There followed the usual scenes of rape and violence. The next morning all Germans had to report for work. Czech partisans established their HQ in Kaunitz College, where the city's leading Germans were beaten and tortured. Sometimes they were forced to go on all fours and bark like dogs. When the Czechs had finished with them they were delivered to the hospital, where they were thrown into a cellar. A Red Cross nurse examined a German who had indescribable wounds to his genitals. Before he died he was able to explain his crime: he had sold vegetables to the Gestapo.[57]

At 9 p.m. on 30 May began the Brno Death March. It was the Feast of Corpus Christi, normally a day for solemn processions, and the largely Catholic Germans did not fail to draw comparisons. The 25,000 marchers had fifteen minutes to pack a bag and to assemble in the Convent Garden, where they spent the night. At dawn they were driven into the courtyard and relieved of their valuables before marching to the camp at Raigern in the pouring rain. The procession included inmates of the old people's home, the hospitals and the children's clinic and one Englishwoman who had been married to a local Nazi. Her case naturally excited the interest of the *Daily Mail* correspondent Rhona Churchill, who filed a story on 30 May.[58]

Stragglers were beaten with truncheons and whips and those who failed to get up were shot and their bodies stripped and plundered. Survivors were strip-searched before being driven on to a camp at Pohrlitz, about halfway to the Austrian border.[59] The Red Cross nurse claimed that a thousand had already died. Another said that the camp claimed a further 1,700 lives. One mother recounts that two of her three children died on the march.[60] The marchers were lodged in a car factory. The younger women were raped by the guards. Those still capable of walking were pushed on to the border the next morning, leaving behind about 6,000, who were thrown into grain silos. The Red Cross nurse stayed with them, and her reports do not make pleasant reading. It may be that some of the atrocities committed have been exaggerated in retrospect, but there is more than enough corroboration to make it clear that the Czechs behaved with in-human cruelty.

The Pohrlitz camp was evacuated on 18 June. Sixty to seventy people had been dying daily, largely from typhus. Nutrition consisted of stale bread and rotten root vegetables. The Russians came every night at 7.30 and stayed until 2 a.m. They raped the women, even a seventy-year-old. When the Red Cross nurse tried to protect a tender eleven-year-old, she herself was taken away to 'suffer the consequences' and was raped by five soldiers. Another witness said that the youngest raped was seven years old, the oldest eighty. Some of the healthier ones escaped and made their own way to the border. It was evidently desired that Brno should be free of Germans in time for Beneš's five-day visit in July. As it happened, the Czechs had failed to round up all the Germans, while others who had broken down on the march were returned to the city. When Beneš arrived they were forced out into the sand dunes without food or water. Many died, others went mad.[61]

The first to leave Pohrlitz were the sick, who were driven away and dumped in the marshes by the River Thaya on the Austrian border. No one knew they were there and according to the Red Cross nurse they starved to death. The corpses were photographed and shown in newsreels in Britain and the United States. The Czechs responded by saying that they had been killed by the Austrians. There was another massacre at Nikolsburg, where the bodies of 614 men were thrown into a mass grave.[62]

Iglau and Kladno

The German-speaking pocket around Iglau (Jihlava) in western Moravia was also a sore subject for the Czechs. When the town fell on 5 May it was the signal for a mass suicide of Germans: as many as 1,200 took their lives, and perhaps 2,000 were dead by Christmas. Between six and seven thou-sand Germans were driven into the camps Helenental and Altenberg. When Helenental was closed, the inhabitants were plundered and herded south towards the Austrian border. Some 350 people are said to have lost their lives on the way. They were detained in another camp in Stannern where hundreds more perished.[63]

The Germans in Kladno were subjected to the full severity of the Revolution from 5 May onwards. Erika Griessmann's father was taken away and never returned. She herself was beaten for refusing to tell the RG where the family jewellery was buried. A few days later she saw Germans being chased across a field like hares, gunned down by partisans with sub-machine guns. Her family was thrown out of their house on the 9th and made to run the gauntlet down their street while the crowd lashed out at them. She spotted some of their neighbours weeping at their windows at the sight.

They joined a group of refugees. Many of them were bloody, after Czechs had hurled grenades into their midst. For the second time the seventeen-year-old Erika heard that she and the better-looking Germans would be raped by the Russians. They apparently had first refusal. The Russians, however, treated her well. She fainted, and was pulled into a car by the hair. She woke on a sofa bound hand and foot. Five high-ranking Soviet officers asked her if she were hungry, and where she wanted to go. She said she wanted her mother. They took her to the football stadium where she found her mother and younger brother.

After threatening to shoot them all, Czechs took the Germans to Masshaupt where they had to stand in a ditch while a crowd spat on them and pelted them with stones. They were then returned to the football sta-dium on a lorry. There were German soldiers lying all around with bullet wounds in their stomachs and heads. Erika's party were strip-searched and taken to a barracks. Bodies were strewn everywhere, even small children whose parents had cut their throats to save them from fur-ther tortures.

On the 10th they prepared to march. Before the gates of the barracks a jeering crowd had assembled. A Czech read a speech: all Germans were criminals. Hand grenades were once again tossed among the refugees, pro-ducing another bloodbath. A Czech priest appeared to administer the last rites. Many of the dying refused his blessing. Erika and her mother man-aged to get into an ambulance and someone gave Erika a Red Cross nurse's hat. Russian sentries accompanied the German wounded as they left Kladno. One of the Russians recognised that Erika was no nurse and demanded she go with him. The injured in the ambulance took her side. He then requested either Erika or their watches. The heavily wounded German soldiers gave the Russian their watches and rings and Erika was bought free. That way they reached comparative safety in the American-occupied zone.[64]

The American Zone

It was the Americans rather than the Russians who liberated western Czechoslovakia. Whatever the Bohemian Germans might have wanted to believe, however, the Americans did not meddle in the activities of Czech partisans. The most that can be said is that the expulsions from their zone were generally more humane than those that took place east of the line.[65] They finally left in December 1945.

One woman did however report that Americans helped her cross the border; in another instance a woman was returned to Brno from Germany as a Czech national, and as a German had to suffer the consequences. In Bory Prison in Pilsen, the torture stopped when the Americans came to inspect, and started again the next day. The writer Ernst Jünger had a letter from his friend Sophie Dorothea Podewils on 10 October 1945. She had been in the Pilsen prison. 'What took place in the German and also in the Hungarian part of Czechoslovakia is a tragedy that is only comparable to what the Jews had to bear here.'[66]

In Mies near Marienbad, Czech partisans and American soldiers searched German houses together. Later the partisans shot twenty-five Germans in their camp. Elbogen (Habartov) was the seat of the Control Commission, which granted permission to Czechs to cross to the other Allied zones, but its decisions were not always respected by the partisans.[67] Franz Weinhand was picked up by the militia in Gfell and taken to the castle in Elbogen. He and his fellow Germans screamed so loudly during their whippings that they began to annoy the American sentries a hundred metres away. One of them fired his machine gun at their window. Two days later members of the American Commission arrived at the castle and took photographs of the Germans' naked bodies. Weinhand and the others dared not say a word for fear of reprisals. After four weeks the Americans took the political prisoners to Landshut in Bavaria. In September they were sent back to Czechoslovakia.[68]

In Schlackenwerth a German clockmaker called Müller was tortured to death. He came from the resort of St Joachimsthal (Jáchymov), where a Herr Steinfelsner, the owner of a sawmill, was hanged before the town hall in the presence of the townsfolk. The body hung there until some Americans came by in a jeep and forced the partisans to take it down.[69] In Bischofteinitz (Domažlice) the usual scenes occurred when the men were rounded up. Thirty-five of them were called out and butchered. In Blatna a girl who had dallied with the Americans even had her head shaved after their departure. The Americans were also in Chodau (Chodov), where the luggage of departing Germans were plundered almost as systematically as they were across the border in Poland.[70]

There were Czechs working and living in German areas, and Germans in the towns which lay in the middle of largely Czech areas. České Budějovice or Budweis in south-western Czechoslovakia was in the Czech heartlands. Until the nineteenth century the Germans had dominated the town. There was still an active minority in 1945, who were put to work in the mines. Most of the atrocities took place around the labour exchange. Large numbers of Czech women cheered as the Germans were beaten bloody. The priest, Pater Joseph Seidl, was one of them – he had apparently committed no other crime than being German. The beds in the military hospital were taken over by the Czechs. One severely wounded soldier was given a lethal jab. SS men aged between eighteen and twenty-one were dragged into the courtyard and beaten to death. In Pilsen, another largely Czech city, Franz Wagner, a former communist who had spent a term in Dachau, was robbed and beaten up before being expelled from the country.[71]

Freudenthal, Freiwaldau and Bilin

Reports indicate that Czechs particularly loathed German innkeepers and physicians. Innkeepers perhaps looked down on Czech customers, and physicians either refused to treat Czechs or were suspected of being involved in Nazi genocide. Carl Gregor was a general practitioner in Freudenthal (Bruntál) in the north-eastern sector of the Czech lands. He was taken to the Freudenthal camp and accused of having murdered 150 foreigners. He laughed off the accusation, and was tortured by eighteen men who beat his back so badly that the skin burst on his buttocks.

In Freudenthal all the inmates had to witness the executions, which took place behind the barrack block. Gregor's knowledge of Czech and Slovak meant that he had to translate the orders given by the commandant. On one occasion twenty men had to dig their own grave and then climb in. They were shot in the back of the head. One man had to be shot three times, yet he was still alive when the prisoners filled in the grave. The excuse for this slaughter was an accident with a grenade that killed a Russian. The Czechs then told the Russians that the death had been the result of a German-laid time-bomb and demanded that a hundred hostages be shot in reprisal. The Russians allowed them to kill just a score.[72]

In Freiwaldau (Jeseník) they marched the camp inmates to the border and pushed them into Germany. The ordeal took seventy-two hours, while the Germans were beaten with whips and pistol butts.[73] Alfred Latzel was the proprietor of a large sugar refinery and farm. On 20 June he was dispossessed and warned that he would have problems were he to remain in Czechoslovakia. He felt he had done no wrong and decided to brave it. He was taken in for a short interview by the local police, at the end of which he was delivered to the Camp II Jauernig – a former RAD or Reichsarbeitsdienst camp. Latzel learned much later that he had been incarcerated because he had allegedly denounced communists during the Third Reich. He denied it. At Jauernig, the gaoler was a German communist. German denouncers were also present at the torture sessions egging on the others.

After four days Latzel was taken to another camp in an old work-service barracks at Adelsdorf, a former POW compound. Here his father-in-law, the estate owner Dr Erich Lundwall, was the representative for the prisoners. The partisan guards wore old SS uniforms, although they sported red stars in their caps together with the letters KTOF – Koncentrační Tábor Okres Frývaldov (Concentration Camp Area Freiwaldau). The same legend hung over the door of the camp, but later this was changed first to 'internment camp', then 'collection point for internees'. The restructuring of the Freiwaldau camps by the authorities in Prague was not popular with the partisan guards. In the period of the wild camps, the partisans not only wielded power, but allegedly amassed quantities of valuables, food and drink, some of which might have been intended for the prisoners. New arrivals were worked over by the guards, beaten with whips and rifle butts. Latzel describes two boys of fifteen or sixteen who tried to escape and were brought back to the camp by their own communist fathers. They were slowly tortured to death after swastikas were carved into their buttocks. They were finally shot in front of two prisoners chosen from each hut. A Nazi greengrocer was selected for special treatment. He eventually vanished. It was assumed he had been killed. The guards also enjoyed whipping a seventy-year-old man. After each stroke he had to say 'Děkuji!' (Thank you!).[74]

Once the camps were taken over by the regular gendarmerie, the brutality was moderated, if never exactly stopped. The bourgeois Latzel was given unusual work to do outside the camp. He ploughed the fields and worked in the woods and factories; he plundered farms and factories and dismantled machines. Nothing was ever entered in an inventory. The food improved with time. To a diet of dried-potatoes-and-water soup unbelievable delicacies were added: vegetables and pearl barley and, once a week, meat. Every now and then there was jam, and cakes at Christmas. Eventually there was even a visit from a priest, though he was not allowed to deliver a homily, and some amateur dramatics were permitted, as well as a cabaret. Some mild, anti-Nazi propaganda appeared, such as an obituary for the Third Reich that was intended to be witty. The Nazi Karl Froning thought it tasteless and silly. When they were shown films of the Nazis' victims they thought they were falsified (a common enough reaction at the time) – 'most of us had seen enough of these atrocities ourselves and suffered them on our own bodies'.

There was a third camp for men in the Freiwaldau area at Thomasdorf; a fourth, Biberteich, housed around 300 women. Karl Schneider spent a gruelling fourteen and a half months at Thomasdorf after he was accused of shooting a Czech. He was tortured and had the usual beating from another prisoner, Franz Schubert from Niklasdorf. Schubert did not hit him forcibly enough and was clouted so hard as a result that he fell dead to the ground. The same night the Czechs killed two others after hours of torture. One of them was a boy of fifteen or sixteen. The commandant greeted the new arrivals with the usual smashing of heads and limbs. When one was seen to bleed profusely he remarked, 'German blood is no blood, it is pig's shit!' The commandant's name was Wiesner, which suggests he might have had some of that non-blood himself.

The Pg and SA member Karl Froning was the former administrator of Thomasdorf in the days when it had contained Russians. He seems to have fared reasonably well by comparison to others, possibly because some of the Czech passion was spent by the time he arrived in the camp in July. He remembered the Czech lessons in the open air, calculated to humiliate Germans who had always refused to learn that language. Effusions of violence were not unknown, however, and the guards had a particular animus towards a Freiwaldau physician called Dr Pawlowsky, who was obliged not only to lie in his own excrement, but to consume it too. He eventually collapsed before his torturers and died. In four weeks, Froning estimated, some 10 per cent of the 200 inmates died from one cause or another.[75]

In Bilin (Bilina), north-west of Prague, they had the good fortune to be taken directly to the border without being subjected to a Czech camp. Anton Watzke nonetheless saw appalling scenes along the way with the Czech *soldateska* killing German women. They even shot the priest. In another instance the witness Adolf Aust remembered seeing a man shot who had paused to relieve himself.[76]

Brüx, Saaz, Komotau, Aussig and Teschen

It was the Poles who liberated the town of Teschen (Děčín) in the north on 10 May. For five days they raped, looted, torched and killed. A grocer was taken off to the water tower and thrown in. They shot at him and missed. Finally one of the Poles fished him out, saying he had done well and his life was saved. The Poles reportedly killed scores of POWs; the rest were taken to the camp at Jaworczno where they were sent down the mines. Other Sudeten Germans were deported to Glatz in Silesia, which had been awarded to the Poles. Here they went through their agonies all over again until they were re-expelled with the Silesian Germans – this time to the new slimmed-down 'Reich'.

According to Franz Limpächer, there was just one Czech in his village of Kleinbocken: Stanislaus Mikesch had moved there from Kladno, married a German girl and become a great enthusiast for Hitler. After the arrival of the Poles he re-emerged wearing a good many red stars and announced that he was now the local commissar. He immediately confiscated his neighbour's belongings. More Czechs arrived from Prague, Tábor and Pardubice and took over the houses of the Germans.[77]

In the small town of Brüx (Most) near by, Dr Carl Grimm was attached to the Czech police as a doctor for Germans. He said Brüx had 30,000 inhabitants, of whom two-thirds were Germans. Some of the worst raping and pillaging was carried out by Russian DPs who had been brought in to work at a local dam. Part of Grimm's work was to certify the causes of death, and he therefore took note of the number of suicides in the months of May, June and July. At its high point, some sixteen Germans committed suicide daily, often entire families. Few could shoot or gas themselves as the Germans had been obliged to hand over their weapons and their gas had been cut off. Most had hanged themselves from whatever convenient perch they could find for that purpose. Grimm thought the total number of suicides amounted to between 600 and 700 – about 3 per cent of the German inhabitants.

Grimm's work with the local police delayed his imprisonment. The other Brüx men were taken off to a camp at Striemitz, half an hour away on foot, while the women were taken to the Poros glassworks in Brüx itself, from which a thousand were eventually marched to the German border at Deutschneudorf. Some of the men were put to work in the mines and at the hydrogenation works. Others were taken to Concentration Camp 28 at Maltheuren.[78] Germans who worked in heavy industry were often protected by the Russians who requisitioned the factories. When the factories were handed over to the Czechs, the Germans who worked there were put into Camp 27. German mine directors were shot: Czechs had been forced to work there during the war.

Householders were simply at the mercy of Czechs who appeared at the doors and forced them out. Apart from a thirty-kilo suitcase (which would be stolen from them anyhow), they were allowed to take nothing with them. The Czechs were protected by soldiers who then took the Germans off to 'evacuation camps' like Negerdörfel in Brüx, which had formerly been an anti-aircraft barracks. Some of them were quickly invalided out to Germany. The worst treatment was naturally meted out to former Nazis, together with the owners of important buildings or impressive houses. They were either taken to Camps 27 and 28 or locked up in the barracks, the police HQ, the local court or Striemitz. Once again the men had to box one another, with the guards standing by to make sure they hit hard.

The terror in Brüx started late, on 1 August. The rest of the German men were rounded up, beaten and marched off to Camp 28. Grimm gives a full list of the camps in the borough of Brüx: 17/18 and 31/32 near Maltheueren, Rössel camp and Camp 37 near Brüx itself, 22/25 at Niedergeorgenthal and 33/34 at Rosenthal. These camps provided workers for the hydrogenation works, which normally employed 35,000 workers. There were also camps for the mines, which employed a further 25,000, but Grimm didn't know their names. He estimated that there were around thirty camps in all in that part of Czechoslovakia. During the war, the mines and the dams had been staffed by foreign workers – Dutch, French, Italians, Croats, Bulgarians, Poles, Ukrainians and Russians. Now they were to be replaced by Germans.

Grimm himself was in Tabor – or Camp* – 28, with a fluctuating population ranging from 500 to 1,400 souls. The inmates were not just from the local towns and villages of the Sudetenland; there were Germans from the Reich too and Hungarian Germans. The camp was made up of wooden huts, with around thirty men to a cell. The fury of the Russians and Czechs had not abated. In the interests of maintaining health, fifteen men who were suffering from tuberculosis were shot. Beatings were a matter of course and the work was gruelling enough: eighteen hours a day at the hydrogenation works with six hours' sleep. Work was a two-hour march away, and a two-hour slog home. The march was all part of the planned humiliation. It was led by two 'court jesters', one wearing a top hat and the

---

* Not to be confused with the town of Tábor.

other a Prussian *Pickelhaube*. The prisoners with white swastikas and 'KT 28' on their backs had to sing German nationalist songs. One of the jesters came to a sticky end when the 'Kadle' (commandant) Vlasak tried to shoot through the top of his hat as a joke, and hit him in the head by mistake. When he was laid out in his coffin he was found still to be alive and was shot two more times through the heart.

'Kadle' Karel Vlasak liked to be called 'Tgyr' or 'Tiger'. The prisoners had their own name for him: 'The Beast of 28'. He walked around the camp with a revolver in one hand and a *nagaika* or cat-o'-nine-tails in the other. He liked to strike the prisoners with his entire forearm. When they fell, as many did, he would kick them in the stomach and the testicles. His compatriots cheered at the sport. Eduard Kaltofen recounts a story of his beating a crippled solder to death with his own crutch. On another occasion four men had to prepare their own coffins before they received a shot in the back of the head. Vlasak was later arrested – not because of his behaviour towards the prisoners, but because he had taken property from them and not handed it over to higher authorities.[79]

The occupation of the famous hop town of Saaz (Žatec) and nearby Postelberg (Postoloprty) followed similar lines. On 9 May the liberating Russian armies raped and shot a few of the overwhelmingly German citizenry. Some Germans hanged or poisoned themselves, others vanished. The Russians were replaced by Czech soldiers under General Svoboda on 2 June. In the meantime, the locals had been praying that the Anglo-Americans would step in to create some sort of equitable division between the Czechs and the Germans. That never happened. On the 3rd it was decided to rid Saaz of its Germans. Before the war there had been some 16,000 people in the town. Five thousand men and boys were herded into the market square. Anyone who struck the Czechs as unusual was savagely beaten. The men were then marched off to Postelberg fifteen kilometres away, where the population had already been evacuated. The journey took two hours. If a man collapsed he was shot – boys in front of their fathers, fathers in front of the boys. The Saazer males were installed in an old barracks building. Another 150 men were left behind in Saaz Prison where they were subjected to more sophisticated brutality. They were taken off to Postelberg later that day, leaving only the anxious womenfolk behind.[80]

The following day there was a small-scale massacre in the Postelberg Barracks. A detail was formed to bury the dead in gravel ditches that would from now on serve as the camp latrine. The men were then robbed of any valuables they had about them. Later a detail went through the prisoners to locate doctors, pharmacists, priests, members of the important professions, useful skilled workers, half-Jews, men married to Jews and any former inmates of German camps. They were transferred to the camp in Saaz.

The hoi polloi spent the night in the stables. In the morning the doors were opened with a cry of 'Rychle, rychle!' (Quick, quick!). Those who tarried were gunned down. The dead and wounded were tossed into the latrine. The remaining men were sifted politically. All members of the SS, SA, Nazi organisations, the Wehrmacht and the National Socialist Party had to come forward. The shootings continued throughout the day and night. Five boys of around fifteen who had tried to escape were beaten bloody with whips and executed before the eyes of the others.

The survivors, numbering perhaps 275, were crammed back into the stables. It was four days before they received any bread and by then some had gone out of their minds. When the doors were finally opened, one of the men emerged stark naked and pranced around like a ballet dancer. A German captain begged the chief torturer, Police Captain Marek, for the right to die like a soldier. Marek made him kneel down to shoot him in the back of the head. He fired and missed. The German officer turned and said, 'Shoot better!' Marek took two more attempts to finish him off.[81]

For the former soldier Ottokar Kremen from Komotau (Chomutov), the Russians were sweetness and light compared to the Czechs. Returning from the army on 7 May, he found the town occupied by Russian soldiers. They assured him they would not be staying long and allowed him to take away some clothes. When he discovered that his bicycle had been stolen while he was inside, the Russian major commandeered a motorcycle from another Russian and gave it to him, together with a laissez-passer in Russian. Kremen then went to his sister-in-law's house in the nearby village of Gersdorf. He was not alone in finding the Russian soldiers more understanding than the Czechs. Dr Siegel in Theresienstadt said the Russians were often 'notably more decent'. A Russian doctor treated the wounds of those that came out on work details and helped others to flee. Siegel used to tell girls who wanted to escape the misery of the nightly rapes to make friends with a Russian and clear off with him.[82]

Nearly a month later, at the beginning of June, the Czechs came to Gersdorf and arrested Kremen. He was interrogated and asked whether he had been in the SS, the SA or the Party, all of which he denied. The Czechs seized the motorbike and everything else they could find and took him to an inn where he had to box other Germans. Then he was escorted to the former Hotel Weimar in Komotau where he was locked up in a room with sixteen others, including an eleven-year-old boy who was later shot with his father, the owner of the local bell foundry. They were taken from the hotel-prison to the camp that had been set up in the former Komotau State Farm. As they left, a Czech held a bust of Adolf Hitler and they were told to salute it. Kremen heard one Czech say to another that anyone who made the so-called Hitler Greeting would be shot. Kremen told the others and no one raised their hands. At the camp they had to strip. Any good clothing was carted off and they were given rags that had belonged to those who had already perished; very often they were covered in blood. Kremen was led to a large room with seventy-eight other men. They were drilled all day – including men of eighty. Anyone who did not march properly was beaten.

Kremen found his knowledge of Czech useful. He was able to take over the drilling, and at his own request he taught the prisoners Czech, which meant they could sit down for a while. The SS and SA members were later picked out, beaten up and shot. The other men had to clean up the yard and scatter sand on the blood. The survivors were then sent to the 'infamous' concentration camp in the former French POW camp at Maltheuren. But Kremen and a few others were spared. They were put in the old glassworks: him, a doctor called Lockwenz, an engineer, an Austrian who was known to have shown goodwill towards Czechs, a Yugoslav, a staff captain from the Czech army and a local postman. The Austrians and the Yugoslavs were sent home. Meanwhile the glassworks filled up again with more Germans, so that the inmates totalled 360 men and eight women. A lot of local worthies were among them: directors of local industries, including the sausage maker, who was later beaten to death, a priest and a gamekeeper, who also perished. They were put to work on the railways, with Kremen as interpreter. While he was at work, Kremen met a young Czech railwayman who had been offered a three-room flat in Komotau. He had refused. He didn't want someone else's flat. 'Where will it all lead?' he said. 'I am not going to take any of the flats here, they have all been stolen.'[83]

Back in the camp the beatings and torture continued. One Latvian could hardly make himself understood, as he knew little German and less Czech. He claimed that his membership of the SS was an accident. He was shot. A German colonel who had served in the Czech army until 1924 was beaten to death. A geometer who had a Polish-sounding name also died a hideous death. There had been little love lost between the Czechs and the Poles since 1938, when the Poles had seized the moment of the Czech diplomatic defeat to march into the Teschen area and appropriate it.

Kremen had been lucky he was not in Komotau when they celebrated the Revolution there. All the men aged between thirteen and sixty-five were made to assemble in the square. There were between five and six thousand in all. The area was then cordoned off. The men had to remove their upper garments to see if there were the usual SS markings. Anyone found to have the tattoo was stripped naked and beaten to pulp. One young, blond boy put up a fight. They prized open his legs and destroyed his genitals before beating him to death.

The survivors were marched out through Görkau, Eisenberg and Kunersdorf. On the way they passed a half-dead local official who had been strapped to a telegraph pole. They spent three nights in Gebirgsneudorf before moving on to Brüx and Maltheuern. Here they were given their first food for four days. The Germans worked in the hydro-electric works. When the anniversary of Lidice came round the camp commandant personally slaughtered the Komotau optician and his two sons and another boy in front of one another. Germans were forced to beat each other up. Their Calvary came to an end when 250–300 of them were sent to Germany in August 1945.[84]

The Czechs indulged in a little orgy of shooting in the small town of Duppau near Kaaden (Kadan). First they shot the soldier Franz Weis and threw his body on to the town square; shortly afterwards it was the turn of two SS men who had been invalided out of the army, Josef Wagner and Franz Mahr. The headmaster of the secondary school, Andreas Draht, and his assistant teachers, Damian Hotek, Franz Wensich and Rudolf Neudörfl, were next in line. The Czechs then turned their attentions to the chief postmaster, Karl Schuh. The men who carried out this little massacre were Captain Baxa and Lieutenant Tichý. In the village of Totzau close by they killed thirty-four Germans because they found arms, although permission to keep them had apparently been granted by the American Army Command in Karlsbad. In another place they shot the wife of the roofer Holzknecht because she looked out of the window at the wrong moment. In Podersheim they killed the farmer Stengl, and another eighty Germans were massacred in the Jewish cemetery. None, according to the witness Eduard Grimm, was associated with the Nazis. Josef Jugl was accused of being a Werewolf, and hauled off to the camp at Kaaden. On the way the Czech guard took pity on him. 'Kaaden Prison bad,' he said, 'you still young.' He told him to scarper, and Jugl did.[85]

On 30 July there was an explosion in Aussig (Ustí nad Labem). The Svoboda Guards had arrived that night in the town, forcing the Germans to wear white armbands and walk in the gutter. About 300 young men from Prague turned up. At about 3.30 a.m. the eyewitness heard a terrible bang, and thought a cupboard might have fallen over. He climbed on the roof and saw smoke billowing from somewhere behind the Marienberg: it was a huge ammunition dump, filled with captured German weapons. Later the Germans were accused of having sabotaged it. He went out on to the street. Luckily he wore no armband, for the explosion was also the signal to attack the Germans with whatever weapons came to hand. As the town commander allegedly put it: 'Now we will start the revolution against the Germans.' He saw men and women with prams thrown twenty metres off the bridge into the Elbe and then shot at by the SNB guards with machine guns. Any that managed to reach the bank were beaten with iron bars. Eventually some Russian soldiers succeeded in clearing the streets and a curfew was established. About 400–1,000 people had been killed.[86]

Anti-fascists did not necessarily have any advantages. As one Czech told Herbert Schernstein, 'Němec jest němec' (A German is a German). Schernstein had just returned to his home town after seven years in concentration camps as a communist. He had endured Theresienstadt, Sachsenhausen and Ravensbrück. His friend Willi Krebs, who had been the founder of the Prödlitz Communist Party, had been robbed of his shop.[87] Near Aussig were the concentration camps Lerchenfeld and Schöbritz. Heinrich Michel was actually working as a policeman for the newly appointed police director Douda when he was arrested on 16 May. Douda was a Muscovite who had been employed in the local gym. He had gone to Russia in 1938 and therefore had the complete confidence of the new regime. After insulting Michel, he had him thrown into a cell in the courthouse prison with a painter, a gunsmith, a lawyer and others. On the second day the cell began to fill up. One man brought a 'bestial stench' with him. It soon became clear why: he was seeping excrement from his trouser legs to his collar. When they undressed him they found no appreciable part of his body that was not covered in blood. He had been caught trying to escape and suffered the consequences.

After drinking three-quarters of a bottle of schnapps, the lieutenant commanding decided he would show them how to treat an SS man. The doors to the cells were thrown open, including that housing the SS. He chose Willi Künstner, an honorary member of the SS and personnel manager of the firm of Schicht, a major employer in Aussig. He was so badly beaten that he had to be taken away to hospital where he died without regaining consciousness. The courthouse gaol was the feeder for the local concentration camps. Michel was taken to Lerchenfeld where he was made a kapo. A former Luftwaffe camp that had been manned by Hungarians and wrecked by the Russians during their advance, it was run by a Commandant Vrša. All new arrivals had to sing the 'Deutschland-slied' and SA songs while a picture of Hitler was paraded before them. Then they had to run a forty-to-fifty metre gauntlet while they were lashed with bullwhips. SA men received an extra twenty-five stripes on the bottom.

With time the population of Lerchenfeld camp grew to 3,500. Michel himself was severely beaten by a Czech guard. When he asked him why he had treated him that way the guard said it was because he had once reported him for stealing a cake when he was twelve years old. When the Russians took over Lerchenfeld in October, the inmates were moved to Schöbritz. They had to build the camp themselves and that meant spending the first night in the open air. In Böhmisch Leipa (now the 'Czech' Česka Lipa), a camp was erected for around 1,200 Germans. In the savagery of the Czech takeover the innkeepers of the area seem to have come out badly, while the local Landrat or councillor had his face pushed in his own excrement until he died from that and other beatings. Two hundred and fifty-one prisoners perished within twelve months.

Theresienstadt

The most notorious camp in Czechoslovakia was Theresienstadt, the Nazis' show camp where inmates had been required to purchase living space in a 'model ghetto'. Many of Germany's, Austria's and Czechoslovakia's most famous or most talented Jews had been holed up within the eighteenth-century walled town. They died in droves, either from neglect or when they were shipped out to Auschwitz or Treblinka.

On 5 May 1945 Theresienstadt was taken over by the Red Cross. The commandant, Karl Rahm, tried to escape and the last Jewish administrator (the Jews had their own governing body) tendered his resignation.[88] A typhus epidemic kept the prisoners in the ghetto for the time being. The Czechs saw a new use for the citadel: it would be filled with Germans. Some were put to work tending the sick Jews. On 24 May there was a delivery of 600 Prague Germans of both sexes, including Red Cross sisters from the clinics. They were taken to the Little Fortress about a kilometre away from the fortified town. It had a long, dark history. It was here that the murderers of Archduke Francis Ferdinand – Princip and Čabrinović – died in 1918. They had been too young for execution and had succumbed to TB.[89] In Nazi times the Little Fortress had been largely devoted to political prisoners. The SS had their amenities there, including a swimming pool and a cinema. In 1943 the Little Fortress was expanded with the construction of a fourth courtyard. The 600 Germans were taken there.

The prisoners were separated into four groups: men, youths, children and women. The entrance was through a low archway covered with grass. Once inside the dark tunnel leading to the cells the RG lashed out at the men with truncheons, beating them to the ground. Anyone who failed to get up was *fertiggemacht* (finished off). In the courtyard they had to run the gauntlet. Those who fell were dealt with in person by the Camp Commandant Alois Pruša, who beat in their kidneys. He was occasionally assisted in his work by his daughter Sonja, a girl of around twenty. Another source attests to his having two daughters, both equally brutal. One boasted that she had killed eighteen Germans with her own hands. Pruša's own viciousness might have been explained by the fact that he had been detained in Theresienstadt by the Nazis. Another inmate, Eduard Fitsch, maintained that the guards were all former concentration camp prisoners.

Those who had been 'finished off' breathed their last in their own appointed cell. Between fifty-nine and seventy of the 600 died in those first few hours. Two hundred more succumbed in the next few days. Pruša and his assistant Tomeš did not give much hope to the survivors, who were told that those who had entered the Little Fortress would never leave it. All their papers, photographs and other – non-valuable – effects were put on a heap and burned. The man who commanded the fourth courtyard was a Pole called Alfred Kling. He claimed that he was an expert in killing and could simply decide by the number of strokes how long a victim would survive his beating. As he put it, 'We have reduced you to such a state in two months that the Gestapo would have needed five years to achieve.'[90]

Dr E. Siegel, a Czech-speaking general practitioner working for the Red Cross, was subjected to the full initiating ceremony. Not only was he beaten, but there were attempts to dislocate his arm and break his bones. A truncheon was placed in his mouth to knock out his teeth, and he was told to confess he was a member of the SA – which he continued to deny. When they had finished with him he was thrown on a concrete floor in a pool of his own blood. There he lay for three days until a Czech 'colleague' visited him. This man picked him up by the hair and dashed him to the ground again. He still failed to die.[91]

Siegel was made camp doctor. Not that he could do much for the moment. As a result of his torture he could neither stand nor sit. With his left hand he needed to hold up his head, otherwise it fell on to his breast –

so badly damaged were the muscles in his neck. His left eye functioned only when he looked straight ahead, and he could hardly hear as a result of the blows to his ears. His heart gave him trouble, but another doctor was able to give him some injections. They were not short of medicaments – according to Siegel, they lay in heaps around the former ghetto.

Once he was able to walk again, Siegel was ordered to kill a number of allegedly elderly prisoners in Cell 50 by lethal injections as it would be a pity to prolong their agonies. He tried to get out of the order, even going so far as to hide the poison. In the account he wrote later, he says he was saved by a visit to the camp by a Czech doctor who proposed the creation of a typhus ward. Siegel was put in charge. It was set up in the old SS cinema on 6 June. Later he had the chance to look into Cell 50 on his rounds. He discovered its occupants to be aged between sixteen and eighteen, and apparently members of the SS. Many of them had freshly amputated legs and dislocated joints. Their bandages had come off and their stumps were septic. They were so thickly crammed into the cell that their bodies touched. They begged for their dressings to be changed, but Siegel was forbidden to touch them or mention that he had seen them, lest he be locked up with them himself. He said that these miserable boys were Pruša's pride and joy, that he would literally jump around like a clown at the sight of them – although he was careful to show them only to his special friends and not to the authorities from Prague.

The hundred or so children under twelve had a special building to themselves. At first this was used for propaganda purposes as there was a courtyard for them to play in and a place to hang out their washing. Journalists were brought to the camp to see the children and note how well they were treated. It was a case of history repeating itself: there was a famous film produced by the Nazis in Theresienstadt, made to show the outside world how humane it was. At the onset of winter, however, the children were not so happy, because their quarters offered them little or no protection from the cold.

Pruša maintained that everyone in the camp was a member of the SS or the Gestapo. When the Russians expressed doubts about a number of boys aged from twelve to fourteen, he replied that they were detained as the children of SS or Gestapo men and that one of them had managed single-handedly to kill eleven Czechs. A similar story was retailed by the Czech Ministry of the Interior: Theresienstadt contained only SS, despite the fact that half its inmates were women of ages ranging from suckling children to one old lady of ninety-two. There were also a number of blind people who had been brought to the Little Fortress from Aussig after the massacre.

Much of the savagery stopped when Pruša was replaced by a Major Kálal, who had no time for Germans but had, at least, a proper soldier's dislike of torture.[92]

Pankrác

One September evening in Pankrác (Pankratz), Hans Wagner had a little performance to distract him from his sufferings: public executions. A gibbet was set up outside the prison. Children stood on the cars to get a better view of the hangings and there was a crowd he estimated at some 50,000. After each execution they cheered.

The first in line was Professor Josef Pfitzner. He was followed by an SS Gruppenführer Schmidt from Berlin. Next came the lawyer Franz Schicketanz, who had prepared the case for the Sudeten Germans presented to the British mediator Lord Runciman in 1938. Then it was the turn of Dr Blaschtowitschka of the German Special Court. His father, the president of the Prague Senate, died of hunger a few days later. Among the other victims that day were Dr Franz Wabra, who headed a unit for internal medicine at the hospital in Beraun, and an insurance official called Straněk. The Czechs were killing some of their own collaborators: General Blaha, the founder of the Society for Czech–German Friendship, together with its president, Richtrmoc and its chief executive, Major Mohapl. The first two were condemned to death. Mohapl was sent down for twenty years.

The most prominent denizen of Pankrác was Karl-Hermann Frank. Wagner saw him exercising in the yard every afternoon. The former Reichsprotektor had been handed over by the Americans and was publicly hanged on 22 May 1946. At the beginning of 1947, another group of German Czechs were strung up: Ernst Kundt, Hans Krebs and Hans Wesen. The leading doctor, Karl Feitenhansl, was sentenced to life imprisonment. The cases against Rudolf Jung and Dr Rosche were dropped – both had already died from hunger in prison.

There were German Jews in Pankrác too. Dr Karl Loewenstein, once a prominent Berlin businessman and former marine officer, had been in charge of the Theresienstadt ghetto police. The Czechs accused him of collaboration, assisting in the deportation of two Jewish policemen to Auschwitz. Loewenstein remained fifteen months in the prison. He was cast as a 'typical Prussian officer' who fulfilled his duties with an unbending zeal. He remained in Pankrác despite letters of protest from the Jewish leader Leo

Baeck in London and others. He shared a cell with other Germans, chiefly SS men. There was so little food that the prisoners ate grass and eggshells. In March 1946 the Czechs finally decided that the accusations were groundless: Loewenstein was simply a disciplinarian who had done more to alleviate the sufferings of the Jews than to aggravate them. He was released from Pankrác but not freed. He went to the camp at Leitmeritz (Litoměřice), where once again he was surrounded by the race that had locked him up in the first place and slaughtered his friends and relations. He was not released from his Czech captivity until January 1947.[93]

Torture

Torture appears to have been the rule. In Prague, Johann Schöninger, who had been based in London before the war, was hit with iron bars and had nails driven into his feet. His assistant, Schubert, was beaten to death. In Domeschau Johann Rösner had lighted matches pushed under his finger-nails. In Komotau, the torture seems to have been similar to the rack. A Waffen-SS man's penis and testicles had been so worked over that the former had swollen to 8–9 cm thick and the latter were septic. The whole area round to his anus was filled with pus and stank. In Theresienstadt one woman observed a female SS member being forced to sit astride an SA dagger: 'I can still hear her screams.' The chief torturers in the Little Fortress were two guards named Truka and Valchař. Guards used a variety of instruments for beating and lashing their victims: steel rods sheathed with leather, Spanish pipes, rubber truncheons, iron bars and wooden planks. In Klattau (Klatovy) one man had wooden wool soaked in benzene put between his toes and set alight so that it burned his sexual organs. Siegel thought they must have had orders from above, because the methods used in all Czech camps were broadly similar.[94]

The first time the activities of the Czech torturers ever came to court was in Germany itself, with the trial of Jan Kouril, one of the most brutal guards at Kaunitz College. Kouril had later been assistant commandant of Kleidova camp. He made the mistake of trying to sell gold fillings to a German dentist in Munich. The dentist recognised him as one of his tor-turers, and Kouril was tried and sentenced to fifteen years in prison by a court in Karlsruhe. During the trial the grave-digger from the College gave evidence that 1,800 bodies had been removed, including the corpses of 250 soldiers. While Kouril could find not one witness in his defence, 200 came forward for the prosecution.[95]

In June 1945 a law was introduced to stop beatings in the camps. It was not always heeded, but it alleviated some of the sufferings. The Czechs also punished commandants and warders who overstepped the mark. By all accounts this had less to do with the prisoners than with the pocketing of their effects. Dr Siegel tells us, for example, that the 'monsters' Pruša and his two daughters, as well as Kling and Tomeš and others from Theresienstadt, were tried in the court in Leitmeritz.[96]

Expulsions

The end of the nightmare was the beginning of another: the march to Germany or Austria. The deportations were sanctioned by Article 13 of the Potsdam Accords, although it was stipulated that the expulsion of the civilian populations should take place in the most humane manner possible. Hans Freund went to Dresden in the blistering heat of June 1945. No water was provided and many of the older Germans died.[97]

It went relatively smoothly for Margarete Schell, who found herself on the same train as her mother and stepfather. She arrived in Hesse 'a beggar, homeless, outlawed – but free!' They had been allowed to take just thirty kilos of possessions with them (later this was increased first to fifty then to seventy kilos) and were assigned to a numbered goods wagon. In each car there was a little stove to warm them, but not enough room to lie down. Right up to the last moment there was a worry that the Americans were not going to let them in. They were Czechs, not 'Reich' Germans after all.[98]

The expulsions did not cover all Germans. Some were left to rot in Czech prisons. Alfred Latzel's father-in-law, for example, was sentenced to eighteen years by a People's Court in Troppau, to be served in Mürau bei Hohenstadt, a medieval castle once the most dreaded prison in the Austro-Hungarian Empire. During the war it had been used to house Czechs and Polish prisoners suffering from TB. The death rate had been alarmingly high. Other Germans were retained after 1946 to work in the mines or forests. The People's Courts were painfully reminiscent of their namesakes in Nazi Germany: justice was summary, death sentences ten a penny, life imprisonment was an option, otherwise the culprit received five or ten years in the mines. Max Griehsel had worked at the main office of the DAF, the Nazi forced-labour organisation. He received a five-year sentence. The trial was over in ten minutes.[99]

The Sudeten communists, who had never supported Henlein and who had suffered under the Nazis, fared no better. Like the new Poland, Czechoslovakia would not suffer minorities (except Slovaks). About 10,000 of them were expelled. It was a rare example of a deportation that followed the rules laid down at Potsdam. It was orderly and relatively humane.[100] Less so were the first organised shipments of non-communist Germans in the summer of 1946: pictures show some of the 586,000 Bohemian Germans packed in box cars like sardines.[101]

The behaviour of the Czechs and Hungarians created more frustrations for Lucius Clay. He was worried about the definition of 'German' in February 1947, especially as a number of pure Czechs were seeking refuge in the West to escape from the communist shadow that had been cast over their country. The expulsions were suspended for a time. When the Soviet-inspired communist coup took place in 1948, many Czechs followed the path of the Germans across the border. They became refugees in their turn. As Clay was quick to point out, they were 'not loved in Germany' as a result of the expulsions.[102] From Hungary came 'Swabians', a development which perplexed him.*

The process was revived on 1 September 1947 at a rate of twenty trains arriving from Czechoslovakia every month.[103] At the end of the official expulsions the Americans asserted that they had received 1,445,049 Czech Germans to settle in their zone, of whom 53,187 were anti-fascists; the Russians had accommodated 786,485, including 42,987 anti-fascists. The rest came in dribs and drabs, as many were still held to work in the mines. In 1950 the Czechs admitted to having 165,117 German-speakers, but the figure was probably somewhere between 210,000 and 250,000. The expulsions had caused an economic crisis in Czechoslovakia. Despite the pickings for the Czechs, whole villages remained empty and the fields around lay fallow for want of labour.[104] It is thought that 240,000 Germans, German Bohemians and Moravians died at the hands of the Czechs.[105]

The Hungarians began to expel their Swabians on 1 November 1946. The Germans were spread throughout the country and at first no one thought of them as suspicious. Many were dragged off to Russia to work in Siberia, along with Hungarian men – the Russians could not so easily tell the difference. Then the minister president Béla Miklos decided that the Germans would be sacrificed in the interests of better treatment for

---

* 'Swabian' is a Hungarian word for an ethnic German. In 1910 they had been nearly 10 per cent of the population, but by the census of 1941 they were down to 4.8 per cent (719,449 people). The principle denominations were Bannater Schwaben, and Batschka-Deutsche from the Balkan areas, as well as the Germans on the eastern side of the Neusiedlersee around Ödenburg (Sopron) and the Schwäbische Türkei.

Hungary. He would distance himself from his former German ally. A wide-ranging land reform was instituted and Germans were interned, as the Russians themselves had suggested in the spring of 1945.[106]

In May 1945 the authorities in Hungary identified between 200,000 and 250,000 Germans they wanted to expel. They were to be allowed up to 100 kilos of luggage. The Americans had allotted them an area near Württemberg. The process continued until August 1946 when the Hungarians began to lose interest and some Germans came out of hiding.* Not all had been banished by any means.[107] The terrible winter led Clay to suspend the process until the spring. Already 168,000 had settled in the American Zone. The usual reports came in of their miserable state. According to the American journalist James K. Pollack, they too had been robbed down to their wedding rings and arrived wearing all the clothes they possessed.[108] The number of refugees in the American Zone was becoming a problem. Clay wanted to send some back across the Oder–Neisse, but that was impossible. For six months of 1946 he had suspended the reception of ethnic Germans into the American Zone because he did not feel the expulsions complied with Potsdam's call for a 'humane and orderly' resettlement. This was a double-edged sword, as it prolonged the misery of the poor souls trapped in the east.[109]

Romania was also ready to evict its 600-year-old German community (there had been 745,421 German Romanian nationals in 1930). Border changes at the so-called Adjudication of Vienna had shifted some of them on to Hungary, but there were still over half a million Germans, mostly in the Banat and the Siebenbürgen. In one town, Braşov or Kronstadt on the western side of the Carpathians, they formed a slender majority. Hitler had already launched his plans to move them to the Reich, a scheme that had its echoes in the policies of the Federal Republic after the war. The Romanians were less harsh to their Germans than other central European countries were, although they were briefly interned; they were well treated on the whole.[110]

There were also major expulsions from Yugoslavia, where there were more than half a million Germans in the census of 1921. Many of these were in Krain, which contained the German-speaking pocket of Gottschee. The 35,000 Gottscheer had already fallen victim to Hitler's alliance with Mussolini, as the western half of Slovenia had been annexed

---

* They kept themselves aloof, generally in small communities such as Villany on the southern border, and rarely dared to speak German. In the author's experience many of their children have only a rudimentary knowledge of the language now.

by Italy in 1941. In the winter of 1941 to 1942 they had been resettled in Lower Styria and in Carinthia in an instance of 'ethnic rationalisation'. Those Germans who remained behind in 1945 were pushed into camps such as Gakavo, Kruševlje and Jarek (the latter took in most of the Batschka Germans), while Rudolfsgnad and Molidorf were reserved principally for Germans from the Yugoslav Banat. In Rudolfsgnad nearly two-thirds of the 30,000 or so inmates died of typhus. About 6,000 more died in Jarek.[111]

Czechs continue to deny that any wrong was committed against the German Bohemians after the war, but they have a word – odsun, 'spiriting away' – which is used to describe the ridding of their land of Germans at the time. There was no exchange but expulsion 'without ifs or buts'.[112] It is described not as an act of revenge, but as an 'historic necessity'. There were a few voices raised against the process at the time; notably two Catholic papers Obzory and Lidové Listy and the journalist Helena Kozeluhová, who was eventually required to emigrate.[113] Then came the communists, and with a brief hiatus for the Prague Spring there was an official silence about the matter. Some exiles from communism did mention it, however. One of these was the former minister Jaroslav Stránský, the uncle of one of the Prague torturers, who had fled to London. Blame was laid at the feet of the communists.[114]

5

Home to the Reich! Recovered Territories in the Prussian East

The recommendation that the expulsion of the German-speaking people from Poland, Bohemia, Hungary and Rumania – about twelve million in all – and their resettlement in the overcrowded ruins of Western Germany should proceed in an 'orderly and humane' fashion was somewhat reminiscent of the request of the Holy Inquisition that its victims should be put to death 'as gently as possible and without bloodshed'.

Golo Mann, *The History of Germany since 1789*,
Harmondsworth 1987, 812

If the expulsions from Czechoslovakia and the banishment of German communities from other areas of east-central Europe involved transferring huge numbers of people, they were a drop in the ocean compared to the deportations from *within* Germany's pre-1937 borders. For hundreds of years Germans had lived east of the River Oder, sometimes in regions such as Pomerania, East Prussia and Lower Silesia, where the population was almost exclusively Teutonic, or in areas of mixed population such as Great Poland, West Prussia and Upper Silesia. At Yalta the decision was made to award these regions to Poland, with the exception of East Prussia, which was divided up between the Russians and the Poles. The inhabitants faced an uncertain fate: banishment by death march. It was the end of an ancient civilisation – of hardy peasants, of German merchants and academics in their own quarters and universities, of German nobles maintaining their culture in Slavic lands.*

---

* The list of those to be expelled runs to 16.5 million people: 9.3 million within the 1937 Reich borders and 7.2 outside. There were 2,382,000 East Prussians, 1,822,000 East Pomeranians, 614,000 in Brandenburg east of the Oder, 4,469,000 Silesians, 240,000 in Memel and the Baltic States, 373,000 in Danzig, 1,293,000 in Poland, 3,493,000 in Czechoslovakia, 601,000 in Hungary, 509,000 in Yugoslavia and 785,000 in Romania. The Russians were not planning to export their 1.8 million Volga Germans, but they were due to be resettled.

Apologetic German historians are keen to point out that the Nazis had provided their own precedent for the terrible deportations that followed Germany's defeat. Europe's Jews had been 'transferred' to the so-called General Gouvernement (the puppet state set up by the Germans in Poland) or the Baltic States, where they were liquidated. In two instances of Hitler's pragmatism, the German-speaking population of the Baltic States had been encouraged to come 'home to the Reich' to allow Stalin a free hand, and the South Tyrolean and Gottschee Germans in Slovenia were also transferred to allow Mussolini to consolidate his territory. Poland was to be partly Germanised, above all in the Warthe and in Danzig–West Prussia. Over a million Poles were resettled.[1]

The Nazis aimed for the 'creation of a racially, spiritually, nationally and politically unified German population'. All those elements that could not be Germanised had to 'be ruthlessly swept away'. This was the nasty idiom of the Treaty of Versailles, which championed nation states. The idea had gained a doubtful respectability in the Bulgarian–Turkish exchange of populations of 1913. Churchill expressed his approval in the House of Commons in December 1944, saying that the expulsion of the Germans was a satisfying and lasting means for ensuring peace.[2] The San Francisco Conference at the end of 1944 made it clear that German expellees were exempted from international aid. No one was to be allowed to interfere.[3]

The post-First World War regimes of the new east-central Europe had all longed for racial purity, and to some degree persecuted their minorities.* Whole villages had been emptied of Germans in West Prussia in the wake of Versailles. Possibly because half of East Prussia was now Soviet property, no effort was made to keep any of the Germans alive. There are striking similarities between the way the population of East Prussia was handled and the deliberate starvation of the Ukrainian kulaks in the early 1930s. The rations received by East Prussians did not contain enough calories to sustain life. They were notably smaller than the already pitiful amounts of food doled out to Berliners.[4]

The East Prussian ordeal was to last until 1948, when trains brought the last bedraggled remnants of the population into Berlin. Most would try to forget what they had suffered in the intervening years – not just the brutality and rape, but also the plagues, disease and vermin that had been their daily lot. Deprived of soap, they were as much the victims of lice as of their

---

* After the Second World War the Poles demanded the return of their countrymen in the Ruhr, many of whom had lived there for generations.

Soviet conquerors, and lice brought typhus. As no water was available, the Königsberger drank from infected wells and bomb craters and fed on sparrows and mice when they could, or on discarded potato peelings and trash from Russian kitchens; boiled ox bones and cattle pelts, glue and the carrion of dead and buried animals.

Graf Lehndorff woke up in Soviet captivity on his thirty-fifth birthday, 13 April 1945. One of his fellow prisoners around the potato pot had a piece of bacon that she shared with him. Despite the freezing cold of an East Prussian spring this proved the calm before the storm. He spoke to a Polish interpreter who had lived in Königsberg for two years and had made a decent living. He informed Lehndorff that he would be sent to Moscow or Odessa to work in a Russian hospital.[5] The kid-gloves approach was discarded within hours. Lehndorff learned that he had been classified as 'dangerous'. The women were taken off to be raped and the men piled on top of one another in a hollow in the ground. It was bitterly cold and there was still a good deal of snow about. 'Cold is much worse than hunger, in your wet things, you try as much as possible, not to move.' The one consolation in the spectacle of burning buildings all around him was that it aroused the thought of heat. The animals had all been driven away or killed. The only ones that remained were a few half-mad dogs.[6]

The men were brought to their feet and together with the women were marched along the road to Rauschen. In better days it had been a seaside resort popular with people from Königsberg. Hans Lehndorff took advantage of the lackadaisical Russian guards and fled into the woods. Once he had shaken off his pursuers he sat down and enjoyed a moment of reflection. Less than a year before he had met his cousin Heinrich Lehndorff, who had tried to convince him to join the opposition to Hitler. Graf Heinrich Lehndorff had been arrested after the July Plot, but like Hans, had slipped away from his guards – in this case the Gestapo – and gone on the run. He was ultimately betrayed, however, and hanged with the others in Plötzensee Prison in Berlin.[7]

Hans Lehndorff was also caught. He was put in a barn with a number of old people, women and children. They were the remnants of the population from the villages within a twenty-kilometre radius. Their shoes were worn through, their clothes in shreds, and they were covered in filth. Many of the younger children had already died, but there was no time to mourn – Lehndorff thought that that might be years in coming. Meanwhile they looked after their surviving offspring as best they could. The women were still prey to the Russians, who took them away from their children and raped them in a house by the roadside. The Germans were moved along. On the road to Rauschen, Lehndorff met a woman pushing an old, blind man in a wheelbarrow. He didn't like the Russians in Rauschen; he wanted to go to Königsberg. Lehndorff didn't have the heart to tell him it was worse there.[8]

It was 20 April – the Führer's fifty-sixth and final birthday. Pillau had yet to fall and was being subjected to a heavy artillery bombardment. Lehndorff was taken to Rauschen. The prisoners were quartered in a motor-repair workshop and taken off for interrogation. On the 21st the Russians told Lehndorff to 'Go home!' He was not fooled: it would be only a matter of time before they picked him up again. Where was home anyway? He went to Palmnicken with a fifteen-year-old boy called Helmut. The next day he was arrested again.

Lehndorff was taken to Rothenstein camp, a former barracks which had come through the war unscathed. He was put in a hall containing some 3,000 other souls. He learned that the daily ration consisted of a cup of groats and a slice of bread. There was no water. There were no latrines. His neighbour made a little space for him and gave him two coffee beans. To his relief someone recognised him and he was fetched and taken to the doctors' compound where he was looked after by the sister. She cleared up the mystery of the lavatorial arrangements: it was the space between two barracks blocks. Dysentery had broken out and many of the prisoners collapsed and died as they squatted in the alley. Once again Lehndorff permitted himself a reflection: 'to have lived one's life and to croak in this place, literally in the shit!'[9]

The dead were taken away and laid out before the guard post. When the Russians began to worry that they too might catch the infection that had killed the prisoners, they earmarked an area of the camp for the sick. On the first night of the new arrangements, thirty-six people died. One was found dead sitting on a bucket. The other prisoners descended on the dead to strip them of their clothes, so it was difficult to establish their identity.[10] On the day that Hitler took his own life, Lehndorff delivered a camp inmate of twins: 'Life goes on, as it is so aptly said.' Both children later died of hypothermia.[11]

The Russians were weeding out the Nazis by means of interrogation. The big fish had either fled via Pillau or had committed suicide; what remained was decidedly small fry. Confessions were beaten out of the men, and many died. Those Pgs that survived were taken to holding camps in Gumbinnen or Insterburg before being marched off to the Soviet Union. Someone informed Lehndorff that there were a number of Old

Masters being kept in a damp room in the camp, which would be ruined if no one did anything about them. Lehndorff was unsympathetic: 'Let them be used for temporary window-panes, or find some useful end in an oven.' He was more impressed by the bravery of the women: 'It is always astonishing what man will put up with.' That day he heard that the war was over.[12]

A daily grind set in at Rothenstein camp. Lehndorff was the doctor once again, a man you needed. If you are wise you don't kill the doctor. A Russian woman came to him for treatment. She had also been raped, and now she had VD. In gratitude she brought him food – margarine for the potato soup. One woman he treated – known only as Wanda – had been raped 128 times. They brought in an old man who was so covered in lice that he looked like an ant-heap. He turned out to be the local railway director. He died an hour later.[13]

At the beginning of June, Lehndorff had a surprise visit from Doktora. She was still working at the German hospital and nurtured plans to get her friend out of Rothenstein to work alongside her once more. There were a thousand Germans being treated in the former Finance Department in Königsberg. The Nervenklinik had been turned over to those suffering from plague. When typhus broke out the victims were taken to the hospitals in the Yorckstrasse and the Elisabeth Krankenhaus. There were 2,000 cases lying two to a bed, four in the case of children.[14]

Doktora brought him wheaten biscuits. Three days later she was back with Lehndorff's rucksack filled with his things. They included a pistol with fifty bullets. This was carefully hidden. After that she came almost daily.[15] The commandant allowed him out one day, and he went foraging looking for medicine. 'The city is really fantastic. The eye no longer attempts to reconstruct it, but rather allows itself to be overpowered, drawn in by the entirely transformed landscape.' He found the red-rimmed glasses in which he had drunk his last glass of Martell cognac. As the Russian car took him back to the camp he spotted Doktora on the city walls, picking flowers to take to him.[16]

In the middle of June Lehndorff was released through Doktora's intervention and was allowed to work with her in the German hospital. The Finance Department was one of the few undamaged buildings in the city. There was food of sorts – a grey pea soup, typical of East Prussia.[17] The summer was slightly better, when grasses and dandelions could be gathered by the roadside, rye grains could be filched from the fields and mussels from the overgrown city pond. The idyll did not last long. Once again it is difficult to avoid the impression that the Russians were hoping that the

Germans would die, to rid themselves of the responsibility of feeding and repatriating them, although a little fat was made available for children. Lehndorff's German hospital was turfed out of the Finance Department. They had twenty-four hours to move 1,500 patients into the old Barmherzigkeit – the Hospital of the Sisters of Mercy.

The chief problem was famine now. Lehndorff was forever seeing patients suffering from oedema who were skeletal from the waist upwards, but whose legs were filled with water. The only solution was to amputate, but how were the Germans to live in post-war Königsberg without legs? Was it not better just to let them die? 'Famine leads to a remarkable death. There is no fight. The sufferer gives the impression that death is already behind them.' One woman was brought to him who had lain ten days in a market garden eating unripe blackcurrants. She was completely blocked up. She nearly died while Lehndorff endeavoured to sort her out. Blackcurrants were quite a boon that summer – there was a glut of them in the allotments behind the now ruinous houses.[18] Somehow the hospital acquired three cows, providing valuable milk, for the children in particular. It was not long, however, before they discovered that the throat of the best milker had been cut. Later the animal's udder was found floating in a vat of soup. Officially the hospital received thirty-five kilos of meat daily, but the Russians interpreted this to encompass heads and feet, hooves and horns. One recipient of the precious flesh was the dying mother superior, who had had to live through the worst of it while her nuns were constant prey to the Russians.[19]

There were plenty of books in the ruined houses, and literature was consolation for some, but there was next to no food. Cases of cannibalism were reported, with people eating the flesh of their dead children. Of the 73,000 Königsberger alive in June 1945, only 25,000 survived the experience.[20] Hermann Matzkowski, a communist sawmill worker the Russians installed as mayor of the Königsberg suburb of Ponarth, reported that 15,000 Königsberger had disappeared or died in the main prison during May. On 20 June 1,000 people were beheaded before his eyes.[21]

Lehndorff and Doktora made an expedition to suburban Preyl. They had no shoes and went barefoot. On the way they plucked cornflowers – the floral symbol of Prussia. Russians were supplementing their diet by fishing in the vast Schlossteich that provided water for the city. Later Lehndorff saw two boys swimming in the pond. Given how malnourished they were, he was amazed by their energy. When he told them not to swallow the water, they replied in a matter-of-fact way: 'Oh, what does it matter how we die, no one is going to get out of here!'[22]

When they reached their goal they found the house of Doktora's relatives burned out. She began to cry. They hitched a lift to Juditten in the suburbs where Doktora's house was. There were Germans living in it. When Doktora tried to enter they attacked her. Lehndorff's beloved was losing her will to live. She discovered that she was infested with lice – the final indignity. When he went to see her in the morning she had taken poison. Lehndorff was shocked at his lack of emotion. He too would find a more appropriate time to mourn.[23]

Autumn 1945 arrived. There were rumours that the Königsberger were to be shipped west under Western supervision, typhus cases first. Hopes were temporarily raised. The news caused a drop in prices for winter clothes as the city-dwellers thought they would be out before the bad weather started. A woollen jacket could be obtained for six potatoes, a coat for a tin of meat. You had to be careful, however, as fraudsters had found a way of replacing the contents of tins with clay and leaves. Meanwhile the ripe corn rotted in the fields as there was no one to harvest it.[24]

The fate of those living in the villages was no kinder than that of the Königsberger. The distinguished journalist Gräfin Marion Dönhoff was the daughter of one of the region's great magnates. The family home, Friedrichstein, was the local Versailles. In 1945 it was burned to the ground. In 1947 Gräfin Dönhoff received her last letter from home. It described what had happened in her village when the Russians came. They arrived on a Tuesday, setting fire to various houses and shooting two old coachmen and the bell-ringer who summoned the workers to the fields. Her correspondent wrote:

> A few days later they shot Magda Bohaim, Lotte Pritt and her child and Grandma Plitt; in Wirrgirren they killed five workers on the estate and the forester Schmidt's wife, who took eight days to die and must have suffered terribly. Old Plitt then hanged himself. In February they began the transports to the Urals. My husband went with them; as did the innkeeper Dreier and his daughter Ulla, Stellmacher's two daughters, Frau Jung, Frau Krüschmann, Frau Oltermann, the four Marx girls, Christel and Herta Heinze and the smith's daughter. I received news from Karl Marx [sic] a few months ago that my husband and most of the others died in the Urals. You can see how death has moved into our little village. First of all the lads all died at the front and now the old, and even the girls.[25]

Typhus had cut a swathe though the population of the village. Sister Hedy, who had nursed them through the epidemic, had now been ill for a fortnight. They had all had to change their lodgings many times, as more and more surviving buildings were requisitioned by the Red Army.

Marion Dönhoff's correspondent had lived at the mill, until her lodger, the *Oberinspektor* (senior estate manager), had been shot in the stomach, and she had moved back into the village in fear for her life. She took the wounded man to the hospital in a wheelbarrow. 'The women from Wittgirren lent a hand, for it was no easy task, moving the heavy old man who was suffering from terrible pains. We laboured for four hours. At the [parish] boundary he asked us to stop, saying "Women, let me see my beautiful Quittainen* once more."' He was dead by the time they reached the hospital.[26]

The way to survive was to work for the conquerors. Marion Dönhoff's informant was one of them. The only ray of light in her slavery was the sight of Sister Hedy's two-year-old daughter while she waited for permission to go to the new Germany across the Oder. The Soviet authorities were gradually repopulating their new territory, but there were a few menial jobs to be performed. There was a little work to be had in the hospitals and factories, and there was an industrial outfitter and a baker where casual labour was required. Germans worked in the power stations and in the carpenters' workshops until they were replaced by Russians. One man made a living by selling the books he dug out of the rubble. A number of priests and pastors continued to operate in Königsberg, as their work – particularly for orphaned children – was tolerated by the Russians. Nine of the clergymen died of starvation or dysentery; three were killed.

On 4 July 1946 Königsberg lost its ancient name. It became Kaliningrad. With the change of nomenclature came Russian physicians to replace the Germans operating in the hospitals, and Russian workers took over from the Germans in the factories. A few roubles could be made from teaching the Russians German or to play the piano. A sort of calm reigned in which Germans could read their own newspapers, listen to broadcasts in their own language and send their children to their own schools. There was even a German Choir made up of doctors, nurses and others at the Yorck Hospital.

This lasted until repatriation began in the summer of 1947. The transports took off in earnest on 22 October that year. On 10 September Ruth Friedrich recorded the arrival in Berlin of 6,000 Königsberger, people who had lived on carrion and rubbish and were 'more cattle than human beings, more dead than alive'. Their advent in the capital was followed by the last remnants of Breslau's German population.[27] By the time they had

---

* Village near Preussisch Holland. The Schloss by Jean de Bodt survived, and was even restored in the 1980s.

finished, no Germans were left in what had been Königsberg. A 700-year history had drawn to a close.*

Country Life

Hans Lehndorff had left Königsberg two years before the transports removed the remaining Germans, because he had heard a rumour that he was about to be arrested. He made a wise choice even if the story was false: on 6 and 7 November 1945, the Russians celebrated their Revolution by beating the Germans bloody and raping the women again. One of the victims was Mayor Matzkowski's seventy-one-year-old mother. The only women spared were those carrying Russian babies.[28] As Lehndorff fled through the shattered streets he watched Russian soldiers clearing Germans out of their houses near the Friedland Gate. From now on they had to live in the allotments. He wanted to reach the Polish half of East Prussia and find out what had happened to his family, particularly his mother, who was the daughter of the right-wing political wheeler-dealer Elard von Oldenburg-Januschau. In Hanshagen he was taken in by two old ladies who revealed their hidden hens. He hadn't seen a hen for six months. They put him to bed and fed him on wild mushrooms. Later he found boletus mushrooms in the woods and ate them raw with sugar.[29]

He headed for Ponarien, near Allenstein, where some of his relatives had lived. Near their estate he ran into the retainer Preuss, who gave him the usual news of rape, murder and suicide. Poles had moved into the big house, but he found his aunt, Frau von Stein, living in the gardener's cottage. She had initially left the house to make way for the Russian commandant, who had since pursued the war to the west. Finding his mother's sister was a source of great joy: 'To see a person again now who belongs to me, after all that has happened, is like a foretaste of our reunion in heaven.'[30] He learned of his cousins: two of Frau von Stein's daughters had been interned with their father; the sons had been at the front and she had no news of them. The women, his aunt included, had developed a *modus vivendi* with the Poles. They worked as agricultural labourers in the fields and received in payment half a litre of skimmed milk every day. The women brought home two basketfuls of potatoes. These were sorted by

---

* Yet when the author visited the city in 1992 a tiny band of Germans had somehow managed to re-establish themselves in Kaliningrad, and even had their own church and pastor. They were naturally one of the first stops for the many *Heimatgruppen* who wanted to visit the city where they had been born and grew up.

variety in order to make the diet less monotonous. The furniture from the big house was being gradually broken up to feed the fires.[31]

It seemed better to stay put for the time being. Lehndorff heard of the perils of deportation to Germany, of the brutality of the Polish guards and of the marauding bands that robbed the refugees in the trains. In November 1945 CARE parcels began to arrive from America, providing some extra food for the starving Germans.* Together with what he could glean from grateful patients, the small German community in Ponarien could survive.

Danzig had been one of the first German cities to fall. On 3 May the German men inhabiting prisons and camps were brought out and marched down 'Victory Alley'. All men aged between sixteen or seventeen and fifty-five were required to go to Russia and work. The women came out to watch the departure of their menfolk, and strewed the streets with spring flowers. Of those men (and a few women) who were taken from Gleiwitz in Silesia to Rudlo near Stalino, many were to die before they reached their destination. Their bodies were stripped naked and buried by the side of the road. Most of the men of Gleiwitz were put to work in the mines. The lucky ones returned to a town depopulated of Germans in October. Many failed to return at all. Of the Gleiwitzer a third of the 300 men died.[32]

The large camp of Laband in Silesia held between 30,000 and 50,000 men, most of whom were deported to Russia to work in the Siberian mines. Few had returned by the end of 1946. The lucky ones escaped the mines and worked on large *kolkhoz* farms instead.[33] In Gleiwitz, Hans-Günther Nieusela's father was marched off to Kazakhstan, and did not return until 1948.[34] German and Polish women were impressed into clearing the streets of rubble. Reusable bricks were set aside, establishing the pattern for other German cities. Even the Jews from Stutthof camp were made busy with restoring Danzig's beautiful façades. More than 60 per cent of the city had been destroyed.

At the end of May a Special Commission had been convened to 'Polonise' the place names in the district. Langfuhr – 'long drive' – was somehow rendered as Wrzeszcz, or 'you scream'. The place names were altered some two months before the Allied leaders met at Potsdam. It was clear that the conference would not alter the *de facto* situation.

For the most part the famous Junkers lived in large if modest manor houses and farmed their own estates. There were relatively few grand

---

* See below p. 374.

houses or absentee landlords. The grandest of all were the Grafen Hochberg or Princes Pless, who lived at Fürstenstein in Upper Silesia and owned a large chunk of the coal mines. Their estates had been split between Germany and Poland after the First World War, and a prolonged legal dispute had robbed the last prince – Hansel Pless – of most of his income in the 1920s and 1930s. During the war the castle was inhabited by Magda Goebbels's lover, Gauleiter Karl Hanke, who carried off anything of value he could find once the Russians appeared on the horizon.

The Russians arrived on 5 May. Later, the last chatelain, Paul Fichte, went back to the castle to survey the scene:

> I crept over to Fürstenstein to see what went on . . . Everything broken up and robbed, our flats were totally empty, all windows broken. All inhabitants were expelled by the Russians so that Fürstenstein could be pillaged, it didn't look as if humans had been there, indescribable. The beautiful fountains on the terraces are broken, the Donatello Fountain was pulled down. The library was loaded to go to Moscow. The most valuable books, even the Sachsenspiegel [thirteenth-century book of law], had been walled in but they were found and burned. The old castle also burned down.
>
> Now the family mausoleum was also plundered, the sarcophagi broken into, the contents thrown around. We had quickly buried Princess Daisy outside the vault, but she was dug up and robbed. Scholz had planted such pretty flowers on her grave that it attracted attention. We reburied the Fürstin [princess] straight away . . . But the mausoleum had been broken up and couldn't be closed again. Now a migration of people to the mausoleum began. Everyone wanted to see what it was like inside, most of them became scared and ran off, for the contents of coffins lay on the floor. The skeleton of a Fürstin *née* Kleist we couldn't find any more, only the head lay there. Andersek from the stud shot himself and his family. The stable boys buried their bodies behind Kummer's goat shed.[35]

The Poles made off with the late princess's jewellery.

Käthe von Normann heard a rumour that Berlin and Stettin had fallen on 5 May and that both Hitler and Goebbels had committed suicide. The next day she had news that Germany had laid down its arms. The Frenchmen billeted in the same house celebrated with barley coffee and began to sing. Rumours were running wild. On the following day she heard that Pomerania would remain German as far east as Stolp, and that her family had a chance of hanging on to the Barkow estate. Uncertainty meant that a lot of people who had fled at the appearance of the Russians made their way home again. More than a million people did this, only to be driven out, once and for all.[36] The stories were confirmed by a Polish policeman on the 8th. That night the Normanns sang the Leuthen Chorale: 'Nun danket alle Gott!' Since Frederick the Great's time it had been Prussia's unofficial national anthem.

As Lehndorff had discovered, the French were generally sympathetic to the defeated Germans, despite the indignities they had suffered during the war: 'their opinion of the Russians and the Poles is just as bad as ours'. One of them, a tall, blond young man, gave Frau von Normann a present of some much needed clothing material. He wanted a crust of bread in return, but she had none to give, just a little butter and a liver sausage. He told her that the French had been hiding a few German noblemen in their ranks. She thought he might also have been German.[37]

The big city of Breslau had yielded only on the 6th. Two days later the war officially ended. It made little difference for the survivors. On the 9th a party of thirteen Poles arrived to claim the city for their country. They moved into a house on the Blücherstrasse and set up a Polish eagle over the door. On the 10th more Polish pioneers joined them, together with a group of men from the Polish Office of the Public Security.[38]

On 13 May a delegation of 'Lublin Poles' headed by Bolesław Drobner travelled to Sagan in Silesia to report to their Soviet masters. Edward Ochab had already been appointed plenipotentiary for the euphemistically named 'Recovered Territories'. Such men were as much 'Muscovites' as the German communists who landed outside Berlin as the Red Army took the city. They assumed power with nil popular support; their mandate based on nothing more than Soviet patronage. Their claims to much of the Recovered Territories derived merely from Soviet policy.[39]

The Russians and Poles divided the spoils, with the best bits naturally going to the former, which resulted in their occasionally coming to blows over the booty.[40] Meanwhile the Red Army was still scavenging, with no regard for leaving any useful equipment behind for the puppet state they were setting up in Poland. In some instances the Poles and the Germans made common cause in order to preserve something that would otherwise have gone east.[41] The Poles also fell out with the Czechs over the Teschen pocket of Silesia.

In Neustadt in Upper Silesia a thousand head of cattle went east, leaving around a score to feed the locals. The harvest for 1945 was confiscated.[42] Treks had been straggling through the towns and villages of the region for months now. At first they were made up of Germans from the General Gouvernement who had fled at the Russian advance. Now they were joined by the Silesians themselves. Some Upper Silesians fled to the Sudetenland, like the doctor Theofil Peters from Pitschen who went to

Leitmeritz before the Czechs threw him out. It might have been worse for him: he was opting for the fire in preference to the frying pan.[43]

Later in May Käthe von Normann heard that the British and the Americans were already releasing POWs. This was not true, but it gave her leave to hope that her own husband might return. The absence of men was a torture to the women in more senses than one. They were nightly victims to Russian bands, which, even if they did not succeeded in capturing their quarry in the form of female flesh, food or valuables, nonetheless shattered all hope of sleep. After the troops had been there a few days, the attacks died down, but each new billeting renewed the problem. When Frau von Normann decided to go to the local town of Plathe to receive treatment for blood poisoning, she learned that the German doctors had been replaced by Russian and Polish medics who were not allowed to treat Germans. She found a German doctor in a pitiful state in her own flat – she had a three-year-old daughter, and was pregnant with another, Russian baby.

In the vicinity of Stolp in eastern Pomerania the Krockows and the Puttkamers were less well informed than the Normanns. The first indication they had that the war was over came a fortnight later at Whitsun. The Russians paraded through the villages shooting into the air and shouting, 'Woina kaputt! Woina kaputt!' Whether it was true or not, no one could tell. They had no newspapers and no wireless sets. Even if they had managed to hide a wireless, there was no electricity to make it work.

The Pomeranian gentry heard a good deal about 'Russki kultura' which decreed cleanliness and order in the villages and towns behind the Oder–Neisse Line. Pigs had to be scrubbed until they gleamed. Pomeranians of all classes were put to work cleaning the pigsties or milking the cows (until they, like so much else, went east), and sometimes they earned a crust of bread for their pains. A squire's wife like Käthe von Normann had to learn how to milk a cow, although she had to admit that she was less proficient at it than the meanest peasant girl.[44] Many of the cows were sick, suffering from foot and mouth disease, and looked bad. When the cattle were driven off to Russia Frau von Normann was relieved of the chore of looking after them and producing milk and butter. In Ermland, where Lehndorff was holed up, there were a few well-concealed hens, and here and there a 'milk-ewe' or a pig hidden in a cellar, but the situation there was much the same.[45]

Yet the formal relationship between squire's wife and peasant woman continued for the time being, despite the fact that both were very much in the same boat – preyed upon by Russians and Poles, and, when not sexually molested, obliged to work as their slaves. Käthe von Normann thought it inappropriate that one former worker should call her 'gnädige Frau' rather than Frau von Normann. She thought the use of 'my lady' silly when they were both milking cows, feeding pigs or mucking out sties together. But the old forms of address died hard. Even when Frau von Normann was finally banished from the family fief, pushing her few belongings on a cart towards a transit camp, she called out to the coachman of her nearest grandee neighbours to 'tell both the baron's daughters that we have all been told to leave Barkow!'[46]

The male sex was restricted to old men and boys. Even in May, a few ancient landowners were still living in their houses, often protected from the Russians by their former workers. The wisest policy was to stay away from the manor or its ruins, and as much as possible to disguise yourself as a peasant. All agricultural instruments and machines had been carried off. The fields were lying fallow for want of implements to farm them. Between Dangeröse and Stolp the railway lines had been taken away and there was no access to the provincial capital. Lehndorff had a similarly frustrating journey when he attempted to get to the town of Allenstein. The Russians had already carried off one set of lines.[47]

The suicides continued. In the village of Horst, Käthe von Normann heard that the sixteen-year-old Christel M. had been repeatedly raped by the Russians. The next day she drowned herself in the Stau Lake. In Ermland a woman responded to her daughter's abduction by the Russians by revealing the presence of all the concealed girls in the village.[48] Frau von Normann was even more distressed when she heard her eight-year-old son Henning say that Christel had done the right thing. Leni S. poisoned herself and her 'cute' children, but a Russian doctor brought her back to life – but not her offspring. Frau von Normann wondered whether he had really done her a service.[49]

Death could come at any time. An old couple in the Krockows' village, were chased into an icy pond and forced to stay there until they drowned; a man was tied to a plough and driven until he fell, then finished off with a submachine gun. The nobles were often the first to go: Graf Lehndorff's mother and brother were killed by the Russians as soon as they learned who they were. The lord of Grumbkow, Herr von Livonius, had his arms and legs cut off and was tossed into the pigsty to be eaten by its denizens. Frau von Normann's neighbour, Baron von Senfft, was found beaten to death in a swamp in June. He was still dressed in his coat and shoes. His orphaned daughters had been to see her just the day before. They were living in the coachman's house and working in the garden. Frau von

Thadden-Trieglaff, of the family of Bismarck's pietist friends, was still living unharmed, however, in the village of Vahnerow. She and her daughter inhabited one wing of the manor while the Russians inhabited the rest with their cows.

Another Fräulein von Thadden together with a young Seckendorff girl brought Käthe von Normann news of the fate of other local Junkers. The von der Marwitzes from Rütznow, famous from the time of Frederick the Great, had seen their manor burned to the ground, and the father shot in Greifenberg. Frau von der Marwitz had been put to work with the cows, and was in a pitiful state, weighing under thirty-five kilos. The Blanckenburgs had a similar tale to tell. Property no longer had any real meaning. Lehndorff was not upset to find shirts embellished with his relatives' monograms on the bellies of his patients. When he treated the Polish commandant he sent him home on a horse with a valuable package that included money, white bread, eggs, stockings and a shirt bearing his uncle's initials.[50]

The women, children and the few remaining men assembled at the sound of a bell at 6 a.m., seven days a week. For their labours they were given a little skimmed milk and 250 grams of corn a head (150 grams for non-workers and children) to make bread. This was far less than the Berliners, but then there were no Westerners around to monitor what was going on, and no propaganda war to win. There was no meat, butter, curds or vegetables to be had, but this was the country, and diets could be supplemented by the odd wild boar or stag, fish from the many lakes and wild mushrooms. Lehndorff even found some morels.[51]

Working for the Poles

The Polish Miliz also materialised – a cross between a militia and a police force. It was variously reported to be made up of young boys of nineteen or twenty who had been in the German 'work service', KZler or partisans.[52] Their desire for revenge made them even more ferocious than the Russians.[53] They took over the job of rounding up Germans from the Russians. Women and children were herded towards Germany, while any remaining men were put to work.[54] The shops in Käthe's local town of Glowitz were now also in Polish hands, and accepted złotys, not marks. The inhabitants of the villages began to form the impression that they were living in an inverted version of the Nazi General Gouvernement. Even in October, inhabitants of Eastern Pomerania had no idea whether their 'zone' was German or Polish.

Faith was deep-rooted in the old Prussian East, particularly among the Pomeranian and East Prussian gentry, where there was a tradition of Pietism exemplified in the journals of Graf Lehndorff. Käthe von Normann's diary reveals a profoundly religious woman who gathers her children around her in daily prayer and sings hymns with them. Every night their missing father is remembered in their orisons. Apart from marauding Russians, hunger and the strains imposed by forced labour, the Normanns seemed to suffer most from lack of shoes. What they had formerly possessed had been taken by the Russians, and the children's feet were growing. Two pairs of stockings replaced shoes, but they were torn and filthy and no protection against the pelting rain of a Pomeranian spring.

Many of the Poles who settled on German land were refugees themselves, driven from their homes east of the Bug, which was now to become Soviet territory. In May offices were recreated in Breslau to find housing for the expellees. On 6 July, eleven days before the conference opened in Potsdam, the first 800 Germans were expelled from the city.[55] For the time being the Germans cleared rubble, buried bodies and cleared mines. The Soviet authorities had little consideration for the Poles, even those who had been slave labourers under the Nazis. Some were packed off to the mines at Waldenburg.[56]

The Potsdam Conference that summer proved an acute disappointment for the Germans marooned east of the Oder and Neisse rivers. The Western Allies turned a blind eye to the Poles as they reshaped their domain. At first the Germans welcomed the news that the Poles were to be their masters – 'that, instead of the "Godless" Russians, from now on the Catholic Poles had taken over the regime'.[57] The level of 'Polonisation' came as a shock to every German. In the cities German 'antifa' groups emerged to help in the work of denazification only to discover that the Poles wanted them out too.[58] New names had to be found. Henceforth Breslau was 'Wrocław' – like 'Gdansk' a name so obscure it was new even to the most fanatical Polish nationalists. On 15 May the bishop of Katowice, Stanisław Abramski, visited the priests of the Breslau Cathedral Chapter to tell them that Poland would brook no racial minorities.* 'Breslau and Stettin are to become thoroughly Polish; Lvov with its university is coming to Breslau; Wilna with its university is moving to Stettin.'[59]

* This was true only up to a point: half a million largely Catholic Germans remained in Upper Silesia, because the Poles refused to recognise their nationality, and there were the 'autochthones' in East Prussia. Most of these left before the 1980s. As many as 30,000 remain around Olszstyn.

Each of Breslau's fine, red-brick medieval churches was to be invested with the traditions of a church in Lvov. In all four and a half million ethnic Poles were to be resettled in this way. On 12 August 1945 the Polish primate Cardinal Hlond arrived to break the news to the German Catholic clergy that they were not welcome either. When Father Helmut Richter received a pastoral letter on 11 October 1945, half of it was in Polish, a language he couldn't read. Latin would have been a more obvious choice. Father Joachim Konrad delivered the last German sermon in the Elisabethkirche on 30 June 1946, closing the German chapter in the history of Breslau. The Catholic hierarchy (both in Poland and in the Vatican) behaved in a particularly craven way – the Church had forgotten about universality.[60]

In Danzig, too, the German clergy were told to leave as early as July 1945. Masses were celebrated in Latin, so inside the churches there was no apparent persecution for the time being. The bishop was, however, informed that all Germans had to leave Danzig as the Polish Miliz went from street to street clearing the last Germans out of their houses. The bishop objected that this meant Reich Germans, not Danziger. He was put in his place: it meant the Danziger as well.[61]

The monks in the Benedictine monastery of Grüssau fared no better. The massive baroque building had been a favourite stopover for Frederick the Great during the Seven Years War. In 1810 the monks had been cleared out, but a religious community from Prague had settled in the buildings after the Czech government had dissolved the abbeys in their new state in 1919. The Nazis had thrown them out in their turn and they had taken refuge in a nearby nunnery. Now it was the Poles' turn to expel them. Because they were 'Germans', only one monk was allowed to remain – he was from the South Tyrol.[62]

At the end of 1945 there were still 300,000 Germans in Breslau. They outnumbered the incoming Poles by five to one. Nine months later the position was reversed. By March 1947 the Germans comprised less than 10 per cent of the population. Because all Silesian roads led to Breslau, there was little hope of avoiding the city of rubble, and the arrival of more forlorn Germans was seen as a further pretext for plunder.[63] While the politicians bargained their city away in Potsdam, Germans were dying at a rate of 300 to 400 a day. Some of these were suicides, but we learn that the number would have been significantly higher had the Germans had access to cooking gas. A few months after the city fell infant mortality had reached 90 per cent. The Russians and the Poles had made it clear they were not in a position to feed the Germans, but a little was dished out all the same – German rations amounted to half to a third of that given to the others. The złoty's exchange rate with the Reichsmark began at parity, then was pegged at two marks. Exchange remained at best capricious. By the summer the Poles were operating a black market in the city, and Germans could trade their last articles of clothing for food. A good dress, for example, could yield between one and a half and two kilos of butter.[64]

The Germans had to make way for the Poles as they arrived. For those children who possessed good health there were exciting times to be had among the ruins. Twelve-year-old Friedhelm Mondwurf, for example, would sing songs for the Russian soldiers and then beg for food. His parents were appalled when he came home with a sack full of *klebba* – black rye bread – but they could see the advantages. The boy also went out to the old allotment, which had been mined, and pulled the fruit from the family trees, although the area was littered with dead soldiers.[65] Again the old contempt for the Poles materialised. The priest in Alterode near Breslau expressed the view that 'The Pole is with few exceptions completely subject to the demon drink.'[66] When Ukrainian and Galician Poles came to Gleiwitz and kicked the Germans out of their comfortable homes, Hans-Günther Nieusela commented that they preferred houses with bathrooms: 'in these places they like to keep their goats and poultry'.[67]

As the Poles came in, Germans were evicted and resettled in the cellars of ruined houses in what were ghettos in all but name. Typhus and diphtheria raged, killing many children. Medicine to deal with the epidemic was made prohibitively expensive to the Germans. Father Helmut Richter reported that a Polish doctor (who was actually no more than a nurse) was injecting typhus cases with carbolic. When asked why, she said it was because they were going to die anyhow.[68]

Rural Silesia

Every Silesian town went through the same process with more or less the same degree of savagery. In the Catholic areas of Upper Silesia the churches and their ministers were an obvious target. In Preussisch-Kramen Poles broke into the church and prised open the tabernacle. The dove above the altar was shot down and the saints decapitated. In June 1948 they deported the priest, but the villagers evidently looked Polish enough, and were allowed to remain for now.[69] In Ritterswalde near Neisse the priest was shot, but not killed, at the altar of his church. Sixteen other Silesian priests were killed.[70]

Klosterbruck in Kreis Oppeln is a particularly well-documented case. The Russians arrived on 21 January 1945. The priests and local nuns had taken refuge in the convent chapel together with a young woman and her child. The usual rape and pillage went on in the streets outside. Any woman who refused to lie down was shot. The priest whose account we have was contemptuous of the Russian conquerors. 'Go back to Russia,' he wrote, 'and sit outside your wattle and daub cottage, chew sunflower seeds and you will become amiable again.'[71] Some were not so bad: a Muslim officer, 'a good chap', brought them a bucket full of soup and some sugar after they had slaughtered the hogs; but then a crazed older officer took a nun behind the altar and tried to rape her. He was interrupted by a younger officer who seized the man and had some soldiers throw him out like a bag of flour. A guard was posted at the door to the chapel. On Ash Wednesday that year the girls paid particular attention to the practice of smearing themselves with ash. They wanted to make themselves look old and ugly.

This did not help the nuns, who had now become the object of Russian attentions again. At the beginning of Lent four of them were taken off and raped. The Poles arrived on 14 March and banned the use of German. 'Satan is back!' wrote the priest. 'The new Satan seems almost more dangerous. He claims to be Catholic and keeps talking about Czestochowa.'[72] Three days later all the nuns who had been spared were raped, including one of eighty. For some of them the new experience was coupled with a further unpleasantness: venereal disease. The Russians now proudly claimed there were no more virgins in Klosterbruck. The plight of the nuns was particularly galling in that the new Polish doctors refused to treat Germans. Some of their torments came to an end when they were expelled on 25 May.[73]

Ukrainian Poles arrived in the wake of the Miliz. They had been driven out by the Russians. The priest thought them 'good people'. Upper Silesia was considered a special case because the population was mixed German and Polish and almost entirely Catholic. For Poles it was an article of faith that they were all Poles, and in many cases only pretending to be German. It was an evident reversal of the Nazi policy, which had stressed the 'Germanity' of Upper Silesia at the expense of the Poles. *Wasserpölnisch* – the local patois – had been banned since the 1930s. In consequence the children no longer understood it.[74] It was useful to know Polish after the population was banned from speaking German. As Ursula Pechtel reported, 'A single German word would have been sufficient to have us thrown into a Polish extermination camp.'[75]

In Schönkirch near Oppeln, in the more German part of Upper Silesia, the Russians spent all day calling for 'wodka', 'cebula' (onions), 'ogorki' (gherkins) and 'panienka' (girls). They had no apparent preference, as long as whichever one it was came 'dawaj, dawaj' (quickly). The locals cunningly set to work distilling vodka. With one to two bottles they could buy back a stolen cow; with two to three, a horse. Of course they were promptly stolen again.[76] In Hindenburg, the Poles arrived bringing along the old name, 'Zaborze', for the town, and proceeded to strip it of anything the Russians had left. Their zeal exceeded even that of their patrons. Many of the Germans pretended to be Poles in order to hang on to their property. In some towns like Schönwald, the expulsions took place in three waves: at the end of October 1945, in June 1946 and in May 1947.[77]

Like Hans Lehndorf, Theofil Peters in Pitschen found that being a doctor could save your life, or at least postpone death a while. The Russians were grateful for the services he performed and brought him bottles of schnapps. On 2 October 1945, however, he was expelled with the rest. A member of the Miliz arrived at his door to tell him, 'You will be expelled on the basis of the Potsdam Accords.' His medical instruments were 'confiscated, property of the Polish state'. He was loaded on to a goods wagon where his last few possessions were taken from him. Peters pleaded for his stethoscope, but they wouldn't listen. 'You don't need a stethoscope for Hitler any more, you German pig!' said the militia man, and punched him in the face.[78]

He spent twelve days on the train, shunting around Silesia. Twelve people died in his carriage. The bodies were unloaded at the next halt. Finally the odyssey finished some twelve kilometres from Görlitz, the crossing point for Germany. The people were too weak to walk, however, and were foully treated by militia men wearing second-hand SS uniforms. Two thousand Germans had to line up for a last body search. Peters was given the job of loading the dead on to a dog cart and taking them to the Neisse. 'In communist Poland,' they told him, 'nobody dies of hunger.'[79]

Officially classed as 'autochthones', Upper Silesians were given the chance to 'opt' for Poland. There were advantages to this: Irene Zelder's aunts in Ratibor told her 'they had "opted" for Poland in order to live, because it was the only way to obtain ration cards'.[80] There were disadvantages too: if you opted for Poland you could not 'go to the Reich'. Many Germans were stuck in Poland and therefore unable to join their families. This was the case with Hans-Günther Nieusela's two sisters, who were not able to leave until 1955.[81] One Upper Silesian who was not given this choice was Carl Ulitzka, the 'King of Upper Silesia', who had spent much of the war in Dachau. He was expelled by the Poles, because in 1919 he had led the resistance to Polish annexation in the wake of Versailles. The Miliz took brutal revenge on anyone suspected of having stymied their attempts to annex Upper Silesia in 1919.[82]

Opting for Poland did not necessarily protect you from Russians. As in rump-Germany, the most dangerous run for a woman was the journey to the pump to fetch water. The Russians lay in wait, hiding in the shadows ready to pounce. Irene Zelder had a disagreeable experience with one soon after her return to Ratibor, but managed to get home and lock the door after abandoning her pail in the street. The Russian hammered on the door with his rifle butt shouting, 'Wodka! Panienka!', but he eventually gave up when no one complied.[83] The acute time for rapes was the two months from mid-March to mid-May 1945. Girls were generally safer in the villages than in the towns, where typhus also raged and carried off significant numbers of Germans.[84]

Neisse – 'the Silesian Rome' – was 80 per cent destroyed in the shelling. When the Russians arrived they robbed the city's many churches and, according to a priest, raped nuns as many as fifty times. The expulsions began in the middle of June, but some of the citizens were locked up in a grim fortress constructed in the time of Frederick the Great.[85] Neisse's fort was one of the six concentration camps operated by the Poles in Silesia. The others were in Breslau (Kletschkau Prison), Glatz, Lamsdorf, Trebnitz and Wünschelburg. Lamsdorf (now called Łambinowice) between Oppeln and Neisse was the most notorious of the camps. Heinz Esser, who acted as an unofficial camp doctor, called it an 'extermination camp'. There were 6,488 violent deaths, 828 of them children. Many of those who were not beaten died from disease, starvation or cold, or from a combination of the three. The priest who left the account related that the 'commandant' was a youth of eighteen. His years were evidently the only tender thing about him.[86] Esser does not provide any indication of the man's age, but gives his name as Cesaro Gimborski,* and added that he was assisted by about fifty members of the Miliz. The most brutal of these was the sixteen-year-old executioner's assistant Jusek who murdered 'to order', until he too was brutally killed by his peers.[87]

The ferocity of the guards might be explained by their schooling – some, at least, had recently been released from German camps. Their methods were certainly reminiscent of Dachau or Buchenwald.[88] There were 'morning exercises' during which many of the older, half-starved

---

* There were unsuccessful attempts to bring Gimborski to trial in the 1960s.

inmates predictably collapsed. Men were beaten to death for trifles: a teacher for wearing spectacles, a mayor because he was tall and therefore might have qualified for the SS. Men and women were stripped naked and forced to perform sadistic acts on one another or eat excrement; girls had to press burning banknotes between their legs. There were many small children in the camp. Some of these were later taken away and given to Polish foster parents.[89]

There was virtually no food. Esser says they were given three or four potatoes a day, a total of 200 to 250 calories. He recalled one day, 8 June 1946, when the figure soared to 530 calories, because there were so few inmates in the camp.[90] Ursula Pechtel from Hindenburg in Upper Silesia drew a short straw and was packed off to Auschwitz. She worked in the factory of the chemical conglomerate IG Farben, dismantling the machines for the Russians. They were savagely beaten by the guards and at night the women were sent up as entertainment for the officers. Max Marek had been in Neu-Schönau camp near Zittau before he too was sent to Jawiszowice work camp near Auschwitz. This was named Jawischowitz by the Nazis: it was one of the Auschwitz satellites built in 1942, in this case to serve the mines at Brzeszcze.[91]

In Beuthen there were rare reports of kindnesses on the part of the conquerors. The Russians would give the children food, and even rides in their lorries. There was the usual black-comic spectacle of Russians learning to ride bicycles and falling off, then taking it out on the inanimate machine. One Russian in Beuthen expressed his bewilderment at the Germans going to war: 'Why you war? In Germany all there. In your country you can rob from a house more than a whole village in ours.'[92]

In Eastern Pomerania Libussa von Krockow was at first unaware of the incursion of the Poles. She became conscious of them only when she applied to the Russian commandant to move into the gardener's cottage on the family estate after the Schloss had been burned to the ground. The commandant had told her to apply to the Polish 'mayor'. The only Poles she had noticed up to then were prisoners of war or forced labourers working on the farms. Now the farms were being turned over to them, so that servant had become master, and master servant. Ermland was on the old 'West' Prussian border and there had always been more Poles. The Germans were Catholics who spoke some Polish. They hoped to be able to cling to their homes by keeping their heads down.

Käthe von Normann found the Poles more sympathetic. Their military units had actually fought alongside the Russians near the town of Plathe, and Polish officers had kept her informed of what was going on in the

Russian camp. The Poles rounded up the last of the men – anyone who had enjoyed a smidgen of authority in the old days, and any nobles who had been missed by the Russians. In the case of Jesko von Puttkamer, he was taken to Stolp and thrown into the former Gestapo prison, with ten or twenty to a cell, just two beds and virtually no food. His stepdaughter had to walk thirty kilometres to bring him an occasional crust of bread until he was transferred to Danzig, out of her reach.

Food, never plentiful, dwindled to nothing. People survived by scrumping and theft. Potatoes, introduced to Pomerania by Frederick the Great, became the delicacy. Frau von Normann had to provide milk, butter and eggs for the mayor and garrison; anything remaining was for the Germans. Generally, however, there was next to nothing left over. Even so, with her little butter, milk, eggs and corn, she was well off compared to urban Germans. In the autumn the pitiful amounts of milk given out to nursing mothers were stopped. Germans who broke the law by trying to sell goods were put in the stocks. Poles were incited to spit on them, but generally merely voided their rheum on the ground.

Treks

Silesia was to be made free of Germans and that meant gathering up what you could carry and heading west. On 5 October 1945 intelligence reached General Clay of the plight of the German refugees from east of the Oder–Neisse and the Sudetenland. The figure of 9,000,000 he felt was conservative, it was probably more like ten. Of these he assumed that 65–70 per cent had already been deported. Of these, three-fifths had settled in Saxony, a sixth in Brandenburg and a sixth in Mecklenburg. 'Undoubtedly a large number of refugees have already died of starvation, exposure and disease.' Many were 'deported by force . . . others fled from fear'. They all converged on Berlin, where there were around forty-five camps. The numbers knocking on the doors of the old capital amounted to between five and six hundred thousand a month. Over 40 per cent of these were children, 'many of them without parents'.[93]

From 20 February 1946 the British demanded (and the Poles agreed) that the deportees be placed at assembly points and that trains and ships be laid on to collect them at fixed times. The size and weight of the luggage was to be predetermined. They were to be permitted to bring food for the journey and money. The Poles had to provide disinfectant. Seriously ill Germans or pregnant women could not be moved. In the case of the latter they had to remain if within six weeks of their confinement. If one member of the family fell ill, all of them had to remain behind until he or she got better. It was very high minded, and quite ineffectual. At the end of December 1946, the junior minister responsible for German and Austrian affairs, John Hynd, had to admit to the House of Commons that twenty trains had recently arrived in Berlin without heating. On one of them twenty corpses were found and 160 people suffering from frostbite.[94]

It was time to leave, but the decision to make the trek west was not an easy one. You risked losing all your possessions, further physical abuse and death. The worst danger was for small children, who often died *en route*. As early as the third week of March 1945, Käthe von Normann had seen one trek come to grief when they were shot at by the Russians and forced to return to the village. In May even those Germans who had made considerable progress towards to the west were returned to the villages they came from. Frau von Normann received a new family at Whitsun, who stole her little remaining soap. She wondered if she too could return to her manor house. She was eventually sent back to Barkow, but only after she had been denounced to the militia by one of her fellow Germans. She never discovered her crime. In Barkow she had the advantage of being among her own people, and the two Polish estate workers who now had the job of running the place looked after her and the children.

The Puttkamer-Krockows determined to go to the provincial capital, Stolp, to find out whether there was a legal means of escape. They walked the ten kilometres in a morning. The sign announcing the town had been crossed out, as it had already been awarded a Polish name: Słupsk. At first sight, not much had changed on the Bismarckplatz, except that the Iron Chancellor had been knocked off his pedestal and beheaded. Inside the old city, however, it was a scene of desolation: rubble lay all around and the Gothic cathedral had been gutted. There had been no bombing. The Russians had wrecked Stolp. They found a man in authority. To go to the 'Reich' they needed permission from their Polish mayor and an attestation that there were no known charges against them. They could pack one suitcase only and take provisions for three days. It was a while before permission was granted. Another winter was to be spent in the new Poland. The nights were long, there was no light, but then there were no books to read. They amused themselves by remembering epics, but they stayed clear of Prussian patriotic poetry – celebrating victories such as the Battle of Sedan was meaningless now.

News came in curious echoes, which might have had a bearing on the truth had anyone known how to interpret it. In Barkow on 27 May 1945 they heard stories that the Allies had fallen out, and that American troops had landed in Stettin and Danzig. The inevitable fall-out between the Allies was still as eagerly desired in Pomerania as it had been by Goebbels in Berlin in the last days of the war. On 12 March 1946 Lehndorff heard that the Russians were in a warlike mood. Stalin had made a critical speech against Britain.[95] A month later new rumours circulated through the Polish police which gave a more accurate picture of their fate. The towns of Greifenberg and Plathe were to be evacuated, and Cammin had already been cleared of Germans. The Greifenberger were indeed expelled with just 15 kilos of kit, and left for days to forage in the Cammin woods before they were rounded up again.

The Silesian expulsions were now in full swing. As the bishop of Katowice had put it, 'The sooner they leave of their own free will, the better it will be for them.'[96] Except that free will played little part in the process. Officially Silesia was to be 'German-free' by June 1946. In reality the Poles wanted to hang on to industrious artisans for a little longer yet.[97] Streams of civilians were forced from their homes at gunpoint from the ancient German towns of Görlitz, Glogau, Sagan and Liegnitz late that spring. Every form of locomotion was brought into service: prams were a popular way of transporting a few bare necessities. One witness saw a cart being drawn by six children, with a pregnant woman pushing from behind. The destination was the Lusatian Neisse, which formed the new *de facto* border. The town of Forst served as an assembly point for crossings. Here they were held back until the Poles could rob them of the little they still possessed.[98] The authorities in Görlitz on the German side were desperate to keep them out of the town, as they had no food for their own people, something which exacerbated the misery of the expellees. Meanwhile Polish border guards combed the columns for young girls, who were to be retained, ostensibly to help bring in the harvest. While the Germans waited at the river, they left messages on trees, indicating to friends and family which way they were heading, and who they had lost.[99]

Grünberg in Lower Silesia suffered because of the amount of alcohol in the town. Not only had it been the centre of Silesia's small vineyard area, but the Nazis had made it their repository for wine – still and sparkling – and cognac, which they had shipped in from Hamburg, Bremen, the Rhine and the Mosel. The brutality inspired by the contents of the cellars led whole families to commit suicide. One priest estimated that a quarter of the population died in this way. The Poles came on 12 May 1945. On 24 June the remaining population was informed that they had six hours to pack their bags.[100] In June and July that year a total of 405,401 Germans were expelled. The last official expulsions occurred in 1950 when 1,329 Germans were thrown out of Swinemünde.[101]

While the stench of death and brutality pervaded the German regions east of the Oder, one old German was allowed to live unmolested in his home. The new Soviet–Polish masters in Silesia showed a remarkable reluctance to expel the Nobel Prize-winning playwright Gerhart Hauptmann, who had lived in a palatial villa on the Wiesenstein in the small village of Agnetendorf in the Riesengebirge since 1902. The Riesengebirge* had been 'Germany's air-raid shelter' and the Foreign Ministry had been evacuated to a ski-resort in the mountains. The old man was counting his days surrounded by the works of art he had collected over the years: the bust of Goethe by David d'Angers had pride of place in the Paradise Hall with its murals by Johannes Avenarius.† Hauptmann ambled about wearing a frockcoat with his order Pour le Mérite in his lapel.[102] He had been in Dresden on Valentine's Day and had been badly knocked about by the blasts from the bombing. Months later he had still not recovered.[103]

Hauptmann's amanuensis, the writer Gerhart Pohl, went to see the Soviet commander in nearby Hirschberg. The streets were festooned with posters repeating Stalin's comforting words: 'Hitlers come and go . . .' Pohl explained that Hauptmann was living in his old house up in the mountains. The officer expressed surprise: 'Hauptmann, the author of *The Weavers?*' The first collected edition of Hauptmann's works in Russian had been published as early as 1902. As a Russian major told Pohl (with a degree of hyperbole for all that): 'Every schoolchild in the Soviet Union knows the writer of *The Weavers.*' Visits by literary-minded Soviet officers began soon after. Hauptmann dealt with them patiently and flattered them with his admiration for Tolstoy and Gorky.[104]

A Polish professor came to see him from the Ministry of Art and Culture in Warsaw. He was Galician, and spoke German fluently with an Austrian accent (Galicia had been a part of the Austro-Hungarian Empire until 1918). He told Hauptmann, 'Germany's fate is hard, but not entirely undeserved. Think about the horrors perpetrated against my people. These are undeniable facts . . .' The professor returned to his ministry to arrange for Hauptmann's protection. The papers arrived on 7 August, five days after the break-up of the Potsdam Conference.[105]

For a while Hauptmann's presence rallied the inhabitants of the nearby

---

* The 'giant mountains' (*sic*) rise to over 1,600 metres.

† (1887–1954). Avenarius was an expressionist painter famed for his illustrations to Hauptmann's works.

artists' colony of Schreiberhau, where the Germans continued to live by selling off their possessions to the Poles. Ruth Storm sold her foalskin coat for 500 złotys and managed to procure two kilos of bacon, a pound of butter and a smoked sausage. She supposed that they were left in peace because Hauptmann received visits from foreign journalists.[106] It was a brief respite. One day in the street Pohl recognised an old man in a dressing gown as one of his former teachers. It was Eugen Kühnemann, the biographer of Schiller. He had been robbed of all he owned and turned out of his house.[107]

Hauptmann continued to live on the Wiesenstein with his Polish protection papers. No one was allowed to enter Haus Wiesenstein or its grounds on pain of punishment. That didn't always stop them. Some heavily armed Russian soldiers explained that they meant no harm: 'Wir nicht machen bum-bum ... Nicht machen zapzerap, bloss mal gucken. Du erlauben bitte?' (We no make bang bang ... no do stealing, just have a look. You permit please?).[108] Some bogus journalists forced their way in on one occasion and ran about the place pocketing small objects. 'Suddenly they stood in the Biedermeyer Room ... before the old man ... "Come closer, gentlemen! Your youth cheers my ancient heart. You wanted to visit my house at an unusual hour. You have had your wishes come true. How might I help you now?"' Pohl sought clarification of Hauptmann's position in the midst of all this harassment, and like many other Silesians he wanted to know what the future held for them. He decided to pay a call on Johannes R. Becher in Berlin. The future East German minister of culture chainsmoked nervously, while Pohl tried to pin him down. He mentioned the Potsdam agreement: that Silesia was under Polish administration until the peace treaty. Did that mean it would return to Germany? 'Mann, verlassen Sie sich darauf nicht!' (I shouldn't put your faith in that, old man!).[109]

Becher consented to visit Hauptmann on the Wiesenstein. He wanted to win him over for his Cultural Alliance and Germany's literary renewal. It was not easy to get there. There were no trains, and he and his Russian friend Grigori Weiss had to set out in two cars followed by a lorry containing food and benzene. It took two days to reach Agnetendorf. Hauptmann told the poet, 'I am an old man, I have no more ambitions, but the fate of Germany concerns us all.'[110] He nonetheless pledged his support: 'I will go along with you ... That is my national duty. Together with my people I shall dedicate all my last strength to the business of Germany's national renewal.'[111]

He resisted all moves to shift him across the border, however – he wished to die in Silesia. The chief concern was the dwindling stock of brandy in Haus Wiesenstein. The old man was used to a life-saving glass every day, and now there remained just a few drops left in the last bottle. Becher and Weiss decided to do Hauptmann a last good turn and headed into Liegnitz to see the Soviet commander. Naturally this Russian knew Hauptmann by reputation too: 'In the evening we returned to Agnetendorf with a whole car full of food and with twenty bottles of cognac [sic] of the best Caucasian brand.'[112] Hauptmann finally expired on 6 June, three days after uttering his last words 'Bin – ich – noch – in – meinem – Hause?' (Am I still in my house?). The Poles preserved the great man's residence, turning it into a children's home. His body was expelled along with the living and the dying. Contrary to his wishes he was buried at Hiddensee on the Baltic coast.[113]

Transit Camps

The Normanns received their marching orders on 29 June 1946. Barkow was to be evacuated within two hours. The 200 or so inhabitants were to pack for two weeks. Accompanied by Polish soldiers and policemen they went as far as Plathe in the gruelling heat. The first stop was to be Wollin, where they were to stay in a camp until they could be shipped across the Oder.

Transit camps like Wollin existed all over the new Poland. Once notified, Germans had to assemble in their town or village squares with one suitcase. Some Poles were worried what the outside world might think of them: Lehndorff was asked to speak to the 400 Germans in his camp to explain that their treatment had been ordered from above, and that it only imitated what the Germans had done to the Poles.[114] For the people of Breslau, the camps were at Freiburg Station and Kohlfurt. Once the railways were ready to handle them, they were put in bolted railway trucks to be taken west. For those living in the depths of the country, the journey to the transit camp was an ordeal in itself. Frau von Normann's cart lost a wheel in the next village, but she was lucky to find help from the old Polish village policeman, Dombrowski, whose wife she had protected from the SS. He loaded her belongings on to his bicycle. The twenty or so Polish soldiers who accompanied the troop were not too hard on the refugees in general.

Treks of this kind were hindered by disputes between the Russians and the Poles. When Frau von Normann's posse arrived in the village of Trieglaff, the Russian garrison ordered them back to Barkow, blocking off the road with men brandishing machine guns. Night fell and the refugees squatted together on the road. Then came the order to return. It had all been for nothing.

Home to the Reich

The Krockows' decision to leave was prompted by an unseasonal descent by a pack of Russian soldiers demanding 'Uri!' The watches had all gone months before. One of their number panicked, however: she knew of a watch. It was up in the attic. It had belonged to Robert von Puttkamer, Libussa von Krockow's grandfather, a right-wing minister of the interior whose sacking in 1889 had been the only successful action of the so-called liberal empire of the Emperor Frederick's English-born wife Vicky. The watch had been a present from Emperor William I, and it had the imperial signature engraved on the cover. The loss of this one last contact with a more glorious past prompted them to make the journey. Libussa would go first, to see how the land lay.[115]

On 20 November 1945 the Allied Control Council had worked out the finer details of the Potsdam Agreement. The 'orderly and humane' deportations were to go ahead. The first tranche covered 3.5 million Germans from the east. Of these one and a half million were to go to the British Zone and the other two to the SBZ. Another two and a half million were coming from Czechoslovakia, half a million from Hungary and 150,000 from Austria. These were to be housed in the Soviet Zone (750,000), the American Zone (2.25 million) and the French Zone (150,000). A year later the British Zone had grown by 3.1 million souls, the American by 2.7 and the Russian by 3.6. Berlin's population had risen by 100,000 and the French Zone had taken in 60,000. The population of Germany in its reduced state had grown by 16.5 per cent.[116]

By mid-winter 1946 Stolp possessed a proper office with 'Emigration' written in German over the door and an official who spoke the language without a hint of accent. Forms had to be filled in using the new Polish names: Rumbske (which was Slavic anyhow) had become Rumsko; Pommern or Pomerania, Pomorze. The applicant had to swear that he or she was leaving of his or her own free will, and would not return on pain of punishment. The certificate cost 150 złotys. That was two months' wages for Lehndorff, once the Poles began to pay for his services. A kilo of bacon cost 400 złotys, and 500 grams of sugar, 90.[117]

It looked deceptively simple: there was a train leaving that morning at

10.14 arriving in Stettin at two. From there it was only an hour or two to Berlin. The ticket cost another 150 złotys. Already half Libussa's money had been spent. She was taken to a cattle truck, the door was pulled open, she was pushed in, and then it was slammed shut. In the gloom she began to pick out the shapes of other refugees – women, children and old people. The train stopped at the main towns: Schlawe, Köslin, Belgard. With every halt the door flew open and more refugees were crammed into the crowded space. It was dark by now. Then it came to a stop. A shot rang out. Then there were more shots.

> The door was ripped open – cries of terror, lanterns flickering, a horde surging in: wild figures dimly glimpsed amid the chaos and the confusion, men, but also youths and women, savage women, perhaps the worst of all, screaming, slavering, striking, snatching. More pistol shots, right over out heads, booming like cannon in the small space, numbness, knives and axes, fists, kicks, feet trampling over bodies, and always this bellowing, and the cries of fear and pain. Suitcases and crates, boxes and bundles, sprouted wings, flew up in the air and out of the door. The horde followed them out, and the door banged shut.[118]

The bandits had done their business in a matter of minutes, perhaps five at the most; but it was just the first attack. At one point militiamen opened the door and pretended to be concerned. When the Germans said they had been attacked, the men laughed. As they no longer possessed suitcases, the next wave went for the clothes on their bodies, stripping off coats, jackets and dresses. Libussa lost her precious rucksack in the second attack, her złotys in the third and her boots in the fourth. The train stopped in Stargard. So much for the timetable: they reached Scheune, near Stettin, in the middle of the night.

Stettin, on the left bank of the Oder, had been awarded to Poland, but many would have seen it as a safe haven. It was anything but. After the train had been shunted around for a while the doors were opened and everyone ordered out. There were guards with submachine guns ordering them to line up in twos. It was snowing hard. A crowd of some 400 was marched towards an old sugar factory, and beaten with rifle butts to make them move faster. One girl understood Polish. She told Libussa that anyone caught with letters would be punished, as a spy. Libussa tore up her letters and threw them into a hedge. The Poles did not want the world to know about life in the Recovered Territories. The sugar factory offered no more than a concrete floor and broken windowpanes, with a couple of full buckets for bodily needs. Dawn came, they waited, then sunset. The Poles 'needed darkness for whatever they had in mind'.[119] The Germans were marched out in pairs. They were beaten with rifle butts again until they reached a hall half lit by candles. Behind a table sat an official. He had a book in front of him and a pile of valuables. They were told to strip naked and throw their clothes to two men who were ready with knives to discover any hidden valuables. Libussa lost her last RM2,000.

They dressed from the pile, lucky to find something of their own. Then they had to sign the book that their money and valuables had been lawfully deposited. Libussa managed to steal a bit back while the attention of the official at the desk wandered over to two women stripping on the far side of the room. As they left, more militiamen examined them by lantern light, sizing them up. Fearing the worst, Libussa escaped through a window and hid in a ruined tank until dawn. Then she saw her fellow passengers coming out of the sugar factory. She caught up with them as they marched back towards the railway line. They had been robbed of all but a few rags. Women were sobbing hysterically. There was a train, and an old-fashioned German conductor in a uniform with a cap: 'All right, it's all right, everything's going to be all right . . . Climb aboard please, all aboard, we're leaving soon, going home.'[120] The refugees admitted they no longer had money for tickets. The conductor assured them that this time it was free. The train took them to Angemünde, where they all had to get out. A Russian gave Libussa a piece of bread. Then a new train was put together to take them to Berlin.

Libussa von Krockow's experience was not the worst. The refugees were often packed so tightly that they could not move to defecate and emerged from the trucks covered in excrement. Many were dead on arrival.[121] During the winter months the near-naked expellees literally froze to death. Women went insane as they watched their children die and they had to be tied up with rope to prevent them from clawing the other passengers. When they arrived in the remains of Germany they tried to carry off the corpses of their infants; they didn't want to believe they were dead.[122] One of the Germans reported that her baby had been dashed against the wall as it had come between her and her rapist. Children had been robbed of their swaddling clothes and allowed to freeze to death.[123]

Libussa had still not had enough. At the end of March 1946, together with her friend Otti von Veltheim, she decided to go back and rescue the remaining members of her family. After crossing into the Russian Zone, they reached the comparative safety of Zehlendorf in the American Sector of Berlin. Near the old Stettin Station they found an East Prussian girl who had an impressive document in Russian that allowed her to go 'home', although where 'home' was was not stipulated. It cost them a packet of

Luckies. There were no more friendly Russians in the railway station in Angermünde, just Russians with their minds on rape. Libussa and her friend escaped again. They found a friendly Russian commandant who assured them, 'Poles bad. Very, very bad. But Russians good. Just ask Russians. Russians always help against Poles.'[124]

After an initial reluctance to countenance the trip, they had won over the reluctant German railwaymen who were due to drive the train to Stettin. It would be a chance to put one over the Poles. Potatoes stolen from the Russians were cooked up in the locomotive steam and after an hour or two the signals turned green and the train set off. The Russians tried their luck with the girls, but accepted their rejection manfully enough and carried on protecting them from the Poles until the train reached Stettin harbour and the sugar factory. The Russian lieutenant even escorted them past the Polish guards outside the free port, before leaving them to fend for themselves in the bombed-out city.

Stettin was not yet cleared of Germans. They could be recognised by the tatters that served as clothes and by their furtive looks. Libussa and Otti found an old lady who offered them a room and very soon after a purported Graf Heinrich Kinsky from Prague who was working as a lorry driver for the Poles. German POWs who were fitting up the building for the Polish authorities provided them with furniture, heat and bedding. The next morning, however, the count disappeared, never to return. They found a less fabulous lead in a Polish railway official from Posen, who had fought in the German army in the First World War and who had been in the Polish resistance in the Second. He obtained tickets for them to Stolp and issued them with a couple of Polish newspapers as camouflage.

The journey went relatively smoothly. When the militia arrived they feigned sleep. The only really tense moment came when they lit up their Luckies and the unfamiliar smell appeared to arouse suspicion among their Polish fellow travellers. One was bought off with a cigarette. The journey to Stolp, which had taken the Royal Prussian Railway a mere three and a half hours, took the new Polish authorities closer to ten. When the train reached the outskirts of the city, they panicked and rushed for the door. One of the passengers said to them in German, 'Try the other side, Fräulein!' The women froze, but the Poles in the carriage were laughing. In a chorus they said. 'Auf wiedersehen!'[125]

Libussa waited for mid-summer to bring the rest of the family back to the 'Reich'. By then a new administrator had arrived and gone to live in the manor house in Zipkow. The women found him courteous, and he spoke excellent German. Indeed, much was familiar in his office: the desk was from Libussa's house and on the wall was a portrait of one of the Glowitz Puttkamers. The Pole asserted that the reason he had hung it there was that he numbered Puttkamers among his own forebears. Likewise Lehndorff was able to impress Polish officials that his family had once borne the name Mgowski, and he was issued with a pass in that name.[126]

The sympathetic – and aristocratic – Polish official had friends in the railways in Stolp. The mood was changing in Poland. A camp had been set up at Neu Torney near Stettin to process the refugees. Attacks on the trains had come to a complete halt, he maintained. The Germans from Pomerania were to be taken to the British or Soviet zones; most wanted to go to the latter. The British authorities were horrified by the physical state of the Germans when they reached the end of their journey. In April 1946 they issued a formal protest, and began to refuse to accept refugees under these conditions. In December they stopped accepting refugees altogether.

Whole villages were being shipped out now. They all had to wait at assembly points until the order came to join the train. The train Libussa and her family took required two days and two nights to travel the 237 kilometres to Stettin. They were allowed out at the stations, and there were indeed no attacks. The end of the journey was a DP camp. There Libussa found her friend Otti and her relatives, one of whom had already gone out of his mind. They spent three weeks in the camp.

When in mid-March 1946 Käthe von Normann heard that her deportation was nigh, it was time to pack and conceal the last remaining objects of value. Cushions were suspended from the rucksacks so that they could travel more comfortably in the cattle trucks, and a bucket was found, for the long hours in the train. A gold pin was hidden in a matchbox, rings wrapped in wool, necklaces sewn into bags or concealed in the food. A pearl necklace was rolled in oats, a wedding ring sewn into one of her son's clothes.

They left on Good Friday. They walked to Greifenberg where they were taken to a camp beside the railway line. The train departed on Easter Sunday with some twenty refugees to a truck. Someone had the good idea of securing the doors with wire from the inside to prevent the bandits from opening it. This proved wise, because there were attempts to rip it open as the train went slowly. The Polish guards obliged them to sing. They opened up with 'Eine feste Burg'. They came to Kreckow, a suburb of Stettin, whence it was a two-kilometre hike to the camp. They were driven on by militia men who threatened them with rubber truncheons. The following day they were all beaten on their way to the luggage inspection: 'the children were beside themselves with terror'.[127] At the counter the Pole failed to locate Frau von Normann's remaining jewellery. They seemed more interested in the bacon that others were carrying. Leaving in May 1947, Hans Lehndorff seems to have had a reasonably easy time of it, or maybe it seemed like nothing after everything he had been through in the previous two years.

Käthe von Normann had suffered much, but possibly the greatest sufferers had been the East Prussians. One transport that left in 1945 crammed 4,500 people into forty-five cattle trucks. In the witnesses' wagon there were 116 men, women and children. The train took eleven days to reach the new German border. During that time there was robbery upon robbery and two or three people died every day. The Poles did not just strip them of their possessions; they took the young girls as well.[128] A third of the East Prussians were dead by the time they reached their homeland. On 28 October 1948 a survey was carried out among young East Prussian girls in Rüdersdorf camp. There were 1,600, most of them country girls who had been taken to Russia before being brought back to Germany. Between 50 and 60 per cent had died on the way, and more had perished since. Their average age was 19.7 years and their weight 45.38 kilos. Most no longer had monthly periods; 48 per cent had been raped, 20 per cent more than ten times and 4 per cent over a hundred times.[129]

Back in the train that night, plunderers descended on the Normanns and the other impotent refugees, trying to steal their cases. They waited two days and then were marched back to the station and driven back into the cattle trucks. The train set off towards Scheune, where Libussa von Krockow had had such terrible experiences. From there a train took them directly to Pöppendorf near Lübeck in the British Zone. The British Zone was also the principal destination for Silesians heading west.[130]

Nor was the search for valuables as draconian as it had been. When Libussa crossed the border for the second and last time she had managed to conceal some family effects in a false bottom to her daughter's pram. The effects of camp food on the baby's stomach had been so terrible that the official declined to search it. To their glee, the train took them to Lübeck in the British Zone. At Lübeck they arrived to find that tables had been set up under the trees and that hot soup was being served to adults and porridge and hot milk to children. Bananas were handed out to the children afterwards. One of them, suspicious of this novelty, refused: 'What the farmer don't know, he don't eat.'[131]

It was the same treatment that Käthe von Normann had received. After all she had experienced, Frau von Normann was speechless. A British officer went between the tables offering seconds. The women were so unused to this solicitude that they burst into tears and tried to kiss his hand. It was not the satisfactory food that relieved them so much, but the feeling of security: 'We were human beings again, and treated as human beings. Who can understand this feeling? To be honest, only those who had been through the many months of horror we had suffered, and from which we had now escaped.'[132]

PART II
Allied Zones

Prologue

Germany was formally divided into zones on 5 June 1945. They were of course clumsily drawn and certain industries became largely unworkable as a result. Spinning was in British Westphalia, but weaving was in Russian Saxony; cameras were made in the American Zone, but the optical glass came from the Soviet, and the shutters from the French; the Americans had 68 per cent of the car industry; while the Russians had all the kaolin needed to supply the various porcelain manufactures that were the pride of the old German *Residenzen*.[1] They were very different parts of Germany. As far as the Western Allies were concerned, the joke ran round that the Americans had been given the scenery, the French the vines, and the British the ruins.[2]

The Allies squatted in their zones offering greater or lesser degrees of co-operation with their neighbours. The Anglo-Americans worked reasonably well together and, as comrades in arms, they went on to create Bizonia at the end of 1946 by uniting their zones. This became Trizonia when the French finally agreed to the merger. The French saw their piece of the German cake differently – almost as a conquered fiefdom. Naturally the Russians would brook no interference with their slice and their purposes were more similar to the French. What concord existed came at the meetings of the Allied Control Council in Berlin, which met for the first time on 30 July 1945 and issued its initial proclamation exactly a month later. The ACC convened three times a month, bringing together the four 'elements', as they were called, on the 10th, 20th and 30th at the old Kammergericht in the American Sector. During the Third Reich this was the seat of the notorious Volksgericht or People's Court, which had tried offences against the state and had handed down huge numbers of death sentences.

After Potsdam the Kommandatura was set up in the Luisenstrasse in Berlin. It was the one Russian word that was palatable to all the Allies. That the Soviets took precedence was clear to all and sundry: the Western Allied flags had second place under a giant red star and hammer and sickle. The Russian commandant was General Gorbatov, while Zhukov's chief of staff, General Sokolovsky, sat in on the meetings. The British representative was General Lyne. The spadework at the ACC was done by the deputy military governors or DMGs, leaving the governors proper to deal with their governments. Each meeting was chaired by a different power, which also provided the 'light refreshments' that followed. They generally were light, except when the Russians were the hosts. The first British DMGs were General Sir Ronald Weeks (who retired through ill-health in August 1945) and General Sir Brian Robertson. The French sent General Koeltz, followed by General Noiret. The governor, Pierre Koenig, came to Berlin 'as seldom as possible'.[3] Clay was the Americans' emissary. The DMGs also regulated the work of the 175 different committees. A DMG typically spent the mid-week in Berlin and the weekends in the zone. It was different for the Soviets of course: Berlin was *in* their zone.

6

Life in the Russian Zone

Die Preise hoch
Die Läden fest geschlossen.
Die Not marchiert mit ruhig festen Schritt.
Es hungern nur die kleinen Volksgenossen,
Die grossen hungern nur im Geiste mit.
Komm, Wilhelm Pieck, sei unser Gast
Und geb, was Du uns versprochen hast.
Nicht nur Rüben, Kraut und Kohl
Sondern was Du isst, und Herr Grotewohl.

The prices high
The shops are firmly shuttered
Famine looms with steady marching pace
Only poor comrades eat their bread unbuttered,
The bigwigs are quick to stuff their face.
Come Bill Pieck, and be a gent:
Give us some of what the Party's sent.
Not just turnips, swedes and weeds
But the things old Grotewohl thinks he needs.

Popular song. Quoted in Norman M. Naimark, *The Russians in
Germany – A History of the Soviet Zone of Occupation, 1945–1949*,
Cambridge, Mass. and London 1995, 389–90

The Russians created their occupation zone or SVAG on 9 June 1945.
Even after they had ceded a large part of their zone to the Poles the
Soviet authorities could congratulate themselves: they had done well. They
had just under a quarter of Germany's pre-war industrial base; 50 per cent
of the country's 1936 tool production; 82 per cent of office-machine
manufacture; 68 per cent of textile machines and 25 per cent of car production. They controlled 24 per cent of the population, but – alas – only

2.2 per cent of the coal. This was the sticking point at Potsdam, which had failed to iron out the differences between the Allies.[1]

The Soviet authorities quietly established a civilian regime in their zone on 27 July, appointing German civilians to ministerial portfolios in transport, finance and industry. Stalin was careful not to go too far, and antagonise his new subjects. From the start there were hearts and minds to be won. He had told his satraps that they were to create national fronts with bourgeois parties even though their own system only allowed for a one-party state. Communists in Germany were to talk of 'democracy', not of socialism. He was pragmatic on the question of satellite regimes in Germany or Austria: perhaps they would come with time. He was torn, however, between the idea of a satellite state in eastern Germany and his desire to get his hands on the Ruhr. He overestimated the 'anti-fascists' and underestimated the lure of Bizonia. He restrained Tito and the Greek communists who he thought would endanger good relations with the West. It was not the same in Poland, which he wished to control without interference from his wartime allies.[2]

Marshal Zhukov was placed at the head of the administration in Karlshorst – 'the Berlin Kremlin' – assisted by his deputies Sokolovsky and Serov. S. I. Tulpanov ('the Colonel' or 'the Tulip') was placed in charge of propaganda, but he was an economist by training – the Russian version of Ronald Weeks. The Russians spread themselves out in the old military engineering school. The intelligence officer Gregory Klimov says that his boss, General Shabalin, had a desk 'the size of a football field'.* Zhukov liked to see himself as a friend to the Germans. Unlike many German communists, he made no attempt to deny the rapes. He blamed them on the demoralisation of his troops, acts that were very different from the crimes perpetrated by the SS in Russia.[3] In the spring of 1946 Zhukov was replaced by Sokolovsky – the battle commander by a pen-pushing desk general. The Soviet commander had far less power than Lucius Clay and had to cope with Stalin's whims. Stalin was 'opaque': his policy directions could be interpreted in a number of ways. It was not easy to know when he would intervene and in what way. Another problem the commander had to reckon with were the activities of the secret service organisations, the NKVD/MVD, the GPU and Smersh. These were independent of the military governor's control. Smersh, for example, had the job of investigating German civilian employees.[4]

The SBZ had a panoply of bewildering organs, including GlavPurkka

* Compare Eisenhower, below p. 227.

in charge of political re-education which ran the newspapers and went into the POW camps to convince the soldiers of the need for socialism.[5] Under Stalin's 'divide and rule' policy, it was always difficult to know who was in control. There were, for example, 70,000 *demontagniki*. Klimov came across some strange Russian troops in weird uniforms, and learned that they were 'dismantlers': 'They are all dressed up as colonels and lieutenant-colonels, but they've never been in the army in their life.'[6] The different Kommandaturas in Berlin, Dresden, Halle and Leipzig reflected the views of their commanding generals and were often at odds with one another. The Thuringian command, for example, was harsh, while the Saxon was liberal. The generals could be sacked and dishonoured on charges of degenerate behaviour. This normally meant keeping mistresses. From mid-1947 it was official policy that any general who was caught living with a German woman would be sent home. By this time all Jewish officers had returned to Russia, as their presence had been deemed inappropriate.[7]

Colonel-General Nicholas Bersarin had something of a hero's status for Berliners, doubtless helped by his untimely death in a motorcycle accident at the age of forty-one. He was credited with doing all he could to promote the rebuilding of the city. He made the production of mortar-producing Rüdersdorfer Kalkwerke available to Hans Scharoun as a personal gift and gave the architect considerable patronage. He also put the internationally famous surgeon Ferdinand Sauerbruch in charge of health, Furtwängler of music and Eduard Spranger of the university. Later the Americans arrested and imprisoned Spranger for a while in Wannsee. It was not the first time he had tasted food in gaol – he had been inside after the 20 July Plot – but this time no one could see a good reason for his arrest, except possibly that the Americans resented his attempts to revive university life in the Russian Sector. Bersarin was passionate about trotting, and revived the race-course at Karlshorst for his favourite sport. Before 1945 Karlshorst had been famous for its steeplechase. When Bersarin died red flags were hung at half-mast all over the city. Ruth Friedrich heard of his death from a paper-seller on the Potsdamer Platz. When she got home Leo Borchard told her it was a personal misfortune: 'He promoted art like no other.' His motorbike ran into an army lorry. The driver of the vehicle shot himself.[8]

In the first days Jews and communists were deemed the most trustworthy administrators. Appointments were often capricious. The Russians would find some apparently uncorrupted soul and tell him, 'You are now mayor!'[9] But it was not always easy to see who was uncorrupted, and a lot of criminals and thieves were placed in positions of authority. In several instances, writers were made mayors of the communes where they lived, and not necessarily communist ones. Rudolf Ditzen (better known as Hans Fallada, the author of the popular novel *Kleiner Mann was nun?* – Little Man, What Now?) was put in charge of Feldberg in Mecklenburg for eighteen months. His ex-wife had been raped by the Russians, but he told his constituents, 'The Russians come as your friends.' Günther Weisenborn was made mayor of Luckau after emerging from the local prison,[10] while another writer, Hans Lorbeer, became head man in Pieskeritz. When Margret Boveri went to Teupitz in the Spreewald at the beginning of May she found that the Russians had left a Herr Susmann in charge. He was above suspicion, being both a Jew and a communist, but that had not prevented the Russians from stealing his bicycle – three times – despite an official document stating that he needed it for his work.[11]

After Potsdam, the antipathies between the West and the East became more open. The British complained that the Russians had stolen half the railway lines to Hamburg and demanded that the second set be put back. In revenge the Russians plundered the trains and sealed the borders so hermetically that it cost RM100,000 to make the illicit crossing.

Once the dust had settled, the Russians' stooges were ready to put through land reform – very largely on their own initiative. It was introduced in the autumn, and the big estates were broken up. Wolfgang Leonhard accompanied the leading German communist, Walter Ulbricht, on a trip to the country where he canvassed opinion. They stopped in a small village and Ulbricht addressed the inhabitants. The peasants responded with silence.[12] Some of these reforms appear to have been in conflict with Stalin's instructions to play the communist card sparingly, but they proved popular with many Germans who had grown up believing the Junkers to be the embodiment of evil, and who also wanted their share of the land. The Russians were particularly hard on the nobles, setting fire to their manor houses and raping or killing the inhabitants. Margret Boveri assumed that the old Junker class was now extinct, and regretted it, as 'there were a good many decent sorts among them'. Elvira von Zitzewitz, who belonged to one of the oldest Prussian families, had told her that her parents had been wiped out in Templin, and others of her Berlin acquaintance had a similar tale to tell.[13] While they were not exactly extinct, they had suffered. One study of under 9,000 Junkers showed that nearly 5,000 died fighting in the war, with another 1,500 killed in other circumstances in 1945. Fifty-eight had died after the 20 July Plot, leaving just over 2,000 survivors in May 1945. Of these another 500 died in detention and the same number committed suicide. Around 15 per cent survived to make their way to the West. Whole families resorted to suicide. In Mecklenburg, which had a reputation as the most feudal region of Germany, thirty noble families were destroyed in this way.[14]

Owning lots of land could have you placed in one of the nastier Soviet camps on the island of Rügen. Initially this meant unseating the remainder of the East Elbian nobility whose lands lay west of the Oder and Neisse rivers, but the Russians might have been vaguely thinking of the need to find room for the refugees from the east. In official East German terminology, these were not *Flüchtlinge* (refugees) but *Umsiedler* (resettlers). The first agrarian law, passed on 3 October 1945, was an excuse for plunder: all estates over 100 hectares were to be sequestered. Another 7,000 people were thus made homeless in one fell swoop.[15] In 1946 the physical substance of what remained was more or less effaced, so that the Schloss or Herrenhaus that lay at the centre of the feudal village of old disappeared from the map – unless, that is, some other use could be found for it as a club for Party functionaries or secret policemen, a mental hospital or a home for handicapped children.[16]

As one recent historian has written, the Junkers played 'a central role in the demonology of the Nazi regime'. The Russians equated them with Nazis, and their German stooges made sure agrarian reform was at the top of the agenda. Communist Party chairman Wilhelm Pieck coined the phrase 'Junkerland in Bauernhand' (The gentry's lands in the peasants' hands).[17] By 1947 there were 477,000 peasants tilling the new *kolkhoz* farms.[18] Some people refused to heed the signs. One of these was Hans-Hasso von Veltheim, a cosmopolitan intellectual with friends in high places around the globe. He lived in his country house, Ostrau, near Halle. It was the Americans who were the first to 'liberate' him. They placed a guard of honour on his land. When the Soviet army took over, they too accorded Veltheim the honour of a guard and offered him a professorship at the University of Halle. He declined. He had refused to believe he was in danger before the authorities grabbed his land. Now, extremely ill, he decided the time had come to flee to the West, rather than end up dying in prison like other landowners. He had looked on while a mob, whipped up by the Russians, pulled down the ancient trees in his park and broke open the coffins of his ancestors to hang the skeletons from the branches.[19] Those who, like the Grand Duchess of Weimar, threatened to resist the impounding of all their worldly goods were threatened with the Russians. Franz Sayn-Wittgenstein's uncle Prince Günter von Schönburg-Waldenburg was not only robbed, he was packed off to Rügen. Many of them died from hunger and brutality. When Prince Günter finally escaped to the West he started a new life as a language teacher.[20] Once the nobles quit their houses they were festooned with congratulatory banners: 'Junkerland im Bauernhand'.[21]

The Soviet authorities were not merely destructive; nor were they only thieves and rapists. Money was reintroduced as early as 8 May and – in theory at least – Soviet soldiers had to stop pillaging and pay for their purchases.[22] The work of clearing the rubble in the towns and cities may have been a punishment, but there was sense behind it: only once the smashed bricks and mortar were cleared could communications be restored. In the first nine months of their occupation of Berlin, the Soviets restored nearly 200,000 homes. In this they had the support and assistance of Scharoun. They put back the tramlines, and the S-Bahn reopened as early as 30 May.

The Russians began to promote the arts in Berlin that same month by creating a Kammer der Kunstschaffenden or Academy of Creative Artists under the presidency of actor–director and star of *Der Golem* Paul Wegener. The Academy had departments dealing with music, writing, theatre and cinema. It had its own 'star chamber' with powers to rehabilitate National Socialists.[23]

Scharoun tried his best to preserve some of the city's shattered monuments, such as the Schloss and the Reichstag.[24] For some time the future of the damaged Prussian monuments hung in the balance. The Berlin Schloss, the oldest parts of which dated back to the fifteenth century, and which had been remodelled by the baroque architect Andreas Schlüter, had been badly shelled during the Russian advance. Many parts were reparable, but a debate soon grew up about the desirability of preserving relics of Prussia's militaristic past. For the time being the White Hall of the Schloss was patched up and used for exhibitions. The best remembered of these was 'Berlin Plant' or 'Berlin Plans', which opened on 22 August 1946. It was organised by Scharoun himself and pointed the way forward to the reconstruction of the city. It also made the case for keeping the modernised carcass of the Schloss. Three months later the exhibition was replaced by 'Modern French Painting'. This was to show Berliners the sort of paintings that had been denied them as 'degenerate' by the Nazis. On 21 December an exhibition organised by the earlier, avant-garde National Gallery director Ludwig Justi displayed the contents of some of the Berlin museums. Many of the others were in the process of travelling east – to Russia. The last exhibition to be organised in the ruins of the Royal Palace commemorated the Revolution of 1848.[25] Scharoun argued the case for keeping the

Schlüter courtyard of the Schloss, if nothing else. In the end the ruling SED not only decided against restoration, they actually destroyed the monuments, starting with the Berlin Schloss in 1950 and continuing with the Potsdam Schloss a decade later. The remains of the Garrison Church in Potsdam were destroyed in 1968.[26]

The preservation of Nazi monuments was also a sensitive issue. Speer had been pleased to observe that his New Chancellery was still there. It was, however, condemned: like all the surviving buildings on the western side of the Wilhelmstrasse, it was demolished to make it easier for the Soviets to patrol their sector. A photograph taken in April 1949 shows one wing of Speer's gigantic conception being torn down. The stone was used to build the huge Soviet monument in Treptow Park.[27] In the interests of 'security' the Russians also pulled down all that was left of their side of the Potsdamer and Leipziger Plätze.

On the other hand demontage took its toll. Before the Western Allies established camp in Berlin, more than a hundred companies were shipped east. Berlin lost around 85 per cent of its industrial capacity, including such weighty names as Siemens, AEG, Osram and Borsig. As demontage the Russians took away a very large chunk of the industrial base of what had been one of the most highly developed parts of Germany. By the autumn of 1945 they had already dismantled 4,339 of the 17,024 major installations in their zone.[28]

Fritz Löwenthal was another Muscovite who returned to the SBZ in 1946. As a communist lawyer he was placed at the head of a legal commission. He fled to the West on 25 May 1947, taking with him a fat dossier detailing crime and corruption in the Soviet Zone. His account amounts to an indictment of the Soviet authorities, and a justification for the young idealist's flight. Nazis were creeping back into positions of authority and all sorts of unsuitable characters achieving local power-bases as a result of toadying to the Soviet rulers.

The local judge at Lieberose, for example, turned out to be a former cook called (of all things) Bütter. On 3 January 1946 he was delivered up to the police in Potsdam accused of fraud. A week later he was found hanging in his cell, but the apparent suicide was contradicted by the state of his corpse – he had had his head beaten in, to stop him giving anything away at his trial.[29] At Forst on the Neisse, there was a flourishing trade in contraband across the new border with Poland. Germans, Poles and Russians were all involved, and the need to prevent the military poking their noses into the smuggling trade resulted in at least one murder. Elsewhere in

Germany corrupt Soviet officials sold grain to the Germans. Another German who was able to hoodwink the Soviets into believing she was anti-fascist was Sonja Kloss, the mayoress of Kolberg bei Storkau. She turned out to be a former SS interpreter who was protecting her lover, an erstwhile senior SS man.[30]

Anyone was in danger of being denounced, as most people had a skeleton in their closet. Muscovites and others who had co-operated with the Soviet authorities in Russia were generally above suspicion. In the sleepy town of Ruppin in the Mark Brandenburg, Landrat Dietrich had denounced the teacher Schulze in Gransee, whom he accused of having been an important leader in the Hitler Youth, and of seducing young boys. Dietrich owed his position of power to the fact that he had been on the committee of the Free Germany movement as a POW in Russia.[31] In Oranienburg the local dictator was the senior judge, one Fandrich, who uncovered a former Wehrmacht paymaster hiding in his parish and had him consigned to the concentration camp at Sachsenhausen which 'the Russians had brought back to life'. It is not known if he ever re-emerged. Fandrich, who employed his son as a spy, was not all that he seemed: he was not a jurist, and he was not even German. He spoke fluent Russian and had fought in the Russian Imperial Army in the First World War. He had later lived as a merchant in Warsaw. Like many people who achieved power in Germany just after the war, Fandrich was a KZler. He had been in Sachsenhausen himself, where he had worn the green badge of a criminal. His position in the Soviet Zone allowed him to amass hordes of treasure handed over by those who did not want their past examined in detail. On those who were less considerate, he imposed prison sentences. By January 1947 he had become over-confident of his position with the Russians. An order was issued for his arrest, and, although he was given time to flee, he felt he was not in danger. He was later put on trial and received a five-year sentence.[32]

Many criminals posed as 'victims of fascism' in this way, like Werner Stahlberg, who had been released from the prison in Brandenburg, but who had been a common criminal. A band led by a Russian-speaking German Balt named Schröder carried out seventy-eight robberies in a 'blue limousine'. They even robbed hospital patients of their valuables. Schröder had begun his life of crime when his friend and protector 'Dr' Werner Zahn, Oberbürgermeister of Potsdam, was arrested. Zahn was another conman who had invented his doctorate. Before the war he had sold cinema tickets.[33]

Löwenthal lifted the lid on Thuringia. Goethe's Ilmenau* was in the hands of Paul Flieder, a former communist who had nonetheless achieved high rank in the SS. With him installed in the town hall, fifty-one former Nazis found gainful employment. In Weissensee near Erfurt power was in the hands of one Hitkamp, another purported 'victim of fascism' who ran a robber-band, conducting house-to-house searches and confiscating property. In Eisenach the CID (criminal police) officer Kirchner turned out to have nine convictions of his own, while Reinhold Lettau, the police president who hired him, was an old Nazi. There could be tough sentences and quite arbitrary killings for anyone who fell foul of the Soviets. The Military Tribunal in Thuringia arraigned one man for being an intimate of the former Gauleiter, Sauckel, on the strength of a round-robin found in his home. In truth he was only the local Party cashier. He was tried by Russian officers in the cinema and sentenced to be hanged. His sentence was commuted by Stalin: he was shot instead.[34]

In Saxony, Karl Keller, the Bürgermeister of Zschieschen, was another 'green' who had spent eight years in a concentration camp and could boast thirty-two offences of theft and fraud. He was one of the lucky ones who got out: the prison population – many of them rounded up after the end of the war – was dying. When informed of the fact the Soviet commander, Lieutenant-Colonel Jakupov, dismissed the matter as 'humanitarian whingeing'. Another Russian officer complained of naked Germans coming across the border from Czechoslovakia. They had been stripped, then pushed over the frontier. The officer said the best he could do was put them in a cellar. He had no clothes to give them. Some Russian officers were living a good life. A Major Astafiev was reported enjoying a regime unknown to tsarist courtiers or boyars: he had a woman to roll on each stocking in the morning and another to hand him his dressing gown.[35] When in March 1947 the Soviet authorities pushed through land reform in Saxony, 300,000 hectares were nationalised, but only 50,000 were handed back to the peasants. The rest remained in the hands of the state. Meanwhile life was cheap in Saxony. When on 16 February 1946 the Russians decided that informer Helene Mader was no longer useful to them, the killer Zimmermann was paid the princely sum of 500 cigarettes.[36]

In the new state of Sachsen-Anhalt, in Niegripp near Burg on the Elbe, Josef Conrad passed as a political prisoner during his time in a concentration camp. The Russians were happy with his credentials and made him

---

* The poet walked in the woods near by, as the town belonged to Weimar. It was here he wrote 'Über allen Gipfeln'.

both Bürgermeister and police chief. They also gave him a gun and told him to round up the former Pgs and liquidate them. Conrad engaged a waiter with a record for theft named Walter Kraft and together they killed the teacher Seewald, the treasurer Dehne, the landlord Fabian and the agricultural worker Helmrich by putting a bullet in the backs of their heads. Their bodies were robbed.[37]

Rural Mecklenburg had formerly passed for the most reactionary corner of Germany. After 1945 it was the 'most bolshevised', according to Fritz Löwenthal. The head of the military government, General I. I. Fediunsky, lambasted the Germans for their lack of efficiency. The Germans were 'shirkers'. One local Soviet commander, Colonel Serebriensky, he dubbed 'the prompter at the Schwerin pocket edition of the Moscow world theatre'. Everything passed under his nose. It was presumably the colonel who caused the disappearance of Willi Jesse, the provincial secretary of the SED for Mecklenburg. Under his rule middle-class Mecklenburgers were held back. At school they were not allowed to progress beyond the ninth class or attend university. Some locals prospered under his reign, like the notorious Wilhelm Stange, Landrat in Usedom, who exploited his office to line his pockets.[38]

Not all so-called communists were crooks, but there was no shortage of people who came out of the woodwork in 1945 to claim that they had been persecuted by Hitler's regime, and who demanded privilege as a result. The Muscovite Ackermann wryly observed that 'It turned out that in the Soviet Union there were fewer Bolsheviks than there were in Hitlerite Germany.' These former communists were jealous of the Wehrmacht officers who were given positions of authority under the Russians, especially those who had fought in Spain, or who had been in a concentration camp, or both.[39]

Although the raping of German women had abated in the summer of 1945, it had not stopped. There was a fresh outburst of wild raping when the occupation lines were redrawn in June. The Russians moved into parts of Saxony and Thuringia where up till then the women had lived in comparative safety. There were a hundred rapes in Zerbst, the town that had seen the birth of Russia's great queen, Catherine, and similar numbers were reported in Halle and Weimar. In Weimar a Russian lieutenant walked into a barber's shop and proceeded to rape the cashier in front of the customers. Two other Russian officers had to be found before 'this animal could be overpowered'.[40] Despite the availability of abortions, many half-Russian children were born. In the US Ralph Keeling of the Institute of American Economics in Chicago thundered against the Russo-German bastards and envisaged 'Bolshevised Mongolian-Slavic hordes'.[41] Apart from the soldiers, there were around two million former POWs and forced labourers from Russia who had formed into gangs and robbed and raped all over central Europe.[42]

Real security was achieved only when the Red Army was garrisoned in barracks buildings in 1947–8. Even later the Russians took over whole areas of towns, throwing the inhabitants out on to the streets. From mid-1945, however, Russians caught raping women were liable to punishment. They might even suffer execution. Some were shot in the act, adding a further trauma to the victim of the sexual assault. A scale of charges was introduced in the summer of 1945, with ten days for debauchery and four years for aggravated rape. No German could report the crimes, however. When a group of young Germans prevented a rape by beating up the culprit, they were arrested and charged with being Werewolves. It was only in 1949 that Russian soldiers were presented with a real deterrent, with ten to fifteen years for simple rape and ten to twenty for raping a child, and for group or aggravated rape.[43] The east Germans had been allowed their own police, but at the beginning these men were armed with nothing more potent than clubs and they were not encouraged to step in when the crime was being committed by a Soviet soldier. They were given a small number of guns in mid-1946.

The other continuing nightmare of the Soviet Zone was that the pillaging seemed unending. In Karlshorst pilfering was tolerated within certain limits and according to rank. A squaddie might steal a watch, a junior officer an accordion, but woe betide any of them who took more than he should. Cars were useless – 'you couldn't hide a car' – and besides, it would have been nabbed by a superior officer.[44] Some choice things did get stolen, especially if they could be consumed on the spot. One MVD officer, for example, boasted of having some of the finest wines from Göring's cellar.[45]

Worse than the full-scale removal of the industrial base of the land was the abduction of men and women to develop industry in the Soviet Union. Some of the more vital scientists had surrendered to the West; the scientists who had created the V1 and V2 missiles at Peenemünde, for example, gave themselves up to the Americans in Bavaria. The Russians also found some useful personnel and they were prepared to overlook a man's Nazi past if the scientist were prepared to work for them. They also lured them over with the promise of better housing. Technicians working at the Oberspreewerk in the west were offered homes in Hirschgarten near Köpenick.[46]

At first the Russians were successful in attracting scientists. The Germans were less enthusiastic when the round-ups began. They took place two days after abortive elections on 20 October 1946, when the SED had been soundly beaten. Soldiers came at 3.00 a.m. to deport all the leading electricians, toolmakers and engineers. The men and women were informed, 'By order of the Russian High Command you have been mobilised for work in the Soviet Union. You are to leave at once, with your family. Your furniture and personal belongings will be moved to your new residence. The length of your stay will not exceed five years.'[47] The size of the operation meant that they had not finished by five that afternoon. One of the places the Russians cordoned off that morning was Hirschgarten.

The Russians were able to take their pick of the skilled workers from GEMA (which manufactured range-finders and sights), ETEM (which made guidance equipment), AEG Kabelwerk (which created radio transmitters), OKG-4 (which made automatic pilots) and Askania (the radar manufacturers). Some of the Germans refused to go. In Halle they literally had to be clubbed into submission. Ninety-two special trains were laid on to transport the 5,000 men, women and children. Some of them were indeed back within five years, some came back in 1953. A few stayed until January 1958, about the time the first Sputnik went into orbit. German scientists were the fathers of both missile programmes, American and Russian.[48] The SBZ did not necessarily approve of the kidnapping of these vital workers, but they had no control over the military. An attempt was made to stop the dismantling of Zeiss and the Schott optical works, but it was to no avail.[49]

The Russians also seized Walter Riedel of the glassworks of that name in Czechoslovakia. Riedel had invented fibreglass and worked on lenses and prism glass. His large-size picture tubes were used by the Luftwaffe as monitoring devices during the war. The Russians deemed Riedel a scientific VIP and 'invited' him to go to Russia after the war. He worked in a laboratory for a decade before he was allowed to go home. His firm had been seized by the Czechs. His son, Claus, had escaped detention in Austria and with the help of the Swarovski family was able to start up the family business again in Tyrolean Kufstein.[50]

Until 1946 it was theoretically impossible to cross into the Russian Zone without an 'Interzone Pass'. It was a risky business, not least because of the danger of arrest or, for women, of rape by border guards. Despite that many people braved the unmanned 'Green Border' in order to reach their families. Margret Boveri crossed to her native Franconia, and Ursula von Kardorff managed to make it from Berlin, despite being shot at by Russian border guards. Some guards were more accessible, and were bought off with bottles of schnapps. The first sight of Russian rule in the east came as a shock. Germans wishing to travel had to get used to sitting on the roofs of trains, while Russians in clean uniforms occupied the half-empty carriages. In tunnels you learned to lie flat and keep your head down. The station signs were written in Cyrillic script, and policemen's hats were embellished with the red star.

The life of the Gulag could be experienced in the Erzgebirge on the Czech border. This was another part of Germany that had originally fallen to Patton's soldiers. The Americans retreated to Mulde on 12 May, but the Russians were slow to take their places and did not get there before the end of June. The Russians learned that the region contained uranium ore. This was an important discovery as 'the Kremlin urgently requires atom bombs for its peace policies'. Initially 10,000 men, later 20,000 men and women, were forced to work in the mines; many of them were ethnic Germans from Hungary who were driven to work with kicks and beatings, and cries of 'Davai! Davai!' (Come on, move). Some of the women were whipped.

At the beginning of 1947 the whole western half of the region was cordoned off. More and more forced labourers were brought in. Some 20,000–30,000 Saxons were not deemed enough and recruiting offices were set up throughout the SBZ to procure the 75,000 men the Russians felt they needed. POWs returning from the east were sent straight off to the Erzgebirge, where they lived in makeshift barracks and tent camps similar to the places they had just left. The camps were at a great distance from the mines, and the workers had to rise at 3 a.m. to start the three-hour journey to the pithead. The work brought the men into contact with carcinogenic material and 20,000 people are believed to have died prematurely as a result of working in the mines. As it was eight men died in one week. The results were positive for the Soviets, however: on 23 August 1949 they were able to detonate their first atom bomb, using uranium from the mines at Wismut.[51]

In May 1945 the purging and recreation of the police force was the most important item on the agenda. At first the force was dominated by unarmed Socialist Party members, as the Allies had stipulated that the Germans were not to be issued with weapons. This made them vulnerable to the bands of armed bandits. K-5 was the name of the political police which took over some of the functions of the Gestapo and would turn in time into the Ministry of State Security, or 'Stasi'. The man behind it was Erich Mielke, a communist who had fled to Moscow after killing a policeman. There were already over 80,000 police in the SBZ by September

1947.[52] If Mielke's Stasi was to be the recreation of the Gestapo, another Nazi institution was to be rapidly dusted down and put back to work: the Hitler Youth. The youngish Erich Honecker was given the job of forming the FDJ, or Freie Deutsche Jugend.

Even more sinister were the many camps and prisons. Some of these had been simply carried over from Nazi times, like Sachsenhausen and Buchenwald. The Russian general Dratvin explained the facts to some British visitors: 'The [Nazi] camps have been liquidated, but the buildings are being used for housing fascist criminals who have committed crimes against our country.'[53] The traditional Nazi camps were joined by new creations like Hohenschönhausen in Berlin, which was also in a Soviet residential ghetto. It was here that Otto Grotewohl, SPD leader in the Soviet Zone, lived surrounded by Russians and barbed wire. Then there was Jamlitz was near Lieberose in the Uckermark, Forst in the Lausitz, Roitzsch-Bitterfeld, Frankfurt-an-der-Oder, Ketschendorf near Beeskow in the Mark, Neubrandenburg, Mühlberg on the Oder, Bautzen, Altenhain (which was used for Russian deserters and former members of Vlasov's army), Stern-Buchholz near Schwerin and the old POW camp at Torgau which had been turned into a political prison. Hardened cases were transferred to the Soviet Union.

The new (and old) camps were called 'Spetzlager', or 'special camps'. At Christmas 1946 there were 15,000 prisoners in Buchenwald and around 16,000 in Sachsenhausen. Sachsenhausen, or Spetzlager no. 7, was closed down in the early 1950s. Later fifty mass graves were discovered there which were thought to have been dug after the war, containing around 12,500 bodies. Most of the dead had perished from hunger or disease; about thirty-five to forty inmates died every day in the winter of 1946–7. Death began with the over-sixties, who perished from dropsy. When they had succumbed it was the turn of the fifty-year-olds. In the winter of 1946 to 1947 even the forty-somethings died in droves. Camp 3, Hohenschönhausen had about 3,000 prisoners, Fürstenwalde 6,000, and Camp 4, Bautzen 18,000. Russian estimates show that, of the 122,671 Germans who passed though the camps, 42,889 died – that is, more than a third. Only 756 were actually shot.[54]

German figures are roughly double the Russian tally: 240,000. Of these a higher figure of 95,643 perished – over 40 per cent. In these revisions there were 60,000 prisoners at Sachsenhausen, of whom just over half died; a little over 30,000 at Buchenwald, where a little under half did not survive the experience; and 30,000 at Bautzen, where 16,700 died.[55] Anyone who was suspected of Nazi sympathies was liable to incarceration;

and a good many monarchists and conservatives were thrown in too. The chief sugar manufacturers – twelve in all – were sent to a camp. One survived. Quite a lot of young people who had been in the Hitler Youth or the girls' equivalent, the BdM, were sent to the camps. For the major landowners and Junkers there was Rügen.[56] Added to the perils of life in the Russian concentration camp, *Nacht und Nebel* abductions had claimed another 5,431 Germans by November 1947, of whom 1,255 were youths.[57]

For all its dangers the Soviet Zone, like the Democratic Republic that succeeded it, offered a sort of daily life provided the citizen was not too demanding. There were times when the inhabitants of SBZ were better fed than the Germans in the West, but this did not prevent them from complaining, as in this parody of the nationalist anthem 'Deutschland über alles':

Deutschland, Deutschland, ohne alles	Germans, Germans lacking everything
Ohne Butter, ohne Fett	Lacking butter, lacking fat
Und das bischen Marmelade	The modicum of marmalade
Frisst uns die Verwaltung weg.	Is mopped up by our brass hats.
Hände falten, Köpfe sinken,	Bow your head in humility,
Immer an die Einheit denken.	Lie back, think of Unity.

Culture

Two heroic figures emerged in the Russian Zone to promote a brief flowering of the arts after May 1945. They were Johannes R. Becher and the Russian art historian Colonel Alexander Dymshitz. Becher was just behind the front line, ready to implement a policy elaborated in Moscow, but once again it was not necessarily an exclusively Marxist–Leninist approach. As early as 30 April 1945 Ulbricht issued a list of writers who were welcome to publish in the Soviet Zone. They were all exiles from Nazism: Anna Seghers, Lion Feuchtwanger, Thomas and Heinrich Mann, Arnold Zweig and Bertolt Brecht.[58]

The Russians actively promoted not just socialist theatre, ballet, opera and cinema; they promoted bourgeois arts as well. This was in keeping with Anton Ackermann's programme penned in Moscow in June, that the Soviet system was wrong for Germany, and that it needed to be reorganised on broad, anti-fascist, democratic principles instead. The programme had to be in place before the Western Allies arrived for the meeting in Potsdam. For the first three years after the war, there were no real cultural divisions in the capital, and the Soviet Zone continued to take the lead in cultural matters.[59] Becher returned to Berlin after twelve years and three months of exile on 11 June 1945. Ulbricht had approved his role; he was 'necessary for the work among the intellectuals'.[60]

Becher found his house in Zehlendorf intact, if not quite habitable. He went off to live in Dahlem, in the home of the Nazi banker Emil Georg von Strauss. He immediately began to invite old friends over to discuss getting intellectual life going again in the city. This was to become the steering committee for the Kulturbund zur demokratischen Erneuerung Deutschlands (Cultural Alliance for the Democratic Renewal of Germany). It was meant to function in all four zones. Becher put down his thoughts on Berlin in a letter to his wife Lily, whom he had left behind in Moscow. 'It is really enough to make you howl . . . and Berlin is Berlin. Despite everything you are not coming back to a strange place. Children sing German, mothers speak German – and the trees on the streets and the green on the balconies – I am *overjoyed*, my most beloved, and the only galling thing is that you are not beside me!'[61] On 3 July the Alliance was launched at a party for 1,500 people in the hall of Broadcasting House in the Masurenallee. Becher spoke: 'We have enough German tragedies in our history, more than enough, now we want to finally bring an end to German tragedies . . .' In the next two years he went a long way towards creating that renewal until the Cold War made bourgeois writers unwelcome in the SBZ.

As the Allies prepared to celebrate their meeting in Potsdam, the Russians reopened the Variété Theatre and in a cinema opposite they screened the film *Dr Mamlock*. Where no specific building existed, the Russians turned over municipal premises to theatre and cinema. A triumphal arch had been set up in Berlin's Frankfurter Allee, which was later to become one of the showpieces of Stalinist architecture. As part of the festivities Wilhelm Furtwängler gave a concert in which Mendelssohn's music was played.* All these events received the hearty approval of Bersarin. Few Berliners, however, knew they were happening. There were as yet no newspapers, and communication was by word of mouth.

The Soviet cultural supremo was Colonel Sergey Tulpanov, head of the Political Department of the Soviet Military Administration. He wanted to prove that the Russians were not quite as barbaric as May 1945 had seemed to suggest.[62] They tended to look after the German artists and show them respect, while the Western Allies cavilled, treated them like unrepentant

---

* Mendelssohn's music had been taken out of mothballs by Leo Borchard. See above p. 120.

Nazis and refused to shake their hands. Tulpanov was a huge, ursine presence, whom George Clare compared to Hermann Göring, many of whose cultural offices Tulpanov had taken over. By April 1946 more than a hundred theatres had opened in the SBZ, performing classics such as Lessing's *Nathan der Weise*, Molière's *Tartuffe* and works by Offenbach, as well as Russian pieces. Tulpanov was abetted by Dymshitz. It was Dymshitz who was behind Die Möwe, the artists' and writers' club that opened in the old Bülow Palace in the Soviet Sector and provided literary and artistic Berliners with a decent meal, comfort and rest. Later they had the premises of the old Berlin Club that Becher turned into an artists' colony with the parquet from Hitler's Chancellery. Here authors ate unrationed food and kept out of the cold.[63]

Dymshitz was a highly cultured man of Jewish origin from St Petersburg. He had grown up in a house with a Steinway and a library. He had spoken German, French and English from childhood and attended the German Reform School, the best in the city before the Great War. He went on to develop a fondness for the avant garde as a student in the 1920s. He had little rapport with the Anglo-Americans, but he had a certain amount of support from the French cultural boffin, Félix Lusset. When the Anglo-Americans outlawed Becher's Kulturbund in their sectors, Lusset refused to follow suit.[64]

Like Göring, Tulpanov could tolerate satire provided he found it funny. He revelled in the performances of Günter Neumann, who was reviving Berlin cabaret at Ulenspiegel in Berlin. Like the Schaubühne in Munich, Ulenspiegel was a stage licensed to poke fun at the Allies. Even the Nazis had tolerated some small degree of satire in this form. As George Clare put it, Neumann lashed out at all the Allies, but without a 'trace of German self-pity'. He poked fun at frat, and the desperation to which German girls were driven by hunger:

> Johnny took me like a lady
> And we traded – nothing shady,
> Two pounds of coffee so I'd do it,
> Fruit-juice cans so I'd renew it.
> Hot we got with burning skins
> For a couple of corned-beef tins
> But for chocolate – Hershey bar
> I went further much than far.

Carl Zuckmayer admired the Russian contribution to the arts at the time. The most prestigious theatre in the Russian Sector was the

Admiralspalast, which had survived the bombing unscathed and now played host to the State Opera. Zuckmayer found the singers less impressive than their counterparts in New York, but on the other hand he was very struck by the talents of the young directors and artists who designed the performances.[65] Of the Western Allies, only the American theatre chief Benno Frank came anywhere near him. He had been a prominent German Jewish actor and director before 1933. Their British counterpart was Pat Lynch, a Cork-man and one-time prepschool master with a fondness for Wagner. It was only much later that the Westerners learned by their mistakes and began to open cinemas and theatres in their sectors.[66]

Becher's office as president of the Cultural Alliance was in Schlüterstrasse 45, just off the Kurfürstendamm in the British Zone. The honorary president was Hauptmann. When Hauptmann died and the Poles could finally dispose of his corpse, Becher, Tulpanov and Pieck travelled to Stralsund on the Baltic coast. Becher pronounced the obsequy over the late writer's coffin: 'According to your wishes, may you be laid to earth before sunrise, to become a symbol of German promise! May your decease become the turning point.'[67] Schlüterstrasse 45 had an interesting history.* After the Nazi cultural association, the RKK or Reichskulturkammer, had been bombed out of its premises in the centre of the city, it had moved here. The building still contained all the files relating to artistic activity in the Third Reich, and, in the basement, the painting collection of the Jewish community. Now it became the rallying point for the starving artists of the occupation who came to Becher for shelter and ration cards.[68] In Becher's time the house contained the 'Spruchkammer', a sort of Star Chamber where German artists were examined for their reliability by a panel composed of the four powers. It was headed by the British major Kaye Sely – born Karl Seltz in Munich.

Becher's success was so great at this time that even Thomas Mann condescended to come to him to request a favour for one of his wife's relatives, Hans von Rohrscheidt, who was being roughly handled by the Soviet authorities. In return Becher wanted Mann to bring his influence to bear in getting CARE packets for his writers. Becher was trying to bring them all home: Döblin had returned (he was in Baden-Baden, working for the French) but Anna Seghers, the Manns, Herzfeld and Feuchtwanger were all hesitating. It was the time of the well-publicised dispute between Thomas Mann and two writers who had stayed in Germany, Walter von Molo and Franz Thiess. Thiess had said it was natural to remain in Germany, and

---

* And future: it is now the popular Hotel Bogota.

pointed out that it had been harder to remain than to enjoy a comfortable life in exile like Mann. Mann's son Klaus called Thiess 'repulsive': he had come to terms with the Nazis and earned a packet working on film scripts. Becher tried to pour oil on the troubled waters, issuing another invitation: 'Come home, you are expected.' On 22 November 1945 he launched an appeal to the émigrés. He did not share Mann's view that books published during the Third Reich were worthless, and refused to allow his writings to appear in a volume of exile literature. He saw no virtue in exile: it was 'bitter necessity', no more. It was an attitude that made him unpopular with those who had emerged from the concentration camps.[69]

With Becher at the helm, and with the backing of Tulpanov for the time being, the Soviet Zone took a pragmatic approach to denazification in the arts. Zhukov had not believed that Hauptmann had resisted the Nazis, but he had given him his entire protection, keeping both his own soldiers and the Poles off him while he eked out his last days. The Americans were after Furtwängler's blood. He had been a Prussian state councillor under the Nazis – a wholly honorary position given out to a few cultural and intellectual worthies who toed the line.* Furtwängler had taken refuge in Switzerland at the end of the war, partly as a result of his fears for his safety. He had been close to some of the men who were executed after the July Plot. As the war drew to a close the Swiss had turned on him and he had fled to Austria in the autumn of 1945. He was summoned back by the Russians in February 1946 to take over his old job at the Berlin Philharmonic. Up to then the reins had been held by Leo Borchard, and by the temperamental thirty-three-year-old Sergiu Celibidache.

'Celi' had taken over the Philharmonic just six days after Borchard's death. He was even more obscure than his predecessor: an unknown Romanian who had arrived in Berlin in the mid-1930s to study composition under Heinz Tiessen. Before he was relieved of his post by the triumphal return of Furtwängler, 'Celi' conducted the BPO no fewer than 108 times. The Allies saw him as a 'political virgin' and, while disputes raged about all the other conductors who were to some extent tainted by Nazism, there was no argument about him.[70]

As the Philharmonie had been gutted, 'Celi' performed in the Titania Palast in Berlin-Steglitz,† the Theater des Westens by the Zoo, the Radio Station and other intact buildings in Dahlem, Tegel and Wedding. He also

---

* The process of humiliating the great conductor was admirably dramatised in Ronald Harwood's play *Taking Sides*.
† A modernistic cinema constructed in the 1920s. It is still there, although it was severely altered in the 1960s.

performed in other German cities standing in for Furtwängler, who was the subject of particularly petty attacks by Allied officials – chiefly American. Before Furtwängler could perform in the Western Allied Zones, he had to receive his *Persilschein* – a clean bill of political health – in Vienna, Wiesbaden and Berlin. Vienna presented him with few problems, but at the American HQ in Wiesbaden they were reluctant to exonerate him. There was a persistent clamour from back home, especially from Thomas Mann's daughter Erika. He could only proceed to the higher court in Berlin in December 1946. He was finally absolved in April 1947. During that time Celibidache stood in for him, but according to Furtwängler's widow relations between the two of them were always good.[71]

Furtwängler returned to Berlin in a Russian aircraft on 10 March 1946, landing at the Adlershof airfield in the Soviet Zone. He was received in all pomp by Becher. The Russians provided him with the Pheasantry, his old grace-and-favour residence in the park at Sans Souci in Potsdam. His faithful housekeeper was waiting for him, and so was his piano. The West objected to his performing, however, and his appearance at the concert in the Radio Station had to be scrapped. That day the orchestra was directed by Celibidache.

Furtwängler had already been cleared by a denazification court in Austria and thought that the pardon would be granted automatically in Berlin. The Americans in the person of General McClure, however, were not prepared to give in so easily and they reminded the other Allies that Furtwängler needed an American licence to perform at the Philharmonie, which was in their sector, and that all Prussian state councillors had been banned from public life under Control Council Directive No. 24. This didn't much impress the Russians, who offered Furtwängler the directorship of the Lindenoper, which lay in their territory. They even whipped up a press campaign to bring him back, embellishing their *Berliner Zeitung* on 16 February 1946 with the headline 'Berlin calls Wilhelm Furtwängler'. The conductor refused to be wooed. Knowing that acceptance meant kissing goodbye to the BPO, he declined the offer.[72]

Furtwängler had never been a Pg, but there were plenty of conductors who had: Karajan, Knappertsbusch, Krauss and the chief conductor of the Berlin City Opera, the Austrian Leopold Ludwig. Ludwig had denied his Party membership on the *Fragebogen* and had been sentenced to a year's imprisonment by the British Military Government. Ludwig was not only a Pg – like Karajan he had joined in Austria where membership was illegal.[73] Knappertsbusch had actually been a protégé of Eva Braun's, who was attracted to the conductor's 'boyish good looks'. Hitler had not held him in high regard, claiming he was 'no better than a military band-leader'. The Führer did not like Karajan either, because the conductor did not use a score and failed to spot the errors of the singers. He would have pushed Karajan aside had he not been protected by Göring. Such was the Third Reich.[74]

The Russians ceased any pretence at taking denazification seriously for the arts scene. The civilised Captain Alexander Gouliga was replaced by an obstreperous Sub-lieutenant Levin who apparently did not even speak German. The Allied culture boffins had their last meeting with Gouliga in the House of Soviet Culture where a splendid feast had been prepared: goblets of Crimean champagne were served by two old German waiters with Hitler moustaches 'who looked like a couple of ex-Gauleiters recently released from a Russian internment camp'. After the sparkling wine came vodka and beer. Salads were succeeded by smoked fish and caviar, caviar by stuffed eggs, cold meats and sausages – and those were just the *zakuski*. Bortsch and stroganoff and orange cream rounded off the feast.[75]

As far as opera was concerned, both the Städtische Oper and the Lindenoper had been outhoused due to bomb damage. Berlin's City Opera was now in the Theater des Westens, while the Lindenoper was in the Admiralspalast in the Friedrichstrasse. Although the former was in the British Sector, the audiences for both opera houses were principally Russian. Neither was open to mere Germans. The night George Clare went to the Theater des Westens in 1946 there was a handful of British officers and two NCOs (himself and his friend), together with a 'sprinkling' of Americans and a 'pride' of Frenchmen. The rest of the audience was made up of Russians and their wives. The Soviets allowed officers to import wives and children, which was forbidden for the time being among the Western Allies – hence the need for frat.[76]

As ever, music had a powerful effect on the Berliners, who had braved the bombs to hear the BPO perform during the war. Margret Boveri remembered her first concert after the war. She heard a choral work of Bruckner's in a 'ruinous hall in [Berlin-]Zehlendorf'. It gave rise to floods of tears brought on by years of suppressed and concealed emotions.[77] When after two years of trials Furtwängler received his *Persilschein* on 30 April 1947 and was able to conduct 'his' orchestra once again on Whit Sunday (25 May), the audience clapped for fifteen minutes, summoning him back to the rostrum sixteen times. It had been an all-Beethoven pro-gramme – the overture to *Egmont*, and the Fifth and Sixth Symphonies. Erika Mann carped: it was not the old Philharmonic, but the purged version that had survived the Third Reich, and even then it had been under-rehearsed. The conductor replied to her father, modestly pointing out that fifteen minutes' applause was not unusual for Beethoven in Berlin.[78] One Jew who wholeheartedly stood by Furtwängler throughout the crisis was Yehudi Menuhin. Menuhin, who performed the Beethoven violin concerto with the conductor on 28 September 1947, was anxious to break the boycott of Furtwängler in America. He demonstratively gave the conductor his hand, and was treated as a traitor in America as a result.[79]

Brecht, Eisler and Heinrich Mann looked on from their places of exile, but theatre prospered. Many theatres had been spared the Anglo-American bombing, and Berlin was in a position to put on plays from the start. Hilde Spiel was awestruck: 'What remains is the world of the theatre. Only here do they [the Berliners] continue to eat and drink, love without worry and die without cause, swagger, croon, charm, laugh. Only here do the porters still strut about and the candles still flicker in ornate chandeliers, only here do the cigars glimmer and the wines flow.'[80]

The Hebbel Theatre performed the *Dreigroschenoper* from 8 August 1945. A few days later Ruth Friedrich went along to the 'Saarlandstrasse, alias Stresemannstrasse, alias Königsgrätzerstrasse' – her litany of purges did not include the last one: the Hermann-Göring-Strasse – and found an immense queue and the idea of 'beggar's opera' right and fitting for the Berliners. The line 'Grub first, then morality' seemed particularly apposite to Ursula von Kardorff when she went at the beginning of October.[81] The Hebbel Theatre also honoured the poets and writers of the 'System time' – as Hitler dismissed the Weimar period: Toller, Tucholsky, Brecht, Heinrich Mann, Erich Mühsam, Lion Feuchtwanger, Leonhard Frank and Ludwig Rubener.[82] The Hebbel, however, was not all it seemed: it was in the American Sector. Brecht was not altogether kosher as far as the Russians were concerned. 'Grub first, then morality' did not suit them; they wanted it the other way round. It did not accord with notions of collective guilt either. Brecht would have to wait for his reconciliation with the Soviet authorities.[83]

The most famous man of Berlin theatre, Gustaf Gründgens, was another state councillor, and was suffering from the same blanket ban as Furtwängler. Once again, the Russians took no notice, and restored him to power as *Intendant* at the German Theatre. Gründgens might have been deemed to have suffered enough already. He had been arrested as *Generalintendant* of the Prussian State Theatres, because – it was said – his Russian captors had believed his rank to have been a military one, and spent nine months in Russian camps. Colleagues had finally persuaded

Bersarin that Gründgens was no soldier, but the difficulty then was to find him: the Russians kept no reliable records of the people interned in their camps and gulags. Once freed, he became a Russian baby and benefited from their aegis, to the degree that they denazified him themselves on 27 April 1946, and declared his character without a stain. Gründgens returned to work, despite all attempts on the part of the Western Allies to prevent him. His first role was in Carl Sternheim's satire *Der Snob*. It was a great occasion; 'an event, the most important by far in early post-war Berlin's social and cultural life'. Despite the poverty that raged all around, ticket-touts were able to charge up to RM1,000 for a seat.[84]

Becher wanted to make the Soviet Zone a refuge for all writers. Authors were given category-I ration cards. He rescued Rudolf Ditzen, tried to wean him off the alcohol that was killing him and provided him with a theme for a novel so that he might start work again. Ditzen's young wife was addicted to morphine, which was provided by another writer, the poet and physician Gottfried Benn, who like Ditzen–Fallada, had made no attempt to emigrate after 1933.[85] The Ditzens were found a place to live in the Soviet enclave of Pankow and were even brought toys and a goose at Christmas – all of which failed to prevent a drunken Ditzen from having a go at the Muscovite Party chairman Pieck at a drinks party that month.

The rehabilitation of writers like Ditzen in the Soviet Zone led to a set-to with the Anglo-Americans and JCS 1067. Ditzen–Fallada was anything but squeaky clean, and had earned a handsome crust under the Nazis. The British denazifiers sniffed and the Western press cavilled. In Munich the writer Hans Habe called one of his novels a work of fascist literature. This led to difficulties in obtaining a licence across the Elbe and in resuming contact with his publishers abroad.[86] The Russians also cast a surprisingly benign eye over publishing in their zone at first. For more than forty years the Aufbau Verlag shone a beacon of light – sometimes bright, sometimes dim – from the former premises of the bank Delbrück, Schickler & Co. in the Französischestrasse.* The house was created on 16 August 1945, under Becher's protecting hand. Becher had been planning new publications even in his exile. Less doctrinaire than most of his colleagues, he believed that the Germans had to admit collective guilt, but was less literal in his interpretation of the Soviet canon. He ensured that the press received the necessary licence from the Soviet authorities. The running of the press was taken over by another Muscovite and long-term Communist Party member, Erich Wendt, in 1947.

---

* From which it was evicted when the building returned to its original owners in 1995.

Becher was elected to the central committee of the SED in April 1946, but some people in the Berlin Kremlin did not believe he was a Marxist–Leninist at all. He certainly did not turn up to all the meetings. The 'Tulip' had abandoned him. As Tulpanov put it tactfully after Becher's death, in Berlin 'Nothing remained of the modesty of the war years. He was at home, completely at home, and he quite naturally expressed the view that he knew better than we did how to order the German house.'[87] Becher was still protected by Vladimir Semionov and Dymshitz. Dymshitz told Tulpanov that the Cultural Alliance was not meant to be an ideological organisation. Tulpanov stayed his hand for the time being, but Alexander Abusch was placed beside the poet in the organisation as the head of the 'ideological division', to keep an eye on him. The SBZ made sure that the press could dip into Russian reserves of paper and board for the book covers. Once again it was Dymshitz who restrained the censor, Captain Filippov. In 1945–6, only one book fell foul of the Russian authorities, and that was Günther Weisenborn's *Berliner Requiem*. Here not even Becher's intercession could persuade the Soviets to allow publication of a work that centred on the misery of the Berliners in the first post-war days.[88]

The Aufbau Verlag's earliest publications were Becher's *Manifest des Kulturbundes zur demokratischen Erneuerung Deutschlands* and the first number of the cultural and political periodical *Aufbau*. Neither was calculated to run counter to the ideals of the Russian Zone or to excite the censor Captain Filippov. A year later the Kulturbund published its own weekly in *Sonntags*, with a print-run of 200,000. The Aufbau, however, was not just a printing press for radical texts: before the year was out it had published eleven books, including works by Georg Lukács, Max Hermann-Neisse, Theodor Pliever – whose documentary novel *Stalingrad* achieved sales of 177,000, not including those sold under licence to West German houses – and Heinrich Heine, all of them authors who had the distinction of being banned by the Nazis. Heine was the only dead author, and the most eminent of them all.[89]

Becher came to the conclusion that Aufbau should not be the publisher of exile-literature, so in 1946 he changed the policy to include writers who had remained in Germany throughout the Nazi years, but who were not tarred with the brush of Nazism. They included Ernst Wiechert, Hans Fallada, Gerhart Hauptmann and Ernst Niekisch. As Germany polarised at the onset of the Cold War, some of the non-communist writers were pushed out of the list, while others chose to remove themselves.

Censorship was formally introduced by the Russian authorities in

January 1947, but that year the Aufbau was still printing works by non-communist authors such as Egon Erwin Kisch and Lion Feuchtwanger, as well as Victor Klemperer's study in the Nazi abuse of language, *LTI*. The Aufbau only became wholly ideological in its policy once the Western Allies put through currency reform. Among other things, the move meant a serious loss of income for the East German publishing house. After 1948 the size of the editions diminished considerably. Many of the Aufbau authors also belonged to the Cultural Alliance. Other members included Anna Seghers, Ricarda Huch and the painters Otto Nagel and Karl Hofer.

One of Becher's projects was to create a new artists' colony at the sea-side resort of Ahrenshoop as the Cultural Alliance's Summer Academy on the Baltic. The Nazis who had been living there were flushed out and a children's home was created so that writers would be unencumbered with parental duties. Becher wanted to build up a new, anti-fascist intellectual elite.[90] The desire to 'make Germans out of Germans' by reintroducing them to their art and literature – some of which had been banned under the Nazis – sadly gave way to more blatant Soviet propaganda after 1947 and Becher was unable to contain the ideological tide. Performances of Schiller and Mozart were replaced by Pushkin and Gogol, Chekhov, Rimsky-Korsakov, Tchaikovsky and Chopin. That might have been toler-able in its way, but soon that too was pushed aside in favour of modern plays which stressed the value of Soviet culture and the evilness of its Western equivalent. Plays had to show the Soviet Union in a positive light. Even Becher came under suspicion for a while until he saved his skin by writing a few poetic encomiums to 'the great Stalin'. The drama put on after 1947 was every bit as tedious as the American plays performed in the US Zone.[91]

On 21–22 May 1946 the Cultural Alliance held a congress with Tulpanov present. Becher sailed close to the wind again. In a speech he questioned Soviet policy: 'demontage and reparations make most people doubt whether they will still be able to lead a tolerable life'. He called for more responsibility to be given to Germans to govern their own lives. The speech did not go down well.[92] He pushed on regardless. The first German writers' congress was held in the Hebbel Theatre (in the American Zone) at the beginning of October. As many as 250 writers came, including Ricarda Huch, but some of the fleurons still evaded his grasp: there was no sign of the Manns, Brecht or Feuchtwanger. Becher called for unity – there was no peace without it. A split Germany was not a Germany at peace. He revealed his hand as an idealist for a united Germany. The congress was the first and last of its kind.[93] Two years later the Cultural Alliance held a congress which brought together artists and writers from East and West to denounce McCarthyist America.[94] The Western Allies had already disowned Becher, and they kicked him out of the Schlüterstrasse at the end of the year.

The crack was coming and many of the writers who had found a *Gemütlichkeit* in the Soviet Zone were leaving: Plievier went to Munich, Ricarda Huch to Frankfurt-am-Main. Becher was unfairly accused of being behind the abduction of the journalist Dieter Friede. He was having to defend the system more and more. When Eugen Kogon (who had been in Buchenwald) compared the Russian camps to the Nazi ones, Becher told him the comparison was absurd. The Western Allies refused him a pass to travel in their zones. At the end of the year Pieck was describing Becher as a 'political ignoramus'. Becher offered to resign in December. His letter was signed pathetically 'Mit sozialistischem Grüss!' (With socialist greetings!),[95] an unfortunate reminder of the Nazi formula. He had been broken; he was one of the first great casualties of the Cold War.

7

Life in the American Zone

They send us chicken feed and expect us to say thank you.
Johannes Semler. Quoted in Volker Hentschel, *Ludwig Erhard,
ein Politikerleben*, Munich and Landsberg am Lech 1996, 51

The American Military Government in Frankfurt-am-Main was housed 'in the conquerors' part of the city' in one of the sand-coloured skyscrapers beyond the main railway station which made up the HQ of IG Farben and which appeared as an oasis in the middle of the rubble. You needed a special pass to approach it and, if you were lucky enough to discover a way in, you found it filled with what the American novelist John Dos Passos refers to as 'chicken colonels'* or pen-pushers.

Dos Passos had lunch there in November 1945. A German maid called them to the table. He ate venison steak and drank first-rate burgundy[1] – a very different bill of fare to that endured by the helots who milled about outside, fetching twigs in prams to heat their stoves. They called the place 'GI Farben Haus' and gave it a wide berth. Visitors might catch an occasional glimpse of the god of war himself, General Eisenhower, accompanied by his Irish mistress Kay Summersby. With some exaggeration excused by the passing of time she wrote that the IG Farben building was 'a small city in itself. It was very elegant – lots of marble and fountains and indoor flower gardens, great curving staircases and very luxurious offices, several tennis courts could have fitted into Ike's office.[†] Bouquets of fresh spring flowers were placed in our offices every day.'[2]

The Russian Gregory Klimov had reason to visit the American HQ, where he wanted to talk to Clay. He was struck by the slovenly attitude of

---

* Not to be confused with the Colonel Harlan Sanders of Kentucky Fried Chicken fame. Colonel Sanders was a 'Kentucky Colonel', a purely honorary rank he shares with the author.

† In her earlier and more respectful volume, *Eisenhower was my Boss* (235), she says the office was 'large enough for an auditorium'.

the black troopers, who had their cheeks wadded with gum. 'The privates stretched themselves out with their feet on the desk while the generals tore around like messenger boys.' Eventually he met a 'long-nosed little soldier' who turned out to be Clay – 'He wasn't a general, he was an atom-bomb.'[3] James Stern was struck by the cute Americanness of it all, particularly the mess, where the officers pecked at coleslaw and drank iced water. Homesick Americans could also assuage their spleen with ice-cream. Stern's friends in Frankfurt were unimpressed by the authority that watched over them, filling them with the breath of democracy. 'Das Pharisäer Ghetto', they called it, 'The Ghetto of the Pharisees'.[4]

Before he left Frankfurt Dos Passos had a chance to look round and sit in on a local American Military Government meeting. 'Frankfurt resembles a city not so much as a pile of bones and smashed skull resembles a prize Hereford steer.' Yet people seemed to be rushing about the streets, doing some sort of business: 'They behave horribly like ants when you have kicked over an anthill.' At the meeting he heard the reports. Frankfurt was receiving 2,000 new residents a week; flats were being revamped for them; there had been five black-marketeers arrested and fish was arriving from Bremen . . .[5]

America's great battlefield generals in the Second World War had been Eisenhower, Bradley and Patton. Patton captured the imagination not only of the Americans, but also of the Germans, making him a sort of American Rommel. He could hardly be restrained from going on to take Prague before the arrival of the Red Army, using the Czech Uprising as an excuse. He claimed, improbably, that the Russians would stop it – 'These patriots need our help!' – when the Soviets had very largely conjured it up. What he meant was that he wanted to take Prague for the West. He was no friend of the Russians. When a Russian came to him with a pettifogging complaint he shouted, 'Get this son-of-a-bitch out of here!' Zhukov was dismissed as a 'comic-opera covered with medals' and Patton was exceptionally proud to report that he had drunk a Russian general under the table. In this respect his views were similar to those of Mark Clark, or even Lucius Clay. 'On to the Oder!' he intoned.[6]

His attitude to the Germans amounts to a metaphor for the American occupation. At first he was toughness incarnate. He famously displayed his attitude – and more – by urinating in the Rhine on 24 March 1945 ('I have been looking forward to this for some time'),[7] and after throwing up at Ohrdruf not only ordered that local populations should be punished for what had gone on at the camps in their neighbourhoods, he wanted simple American servicemen to see the concentration camps. His attitude soon began to change, however, and it changed more quickly and went further than any of his colleagues. Like Clay he had no truck with the no-frat order, and he was clear in making a difference between Germans and Nazis: 'All Nazis are bad. But not all Germans are Nazis.'[8]

He was made military governor of Bavaria and set up his HQ in the former SS officer training school in Bad Tölz. On 22 September he blotted his copy book by appointing Nazis to administrative roles within his Bavarian command and marginalising their criminality – all in defiance of JCS 1067. He backtracked a little, saying that he was employing Nazis because he needed to retain his own men to fight, and because they hadn't yet found anyone better.[9] A week later, Eisenhower relieved him of his command.[10] It may have been that Patton thought the authorities were being ridiculously harsh about the run-of-the-mill Pgs, but there was something more sinister besides. He was prone to antisemitic utterances. Morgenthau and Baruch were exercising a 'semitic revenge on Germany', while the Jewish DPs were beneath contempt, or 'lower than animals'.[11]

He visited Camp No. 8 at Garmisch-Partenkirchen in September, which was said to contain among its nearly 5,000 inmates the 'cream' of the black – Totenkopf – SS which operated the concentration camps, including guards from Dachau and Buchenwald (those who had not been killed while the prisoners were liberated). He was told that some of the people there were not even Pgs, let alone criminals. At this moment Patton was heard to utter in frustration, 'It is sheer madness to intern these people.'[12] There is no doubt that he meant it. On another occasion he said, 'We have destroyed what could have been a good race . . . [and replaced it with] Mongolian savages. All of Europe will be communist.'[13] His conciliatory attitude towards the SS prisoners must have led to the rumour that he had told the camp commanders to behave more decently towards their captives. A few months after his dismissal he was injured in a car accident on his way to a pheasant shoot near Mannheim. He died in Heidelberg on 21 December 1945.[14] There have been conspiracy theories.[15]

After Eisenhower went home, the American commander in chief in Germany was General Joseph T. McNarney. His deputy was Lucius B. Clay. Clay, who replaced McNarney as commander of European Command in the spring of 1947, was an instance of one of Westpoint's great strengths, something that neither Sandhurst nor Woolwich has ever seemed capable of producing – astute political officers. He was a southerner who had spent seventeen years marking time as a first lieutenant in the engineers. He missed action in the First World War and never commanded anything with greater firepower than a desk. Yet he was one of a handful of outstanding figures of the immediate post-war period. Together with his political adviser Robert Murphy he refused to concede where his political superiors were prepared for retreat on all fronts.

Clay had abandoned any pro-Morgenthau feeling he might have had by 26 April 1945. He was already keen to relaunch German industry.[16] His guru was James Byrnes, and he must have profoundly regretted the latter's departure as secretary of state in January 1947. Three months later Clay confirmed his discipleship in a letter. Byrnes's Stuttgart speech, in which he announced a new deal for Germany, served as his model: 'Every word that you said at Stuttgart became a part of my "Bible" for Germany . . . It was a living document of hope. I am not pro-German but I hope with all my heart that in our political warfare with USSR we do not forget that here in Germany we have 70,000,000 human beings to remember.'[17] Clay realised that his role was to make propaganda for the West. As he told General Draper in Washington, 'we do propose to attack communism and the police state before the German people, whereas in the past we have confined our efforts to presenting the advantages of democracy . . . Our political objectives are to promote democracy which must mean to resist communism.'[18]

At first civil administrations were created in a similarly haphazard way to the Russians. The soldiers who occupied a town or village looked for someone who was untainted by Nazism. In the writer Ernst von Salomon's local town they asked the parish priest, who suggested that the pre-1933 mayor had done a good job. The former mayor confessed, however, that he had subsequently joined the Party. The Americans turned a blind eye to that and asked him to appoint seven councillors. He told them frankly that he would be hard pressed to find seven decent men who were not members of the Party, so in the end they had a council that contained more Nazis than it had during the Third Reich.[19]

America disposed of a large body of linguists. These were either German Americans from the Mid-West or German or Austrian Jews – often recent arrivals in the States – Czechs, Poles and other educated Slavs who had lately established themselves across the Atlantic, or soldiers who had simply acquired the language. There were German writers in uniform, like Klaus Mann, Hans Habe, Stefan Heym and Georg Stefan Troller, most of whom worked in intelligence or propaganda. Saul Padower, whose job was to interview prisoners for the Psychological Warfare Department, spent his early years on the Elbe. Padower thought his colleague Joe hailed from Nebraska – although his fluent German should have rendered him suspicious – but when they reached Bavaria Joe suddenly grew pensive. He said his parents lived near by. They drove to his village and entered the house. Joe poked an old man in a chair whose pipe dropped out of his mouth. He asked the man if he knew who he was. The man had a stab, got it wrong and tried again. This time he recognised the son who had left them at the age of twelve: He turned to his wife who was knitting: 'Hoer mal Du . . . onser Sepp ist hier, doss ist onser Sepp!' (Hey, listen you, our Joe is here, that's our Joe!).[20]

American linguists were not always so politically reliable – some 70 per cent of US army linguists had German relations like Padover's Joe–Sepp. Salomon's friend the Austrian lawyer Diewald was astonished to find that the local American commandant was Chinese, but his amazement was unsurpassed when he discovered that the man not only spoke perfect German, but was a great admirer of the 'As-As', as he called the SS.[21] Distrust, and the fact that many were only FOB (fresh–off–boat) Americans, meant that only sixty-five out of 1,500 exiles figured in Military Government, but that was still more than in the SBZ, and the British did not believe in making the oppressed victors.[22]

James Stern arrived in Germany in the spring of 1945. As the aircraft came in to land he glimpsed Koblenz and the Deutsches Eck, where the Rhine and the Mosel meet. He was appalled at his first reacquaintance with the country that he had first known as a teenager learning German: 'Sections of a shattered bridge stuck up out of the mud-coloured water and a castle sat perched on top of the vine-terraced hills. Then the plane dropped, and we looked down into rows of burned out-houses – just shells of houses, without roofs or rooms, You looked down between their four walls to their ground floors, on which there lay either nothing or else a mound of smashed brick, smashed sticks of furniture and garbage.'[23]

Carl Zuckmayer returned an exile from his native land in the autumn of 1946, just before the great chill. He had emigrated to Switzerland after his works were banned by the Nazis. In 1939 he became an American citizen. At the end of the war he was living on a farm in Vermont and making his expertise on German life available to the War Office. In July 1946 he became the head of the European unit of the CAD (Civil Affairs Division). He resigned in May 1947, deeply disappointed by everything he had seen during a winter in the land of his birth.[24] The occupation was eighteen months old, and he found that his former countrymen viewed the Americans with mixed feelings. There was 'a little hatred, some disappointment and a bit of reasonable, grateful recognition'. What hatred there was existed chiefly in the hearts of stupid Germans, he thought, men and women who refused to take responsibility for what had happened.[25]

German attitudes to Americans were coloured by lack of contact; and lack of contact meant lack of influence. The Americans tended to live in their own compounds, or to requisition large sections of the extant middle-class suburbs of the bigger cities. This was the case in Wiesbaden, where they moved into the smart quarters on the heights above the town. The compounds were often ringed by barbed wire, making them into little fortresses announced by the legend 'Entry Forbidden to Germans' – a sign with a conscious or unconscious allusion to recent German exclusivity towards the Jews. The Americans bought from their own shops, went to their own schools and spent the evenings in their own clubs. When they wanted to know the news, they read it in the *Stars and Stripes*.

Zuckmayer believed it was important for Americans to go out and meet Germans, particularly young Germans. Many German boys, he felt, were reticent about making contact with Americans, but he held out hope for the girls. By that he did not mean frat, but beneficial contact through discussion groups, possibly on Sundays. The most dangerous group of Germans were those who were most hard done by: those who remained homeless and out of work, and who spent their days idling, looking for trouble, or for something to steal.[26]

The American Zone had been fixed long before the end of the war, but on 12 December 1945 the US increased the size of its holdings in Germany by taking over the Bremen pocket from the British. The Americans needed a port to unload supplies for their forces. The news was bad for the famous Rathauskeller, as US forces adhered to their right to plunder supplies of wine. Whether the British had helped themselves to the world's most famous collection of German wine first is not clear from the official history. Nearly 100,000 bottles were plundered before an order was received to deliver a further 300,000 to the American army. German civilians were no longer allowed to use the cellar and it was turned into an officers' mess. American officers could buy wine, but no one restocked the cellar, and because many American servicemen were not keen on German wine, whisky was served under the ancient vaults.

The Americans may have drunk up many vintages from the nineteenth century, but they left the two most famous wines alone: the cask of seventeenth-century Rose wine from the Rheingau and the twelve barrels of eighteenth-century Apostle mosel were sealed and apparently left untouched. On 15 October 1948 the cellar was handed back to the town hall at a solemn ceremony at which the mayor, Wilhelm Kaisen, and the head of the American military, Thomas Dunn, were present. There were many toasts, so perhaps it was not so solemn by the end. All the Allies helped themselves to wine. For the owners of prestigious estates and cellars, the important thing was to protect the most highly prized bottles. At Maximin Grünhaus on the River Ruwer, for example, the current owner's grandmother used to find an excuse to visit the building, which had been taken over by the Americans. She was a corpulent woman, who used to dress in wide skirts for the occasion. Once she had found her way down to the vast formerly monastic cellars, she would pick up some bottles of the best wines and hang them with cords under her clothes, thereby ferrying them to safety.[27]

The cession of Bremen was an instance of Anglo-American co-operation. In general the British and the Americans worked together from the beginning, although the Americans often looked down on the British, and vice versa. John Dos Passos cites an instance of a man requiring a spare part for his Opel. He was told he needed to obtain it from the British Zone, but it was no problem – 'we have good co-operation on things like that'. Someone asked about the French: 'If anybody knows any way of getting anything out of the French Zone they haven't told me about it.' Finally the Russians were mentioned. 'We don't talk about the Russian Zone' was the answer.[28]

Due to clever planning and relocation, a lot of German industry had survived. Clay put the figure as high as 25–30 per cent, but he did not think the economy was ready to start up again in June 1945.[29] The Americans had come through the war with their wealth, and they turned their noses up at the idea of demontage. Clay understood what that meant for his country all too well: 'rolling stock, livestock and agricultural implements required for a minimum economy in Germany and which if not available would result in increased imports into Germany, would militate against the ability of Germany to pay reparations and inevitably result in calling on the US for relief'.[30]

Zuckmayer was able to witness the first steps taken to re-establish a professional life in the ruins. He met a young dentist and was intrigued to know how he would practise his skills in a broken city. He located the surgery in an area filled with the usual heaps of rubble. The ground floor was filled with heaps of masonry but an emergency staircase had been built to give access to the first floor, and on the second a dozen families and their sub-lessees were living in a few patched-up rooms. From there another exposed stairway took him up to the remaining rooms of the house where four dentists had established their practice. Only two of the rooms could be heated, and the surgery's hours were limited by the caprices of mains electricity that came on and went off with distressing regularity. During the hours that the surgery functioned, it was overrun by patients who lived in the rubble all around. The nurses were sometimes engaged as assistants, sometimes as builders helping to render the other rooms inhabitable. They looked pale and thin, but not exhausted. When they saw Zuckmayer they did not ask for cigarettes or food – they wanted books. The dentists themselves had all suffered personal tragedies, their families killed in Allied raids. One had lost a leg. One was waiting to marry his fiancée, who was due to walk to Berlin from East Prussia. Her father had been killed and her mother had committed suicide.[31] For others, the full story was only then coming to light. There was a cleaning lady who worked at Zuckmayer's Berlin lodgings, for example. She was actually a pastor's wife, but the clergyman had been called up by the Volkssturm in the last days of the war and had subsequently disappeared. She had three children, two boys in their teens and a baby boy born towards the end of the war. For their sake she had to work. She had always insisted that her husband would return. Then news came that his body had been found in the Grossbeerenstrasse in Glienicke in the far north of the city, and had been positively identified. It had lain among the ruins for nineteen months. The elder children had known their father was dead. Once she had heard one of them praying: 'Lord, make us loyal and brave to the end, like him.' It was two hours' walk from Zuckmayer's boarding house to the place where her husband had met his end, but she still insisted on going, and going on foot. Until that moment she had been utterly stoical about her fate. Now, finally aware of how hopeless her position was, she broke down: she wanted to leave Germany – 'this damned country'. Then she recovered her composure and set out on her trek to Glienicke.[32]

American GIs had been fed a good deal of propaganda at home and on the way. They had drunk deep from the films of Frank Capra, and had read the articles of Emil Ludwig, Louis Nizer and Siegrid Schultz; they had heard Dorothy Thompson. They had been equipped with copies of the *Pocket Guide to Germany*. From the first moment they walked on German soil, they expected to be attacked by Werewolves. They were nervous of Germans – civilians and soldiers alike. Despite all this, surveys at home revealed that Americans were more anti-Japanese than anti-German: German Americans were and are a sizeable part of the US population.[33]

The order banning frat contributed to the Americans' brutality towards the conquered Germans. Public opinion favoured punishment and Eisenhower had made it clear that there was to be no billeting of American soldiers with German families, no mixed marriages, no joint church services, no visits to German homes, no drinking with Germans, no shaking their hands, no playing games with them, no exchanging gifts with them, no dancing with them, going to their theatres, taverns or hotels. The penalty was a $65 fine or a court martial.[34]

Propaganda had taught the soldiers that Germans – particularly German soldiers – were subhuman. In the autumn of 1944 the Americans burned down the village of Wallenberg because they had encountered resistance. In the spring of the following year they liberated their first concentration camp at Ohrdruf. Eisenhower was quick to seize on the importance of the camp in raising American morale and ordered his troops to visit it. Pictures from the camps were also distributed to soldiers. The Germans were to be treated no better than dogs. Indeed, in some instances dogs loomed large. A Frau Sachse told Salomon of a potentially dangerous moment that occurred when her four-year-old daughter had heard that an American officer's pet was called Hitler. 'All dogs are called Hitler,' he told her. The bemused child replied, 'My dog's called Ami [Yank]!' The mother dragged the child away before the American could respond.[35]

Salomon gives a highly coloured account of the fate of his *Wehrpass* at the hands of a GI – this was the document that showed he was officially excused from military service. In his south German village a sentry post had been established in a tent:

one day as I approached the tent [I] saw a man seated on the stool[.] I auto-matically put my hand in my breast pocket. Sitting there outside the tent, his eyes glued on a plump girl leaning on a fence, he was whistling a tune of the type the Americans called 'long-haired'. This man in his tight-fitting American uniform attracted my attention because on his left lower arm he wore no fewer than three wrist-watches, while his lapels were decorated with a great number of those little gold brooches containing brightly coloured stones such as peasant or servant girls wear in this part of the world. As I drew near him, this man, scarcely taking his eyes from the plump girl, signalled me with an inclination of his head to approach. He took my *Wehrpass*, glanced though it in a bored fashion for a few seconds, and then, with a slow and satisfied gesture, tore it in four pieces which he proceeded to drop into the gutter. While doing this he did not for a moment interrupt his long-haired whistling.[36]

James Stern met a heavily pregnant Frankfurt woman near Kempten in the Allgäu. She was walking home from Rome, where fascists had allegedly shot her husband. Stern asked her if she had come on foot all the way from Italy. She said she had had a bicycle, but an American soldier had stolen it together with her bag and luggage. The Englishman Stern refused to believe the story – Americans did not behave like that. It must have been a German in a stolen uniform.[37] The Americans' fear of Werewolves showed in their treatment of the civilian population. They were allegedly at their worst in Bavaria. The half-American journalist Margret Boveri thought the Americans particularly ignorant of Germany, a sentiment that was confirmed for her during her time in internment across the Atlantic. They had not taken the time or the trouble to look into National Socialism, for the good or the bad.[38]

The American authorities continued in their attempts to stop their soldiers listening to the siren calls of Germans. When US troops entered Frankfurt they were even prevented from speaking to the 106 remaining Jews. Before the war there had been 40,000. The American Forces Network put out anti-frat broadcasts: 'pretty girls can sabotage an Allied victory'. Some German women from Stolberg were prosecuted for attempting to woo GIs, although the trial turned into a farce. The first dent in the armour of American anti-frat policy came when the rule concerning small children was relaxed. The next exception concerned public contacts with Germans. The ban was lifted altogether on 1 October 1945. The last remaining stones in the edifice were interdictions concerning billeting and marriages with Germans.[39]

German men, such as there were, received a cold shoulder from their women. Poorly nourished, dressed in rags, penniless and morally suspect, they did not have the heroic smell of the conqueror. Carl Zuckmayer spoke to two pretty waitresses who worked in an American mess in Berlin. Neither would have anything to do with German boys. As one put it, 'They are too soft, they are not men any more. In the past they showed off too much.' The other described German men as 'worthless'.

The Americans were everything now, the Germans nothing. Natives who were taken on by Allied garrisons sometimes succumbed to the temptation to be high and mighty with their less fortunate countrymen. Some of the worst were the waiters and waitresses who worked in the messes. For them, the qualification for membership of the human race began with the right to shop at the American PX or the British NAAFI. Really superior beings were adorned with the officers' pips of a foreign army. Zuckmayer was naturally interested in this phenomenon. As the author of the successful play *Der Hauptmann von Köpenick* he had explored the old German, or rather Prussian, respect for uniforms, which had made the reserve lieutenant the metaphor for an arriviste in Wilhelmine society. Zuckmayer was not impressed by these sycophants who chewed gum, and said he believed that an unreformed young Hitlerite made better material for the new Germany than some toady who clicked his heels at the sight of an

American sergeant or captain.[40] In Heidelberg he discovered that there was no room at the inn for his driver, the latter being a German working for the military government. The German hotelier told the writer that his driver had to sleep in the car – he was not allowed to give beds to Germans.[41]

When they weren't working they went to a nightclub called Feminina in the ruins of the Tauentzienstrasse in Berlin's New West. There were prostitutes there who served the Allied soldiers; the waitresses from the mess were not averse to selling their bodies either. In the Feminina the girls met men of the right sort who later took them off to a 'black' nightclub and were prepared to shell out a few hundred marks for a bottle of champagne. One of the girls would take her men home to the flat she shared with her parents. Her father was a civil servant. Zuckmayer was anxious to learn whether they knew what their daughter was doing – 'Naturally, that is unavoidable, as our rooms are too close to one another. But the old folks say nothing, in the end I pay my own rent.' The playwright reflected that after the First World War the parents would have thrown their daughter out on the street, or taken their own lives from shame. Now they just turn the other way and pretend not to notice.[42]

Understandably, civilians were shot as Germany was invested in the spring in 1945, either deliberately or by accident. This happened above all in the east, but it was a relatively frequent occurrence in the west as well, and the victims were not always Germans – sometimes soldiers succeeded in killing some poor foreign worker as well. Billeting soldiers was an anxious moment for families who were already harbouring refugees from the devastated towns and cities. The invading armies appeared pitiless. German armies compared the behaviour of French troops unfavourably with their own in occupied France.[43]

When Margret Boveri finally arrived in Bamberg after her long trek on 2 September 1945, she was relieved to find the city largely undamaged. Only the bridges were down. Also there was food to be had – bread, butter, cheese and soup made from meat stock. On the other hand the Americans drove around with a great show of force. Everywhere there were armed guards.

Carl Zuckmayer came rapidly to the conclusion that American policy was wrong-headed. In his report to the American War Office he advocated removing the propaganda role from the army and reinvesting it in the State Department. The problem was that he and his fellow left-wing German and Austrian émigrés were falling increasingly under the suspicion of communism, so that the American authorities tended to hold them and their suggestions at arm's length.[44] There was also backbiting within the émigré group in the United States, with the Manns retreating into their corner and pouring scorn on the efforts of others to restore culture in Germany. According to Zuckmayer, Thomas was not the worst of them, but he stood too much under the influence of his hot-headed daughter Erika.

With time, however, the Americans ceased to heed the injunction against frat. GIs empathised with the Germans, whose lives and values seemed similar to their own. As one soldier put it, 'Hell! These people are cleaner and a damn sight friendlier than the frogs . . .' The feeling that contact with the natives could have its pleasant side was compounded when American servicemen began to sleep with German women. *Life* came out with a variant on the old line about fires and chimneypieces: 'You don't talk politics when you fraternize.'[45]

American policy on the ground changed with new directives from Washington. On 6 September 1946 James Byrnes delivered his now famous speech in Stuttgart that announced an about-turn in US policy towards the conquered Germans. The Russians were now the principal enemy. On the advice of George Kennan, the ambassador to Moscow, and Clifford Clark, the special adviser to the president, who continued to warn of Soviet Russia's expansionist desires, Truman decided to fight the growing threat of communist tyranny. The president's speech of 12 March 1947 marked the 'official' beginning of the Cold War.[*] The phrase derived from the title of a book published that year by Walter Lippmann.[†] On 7 July George Marshall, who had succeeded Byrnes as secretary of state, replaced the controversial Directive JCS 1067 of 17 July 1945 that forbade frat. Directive JCS 1779 advocated the creation of a 'stable and productive Germany'. The Morgenthau Plan had also been laid to rest.

The émigrés were almost all disappointed by the American policy. Marxists like Franz Neumann felt that the Americans had also failed to exterminate the ghost of National Socialism and that they would never succeed in introducing stable democracy. John Herz, who worked with Neumann at the Office of Strategic Services, was equally critical: 'Too ambitious, because it started with the nonsensical idea of showing up every German by means of the *Fragebogen*; and not thorough enough, because at the same time we were content to give accreditation to the mayor and the priest – who were doubtless Nazis – and allow them to walk away.' Herz

[*] Or one of them: see below Chapter 19
[†] *The Cold War: A Study in US Foreign Policy.*

had advocated the drawing up of lists of Germans who were 95–100 per cent sure anti-Nazis.[46]

Other exiles were harder hitting about American policies. Volkmar von Zühlsdorff had emigrated to Austria in 1933, departing for America later. He left with Prince Hubertus zu Löwenstein who ran a republican youth group in Brandenburg for the Social Democrat Reichsbanner organisation, which vowed to defend the Weimar Republic from its enemies. Zühlsdorff wanted to help with the rebuilding of Germany. He expressed his outrage in correspondence with his fellow exile Hermann Broch, the Austrian novelist. For Zühlsdorff the Potsdam Declaration was a major crime that had been based on the Ribbentrop–Molotov Pact and the Nazi–Soviet Fourth Partition of Poland: 'Cutting off large, purely German regions is no less a crime than the earlier annexation of Czechoslovakia. The complete expulsion of the German population is a ponderous, international crime.' Broch was not opposed to such views, but pointed out that protest against Potsdam meant war with Russia. The crime could never be resolved. Zühlsdorff felt that Nazism was burned out by 1945, that the German people were ready for a complete change. Instead they had been treated to 'the propaganda of hate'. What they needed was 'liberation, reason, peace and human rights'.[47]

Dorothy Thompson had been close to the hanged resister Helmuth James von Moltke during her time as a journalist in Berlin. She knew Germany and its people well, she was a fanatical opponent of collective guilt, and after the war she continued to press for reasonable policies. Her views resembled those of the writer Ernst Jünger in his essay *Der Friede*. Directly after the war she toured central Europe with her husband, the Prague-born painter Maximilian Kopf. She was particularly struck by her visit to Dachau, where she was able to view the commandant's house and see that he possessed an edition of Goethe's works, loved children, music, art and literature, and lived, to all extents and purposes, a normal family life.[48]

The Russians linked food distribution to work, encouraging the business of clearing up. In the American Zone no one worked because there was nothing to buy. Soon that position reversed itself and the Russians fell behind. Russians were also notorious for their light fingers – wristwatches were always at risk, but the French and the Americans were not so loath to steal the odd souvenir, or even a watch or three. American official theft was carried out on a massive scale when it came to seizing scientists and scientific equipment. This received governmental sanction as 'Operation Paperclip'. During their few months in the famous lens-city of Jena, the American military government or AMG nabbed eighty scientists between

22 and 25 June and obliged them to make their way to the safer, US areas of occupation in the west.[49]

The Anglo-Americans were not uninterested in plunder. Margret Boveri thought the Russian reputation was unfair. True, they had stolen a good deal, but the Western Allies stole objects of greater worth. The British received the best press. They were the 'quietest, slowest and most understanding'.[50] Sometimes they paid. James Stern recounts a visit to a black market in Kempten where he was received by a dirty greasy little black-marketeer who tried to sell him some sweet Mavrodaphne. 'We are not ladies . . . and we want wine . . .' said Stern firmly. Through an open door, however, he saw something more interesting: some cases of 1939 Pfalz wine. A second man said they had been ordered by the Military Government, but thirty marks seemed to do the trick and the Englishman went off with a couple of cases.[51] The Americans and the Russians were also trading. James Stern got wind of exchanges of gems for cases of cognac or American cigarettes.[52]

Nor were all the rapes committed by the Russians. In Salomon's local town, he claims half a dozen women were raped as the Americans took possession of place and people. Nor was his indictment so far fetched – the figures bear him out. Rape charges in the US army rose steadily, from 18 in January 1945 to 31 in February to an enormous 402 in March and 501 in April, once military resistance had slackened off. With peace the rapes petered out: there were 241 reports in May, 63 in June and 45 for each month thereafter. About a quarter to a half of these reports resulted in a trial and a third to a half of the trials to a conviction. A number of American servicemen were executed, proportionally higher than any of the other occupying powers.[53]

One reason there were fewer reports of rape was that there was far more consensual congress. German girls would have sex for food or cigarettes. You didn't court a German woman with flowers – a basket of food was more welcome. The Americans were attractive to the Germans, because they had not suffered the deprivations of war in the same way. Few were crippled, and they were taller and more athletic. Every now and then the Germans took it out on the women who spurned them in favour of the occupiers. It is not hard to imagine the feeling of impotence of the rare young German who saw his girl making for the American garrison on the promise of sweets and cigarettes. Zuckmayer believed that this and the brutal confiscation of property by the military made the Americans unpopular. He alludes to an incident in the Munich suburb of Harlaching in the perishing cold of December 1946.

The hatred of the conqueror, however, had no political overtones, and was by no one politically exploited; and if there was grumbling about the behaviour of the *Amis*, there were always people to remind the malcontent that he would be shot in the Russian Zone, worse fed in the British, and face more corruption in the French. The American Zone was the easiest place to obtain cigarettes as well.[54] The liaisons naturally resulted in children. It is estimated that 94,000 *Besatzungskinder* or 'occupation children' were born in the American Zone under military government. The Germans joked that at the next war they would not need to send soldiers, just uniforms. These children – wanted or unwanted – often caused distress, as there were no paternity orders issued against the servicemen. The situation must have been alleviated in December 1946 once marriages were finally permitted. The American soldiers were not slow to show their enthusiasm. There were some 14,000 GI brides brought home from Germany, a figure only exceeded by Britain, which saw nearly 35,000 of its girls go home with the American troops. For Ruth Friedrich and her friends these German brides were 'rats leaving the sinking ship'.[55]

There were 42,000 American blacks in the forces of occupation. They were particularly enthralled by the Fräuleins – women who were more prepared to sleep with them than people back home. They were, as one writer has written, 'early and enthusiastic fraternisers'.[56] During the first years of the occupation. between two and three thousand mixed-race babies were born – about 2 to 3 percent of the *Besatzungskinder*. In Bendorf on the Rhine the Russian Elena Skrjabina encountered ten 'half negro' babies that had been brought in for adoption: 'These soldiers quite willingly go with German girls, the girls are available for all types of rarities such as coffee, chocolate and so forth.' The only problem was that the arrival of the coloured child caused anger in the girl's family, hence the fact the children were being offered for adoption.[57] Another problem was VD. An American source related that over three-quarters of the black solders were infected. Relationships between black soldiers and German girls caused friction with the natives, and with white American soldiers too. The consequence was 'bitter hatred among German men. Many of our own [US] soldiers feel almost as strongly about it.'[58] In Asperg in Bavaria there was an incident at a dance when a fight broke out. A white soldier was killed and four others wounded. Three blacks were sentenced to death as a result.[59]

German racial tolerance clearly surprised American blacks. A black musician came to see Leo Borchard in Berlin and talked to him about Bach. Borchard sent him off with a score. The musician told Borchard, 'We are the most despised people on earth. We are even more deeply despised than the Jews, or . . . or the Germans.' He said that people came to his concerts not to hear him play, but to see the novelty of a black man playing classical music.[60]

With time and with the increasing unease between the Western Allies and the Russians, the Americans sought to win over the hearts and minds of the conquered Germans. From a policy of forbidding fraternisation, American soldiers were actively encouraged to look after vulnerable Germans, reserving their wrath only for the more obvious culprits. In Bad Kissingen, for example, Prince Louis Ferdinand of Prussia was able to come together with a Captain Merle Potter to create the first German American Club in 1946. Louis Ferdinand was the grandson of that famous militarist, Kaiser William II, who would certainly have failed the test of the *Fragebogen*.[61]

Political Life

While the British were keen to see the Germans issued with a good, workable constitution that would prevent them from falling into bad ways in the future, the Americans were obsessed with the need to introduce their brand of government: every German was to become a good democrat. Once the Germans had democracy, they would never be tempted by totalitarianism again. The fact that they had already had democracy, and that it had dramatically failed in 1929, seems to have been unclear to people such as James Stern's colleague 'the Professor'.[62] This attitude led to a deal of absurdity in the Americans' pursuit of fairness in the newspapers they licensed: the *Rhein-Neckar-Zeitung* had to offer leading articles from all four main political parties, including the communists. One of the movers and shakers in post-war Bavarian politics was Josef 'Ochsensepp' Müller. Müller returned from Capri in the middle of June 1945 having established a relationship with the Americans that would stand him in good stead. The American authorities allowed him to establish a base for anti-Nazi politicians in Munich that would form the nucleus of a new political party. The men met on Wednesdays. To observe the proceedings the Americans sent along Dany Weiss, a Jew who had lost his entire family in the east. The idea was to establish a party that would cross Christian lines, and not be entirely Catholic like the old Centre Party.* Müller also recruited the leading

---

* It is a moot point whether the CSU is really seen as anything other than a Catholic Bavarian force.

political figure in Franconia, Adam Stegerwald, and the trades-unionist Franz Wegner.[63]

Müller's ideas echoed those of Jakob Kaiser in Berlin: Germany needed to learn from the primitive Christians. If their teaching was followed there would be no need for communism or socialism. It was an idea he had developed in the Hotel Paradiso in Capri, in conversation with the American naval officer and Mormon, Dale Clark. These sun-baked discussions sired the Christlich-Sozial Union or CSU.[64] A few monarchists were easily pushed to one side. Their leader, Eugen Graf Quadt-Isny, had unfortunately had himself photographed in SS uniform in the company of the leading Nazi 'beasts' after the dissolution of his own Bayrische Volkspartei or BVP.[65] The Americans licensed the CSU on 8 January 1946.

The Americans insisted that denazification be carried out with a toughness absent from the other zones. Fritz Schäffer, a former head of the BVP and an old Dachauer, was their first nominee as minister president of Bavaria. He then fell foul of the Americans because he failed to pursue former Nazis with the right degree of enthusiasm, even if they already had 46,000 in the can by 3 October 1945. Clay thought him insufficiently liberal and had him sacked.[66] Not even Müller was immune, he who had been in Flossenbürg and Dachau, had almost been shot, and had witnessed some of his closest friends being beaten, tortured and murdered for their opposition to Nazism. As a former member of military intelligence he had belonged to a 'tainted' organisation. Through the new minister president, the 'remigrant' Dr Wilhelm Hoegner, and his 'special minister' for denazification, the communist nominee Heinrich Schmitt, Bavaria established 'Spruchkammer' or special courts. They were staffed by non-professional judges reflecting the parties in power in the Landtag, or local parliament. Müller's view was encapsulated in a joke that was doing the rounds at the time: a former street-sweeper passes a man ineptly cleaning the pavements on his old beat. As he stares at the new cleaner, the latter shouts out, 'I have to clean the streets because I was in the Party!' The former cleaner shouts back, 'I am not allowed to do it, because I was in the Party too!'[67]

One outstanding figure who joined Hoegner's government was Ludwig Erhard. He was from Fürth in Franconia, making him a sort of Bavarian. After a chequered academic career as an economist he found himself unemployed when the Americans came in and volunteered his services in his home town. He had no Nazi track record and he was popular with the Americans. When Schäffer's government fell in October he was appointed minister for trade. He was not a member of any party and his career in the

Bavarian government came to an end a little over a year later. He went back into academic life as an economics teacher at Munich University.[68]

The Americans fished him out again to make him one of seven members of the Economic Council in autumn 1947. Erhard became president of the Special Commission for Money and Credit. Germany had somehow to stabilise its currency, which had no credibility. The Reichsmark, which was still circulating, was causing terrible inflation. Erhard's idea was that the quantity of money in circulation needed to reflect the quantity of goods on offer in the marketplace. This way prices could be made constant and there would be something to buy.[69] Erhard's formulations became the basis for the Homburg Plan for a market economy which was published on 18 April 1948. Erhard himself became the head of the economic administration in Bizonia after Johannes Semler's well-publicised faux pas in describing the American food aid as 'chicken feed'.[70]

Culture

Culture became a way to reinstil notions of civilisation in the renegade Germans, but at first it was also used to punish them. One of the high temples of German art, the Festival Opera House in Bayreuth, was singled out for special treatment. After all, in American eyes Richard Wagner was a prototype Nazi, his music was banned, his house destroyed by bombs and his daughter-in-law threatened with a labour camp. In the circumstances the natural thing to do was to give the Bayreuther some real, democratic culture: variety shows and revues were put on for the troops in the same building where – the summer before – weary and invalid troops had watched *Siegfried* or *Götterdämmerung*.

When the American authorities put on an opera, it turned out to be *Die Fledermaus*. Meanwhile the Festival Restaurant was baking between 12,000 and 15,000 doughnuts a day. A programme for 12 December 1945 shows that the Bayreuth Symphony Orchestra were billed to perform 'Music You Love to Hear', conducted by the elderly operetta composer Paul Lincke, who had written hit songs like 'Berliner Luft' before the Great War. Not all Americans, however, were unmoved by the heritage of the Wagners. The critic Joseph Wechsberg found his way into the Opera House and saw that the stage was set for *Die Meistersinger*. He sat down in Hans Sachs's chair and sang the monologue 'Wahn' (delusion) to an audience of one – the carpenter who had come out to listen.[71]

Wieland Wagner hoped to enlist Toscanini to come to the aid of the

theatre and of his grandfather's legacy. The Italian conductor had been vol-
ubly anti-fascist and was in good odour in the United States. The Opera
House was an 'unprotected shrine'.[72] As for the Wagner home, Wahnfried,
the ruined house provided a backdrop for American dances and summer
parties. There were reports that GIs had been seen dancing the jitterbug on
Wagner's grave.[73] With time it became clear that the Wagner legacy could
be saved, providing it was purged of its flirtation with Nazism. Oskar
Meyer, the new mayor of Bayreuth, ensured that some serious, non-
Wagnerian operas were performed under the sacred roof, even if he wanted
to send Winifred Wagner to a labour camp for five years. The three children who had remained behind in Germany were all tainted by Nazism to
a greater or lesser degree. There remained only the émigré Friedelind.

If the Americans were not as active as the Russians in promoting culture,
their zone was not a complete backwater. Prince Franz Sayn-Wittgenstein
remembered seeing *As You Like It* performed by the Shakespeare
Company – the forerunner to the Royal Shakespeare Company – in
Wiesbaden. Later he saw Carl Zuckmayer's play, *Des Teufels General*, based
on the life of the Luftwaffe general Udet who committed suicide in 1941.
Sayn-Wittgenstein became so enraged at the scene when the general is
confronted by an SS officer that he leaped to his feet and shouted, 'Hauen
Sie doch dem Schwein eine in die Fresse!' (Go on, give the pig a punch in
the gob!). His neighbour sought to calm him down in the local dialect: 'Ei
beruige Se sich. Es ist nur auf der Biehne' (Come on, calm down. It's only
a play).[74]

Part of Zuckmayer's job was to report on the state of theatre in the
American Zone. He was impressed by what he encountered in Berlin:
'with what seriousness, passion and enthusiasm theatre is performed in this
undernourished and freezing city, how much theatre is fought for,
attended and loved, spoken about and criticised – the whole gamut of
artistic events and projects theatrical and operatic – and, thank God, free
cabaret as well, [cultural life in Berlin] reveals a spiritual, intellectual and
physical vitality that could not be stamped out by robbing the people of
liberty for twelve years nor by the consequences of a collapse without parallel, nor by dividing [Germany] into four zones.' Not only did Berliners
appear to live and breathe theatre, they were prepared to forgo much of
their paltry livelihood to attend. In the west you could see people with
money to spare, but in the north-east, 20 per cent of the population
attended performances, although the entrance ticket cost them as much as
they would pay for a small amount of pork dripping or a few grams of
butter on the black market.[75]

Looking into theatre meant liaising with the actor–director Benno Frank, who headed the music, theatre and cinema section of the ICD or Information Control Division. His assistant was the Eric Clarke who in civilian life had been the administrator at the Metropolitan Opera in New York. One, fairly unsuccessful policy was to make German troupes act translations of American plays that were seen to have propaganda value, but which offered no criticism of American life. Some of these were of undoubted interest, such as those by Thornton Wilder, others were less so – Elmer Rice's *The Adding Machine*, John C. Holm and George Abbott's *Three Men on a Horse*, Paul Osborn's *On Borrowed Time*, Samuel Behrman's *Biography*, William Saroyan's *The Time of your Life*, Clarence Day's *Life with Father* and Lillian Hellman's *Watch on the Rhine*. The latter caused grumbling in Vienna when it was put on by Ernst Lothar with his wife, Adrienne Gessner, playing a leading role. It was a play about the opposition to Hitler, but the audience felt the author was uncertain of her ground.

The heavy-handedness of Allied theatre policy led to a conference in Stuttgart at the end of February 1947, when it was decided to allow German theatre more freedom to perform plays it chose and to direct them the way it wanted. There had been a successful interaction between the French and the Americans in Stuttgart, which is not far from the ancient university town of Tübingen in the French Zone. Newell Jenkins, the far-sighted American theatre officer for Baden-Württemberg, had encouraged these exchanges. Jenkins and William Dubensky were also successful in 'liberating' the theatres in Stuttgart and Wiesbaden that had been requisitioned by the American army. They were turned over to their original use. There had also been a successful exchange between the Americans and the Russians in Berlin, but that was once again due to Dymshitz. In the American Sector it was the Hebbel Theatre that led the way, while the Russians encouraged performances in the Volksbühne in their own sector.

The usual physical problem beset theatres in the American Zone: 60 per cent of them had been destroyed in the bombing. Added to the lack of premises was a paucity of actors and directors, many of them having either voted with their feet in 1933 or perished in the camps. Theatre was nonetheless best represented in the American Zone. The Western Allies controlled 70 per cent of the theatres, and in Bizonia the Americans led the British by six to four. A little bit of invention was necessary. In Munich the theatre had been destroyed, and performances took place in the Fountain Court of the badly damaged royal residence. One thriving part of the Munich theatre was the Schaubühne cabaret which was directed by Erich

Kästner, the author of the Berlin novel *Florian*. The Americans made him editor of their *Neue Zeitung*.[76]

Zuckmayer also filed a report on the film industry in the American Zone. It appeared that Germany had become a dumping ground for Hollywood, and not enough was being done to help revive the native German film industry that had come under Goebbels's control during the Nazi years and had naturally been used chiefly for propaganda. The German people lapped up the films they had been deprived of during the Third Reich – that is, all except the bigwigs, who had continued to watch them in their specially constructed home cinemas.* German films were subjected to censorship, sometimes as a result of over-sensitivity on the part of the American authorities. An example of this was a film on the life of Louis Pasteur. It showed a group of Russian refugees being injected with a rabies vaccine. The Americans thought it would remind people of the experiments carried out in the camps and cut the scene. Such films that were made under the American aegis were often as tainted with propaganda as those of Dr Goebbels. They familiarised German audiences with the problems Jews faced in reaching Palestine, or the living conditions of DPs. Zuckmayer felt they should sponsor a film on the German opposition.[77]

Zuckmayer was present at a performance of his most popular play *Der Hauptmann von Köpenick* in Heidelberg, and was surprised to find a small number of young men wolf-whistling. After the play was over he challenged one of them to explain his behaviour. The play had been particularly despised by the Nazis because it had poked fun at the Prussian respect for army uniforms. Zuckmayer discovered that the whistlers were mostly ex-officers and students, and in no way standard louts. They had gone to voice their disapproval of plays that devalued German 'culture'.

Zuckmayer's role was also to promote American culture and democracy, and he invited the hecklers to come to see him, and discuss whatever it was that annoyed them so much about his play. In Bavaria he was engaged to speak to some of the older children in a Gymnasium about the benefits of democracy. He was wary, however, of presenting his talk as such, for fear that the children would see him as a mere spouter of American propaganda. The children were by no means taken in by the American profession of disinterested benevolence. They wanted to know why half the seminars at Munich University had been closed. They also revealed that

---

* They were popular with the 'lofty animals' of the Party: Martin Bormann had one in his house in Berchtesgaden and Goebbels one in his Berlin home.

some of the children had been threatened that they would get their come-uppance and suffer ostacism and physical violence once the occupation was wound up.[78] The author had to duck the 'Gretchen Question'* on his many appearances on the podium. Germans were well aware of the position taken by Thomas Mann, and of the intransigently anti-German pose struck by Mann's daughter Erika.

Zuckmayer proved a remorseless critic of American policy until he was brought down by a heart attack in December 1948. He had always been adamant that he would not go to Germany to boss Germans around while posing as an American officer. He wanted to bring the Germans books, especially those (like his own) that had been banned since 1933. He was convinced that love was a stronger emotion than hate, and that the Germans needed encouragement, not the lash. He intended to make a film about the Nuremberg trials, but in this he was thwarted and pipped at the post by Stuart Schulberg, who headed the film division of the ICD in Berlin. He had disapproved of the way the trials had been run, and felt that the real trials took place in the hearts of Germans.[79]

There was at least as much enthusiasm for books as theatre, and the dramatist contended that if the publishers were merely given enough paper they could instantly sell everything they brought out. The Americans sensed this and created libraries in the form of twenty-six Amerika Häuser and 137 reading rooms. In Berlin-Zehlendorf, Zuckmayer discovered the publisher Peter Suhrkamp, who had run the illustrious house of Fischer before the war, and was to create Suhrkamp in Frankfurt-am-Main in 1950, one of the most influential publishing houses of post-war Germany. Suhrkamp had been allowed to move from Potsdam in the Russian Zone and set up in comparative comfort, although the frigid winter of 1946–7 hit him as hard as everyone else, especially after his pipes froze. Suhrkamp had had anything but an easy war. An opponent of Hitler, he had been tangential to the so-called Solf Circle around Hanna Solf, the widow of the last imperial foreign minister Wilhem Solf, and had been denounced by the same Swiss Dr Reckzeh whose testimony resulted in them all being thrown into Ravensbrück concentration camp and the execution of two of the set, the Red Cross nurse Elisabeth von Thadden and the diplomat Otto Kiep. He had been badly treated in the camp and sustained serious injuries to his back, as well as a near mortal inflammation of the lungs and the skin covering his ribs.[80]

---

* In Zuckmayer's case the question was whether he was still a German, and whether he would consider coming back to Germany to live.

The American Zone also silently (or almost) played host to Group 47, the first post-war school of German literature. The group was the brainchild of Hans Werner Richter, whose attempts to create a magazine *Der Skorpion* were snuffed out by the American censors. The aim was to turn their backs on everything the Nazis might have taught them: existentialism was fashionable, and the name of Sartre a leitmotiv in their discussions. Magical realism reared its head in the writings of Wolfdietrich Schnurre. One of those early movers and shakers was Nicolas Sombart, the son of the famous sociologist Werner Sombart. Every six months the members met to read their works in progress in various bucolic spots around the zone. Very soon the group began to attract some of the bigger names in post-war German literature: Alfred Andersch, Martin Walser, Günter Grass and Heinrich Böll.[81]

It is probably not surprising that one particular man in an American uniform was very interested in discovering illustrious fragments of German culture, and that was W. H. Auden. One night James Stern returned to hear Beethoven being performed in the *gute Stube* of the house he shared with the British poet in Nuremberg. It was a Herr Ledenfels, once the most famous performer in the city. Auden had picked him up somewhere on his rounds.[82]

8

Life in the British Zone

No German is *persona grata* with Mil. Gov.
A British officer. Quoted in Charles Williams,
Adenauer, London 2000, 296

British Military Government

The British 'element' in the occupation of Germany was required to administer 23,000,000 souls. It was formally governed by a junior minister, the Chancellor of the Duchy of Lancaster, who was responsible for both German and Austrian affairs as head of the Control Office for Germany and Austria, or COGA. Originally this fell under the Civil Affairs Division of the Ministry of War, as the Foreign Office disowned it. Later, when Lord Pakenham was minister, he was given a room at the Foreign Office, which brought him closer to the foreign secretary, Ernest Bevin, physically at least. The first minister was John Hynd, a former railway clerk and trade unionist, who had only been an MP since 1944. It seems his choice was suggested by the fact he had taught himself German. For obvious reasons his department was called 'Hyndquarters'.[1]

He was shunted on to pensions and replaced by Lord Pakenham, a quondam Oxford don who was to achieve household fame as the Earl of Longford, campaigning against pornography and in favour of prisoners. The left-wing British publisher Victor Gollancz thought Hynd a good fellow: 'There is no humaner man in British public life,' but it is clear that he also thought his humanity of no avail when those above him refused to change British policy.[2] He had less time for Frank Pakenham, who made a speech in the Lords that was 'a model of feebleness and futility'.[3] The real problem was not the quality of the men the government put in to look after Germany, but the amount of power accorded to them to put things right.

According to his own short and self-deprecating account, Pakenham believed that he had been appointed because he was a Catholic, and a majority of the Germans in the British Zone shared his religion. This is unlikely to be true: although there is a majority of Catholics in the Rhineland, they are not super-numerous in the Lutheran bastions of Lower Saxony or Schleswig-Holstein. He was appointed in the spring of 1947: 'I was filled with passionate Christian desire to see justice done to this broken people.' He was taken to a school in Düsseldorf where some of the three million children in the zone were fainting from hunger. He told them, 'Never believe the whole world is against you, you're absolutely right to be proud of being German.' Pakenham later claimed that the government reined him in after that, but he nonetheless visited Germany twenty-six times during his period of responsibility.[4] He did not convince everyone that his intentions towards Germany were utterly benign, however. Franz Sayn-Wittgenstein was outraged by a conversation with him in Frankfurt during which he appeared to extol the virtues of the Morgenthau Plan.[5]

If Hynd and Pakenham lacked real power it obviously resided with the foreign secretary, Bevin, and his deputy Hector McNeil, the minister of state. There was precious little sympathy for the Germans at the top. Prime Minister Clement Attlee was quite open about it – he disliked the lot of them, but he and his wife had once had a nice German maid. Bevin had not forgiven the German socialists for voting war credits in 1914: 'I try to be nice but I 'ates them really,' he said.[6] The first military governor was Sir Bernard (later Viscount) Montgomery, with General Weeks serving as his deputy. Weeks established a precedent, intentional or otherwise, of planting men with industrial experience in positions of power in occupied Germany. Apart from a distinguished record in the First World War, he had only ever been a part-time soldier, and had risen to become chairman of Pilkington's glassworks in 1939. During the Second War he had been appointed to the General Staff, becoming its deputy chief in 1942, 'a unique position for a citizen soldier'.[7] It is unlikely that his dual experience was overlooked in his selection. Britain's attitude to post-war Germany was to some degree a reflection of its penury. It wanted the fastest possible economic recovery prior to Germany's being granted independence.[8]

Montgomery was replaced by the former head of Fighter Command, Marshal of the RAF Sir Sholto Douglas, in 1946. Douglas had been head of BAFO, the British forces of occupation. Like Weeks he was a university-educated man and had sung in the Bach Choir before the war. He had also been in the war industry, having quit the RAF during the inter-war years to work for Handley Page. Douglas presided over the dismantling of the

Luftwaffe and oversaw the British entry into Berlin. He expressed a desire to reintroduce 'normal life' into Germany, and although one of his first duties was to approve the Nuremberg sentences, he had grave doubts.[9] He resigned in October 1947 over the Bückeburg affair.*

His successor was General Sir Brian Robertson, whose father Sir William had been military governor in Germany in 1918. Robertson was born in Simla, and on his mother's side he came from a long line of Indian Army soldiers. India and the Raj provided some of the inspiration for the British in Germany. The British sense of innate superiority over their former enemy was not lost on the Germans, who grumbled that they had been turned into a *Kolonialvolk* – a colonial people like the Indians. At the beginning, some Germans had even connived at a subservient role, pre-sumably because they believed they would be treated better that way. There was a move by some politicians in Hanover to reinstate the old king-dom, divorced from Great Britain when Queen Victoria ascended the throne.† That way Hanover would be part of the British Empire, and not of a defeated Germany.[10] Robertson had been educated at the same Charterhouse School as Weeks before attending the Royal Military Academy at Woolwich.‡ He was commissioned in the Royal Engineers – a background he shared with Clay. Unlike Clay, however, he had seen ser-vice in the First World War and emerged with an MC and DSO. Between the wars he had taken leave from the army to become managing director of Dunlop in South Africa and had befriended Jan Smuts. His role in the Second World War was largely administrative. He became deputy military governor in succession to Weeks. After the Bonn government was created in 1949 he stayed on as UK commissioner for a further year. Bevin worked well with Robertson, who kept him abreast of what was going on by weekly letters. The official history says Robertson was a 'firm but com-passionate' interpreter of British policy.[11]

Montgomery, Douglas and Robertson had the power of life and death without any interference from Westminster. They ruled with the aid of the Control Commission Germany, or CCG. This was jestingly known as 'Charlie Chaplin's Grenadiers' or 'Complete Chaos Guaranteed'. It had a gigantic staff of nearly 25,000, five times as many as the American contingent, and was reportedly venal, overpaid and riddled with scandal. British officers serving in occupied Germany were sent to Bletchley for a course. According

---

* See below p. 390.
† Under Salic Law a woman could not inherit the throne of Hanover.
‡ There may be a case for seeing a Carthusian 'mafia' at the heart of British Military Government. Robert Birley (see below) had been headmaster of Charterhouse since 1935.

to George Clare there were superficial lectures on German history and classes on the function of the Control Commission. The potential officers were a mixed bunch, including many women speaking excellent German. Only about a fifth of the recruits dealt with administering Germany; the rest was made up of senior officers who served in its 'swollen bureaucracy'.[12] In April 1946 the men were joined by their wives and families, further inflating the household and leading to the requisitioning of yet more undamaged homes. In Münster only 1,050 houses remained undamaged of a total of 33,737. The occupiers promptly requisitioned 445 of them – over 40 per cent.[13] After Indian independence Germans feared that they would receive all the former ICS (Indian Civil Service) men, some of whom might in fact have been an improvement. There were some able administrators in the CCG such as the banker Sir Vaughan Berry in Hamburg, who had studied in Germany and knew the country and its people.[14]

Victor Gollancz objected to a *Herrenvolk* mentality he saw among British officers, and to the contrast he saw between the accommodation and food in the officers' mess and the miserable, half-starved hovels outside. Much of Germany was uninhabitable. The military governor had a modest HQ in Bad Oeynhausen, where all the inhabitants had been cleared out of the spa town to make way for the British, and a country house in Melle; but there were plans to build something more grandiose in Hamburg. It was to be a vast military and social headquarters, presumably to rival the Soviet HQ at Karlshorst or its American counterpart in Frankfurt. The complex was to include hotels and clubs, as well as lodgings for married and unmarried officers. Had it gone ahead, an estimated 38,200 Germans would have lost their homes. The district governor, Vaughan Berry, was vehemently opposed to the project, and, given the state of British finances at the time, it must have seemed like so much pie in the sky.[15]

Au fond the British believed more in re-education than in denazification and the story of the re-establishment of schooling and university education in the zone was one of its great claims to fame. Robert Birley took a couple of years off between the headmasterships of Charterhouse and Eton to reorganise schools in the British Zone. As an historian he was well aware that there was no precedent for the Allied position in Germany: 'We occupied a country without a government and from the outset our occupying forces had not only to prevent the revival of a military danger, they had to rebuild a community.'[16] Birley was evidently shocked by the godlessness of the Nazi state. He had been to Brno, and seen the chapel in the Spielberg fortress above the city. The SS had turned it over to paganism. The altar had been mounted by a giant swastika containing a copy of *Mein Kampf*

and an immense eagle decorated the wall in the place of a reredos. The
British needed to change the minds and outlook of the people who did
such a thing, and who had suffered a 'complete moral collapse'. Birley
stressed, however, that the German malaise was not an isolated phenomenon but another manifestation of the 'diseased condition of western
civilisation'.[17]

Nothing was easy: the three Rs took a back seat to the three Fs (food,
fuel and footwear) and the three Ps (pens, pencils and paper). Birley
thought shoes the greatest of these.[18] He took heart when he saw a
German desire to get on. In cities laid waste by bombing he saw young
men as old as twenty-three trying to pass their *Abitur* to enter a university.
They were so many 'Peter Pans', utterly ignorant of anything other than
what their National Socialist instructors had told them. Many had been in
the Wehrmacht. These were prevented from entering higher education
before February 1947. And yet the British were forced to impose a *numerus
clausa* until 1949. The lack of places was down to the wrecking of the
buildings by bombing and the long-drawn-out process of screening all
university teachers though the Public Safety Branch (the name perhaps an
unintentional evocation of the French revolutionary terror).[19]

Birley wanted to restore the love of freedom and a readiness to accept
personal responsibility. The most important men for the task, he thought,
were philosophers, and he pointed to the sterling work done at St Michael's
House near Hamburg. It may have been a coincidence, but at the precise
moment when Wehrmacht men were finally allowed to enter the universities, the dean of the faculty of philosophy at Cologne University appealed
to those who had emigrated to return to the department.[20] It was not so
much the philosophers, however, who tried to reform the German mind
as historians like Birley and Michael Balfour, who had been a friend of the
late Helmuth James von Moltke of Kreisau. Balfour was made director of
Information Services within the British Zone in 1946. He made it clear
that he needed to move quickly: 'We are not in Germany forever.'[21] As it
was, he lasted only a year.

One of the most successful British efforts at re-education was Wilton
Park in Buckinghamshire, a former POW camp which had been turned
over to residential courses for Germans run by Heinz Koeppler, Koeppler
was a German who had left his country to study at Oxford in 1933, and
had never gone home. The style was derived wholly from Oxford and
Cambridge – something utterly new to even the most privileged students
at the German universities. They were waited on at table, received tutor-
ials and were allowed to discuss issues freely. The idea was to make men

ready for public life and to create a new non-Nazi elite. 'Respectable' Germans such as the socialist Kurt Schumacher, Bishop Dibelius, Pastor Niemöller and Archbishop Frings also addressed the students.[22]

Another distinguished historian, the expert on the Reformation A. G. Dickens, was editing the *Lübecker Nachrichtenblatt*, aided by the inevitable Viennese Jew.[23] There weren't so many German-speakers around, apart from these specialised historians. Another purveyor of British civilisation was the British Council. Its well-meaning, bumbling approach is carica-tured in Wilfrid Hyde White's role in *The Third Man*. The screenplay for the film was written by Graham Greene, whose brother Hugh Carlton Greene ran the NWDR radio in occupied Germany. The latter expressed a view in total opposition to that of Vansittart, one which was closer to Balfour: 'I am here to make myself superfluous.' He too thought the Germans merely needed re-education. Kaye Sely and George Clare inter-viewed German denazification candidates in Greene's office, while Greene sat on the sofa to make sure they were fairly treated. Greene had saved a little treat for himself: a magnificent car, the Maibach Tourer that had for-merly belonged to Karl Wolff, Himmler's chief of staff.[24] Greene took over from Rex Palmer as broadcasting controller to the British Zone. Palmer had been a disaster – he had run children's radio before the war, and it showed.

The British needed to take stock of their zone. They had the largely empty farmlands of Schleswig-Holstein, the industrial and farming areas of Lower Saxony, and the industrialised but also highly cultural region of the Rhine and the Ruhr. The area had been very badly damaged by bombing. Cologne was 66 per cent destroyed, and Düsseldorf a staggering 93 per cent. Aachen was described as a 'fantastic, stinking heap of ruins'. The British reordered their domain, creating Rhineland-Westphalia by amalga-mating two *Länder*. The French responded with Ordonnance 57 which gave birth to Rhineland-Palatinate in August 1946. Naturally suspicion was aroused again over the motives of the French. People imagined they were trying to create independent German states before annexing them to France.[25]

The most glamorous posting was Berlin. The military train took the sol-diers into Charlottenburg Station, which was their introduction to the city, if they were not lucky enough to fly into Gatow. British soldiers in Berlin wore a flash on their sleeve. It was a black circle rimmed with red – 'septic arsehole' they called it. British Control Commission's headquarters in Berlin was in 'Lancaster House' on the Fehrbelliner Platz. George Clare described it as a 'concave-shaped grey, concrete edifice' in the style of

Albert Speer. Under the British Control Commission there were detach-
ments in each of the boroughs under British control, together with a
barracks and an officers' mess. There were messes all over the British
Sector. When George Clare reappeared in officer's garb on his second
tour of duty, he was assigned to one on the Breitenbach Platz which was
large and lacked social cachet, and resembled a Lyons Corner House.
British Military Government was a large yellow building on the Theodor
Heuss Platz. This was the former Adolf Hitler Platz in Charlottenburg, the
name of which was changed to Reichskanzlerplatz until it was realised that
Hitler too had been chancellor. On the other side of the square was the
Marlborough Club, where officers could be gentlemen. For the Other
Ranks there was the Winston Club.[26]

Germans had to receive permission to enter HQ Mil. Gov. This was not
issued to former Pgs. The rules were bent only if the person was of interest to the British – that is, a scientist, a pre-1933 politician or an expert
technician. A German editor seeking permission to start a magazine (such
as Rudolf Augstein with *Der Spiegel*) or an entrepreneur looking to put on
a theatrical performance had to take his suit to the Berlin Control Unit in
the Klaus Groth Strasse near by. The path to redemption in all cases was the
Fragebogen. The forms had to be filled in, and any membership of Nazi
organisations checked out. With time minor Nazis were let off the hook.
As far as soldiers were concerned, the Wehrmacht members who were not
already languishing in a POW camp were fine. The SS was divided into
grey and black. Blacks (Totenkopf) were interned, greys (Waffen-SS) were
released. Eventually the British authorities learned that separating black and
grey was not so cut and dried.[27]

The life of an interrogator was filled with unexpected surprises: charm-
ing young men who turned out on closer examination to have been
inveterate Nazis, and rebarbative Prussian militarists who, it transpired,
were anything but. Clare had a visit from the widow of the General Carl-
Heinrich von Stülpnagel who wanted to join her daughter in the British
Zone. He eventually recalled that this general was the one who had locked
up the Paris SS and the Gestapo on 20 July 1944, who attempted suicide
when the Plot failed but managed only to blind himself, and who was
gruesomely hanged with the rest. Frau von Stülpnagel would not hear of
special pleading: her husband was just a German, doing his job.[28]

Despite the lordly nature of their approach, the British had a reputation
for being more decent people than the other Allies, but that did not mean
they were without sin. Len Carpenter, an escaped POW who had holed up
in the Neue Westend of Berlin until the arrival of the Allies, ran a

successful business as a black-marketeer and pimp (unpaid, he assures us) to the British occupation forces.[29] In November 1947 Speer described one of the British guards in Spandau who had arrived drunk for work: 'He boasted to his fellows of the vast amount of beer he had drunk, and hinted at pleasant company.' The party had ended only three hours before. Speer lent him his bed so he could sleep it off and patrolled the corridor lest a superior officer appear. The man was still unsteady on his feet hours later.[30]

One of the oddest briefs given to the British army occupying Germany was to punish its very soil. This was the case with the island of Heligoland, which had been British for most of the nineteenth century, but which had been acquired by the Kaiser in 1890 in what he saw as his first foreign political coup.[31] The island had been heavily armed during the 'Kaiser' Reich, and in Nazi times it bristled not only with guns, but also with submarine docks. The RAF destroyed most of the defences as well as the town in a raid of 18–19 April 1945. On 11 May, the Royal Navy made a foray across the waters of the Baltic to see what was left. Despite the pulverising the island had received during the war, the U-boat shelters were undamaged, as was the network of tunnels under the island together with the diesel trains that plied them.[32]

At Potsdam it was agreed that Germany was to be completely disarmed and that all German fortifications were to be destroyed. For the British that meant primarily the naval forts on the Frisian Islands and Heligoland. British High Command calculated that they would need 48,400 man hours and 730 tons of explosives.[33] They began to prepare for Operation Big Bang. When this occurred two years later, on 18 April 1948, it was a literal case of over-kill. Having decided presumably that the previous estimate had been too low, the British set off 7,000 tons of munitions in what was described as the 'greatest non-nuclear explosion in history'. A huge 'cauliflower' of smoke shot up 8,000 feet from the catacombs 180 feet below the surface of the rock, but once the skies cleared it was apparent that instead of eradicating the hated island, they had destroyed a mere 14 per cent of its surface.[34]

For several years the RAF and the American air force based in Britain continued to use the island as a bombing range. Preparations were made to test the British atom bomb there and trials were made of chemical weapons.[35] The idea of using the island for nuclear tests was finally abandoned out of consideration for the population of Cuxhaven, which was only thirty miles away. The German fishermen who had previously caught lobsters off the islands were at last allowed to return to their homes in 1952, largely as a result of a campaign launched by a young theology student,

René Leudesdorff.[36] The RAF had proved very reluctant to hand over their toy.

Many Germans – above all German women – went to work for the Allies. The sculptress and later nun Tisa von der Schulenburg had fled her native Mecklenburg, leaving behind her the ancestral manor of Tressow and Trebbow, the Schloss where she had lived with her husband, C. U. von Barner. Tisa settled in Lübeck in the British Zone and went to work as a secretary to Heinz Biel, the half-English industry officer in the Military Government. She endured the endless complaints and applications, the dispossessed seeking to repossess, the petitions to restart local businesses from Niederegger Marzipan and Schwartauer Marmalade to the aeronautics company Dornier and the porcelain manufacturers Villeroy and Boch.

Her boss did not impress her. Had he been purely German, she thought, he would have rushed to join the Party. Like most other thinking Germans, Tisa was infuriated by the *Fragebogen*. She had flown in the face of her noble, Nazi father, married a Jew and gone to England before the war to become an artist.[37] She left to serve as a social worker in a British military depot in Glinde near Hamburg. There were two thousand German civilians there, 'flotsam and jetsam from every party and province. The former leading lawyer and a man who had been consul in Australia mucked in with merchants and workers; it was only about survival, income and bread.' The only question they asked was 'How do I survive?'[38] The British had promised to give her officer-status and she was responsible to the major commanding. That Christmas the British tried to inject a bit of party-spirit into the depot: 'the English [*sic*] failed to understand that we had no desire to dance, we had no desires at all; not to dance or to sing'. The soldiers fed hundreds of children. One of the sergeants told Tisa: 'The kids bit into the oranges and ate them skin and all, like apples.' Tisa not unreasonably concluded that these children had never encountered oranges.

The situation deteriorated with the weather that winter. The zone had never been self-sufficient. Even before the war it had produced only half the food it needed.[39] Two workers froze to death for want of warm bedding. Tisa managed to locate 200 blankets for 2,000 people – a find that was bound to cause more trouble than it cured. At midday the workers received a thin, evil-smelling soup. An hour later they were hungry again. A hundred men were suffering from dropsy. Big men weighed no more than fifty kilos. One of the British officers allowed them to take the leftovers from the mess – although this was highly illegal. They procured an oven, milk and potatoes and in time they were able to lay on a supplementary meal at midday. The men began to put on weight again. They were over the worst.

Sometimes they walked the fourteen kilometres to Billstedt where there were trains to Hamburg. Trams took them through vast expanses of ruins. Even four years after the end of the war the sight of Hamburg moved the American diplomat George Kennan to reflect on whether it had all been worth while: 'Here for the first time, I felt an unshakable conviction that no momentary military advantage . . . could have justified this stupendous, careless destruction of civilian life and of material values, built up laboriously by human hands over the course of centuries for purposes having nothing to do with war.'[40]

It was this barren townscape that struck Victor Gollancz during his time in Hamburg. He stayed at British officers' messes and marvelled at the copiousness of the menus; he went to the town hall and drank rare bottles of 'magnificent hock' which a careful concierge had rescued from the Nazis.[41] In a hovel he came across the stoic spirit of the north German as they eked out their days under a picture bearing the legend 'Lerne leiden ohne zu klagen' (Learn to suffer without complaint). It showed a picture of the Emperor Frederick, who died of throat cancer ninety-nine days into his reign.[42]

The British were not frank about demontage. In theory they washed their hands of it, but demontage was carried out in the British Zone on behalf of client states. German industrial installations were shipped out to Greece and Yugoslavia – which received equipment from Krupps.[43] Demontage was controlled by the Allied agreement of 24 January 1946 which established the Inter-Allied Reparations Agency, or IARA. America had ended the Lease–Lend Agreement six months before and presented Britain with a colossal bill, demanding cash on the nail. The British press was antipathetic to demontage, and the Americans were shocked at every British attempt to remove plants. Some of it could be written off as 'booty' which was not controlled by IARA, and in other instances it could be excused by the need to dismantle Category I War Plants (that way they were able to take home much-needed naval installations).[44]

The Soviets were desperate to grab what was left of the Ruhr. The British were supposed to hand over 10 per cent of what was produced. After 1948 those deliveries were stopped. Krupps in Essen was the property of all the Allies, but Clay in particular was keen to keep the Soviets out. Parts of the Krupps empire had fallen to the Poles in Silesia and the Russians in Magdeburg. Jet planes, wind tunnels and other interesting bits of military equipment were lifted out of the country as quickly as possible. In other instances Category I was stretched to include plants that might later offer competition with British industries. The Germans smelled a rat and suspected that they were seeing the implementation of the Morgenthau Plan. This led to attacks on CCG officials. Once or twice the British actually started up a valuable branch of German industry. One case in point was Volkswagen in Wolfsburg. The Nazis had intended their 'People's Car' or 'Kraft durch Freude Auto' (Strength through Joy car) to become the property of every decent German, and money was docked from their pay for that purpose, but by the time the war started only two had been built and the factory was turned over to war work. The British started the project up again, with Major Ivan Hirst at the wheel, and made 10,000 'beetles' before October 1946 largely for their own needs. The car became 'the wheels of the British occupation'.[45]

Gollancz watched demontage in the Ruhr and in Hamburg Docks. The removal of Hoechst from Dortmund threatened to ruin what was left of the city. In Hamburg large parts of the Bloem and Voss shipyard had been blown up. It was a short-sighted policy that removed the possibility of work for the starving people, and wantonly destroyed useful property. Despite statements by Hynd, Germans were being turned out of their homes. There was a terrible shortage of space: in Düsseldorf the average home amounted to 3.2 square metres. Meanwhile the British swanned around in an ugly way (although they did not force the Germans to walk in the road like the French). 'The plain fact is that there are two worlds in Germany today, the world of the conquered and the world of the conquerors. They meet at the peripheries, but their hearts beat in an inhuman isolation.'[46]

Tisa von der Schulenburg's sister-in-law Charlotte found a moment to return to her late husband's family house at Trebbow while the British still clung to the westernmost reaches of Mecklenburg. She reported to the CO, whom she found in one of the guest rooms looking out on to the lake. Over his head hung a portrait of Charlotte herself and the children. She waved the pass she had obtained in Plön. 'Ah, the lady in the painting,' he responded laconically. Everything had been moved by the refugees and soldiers and nothing looked right any more. She was not allowed to take the children's beds, but she did find the family porcelain – Meissen, Nymphenburg and Schlaggenwald – and by a ruse was able to enlist some soldiers to carry it out to the lorry she had got hold of. She found the beds she was looking for in the forester's house, as well as Fritz-Dietlof's armchair. She was able to retrieve a typewriter, a gramophone and some of her bedlinen. That night she and the children ate their frugal soup off the finest china. The next day was 28 June and the British yielded their toe-hold in Mecklenburg to the Russians.[47]

Ten-year-old Karl-Heinz Bohrer had seen little of the occupying armies since he was 'liberated' by American troops at Remagen. At the end of 1945 he was taken to Cologne to visit his estranged mother and the doctor she lived with. He had left the Rhineland city in 1943. Now it was completely transformed. In the centre not a single building was intact. As there was no shelter in Cologne, he went to live in southern Westphalia. At once he was aware of the British. They had already put their stamp on German life, in the same way as the other occupying powers. He recalls the pleasure of tinned sardines, white bread and black tea. The British army seemed to him to be more professional and 'more military' than the American. Its soldiers were calm, where Americans were noisy; he felt he had nothing more to fear. At school they learned English.

In the winter of 1946–7, Karl-Heinz was taken to the cinema for the first time by his Irish grandfather. He saw Laurence Olivier's *Henry V* in English, with German subtitles. He cried with happiness at the end, and had to be taken three times. He fell in love with the English language, which became an important factor in coming to terms with occupation. Looking back on the time he felt that the British pursued a sensitive but unflashy cultural policy in their zone.[48] For him, growing up in the west, a new orthodoxy was developing. Intellectually the period was informed by Jaspers, Habermas ('German history starts at Auschwitz') and Professor Heimpel of Göttingen. Hartwig von Hentig and Georg Picht proved influential pedagogues. Education was much discussed and the writings of Schiller invoked. Germans were not to get into the same mess again. The Nazis were temporarily cleared out of the universities, but those establishments remained otherwise unchanged until 1968. For him the outstanding political figure of the time was Carlo Schmid. What was to become West Germany sought to identify with the West.

The Beginnings of West Germany in the British Zone

In the Rhineland the former mayor of Cologne, Konrad Adenauer, had been forced into retirement by Hitler's men. He went on prolonged gardening leave, and resisted all attempts to become involved. He was suspicious of the July Plot against Hitler, but was imprisoned all the same. The Nazis had known what they were doing in the last months of the war. They executed some 5,000 people who might have created the cadre for a

post-Hitlerian Germany. Very few of those killed had any direct involve-
ment with the July Plotters. The bloodbath was intended to create a
political vacuum.

Cologne's proximity to France meant that Adenauer was liberated rather
earlier than any politician in Berlin. American tanks were seen in his home
village of Rhöndorf as early as 15 March 1945. The following day two
American officers arrived at Adenauer's door to ask him to resume the
office of mayor of Cologne. To their surprise he refused: he had three sons
away at war, and he feared reprisals. He must have been aware of what had
happened to the mayor of Aachen (he had been murdered). In his heart of
hearts, however, he might have already been eyeing up a bigger job: that of
post-war German leader.[49] Adenauer was put under some pressure to
change his mind. One who wanted him to take up the offer was Josef
Frings, the German primate and archbishop of Cologne. He was interested
in the idea of rebuilding the city, the medieval core of which had been
smashed by the 1,000-bomber raid. The ever-cautious Adenauer agreed to
run Cologne once hostilities were over, and he took up his old job on 3
May. In his earliest statements he was already seeking to make Prussia the
scapegoat for the failure of German democracy, even if it had been as a
Prussian that he had been elected mayor of Cologne and a member of the
Herrenhaus (or House of Lords) in 1917.

He was flattered that the Americans appeared to hold him in such high
esteem and had placed him at the top of their 'white list', although – as a
recent biographer has pointed out – this might have had something to do
with the fact that his name began with A.[50] After a while, the Americans
lost their glamour in his eyes: he found them childish and was relieved
when authority in the region passed to the British on 21 June. His relief
was premature, however – there was to be no repeat of the more courteous attitudes of 1918. The ban on frat was still in force, denazification was
on the cards, and – as one British officer put it – no German is *persona grata*
with the military government.[51] What is more, the British were the slowest of the Allies to allow the Germans to express themselves politically.
Montgomery made a promise to restore party politics on 6 August 1945,
but it was not until 29 September that parties became legal again.[52]

The French may have started as the poorest and least regarded of the
victorious Allies but it turned out that their plans to atomise Germany tal-
lied with the eventual solution to the problem. What they were proposing
for the Rhineland had possibilities: there you could erect a state that was
Catholic, free-market driven, anti-Prussian, federalist and dominated by the
Rhenish upper-middle classes. The European and German division along

ideological lines was no more or less than a foundation to build on. The German state would be made in the west and act as a sponge that might absorb the other parts of Germany at a later date. This was summed up by Wilhelm Hausenstern, ambassador to Paris at the time of the founding of the Federal Republic: 'Adenauer conceived the Federal Republic on the Rhenish, or even Lower Rhenish Axis.' The Rhine was the natural centre point for the new Europe, the link between Germany and western Europe. It was an ore that was a conglomerate 'Catholicism and liberalism, north and southern Europe, French lifestyle and Prussian virtue'.[53]

The mayor wanted to readjust the balance, above all by concluding a sort of concordat with the French. Prussia had had only a marginal role in the Holy Roman Empire, and Adenauer now chose to make his vision of Charlemagne's Europe into the foundation stone for Germany's future. Prussia had become a monster to him – he attributed to it all the vices of the Nazis, despite the fact that Prussia (which had amounted to two-thirds of pre-war Germany) was notably under-represented in Nazi Germany, and that most of the leaders of the movement came from the Catholic south and west. One of the most pungent – Joseph Goebbels – was a man from his beloved Rhineland. Adenauer was singing a tune that appealed to the Control Council: they too were keen to make Prussia the black sheep that had led Germany astray. It was a convenient argument anyway, because much of the Prussian heartland had been lost to Poland and Russia at Potsdam. Adenauer could clearly put it on with a trowel if he had to – but he didn't have to. On 25 February 1947, the Control Council issued its Law No. 46: 'The Prussian State which from early days has been a bearer of militarism and reaction in Germany has *de facto* ceased to exist.' Its remaining agencies and institutions were scrapped in 'the interests of preservation of peace and security of peoples and with the desire to assure further reconstruction of the political life of Germany on a democratic basis'.[54]

It seemed that there was a possibility of an agreement between Adenauer and the Allies, but the British frustrated him at every turn. It was then that he turned his attention to the French. They too were victims of the Allies, perhaps – their vanities were also wounded. But for de Gaulle, they might have had to brook the ignominy of military rule from London. The Yalta Conference had carved out a small corner of Germany to be ruled from Paris. Adenauer pinned his hopes on its expansion to cover Cologne, as de Gaulle was agitating for a larger slice of the cake. In the summer and autumn he had a number of meetings with the French arranged by his friend the Swiss consular official 'Uncle Toni' Weiss. The idea was

Germano-French economic co-operation in the Rhineland. He suggested that Germany should be broken up into three small quasi-autonomous states. Naturally he would be the ruler of the one that centred on the Rhineland.[55]

Weiss's undiplomatic wheeling and dealing caused anger in Berne, and Adenauer's flirtations annoyed the British. They may have known little about his meetings with the French, but they were aware that he was holding talks with politicians in Bad Godesberg and Königswinter aimed at creating the political party that would be the Christian Democratic Union, or CDU, of the post-war German right. His adversary was the head of the British Military Government in North Rhine Province, Brigadier John Barraclough, who thought Adenauer increasingly unreliable politically. Barraclough was a tough soldier, but not necessarily a shrewd political analyst. On 6 October Adenauer was summoned to appear before Barraclough and two other officers in Cologne and was denied even the right to sit down in their presence. They read out a letter dismissing him from office. He was to be banned from all political activity and was to leave Cologne as quickly as possible. This put a temporary end to his dalliance with the CDU, for which he was an obvious leader. Adenauer felt grossly insulted.[56]

The British clearly believed that Adenauer was incompetent. Cologne lagged behind the rest of North Rhine when it came to the business of clearing up and sanitising the city. As the director of Military Government, General Gerald Templer, put it, 'The city was in a terrible mess; no water, no drainage, no light, no food. It stank of corpses.'[57] The decision to sack Adenauer was regretted almost immediately. In Berlin, Noël (later Lord) Annan, then a colonel serving in the Political Division of the Control Council, saw that an awful gaffe had been committed, and both he and Captain Michael Thomas* were anxious to mend fences. Perhaps fearing loss of face, Barraclough was not prepared to reinstate Adenauer, but very soon the British allowed him the opportunity to indulge in politics again, albeit only within the limits of the city of Cologne. During the crisis, Annan went to see a badly shaken Adenauer. He broached the issue of the politician's attitude to Britain. Adenauer replied that he was not anti-British, but that 'he found difficulty in seeing Britain as a European state'.[58] As a result of the interview, the ban on Adenauer's political activity was completely lifted, and he was free to come and go in Cologne whenever he pleased. He could now play his role in the founding of the CDU.

---

* The former Ulrich Holländer, son of the Berlin writer Felix Holländer. As a Jewish refugee he had served in the British Pioneer Corps.

Adenauer had rivals for the time being. Some of the July Plotters survived and were popular with the German people and, more important, with the Allies. The Christian trades-unionist leader Jakob Kaiser, who based his 'Christian socialism' on the Sermon on the Mount, [59] the former Centre Party politician and minister Andreas Hermes, and Adenauer's later foreign policy adviser Herbert Blankenhorn had been part of Helmuth James von Moltke's Kreisau Circle, which had looked forward to the dawn of a new Europe. At Moltke's Schloss at Kreisau in Silesia they discussed dropping notions of hegemony in order to dig out the roots of war. Germany had been perceived as a European counterweight to the United States as early as 1942.[60] The French right had also listed towards the idea of a united Europe during the Collaboration; they recognised the *fait accompli* of occupation.

Kaiser's views did not prevail in the infant CDU, however, because he saw the French as the enemy. The French consistently opposed German unity, which they saw as an attempt to restore the venomous Reich. Adenauer, on the other hand, envisaged working with the French from the beginning.[61] Kurt Schumacher, head of the SPD in the British Zone, thought the French the enemy for different reasons: they wanted to bleed Germany of its resources.[62] Andreas Hermes was in an uncomfortable position, fronting the fledgling party in the Russian Zone. Adenauer's task was to assert his authority in the British Zone and to take control of the Party.

Hermes was expelled from Berlin for opposing the Soviet policy on land reform. That meant that Adenauer's chief rival was Kaiser in Berlin. Kaiser was backing the wrong horse in the old Reich capital, which was to be sidelined and virtually eliminated from post-war German politics. Adenauer was not averse to using pure fabrication to do down his political enemies. He claimed that Kaiser had been holding talks with Soviet officials and former Wehrmacht generals, which was enough to discredit him with the Party. Adenauer's position was shored up by the arrest of 600 members of the Party in the Soviet Zone in August 1947.[63] In the end it proved very easy for him to grab the presidency of the CDU in the British Zone and see off any possible challenge from Hermes.

On the left, Adenauer's rival was Schumacher, a First World War veteran and front-line socialist politician. He came from Culm in West Prussia and was the very model of a Protestant Prussian. His mentality contrasted with that of Adenauer. There was none of the cosiness of the Rhineland. The Culmer was always on the battlements, watching out for the arrival of the enemy. He had lost an arm fighting for Germany only to be rewarded by nine years, nine months and nine days in Hitler's camps, including an eight-year stint in Dachau. His solid principles and experience during the Third Reich made him one of the very few German politicians with spotlessly democratic credentials.[64] He felt very much alone at first: his colleagues, the fighters, were all dead. The concentration camps, the bombing and the 20 July Plot 'have swallowed so many of us'.[65]

He was soon seen as a potential post-war German leader, but he fell by the wayside when West Germany moved to the right. As the leader of the SPD in the Western zones, he might have been expected to find favour with the ruling Labour Party in Britain, but he was not impressed by British socialists. The British nonetheless felt responsible for him. When he went to Berlin in February 1946 he was provided for: 'The visitor from Hanover travelled in a British aircraft, slept in a British bed, had a British car with a British escort at his disposal and was for the duration of his stay in Berlin accompanied by a British officer with a revolver at the ready.' This British patronage was later used by Adenauer to suggest that Schumacher was a Labour Party puppet.[66]

The SPD was splitting in two. The leader in the Soviet Zone, Otto Grotewohl, was taking his faction into the new communist–socialist front, or SED. It was not a road Schumacher was prepared to take. He had seen the communists wreck Parliament in 1932, at the time of the *Preussenschlag* which brought down the Prussian state government and opened the way to Nazism. His soulmate in Berlin was Gustav Dahrendorf, another 'red' who had done time in a concentration camp, and a bitter opponent of the SED. The British had been hedging their bets. At one stage they were wooing Grotewohl, or 'Jugo' (*der junge Gott* because of his imposing build and striking looks). The Russians were using both stick and carrot: to bring over the socialists. Dahrendorf's son Ralf, later a British peer, remembered the carrot: it came in the form of 'pajoks', food parcels at Christmas.[67]

In Berlin that winter Schumacher had talks with Hynd and the political advisers Sir William Strang and Christopher Steel, and with Clay and Murphy. The British thought the Russians would kidnap him. He was evidently a man who inspired protection. Dachau had wrecked him physically, a fact that was further compounded by his hunger strike at the concentration camp. His assistants combed the black market for milk and butter which they thought would assuage his delicate stomach. Yet Schumacher did little to help by his diet of black coffee and cigarettes.[68] This austerity was not everyone's cup of tea. Like many Prussians, Schumacher lacked charm. That was where Carlo Schmid came in. He had the social graces Schumacher lacked, and could bring the SPD into Germany's shabby drawing rooms. The half-French Schmid was deemed to be at home any-where: talking about Baudelaire, writing poetry, dealing with points of law as a professor of jurisprudence or eating with the former rulers of Württemberg off the finest china.[69]

Schumacher may have taken up the British offer of protection, but he was bitter about the Allies, whose reputation was less than spotless in his eyes. He thought the idea of collective guilt an abomination. Writing to Hans Vogel, he vented his ire:

> You could not imagine what a frightful effect the propaganda attempt to impose 'collective guilt' on the German people has had on the German opponents of Nazism. The men and women in our country who even before 1933 risked so much in the fight against Nazism and Big Business, who after the assumption of power, at a time when the present victorious powers were still concluding state treaties with the Hitler regime, were working underground and were being put in prisons and concentration camps; they should recognise their guilt. They must do this in no way and in no circumstances.

Schumacher felt himself personally defamed by the notion of collective guilt.[70]

Adenauer and Schumacher were mutually antipathetic. The Protestant Prussian was for a central administration, the Catholic Rhinelander for a federal state. They had difficulty speaking to one another. Michael Thomas saw it in their lifestyles: Adenauer was *gutbürgerlich*, while Schumacher worked from a bombed-out building, and yet his talk was coloured by wit and irony. The British brought the two men together in Hamburg in March 1946 to tell them they were going to merge the states of North Rhine and Westphalia in response to the Russians introducing a one-party state in their zone. Adenauer remembered Sir Sholto Douglas making his entry to 'drum rolls and the blast of trumpets'. It was all very colonial: the Germans might speak, but the British kept all the power in their own hands.[71] They appointed an old schoolfriend of Adenauer's, Rudolf Amelunxen, to head the administration. Adenauer remained aloof, as he did when the CDU was asked to form part of the governing party in the Landtag. In reality the new Nordrhein-Westfalen was Adenauer's dream: one of the three quasi-independent states he had imagined for Germany. He would pick up the western German remnants of his detested Prussia, and the centre of gravity for Germany would be shipped several hundred miles to the west. Schumacher was appalled.

Adenauer had not been singled out – the British behaved in a super-cilious way towards several German post-war politicians. One was Karl

Arnold, Oberbürgermeister of Düsseldorf. He was second only to Adenauer in the CDU and minister president designate in Nordrhein-Westfalen, but he failed to grab the top job because he was too modest and believed his time had passed. Victor Gollancz called him 'one of the half dozen best Germans I met'.[72] George Clare had arranged to meet him at his Berlin mess, but the mess butler informed him that Germans were not allowed. Not only had they not let him in, they had left him outside in the cold. This occurred in March 1947, some eighteen months before the restoration of the German state.[73]

Culture

The British management of the arts was closely bound up with weeding out Nazis – an admirable aim in itself, but one which had very little to do with promoting cultural activity. It became increasingly obvious, as well, that the British were netting just the small fry, and there was more and more grumbling at home. The complaints about the denazification policy eventually spread to the Germans, who were annoyed to see the Party big-shots go free while the authorities continued to harass rank-and-file members who had done nothing monstrous.[74]

The British did a few things well, if half-heartedly. They had their own version of the Russian culture club, Die Möwe. It was a requisitioned villa in the Branitzerplatz in Neu Westend where they could entertain screen and theatre people over a whisky. The club had its own chatelaine in the person of Else Bongers, a former dancer who had suffered under the Nazis.[75] The British also sponsored performances of the Berlin Philharmonic Orchestra and operas at the Volksoper in their sector. Just like for Margret Boveri, the first post-war concert proved a memorable event for the Kaiser's daughter, Victoria Louise. In her case she heard the Berlin Philharmonic play in Celle. Celibidache was conducting. As there was no other room available, they used the riding school of the town stud, and the podium was set up in the same place as they had once trained the celebrated Celle stallions, while the chairs were laid out in the sand of the riding school. Music 'tore us away from the murkiness of our everyday lives and lifted us into the sphere of the pure and beautiful. It was like redemption.' Wilhelm Furtwängler might not have expressed it better himself.[76]

9

Life in the French Zone

When they at last reappeared, their faces looked as white as the slips of paper they carried in their hands, and they were speechless. They had spent that half an hour arguing with three stubborn, disinterested little bureaucrats already half asleep with wine. The men had carefully examined, or pretended to, every paper in their possession and then insisted on their filling out a sheaf of forms. Only after these had been carefully read, checked and rechecked were four Americans given permission to inhabit two rooms in Stuttgart for the night.

James Stern, *The Hidden Damage*, London 1990, 104–5

France's German policy looked suspiciously like a return to Cardinal Richelieu and the Thirty Years War. The French were largely indifferent to the question of whether a German was a Nazi or not, or whether he needed to be cured; it was enough to be a German.[1] They wanted a fragmentation of the enemy who had invaded their territory three times in under the century. The man they installed to enforce their will on the ground was a hero of their African wars, General Pierre Koenig – Scipio Africanus. Unlike Scipio, however, Koenig was anything but patrician. His civilian sidekick could not have been more different: Emile Laffon was a brilliant lawyer, a member of the resistance and an intimate of de Gaulle, albeit a socialist.[2]

The French were not free of the sort of behaviour more commonly associated with the Russians. Even after the scandals of Freudenstadt, Stuttgart and Vaihingen, James Stern heard the testimony of a half-Jewish woman friend in Seldau in Bavaria. The husband was away working in his hospital in Munich when the French Moroccans arrived at the farmhouse. They left the woman alone – 'by some miracle they didn't touch her' – but the whole house was looted and most of the furniture smashed. They killed the livestock and stole whatever they could carry.[3]

Initially the French were deeply unpopular in Germany because of their insistence on coming as conquerors. As far as the atrocities were concerned, they adhered to the policy 'Never apologise, never explain.' They had their grievances: the bits and bobs of Germany that they had received off the Anglo-American plate continued to make little sense. They had 64 per cent of Baden[4] – the *Residenz* in Baden-Baden but not the capital, Karlsruhe. In Württemberg they had Hohenzollern, the minuscule former territory of the Catholic cousins of the rulers of Prussia and Germany. It was significant that the capital – it hardly merits such a grandiose description – Sigmaringen had been the last seat of Pétain's and Laval's Vichy government. The French ruled Sigmaringen, but not the coveted Stuttgart, and they had large amounts of the Rhineland, including Mainz – but not Cologne or Frankfurt.

They came into formal possession of the 'Brassière' in July 1945. Unlike the Americans, who requisitioned entire areas and fenced them off from the German population, the French sequestered good houses and villas but erected no fences. In Baden-Baden they put their administrative bodies in the best hotels of the spa town.[5] Military headquarters was in Freudenstadt – an extraordinary choice of location – but one that was, perhaps, in keeping with their possession of Sigmaringen: they were the best custodians of their own secrets. They continued to voice their disgruntlement, and tried to swap their portion of Württemberg for the rest of Baden, which would have afforded them not only a big town in Karlsruhe, but also a territory that was contiguous with their border, but the Americans were not willing to do the deal.[6] The Americans wanted the whole motorway that went from Karlsruhe to Munich, via Stuttgart.

Proportionally speaking, the French were the most densely populated of the Western occupiers: they had eighteen men for every thousand Germans, the British had ten, the Americans three. They set about the business of denazifying, politically re-educating and punishing war criminals while assuring the population that they would have a 'bearable standard of living'.[7] They also punished at least some of the rapists of Freudenstadt and Stuttgart. Nothing was said to the locals, but the soldiers were informed that such acts were not to be tolerated, and death sentences were handed out.[8] Being kind but firm was meant to conceal a darker purpose – the French had not forgotten their aims to sever parts of western Germany like the Rhine, the Ruhr and the Saar, and they wanted to encourage provincial loyalty above all. They were frustrated in their attempts to prise the Ruhr away from the British. Meanwhile they transferred what resources they could to France, and rounded up all available manpower for their own version of the STO, the *service de travail obligatoire*, by which the French had been forced to work for the Nazis.

The Soviet example of cruelty towards the Germans was one reason for the milder treatment they received in the ZOF, or Zone d'Occupation Française. There was a conflict between the two wings of the administration in Baden-Baden, or 'Little Vichy' as the French communists rendered it, Vichy also being a spa. The communists were alluding too to the fact that there were quite a few Vichy men lying low in occupied Germany. The military chief Pierre Koenig was anxious to be tough, while his civilian counterpart Emile Laffon believed that occupation meant reform, a difference of approach that led to frequent fights. The French took all they could: between 1945 and 1947 some 45–47 per cent of the ZOF's exports left for France. Their sale in France made the ZOF a healthy profit of eight million dollars, while the Germans were subjected to heavy taxes, strict rations and a wage freeze. On the other hand the inhabitants of the ZOF could boast some advantage over, say, the inhabitants of Brandenburg or Thuringia: they had a free press, democratic elections and the right to an education that stressed French and European cultural achievement.[9]

The Germans did not entirely acquiesce in French rule, especially given their supposed conquerors' insistence on their 'right to plunder' and their view that 'le boche payera' (the Hun will pay). The half-French professor of law Carlo Schmid in Tübingen knew how to play the fish. He was quickly made chief of the ZOF's Democratic Union and, when governments were formed in the French provinces, he became minister president of Württemberg-Hohenzollern.[10] Schmid was an outstanding politician, the father of the basic law (the Federal Republic's constitution) and no French stooge. Within the SPD he appeared to be a federalist, but was rather vague about this when challenged.[11] He fought for German rights: 'Democracy without sovereignty is a contradiction in terms,' he told his audiences. He also railed against the terrible demontage in the zone. He was not alone. In October 1947, for example, there were strong objections to cutting the electricity at Tuttlingen Hospital between 7.30 a.m. and noon and again from 4 p.m. to 8. It was pointed out that operations were being performed and babies born. On 21 June that year the Baden minister of economics Dr Lais had complained 'before God and humanity' that more machines were being dismantled and taken to France.[12] 'Unlicensed requisitions' amounted to somewhere between fifty and seventy million Reichsmarks in pre-war values. Ludwig Erhard estimated the value of the machinery going west at RM180 million in 1945–6 alone.[13]

Sometimes the French showed themselves more pragmatic than the Americans. Where the latter had sequestered IG Farben and banished the directors, the French allowed BASF in Ludwigshafen to remain as it was. On the other hand they made no bones about pocketing a chlorine business in Rheinfelden, a viscose business in Rottweil, the Preussag mines or the chemicals group Rhodia in Freiburg-im-Breisgau and awarding them to French concerns. In Friedrichshafen they shipped out everything useful in the Zeppelin works and did much the same at Dornier and Maybach.[14] Clay voiced his frustration at the French 'living off the land' in Baden-Württemberg, but it was to some extent an expression of a more old-fashioned attitude to war and conquest, where naked self-interest played a large part.[15]

The French too managed to pick up a few scientists, whom they wanted for their missile programme. There had been a research institute outhoused at Biberach in their zone. The Germans were lured over to work for them by the promise of excellent conditions. They could live in Germany and work in France. There was Kehl opposite Strasbourg, and Neuf Brisach on the other side of the Rhine to Alt Breisach. One of the scientists, Helmut von Zborowski, invented the coleoptor, a pioneering VTOL aircraft.[16]

Reading Elena Skrjabina's account of life near Koblenz in the French Zone, you would believe all was sweetness and light. The French had not been present at Yalta, and had made no promises to return Russian nationals. A Soviet commission for repatriating Russian citizens had been set up in a nearby castle, but Elena was spared the consequences of Operation Keelhaul, which probably saved her life. She had spoken French from childhood, and this evidently made her sympathetic to the officers of the garrison. They arrived at the beginning of July 1945 and a few days later she was helping their cook procure veal for the 14 July celebrations. The Russians quite naturally fared better than the Germans, who were being rounded up for heavy labour in France, but not all Germans by any means suffered in this way, and returning soldiers were allowed to go back to their homes.[17]

When Karl-Heinz Bohrer went to school in the Black Forest, he came face to face with life in the French Zone. At the outset the French were the most hated of the four occupying powers. They threw their weight around, requiring Germans to walk in the roads in the university city of Freiburg-im-Breisgau. Karl-Heinz had heard reports of atrocities carried out by Moroccan troops. The locals laughed at the operatic uniforms. The French wanted to have their revenge for the German occupation, and the Germans resented the political imposition of French 'victory'. That changed with time. For Karl-Heinz the next few years were marked by an awakening, political and erotic. He read Eugen Kogon's book *Der SS-Staat* which was pretty well the first in German to examine the machinery of Hitler's terror. He discovered French culture, first of all in the little cinema in the tiny village of Bickendorf near his school; he saw *La Belle et la bête*, *Les Enfants du paradis*, *La Mort de Danton* and *Sous les toits de Paris*. Among his neighbours, France – Paris in particular – became chic. The antipathy to all things French disappeared. Boys wore Basque berets and hung French posters in their dormitories. They longed to be accepted by the French.[18] That was a long time in coming. Paul Falkenburger, a Frenchman who taught at Freiburg University, recalls that it was not until 1947 that there was any meeting between young Germans and French, and that that first occasion took place in Titisee in the Black Forest.[19]

Berets became a potent symbol for post-war German youth. Ruth Friedrich saw them cropping up like mushrooms in Berlin: 'Anyone who felt they had something to say wears a black beret. There have never been so many berets in the city. They are the Phrygian bonnets of the first post-war weeks in Berlin.'[20]

The French acquired the Saar at the four-power conference in Paris in April 1946. They were once again the keenest to return to the *Kleinstaaterei* – the system of small, impotent states that had been Germany before 1806 – and to this end were reluctant to join Bizonia. French attitudes to Germany changed radically after the end of the war. At first they wanted merely to milk the country, but soon they saw the point of wooing the defeated Germans. President de Gaulle did this as early as October 1945 when he visited the ZOF and spoke of the need to return to ordinary life, to reconstruct the economy. The Germans and the French had to work together 'because we are Europeans and Westerners'.[21] Of course the reason for this was de Gaulle's spat with Moscow. The Soviet leaders had gone cold on him, and he could no longer rely on the Russians to get his own way.

De Gaulle was still insisting on a veto for the central agencies at the Control Council. Koenig was happy to take on the role of opposing any attempt to reunite Germany, which removed any chance of a centralised railway system and trades union movement. Koenig came up against Clay, who was anxious to re-establish sovereignty so that American troops could go home. Here the French became the unconscious allies of the British, who feared just that – an American departure. Clay was tempted to proceed without France, which was deliberately segmenting Germany.

At the New Year of 1946 de Gaulle insisted that Germany be re-created as a confederation, not a Reich. As the barometer dropped the French were as pitiless as ever in their demands for coal. Production in the Ruhr had fallen to 12 per cent of the 1943 level. In June 1945 the British commander Montgomery had insisted that the coal be kept in Germany 'to prevent . . . unrest and disorder'.[22] At the Conference of Foreign Ministers (CFM) in Moscow in December French demands for coal went up again. They required annual shipments of twenty million tons from 1947. Once again they dished the idea of central agencies by rejecting the suggestion that there should be a central body looking after finance. Koenig was prepared to accept a German commission of experts, providing that it did not operate west of the Rhine (which the French hoped would fall to them). Clay could scarcely conceal his annoyance at the Control Council.[23] It was suspected that he intentionally disrupted shipments of wheat to the ZOF.[24] Later he quite openly proposed stopping deliveries. Clay was slow to decide that the real danger to peace came from Moscow, not Paris.

The central-agencies argument was eventually won by the French when, as the Cold War broke out, the British for one saw the possibility of centralised, Berlin-based bodies falling into the hands of the Soviets. The French remained at odds with the policy of the Anglo-Americans, however. Their view was that the German economy should serve their needs, while the Russians wanted to hold it down; as far as London and Washington were concerned, Germany should have been allowed to enjoy reasonable levels of industrial activity. To this end Clay halted the dismantling of industrial sites in his zone in May 1946.[25]

France had a chance to show off in July and September 1946. First came the Paris CFM and later, also in Paris, the much vaunted Peace Conference that was no such thing. The mood among the victorious Allies had changed once again after Churchill's Fulton speech that March. The former prime minister's sabre-rattling was not popular at first: his American audience thought he was showing himself an imperialist. It was now the turn of Soviet foreign minister Molotov to try to seduce the Germans. In July he issued a critique of the Western Allies, interpreting the French *idée chérie* of detaching the Ruhr as 'agrarianisation' in the spirit of the loopy Morgenthau Plan. Such measures would only breed a spirit of revenge. The Allies needed to render Germany a peaceful, democratic state.[26]

In 1946 the outstanding French figure of his time, the apostle of Franco-German reconciliation Robert Schuman, entered the lists.[27] Schuman seemed almost fated to play his role. He had been born in Luxembourg in

1886, and went to school there before attending four German universities. He became a lawyer in Metz, in German Lorraine, on the eve of the First World War. After the war he represented a Lorraine constituency in Paris, now that the province had returned to France. In 1946 he was made minister of finance under Bidault and, shortly after that, foreign minister. For nine months from November 1947, he was president of the Council, or prime minister. His tenure corresponded to the early period of the Berlin blockade.*

At first Schuman's line echoed that of de Gaulle. He coveted the Ruhr and opposed German unity, stressing the need for a federal German state. Germany in a segmented state was less dangerous. Yet he was clear that Germany needed to be brought back as an equal partner to play its role in the concert of nations. Provided it could accept its 'harmless', federal structure, Schuman was prepared to see it released from the doghouse. He also knew that individual European nations had little chance in competition with the great power blocs: the United States, the Soviet empire in eastern Europe and the British Empire. They needed to federate themselves in order to succeed. The first step towards the European Union would be taken with the formation of the Council of Europe at Strasbourg in 1949. It was at the then German Strasbourg University that Schuman had presented his doctoral dissertation.[28]

The Anglo-Americans were proceeding towards Bizonia: the merging of their territories which the British believed would cut costs. The pro-Soviet ministers in the French cabinet kept France out of the arrangement. The Paris Peace Conference was held at the Palais du Luxembourg, but although it was billed as an assembly on the scale of the Versailles conference that had followed the First World War, in reality it was empowered only to deal with peripheral issues, settling border questions in Italy and eastern Europe.

In September 1946 it was James Byrnes's turn to wag his finger at the Russians in Stuttgart. Germany, according to the US secretary of state, was an economic unit, and the aim was economic revival and democratic self-government. American troops would stay in Germany until Germany was secure. Byrnes's peroration was followed up by Bevin's in the House of Commons, which alluded to the presence of PCF (Communist Party) ministers in the French government. The Ruhr was not up for grabs, and Britain and America were ready for Bizonia. The American economic adviser General William Draper proposed that the French enter Trizonia as

---

* See below Chapter 20.

a means of goading Russia, but the French continued to hold aloof, even imposing a customs wall around their zone in the Saar in December 1946, much to Clay's exasperation.[29]

The French had lowered their demands for German coal. They now pegged their needs at half a million tons a month for 1947, rising to a million thereafter. It was feared that the German economy might catch up with France's. Shipments, however, were fixed by output at the mines: at a daily production of 280,000 tons, 21 per cent could be exported. This would rise to 25 per cent only when production passed 370,000 tons.[30] French demands continued to irk Clay. On 6 February 1949 he wrote, 'Sometimes I wonder who conquered Germany, who pays the bill, and why?' He had a successful meeting with Schuman the following month, however, and expressed an interest in his project for a Western European Union.[31]

Culture

De Gaulle's persistent noises about the Rhineland made most Germans think he wanted to annex it to France. He insisted, however, that French policy was only about security, and that the Rhineland was to be a buffer-zone. Where French intentions were generally treated with suspicion, their cultural policy was a startling success. This was very largely due to Raymond Schmittlein, who was director of culture in Baden-Baden. Schmittlein had been born in Roubaix in the north of France, but his mother was Alsatian and he had cousins on the far side of the Rhine. He was *agrégé* in German, and had studied at the Humboldt University in Berlin, where he met his wife. He had taught at the University of Kaunas and had headed the French Institute in Riga. He was a Gaullist. His solution to denazification was to lure the people away from dodgy ideology through culture.[32]

The famous Weimar novelist Alfred Döblin reappeared in Germany in French uniform and became a literary censor in Baden-Baden. By his own testimony, towering piles of books were placed before him, written either during the war or just after. Suppression had not done wonders for German letters, he thought. With no pun intended (Günter Grass's first successful novel, *The Tin Drum*, was not published until 1959), he wrote, 'At first the only thing that grew on the ground was grass and weeds.'[33] He founded a literary journal, and formed part of the delegation that inaugurated the new University of Mainz. The journey to the inauguration ceremony was an adventure in itself. As they approached the cathedral city they saw the wrecks of factories 'as if brought down by an earthquake' and then the city centre: 'But where was Mainz? All that one could see were ruins, faceless people, twisted beams, empty façades: that was Mainz.'[34] In the old barracks that was now the university Döblin watched civilians and military figures leafing through the translated transcripts of the speeches that morning. There were British and American uniforms scattered along the rows. An orchestra struck up the overture from *The Magic Flute*. Men came in wearing black gowns and mortar boards. Döblin was reminded of a high-school graduation in the United States. The president of the region gave a speech in which he described the new university as the key to the material and cultural revival of the region.[35]

The invited guests from the Anglo-American zones aside, the French kept themselves culturally aloof. Mainz newspapers could not be obtained in Frankfurt and vice versa.[36] French art, literature and architecture remained popular into the 1960s and 1970s, despite the drubbing the Germans received during the first years of the occupation, and the French were not embarrassed to export their talent. In Mainz the French architect Marcel Lods, a pupil of Le Corbusier, drew up the plans to rebuild the city. French culture remained the legacy of the occupation – the rest has been forgotten.

IO

Austria's Zones and Sectors

The 8 May!
The day, the hour when every bell in Vienna proclaimed peace and
the end of the Second World War. I was lying on an upturned fridge,
unwashed and unshaven, covered in filth in my 'partisan uniform' in
a coal cellar in the Plösslgasse in the 4th Bezirk. The door to the cellar
was guarded by a Red Army soldier speaking only a smattering of pig-
German, who played *ad nauseam* the first bars of the Volga Boat
Song – he clearly couldn't manage the rest.

Carl Szokoll, *Die Rettung Wiens*, Vienna 2001, 380

Vienna

On 9 May 1945 Cardinal Innitzer said Mass for Karl Renner's new
Soviet-backed administration. All the working bells in the city were
set to chime and celebrate the end of the war in Europe. Vienna was still
a sad, wrecked city. More than 80,000 homes had been wholly or partially
destroyed and 35,000 people had nowhere to live. For the most part there
was no gas, electricity or telephone. Large tracts of the 1st Bezirk had been
turned to rubble in the last months of the war and in the wild looting that
followed liberation. The commercial Kärntnerstrasse was among the worst
hit. The French commander, Lieutenant-General Emile-Marie Béthouart,
described it as a heap of ruins. At one end the gutted opera house, at the
other the roofless cathedral, the Steffl.[1]

Unlike Berlin, Vienna was still recognisable under the dust and rubble.
The American novelist John Dos Passos came at the end of 1945 and
admitted that the city still 'wears the airs and graces of a metropolis . . .
Vienna is an old musical comedy queen dying in a poorhouse, who can still
shape her cracked lips into a confident smile of a woman whom men have
loved, when the doctor makes his rounds of the ward.'[2]

The Russians were still the real power in the city, and Austrians were required to fetch and carry. When Graf Alfred Sturgkh turned up three-quarters of an hour late for a meeting at the Chamber of Commerce it was because the count had had to unload a delivery of potatoes from a lorry.[3] Anything might happen: in Hietzing people were being thrown out of their houses for the benefit of the Russian garrison. The Margaréthas had to move up to the attic to make room for a general. For the time being they had a courteous colonel lodging with them who brought them flowers and wine and went to the ballet.[4] The former Nazis were proscribed. Most Pgs tried to conceal their pasts, some tried to hide themselves, others committed suicide – such as Josef Schöner's friend the dermatologist Professor Scherber and his wife, who came from Komotau in German Bohemia. Now that German-speakers were being slaughtered with impunity, there was no point in going home.[5]

The cautious Eugen Margarétha thought it wrong to be too black and white about the Nazis. 'However just the measure might be, it is possibly going to come down hard on some individual cases who are decent fellows in themselves . . . men who are hard-working in their domain and indispensable people will be excluded from the economy.' There was a little mutual backscratching to be done. Margarétha's greengrocer in the Naschmarkt wanted him to sign an affidavit to say that he had been a good man – despite membership of the Party. Margarétha received a lettuce for his pains.[6] He had little sympathy for most of the Austrian Nazis. Now they were saying that they had been forced to join the Party, and that they had been compelled to 'torture hundreds of thousands of people to death, to gas them or kill them in some other way! I am not a vengeful sort, but I have no patience when I see and hear these now innocent lambs.'[7]

There was another side to the coin. As the Germans were also well aware, the concentration camps had housed not just political prisoners and innocent Jews or gypsies; they had also been used for hardened criminals. Now all former KZlers were allowed to jump the queue for ration cards, flats and other benefits. Eighteen thousand homes in Vienna were made available to them, as well as to the bombed-out and the homeless. Margarétha's office had had a visit from a couple of former inmates 'who have now mastered the situation and are demanding jobs, accommodation, clothing etc'. They were 'common criminals. Now you can't tell the difference between this sort and the poor devils.'[8]

Subsistence levels had dwindled to next to nothing. There were 1,500,000 people in the city and around forty lorries available to bring in supplies. Rationing was reintroduced on 6 May, and on 1 June the daily intake was fixed by the Russian authorities. The citizens were to have 250–300 grams of bread a day, with 50 grams of fat and 20 grams of sugar. When the refugees came flooding in across the Czech border the situation worsened. Starving German Bohemians and Moravians were not averse to robbing houses in the north-eastern Weinviertel in the hope of finding food. The Viennese looked to the Western Allies for succour.[9]

They were making slow progress. On 11 May the Americans were reported in Amstetten, the Russians had gone into Graz. Later the Americans took Klagenfurt in Carinthia. The British were having to contend with unforeseen changes to their Austrian policy, because in their absence Tito's partisans had moved into Carinthia and made it known that they intended to keep for Yugoslavia part of the territory earmarked for the British Zone. In Vienna on 16 May the mood was very low, because of the delay in seeing Western troops in the city.[10] After a month of looting and rape the Western Allies were needed to raise the tone of the occupation. The Viennese appreciated there might be disadvantages too: the Westerners would seek to control the administration down to the smallest detail, whereas the Russians had an 'Asiatic liberality' coupled with a sloppiness that allowed the inhabitants of their zone to get on with what they wanted.[11] This was evidently the version edited for Austria. The Soviets did not behave like this in Germany. The Austrians were not the enemy, after all. The Russians were very little interested in the Austrian Pgs, for example. The Western Allies might just have dug a little deeper. Some people maintain that the Soviets were more interested in wiping out the opposition, because they impeded the smooth exercise of power in the zone.[12]

As it was, a small advance party from the Western Allies did arrive on 3 June, just 186 of them in 140 cars. Field Marshal Alexander declined to go, and sent Major-General Winterton instead. General Flory represented the Americans and General Cherrière the French. They were spotted in the Lainzer Strasse and covered with flowers. The Viennese received them with jubilation. The Westerners took no notice of this effusion: the no-frat rule was still in force. The story was now ebbing out: the Allies were going to treat the Austrians 'differently', but not necessarily better. The Russians had allotted eleven Hietzing villas for the use of the Western Allies. The purpose of their visit was to work out the partition of the country, but although the Russians plied them with caviar, they proved truculent when it came to showing them airfields.* The Westerners were

---

* The Americans were eventually allotted Tulln, the French Götzendorf and the British the partial use of Schwechat – now the main airport for the city. Eventually the British and the French shared Schwechat.

required to take their leave on the 10th, but did not depart until the 13th. The Russians were keen to reach an agreement – they were fed up with paying for the provision of the Austrian capital.[13]

New problems were emerging for Austria: huge numbers of people were converging on the impoverished country. Around 100,000 Germans from Prague, Brno and southern Moravia were streaming across the frontier with their Czech tormenters in hot pursuit. The subject was on everyone's lips that June. Austria had no border guards to turn them back; the Russians did nothing, and they had no food to feed them with. In Krems in Lower Austria the refugees were deeply resented.[14]

Renner was in favour of letting them in, even if only 20 per cent of them had any claim to Austrian citizenship.* Renner was from Moravia himself, from just outside Nikolsburg,† where many of the local Germans had been massacred.[15] The rest of them, said Schöner, were Reich Germans, or German-speaking Czechs. The communist minister of the interior, Honner, was keen to throw them out, and – when they woke up to the fact that they had another 300,000 mouths to feed – the Russians were too. The question was where could they send them? The Czechs maintained they were leaving their country of their own free will – like those who were quitting Poland.[16]

As regards the German-speaking Czechs, the attitude was less *sauve qui peut* than *on a pu nous sauver!* (and to hell with the rest of them). The future president of the National Bank, Margarétha, had a full report on the expulsions from a Dr Dyszkant who had visited Brno and Prague. Germans, 'but Austrians as well, are being chased away and on the road from Brno to Vienna you see endless columns of refugees in a most miserable state who pluck the fruit from the cherry trees as their only form of nourishment. In Prague you hear not one word of German spoken any more.'[17]

In exchange for the 'ethnic Austrians' Austrians wanted to see the backs of any German nationals left in their country. In 1945 there were 346,000 or them. Ten years later that number had dwindled to 18,600. They were 'treated with no consideration, dispossessed, properly seen to and expelled'.[18] The new foreign minister, Dr Karl Gruber, was one of their most outspoken critics. They had once again asserted their superiority over the 'sloppy' Austrians. Gruber wanted revenge: 'only with difficulty and full of fury did the Austrians put up with the long years of Prussian condescension and meddle-o-mania'. Gruber added that he thought that

---

* They were *all* citizens of Austria-Hungary before 1918.
† Schärf was also from Nikolsburg.

many of the Germans had come to Austria to escape from the consequences of their actions at home. There was possibly some truth in the
assertion, but it sounded like a dangerously familiar game of putting the
Allies off the scent.[19]

Far from showing sympathy for their ethnic German brothers and sisters
in Czechoslovakia, Hungary and Yugoslavia, the Austrians now began to
flex their muscles a bit to demand territory for their martyred state. These
demands did not come from the federal government, but they had the
backing of Gruber, especially in his capacity as governor of the Tyrol. If the
Poles could have some more land, why not the Austrians? The newly
recreated Burgenland still hankered after the city of Ödenburg (Sopron in
Hungarian), which had been awarded to Hungary at Saint-Germain and
had failed to come back with the rest of Burgenland because of a 'falsified
plebiscite';[20] from Josef Rehrl, the governor of Salzburg, came a call to
detach Berchtesgaden and the surrounding region from Bavaria – despite
its ominous past – as well as the Rupertiwinkel, which had been estranged
from the archbishopric of Salzburg in 1809.

When they were not planning a merger with Switzerland (there was
some talk of this in the Tyrol too), the Vorarlberger eyed the Kleine
Walsertal, where the pastures made some of the best Bergkäse; the
Tyroleans wanted their brothers and sisters to the south; Upper and Lower
Austria looked enviously towards southern Moravia and Bohemia, despite
the streams of wretched German-speaking refugees and the certain knowledge that the Czechs were purging the region of Teutons; finally there
were even discussions in Styria and Carinthia about revising the borders,
and not just to fend off the Yugoslavs, who were keen to wrest away areas
of Austria where there were populations of Slovenians. The Carinthians
even mentioned the Kanaltal and Gottschee,* where there were clusters of
Germans who had come adrift from the fatherland and who felt insecure
in the post-war world.[21] Renner gave a nod to the Foreign Office to pour
a little cold water on these territorial claims; Gruber, however, even spoke
of 'reparations'.[22] It is possibly in response that the story is told of the
Germans offering to send back the bones of Adolf Hitler.

Margarétha, who failed to note Hitler's death in his journal, referred to
this overweening self-interest on the part of the Viennese in his entry for
14 August:

The Viennese are not interested in the atom bomb, nor the participation of

---

* The Kanaltal along the Fella river, around the now Italian town of Tarvisio; for Gottschee
see p. 503.

the Russians in the war [in Asia] . . . nor Japanese surrender; all they are interested in are the questions: when will the unbearable demarcation lines within Austria be wound up? When will we be rid of the Russians? When will the new tram lines be finally ready? When are we going to get meat, when are we finally going to have something to smoke? When will we have coal and wood for heating, when gas? When will there be glass for the window panes? The Viennese are not in the slightest bit interested in elections . . .[23]

In London Austria's territorial ambitions were given short shrift. The European Advisory Commission limited itself to the job of dividing Austria up into four zones of occupation. Access to Vienna from the Western zones, however, was held up until June. In the meantime exiled political groups continued to put pressure on the Allies, who in turn paid them scant attention. After Otto von Habsburg returned to Europe in 1944, London was the centre of legitimist agitation. He had not been a sparkling success. His agitation in America had upset the governments in exile and the State Department had had to issue a statement in April 1943 that it had no desire to reinstate the Habsburgs.[24] A leading monarchist was the Jewish nobleman Baron Leopold Popper von Podhragy. In June Podhragy wrote a pamphlet attacking Renner under the title *An Experiment in Socialism* using his pseudonym 'Florian George'.[25]

Renner had laid himself open: he was Austria's 'vicar of Bray', a communist toady who had begun life as a pan-German, a disciple of the same antisemite Schönerer who had exercised a seminal influence on the young Adolf Hitler. In 1918, when Austria had been divested of its subject states, he wanted it hitched to the German Reich. In this he felt much as the rest of his people felt at the time. He had also been implicated in the socialist uprisings of 1919, 1927 and 1934. Podhragy was pro-Dollfuss, the Austrian chancellor gunned down by the Nazis who himself brutally put down the socialist revolt. Dollfuss had also scrapped democracy in Austria, establishing the Corporate State. In Dollfuss's Austria the press was censored and arrest arbitrary.[26] Podhragy might have had reason to suspect that both Dollfuss and his successor Schuschnigg had monarchist leanings. In 1938 Renner had publicly supported the Anschluss with Germany, where other 'German Austrians' had been more reticent about the Nazis.

Renner had been quite open in giving his reasons for supporting the Anschluss and had urged Austrians to do the same. In an article published in London in May 1938 he had accused Dollfuss of 'monarchism and mediaeval clericalism'. 'German-Austria', a word of his own coinage, was and remained in his view a component part of the German Republic.[27] After

April 1945 he did not go back on this and he was as keen as ever to remove the trappings of the Corporate State. He had also become a Russian puppet. American intelligence reported that it was almost impossible to get anywhere near him, as he was always flanked by Russian minders.[28]

Seven years of German rule had wrought many changes. Whereas in 1938 most Austrians would have supported some sort of bond with Germany – not necessarily with the Nazis – in 1945 no one would have openly admitted a pan-German bias. German behaviour in Austria immediately following the Anschluss – the deporting of large numbers of ministers and government officials to Dachau; the brutal revenge against anyone who had been instrumental in repressing the Nazis during the time they were illegal; the confiscation of over half of the Austrian industrial base;[29]* the deportation of the Jews (although many Austrians were not just indifferent here, they actively joined in); the privations of war; the deaths of near ones and dear ones; and finally the capital crime, defeat – had all served to sever any bonds of affection that might have united the peoples on either side of the Inn. If there were pro-German Austrians after 1945, they kept mum or sought some other way out.

The Soviet authorities were playing their usual game and delaying the entry of the Western Allies. As the American commander General Mark Clark put it in the hard-hitting Cold War idiom of 1950: 'They were busy looting Austria at the time, and didn't want to be bothered.'[30] On 4 July 1945 the Allies came together again to decide the form of the Control Council. The Western missions were headed by the DMGs: General Winterton for Britain, General Gruenther for the US, and General P. R. P. Cherrière for France. The Russian commander was allegedly ill,† and the Soviet Union was represented by Colonel General A. S. Zheltov, a political commissar who was high up in the NKVD and who was famed for his entirely negative attitude.[31] Tolbukhin was actually in the doghouse and was replaced by Koniev on the 7 July. Stalin was cross because he had allowed the Red Army to give a negative image of the Soviet Union.[32] Fischer was angling for a German-style SED: a united front of communists and socialists. He had been inspired by the communal elections in France, which had returned the communists as the largest party in the country. Schärf feared that if the Western Allies did not arrive soon there would be a communist putsch.[33]

The zones were not finalised until 9 July. The Soviet Union clung to its

---

* A lot of this would have been formerly Jewish owned.

† Clark says this was Koniev, but Koniev had yet to be appointed.

bastions in the east: Burgenland – abolished by the Nazis and recreated for the Russians – Lower Austria and Upper Austria north of the Danube. The United States faced them across the Danube in Upper Austria, as well as taking on the Salzkammergut. Britain was anchored in the south, with Carinthia, Styria and the eastern Tyrol. France was left with the rest of the Tyrol and the Vorarlberg. As in Germany, this meant some adjustment of the lines. The Russians, for example, had occupied the eastern half of Styria. Margarétha would have expressed the views of most Viennese in voicing his unhappiness at the settlement. The Russian slice of the cake 'meant that the land around Vienna will be further leeched by the Russians, and that we will receive no potatoes, no fruit, no milk, no eggs . . .'[34]

Under the Allied agreement, the city was divided into four sectors like Berlin. The difference was that the 1st Bezirk, which occupied the medieval city bordered by the famous Ringstrasse, was managed by all four powers, a different victor taking on the role every month. Command was represented by four generals who reigned supreme in their sectors, and who administered the 1st Bezirk communally. They were the military commissars, whose presidency was also subject to monthly change. The 1st Bezirk was patrolled by the famous 'four in a jeep': a military policeman from each of the occupying powers.

Beyond the 1st Bezirk, the Allies all had their sectors, each of which included a slice of the inner city within the Gürtel as well as some more suburban areas. The Russians had the old Jewish quarter in the second, and Floridsdorf bordering the Danube, helping them to maintain their control of the waterway, Wieden and Favoriten; the Americans received Neubau, Alsergrund, the Josefstadt, Hernals, Währing and Döbling with its vine-yards; the French had Mariahilf with its famous shopping street, Penzing, Fünfhaus and Ottakring. Their offices were in the old Military Academy. General Béthouart was billeted in the villa of Frau Petznek in Hütteldorf. She was the only child of Crown Prince Rudolf who, after her marriage to a Prince Windischgraetz, had wedded a socialist politician. The Russians had been in the villa before him. They had removed much of the furniture and ripped the crowns off the books in the library. The British controlled Landstrasse, with its important communications to their airport at Schwechat, Margarethen, Simmering and Hietzing.

The Allies were the custodians of Austrian sovereignty. According to the London Agreement, drawn up by the European Advisory Commission in January 1944, they would continue to exercise executive power until independence was restored by a state treaty. The Austrian government had to submit proposals to the four powers, whose decisions had to be unanimous. The Soviet Union fought off the notion of granting Austria its sovereignty for ten years, although it was first suggested by US Secretary of State Byrnes in February 1946, and the project had full British backing. The Russians' pretext for their veto was that the country had been insufficiently purged of its Nazis, although they were notoriously lazy about pursuing culprits.[35]

Renner had never been trusted by the Western powers. His chief rival was the Dachauer Leopold Figl, who was the first to advocate a return to the 1929 Federal Constitution. Figl, patronisingly described by Mark Clark as 'a courageous and competent little fellow',[36] was the first great political figure of the Austrian Second Republic. A *vigneron* from Lower Austria, he had headed the Bauernbund or Peasants' Union before 1938. He had received a rough but effective political education in Dachau, spending a total of sixty-two months in Nazi captivity along with a number of other important political figures in post-war Austria. His hard peasant head proved an asset when it came to dealing with Koniev, and he was often seen reeling out of the Hotel Imperial (requisitioned by the Russian commandant), his belly full of vodka, after some tough trading. Another *Septembriste* was Dr Karl Gruber, who was only *de facto* foreign minister, because Austria officially had no right to conduct its own foreign affairs.

Figl was freed on 6 April 1945. On the 17th he went to the Imperial to make his peace with the conquerors.[37] He emerged as the Landeshauptmann, or governor, of Lower Austria. The Russians had no fondness for Figl, and his conservative ÖVP,[38] but they were hedging their bets, waiting to see if Austria would fall into the communist bloc, and in the meantime they were backing a multi-party system. Just to make sure the Austrians did not have it too easy, however, they also gave credence to Yugoslav demands for reparations and border changes.

Once the Americans had their feet under the desk in Vienna they too took stock of the political situation. Renner had moved out of his old home and into a former SS radio station in the Himmelstrasse in Grinzing. The Americans knew about his pan-German past and his support for the Anschluss. His persistent attacks on Dollfuss had angered Figl, who insisted that the murdered chancellor had been a democrat at heart.[39] The situation was not an obvious one: socialists like Renner had managed to stay out of concentration camps during the Nazi years, while the leaders of the Corporate State – which might have been sympathetic to Hitler had it played its cards right – had spent long, sometimes fatal, spells in Dachau and Mauthausen. It was not until 6 September that the OSS recommended that the American government recognise Renner's regime.

The British were also playing hard to get. On 26 September they told the Americans they were unwilling to recognise Renner because he was too much under the thumb of the communists.[40] The British thought the communists wanted to extend their influence over the whole of Austria. The dashing British political adviser Jack Nicholls (who was known to smuggle women at risk from the Russians out in the boot of his car) had also expressed his doubts about Renner's self-important ways. With time the British fell in behind Clark, whose view it was that Renner had to be given time to clean out his stables and make the government more representative.[41]

The British remained obdurate about their entry into Vienna, the Russians having stolen a march on them once more. They had left the issue to Churchill to sort out at Potsdam, which he had failed to do. Their refusal to advance to their sector was 'almost destructive'.[42] It resulted in Stalin agreeing to feed the Viennese population for the time being, but it was hardly a humanitarian solution, unless the Russians could be relied upon to do it properly. As it was, poor Austria was feeding a large number of strangers. There were around a million refugees within its pre-1938 borders and around 350,000 troops. The bulk of these were Russian, but there were also 50,000 Americans, 65,000 British and 40,000 French. That figure had been reduced to some 65,000 soldiers all told by the end of 1946.

The meeting of the victors at Potsdam in the summer of 1945 failed to rule on the Austrian question. One thing was agreed, however – that in the light of Austria's 'victim' status, there were to be no reparations paid. The French defied this by shipping home some valuable portions of Austrian industry they found in their zone, but the Russians had a better way of dealing with it. The day the conference opened, the *Daily Telegraph* reported the hypocrisy behind Soviet behaviour. The Russians had already carried away every machine, all cars and buses and cattle from the city: 'Austria is free but looted of all that can sustain or rebuild life.' For six weeks there had been no food delivered to the city, and half the newborn children had died. The corpses of the city's defenders still lay under the ruins of the buildings they had fought over.[43]*

The Allies had appointed their own high commissioners to govern their zones. Under these men there were a number of committees dealing with

---

* There were an estimated 9,000 unburied bodies in the city (Adolf Schärf, *Österreichs Wiederaufrichtung im Jahr 1945*, Vienna 1960, 24).

particular problems such as denazification, the restitution of sequestered property, DPs, POWs, military issues and disarmament. Once the Austrian government was recognised after the 1945 elections, the Allied high commissioners were invested with the rank of ministers in their respective governments. In fact, despite the reports in the British press, there was some small degree of co-operation between the Western and Eastern Allies at the beginning, and some of the 'German assets' were run well, while others were handed back to their original owners. The Allies jointly administered the country's oil industry at first, and Marshal Tolbukhin was in favour of the removal only of Austrian heavy industry.[44]

Even the staunchly communist parts of the city in Heiligenstadt had had enough of their Soviet liberators by the summer. For their own part, the Red Army had found it unbelievable that the Austrian communists had managed to live in such *Gemütlichkeit* in their fortress-like blocks of flats. There were homely lace curtains and soft sofas more readily associated with the bourgeoisie. Once the scales had fallen from their eyes the usual scenes of rape and rapine had followed.[45] On 22 July 1945, thirty American cars were spotted in Mauer.[46] Three days later a British quartermaster came to see Eugen Margarétha. He asked the economist politely if he had any room to spare. The Margaréthas volunteered two rooms on the parterre. It turned out that the English were expected the next day. That proved to be yet another optimistic rumour. They had still not pitched up on 5 August. Finally on the 12th a captain in the Coldstream Guards arrived, 'a nice, well-turned-out person', who took pity on them and gave them sandwiches and beer. At the end of the month electricity was restored and the Margaréthas' fridge started to work again, prompting much jubilation in the house.[47]

The world was at peace from the 15th. On the 19th the bedraggled former capital of the great Habsburg Empire received a new monument. A soaring column was set up on the Schwarzenberg Platz in the centre of the city, surmounted by a figure of a Red Army soldier in a gilded helmet. The coy Margarétha, who could not bring himself to talk about what the Russians had been doing since their arrival that spring, said it had already been dubbed 'The Monument to the Unknown Looter'. Most of his compatriots knew it as the 'Unknown Father' or, more coarsely, the 'Unknown Rapist'. The Russians erected their monument just six days before the other Allied commanders moved into their digs.[48]

Koniev had asked the Allies to come to Vienna on 23 August to admire the 'Unknown Father', but he was going to return Clark's hospitality first*

---

* See below p. 309.

and asked him to visit him in his HQ in Baden, the old summer capital. In 1945 it became Soviet army HQ and Russian officers and men moved into holiday residences rendered infamous by the stories of Arthur Schnitzler. The Russians had taken over most of the little spa and fenced off their quarters with barbed wire. Clark was asked to review the troops, then was taken back to headquarters and a bottle of vodka. It was the early afternoon. The Russians were 'obviously prepared for an afternoon of drinking. My party was plied with vodka and there was more liquor on the table when we went to Koniev's for dinner about 5 o'clock.' Clark came to the conclusion the Russians wanted to get them 'plastered'.

Not unnaturally, Clark was put out that Koniev was matching his shots of vodka with nips of white wine. He complained, telling his Russian opposite number that he wanted to drink the same juice as he was having: 'you see, I've got just one stomach to give for my country'. At ten they finished dinner and went to Baden Opera House to see a performance of Russian dancing. Clark had problems staying awake. The dancing was followed by a propaganda film. Then Zheltov insisted they have another meal before they went to bed. Clark went to his cot at four or five. Zheltov said he'd be back at eight so that they could go for a swim. Clark had his black batman wake him at 7.30 a.m. When he set eyes on his commander, he asked, 'Boss, did you drink some of that kerosene too?'[49]

Clark had no personal objection to Koniev, and they got on quite well at first. The froideur of the Cold War only set in the following year, but in his autobiography Clark gives the impression it was there from the start. The American general cites an example of their mutual understanding when he told the Russian his opinion of Fischer: 'I don't like him because he is a communist.' Koniev was completely unabashed. He apparently replied, 'That's fine. I don't like him because he's an Austrian communist.'[50]

The American intelligence officer Martin Herz, who interviewed Fischer in August, understood him better. Fischer was a pragmatic communist. Unlike Ulbricht in Berlin, he admitted that the Russians had raped women during the occupation and that the emergency police they appointed contained 'many of the lowest, criminal elements of the population'. They had been partly responsible for the looting. He was not in favour of the proscription of half a million Austrian Nazis. The number was just too large and doubtless included a great many hangers-on and nominal Party members: 'To outlaw them and make pariahs out of them would not only be unwise, but also unjust.' Fischer admitted candidly that National Socialism was 'a terror machine that worked with deadly precision and exacted nominal acceptance from people who conformed only in order to be able to live'. The Nazi rank and file should be allowed to redeem themselves.[51]

Clark had a little present for the Viennese before he went back to his hunting lodge in Hinterstoder. In a mine in the Salzkammergut the Americans had discovered the crown and regalia of the Emperor Charlemagne. Now they wanted to restore it to its rightful place. Unfortunately that meant the Hofburg, the imperial palace in the centre of Vienna, which was occupied by the Russians. Renner was very much opposed to the Americans letting it go anywhere near the Russians, so they kept it in the vaults of the bank building that served as their HQ.[52] The Americans had armed it as if it were the Pentagon itself.[53]

It was Koniev who put an end to the British intransigence. He announced on 27 August that he would withdraw his command over the Western sectors of Vienna as of 1 September and that these areas would then be 'without masters'. The ploy worked, and the Americans, British and French took up their positions on the first of the month.[54] They could now look closely at Vienna, which had been the Russians' exclusive preserve since early April. Herz noted that 200,000 Viennese were eating at the soup kitchens set up by the Russians.* It was hard not to give the Austrian communists some credit. They were not tainted by their Austrian past, only by their period in Moscow and the uncertainty of their instructions. The socialists were compromised by their support for amalgamation with Germany; the conservatives because they had been part and parcel of the anti-democratic Corporate State. The communists had their 'Immediate Programme' which called for a purge of the Nazis, three-party commissions to weed out fascists in the administration, administrative reform, nationalisation of industry and a democratic foreign policy. It was not meant to be a revolutionary programme.[55]

The first meeting of the high commissioners took place under Koniev's roof at the Imperial on 11 September. Clark thought it a shambles. It was Béthouart's first chance to meet the charismatic American general, who he decided resembled a Sioux Indian. The agenda was based on the four-power arrangement decided in London before the end of the war. The Russians knew exactly what they wanted: mastery of the Danube, the big oilfields at Zistersdorf in the eastern Weinviertel, and the Austrian 'bread-basket' in Burgenland. They already had most of the infrastructure – control of the railway lines, the roads, the airfields and the telephone lines. All

---

* These establishments lived on to the 1960s, possibly later, providing the Viennese with wholesome food at subsidised prices.

international calls passed through Vienna, giving the Russians the chance to monitor and control them. Similarly, the RAVAG, or Austrian radio network, was based in the Soviet Zone. The Soviet forces thus still over-saw important parts of the Austrian economic infrastructure, not just in the east of the country, but nationwide.[56]

From 20 October 1945, the Western Allies thought it prudent to shift the meetings around the corner to the Chamber of Industry on the Schwarzenbergplatz (for the time being, Josef-Stalin-Platz). That meant throwing out the Margaréthas. They found new premises and were helped to move by black American drivers and Nazi forced labourers who were so weak from hunger that they could hardly carry the boxes of files. The Allied sessions took place once a month. They were stiff. For a while the British high commissioner refused to attend because the Soviets would not allow the West to bring in food supplies for the half-starved population. There was a tea afterwards and attempts were made to break the ice. Koniev talked to Béthouart about Balzac, which he had read in Russian.[57]

Possibly his interest in French literature led him to invite Generals Béthouart and Cherrière, together with the civil administrator Alain de Monticault, to a lunch in his Baden villa. Once again the vodka flowed. Once again Koniev had an ulterior motive – he wanted to propose an alliance with the French that would serve both their interests on the Council.[58] The communists were still a power to be reckoned with in French politics, and, of all the Western Allies, the Russians had the most empathy with the French.

All the main receptions to commemorate important Soviet feast days were held in the Hofburg Palace. The feasts were as lavish as those held in the Russian embassy in Berlin. There was copious vodka and caviar and the Russians looked far more splendid in their Red Army dress suits than the Western Allies in their khaki.[59] A certain style and an ability to entertain on an imperial scale may explain the gracious treatment accorded to the former Austrian ruling house. Franz Joseph's nephew Hubert Salvator was told that the Russians would respect his property and person, and he was excused from the duty of billeting officers. Béthouart relates that the Russians even helped him put out his relics on Holy Days of Obligation.

The British HQ was in Schönbrunn Palace, where the commander General Sir Richard McCreery occupied the room that had served Napoleon before him, a fact that caused the French general de Lattre de Tassigny considerable annoyance. McCreery, who had served with the British army in Italy, endured strained relations with Koniev from the outset. Soon after he moved into a villa near the palace in Hietzing the Soviets kidnapped his gardener. He was never seen again.[60]

Each of the four powers was granted an hotel where they could put up their guests. The Russians took the Grand, opposite the Hotel Imperial, where the Russian commandant had his lodgings. It had also been Hitler's favourite on his visits to Vienna. The portrait of the Emperor Franz Joseph had been replaced by one of Stalin. The Americans appropriated the smaller but grander Bristol. The French occupied the Hotel Kummer in the Mariahilferstrasse, and only later moved into the rather more impressive Hotel de France on the Ring. The British were in Sacher's behind the Opera. The Western Allies all sponsored a newspaper which now joined the largely propagandist Russian press consisting of *Neues Österreich*, the *Arbeiterzeitung*, the *Österreichische Zeitung* and the *Kleine Volksblatt*. Now the Americans launched the *Wiener Kurier*, the British *Die Weltpresse* and the French *Die Welt am Montag*.

Clark gradually took on the role of baiter of the Russian bear that was performed by Clay in Germany. He believed the Americans were 'selling Austria down the Danube'.[61] When the Russians staked a claim to all shipping on the river, Clark noted that the vital river barges were in the American Zone in Linz. Linz was on the border with the Soviet Zone, so Clark had them taken upstream to Passau, in the American Zone in Germany. It transpired there were Yugoslav barges among them, and the Yugoslavs began to complain. It was only when Clark had a direct order from the secretary of state, however, that he agreed to hand over the Yugoslav vessels.[62]

The political scene was beginning to move, and it looked hopeful for Austria. On 11 September, the Allied Council gave permission for the re-establishment of the three main political parties: popular, socialist and communist. On 24 September Renner obligingly reshuffled his cabinet to include Figl, leading the Western Allies to recognise his government on 20 October. Renner took the hint and resigned following the elections, which took place on 25 November, eventually becoming federal president a few days before Christmas when the deputies unanimously voted him upstairs. On 3 December his place was taken by Figl.

The results of the first free elections since 1930 were announced on 2 December. There had been a 95 per cent turnout. Margarétha, who was one of the founders of the People's Party, the ÖVP, called them 'brilliant' and with good reason: communist hopes were dashed and his party headed the list with just over 1,600,000 votes, representing nearly half the electorate. The SPÖ, the Socialist Party, won 1,434,898 votes. The communists, the KPÖ, limped home a long way behind with 174,255 or 5.5 per cent. Even in 'Red Vienna' they had come third with just six seats in the regional assembly. The SPÖ did best, with fifty-eight; the ÖVP won thirty-six. The communists achieved just four seats in the Federal Parliament. Women, it seemed, had been their undoing.

Women were now 64 per cent of the electorate, and they had suffered unduly at the hands of the Red Army. The ÖVP campaigned with posters that also showed the Russians in their worst light: 'Ur-Wiener und Wiener ohne Uhr, wählt ÖVP!'* Another ruse was to put up posters telling the Austrians, 'For all who love the Red Army, vote KPÖ!'[63] Missing from the electorate were around a quarter of a million Austrian dead, 600,000 POWs, half a million Nazis and sundry other political undesirables. The ex-Nazis would not have helped the left much. Their half-million votes would probably have gone to the People's Party. Margarétha thought the message would cause relief at home and abroad.[64] He was right. The Americans reported that Austria was now finally aware of the meaning of democracy. The Figl government was recognised on 7 December 1946.[65]

The Viennese were cold and hungry. The larger coffee houses had been taken over by the Americans. Margarétha and his wife had a modest Christmas: festive *Paprikafisch* came out of a tin. The British captain was kind enough to make Eugen a present of a dozen Havana cigars, and in turn he gave the Guards officer a little bottle of cognac.[66] Figl, however, began his rule on fighting form. To thunderous applause he demanded the opening of the demarcation lines between the zones, the restoration of Austrian unity, the return of South Tyrol and the end of the Yugoslav threat to Carinthia. Austria had never been a second German state.[67]

The communists were bitterly disappointed by the results of the elections, although they were granted the concession of a ministerial portfolio which went to Karl Altmann. As their Soviet-controlled newspaper, the *Österreichische Zeitung*, put it, 'We have lost a battle, but we are just at the start of the battle for Austria, and that will be won.'[68] Their failure to endear themselves to the Austrian people may have been behind Koniev's departure: he was replaced by Vladimir Kurasov in the middle of 1946. Just as in the aftermath of the Berlin elections of 1946, the Russians began to show their teeth, creating petty difficulties for the Western Allies wherever they could. As far as the Austrians were concerned, they had learned nothing: the ÖVP were closet fascists misleading the public under a halo of

---

* The pun just about works in English: 'Viennese old-timers and Viennese without timers, vote ÖVP!' The Russians had stolen their watches.

martyrdom (Dachau and Mauthausen), and the SPÖ were tainted by their complicity in the Anschluss. Austria quite clearly could not be trusted to rule itself.[69]

Feeding the Austrians

When Dos Passos visited Vienna at the end of 1945 he was able to have a quick look round courtesy of American army public relations. He attended Mass in the Hofburg Chapel and noted the American, British and French 'gold braid' listening to Schubert. The famous cafés, uncleaned and unheated, served cups of 'mouldy-tasting dark gruel called coffee'. The waiters 'kept up a pathetic mummery of service' providing the usual glass of water, but not the cream, although they still had the jugs. The writer plucked up the courage to ask a waiter what was in the coffee. 'That's our secret,' he was told. He also wanted to know what the Viennese ate. 'Bread and dried peas' was the answer.[70]

The winter had set in, provisions were at an all-time low, and there was no fuel to heat houses and flats. The Allies gave permission for the felling of large numbers of trees. Feeding Vienna remained a Western grievance. The Soviets had made off with the arable land and the roads into the capital. Their zone had produced 65 per cent of Vienna's food before the war. Clark said the Americans intended to give the Austrians 1,550 calories (he said the average American had 3,000), but he admitted that the British had problems matching that figure.[71] As it was, the diet varied considerably across Austria. In Vienna in May citizens received a piffling 833 calories, which they presumably supplemented with fresh fruit and vegetables. In the American Zone it was not much more, and the French complained they had no means of feeding the Vorarlberger or the Tyroleans.

Desperation led the Austrian government to moderate the outward flow of Germans and grant citizenship to one, the Nobel Prize-winning chemist Friedrich Bergius, who had been trying to extract sugar from tree bark. Bergius was also promising to make meat from wood, a project that has now been dismissed as the purest alchemy. Bergius's citizenship becomes all the more scandalous given that he was fully in collaboration with IG Farben during the war, and working for a Nazi victory. He fled to Buenos Aires and died there in 1949.[72]

In order to receive foreign aid, Austria had to prove itself a proper enemy of Hitler. At first it was the Russians who made trouble, charging that the Austrians had not actively sought freedom from Hitler. After the war, it was Yugoslavia that vetoed Austria receiving aid from UNRRA (the UN Relief and Rehabilitation Administration). The aid was only forthcoming from March 1946. The previous December the British Foreign Office had been preparing a new four-power agreement for the administration of Austria that would result in granting the Austrians a degree of self-government, but holding them in check through vetoes. The Allies – particularly the British and the French – wanted to scale down their operations in Austria, for the simple reason that they were expensive.

The agreement was long in the making. At first the British did not tell the other three of the draft; then the Americans opposed it. When it was finally signed on 28 June 1946 it was supposed to last for six months, but in reality it survived until the State Treaty was promulgated on 27 July 1955.[73] The Austrian federal and state governments achieved a greater degree of liberty and were able to use quasi-total power to run their houses. Military government by the Allies was scrapped and replaced by 'control missions'. That the Russians saw the opening of a new era is clear, perhaps, from the recall of Koniev and his replacement by Kurasov. Clark's bugbear Zheltov, however, remained behind.

As much as possible, the Western Allies sought to administer Austria with the help of apparent anti-Nazis. Ulrich Ilg, who had been a minister in the inter-war First Republic, was a typical appointee, much as the gerontocracy had returned to power in Berlin. The French set him up in the Vorarlberg. The British also worked to redraft Austrian law. An important British contribution to the re-establishment of a non-Nazi Austria was BALU – the British Austrian Legal Unit. The body had been formed in 1943 by pulling a number of Austrian lawyers out of the British army and putting them to work in the War Office. In 1945 they were packed off to Vienna where they formed part of the legal department of the Control Commission under the British-born (but of German Jewish origin) lawyer Claud Schuster. Schuster was assisted by George Bryant, né Breuer. BALU itself was run by the Viennese Lieutenant-Colonel Wolf Lasky, who had worked in the town hall until 1938. He was now claiming royalties for legal textbooks sold during the Nazi interregnum. The Austrians took fright and appointed him to the bench, so that he now enjoyed the curious position of being a judge in both Austria and Britain. He never practised in Austria and had no desire to settle there once his work was done. He later worked as a legal adviser to the British in Germany.[74] The British legal division generally advised acceptance of the laws voted by the Austrian parliament.[75]

In March 1947 a poll taken among the Austrians indicated the popularity of the Allies – the Soviets, it seems, were not mentioned. The British were well liked, but the French were no more than 'perfumed Russians'. Mark Clark was singled out for veneration for his tough stand against the Soviets, Figl going so far as to call him 'a legendary national hero'. Dos Passos reported that he would wander around the streets of Vienna accompanied only by an interpreter at a time when the city at night was 'as in mediaeval days' – you went abroad at your own risk.[76] The violence was normally down to the Russians or gangs of DPs. The Austrians voiced their opinions of the various DPs whose camps were scattered over their land: the Jews were liked least, followed by the Poles, Yugoslavs and Russians. Quite a few of these had become lawless bandits, seeking revenge for the indignities of the lives they had led as KZler or forced labourers. The best loved now were ethnic Germans from Czechoslovakia, Hungary and the Balkans.[77]

With little food or fuel, Austria had around 600,000 extra mouths to feed. There were about 170,000 'Danube Swabians', 151,000 Sudetenländer and 15,000 Hungarian Germans, as well as 15,000 Germans from the Siebenbürgen and the Banat and 170,000 Jews. It was only after 1949 that the figures began to drop. The Americans put the DPs into the care of Austrians, but the British thought they were better off under their own authority. The Allies used the RAD camps that the Nazis had built for their forced and volunteer labour force.[78]

A constant stream of German Bohemians and Moravians gushed into Austria. The Russians had a camp for them in Melk on the Danube, but it was grossly overstretched and they ended up becoming a burden to all the Allied zones. The response was to demand the expulsion of 'Reich' Germans. Gruber was particularly vociferous here. By a highly specious argument 'German' was made to mean 'Nazi'. The expulsion of the Germans from the Austrian body would purge it of its former evil. On 1 November 1945 the Americans stopped their ration cards in Salzburg. Austria made a point of celebrating its anti-German past – books were published, for example, that showed how gallantly Austria had resisted Prussia in the Seven Years War.

In March 1947 there were hunger marches in Vienna and Lower Austria. The demonstrators shouted, 'Down with Figl's hunger regime! We want new elections! We are hungry!' There was a sit-in at the chancellor's office orchestrated by the communists. The Viennese police were too terrified of the Soviets to help. The latter even refused to allow the Allied 'four-in-a-jeep' patrols to interfere. The demonstrations were coupled with the failure of Gruber and the Austrians to make any headway towards independence in Moscow.[79]

German Assets

The restitution of stolen property was part of the work of the Control Council. The various Allies pursued property claims pertaining to their own people. The French, for example, were anxious to trace the library of the former prime minister Léon Blum, which had gone missing in Austria. It was last seen in Carinthia, but was never found. As regards stolen Jewish property, restitution was effected only in certain cases and in others the awards were only partial.[80]

Restitution was complicated by several factors. One was that the Soviet authorities were patently uninterested in the fate of the Jews, and were determined to mop up as much property and money as they could. On 27 June 1946 the Russians seized all 'German' assets in their zone in contravention of the Potsdam Accord. It followed on from similar measures taken in Hungary, Romania, Bulgaria and Finland. When the West protested, the Russians contradicted the spirit of the Moscow Declaration and said that the Austrians had 'fought with Germany'.

'German' assets accounted for around a fifth of Austrian industry: more than 62 per cent of Germany's capital abroad. The total sums for other countries – Finland, Poland, Hungary, Romania, Bulgaria and Yugoslavia – totalled 188 million dollars, while for Austria the figure was a staggering 1.5 milliard.[81] Some of these assets had no connections with the Germans whatsoever. Others were businesses legitimately built up and developed by Germans. The Russians interpreted these matters very freely. Of 120 industries taken over in their zone, only 47 were actually 'German'; and of the seventy-six agricultural properties they took over, only one had previously been in German hands. They expressed their intention of taking over the 27,000-hectare Esterházy estate based in Burgenland, for example, which could hardly be described as German and which would have fed (according to the Americans) between 80,000 and 100,000 people. They had 72 per cent of Austria's oilwells and half the country's refinery capacity.[82]

Soviet Russia's determination to grab all German property included businesses that had been filched by Germans from Austrian Jews, who had been either driven into exile or murdered in the camps. The Russians also swiped a lot of things the Germans had stolen from the Austrian government and foreign nationals. The demands for compensation by certain very rich Jewish families such as the Rothschilds were used by the Russians as a justification for their actions, as they claimed that the Americans would beggar the Austrians were such claims to go through. They were much fairer in their approach in that they shared their spoils with the people of their zone. They sequestered the oilwells, although the equity had been mostly held by Britons and Americans before the war. Their argument was that the foreign interests had been legitimately sold to the Germans in 1938 and that the Anglo-Americans had no right to claim them back.[83]

They took what ships they found on the Danube. Some of the companies seized were simply stripped of anything of value that could be sent home to Russia. Others were run at a profit. USIA (Upravleinje Sovetskogo Imuščestva v Avstrii – Administration of Soviet Property in Eastern Austria) was the company the Russians created to administer their spoils. In 1949 USIA was running 250 factories with 50,000 workers and controlled a third of industrial production within the Soviet Zone. These factories made all Austrian locomotives and turbines, half of the nation's glass, fuel and pharmaceuticals and around 40 per cent of its iron. They also had 157,000 hectares of land. The Russians continued to exploit Austria though USIA for a decade and their profits over that period are estimated at over a milliard dollars. The Western Allies protested, but, as no one wanted war, their protests remained hot air.

Russia was anxious to snatch 'German' assets in the west too, but that came to nothing. Not all the industry was in the east. VOEST was originally the Hermann-Göring-Werke in Linz. After Potsdam's ruling on former German property the huge steelworks, one of the most modern in Europe, fell to the Austrian state. In the light of Soviet behaviour in the east, the Western Allies demonstratively waived their right to reparations – in the French case, somewhat reluctantly.[84]

The confiscation of the Zistersdorf oilfields gave rise to an act of resistance by Renner, who refused to sign the agreement.[85] The Russians threatened to report him to Koniev, but he must have known he had the backing of the Western Allies, Clark in particular, who – like Clay north of the Inn – could see the propaganda value in exposing Soviet knavery in this and other instances. Clark also claims to have foiled a Soviet attempt to take over the building of the Ministry of the Interior.

January 1945. The inhabitants of East Prussia have finally been allowed to flee, but the Red Army has cut them off from the Reich at Elbing. In desperation hundreds of thousands make their way across the frozen inland sea or Haff. Russian warships open fire on the ice

The 'treks' began that winter. These Silesians are making their way west in any transport they can find. Note the elegant carriage among the carts and traps

Over sixteen million Germans left their homes, few of their own free will. These Sudetenländer are being shipped out in cattle trucks. The manner of their going was a relief, however, after what many had suffered in the camps

Conditions on the trains were at best primitive. Everything had to be done in the carriages. If they were lucky the Czechs or Poles allowed them to take off the waste

Miserable Sudeten expellees wait to board the train to Germany

Left: Pious Sudeten Catholic hear an open-air Mass on their way to their new lives

Below: Silesians assemble in the streets of their town prio to their expulsion. This was only the beginning of their Calvary: they would often spend weeks in a transit camp where they would face the most abominable treatment. Many died

The Oder at Frankfurt. This was to be the new Polish–German border after the Western Allies gave in to Stalin's demands at Potsdam

For the Jews life in the new Poland and the new Czechoslovakia had few temptations: the ruins of the White Stork synagogue in Wrocław (Breslau) in 1991

Sudetenländer rounded up in Bergreichenstein (Kasperské Hory) push their goods to the assembly camp. They are wearing white armbands to mark them out as Germans

Germans were allowed to take only the basic minimum with them. Here in Bergreichenstein in eastern Bohemia Czech officials inspect suitcases and clothing for anything of value

Note that the guard is wearing a recycled German helmet while his colleague is trampling on the German's possessions

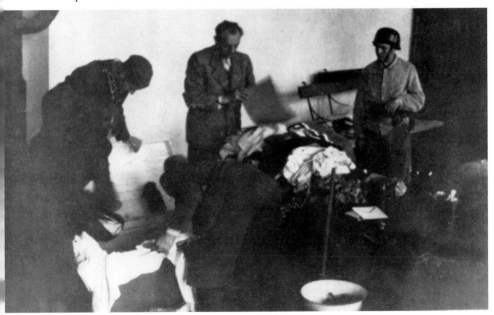

A rare picture of the Little Fortress in Theresienstadt with German prisoners. During the war the Kleine Festung had provided accommodation for the SS and was used for occasional executions of Czechs and Jews. Now the boot was on the other foot

osef Schöner's pictures of the ruins of Vienna. The State Opera House with the Jockey Club
behind. The Jockey Club had taken a direct hit in the last weeks of the war. Hundreds of
bodies lay in the cellars

The Cathedral or 'Steffl' denuded of its high-pitched roof. No one could say precisely who had started the fires: the Russians, the Germans or the Viennese themselves

The Graben shopping street. Life was returning to normal. Note the woman in her traditional *Dirndl*: Austrian dress proved you were not German. (*inset*) The Austrians had been liberated as the first victims of Hitler, but the Allies were not entirely convinced

AN DIE BEVÖLKERUNG DER STADT BERLIN

Um die regelmäßige Versorgung der Berliner Bevölkerung mit Lebensmitteln sicherzustellen, hat das Sowjetische Militärkommando durch den Kommandanten der Stadt Berlin der Stadtverwaltung ausreichende Mengen von Lebensmitteln zur Verfügung gestellt.

Gemäß Befehl des Militärkommandanten der Stadt Berlin, Generaloberst BERSARIN, sind ab 15. Mai 1945 folgende, feste Lebensmittelrationen pro Person und Tag festgesetzt worden:

Brot

1.) Schwerarbeiter und Arbeiter in gesundheitsschädlichen Betrieben	600 gr.
2.) Arbeiter, die in schweren oder gesundheitsschädlichen Berufen tätig sind	500 gr.
3.) Angestellte	400 gr.
4.) Kinder, nichtberufstätige Familienangehörige und die übrige Bevölkerung	300 gr.

Nährmittel

1.) Schwerarbeiter und Arbeiter in gesundheitsschädlichen Betrieben	80 gr.
2.) Arbeiter, die nicht in schweren oder gesundheitsschädlichen Berufen tätig sind	60 gr.
3.) Angestellte	40 gr.
4.) Kinder, nichtberufstätige Familienangehörige und die übrige Bevölkerung	30 gr.

Fleisch

1.) Schwerarbeiter und Arbeiter in gesundheitsschädlichen Betrieben	100 gr.
2.) Arbeiter, die nicht in schweren oder gesundheitsschädlichen Berufen tätig sind	65 gr.
3.) Angestellte	40 gr.
4.) Kinder, nichtberufstätige Familienangehörige und die übrige Bevölkerung	20 gr.

Fett

1.) Schwerarbeiter und Arbeiter in gesundheitsschädlichen Betrieben	30 gr.
2.) Arbeiter, die nicht in schweren oder gesundheitsschädlichen Berufen tätig sind	15 gr.
3.) Angestellte	10 gr.
4.) Kinder	20 gr.
5.) Nichtberufstätige Familienangehörige und die übrige Bevölkerung	7 gr.

Zucker

1.) Schwerarbeiter und Arbeiter in gesundheitsschädlichen Betrieben und Kinder	25 gr.
2.) Arbeiter, die nicht in schweren oder gesundheitsschädlichen Berufen tätig sind, sowie Angestellte	20 gr.
3.) Nichtberufstätige Familienangehörige und die übrige Bevölkerung	15 gr.

Kartoffeln

Für jeden Einwohner	400 gr.

13. Mai 1945.

Bohnenkaffee, Kaffee-Ersatz und echter Tee

1.) Schwerarbeiter und Arbeiter in gesundheitsschädlichen Betrieben: 100 gr. Bohnenkaffee, 100 gr. Kaffee-Ersatz und 20 gr. echten Tee im Monat.

2.) Arbeiter, die nicht in schweren oder gesundheitsschädlichen Berufen tätig sind, sowie Angestellte: 60 gr. Bohnenkaffee, 100 gr. Kaffee-Ersatz und 20 gr. echten Tee im Monat.

3.) Kinder, nichtberufstätige Familienangehörige und die übrige Bevölkerung: 25 gr. Bohnenkaffee, 100 gr. Kaffee-Ersatz und 20 gr. echten Tee im Monat.

Salz

Für jeden Einwohner monatlich	400 gr.

Mengen und Form der Versorgung mit Milch, weißem Käse und anderen Milcherzeugnissen werden nachträglich bekanntgegeben.

*

Verdiente Gelehrte, Ingenieure, Ärzte, Kultur-und Kunstschaffende, sowie die leitenden Personen der Stadt-und Bezirksverwaltungen, der großen Industrie und Transportunternehmen erhalten die gleichen Lebensmittelrationen, die für Schwerarbeiter festgesetzt sind. Die Liste dieser Personen muß vom zuständigen Bürgermeister bestätigt werden.

Sonstige technische Angestellte in Betrieben und Unternehmen, Lehrer und Geistliche, erhalten die Lebensmittelrationen, die für Arbeiter festgesetzt sind.

*

Kranke in Krankenhäusern erhalten Verpflegung entsprechend den Sätzen, die für Arbeiter festgesetzt sind. Kranke, die besondere Ernährung bedürfen, erhalten eine Sonderverpflegung entsprechend den Sätzen, die von der städtischen Abteilung für Gesundheitswesen festgesetzt sind.

*

Die Brotausgabe erfolgt täglich, wobei der Verbraucher das Recht hat, Brot für zwei Tage — und zwar für den Kalendertag und den nächsten Tag — zu erhalten.

Fleisch, Fett, Zucker, Nährmittel und Kartoffeln für den Monat Mai werden entsprechend den festgelegten Tagessätzen in zwei Zuteilungen ausgegeben:

erstmalig für die Zeit vom 15. Mai bis 21. Mai, d. h. für sieben Tage, und das zweite Mal für die Zeit vom 22. Mai bis 31. Mai, d. h. für zehn Tage.

Salz für die Zeit vom 20. bis 31. Mai wird in der Menge des festgelegten Monatssatzes ausgegeben.

Bohnenkaffee und echter Tee wird vom 25. bis 31. Mai ausgegeben, Kaffee-Ersatz vom 21. bis 31. Mai in der Menge des festgelegten Monatssatzes.

Die Ausgabe der Lebensmittelkarten mit den neu festgelegten Sätzen an die gesamte Berliner Bevölkerung erfolgt spätestens am 14. Mai ds. Js.

Bis zum 15. Mai erfolgt die Zuteilung der Lebensmittel, entsprechend den zeitweiligen Sätzen der früher an die Bevölkerung ausgegebenen Lebensmittelkarten, welche bis zum 14. Mai in Kraft bleiben.

The Allies had a duty to feed the vanquished Germans. This notice of 13 May 1945 sets out the rations for Berlin. Four ration cards were issued according to the recipient's usefulness to society. Workers received twice as much as children. Later two more categories were invented including the sixth, hunger card. Needless to say, very little of this largesse was really available

Silesian children arriving in the British Zone in Germany after their ordeals. Many could not believe the benevolent treatment they received at the hands of the Western Allies

These Silesian children could look forward to a new life in West Germany

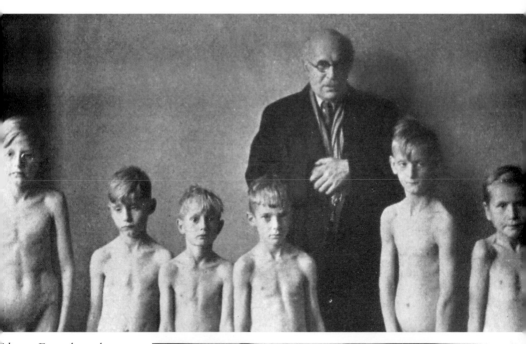

Above: For others the misery was not yet over. The Allied rations did little to allay malnutrition. Here Victor Gollancz presents a powerful indictment of the British treatment of the Germans

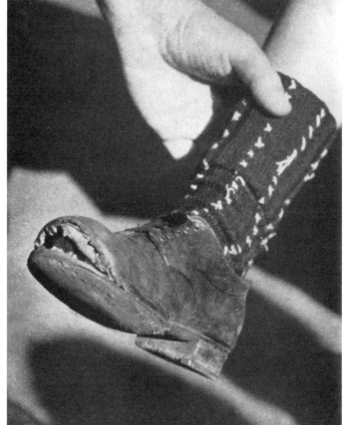

Right: Gollancz was particularly interested in the state of German children's shoes

One of the more positive elements of the Occupation: Sir Robert Birley (here as headmaster of Eton). He felt that what the Germans needed was re-education, not denazification

Lord Pakenham, later Earl of Longford, the second British Minister for Germany and Austria, gets to grips with the problem

Right: The Allies leave a positive legacy. It was the British who revived production of Hitler's 'Kraft-durch-Freude' car. The 'Beetle' was to be the 'wheels of the Occupation'

Right: A rare moment
of Anglo-Soviet co-
operation: Marshal
Koniev and General
Sir Dick McCreery
award the cups at a
race meeting at the
Freudenau in Vienna

Below: Airlift: British
Pilot Officer W. K.
Newell crashes his
aircraft

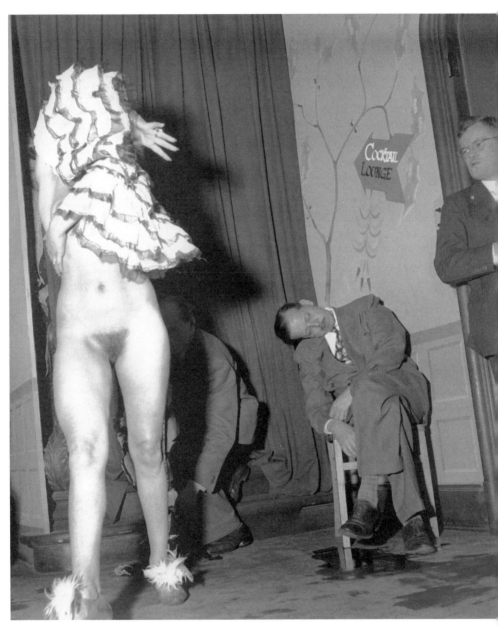

And there was plenty of fun to be had at the expense of the conquered: a drunken American officer sleeps through a striptease in his Darmstadt mess in April 1948

Culture

When Carl Zuckmayer revisited Austria, he was aware of the difficulty of distinguishing between the 'liberated' and the 'occupied' country. Despite control by four powers, Austria had its own administration, and licensing plays for performance was a mere formality. Despite that, the American authorities imposed a number of their own plays on Ernst Lothar, who was the author of the immensely successful novel *Der Engel mit der Posaune* which charted the rise of Nazism in Austria. Lothar (né Müller), who had spent the war years across the Atlantic with his wife, the actress Adrienne Gessner, was an excellent choice as American theatre chief in Vienna and he was given the job of denazifying the Viennese theatre. Naturally he felt bitter. He had told Zuckmayer that the Germans should not feel 'pride' for fifteen years. Zuckmayer commented to his wife Alice, 'How good that he is only going to Austria, and to what is clearly a secondary position!'[86]

Zuckmayer concluded that the Austrian film industry was in a state of 'hopeless confusion'. The Americans had seized control of the studios in Sievering, in the suburbs of Vienna. Some of the old talent was still around, like the singer and actor Willy Forst, who had made *Wiener Madeln* (Viennese Girls) under the Nazis but never released it, because, so he said, he had wanted to save it for a non-Nazi Austria.[87] The composer Egon Wellesz did not return before 1948, and then only for a visit. When he was asked why he had taken so long, he replied no one had asked him. As Wellesz's biographer Franz Edler has said, he was 'The pupil and confidant of Guido Adler and would have made an exemplary successor to him at Vienna University, where he had taught before the war, but after 1945 no one even mentioned the idea.'[88] *Pace* the new mayor of Vienna, Theodor Körner, many people believed that their race was still a disadvantage in Austria. Even as late as April 1948, Alfred Rosenzweig could write to Ernst Krenek in the United States that the Jewish conductor Otto Klemperer had told him he was unable to procure work in Vienna or Salzburg, adding that 'Nazis like Herr Böhm and the Oberstandartenführer Karajan and the like, have got the lot . . .' This was despite Allied meddling in cultural matters, with the Soviets controlling the musical scene in Vienna and the Anglo-Americans making Salzburg their flagship.[89]

Richard McCreery earned a place in the hearts of the old-fashioned Viennese by bringing back flat racing at the Freudenau track in the Prater, even though it lay in the Russian Sector. His action allowed the elite Jockey Club to revive its functions, although its clubhouse opposite the

Albertina had been destroyed by a direct hit in the last weeks of the war. The British had begun by organising racing in the park at Schönbrunn, which lay within their own sector. It was not long before they asked the Soviets if they could use the old course in the Prater. McCreery gave the job of organising it to his chief veterinary officer Colonel Glynn Lloyd. On 27 October 1945 six events were planned. In March the following year funds were found to award prizes. The racing began on 14 April 1946.[90]

As the Russians had had the run of Vienna for months before the Western Allies arrived, they had had the pick of the buildings. The French wanted a palace for their Institut Français. The building on offer was the Palais Coburg, the magnificent residence of the dukes of Coburg overlooking the Stadtpark from its bastion on the old city wall. For some reason the French thought it too remote and coveted the Palais Lobkowitz instead. This had once been the French embassy, and it was across the way from the Albertina in a much more central position. Béthouart succeeded in wresting it from the Soviets in the course of a reception for the twenty-eighth anniversary of the Red Army. The Russians received – and trashed – the Palais Coburg instead.

Once the French were in possession of their cultural turf they could lay on concerts and exhibitions. Musicians like Jacques Thibaud and Ginette Neveu performed in its salons and lectures were delivered by the architect Le Corbusier and the artist Jean Lurçat. The Paris opera company performed *Pelléas et Mélisande* at the Theater an der Wien, the Staatsoper being bombed out. On 24 March 1947 the Comédie Française performed *Tartuffe* and Louis Jouvet's company staged *L'Ecole des femmes*. The Viennese were also treated to French mannerists, fashions from Hermès, the Nabis, Cubism and more, while the treasures of Vienna's museums were exposed at the Petit Palais in Paris.

Soviet Zone

The Soviet Union had always been in favour of occupying the more industrialised east of Austria. On 29 March 1945, as its troops began to cross the border from Hungary, however, it considered the southern regions of Styria and Carinthia as well. A good deal of German industry had been transferred there during the Anglo-American aerial bombardment and there was promise of rich plunder. Taking that portion too would weaken the British and strengthen the Soviet influence over Yugoslavia. As it was the Russians were able to take most of Styria before the British arrived, and help themselves to what they wanted in Graz. Not only was their arrival the signal for Tito's partisans to enter Carinthia, the First Bulgarian Army moved up into positions in the wine region of South Styria around the small towns of Leibnitz, Radkersburg and Wildon.[91]

With Styria temporarily in the Soviet Zone, virtually all Austria's vineyards had fallen into Russian hands. Grape farmers saved what they could at their approach. In Gols in Burgenland the Stiegelmar family put the bottles in the well; the Osbergers in Strass in the Strassertal in Lower Austria resorted to the popular ruse of building a false wall to save their rarest wines. At Kloster Und near Krems, the Salomons put examples of the best vintages into the empty tuns, hoping that the Russians would be deterred by the hollow reverberations when they tapped the casks.[92]

The Russian forces of occupation continued to be wild and uncontained. On Victory in Europe Day the Red Army celebrated by a new burst of looting in the course of which forty-four people lost their lives. Rape was part of daily life until 1947 and many women were riddled with VD and had no means of curing it. Burgenland suffered more than any other region of eastern Austria from the ravages of Russian solders. In Mattersburg the peasants posted guards to warn women when the Russians were about to come among them. And yet there were moments when the people had cause to thank them. For example, it was Soviet troops who built the pontoon bridge at Mautern on the Danube after the other crossings had been blown up, allowing communication to be restored between Mautern and the twin towns of Krems and Stein. It is still there, and locals call it 'the Russian gift'.

The Allied Zones were self-contained units and it was not easy to move from one to the other, and well nigh impossible to get from the Western Allies to the Soviet Zone. Schärf maintained that it was easier to go from the Marchfeld, north-east of Vienna, to Brno in Czechoslovakia than it was to reach Salzburg in the American Zone. From Salzburg it was a simple business travelling to Munich, but much harder to make it to Vienna. To some extent this was intentional: Stalin desired a buffer zone to his satellite states in Hungary, Czechoslovakia and Yugoslavia, and wanted to keep the Western Allies away.[93] The Russians kept a huge army in eastern Austria, based in their HQ in Baden. The command extended all the way to Romania, taking in Hungary.

The camp at Mauthausen lay near Linz in the Soviet Zone. Many French deportees had perished there and Béthouart accompanied several pilgrimages made up of bereaved families. On 20 June 1947 he went with Figl and the education minister Hurdes, both of whom had been incarcerated in Mauthausen. The Russians were notoriously half-hearted in their pursuit of Nazis, and officially left it up to the Austrian civil authorities to hunt war criminals, although they were always keen to accuse the other Allies of sheltering them. In March 1947 they claimed that the British were protecting Nazis in Carinthia. They were still supporting Yugoslav claims to territory in the southern province.[94] The Americans were keeping a record of Soviet anti-Nazi activity: in Krems the Russians rounded up 440 Nazis and put former Nazis to work clearing rubble in Gmünd and Wiener Neustadt.* Half of Wiener Neustadt had been destroyed and there were outbreaks of spotted typhus.[95]

British Zone

The British Zone of occupation was fraught with problems at the start. The Russians were camping in Styria, and emptying the region of any equipment of value; Bulgarians were dug in among the South Styrian vines; and the Yugoslavs had taken large parts of Carinthia. While the Bulgarians were relatively easy to control, the Russians and the Yugoslavs were a nightmare. Firstly the Yugoslavs had taken the Carinthian capital, Klagenfurt, and hoisted their flags over the city. When the local governor refused to fly a Yugoslav flag he was replaced by a more compliant figure. Posters announced that Carinthia was now part of Yugoslavia.† 'National councils' were hastily formed on which Yugoslavs and members of the Slovenian minority sat. The British were helpless. They were in the second city of Villach, forty-seven of them: twenty officers and twenty-seven administrators. Even after the British forces arrived, there were still more partisans than Tommies. 'Shooting was out,' although the Yugoslavs had no heavy weapons.[96]

There was at least one comic moment reported by those pioneering officers in Villach. One of them was reconnoitring in the woods shortly after the British force arrived and ran into a woman in Luftwaffe uniform. She made it clear her unit was running out of food. The British officer followed her to a large underground bunker where women were pushing in and pulling out telephone plugs. It turned out to be the major military exchange for southern Austria. 'They had known perfectly well what was

---

* When Holly Martins goes to the Russian 2nd Bezirk to flush out his friend Harry Lime in *The Third Man*, men can be seen clearing rubble by the Reichsbrücke. It is not said whether they were Nazis.
† A plebiscite carried out in the wake of the Treaty of Saint-Germain on 10 October 1920 had given the region to Austria.

happening, and had assumed that sooner or later someone would come along and give them some orders.'[97]

Carinthia not Styria was the lynchpin of British foreign-political aims in the region. The goal was to prevent Trieste from falling into the wrong hands – that meant Tito. At the end of the war the New Zealanders had been sent to take the port and keep the Yugoslavs out. Trieste was to be granted to Italy in 1947, and in the meantime it was needed to supply the British and Western Allied garrisons. It was left to Field Marshal Alexander to convince the Yugoslavs to withdraw. When they refused, the British printed their own posters, accusing Tito of methods similar to Hitler's. Byrnes's predecessor as American secretary of state, Edward Stettinius, threatened to withdraw aid from Yugoslavia. Alexander used a line of argument that was current at the time and assured Tito that territorial settlements would be left to the 'peace conference'. The Yugoslavs finally consented to leave on 21 May.

Bankrupt, overstretched and reeling from the blows inflicted by the war, the British showed a reluctance to be saddled with Austria. From 1943 onwards they were active in seeking a solution that would mean Austrian independence.[98] By October 1948 the British presence had declined to 7,000 men and a thousand civilians. In March that year Bevin had made it clear that it was 'out of the question to defend Austria'.[99] The British Zone was made up of Styria, Carinthia and a small part of the eastern Tyrol around the city of Lienz. Styria presented the new overlords with a problem of what to do with widespread sympathy for the Nazis, and Carinthia with a quite different conundrum: how to handle a large Slovenian minority. Besides these, there was the nagging Yalta Agreement. The British, like the Americans, had agreed to deport any Russian citizens within their zone of occupation. They had also told Tito they would return Yugoslav citizens who had opposed him.

Styria had been having a rough time under the Russians. At first the locals were merely grateful that the war had come to an end. The future governor, the farmer Anton Pirchegger, recorded the fact in a typically pious, Austrian-provincial fashion: 'Christus lebt und wird wieder regieren' (Christ lives and will rule again). A week later the Russians were banging on his door demanding schnapps.[100] They proved less than welcome. During their tenure, the Russians had raped at least 10,000 women and dragged off anything up to 500 men aged between fifteen and sixty-one to work in Siberia. One eyewitness remembered the terrible scenes of looting, and hearing a German-speaking Russian NCO pronounce one word in justification: 'Vergeltung!' (Retribution!).[101]

While the Russians seized anything that appealed to them, the British sat in Bruck-an-der-Mur and waited until the night of 22–23 July when the Red Army pulled out, to be replaced by the 46th Division of the Eighth Army. The Oxford-educated military governor, the Australian Colonel Alexander Wilkinson, installed his military command in Graz, a town which had expressed a notorious fondness for the Führer. On 24 July General McCreery issued a proclamation from the town hall. The British regime was strict: Wilkinson expressed a certain Anglo-Saxon scepticism when he told his fellow officers that 'some, at any rate, of the Austrians were fairly lukewarm Nazis'.[102] The homes of all the Nazis who had fled the city were confiscated and the British continued the process of denazifying the schools. The Russians had made a fairly lame beginning. Wilkinson's men removed a total of around 400 schoolteachers from a body some 3,130 strong.

The priority was to endow the zone with a stable political leadership. Carinthia had been given a Russian-approved cadre and governor in Reinhold Machold in May, and various self-styled resistance groups vied for recognition. The British now 'liberated them from their liberators'. Wilkinson dissolved the lot. Henceforth Styria would have political parties, not resistance groups. He sacked Machold on 25 November and appointed Pirchinger of the ÖVP.[103] A British observer sat in on every session of the provincial assembly or Landtag from now on and every measure had to be approved. It was very much occupation, not liberation.[104] Austrian law as of 13 March 1938 was to be reinstated, but when that date was challenged (the Corporate State had done a few questionable things, such as bring in racial law in 1935) the 1929 constitution was made the fount of legal authority. A curfew was imposed for Austrians. On 1 August Styria received its own judicial overlord in the form of the jurist Lieutenant-Colonel H. Montgomery Hyde.[105]

The British were occasionally overbearing and arrogant, leaving at least one Austrian in no doubt about who the real 'nation of lords' were.[106] One former British subaltern who entered the zone from Italy remembers thinking that 'liberation' was not quite the word: 'In our eyes an Austrian was just a slightly different sort of German.'[107] The arrival of the British nonetheless gave rise to considerable relief, as the Russians had run the province down. But it was a difficult situation. A local newspaper, the *Neue Steirische Zeitung*, was launched to express the British point of view. There was no food, and there was no transport to deliver bread to the suburbs and outlying villages. It was so warm that summer milk went bad on the carts leaving the dairies. There was very little meat or fat and no sugar. Potatoes were issued at a kilo a week. For anyone who had something to barter, supplements to this meagre diet could be obtained from the black market on the Volksgarten. The British authorities made several attempts to break this up.[108] There was also a degree of lawlessness in what was normally a sleepy province. Over two hundred murders had been committed since the end of the war – about a quarter of these by Russians in incidents connected with rape. The historian Donald Cameron Watt served in the FSS (Field Security Service). During his time in the unit he vetted ninety-two petitions from local women wanting to marry British servicemen; investigated a *Third Man*-style theft of pharmaceuticals; and looked into the festering problem of white slavery in the DP camps.[109]

The character of the administration in the British Zone is lightheartedly summed up by Alan Pryce-Jones, then an intelligence officer in the British army. Austria, he said, was divided into eight zones, each one of them a separate state. Four of these were civilian states, four run by the army. 'In the background is a ninth state, Austria, the chief function of which is to be talked about at meetings.'[110] The government of the British Zone was part of John Hynd's 'Hyndquarters'. John Mair, who served on the Austrian Commission, is quick to point out that there was a huge difference in scale between the Austrian Commission and the German Control Council.[111] Hynd was highly sympathetic but, as in Germany, largely impotent when it came to changing the government line. At a subaltern level he was supported by Sir Henry Mack, as well as by Peter Wilkinson, M. F. Cullis and N. J. A. Cheetham.[112] McCreery went home in April 1946 and was replaced by General Sir James Steele.

The Graz Festival was slightly less spectacular than Salzburg, but it had a solid tradition. The British were careful to revive it in 1945, and that year Karl Böhm conducted and the Grazer were able to hear the voices of Julius Patzak and Elisabeth Schwarzkopf. When the festival was staged the following year, the occupying power lent it a British flavour, and Sir Malcolm Sargent was brought in to conduct Elgar's Second Symphony.[113]

Cossacks *and* Domobranci

In Carinthia the British faced a thorny refugee problem resulting from the Big Three Conference at Yalta. Tito's partisans had been fighting Croats and German- and Italian-backed *domobranci* or home guard in Slovenia. In both cases their Catholicism made them allergic to the ideologies proposed by Tito, and they thought fascism a lesser evil. When the war ended both the Croats and the *domobranci* justifiably feared reprisals. There was the usual spate of denunciations, and the wisest fled north across the revived Austrian border with their families, through the Ljubelj Pass to Viktring near Klagenfurt.[114] According to one source, they went first to Hollenburg on the Drau, where they joined up with a number of Waffen-SS men.[115] Tito's partisans had also crossed the border in order to stake their claim to large parts of Carinthia.

The *domobranci* ran into their first dishevelled Tommies, who promptly exhibited the light-fingered approach most often associated with the Red Army and stole their watches.[116] The British were torn between their sympathy for the Slovenians and their families, and their wartime alliance with Tito's partisans who were now showing their colours by raping and pillaging around Klagenfurt.[117] The *domobranci* thought the British would redeploy them to fight the communists. They had not reckoned with the secret arrangements made at Yalta. Sadly for them, the Cold War had not yet started.[118] On 19 May 1945 the British and Tito's men came to an agreement to repatriate all Yugoslav nationals. No differentiation was to be made. The Yugoslavs were not popular with the British and no one was prepared to stick his neck out for them.[119]

Under the Yalta arrangements, the British in Austria had to deal with 45,000 Cossacks requested by the Red Army, as well as the 14,000 Serbs and Croats who were being reclaimed by Tito. The Cossacks had been recruited by the Germans in southern Russia from POWs, and they had been joined by some former tsarist officers and their families. These last amounted to around 3,000 people. Some of them were not Soviet citizens, and therefore not covered by the Yalta agreement. As POWs they enjoyed protection under the Geneva Convention. This was waived.[120] There was also the fact that most of the Cossacks had been fighting in the SS. Their last assignment was to fight with Schörner's army near Prague. There were 60,000 in the British Zone: 'They wore German uniforms, carried German arms, were commanded by German generals, and were an integral part of the German armed forces.' One thing, however, complicated the humanitarian issue: 'They had with them quite a few women and children.'[121]

Marshal Tolbukhin had asked for the Russians to be sent back and the British had agreed. The deportations were carried out by men of the 46th and 78th Divisions on orders from V Corps, following a brief visit by the minister resident at Allied HQ, Harold Macmillan, on 13 May. On 1 June, they were lured out of their camps in Spittal, Judenburg and Lienz under false pretences.[122] Once they discovered what was going to happen to them they refused to budge, which led to some ugly scenes. Women and children said they preferred to be shot there and then to being handed over to the Soviets. Some of the women tied their children to their backs and jumped to their deaths in the River Drau. Tommies used rifles, bayonets and pickaxe handles to convince them to board the lorries that would take them to the frontier. When a warrant officer was bitten, the British soldiers beat some of the Cossacks unconscious. The Argylls were particularly brutal, to women and children as well.[123] The British also 'returned' some 900 German officers, including the commander, General Helmuth von Pannwitz, who was publicly shot on Red Square in Moscow. The British were forced to use duplicitous tactics in expelling both the Cossacks and the *domobranci*, and this caused them considerable distress.

The British were in a difficult position in Carinthia anyway. All the Allies had confirmed Austria within its pre-1938 borders. On the other hand, it appears that Tito had actually backed down on the issue of repatriating the *domobranci*, but the British proceeded anyhow.[124] There is a suggestion that the commanders of the British Fifth and Eighth Armies acted on their own initiatives here, fearing armed conflict with the local partisans. Nigel Nicolson, a British intelligence officer, later summed the matter up with cold-hearted clarity: 'There were many people who felt "Well, so many millions of young men have died in this war, what does another 30,000 matter?"'[125] No one, including Nicolson, knew the precise number of Cossacks in the British Zone. Only when the moment came to shove the home guardsmen into cattle trucks was he reminded of prisoners being despatched to a German concentration camp. As it was, they were told they were being transferred to camps in Italy, but they do not appear to have believed it. The British brought up tanks to make sure there was no trouble, and searched the men's rucksacks: their last cameras, knives, fountain pens and other valuables disappeared into the Tommies' pockets. The officers were sickened. The Welsh Guards, who had been given the job of forcing the 12,000 men back to their deaths, were reported to be on the brink of mutiny. The matter was later covered up.[126]

American Zone

When the Americans marched into Austria in the spring of 1945, they too saw it less as a 'liberated' land than as 'a part of Germany'. Salzburg, for example, yielded without a fight on 3 May, but the Americans would tolerate no red–white–red flags. They were unsympathetic to Austrian complaints about their treatment and dismissed the stories of widespread rape as 'Nazi propaganda'. The Austrians were an 'enemy people' and they had only themselves to blame.[127] The famous American airman Charles Lindbergh noted in his diary that the American GIs had an interesting interpretation of the word 'liberation': it meant helping themselves to anything they could have without paying for it: cameras, weapons, *objets d'art* – 'even women'.[128]

There were good men in their ranks. Paul Sweet was a university history teacher in the OSS. On 27 June he wrote that military government was inconsistent with the notion of a liberated country: 'the sooner we give Austria back to the Austrians the better'. The OSS took the Moscow Declaration more seriously than some. Sweet outlined the reasons for the American presence – to demobilise, protect DPs and arrest Nazis. There should be a minimum of supervision. Austria was needed to stabilise central Europe.[129] When he had been in the job a few months he changed his mind. Writing to his wife, he said the Austrian people were 'morally and politically bankrupt. The only thing about which they seem to have a firm opinion is that the US should cut loose from the Russians, the sooner the better.'[130]

One of the most curious situations the Americans found themselves facing in Upper Austria was the provisional government set up by Ernst Kaltenbrunner, the Nazi RSHA (Security Service) and police chief, as an alternative to Renner. Kaltenbrunner had assembled a number of industrial magnates and enlisted the support of Schuschnigg's minister Edmund Horst-Glaisenau and the archbishop of Salzburg, Andreas Rohracher. Talks had been held with the mayor of Linz, Franz Langoth, and the Gauleiter of the Tyrol, Franz Hofer. Some Christian Socialists were brought out of mothballs such as Karl Seitz, the former mayor of Vienna, and his Corporate State successor Richard Schmitz. Schmitz had sadly died after his incarceration in Dachau. Figl's name was brought up as well. The Americans had no truck with the alternative government. Kaltenbrunner was hanged.[131]

The US Zone had outstanding political advisers at the second level resulting from the large German and Austrian presence in America itself. None of the other Allies possessed such linguists and experts with a first-hand knowledge of the conquered lands. One of the American experts was Martin Herz, whose father had emigrated to the United States from Moravia but had returned to Vienna, so that his son's entire schooling had been in the city. Herz was deeply involved in post-war planning for Austria. Certain things he found silly or preposterous: the ban on frat was one of these. It was 'distasteful' and 'ineffective'. On the question of Austria's 'liberation' he was of the view that it was a 'psychologically reasonable and effective fiction'.[132]

The American commander Mark Clark has gone down in the annals of the Cold War as one of its biggest personalities, but he did not fall out with the Russians or abandon the idea of co-operation until early 1946.[133] He revived the Salzburg Festival in August 1945, and his French opposite number General Béthouart was helpful in procuring the Clave Quartet and Jacques Février. He hoped to bash McCreery's and Koniev's heads together and make the British agree to go up to Vienna, but the British remained as stubborn as ever and Koniev cried off.[134] Clark entertained in style, lodging his guests at his HQ in Schloss Klessheim (called Schloss Claessens by Béthouart) like Hitler before him. Clark was pleased with Klessheim, and was under no illusions about its previous role as a guesthouse for visitors to Berchtesgaden. It had been 'wonderfully modernised and furnished with art treasures, mostly stolen from France'.[135] The festival was a useful way of bringing the Allies together and impressing them with American hospitality. He invited them all for 19 August. Koniev sent Clark's bugbear Zheltov in his place. Zheltov wanted to see what was left of Berchtesgaden, and they visited it in one of Hitler's own cars.[136]

Clark had a number of issues to discuss between concerts. Before Austria could be allowed its independence again, there needed to be talks on DPs, food supplies (a particularly thorny issue), free elections, and 'German' assets.[137] Lapses were reported in the US denazification programme.[138] With time the Americans came to the conclusion that it was not as easy as it had seemed at the outset. Many of the people they had seen as being as above suspicion were no more than common criminals.[139] In the Salzkammergut Clark made use of a German interpreter who claimed to have been a big-shot in the resistance to Hitler. When the German learned that Clark was to take up residence in Vienna, this man offered him his flat there. Clark says that the locals eyed him with suspicion when they saw him sitting with Clark in his staff car. Counter-intelligence was asked to look him up. It transpired that he was no opponent of the regime, but a senior Nazi, and on the Americans' own wanted list.[140] Clark tells us that he foiled Russian attempts to reclaim their own citizens who were ensconced in DP camps in the American Zone. At one point there was a raid carried out by Soviet soldiers in stolen American uniforms. Clark laid a trap for them and caught them red-handed. There were 750,000 DPs in the American Zone, not all of them Russians by any means.[141] Clark was being less than frank, of course, about the very limited protection that the Americans gave to Russians in their zones in Austria or Germany.

Clark used a great deal of Cold War rhetoric in his account of his time in Austria, but his mission had largely come to an end before the big decisions were made. From 1947 the Truman Doctrine and the Marshall Plan were both designed to stem the tide of communism, by liberal use of both stick and carrot – chiefly financial. Washington's National Security Council was also founded at this time, and it was General Geoffrey Keyes, Clark's successor, who was the man to enact the full range of Cold War options. As he pointed out, 'Prague lies west of Vienna.' The United States needed to arm for the Cold War and for the great 'roll-back' – the reclamation of Europe from the Soviets.[142]

The American authorities were slow to create a proper political structure in their zone. In October there was still no governor appointed for Upper Austria.[143] They had to deal with the chaos in Austrian industry. Some of the bigger companies had had installations all over the country and now found themselves divided up among the Allied zones. The motor manufacturer Steyr was a case in point. The administration was in Linz, in the American Zone, but most of the works were in the Soviet Zone, with the exception of the plant making bicycles and motorbikes, which was in Graz – what was later to be the British Zone. The Graz factory also made tank engines and aeroplane parts, which were naturally of interest to the Red Army. The Russians ensured that they had taken all of these before the British came in July.[144]

Another industrial concern was the Hermann-Göring-Werke, an enormous conglomerate of sequestered businesses established in Hitler's home town of Linz. The works were administered by a Pg called Hans Malzacher, but the Americans were forced to admit that Malzacher was universally popular, not only with the governor, Eigl, and the mayor, Koref, but also with the local communists. The pragmatic solution was to make an exception and leave him in the job.[145]

French Zone

The French Zone, which covered the Vorarlberg and most of the Tyrol, was originally run from French HQ in Lindau on Lake Constance in Württemberg. Despite the fraternising billboards set up by General Béthouart, Austrians and the Germans still nurtured fear and resentment of the French and their colonial troops – the Moroccans in particular.[146] The

French had the usual linguistic problems, as far too few of them spoke German, but they were able to find a few refugees and German and Austrian Jews in their Foreign Legion.[147]

The principal problems facing the French were their attitude towards the Renner government; the form of the constitution created after free elections; the ratification of the constitution; the revision of Nazi statutes; the reorganisation of the administration after the necessary purge of Nazi officials; and how to cope with the thousands of refugees, POWs and Austrian Nazis.[148] The figure who emerged as the clear political leader in the Tyrol was Karl Gruber, who was credited with having organised a cell of military opposition to the Germans in the region. On 1 May 1945 he had managed to close down a number of Nazi organisations in Innsbruck. When the Americans marched in on 3 May they were offered the rare sight of an Austrian city festooned with red–white–red flags. The streets were filled with 'resistance fighters', often armed to the teeth.[149]

The French were also planning to reopen schools and universities in their zone in time for the new academic year that autumn. Before that was done, Nazi staff had to be purged and Nazi texts removed from the libraries. The University of Innsbruck was in a parlous state – all the windows had been blown out and the Faculty of Theology closed on Hitler's orders. The French vowed also to restore liberties: individual, political, of assembly and of the press.

The French were reluctant to discharge all their POWs because they wanted to use them as slave-labourers, as elsewhere.[150] On the other hand there was very little active pursuit of the Nazis. Paul Sweet visited the Vorarlberg in June 1945 and found that no one heeded the ban on frat: 'everything seems to be much as normal'.[151] Instead of the Nazis being locked up, they were attached as unarmed auxiliaries to troop units. Marauding DPs were a problem, the Russians in particular. Theft and murder was not unknown. Two found guilty of killing and robbery were executed by the French in the Vorarlberg.[152]

Two early difficulties that the French confronted were the arrival of Archduke Otto and the South Tyrol. Otto was the eldest son of Emperor Charles, who had abdicated in 1918 and died shortly afterwards. Otto had enjoyed a small émigré following during the war and he now saw his chance to push for a Habsburg restoration. He arrived in the Tyrol in September 1945 and left again at the beginning of 1946. The South Tyrol had been awarded to Italy in 1918 as a reward for fighting on the Allied side. As Italy had fought on the wrong side for most of the Second World War, some southern Tyroleans saw a possibility of returning to Austrian rule.

The Americans moved their troops out of the Tyrol on 7 July, to make room for the French. When Béthouart arrived in Innsbruck on the 18th he found a petition from Dr Gruber referring to the 'bleeding wound' inflicted on the Tyrol with the loss of the southern part of the region. On 4 September there was a demonstration in Innsbruck in which 25,000 to 30,000 people took part, 12,000 of them in their local costume.[153] Archduke Otto arrived on 10 August. Béthouart reported his presence both to his own authorities and to the provisional government in Vienna. According to Béthouart, Renner entertained a degree of nostalgia for the great days of empire and merely shook his head, exclaiming, 'Oh! But if he does nothing political!' Renner put pressure on Béthouart to expel Otto, however, possibly because he had heard that the archduke had been conspiring with Gruber to convince the Western Allies to refuse to recognise his regime. Béthouart replied that he would not fetch and carry for Renner. Otto continued to rock the boat and his two brothers, Karl Ludwig and Robert, were in the French Sector of Vienna flirting with the monarchists in the Federal League of Austrians. Eventually all the Allies with the exception of the French expressed a desire to see the old Habsburg ban re-enacted. Otto received delegations during the time he was under the noses of the French. In the end the provisional government dealt with the problem by reintroducing the ban on the Habsburgs instituted in 1918. By that time Otto had left of his own volition.[154]

The first tranche of Nazis in the Tyrol had been eliminated by the Americans as they conquered the region. They had dealt with the more notorious cases. On 16 May 1945 all the councils in the Vorarlberg were sacked, as they were Nazi to a man. Councillors were appointed by the French until February 1947, when elected councils returned. Half the magistrates had to be dismissed as a result of Party membership, as were seven university professors.

It had been decided at Potsdam that all Germans who had entered Austria after the Anschluss were to be repatriated, together with any German Nazis. The French approached the task with zeal. Taking their cue from the expulsions of pro-German Alsatians after 1918, they allowed the Germans to carry just one case, weighing thirty kilos at the most. Germans were expelled willy-nilly at first, but the pace slackened off in 1946 after complaints from the British and American authorities in Germany that they could not accommodate them all. The French showed how partisan they were by releasing all Austrian POWs.[155] The German minorities in Romania and Yugoslavia had not been included in the discussions at Potsdam, and they naturally gravitated towards Austria as former subjects of the Austrian Emperor. For the time being they were herded together in DP camps.

At the end of 1947 there were still 400,000 DPs in Austria, more than there had been in 1945. The South Tyroleans had been found homes in the Austrian northern part of the province. Many had fled from the Soviets, and the Red Army maintained small staffs with the Western Allies part of whose work was to track down their own people and repatriate them. The British had refused to countenance having Soviet officers in their camp at first, but the Russians had made life difficult for them in Vienna and they had had to give in. The French refused to agree to Russian requests to yield the refugees up.

France's political commitment to its zone in the Tyrol–Vorarlberg quickly slackened. At the outset the governor, M. Voizard, had a staff of 1,600. A year later less than half that number remained. By the end of the decade it had sunk to ninety-three. In 1945 there were thirty-four offices in the Tyrol alone, in 1948 just eleven. Before the French went home, they performed their own demontage, removing 3,000 machine tools and 2,700 tons of different metals to compensate for the 35,000 machines taken by the Germans from France: a greater prize was the testing equipment for jet engines in Kramsach and the wind tunnel at Oetztal, which the French reassembled at Modane. Some French machinery had ended up in Kapfenberg in the British Zone. The British helped dismantle it and pack it up for shipment back to Alsace.[156]

11

Life in All Four Zones

Germany today is divided into four zones and within each there are two worlds: an army of occupation and a conquered people.

The former are not just there to supervise and control, they must also exert an influence; they are meant to stop up the spirit of aggression and nationalism and eliminate it before leading the way to democratic self government; civilisation should heal the smashed and shaken land.

The first question that comes to mind is what do these two worlds know of one another? How do they perceive one another? What is the real relationship?

Naturally no one expects an army of occupation to become an object of love and adoration, and on the other side, a conquered people, whose leaders without question launched the war, cannot expect to be treated at once with sympathy and trust.

But the task of reorientation, even successful administration, requires an atmosphere of trust and respect on both sides.

Carl Zuckmayer, *Deutschlandbericht für das Kriegsministerium der Vereinigten Staaten von Amerika*, Göttingen 2004, 71

Children

As a Viennese Jew returning to central Europe in British uniform, George Clare steeled himself against feeling pity for the conquered. At the railway town of Hamm in Westphalia, his mettle was put to the test by a swarm of infants who appeared under the train windows: 'Eh Tommy . . . Please Tommy vat you got? Chockie, sandvich, sveets?' Clare observed the 'manna from Britain' that was tossed out to the urchins: hard-boiled eggs, sweets, sandwiches, chocolate bars, oranges, apples, even tins of pilchards. The children fought with one another to get at the loot while the soldiers enjoyed the spectacle, like 'throwing nuts to monkeys at the zoo'. Clare went back into the compartment and fetched his haversack rations. He jumped down from the train. The four children closest to the door ran away. 'Hier bleiben!' shouted Clare – Stay here! They turned back, curious to hear a Tommy speak German. He shared out his rations among the four of them. He wondered whether any German had done this in the Warsaw Ghetto and yet he felt that what he was doing was right: 'I could not hate all Germans, as the Nazis had condemned and hated all Jews. No, I neither hated Germans nor – with the exception of the children – did I pity them.'[1]

Many German children had become feral. They had lost one or both parents, or had simply been estranged from them. In the big towns they lived in holes in the ground like the rest, begging or scavenging for food. At least one British high court judge began his life in this way, until he was rescued by a British soldier who took him back to Britain with him and sent him to school. James Stern remembered the vision of these curious guttersnipes, clothed in rags – 'or rather, from head to foot they were perfectly camouflaged in filth, so that until they moved you could not tell they were there'. At the approach of an adult, especially a foreign soldier, they scattered like so many rabbits, disappearing into holes. When they re-emerged they sniffed and stared around them. 'And then you'd see that they carried stones or sticks or bars of iron, and their teeth were black and broken, or that they had no teeth, that one had a single arm, another a crutch, and that the only clean spots on their bodies were the whites of their eyes.' When he looked into their eyes, however, they were no longer rabbits to Stern – they were famished, diseased leopard-cubs 'whose one enemy was man'.[2]

Some of these children had homes, but they nonetheless went out and hunted in packs, stealing what they could from the conquerors. When Stern's major was alerted to some theft from their well-stocked larder, he decided that some children were to blame. The supposed criminals were hunted down to a dung heap where they had their camp and threatened at pistol point. The youngest of the boys was around five. The only evidence they found was a bottle containing some pink petrol: American petrol was dyed pink. That was enough to convict them. The major ordered a search of their parents' lodgings. The flats were searched and at least one of the boys received a clip round the ear from his father, but no contraband was found, and the case against the boys was dismissed.[3]

Nor was it only working-class children who took to crime in this way. Zuckmayer met a certain Frau Doris von M., a former actress married to an elderly Prussian nobleman who kept a boarding house for American visitors to Berlin. 'My son steals!' she told the dramatist. 'And we don't know what we should do about it.' Her son and his private-school-educated friends stole to trade, sometimes for pleasure, sometimes for sport: 'The only true Commandment is the eleventh – thou shalt not get caught.' Jürgen was the boy's name. One day he returned with a pound of sugar that he had bought with cigarettes pinched from a teacher's pocket. He also had some chocolate, taken from an American nurse. He proudly delivered these preciosa to his parents, believing that he had done something useful and that he was contributing to the family budget. He had two pilfered cigarettes for his father and was disappointed when he received no thanks. Jürgen had no religion: 'The Lord looks after the "Amis", because they can afford him. The Ivans don't need any, because they worship vodka. The Germans are too poor for either.'

Jürgen's parents were strict about his thieving, but it was not always so. Others welcomed a wheelbarrow filled with stolen coal or a pound of bacon.[4] For many more indigent Germans they could hardly have done without a little help from their children, particularly teenage boys. Heinrich Böll's short story 'Lohengrins Tod' (Lohengrin's Death) of 1950 is about a boy who is shot at by Luxembourgeois soldiers while stealing coal from a train, falls and suffers appalling injuries. In the hospital they ask if his parents should be informed, only to find out that his mother is dead, and the head of the household is his elder brother. Stealing coal was hardly seen to be a sin: after all, Dr Frings* had actually absolved the coal-stealers from his pulpit.[5]

Children were a considerable problem for the Allied authorities. There were over fifteen million of them in Germany. Of those born after 1930, some 1,250,000 had lost a parent in the war, and 250,000 had lost both. Up to a third had no more contact with their fathers as they were in POW camps, while a further million and a half were refugees from the east, with a little under half that number living in makeshift camps. In the case of a boy arrested for petty larceny in Munich in 1946, it transpired that his mother had been killed in an air-raid in Essen in 1943, that his father was missing in Russia, that he had been billeted with an aunt in Dortmund but had been evacuated to East Prussia. He had moved to Danzig to be trained to operate an anti-aircraft battery where he had been captured by the Red Army. The Russians had released him. He had gone to Berlin, but had been unable to locate the relative he was looking for. He had finally gone to Bavaria in search of food. Many female children resorted to prostitution

* See below pp. 368–9.

to survive. Boys, too, performed a service for Allied soldiers. In Frankfurt their most prominent client was the infamous American major 'Tante Anna' (Aunt Anna).[6]

American schoolmasters thought the appropriate policy was to organise the children in sporting clubs and teach them democracy at the same time. It was believed that baseball and football might instil a sense of fair play in small Germans. The sporting life was lost on many of them, but jazz and dancing tended to succeed where baseball failed: the jitterbug and boogie-woogie were popular with German youth, as were Louis Armstrong and Duke Ellington. Attempts to extend musical re-education to Samuel Barber and Aaron Copeland proved less successful. The Germans had a musical tradition of their own. A camp was established at Compiègne near Paris to train German teachers.[7] The Americans made the mistake of trying to herd German children together in these imitation summer camps. Hitler's *Volksgemeinschaft* had emphasised the community in preference to the individual, and right-thinking German youth wanted nothing of the American idea. They loathed all notions of being 'herded together once again'.

One visionary was Yella Lepman, a Jewish writer born in Stuttgart who returned to Germany in 1945 in an American uniform. From 1946 she built up an international children's library in Munich which she ran until 1957. In December 1945 she went before incredulous American generals to demand cases of books for German children. She stood her ground and eventually received their blessing to import some. In her memoir she describes the sight of young children as she first encountered them playing in the bomb craters before the ruined station. Many were without shoes, and ran around in their socks or barefoot. It was hard to tell the difference between little boys and girls; 'here and there they made an attempt to beg; a ten-year-old with one leg, the other certainly lost during a night of bombing, hops like a lame bird around the American canteen, clapping his hands imploringly. Occasionally a white or black soldier takes pity and throws the child something: a half chewed piece of chocolate out of his pack, a stale sandwich, a few cigarettes to barter: that produces a wild commotion, sometimes a fight, a punch-up.'[8]

CARE packets were the salvation of suffering Germans like Charlotte von der Schulenburg. After the currency reform of 1948 which scrapped the inflationary Reichsmark she exchanged the coffee in the parcels for Deutsche Marks. She also received second-hand clothes from English and American families who had heard of her plight. There was always a party when the parcels came and the maid Klara was proud to take the children into the village dolled up in their not quite new finery. The collars were dazzlingly white, their hairbands freshly ironed.

Another charity organisation for the families of the Plotters was founded by a Swiss doctor, Albert von Erlach. The money was spent on taking the children of the conspirators and giving them a holiday with a Swiss family. Two of Charlotte's children were dressed up in their best tracksuits and clogs and taken to a Red Cross train in Hanover where they were consigned to the care of English nurses. The train took off with little Schulenburgs, Schwerins and Kleists. They came back three months later. One of the Schulenburg daughters had put on seven and a half kilos. She was smartly dressed in grey flannel and wonderful shoes. The other had plump cheeks and a splendid little coat. They called out to their mother, 'We have brought you silk stockings and Nescafé!' The following year two of her other children went and gorged themselves on oranges and chocolate and other delicacies that Germans could only dream of. It broke her heart to lose her children for such a long time, but she had to admit the benefits.[9]

Arts

German literature was set for a flowering after 1945, once the pressure of Nazism had been lifted, and Goebbels's nose pulled out of the pot. Thomas Mann had adopted a typically high and mighty attitude to any literary stirrings that took place between 1933 and 1945: 'A stench of blood and shame attaches to them; they should all be pulped.' Had such pulping come about, it would have been as effective a form of censorship as the Nazis ever used.[10] Mann's comments were occasioned by an invitation to return to Germany penned by the author Walter von Molo in the summer of 1945.

> Please come soon . . . look at the grief-furrowed faces, look at the unutterable sadness in the eyes of the many who did not take part in the glorification of the shadowy side of our natures, who could not leave their homes, because we are talking here of many millions of people for whom there was no other place on earth other than their own land which was gradually transforming itself into a huge concentration camp, in which there would be only different grades of prisoners and warders.

Mann's rigid stance did not make him popular in Germany, and Hans Habe, who had returned to Germany in American uniform and set about castigating his former countrymen, was dismissed as a 'Morgenthau-boy'.[11]

Ernst Jünger's tract *Der Friede* (The Peace) was one of the most important pieces of samizdat literature written during the war, and it continued its illicit circulation after the peace. It was written in 1941 and revised in 1943, when Jünger was protected by the Army Command, chiefly in Paris. The following year Jünger suffered a personal tragedy when his son Ernst was killed near Carrara in Italy. It was Fritz-Dietlof von der Schulenburg who brought a copy of the text back to Germany and circulated it among the opposition. More copies were made in March 1945, and these were distributed in south Germany. The Allies, however, refused to grant a licence to print the book. In 1948 it was published in Paris, Amsterdam and New York and in 1949 in Zurich and Vienna.[12] On 30 August 1945, Jünger had a visit at Kirchhorst: 'In the afternoon Axel von dem Bussche-Streithorst came, a young and severely handicapped major. He brought with him a copy of my treatise on the peace. I have the impression that this is the best known of my writings . . . although no press has printed it, no bookseller has sold it, and no newspaper has published a review. The whole fame of the book rests on a few copies that I gave away.'[13]

Written in Jünger's mystical style, *Der Friede* is a work of great foresight which makes a plea for an honest, workable peace. It is at once clear why the Allies disliked it: it calls their actions – and their peace – into question even before they had formulated the terms. For Jünger the blood of dead solders was the seed that would bring forth corn after the peace; and that corn was for all to share, conqueror and conquered. It must be a peace in which all sides win. Hatred was poor-quality corn. 'The good corn that has here been so finely ground should never be squandered; it must provide us with bread for a long time.'[14] Jünger spared neither side. He talked of the exterminations carried out by the Germans, 'where men were killed like vermin' or 'hunted down like wolves'. 'Dark rumours spoke of horrible agapes where thugs and torturers . . . waded in the blood of their victims.' For the foreseeable future these 'death pits' would remain in the minds of man – 'they are the real monuments to this war like those at Douaumont and Langemarck'.* 'No one can rid himself of guilt.'[15] Jünger cast himself as the 'decent' soldier, the respecter of his enemy, for 'no one can be a hero to his enemy who does not credit him.'[16] Finally, Jünger warned against a merely technical, non-creative peace. Such a settlement would mean that 'tyranny would grow and fear with it, the darkness would spread yet further and in a short while new fronts would open, occasioning new conflicts'.[17]

---

* Douaumont was one of the bloodiest battles in the Verdun campaign; Langemarck near Ypres witnessed the killing of the flower of German youth in October and November 1914.

Jünger had his fans, although they were not often to be found among the forces of occupation. He was also under attack from the exiles. He was the most important German writer to have stayed put, but he wrote no praise of the Nazis, and when the Nazis offered him a seat in their emasculated Reichstag he told them he would rather write a good poem than represent 60,000 dolts. His book *On the Marble Cliffs* was seen as a brave attack on the dictatorship, and gave solace to many opponents of the regime. Klaus Mann nonetheless lashed out at him in *Auf der Suche nach einem Weg*, calling him a 'card sharp who tries to mislead people into believing barbarity was a new way of thinking'.[18]

Like everyone else in public life, artists and writers had to fill in the 133-question *Fragebogen* or questionnaire to determine their degree of collaboration with the regime. Ernst von Salomon sent up the high-minded and clumsy Allied approach in his highly successful book *Der Fragebogen* (*The Answers*) of 1951. Salomon was naturally an object of suspicion to the Allies because he had played a role in the assassination of the Jewish foreign minister Walther Rathenau in 1922. Salomon had been nineteen at the time, a proudly Prussian, right-wing thug who had been at a cadet school when the Great War ended and regretted having been denied the chance to join the scrap and serve his king and Kaiser like countless other Prussian noblemen before him. He was in and out of prison throughout the 1920s, but his first book, *Die Geächteten* (*The Outlaws*) of 1930, brought him into the literary limelight. He became a successful author and screenwriter and one of the darlings of the publisher Ernst Rohwohlt.

Salomon was a Prussian royalist, not a Nazi, but the tone of his books appealed to the country's rulers after 1933. He nonetheless dismissed out of hand their attempts to woo him. When American interrogaters asked him why he had not pursued what would have been a highly successful career in the Party, he replied candidly that he had earned three times as much as a screenwriter as he would have done as a Gauleiter.[19] *Die Fragebogen* was a huge success, selling a quarter of a million copies in the fledgling Bundesrepublik. Having been so severely chastised and humiliated by the Allies, many Germans revelled in its pugnacious treatment of what Salomon saw as American hypocrisy. Liberals, both in Germany and abroad, were not so sure. The Oxford academic Goronwy Rees, who provided an introduction to the English edition, warned readers against the smoothness of the author's tongue, but concurred with Salomon's outraged contention that 'to be convicted of National Socialism was necessarily to be convicted of guilt'.[20]

What annoyed others more was the absence of apology for the deeds of the Nazis, or indeed for some of the spicier moments of the author's youth (even though he had paid his debt), and his desire to turn the SA leader and Nazi ambassador to Slovakia, Hanns Ludin, into a decent man and a martyr to his principles. Despite his diplomatic rank Ludin was hanged, or rather strangled, by the Czechs in January 1948. It took him twenty minutes to die.[21]

But, if some of the arts were to see a flowering, others were dogged by denazification. This particularly affected music and the persons of Germany's two greatest non-émigré composers, Richard Strauss and Hans Pfitzner. Both had been members of the Nazi Reich Kulturkammer and were eligible for internment under JCS 1067. The seventy-six-year-old Pfitzner was put in the camp at Garmisch-Partenkirchen, smack opposite the gates to Strauss's villa, in 1945 and was banned from writing. The ban was lifted the following year, but he had to go before the Spruchkammer or denazification tribunal in 1947. He died in the same year as Strauss: 1949.

Strauss managed to avoid internment. He had never been a Nazi, and on 1 May 1945 described the Third Reich as '12 years of the rule of bestiality, ignorance and illiteracy, which brought about the destruction of 2,000 years of German civilisation'. Then Thomas Mann's son Klaus turned up and tricked him into saying the sort of things that would make Americans believe he was an unrepentant Nazi. But not all Americans shunned him, and famously the oboist and GI John de Lancie commissioned one of his great late works, the Oboe Concerto of 1945. Denazification dangled over Strauss's head too, but he managed to make it to Switzerland. In 1947 he gave a tour in Britain, although his music was still banned in Germany. He was finally cleared in June 1948. He had meanwhile become an Austrian citizen.[22]

The visual arts were also hampered by the perceived need to avoid everything that had been practised under the Nazis: representation was out. Those members of the older generation who struggled on did it with far less conviction, as was plain to see in the poor late works of Dix and Grosz. One exception, perhaps, were the 'unpainted' works of the right-wing artist Nolde, who had gone into 'inner exile' after his paintings had been declared degenerate by the Nazis. The Nazi artists, the sculptor Breker for example, had no appreciable audience now. The coming men were of the Beuys and Baselitz type, the latter literally standing tradition on its head.

The Press

The new papers after the war in Berlin were propaganda sheets put out by the Russian army such as the *Nachrichten für die deutsche Bevölkerung*. The first proper paper was the *Tägliche Rundschau*, which appeared on 15 May 1945, edited by SBZ. It was eagerly scoured in hope that it would give a clue to what the Russians would do next. The next to appear was the *Berliner Zeitung* a week later. Initially this was also the work of the Soviets, but they handed it over to the town hall, and it was edited by Rudolf Hernnstadt, a Jewish journalist who had enjoyed a good reputation before the war. The first paper for Berlin was the communist *Deutsche Volkszeitung*, edited by a Muscovite. This was followed by the socialist *Das Volk*.

Experience and language made German and Austrian *Remigranten* invaluable when it came to controlling and editing the new press. Bernhard Menne became the first editor of the *Welt am Sonntag*, while Erich Brost was his opposite number on the *Kölnischen Kurier*. The Viennese E. H. Pollitzer – or Pollitt – was editor of the *Lübecker Post*. At first he worked under the historian A. G. Dickens before he was allowed to run his own show. Other returned Germans became prominent journalists. Leo Felix, who had gone under the name Felix Field during the war, worked for a number of papers. Peter de (or von) Mendelssohn was the British equivalent of a Muscovite: he had emigrated to Britain and served in the British army and helped the British establish the credentials of German journalists after the war.[23] He was editor of Ullstein's ambitious *Neue Zeit*. In the end this came to nothing, and the first paper free from Allied propaganda was the *Tagesspiegel*.

For a while the Americans founded their 'newspaper metropolis' on the little town of Bad Nauheim. This was the base for two new papers, the *Frankfurter Presse* and the *Frankfurter Rundschau*. The first issue of the *Allgemeine Zeitung* – which was to become the famous *Frankfurter Allgemeine Zeitung (FAZ)* – came out on 7 August 1945, after the break-up of the Potsdam Conference. The editor had instructions from the Americans not to print any stories about Allied discord. Later Peter de Mendelssohn ran that too, before returning to London. The *Frankfurter Presse* got off to a good start, with the letter from Walter von Molo to Thomas Mann and a piece by Alfred Kerr. The Liberal Democrats had their voice in *Der Morgen*. By September, newspapers were popping up like mushrooms. There were 150 of them founded between 1945 and 1948.[24]

The Americans had a considerable success with the *Neue Zeitung* and the glossy *Heute* in Munich. Erich Kästner edited the *Neue Zeitung*, which was controlled by Major Hans Wallenberg, a former Ullstein editor who had emigrated in 1937. Wallenberg was a convinced anti-communist who left the *Neue Zeitung* to work for Springer in Hamburg. The paper was a breath of fresh air in its time, as its aficionados admired the quality of the writing and ignored its propaganda content. In 1947 it was selling 800,000 copies, and Wallenberg believed he could easily dispose of one and a half million. Zuckmayer thought that the Americans could be really proud of what they had achieved through the *Neue Zeitung*.[25] Another prominent 'remigrant' was Hans (Janos) Habe, the son of the Viennese press baron Imre Bekessy.[26] Habe ran parts of the press for the Americans and had to deal with the odd dissenting voice the Americans wanted to ban. One of these was *Der Ruf*, which branded the occupation 'anachronistic, colonialistic and inhumane'. Habe turned to Thomas Mann for support: 'These young people hate their fathers; but they hate the enemies of their fathers even more.'[27]

The Americans were also successful in creating radio stations with a distinct propaganda role. One of these was Radio Liberty, launched on 12 August 1946. Another was RIAS (Radio in American Sector), which came into its own during the Berlin blockade, broadcasting from vans. Clay believed that RIAS did essential propaganda work, and that the Americans should grant it funds to continue.[28]

In the summer of 1947, Tisa von der Schulenburg found work as a journalist in Hamburg. She paid a call on Martin Beheim-Schwarzbach, who worked in the office of *Die Welt* in the city. He had been a chess partner in London of Tisa's first husband, Fritz Hess. The editor, Julius Hollos, was also present at the meeting. She told them she wanted to work as an illustrator on the *Süddeutsche Zeitung*. 'Why not come to us?' they said. She was engaged at RM300 a month, as a writer and illustrator.[29] She focused her attention on the Ruhr, where she sketched the miners in the same way as she had drawn the pits in County Durham in the 1930s. Everyone was suspicious of her. The British thought she was a communist agitator, the miners a British spy. When she tried to cover the 1948 London Olympics for *Die Welt* the British refused to grant her papers. In despair she took the veil.[30]

Where the former owners had been Jewish, newspapers were relatively free from Allied interference. This was the case of Ullstein in Berlin, owners of the *Berliner Zeitung*, the *Berliner Morgenpost* and the *Berliner Abendpost*. Some of the Ullsteins had fled to America and others to

London, where they had created an Ullstein Ltd. The head of the family, Hermann Ullstein, had died in the autumn of 1944. The only Ullstein remaining in Germany was Heinz, who remained alive because of his Aryan wife. Like most Jews married to Christians, he performed hard labour for the Todt Organisation, but fled at the right moment and survived the massacre of many of the others. He surfaced just in time to save the machinery of the press, which the Russians had dismantled but not yet shipped.

Axel Springer was a creation of the British Zone. The successful German weekly *Der Spiegel* began life as *Diese Woche*, the child of the twenty-one-year-old Major Chaloner of the Hanover Information Council. When its editorial got out of hand, it was offered to the Germans and Springer. Springer was given his first licence by Major William Barnetson, later chairman of Reuters. Despite the opposition of some British administrators, Springer rapidly advanced to become Germany's first post-war press baron.[31]

Attitudes to 20 July

The Allies introduced a term for the victims of National Socialism, which should have secured privileges. In practice this did not happen much at first. They were called 'Opfer des Faschismus' (victims of fascism) or OdF. In theory at least Greta, the widow of the poet Adam Kuckhoff who had been executed as a member of the communist-inspired 'Red Orchestra', and Marion Gräfin Yorck, whose husband perished on a gibbet after 20 July, should have received higher rations. The OdFs had their own relief organisation. It was not alone – there was a rival body in the VVN, or Vereinigung der Verfolgten des Naziregimes.

While he was attached to an American unit researching the nature of Nazism, the poet W. H. Auden heard the story of the Scholls for the first time and their touching but ultimately hopeless attempt to resist Hitler: 'Those who condemn the Germans for their lack of opposition . . . should have spent six months here during the war.'[32] Hans and Sophie Scholl, Alexander Schmorrell, Christoph Probst, Willi Graf and Professor Kurt Huber had brazenly printed leaflets attacking Hitler and the war and scattered them throughout the lecture halls of the university in Munich. A branch of this 'Weisse Rose' Movement had been formed in Hamburg too. They had all been beheaded for their pains – and eight more in Hamburg.[33]

Auden and his friends went to see the family of 'Schurik' Schmorrell to learn the story at first hand. It proved a harrowing and emotional moment as the father, mother and sister of the young medical student rehearsed the story of his arrest and execution. The sister, Natascha, had been tortured and lost an eye in the process. This did not protect them from the American army of occupation. James Stern later learned that the Schmorrells, father, mother and sister of a hero of the resistance, had been kicked out of their home to provide accommodation for servicemen and their families.[34]

However much Stern wished to deny the idea of 'good Germans', the subject exerted a sort of fascination for him. Spurred on by what Auden had discovered about the White Rose conspirators, he paid a visit to Prince Fugger von Glött in his vast palace near Memmingen. The prince had been designated governor of Bavaria in the event of Hitler's death on 20 July 1944, as he was connected with the two Jesuit priests who had taken part in the discussions of the opposition. He had been arrested after the failure of the Plot and had been one of the few survivors. As he told his harrowing tale the scales began to drop from Stern's eyes.

The BBC's Hugh Carleton Greene made an early sympathetic pro-gramme about the Plot broadcast on its first anniversary on 20 July 1945. Greene had been a journalist in Germany before the war and an intelli-gence officer during the conflict. After the war he directed the German-language service of the BBC and as control officer for the media exerted an important influence in the intellectual reconstruction of Germany. Ursula von Kardorff, who had been closely connected to many of the plotters, described the programme as 'very fair, no one could have done it better'. From it she learned the sad news of Nikolaus von Halem's death.[35]

German attitudes were more complicated. Until May 1945 these men had been traitors; now ordinary Germans had to get used to the idea that they were actually heroes. For those who had been peripheral to the plot-ters' circle this was not a problem. Ursula von Kardorff was particularly interested to know the fate of Fritz-Dietlof von der Schulenburg. The BBC or the Allied station in Calais had put it about that he was still alive. His wife Charlotte had also held out hope. Immediately after the war she had gone to the British CO in Plön to ask whether there was any truth in the broadcasts. She was received by a Jewish liaison officer who promised to look into things. Later he appeared at Testorf where she was living. 'That was just propaganda' with no foundation in fact, he told her. Her husband had been hanged in August 1944.[36] Also in Lübeck was Fritz-Dietlof's sister Tisa. On the day of Greene's broadcast she suffered a complete nervous collapse: 'The memory of the past year. All the tears that I had failed to shed at Fritzi's death came out unexpectedly in an unstaunchable deluge, I was defenceless. All my brothers were dead. My home was lost.'[37]

One exile who had a fully open mind about the German opposition to Hitler was Carl Zuckmayer. Zuckmayer had been a Heidelberg contemporary of Carlo Mierendorff, one of the chief plotters who had been killed in an Allied bombing raid on Leipzig in December 1943. He had also been a friend of Helmuth James von Moltke, great-nephew of the Great Moltke, Prussian chief of staff in Bismarck's wars, and nephew of the Lesser Moltke, who as chief of staff bungled the German advance in 1914. Helmuth James's manor at Kreisau (a gift to the older Moltke from his grateful king) had been used for meetings and debates by members of the opposition, who were later known as the Kreisauer Kreis, or Kreisau Circle.

Zuckmayer had believed that the Kreisauer were the perfect breeding stock for the new Germany, but he sadly realised all too quickly how comprehensive had been the purge after 20 July. Not only Mierendorff and Moltke were dead, but also his friends the trades-unionist Wilhelm Leuschner and the socialist Theodor Haubach. Some, however, had survived; and Zuckmayer felt they should be hailed, and receive a promise of support.[38] Many of their names had not even appeared in the newspapers – 'the footsloggers, the unknown warriors of the resistance'. Zuckmayer cites one example of a widow whose husband had been arrested in June 1941. More than a year later a neighbour drew her attention to a notice in an advertisement column. It informed her and the rest of the world that the man had been executed for high treason. The widow had lived as a post-office cleaner, but when Zuckmayer met her she had no work and no savings. The only thing she had to live on was a modest sum from the OdF. She was bitter, because the Nazis did more for their people; indeed the judges who had sentenced her husband to death received pensions, and so did their widows. She lived in great solitude, her only pleasure had been her wireless set, but the Nazis had taken that away. She was resigned to her fate: nothing could give her back her husband.[39]

One who survived the general purge was the poet and writer Günther Weisenborn. He had been involved with Harro Schulze-Boysen and the Red Orchestra. The Gestapo lacked evidence against him and his life was spared. He was condemned to life imprisonment. His young wife had endeavoured to maintain contact with him in prison in Luckau. She discovered that he was part of a work detail that was sent out of the prison, so she travelled on the trains that transported the prisoners in order to catch a glimpse of him. She had written and performed music to accompany some of his lyrics, and to attract his attention she whistled one of these tunes. One day she heard the same tune whistled inside the prisoners' carriage, and knew that he was aware that she was near him. When the Russians came they released the prisoners from their ordeal, but immediately they were assigned roles within the zone. Meanwhile the Battle for Berlin reigned, and she could not find a way to him. The Russians finally dismissed him from his job and he rode on a bicycle to Berlin. Their former home had been destroyed by bombs, and he had not a clue where she might be. Later he was riding though an unfamiliar suburb when he saw another bicycle coming towards him: it was her – 'They had found one another in the chaos.'[40]

Jews in Germany and Austria

One way or another, Germany and Austria had lost the Jews, who had been such a noticeable part of their populations. There had been around 450,000 in Germany in 1933. Of these some two-thirds emigrated. The other third perished in the camps and ghettos. In Austria the original figure was around 180,000, with almost all of them living in Vienna. Again two-thirds got away, but the other 65,000 died. Of those whose lives were saved by timely emigration, only a tiny percentage returned. Most of them would have been reluctant to find themselves face to face with the murderers of their friends and relations. But there were Jews in Germany and Austria after 1945 – soldiers and DPs.

Not all Germans had been pleased by the official antisemitism of the Nazi years, by any means. Ursula von Kardorff, who saw a convoy of vehicles emblazoned with Stars of David (they belonged to the Jewish Infantry Brigade) leading off a posse of bedraggled POWs, called it 'divine justice' and recalled the moment three years before when she had seen Jews wearing the same stars cowering in the backstreets of Berlin while German soldiers swaggered around in smart uniforms bedecked with decorations.[41]

By the summer of 1945, the Jews had their own fighting units in Germany. Up to 35,000 Jewish Palestinians signed up for the Brigade – a proper fighting force. For much of the war the British had allowed German and Austrian Jews only to serve unarmed in the Pioneer Corps and many felt profoundly insulted. When former German and Austrian Jews arrived in Germany in 1945 they learned what had become of their relatives and co-religionaries who had stayed behind. They had feared the worst, but few could have imagined that the horror would be as bad as it was. They were still in uniform and very few could do much to help in the circumstances. One exception was Captain Horwell, who became assistant commander of Bergen-Belsen after the liberation, and was able to aid the 10,000 who survived.[42]

Many German or Austrian Jews had distinguished themselves in the fighting and they were to go on to play important roles under the occupation. One who played a significant political part in the British army was Michael Alexander Thomas. At D-Day Thomas was a liaison officer between the British and the Poles. He was much feared by his staff, who he insisted should shower and brush their teeth daily. Such rigour earned him the sobriquet 'the Prussian Baron'.[43] In Germany he was appointed political officer and made firm contacts with leading socialist politicians such as Karl Severing and Rudolf Petersen in Hamburg. He prevented General Templer from banning Germans from wearing military uniforms, as he pointed out they had no other clothes. Templer found this advice unwelcome. Thomas left the army as a result of the insensitivity of his immediate superior, Lieutenant-Colonel Pearson, who referred to him as a 'Jew-boy'.

Thomas was not the only Jew holding high rank as a political officer. In Schleswig-Holstein Major Lyndon was head of the Political Department. Jews also performed important roles in Information Departments – that is, propaganda and denazification. Two majors, Calmon and Kendal (born Knobloch), served first in Austria before being assigned the task of finding war criminals. Major Linford was second secretary to Allied Control Commission in Austria, acting as liaison with the other Allies. His counterpart in Berlin was a Captain Lederer. Kaye Sely was chief of information control, first in Hamburg and then in Berlin. Many of these Jews were academics in disguise. The distinguished historian of Germany F. L. Carsten was the son of a Berlin doctor who had Anglicised his first name (Franz) to Francis. He spent his war at the Political Warfare Executive (PWE) and performed an important role during the occupation as the author of a handbook explaining Germany to British forces.[44]

Many Jews spoke German – although they often refused to use it among themselves, having decided that the language was somehow polluted. Even the Poles used Jewish soldiers as interpreters with the Germans in the so-called 'Recovered Territories'.[45] When George Clare went to work in denazification in Berlin in 1946, he found that all his colleagues were German or Austrian Jews or half-Jews with the exception of the Russian. Sely was from Munich. The American, Ralph Brown, was a Berliner.[46]

The role of the Jews in the British army occasionally caused concern. Kaye Sely showed George Clare a letter from 'Public Safety' accusing the Jews of excessive zeal in denazification, citing the fact that most of the leading lights were former German and Austrian Jews who might be acting from motives of revenge.[47] There were many more Jews in the American army than in the British. The Americans were much more willing to grant commissions to refugees. The British had qualms about using them.

Most of the Jews employed during the occupation worked as interpreters, and a special school was formed to train them in Brussels. An Austrian, Major Reitlinger, who had been in SOE during the war, was the eyes and ears of General McCreery in Vienna. A Viennese, Sergeant R. Rawdon, was interpreter for the Military Police unit who were the first British soldiers to enter Berlin. Not only Jews, however, were used to make up for the linguistic inadequacies of the British forces. Until they realised who they were dealing with, the British and Americans actually employed members of the Nazi Concordia Bureau and British Free Corps the motley gang commanded by John Amery, son of the colonial secretary Leo. Once the penny dropped, the traitors were shipped back to Britain and tried.[48]

The Fate of Jewish DPs

The Jewish survivors who drifted towards Germany in the hope of reaching the West or Palestine were put back behind barbed wire in DP camps. Many children were born in captivity. For the Jewish survivors there was a quandary: once they had achieved a sense of humanity once again and could begin to think about the basics of food and clothing, they needed to decide what their future would be, and where. Could they go back to their old homes in Poland or Hungary? These countries had been more or less cleared of Jews. There were no more friends and relations to welcome them, and wherever they went they would be reminded of the scale of their tragedy. And there was the nasty thought of the gentile neighbour, who might look them up and down, surveying them with a mocking smile that said 'What? Still alive?'[49]

These Jews, who were known as the *she'erit Hapletah* or 'rescued remainder', kept flooding into Germany. Partly this was a result of renewed antisemitic violence in the new Poland, where between 1,500 and 2,000 Jews were killed in pogroms in Kielce and elsewhere in 1945. Occupied Germany was considered the safest place to be. Some 270,000 Jews went to Germany after the end of the war and sought refuge in DP camps. The period before they were to find new homes in Palestine and elsewhere has been called the 'grim aftermath of the Holocaust'.[50]

The British were suspicious about the influx of Jews into Germany. They thought, possibly correctly, that they were intending to use Germany as a springboard to Palestine. The head of displaced-persons operations for UNRRA in Germany, Lieutenant-General Sir Frederick Morgan, thought a secret organisation was behind the arrival of so many 'well-dressed, well-fed, rosy-cheeked' Jews who appeared to have 'plenty of money'. The British began to bar entrance to the DP camps to new arrivals and prevent Jews from going south via Austria. They also introduced a compulsory labour law for the inhabitants of the camps.[51]

At their height there were 184 Jewish camps scattered around Germany: there were eleven in the French Zone, twenty-two in the British and 151 in the American. One of the most famous camps was at Landsberg in Bavaria, where the *Landsberger Caytung* was based. The *Landsberger Caytung*, the most successful Jewish paper of the time, offered practical advice to Jews and reported on the Nuremberg trials.[52] *Caytung* (newspaper) was an example of the Germanified Yiddish spoken in the camps. The *Katzet* was the concentration camp, from the German 'KZ'.

One unfortunate aspect of life in the DP camps was that Jews were often driven in with their former tormentors – Hungarian, Ukrainian, Latvians and Poles who had worked voluntarily in the camps and were now as good as stateless. They formed a rough and often criminal core at the centre of the camp. It was not uncommon for the Allies to assign ex-Nazis to the camps as guards; to add insult to injury, they were armed. The presence of these sentries and the barbed-wire fences around the barracks gave the Jews' new quarters an aspect of the concentration camps they had only recently quit.[53]

The preponderance of Jewish DP camps in the American Zone was no accident: Jews wanted to reach America and found British policy on Palestine unsympathetic. Britain was the principal enemy of the Jews before 1949.[54] From January to April 1946 admissions to American camps ran at around 3,000 a day, with some 2,000 entering camps in the American Zone in Austria. By April there were 3,000 Jews in Berlin, 1,600 in the French Zone, 15,600 in the British and 54,000 in the American. There were six times as many Jews in American-occupied Austria as in the British Zone. By the end of the year there were 204,000 Jews in the parts of Germany and Austria controlled by the Western Allies, 90 per cent of them in the American Zones. It was not always the case, however, that the Americans were more considerate towards the Jews than the British. General Patton expressed the view that they were 'baser than animals'.[55]

The Americans were spending $500,000,000 a year on the camps. There was some question as to whom the Jews belonged. They were hardly likely to want to be Germans, and most of the eastern states disowned them too. They were effectively stateless. As numbers continued to swell, the Americans let in a trickle to the US by slightly loosening their quota in December 1945. The British Dominions, which had been excessively stingy in extending hospitality in 1938, continued to sport the oak. Jews who tried to run the blockade into Palestine were famously intercepted and interned in DP camps on Cyprus. When the Jewish state was established in May 1948 they flooded across the water.[56]

The DP camps in Germany resembled Yiddish-speaking villages. The language acquired immense importance before Hebrew developed under the auspices of the new state of Israel. German was clearly out, unless there was no alternative. After 1949 the state of Israel would ban both German and German music. The pre-war drive to assimilation also ground to a halt. Adolf Hitler had taught the Jews in no uncertain terms that they were not wanted.[57] The camps were as close to the *Shtetlach* as anyone was likely to see after the Third Reich. Indeed, they have been described as the shtetl's last evocation.[58] The Jews remained there until they could find a means of getting to Palestine or the United States. The American quota remained very strict until 1950.

Carl Zuckmayer believed that the Jewish DP camps were keeping antisemitism alive. As the Jews were outsiders or foreigners, the word *Ausländer* (foreigner) had become synonymous with Jew in some parts of the country. A little girl near his house in the Salzkammergut told him, 'Mummy went shopping because she wanted to bake something for you. She needed flour, so she had to go to the foreigners.' Often this meant going to a DP camp where those still lucky enough to own cars often found supplies of benzene.

The Jewish camps were comparatively well provided for, and the surplus was sold off – for a price. Zuckmayer heard the Germans grumble that the Jews were growing rich from their hunger. In a dark corner of the main station in Munich he saw a Jew wearing a kaftan, with a long beard and curls – 'a figure never seen in this part of Germany, but perhaps [visible] in Vienna's Leopoldstadt, in Bratislava, Łódź or Warsaw'.* He had a table, chair and cash register, and scruffy individuals were showing him things

---

* Zuckmayer exaggerates. Such figures were certainly to be seen on Berlin's Sophienstrasse after 1918.

they had in their pockets. A woman told him it was a big jewellery market. The last of the family heirlooms were being transformed into meat, fat or coffee. Some of the gems were obviously stolen.[59]

There were still 29,000 Jews in American camps in Austria at the time, who were given better rations than the other DPs, and unlike the others they were exempted from work. That this caused resentment is something of an understatement, especially as the Jews were prominent in the black market. An Allied report produced a statistic that 71 per cent of Austrians felt no guilt about the Second World War. On the other side the Jews complained too. 'Until you get your things back, you are treated like a beggar. Once you have them back, nobody remembers that you were ever a beggar.'[60]

Resentment of the Jews and their higher rations led to a small riot in Bad Ischl in the Salzkammergut in the summer of 1947. The issue was the milk quota. Angry protesters surrounded the hotel that served as the Jewish DP camp and pelted it with stones: 'Down with the dirty Jews! Hang the Jews!' they shouted. The American authorities acted firmly and one rioter was sentenced to fifteen years. The sentence was later reduced by General Keyes.[61]

There were also 15,000 Jews in Germany who had survived the genocide. One of these was Victor Klemperer, who went back to his damaged but inhabitable house in Dresden dreaming of good wines, food, drives in his car, visits to the seaside and the cinema. Mostly he cherished the fact of raw life, of 'simple survival'.[62] He was one of the 3 per cent of German Jews who owed his survival to an Aryan spouse. Jews tended to be given the pick of the jobs in the Russian Zone. A former 'submarine', the machinist Walter Besser, was put in charge of a hospital in 1945. Jewish leaders emerged from captivity in the concentration camps to found newspapers. Josef Rosensaft had been in Bergen-Belsen, where he married the camp doctor Hadassah Bimko after the war. He founded the first Yiddish newspaper in the British Zone at Belsen, *Undzer Sztyme* (Our Voice). Another was Zalman Grinberg, a doctor from Kovno. He founded the Yiddish newspaper *Undzer Weg* (Our Way), first published in October 1945. In the British Zone Hans Frey started the *Jüdisches Gemeindeblatt für die Nord-Rhein Provinz in Westfalen*. Between 1945 and 1948 there were over 200 publications – books and newspapers – published in Yiddish in Germany.[63]

The camps were mostly old barracks buildings, together with some pukka structures that had been cleared of their German occupants. Quite a few of them were near or actually located in old concentration camps like

Bergen-Belsen and Landsberg. Two training camps for Jews were housed in property that had previously belonged to Julius Streicher and Hermann Göring. Jewish DPs in the American Sector of Berlin were actually lodged in the Villa Minou, where the infamous Wannsee Conference had been held in the first weeks of 1942, and where reports had been delivered on the progress of the Final Solution.[64]

In the main, the camps were not as daunting as they might have seemed from the outside. They had their own schools and courses in Jewish history, Hebrew, Zionism and Palestinian geography – once more attesting to the abandonment of assimilation and the embracing of Zionism in most cases. Political parties were formed, theatres put on Yiddish classics, and concerts were given. Groups of singers such as the Happy Boys sang Yiddish songs. American rabbis were assigned to the camps to look after the spiritual well-being of the inmates.[65]

One of the most notorious DP camps was Bergen-Belsen. Once the British had managed to bring down the death rate it was possible to introduce some degree of comfort into the camp, especially when the inmates were moved out of the old buildings and into the well-appointed SS barracks. That took a while. At first witnesses were horrified to see how dehumanised the former prisoners had become. Many of the Jews were women, and General Dempsey, commanding the British Second Army, recalled seeing one 'standing stark naked washing herself with some issue soap in water from a tank in which the remains of a child floated'.[66]

In theory, at least, the French, Dutch, Russians and Poles in Belsen had homes to go to. The Jews did not want to go back, they wanted to go forward. Once the enormity of their suffering was known, they received special treatment. The British rabbi, Rev. Leslie Hardman, arrived at Belsen soon after its liberation. On Friday 20 April he conducted the first Jewish service there, observing *Kiddush* in the open air. With foreboding he remained behind to eat some *gefilte fisch* with the prisoners. The next morning he woke with excruciating pains and was forced to take to his bed for forty-eight hours.[67] Hardman witnessed some old-fashioned anti-semitism among the British officer corps. One officer exclaimed, 'Bloody Jews! Serves them right!' In general, however, it was more the dehumanising effect of the war that he observed in the British – they had seen too much horror to be able to respond any more.[68]

Part of the process of recovering was for women to begin to take an interest in their physical appearance again. One of the doctors working at Belsen was repeatedly asked by the women whether their beauty would return.[69] For some it would take a long time: the humiliation that had been part of the policy of their Nazi torturers had gone too deep. One Red Cross man recalled asking a woman what her name was and where she came from. 'Me . . .' she replied, 'no name – only number – no country, just a Jewess, do you understand? I am only a dog.'[70] Baths were treated with suspicion. Some of the women had been in the extermination camps, and had learned to fear trips to the shower block. The situation was considerably improved when some old women's clothes were found to replace the prison gear and someone discovered a cache of lipstick. In the words of one of the senior medical officers, 'It was the action of genius, of sheer unadulterated brilliance.' The women were overjoyed. The same officer reported seeing a woman dead on a slab still clutching her lipstick.[71]

By June the atmosphere was wholly changed at Belsen. When the cameramen rolled up it reminded a Red Cross woman of 'a Butlin holiday camp'.[72] The inmates wanted to know about Zionism and Palestine. Ironically Hitler had made them better Jews: assimilation was a dead letter. Even hardened atheists were keen to learn about a religion that had not been practised for a generation.[73] To inject a little morale, concerts were given and the likes of Yehudi Menuhin and Benjamin Britten visited. The women of Belsen rediscovered men. Dancing became popular, although the women were still little more than skeletons. The camps were not just culturally fertile. They were productive in human life. After the genetic experiments of the concentration camps, many Jews feared they were barren. This proved not to be the case. In 1946 UNRRA reported between eight and ten thousand pregnancies in the camps, giving the Jewish camps the highest birth rate in the world.[74]

Incidences of antisemitism were comparatively rare, although a Jewish shopkeeper was threatened in Staubing and locals accused the Jews who inhabited the old concentration camp in Deggendorf of carrying out armed robberies. In Munich the Möhlstrasse had its complement of Jewish shops and there was even a kosher restaurant.[75] The camps had flourishing black markets that led to one police raid on a camp near Stuttgart. In the course of the police action a Jew was killed during a dispute about bootleg eggs. After that the police were banned from entering the camps.[76]

There were occasional incidences of fury directed at the Germans, but they were rare. The greatest act of lawlessness committed by the Jews in post-war Germany was the attempt to kill a large number of POWs in Nuremberg. Abba Kovner, who had led an armed revolt in the Vilna Ghetto, founded the Nakom ('Revenge') Group and conceived the idea of poisoning the drinking water in the city. One member of the group found a job in the waterworks, but David Ben-Gurion refused to allow him to go ahead with the scheme. They turned instead to the camp, where 12,000 POWs were kept, many of them ex-SS or Nazis, and succeeded in poisoning the bread. The prisoners suffered terrible pains, but none died. The perpetrators fled to Palestine and resisted all attempts to make them face justice in Germany.[77]

The afterlife of the German Jews was a long time fading. Behind barbed wire they continued their shadowy existence for over a decade. The last Jewish DP camps closed in 1957.

PART III

Crime and Punishment

I2

Guilt

We experienced the false indignation of other lemurs who came to the
place of lies to dig up the dead and expose the decomposed bodies; to
measure them, count them and photograph them, as it was their aim.
They played the role of prosecutor only to gain for themselves the right
to base revenge and then to satisfy themselves with similar orgies . . .
The hand that wants to help man in all this, and to lead him forth in
his blindness, must be free from sin and acts of violence.

Ernst Jünger, *Der Friede*, Vienna 1949, 21

How Could We Have Known?

'The Allies have ceased to threaten us with bombs, now they speak to
us like a nanny, one who gets on our nerves with her bony index
finger and her shrill old maid's voice. You get the feeling of sitting in a
classroom where you are constantly being told off in such a way that even
the best-behaved pupil will after a short while become obstinate.'[1] Many
Germans reacted to the Allies' revelations with disbelief. Ursula von
Kardorff met a typical old Nazi woman who dismissed their broadcasts as
so many lies. She simply didn't want to believe in the atrocity stories.
When they were shown pictures of piles of corpses in Dachau they said
these were pictures of the dead after the Allied bombing raid on Dresden.
Such was the effect of Goebbels's propaganda.[2] When a Polish Jew told
Käthe von Normann he had escaped the fate of twenty-three members of
his family only by being incarcerated in a Siberian POW camp, the truth
dawned on her. She noted in her diary, 'What a mess was caused by this
fallacious doctrine!' and cursed Hitler for not making peace.[3]

James Stern found in the course of his interviews in Munich that the
responses to the questions about concentration camps varied. One
working-class man asked him how German Americans were being treated.

Stern replied, 'With extraordinary fairness' – something we now know to be untrue. When faced with the atrocities of the German camps, the man's response was measured: if it were true it was 'die grösste Schweinerei die es gibt!' (the most disgusting thing he had ever heard!). A young doctor he talked to, who came from a rich family, referred to the treatment of the Jews as a *Kulturschande* (a national disgrace), but he thought the German occupation of Russia had been carried out with no more brutality than the American occupation of Munich.[4]

Carl Zuckmayer thought there were relatively few of these *Ewig-gestrige* (yesterday's men) who believed their current situation was all down to the Allies and that the Germans had done nothing to deserve it. Rare were the Germans, even in the safety of their broken homes or in the corners of a dim-lit, ill-heated *Kneipe*, who rued the hanging of the defendants at Nuremberg. Most Germans would have rejected the extreme charge of 'collective guilt', however, on the ground that there was very little an individual could have done to stop Hitler's warmongering and killing even if he had been fully aware that it was happening. 'Collective guilt' was also changing its meaning with the opening of the concentration camps. Originally the Germans were all guilty of starting an aggressive war, as their fathers had been in 1914. Now they had all committed, aided or abetted mass murder. Ernst Jünger thought he recognised an Allied agenda: 'The thesis of collective guilt has two interwoven skeins. For the conquered it means "I must atone for my brother's guilt", for the victors it affords practical support for their indiscriminate looting.'[5] Some, like the philosopher Karl Jaspers, however, were prepared to assent to the lesser accusation of 'general responsibility'.[6]

Jaspers in Heidelberg was now the respected voice of post-war German philosophy. He tackled the subject of German complicity in his post-war lecture–cum–essay delivered to the medical faculty: 'The Question of German Guilt'. Doctors had been especially prominent in acts of atrocity against the Jews. He defended the necessary evil of the Allied presence: 'They stop us from becoming bumptious and teach us modesty.'[7] The whole world was wagging its finger at Germany. Not just the victors, but also Germans who had opted for exile. Germans might feel they had other things to think about. 'The horizon has become narrow. People don't want to hear about guilt or the past. They don't care about the judgement of history, all they want is for the suffering to cease . . .'[8] Jaspers warned, however, that 'it is the duty of all us Germans to look clearly at the question of guilt and understand the consequences'.[9]

He had lived in Germany during the war. 'Germany under the Nazi regime was a prison. The guilt of falling into this prison is political guilt. Once the gates were shut, however, a prison break from within was no longer possible. Any responsibility, any guilt, attributed to the imprisoned – whenever it arose – must prompt the question whether there was anything they could do.' In a lecture delivered on 15 August, he returned to the theme, but he was kind to Germany and the Germans: 'Thousands of Germans either sought death or were killed anyway because of their opposition to the regime. The majority of them remain anonymous. We survivors did not seek death. We did not go out on to the streets when our Jewish friends were led away, nor did we cry out until they destroyed us as well. We preferred to stay alive on the weak if justified grounds that our death would not have helped anyway. That we live is our guilt. We know before God what deeply humbles us.'[10]

'The Question of German Guilt' helped to define a form of orthodoxy in the early years of the Federal Republic, even if the author himself thought it the most 'misconstrued piece of his collected works'. One of Jaspers's favourite students had been Hannah Arendt, who had spent the war years in safety in America. She too tackled the question of guilt in her book *Organised Guilt and Universal Responsibility*. Like Jaspers she felt it did not help to tar all Germans with the same brush. 'Where all are guilty, nobody in the last analysis can be judged.' It was an echo of Jaspers's own line that 'It runs contrary to sensible argument to make a whole nation guilty of a crime. The criminal is always an individual.' 'The *collective guilt of a nation* or a group within a nation *cannot therefore exist* and with the exception of political responsibility, there is neither criminal, moral nor metaphysical guilt.'[11] Joseph Frings, archbishop of Cologne, adopted a similar line. As far as the war was concerned, 'The Führer took such decisions on his own and at most consulted his closest advisers.' As regards the atrocities, he maintained that most people had learned about them after the war, from the BBC: 'The German people are much more the victims than the perpetrator of these atrocities.'[12]

Jaspers's wife Gertrud was a Jew, and, although she was to some extent protected through her marriage to the prominent intellectual, by the end of the war she was in hiding. Jaspers nonetheless felt that most of his fellow countrymen were not evil: 'Generalisations about the mentalities and behaviour of millions of Germans in the Nazi era are bound to be of limited application – apart, perhaps, from the generalisation that, for the great mass of the population, the figurative colours to look for are less likely to be stark black and white than varying and chequered shades of grey.'[13]

Zuckmayer was also fairly indulgent. He believed that the tally of Nazis left in German society lay at around 20 per cent – the 'blacks'. The 'whites' were equally represented, with 60 per cent of Germans being 'grey' or fellow travellers. Around 40 per cent of the 'greys' were an acceptable shade, while another 20 per cent were dark grey, verging on black. Zuckmayer thought the percentages given would apply to most countries, and Germany was no worse than them. Thinking back to that time, the literary critic Karl-Heinz Bohrer estimates that 70 per cent of Germans were 'nationalists' in 1945, which meant that they made common cause with the Nazis, even if they said they disapproved of them.[14]

For everyone who had heard stories 'from the east' – transmitted by relatives in the army who had witnessed atrocities – there were equal numbers of ordinary Germans who genuinely knew nothing. One who merely suspected that terrible things were being done was Gertrud Jaspers – who might have experienced the horrors at first hand had the authorities been able to prise her away from her husband. The Allied revelations came as a profound shock to her; they painted a picture she had never imagined.[15]

Re-education through Propaganda

James Stern ran into the American propaganda campaign soon after arriving in Bad Nauheim. He observed the groups of Germans huddled in front of a billboard. At first they were silent, then they began to shake their heads and walk away, but it was no good – the poster was everywhere. 'Who is guilty?' it read. Beneath those words were a number of photographs showing human skeletons, charred bones, prisoners in uniform hanging from gibbets and children dead from starvation. This poster was to be seen throughout the zone.

According to Stern, no German commented. Some moaned, one or two stifled a cry, but generally they looked on in silence before moving away. Another poster in the series answered the question posed by the first: 'This town is guilty! You are guilty!'[16] Others report that, despite the propaganda posters, the Final Solution was very little discussed in the 1940s or 1950s, possibly because images of slaughtered children aroused memories of the Allied bombing campaign which was still fresh in German minds. The Western Allies failed to pursue their quarry after the first campaign. That would fit with the diminishing enthusiasm for trial and denazification. By 1948 it had fizzled out.[17]

The most famous propaganda film of all was the Movietone footage shot at Belsen by the British cameraman Paul Wyand. Even today it remains the most powerful account of the abuse of human life and dignity in the Nazi camps. Wyand turned up at Belsen on 23 April 1945. It is not clear whether the film was intended as propaganda from the outset, or whether Wyand and his crew were there to record what the British were doing to save lives. Wyand interviewed a number of inmates and guards. The latter were humiliated and made to pose in front of heaps of bodies. Dr Fritz Klein, who had been involved in selection at Auschwitz, had been burying bodies for a week. Wyand worked with a Polish interpreter. Klein, who was already half insane from the work he had been forced to do, gave an incorrect answer to a question. When the interpreter relayed this to Wyand, the British beat him with rifle butts. Klein was then filmed in a pit filled with corpses. Sometimes the film had the wrong effect. People found it hard to cope. Alfred Karzin saw it in a cinema in London's Piccadilly: 'many laughed'.[18]

Doubts were expressed about the use of such grotesque images, but one writer has raised the valid point that where we have no pictures we find the slaughter intangible, and easier to forgive. There are, for example, few revealing pictures of the Soviet camps, or of the fate of their victims.[19] There were mixed reactions in America. One obvious target was the large German American population of the Mid-West. Joseph Pulitzer from St Louis was one of them. He insisted that the city's Kiel (*sic*) Auditorium be festooned with photo-murals taken from the camps. Others, such as James Agee in the *Nation* of 19 May 1945, were unconvinced. Agee refused to look at the pictures and questioned their propaganda role, which was to prepare the American people for an 'extremely hard peace against Germany'. The pictures elicited another protest from Milton Mayer in the *Progressive* who spoke of a Carthaginian peace and said 'vengeance won't raise the tortured dead'.[20]

Meanwhile the camps had become the object of a ghoulish voyeurism. The former prisoners continued to die in droves (200 a day in Mauthausen), while journalists, congressmen, senators and soldiers paraded around the huts. At Buchenwald tours began with the iron hook and the crematorium before visitors saw the macabre collection of tattooed-skin lampshades, shrunken heads and pickled organs apparently put together by Ilse Koch. Dead bodies were left around for days for the visitors to see. A tour of a concentration camp became part of the 'ritual of exorcism and revelation in the occupied Germany of late April and early May 1945'. Typical was the reaction of Representative John Vorys who visited the Little Camp at Buchenwald and saw what appeared to be 'absent-minded apes. Many were professors, doctors, writers or generals . . . They had preserved their spirits and had not sunk mentally to the bestial level of their living.'[21]

The Ministry of Information, as the British called their propaganda ministry, were anxious to make as much as they could from the opportunities offered by Belsen. They brought in the local mayors from Celle and elsewhere and showed them the pit full of bodies. SS men and women stood on the other side of the trench and a German-speaking officer read out an indictment. Wyand's cameramen recorded the moment. One of the mayors wept, another was sick.[22]

The Fragebogen *and Denazification*

The *Fragebogen*

The Americans were hell-bent on purging the Nazi evil from the German body politic. Their policy for Germany was constructed on the adamantine plinth of JCS 1067, Clause 6 of which deemed the foremost requirement to be denazification as a punitive measure. The Joint Chiefs of Staff had drawn up the document in wartime, but it had received the support of Roosevelt, who was wallowing in Teutonophobia. As ever, the British limped after the Americans. The French and the Russians went their own ways.[23] With its desire to impose a 'peace of punishment', JCS 1067 was Morgenthau's last legitimate child and survived long after Truman formally relinquished the Plan. It proposed to tear down, rather than rebuild, and to help Germans only when it was necessary to avoid disease or disorder. JCS 1067 was responsible for the inhumane approach of the Americans and to some extent had a knock-on effect on the British in the first months of occupation. There were modifications, however, in that JCS 1067 allowed for some industrial activity in the conquered nation. To surrender to the Americans – as most Germans actively strove to do – was 'a lottery ticket'. At best you might be released before all the other POWs, at worst you might die in the Rhine Meadow mud. JCS 1067 policy was largely overturned by Clay, who was 'very nearly an independent sovereign' in his German house. Clay rapidly came round to the idea that the best way to succeed was to allow the Germans to govern themselves.[24]

The chief instruments of denazification were the *Fragebogen* or questionnaires. They were also the first attempts on the part of the Americans to quantify National Socialism and exclude former Nazis from public life. One American writer questioned the legal foundation of denazification, calling it a 'Nazi or communist concept of jurisprudence'.[25] As many as thirteen million forms were printed and handed out either to those with dubious pasts or to Germans who were looking for employment. The number corresponded roughly to the number of Pgs. Ursula von Kardorff was subjected to a prototype of the *Fragebogen* as early as 7 May 1945, the day the Germans capitulated. Captain Herrell, the commandant in Günzburg, brought out something that looked like a book: he wanted to know if the women had been in the Party or the Frauenschaft (Nazi women's league). She hadn't known there were so many organisations, and the officer reminded her of the Gestapo.[26]

Margret Boveri got her first glimpse of the form on 5 June 1945, and thought the vetting system of her new lords and masters much more complicated that the Nazi one. The questionnaire consisted of twelve pages and 133 questions. It had been handed out to a crowd of doctors to determine if they had belonged to Nazi organisations. If they had, they were banned from practice. Ruth Friedrich saw the form at the same time. It asked a number of questions she could no longer answer with any certainty: how she voted in 1932, the numbers of her bank and post office accounts as well as those of close relations: 'Is one supposed to commit perjury because one has a bad memory?'[27]

Some of their Allied tormenters had sympathy for the Germans' wounded pride. Stern read through the *Fragebogen* and was struck by its 'peculiar German'. He 'wondered how on earth . . . [he] would answer some of these vague, some unintentionally humorous queries'. The Allies wanted to know, for example, whether the bombing had affected the interviewee's health, work or sleep. Information was demanded about insurance and indemnity claims, and more questions about sewage, electricity and drainage. At a house in Munich's Planetta Strasse, Stern interviewed a thirteen-year-old girl and an eighty-eight-year-old man who was 'quite gaga'. One blind man came to the interview accompanied by his wife, who was almost completely deaf, an affliction she shared with her husband. Stern discovered that many Germans had been temporarily deafened by the bombing. The names had been drawn at random, 'à la Gallup'.[28] The idea that all Germans were to be questioned in this way, even those who had been in concentration camps, provoked another outburst of fury from Kurt Schumacher: 'we want a just and objective examination of the facts', he said in Kiel in the autumn of 1945.[29]

Ursula von Kardorff had to wait until the end of July. She was outraged by the 148 (*sic*) questions asked: how much you weighed, scars, distinguishing features, religion (and whether you had quit the Church), titles of nobility, earnings, whether you had worked in an occupied territory. The question about scars was to determine whether you had been a member of one of the wicked duelling fraternities, but they had been banned by Hitler. She found the question about how she had voted particularly absurd: firstly because it was so easy to lie and secondly because Germans were being told that the secret ballot was one of the foundation stones of democracy. In the end they found the form so comic that it put them all in a good mood: 'in the old days it was having a Jewish grandmother that caused problems, now it is having a noble one. And what has the colour of my eyes got do with my political opinions?'[30]

No one escaped. Jünger came home in early September 1945 to find one on his desk. It was marked with the warning 'False information will result in prosecution by the courts of the military government.'[31] Had he known that Bishop Graf Galen, whose sermons had been dropped from British aircraft as propaganda, was also required to fill in the form, he might have felt relieved.[32] In Jünger's literary world, anyone who did not leave and take up residence abroad like the famous Thomas Mann was treated with the utmost suspicion by the Western Allies. One case was Erich Kästner, author of *Emil and the Detectives*. He had been banned from writing under the Third Reich, but that cut no ice with the interrogators.[33] One of the most bizarre examples of the American insistence on the *Fragebogen* was when Emmy Göring was required to fill one in. She, her daughter and her sister were all in Straubing Prison at the time. Her husband was awaiting trial at Nuremberg.

> One of the questions was: 'Did you have a relative or a close friend in the Party with a high position in the Third Reich?'
>
> 'Yes, my husband, Hermann Göring,' I wrote.
>
> 'What post did he have?'
>
> 'He was not in the SS. But the SA. He was *Reichsmarschall*, master huntsman, Commander in Chief of the Luftwaffe ...'
>
> I tried to remember his other titles and ended up by sighing.
>
> 'Why are you sighing like that?' asked an American.
>
> 'I can't remember my husband's titles any more.'
>
> 'Don't worry. Just write: Hermann Göring. We've got enough information on him already.'[34]

The nature of the questions on the form gave a fair indication of the sort of things (besides Nazism) that were offensive to the Allied Military Government. One thing they wanted to know was whether the interviewee had ever hoped for a German victory. Margret Boveri was not slow to point out that in other countries to hope for defeat would be classically construed as treason. After May 1945 it was quite wrong to believe in

German victory, but was it so bad in 1939, or 1940? It recalled the line of Talleyrand, who said treason was a question of dates.[35]

The question that had incensed Ursula von Kardorff was nobility, as enshrined in Question 18. The captain in Jettingen showed her a memorandum in which American soldiers were told how to sniff out a wicked Junker: find out if he had a potato schnapps distillery on his estate. The form required you to state whether you or your wife, your father, mother, wife's father and mother, or either of your grandparents had belonged to an ennobled family. Antiquity of lineage was clearly synonymous with political unreliability and the Junkers in particular were accused of having helped in Hitler's rise to power; and yet, of the people who had taken active steps to dispose of Hitler and his regime – particularly on 20 July 1944 – a very high proportion had been nobles, Junkers in particular. In the winter of 1945–6 the supposition that nobility and Nazi were in some way at one contributed to the lack of fuel. As an American interrogator told John Dos Passos, all the foresters had been sacked because of Question 18: 'von This and von That, big time Nazis, every one'. The *Fragebogen* was the absolute authority, the litmus test. Another officer told Dos Passos 'It's the *Fragebogen*. The *Fragebogen* is the best thing in Germany . . . If they get past this, they can hold any job they want.'[36]

Question 25 was concerned with membership of a student corps. The author of the *Fragebogen* was possibly unaware that the famous student *Burschenschaften* had been suspended at the end of 1935 and not revived until after 1945. The first nail in their coffin had been a drunken student at Heidelberg who had rung Hitler's adjutant to ask him to ask the Führer the correct way to eat asparagus. Hitler was not amused. Not only did pranks of this sort thenceforth go under the name of 'Spargelessen' or asparagus eating, all secret meetings of old members of the fraternities became *de facto* acts of opposition. Later on they proved recruiting grounds for the July Plotters.[37]

The Allies were obsessed with the need to stamp out 'militarism', and any connection with the armed forces was held against the supplicant. A joke ran round that one of the questions on the form was 'Did you play with toy soldiers as a child? If so, what regiment?'[38] The real Question 32 also went wide of the mark. It demanded to know if the applicant had been a member of the General Staff. The German staff officer, with carmine stripes on his trousers, was the intellectual of the army. In 1939 there were 824 of them, of whom 600 served in staff positions. Of these 359 were dead by 1945: 149 had been killed in action, 10 had died of natural causes and 143 were missing. There had been sixteen suicides, mostly in the aftermath of the July Plot, while another twenty-four had been executed for their part in the conspiracy. All in all some sixty staff officers were arrested as a result of the attempt on Hitler's life – that is, 10 per cent. The names included Stauffenberg and Colonel Merz von Quirnheim who both died on the night, together with Colonel General Beck. Others who were executed were Field Marshal von Witzleben and Generals von Stülpnagel, Olbricht and Hoepner. General Staff officers such as the former army chiefs Hammerstein and Fritsch had also been opponents of Hitler and his war plans.[39] The General Staff officer was liable to immediate arrest. He was seen as the symbol of German militarism, and the Western Allies did not want his expertise put at the disposal of the Soviets. On 22 June Radio Hamburg broadcast a speech by Bernard Montgomery saying that all General Staff officers would be imprisoned for life in special camps outside Germany.[40]

The problem remained that it was only once the properly completed questionnaire had been returned and vetted that a German could return to normal life. Until then he was in a sort of purgatory that left him outside the law. If you wanted to get on, you faced the 'inquisition' and filled in the form with its 'sometimes stupid questions', otherwise you were out of work and deprived of ration tickets. If you were not careful, you were declared a war criminal to boot.[41]

Denazification

The American policy was to locate the least objectionable German and give him the work, but insufficient zeal in denazification could still result in important heads falling. Membership of any Nazi Party-affiliated institution was enough to have you banned from office. The American-appointed minister president of Bavaria, Fritz Schäffer, was a known anti-Nazi, but the Americans sacked him because he did not hate all Nazis, and allowed some of them to figure in his administration. Another who fell from grace was General Patton, who had the temerity – indeed folly – to say that the 'Nazi thing is just like a Democrat–Republican election fight'. He was relieved of his command. Elsewhere Patton's approach had been attractively pragmatic: 'we shall need these Germans' was his line, and it turned out to be prophetic.[42] The future German president Theodor Heuss urged restraint. He thought that only 10 to 15 per cent of Nazis were in any way dangerous, and that the Americans were too strict: 'only he who has lived twelve years under the Nazi terror can judge how enormous this pressure was and how much heroism and political insight were required to resist it'.[43] All hints of what Germany had been over the previous twelve years were to be expunged. In one town hall Dos Passos noted the gaps where the pictures of past mayors had been hung. When he asked why, he was told they wore the *Geflügel* (the fowl): the Nazi Party badge.[44]

The right way to denazify Germany was not generally agreed between East and West, and even the Western Allies had their fall-outs. The British were lukewarm, but in their sector of Berlin there was a little show of strength. One of George Clare's first experiences in the city was interpreting for a British officer who was determined to keep a fire chief in office despite his Nazi past. He wanted efficient firemen, and he couldn't give a damn about the man's past. The only problem was that the other firemen were social democrats who had been persecuted by the Nazis and for that reason would not tolerate having one in their midst.[45] In the Ruhr all the mining engineers were dismissed as Nazis. Then there were explosions that claimed hundreds of lives – including British – and General Templer decided that Military Government had been foolish.[46]

Clare's office might have been feared by Berlin Nazis, but in general no one worried too much about the British, and visitors to their zone reported pro-Nazi graffiti they did not see elsewhere. The British attitude was allegedly not to disturb the status quo and to use re-education where possible. The results were not deemed successful in retrospect.[47] The figures, however, do not always bear this out. By September 1946 there were 66,500 Nazis interned in the American Zone, and 70,000 in the British.[48] In Nordrhein-Westfalen alone two and a half million cases were examined. The mill ground very fine and many of these men, and some women, were kept under lock and key and in terrible conditions for years. In general, however, they were either released at the end, or given a trifling punishment. The British had their own problems at home to worry about. Denazification was hardly their top priority. Around 80 per cent of Nazis were exonerated. By that time even the Americans had lost their enthusiasm and there were only 200 of them working in Public Safety, assisted by around thirty-five foreigners. They could not hope to be able to sift the evidence and they had no co-operation from the Russians whatsoever.[49]

The Russians were firm believers in collective guilt and any German was liable for punishment, even death. They set the Germans to work and gave them as little as they could to sustain life. They investigated half a million cases in their zone, around 3 per cent of the population, and, as in Austria, the Pgs were not allowed to vote in the various elections held in 1946. By 1948 they too had lost interest and ended the purge.[50] The French attitude lay somewhere between the British and the Russians: it was less a question of guilt than 'should this man play a role in public life or should he not?'[51]

One of the problems facing the Allies was the scale of the work before them. With twelve million Pgs in their midst it became clear after a while that their original ferocity would be tempered with time and that a lot of small fry would swim free. The Germans, for their part, were more used to the methods used by the Gestapo or the NKVD and assumed that, once caught, they were for the high jump. Allied Military Courts, on the other hand, were snowed under with Nazis waiting to know their fates.[52]

Denazification was a fact of life for all Germans, even dead ones who had been hanged for their part in the plot to kill Hitler. In 1949 Charlotte von der Schulenburg had yet to receive her widow's pension and was having difficulty providing for her children by Fritz-Dietlof. The problem was that her husband had been an early member of the Party, having joined in 1932, a fact that 'was clearly more important than anything that he did afterwards'.[53] Four years after the end of the war Charlotte had to go before a tribunal in Hanover to fight her late husband's corner.

She sat on a bench outside the court waiting for her case to be called. Next to her were Jews and gypsies seeking recognition as victims of the Nazi state. She defended her husband's memory bravely, clutching telegrams from Annedore Leber and Gustav Dahrendorf, but the problem was that a Prussian bureaucrat who had been condemned to death, in the same way as a common murderer, could not expect a pension for his wife. The law had to be changed before Charlotte could have her pension. She did not receive any money until 1952, and that was due to her as the widow of a Third Reich Regierungspräsident – the president of an admin-istrative district.[54]

There was a joke doing the rounds (a variant of it is still told in Vienna): a man comes into a police station and tells the officer that he wishes to reg-ister as a Nazi. The policeman replies that he should have done that a year and a half ago. The man tells the policeman, 'Eighteen months ago I wasn't a Nazi!'

Dos Passos cites an interview with an American lieutenant whose busi-ness it was to interrogate Nazis. 'My people are Jewish . . . so don't think I'm not bitter against the Krauts. I'm for shooting the war criminals where we can prove they are guilty and getting it over with. But for God's sake, tell me what we are trying to do?' The lieutenant continued, 'Hatred is like a fire. You've got to put it out. I've been interrogating German officers for the War Crimes Commission and when I find them half-starved to death right in our own PW cages and being treated like you wouldn't treat a dog, I ask myself some questions . . . Brutality is more contagious than typhus and a hell of a lot more difficult to stamp out . . .' He mentioned Patton and his habit of putting his foot in it, but he clearly approved. 'All those directives about don't coddle the German have thrown open the gates for every criminal tendency we've got in us.'[55] The American hatred for the Germans continued to astound many people. Dos Passos met an eastern European in Berlin who spoke to him in French. The man asked him, 'why do you Americans feel this desire for vengeance? I can understand it in the Russians, who suffered fearful injuries, but your cities were not laid waste, your wives and children were not starved and murdered.' Dos Passos did not have an answer.[56]

For Zuckmayer there was a fundamental error behind the denazification policy: it failed to create a belief in a state of law because it failed to differentiate between the innocent and the guilty. The ideal liberation should have come about through a revolution within Germany. It was not going to be possible to clean up Germany by pushing a large number of its citizens before the courts. There were too many cases, and the witnesses were in many instances unreliable, as they knew they would come under the microscope themselves and the most important thing was to deny everything. The accused were protected – there was evidence of nepotism and intimidation. Denunciations were frequently made out of sheer bloody-mindedness and there were too few judges and lawyers around who were free from guilt.

The courts themselves had a hopeless task. In one Bavarian district Zuckmayer was told there were 11,850 former Nazis who were due to be examined by the Spruchkammer. The president of the chamber estimated that it was going to take between eleven and twelve years to acquit the work. In Stuttgart there were around 80,000 cases. Zuckmayer saw a danger of *renazification* as the suspects were forced to mark time before their cases came up for review. He was for a wide-ranging amnesty for the small fry, who were implicated in no particular crime other than opportunism or ideological commitment.

Zuckmayer gives an example of a minor case – a midwife who had her husband sent to Dachau for two years because he had had an affair with a young girl in the factory where he worked. He later threw a bust of her beloved Adolf out of the window, enabling her to denounce him. When her case came up the husband made a plea in mitigation. She had helped non-Aryans and delivered their children without question and had even waived payment in certain cases. She was a good midwife and performed a service to society. If she had committed a crime it was out of passion. She had also been sufficiently punished: she had lost the man she loved because of the Hitler bust. The judge accepted the plea, and let her off with a fine, and allowed her to continue working as a midwife.[57]

Franz von Papen, a former chancellor who had become a Nazi minister and ambassador, had never been a member of the Party. He had been acquitted at Nuremberg. A new trial was arranged for January 1947. He was to face a panel of seven judges: two Social Democrat lawyers and five members of democratic parties. The seven included two Jews. Bavaria's minister for denazification called on the court to sentence Papen to ten years' hard labour on the basis of his having profited from Nazism. Papen was given eight. His property was confiscated and he was deprived of his civic rights.[58] Schacht, who was tried at Nuremberg alongside Papen, had an ingenious way of wriggling out of responsibility for the crimes of the Third Reich. A paper was produced that had been written at the time of the takeover of the Austrian National Bank by the Reichsbank, of which he was then president. It was a hymn of praise to the God-given Führer written by none other than Schacht. The banker was asked to comment: how did he find it? 'I find it excellent!' said Schacht. He told the tribunal what clever 'deception' (*Tarnung*) it was.[59]

The wives of the leading Nazis were put through a predictably humiliating trial. After leaving Straubing Prison, Emmy Göring was living in a hut near her husband's castle at Veldenstein in Franconia. She was suffering from sciatica and had a high fever. She was nonetheless incarcerated in a rat-infested prison for two weeks along with the wives of Hess, Funk and Baldur von Schirach. The brides of Speer, Dönitz, Neurath and Raeder, on the other hand, were spared this indignity, although Speer's wife Margarete was closer to Hitler than any of them, with the exception of Henriette von Schirach who was the daughter of his hard-drinking court photographer Heinrich Hoffmann. As it was, Frau Göring was able to muster a good deal of testimony from Jews that she had helped them over the years, even if she clearly disappointed the president of the tribunal by failing to denounce her dead husband. She was classified 'Group 2' and allowed to return to her hovel.[60]

Another high-profile case was the English-born daughter-in-law of Richard Wagner, Winifred. There was no doubt that 'Winnie' was besotted with her 'Wolf' – as she and her four children called Hitler – but after 1940 the Führer had avoided her. One of her grandchildren has even gone so far as to say that she had wanted to marry Hitler, and that with her at his side there would have been no war.[61] Hitler kept away from Bayreuth, although he continued to see three of the four Wagner children (the eldest girl, Friedelind, emigrated to Switzerland and the United States, where she fanned the flames against her mother) and exempted the first son, Wieland, from military service as the heir to Bayreuth.

The Wagners all had questions to answer. Verena's husband Bodo Lafferenz had been in charge of the Kraft durch Freude Nazi leisure organisation, and as such had held high rank in the SS. He was shipped off to an internment camp in Freiburg. Wolfgang had not been a Party member and could take refuge behind that fact, even if he had been entertained by Hitler and had been as close to him as the others. Party member Wieland had made himself scarce at the Americans' approach, hiding in the French Zone until the coast was clear. He had been administering the town's 'concentration camp' – an outside station of the more notorious Flossenbürg housing a few score inmates who were involved in technical research for the SS. He never mentioned his closeness to the regime in his remaining years, and set himself up as a hero of a debunking, cultural revolution in Bayreuth. His designs were meant to clear his grandfather's operas of all their nationalist trappings, and as such they represent a major instance of the cultural and artistic purge of the arts that followed the Second World War. The Spruchkammer branded Wieland a 'fellow traveller'. His mother took the rap.

The Americans entered Bayreuth after reducing a third of the town to rubble – including much of Wagner's home, Wahnfried, though not the house of the master's son, Siegfried, which had been called the Führerbau because it was made over to Hitler for his use during his visits to the festival. The Americans moved into the opera house on the Green Hill and created havoc playing jazz on Wagner's and Liszt's pianos. Winifred insisted that most of the damage was done by 'coloured' American GIs, who looted the theatre and shot up the sets with their revolvers. They also amused themselves by dressing up in the operatic costumes. Another story has it that German refugees stole the costumes, and for miles around you could see people fleeing Bayreuth dressed as characters from Wagner operas. The American authorities promptly banned the playing of Wagner's music.[62]

Winifred took on the role of the unrepentant Nazi, although she had performed numerous acts of intercession with the Party to save the lives of Jews and others who had fallen foul of the regime. Almost the first 'Americans' she received were Thomas Mann's son Klaus, and Curt Riess, reporting for the army newspaper, the *Stars and Stripes*. The two Germans in American uniform were getting used to hearing that no one had been aware of the atrocities carried out by the regime, and that everyone had been against Hitler and was proud to possess a '"non-Aryan" granny'. Winifred therefore came as a surprise. First of all she insisted on speaking English to the freshly baked Americans – and was rather more proficient than they were. She made no bones about her friendship with Hitler. She praised his charm, his sense of humour and his good looks. This came from the heart, although she later admitted that she could not resist the temptation to rile the Germans in their borrowed clothes. Mann retired bruised.

The interview brought Winifred Wagner new fame. More reporters pitched up at her house in the Fichtelgebirge. Some wanted to know if she had slept with Hitler. She said no. She told them that Hitler had been misled by Bormann. She clearly possessed a 'stuff and nonsense' charm, and had seen enough of the Third Reich and its puffed-up officials to know how to deal with a few army interrogators. With time she won the conquerors round. One reason was her command of English, which made her an important source of information for the occupying forces.[63]

Meanwhile Thomas Mann had weighed in from his exile in America, publishing his reasons for not returning to Germany. He attacked those who had continued to pursue an artistic life under Hitler. One who felt that he was being indicted was Emil Preetorius, who had designed some of the most famous sets for Bayreuth, and whose anti-Nazi views and friendship with Jews had not only been well known but had put him in danger. Mann gave no credence to the idea of 'inner emigration' as expounded by Preetorius and others. Preetorius's message to Mann was 'My dear friend, you have no idea of the sorcery of terror.' It was an argument forcefully put forward by Furtwängler when he asked Mann why he felt that Germans should have been deprived of the solace of Beethoven during the years of the Third Reich.[64]

Furtwängler's humiliation began on 11 December 1946 in the Spruchkammer in the Schlüterstrasse in Berlin. This was run by the British major Kaye Sely as head of the Information Services Control Intelligence Section. His attitude to denazification was generally more indulgent than that of most gentiles, but it was not going to help Furtwängler much. The first session of the Spruchkammer lasted for five hours before it was adjourned so that more witnesses could be called. Heinz Tietjen, who had abandoned his lover Winifred Wagner to her fate, once again played a questionable role. Now he attempted to cover up for his intrigues at the Lindenoper. He had had enough of the vain Furtwängler and sought to promote the equally vain but considerably more ambitious Karajan. He became Goebbels's stooge in his campaign to discredit the older conductor.[65] Furtwängler meanwhile expressed his astonishment at his treatment considering that he was the only member of the musical establishment to have actively opposed Hitler.*

In words reminiscent of Dietrich Bonhoeffer, Furtwängler said, 'You have to work with the regime in order to work against it . . . Emigration would have been a more comfortable solution in any case.' The Western Allies had plenty of dirt to throw at the conductor. Much of it centred on the critic Edwin von der Nüll, who had made unflattering comparisons between Furtwängler and Karajan, and whom the former had contrived to have sent to the front, where he perished. Nüll had been a pawn of Goebbels. Furtwängler's defence had been limp, and the conclusion of the day was to direct the case to the Allied Kommandatura. Those who had hoped to be able to hear the conductor perform the *Eroica* the next day were to be disappointed.[66]

Behind the scenes there was the constant clamour of the émigrés who were determined to see the conductor as a cultural figurehead for the Nazis. Chief among them was Erika Mann. His old rival Toscanini also played a prominent role. Furtwängler had sealed his fate with many Jewish Americans when in 1936 he had been offered the position of principal conductor of the New York Philharmonic but chose to direct the orchestra of the Berlin State Opera instead. Once again he had been a victim of Nazi intrigue. News had been leaked to the press in order to compromise him with the New Yorkers.[67]

The Americans led the way with denazification, trying 169,282 cases. The Russians and the French weighed in at around 10 per cent of that figure at 18,328 and 17,353 respectively.[68] The British seemed to show very little interest in the matter within their zone, handling a little over 1 per cent of the American cases, at 2,296. Clay had full belief in the process and thought the Allies were doing well. On 5 July 1945 he reported that denazification in the early 'liberated' cities of Aachen and Cologne was virtually complete. In Bavaria and Württemberg, however, it was going very slowly. In March 1948, the Russians made a point of releasing 35,000 minor Nazis from their camps.[69]

Clay had bagged 75,000 Nazis to date. Certain organisations were particularly thick with them. He estimated that the police administration was 100 per cent Nazi; the 'Kripos' or criminal police 60 per cent; the others

---

* He had forgotten Erich Kleiber.

40 per cent.* In the banking world of Frankfurt half those employed were Nazis; that meant 326 people. On the other hand the docility of the post-war Germans struck Clay as it did everyone else: the 'German masses seem totally apolitical, apathetic and primarily concerned with [the] every-day problems of food, clothing and shelter'. They did not quite behave as he expected them to: 'no general feeling of war guilt or repugnance for Nazi doctrine and regime has manifested itself. Germans blame Nazis for losing war, protest ignorance of regime's crimes and shrug off their own support as incidental and unavoidable.'[70]

Clay continued bagging Nazis. In autumn 1945 he had 80,000 in the bag plus the same number of Waffen-SS and 'Schupos' – members of the Security Police who were interned with the POWs. On top of these he had around 75,000 Germans sacked because of their Nazi past, and 9,500 from financial institutions.[71] On 8 December the number of imprisoned Nazis in the American Zone had risen to 90,000, and was to reach 100,000 by the end of the year. Another 25,000 members of paramilitary organisa-tions were lodged with the POWs.[72] It is not clear whether or not most of the SS men had been released. Certainly, most of the Nazis had been released by the summer of 1948. Clay admitted to holding 5,000 prisoners at that time, with some 25,000 more awaiting trial outside the camps. They were all hard-core cases. In September 1947 he turned his mind to the German scientists who had been taken to the US in Operation Paperclip, to work on the atom bomb and the rocket programme. In his opinion they should not have been exempt from trial.[73]

On 13 May 1946 Control Council Order Four was passed. All literature of a Nazi or militarist nature was to be confiscated. Clay was not impressed. He had, by his own admission, been banning and confiscating such books since the arrival of the Americans in Germany. He was particularly keen to replace school textbooks from the era of the Third Reich. It was an under-standable measure, but taken to extremes it could only lead to absurd situations and scenes reminiscent of the Nazi book burnings when over-zealous local councils decided to expurgate their library collections.† It also furthered the confusion – which reigned at the heart of the Control Council – that Nazism and 'Prussianism' were intimately related.[74]

Clay played the game while he was at the helm. In 1948 the Cold War was coming and JCS 1067 was replaced by the less stringent JCS 1779, which advocated economic unity and self-government. Clay was replaced

---

* Given that at a national level the police was *gleichgeschaltet*, or incorporated in the SS, Clay's figures seem conservative.

† See below p. 508.

by his deputy, John McCloy. Times had changed and the former banker was more interested in building a bridge to the Germans. His wife Ellen came in useful in all this: she was German, and a distant cousin of Adenauer's second wife.[75] McCloy himself went to Canossa: he paid a call on Frings and promised the prelate that he would review the sentences passed on German war criminals. The Americans began to release them in droves in 1949 in the interests of good relations with Adenauer's government.[76]

Seen as an exercise in punishing criminals, denazification was a farce. A number of insignificant Pgs were treated with the utmost cruelty while the big fish went free. Most of the minor cases were not ideologically committed anyway. Some of the worst killers, those who sent thousands to their deaths, who carried out the executions in the east as members of police units, or who operated the trains which took Jews to the death camps in the General Gouvernement, were not punished at all; they retired from the police or the railways without anyone having called them to account, and died in their beds.

Nazis in the Austrian Woodwork

In Berlin, the Viennese George Clare was keeping an eye on Herbert von Karajan. He was well aware of the conductor's Nazi past. The impresario Walter Legge came to see them in the Schlüterstrasse to enquire about his status, as he wanted to know if he was permitted to give concerts in Britain. He had been denazified in Vienna, but as Sely told him, 'we always discount Austrian denazification'. Sely later sent Clare off to investigate, giving him the address of the British theatre and music officer Peter Joseph Schnabel – otherwise known as 'MacSchnabel' from his dandified ways and the fact that he had once performed the role of teaching the Cameron Highlanders to ski.

Clare found a room in the Park Hotel in Hietzing, a stone's throw from British Army HQ in Schönbrunn, where his murdered parents had spent their honeymoon. He met Schnabel at Demel's coffee house by the Hofburg. The Austrian Jew was doing a tour of the tables, kissing the hands of the local ladies. It soon dawned on Clare that Allied culture boffins were even more firmly wedded to the local terrain in Vienna than were those in Berlin: there was Schnabel and 'George' the Frenchman, whose Danubian accent gave him away. Also 'one of us' was the US captain Ernst Häussermann, who was deputising for another – Ernst Lothar. Finally the

Russian representative dashed into the meeting late, and bearing a parcel. She had a 'sweet' excuse in her hand: it was a *Sachertorte*. Her name was Lily Wichmann, another Viennese.

Denazification was not a big issue for any of them. For a start Austria had had its own government from the beginning – a privilege granted to the 'first victim'. The armies of occupation were there to enjoy themselves, and that meant music. It would have been a shame, according to Clare, to lock up decent musicians. He looked up a former corporal in the Pioneer Corps who had risen to the rank of lieutenant-colonel. The colonel invited him to the British Officers' Club in the Palais Kinsky. Clare was shocked to see how much the Austrians had buried the past. Pure German *Hochdeutsch* was now out of fashion: everyone did their best to speak in a sing-song Austrian dialect, and men donned Styrian hats and suits, and women dirndls, to assert the cultural differences that occurred once you crossed the little River Inn.[77]

Yet there was still the problem of what to do with the Nazis who so openly contradicted Austria's pose. The Figl government drew up a National Socialist Law which was passed by the federal parliament on 24 July 1946 in the belief that it was in keeping with Allied demands for denazification. It was not: the Russians in particular found it too lenient and the Americans wanted automatic prosecution at the level of Untersturmführer – that is, a second lieutenant in the SS. The Allies made around 200 changes. The American minister, Erhardt, went so far as to suggest the creation of 'concentration camps' for Nazis.[78] These already existed in the British Zone.[*] It was finally adopted on 7 February 1947. Under this law Nazis were divided into two groups according to the power they yielded during the Third Reich. For war criminals there was a special jurisdiction. The categories were similar to those employed in the American Zone in Germany: 'incriminated', 'slightly incriminated', 'not incriminated'. Of the more than half a million Austrian Nazis, a little under 10 per cent fell into the first class. It was assumed that the 470,000 in the second class would be amnestied and returned to the suffrage for the next elections.[79]

Special 'People's Courts'[†] – *nomen est omen* – were established to try Nazis. There was no appeal. The first case came up on 14 August 1945 when four SA men were accused of the massacre of 102 Jews in Engerau. There were seven death sentences passed by the end of the year. It was a

[*] See below p. 455.
[†] The 'Volksgerichthof' in Nazi times had tried the enemies of the state. There were no appeals and frequent death sentences.

modest tally. Where possible the blame was laid at the feet of the Germans. On 30 August William Donovan, head of the OSS, received a report that 63,000 of Vienna's 67,000 Nazis had been tagged. A large number of them were claiming they had been forced to join the Party and wanted their names dropped from the register. Some 5,800 of the city's 'dangerous Nazis' had been gaoled, but another 10,000 were still at large.[80]

When the tally was concluded there was a total of 536,000 names on the register; and 100,000 of these had been so keen they had joined before 1938, when it was still an illegal organisation. Denazification went off at half cock in Austria. From the beginning it was left in the hands of the Austrian government to pursue Nazis, albeit under the gaze of the Allied Bureau. The Americans prided themselves in being the 'most drastic', although the evidence does not necessarily point to that. In October they came under strong criticism when it was reported that the former Gauleiter Scheel had been seen walking about the streets of Salzburg. They were also keen to weed out the 'Austro-fascist' Dollfussites from the ÖVP. The British they castigated as the 'mildest'. Again this is misleading.[81]

On 26 February the trial of Chancellor Schuschnigg's foreign minister Guido Schmidt opened in Vienna. This was the moment to review the behaviour of the Corporate State and to discover who was responsible for the Anschluss. Schmidt had come home from Nuremberg, where he had appeared as a prosecution witness in the case against Schuschnigg's successor Arthur Seyss-Inquart.[82]* The trial lasted 107 days but failed to prove that Schmidt had acted behind the back of his chancellor. There had been much finger-waving on the part of the Dachauer because Schmidt had been spared incarceration in a camp. Although he had been ousted from politics by the Nazis, he was nonetheless made a director of the Hermann-Göring-Werke. He was acquitted.

The efficacy of the courts altered from zone to zone. The OSS reported on a trial in Vienna of four criminals and Jew-murderers: three were convicted and sentenced to hang.[83] As in Germany capital sentences were often commuted. The courts awarded ten death sentences and thirty-four terms of life imprisonment. The tribunals delivered another 13,600 guilty verdicts. The punishments for major culprits were chiefly pecuniary: up to 40 per cent of their property and a 10 per cent fiscal surcharge over a certain number of years. In all Austria 42,000 people were treated in this way. Lighter measures were imposed against a further 481,000. The punishments were fairly trifling, but 72,000 to 100,000 government employees lost their

---

* See below Chapter 16.

jobs. This, it seems, was in no way consistent, and 40,000 Nazi civil servants continued in their functions in the Tyrol and the Vorarlberg.[84] Nazis were debarred from a certain number of professions as well: journalists, university chairs, physicians; they could neither vote nor stand as candidates in elections.

Some of the Allied commanders considered that harsh. The Frenchman Béthouart, for example, felt that the law was cruel to small-time Pgs and that it eliminated valuable experts from the workplace while 'closing the door to national reconciliation'.[85] He does not allude to Austria's Jews, who had been robbed and murdered, and who were wary of a state that had not actively sought their return. Few but the main activists even thought of coming back.[86] After the delusions current during the war years, it was now clear that the majority of the Austrian people were party to their expropriation. Nonetheless, Béthouart pushed for and succeeded in attaining a moderation of the statute that amnestied the youngest Nazis.

Béthouart was not alone in forgetting the Jews. Of the 120,000 or so who had managed to escape from Austria after the Anschluss, only 8,500 had returned by March 1947. With time the number was to go down, not up. There were other Jews in Austria – around 42,000 DPs, living mostly in the American Zone. The Americans made sure they received larger rations than the others: around 2,000 calories as opposed to the standard 1,550. It was said that Austrian antisemitism was the reason why so many Jews were reluctant to come back. The charge was bitterly resented by the mayor of Vienna, Theodor Körner, who said he had issued an invitation to Jewish artists to return. In a dazzling *non sequitur* he said, 'The Austrians are cosmopolitan and therefore not antisemites.' The notion of Austrian antisemitism amounted to 'deliberate lies or thoughtless babble'.[87]

The British approach to the Nazi problem in Austria was markedly different to the approach in the British Zone in Germany, where denazification was at best limp-wristed. The enforcement squad was the Field Security Service or FSS, which had instructions to identify and arrest all those on the pre-prepared Allied lists, and which depended on the Intelligence Corps at home. One former member described the force as a 'secret service in uniform'.[88] Nazi lawyers were suspended – twenty-six in Carinthia and seventy-six in Styria.[89] The FSS also had to deal with brigands, gangs of non-German SS men and Cetniks who terrorised isolated farmhouses close to the Yugoslav border. It had a more strategic role on the Carinthian border, controlling a twenty-kilometre-broad strip otherwise accessible only to residents. This was used not only for the defence of the region against Tito but also to keep the Yugoslavs out of Venezia-Giulia. Those involved in the hunt for war criminals worked from lists drawn up by the Atrocities Committee Austria.[90]

In the British Zone the courts examined the case histories of 31,517 Nazis. Of those only 2,623 were acquitted. The British maintained three internment camps for Nazis at Wolfsberg, Weissenheim and Wetzelsdorf. The first named became a synonym – along with Glasenbach in the American Zone – for the rough treatment of political prisoners. The higher courts dealt with around another hundred cases. These meted out fifty-three death sentences, forty-two of which were carried out.[91] The main atrocities committed in Styria concerned the death marches to Mauthausen at the end of the war. These gave rise to a number of high-profile cases in 1946. The Eisenerz Trial dealt with the SS guards who killed off 162 Hungarian Jews in the village of that name because they were in no condition to make it to Mauthausen. Ten of the eighteen defendants were sentenced to death, and were shot on 21 June.[92]

Shooting gave way to hanging when the gallows was set up in the Provincial Court on 24 September 1946 and eight men were despatched by the British master, Albert Pierrepoint. The British had brought in a Herr Zaglauer and his two assistants to learn the ropes. Pierrepoint expressed his confidence in these hangmen, who were deemed 'now fully competent officially to conduct executions themselves in the approved British manner'.[93] The People's Courts then took over from the British. In Austria as a whole they meted out forty-three capital sentences. Vienna naturally took the lead with twenty-eight, but Graz came second with twelve; Linz, in the American Zone, passed only three; French Innsbruck, none.[94]

The Soucek Case examined by the People's Court dealt with an important group of neo-Nazis. The court also handled the trial of the Leoben Gestapo chief Johann Stelzl and those responsible for the euthanasia programme in the lunatic asylum in Klagenfurt. Four men were condemned to death. Sometimes the tariffs handed out seem light: the main culprit in the Stremer Jewish Murder Case, in which the defendants were proved to have killed fifty Jews, received twenty years.[95] The following year, on 27 February 1948, the Russian general Kurasov proposed a bigger amnesty. The consequence two months later was the law of 21 April which struck 487,000 names from 524,000 on the original lists. This added half a million electors to the roll, most of them on the right.

Once the former Nazis had been included again within the pale of the constitution, a new party came on the scene in the guise of the Union of Independents. Anti-Nazi politicians sought to ban the Independents in the Western zones. The Soviets, however, refused to follow suit, and the Independents promptly took 12 per cent of the vote in the elections of 9 October 1949. The ÖVP once again topped the poll.

Punishment by Starvation

Once it had been decided that all Germans were guilty, the next job was to punish them. Despite the propaganda rations meted out by the Russians in Berlin, the Potsdam Conference decided that the Germans were not to be over-fed. Requests by the Red Cross to bring in provisions were waved aside, and in the winter of 1945 donations were returned with the recommendation that they be used in other war-torn parts of Europe – although the Irish and Swiss contributions had been specifically raised with Germany in mind. The first donations to be permitted reached the American Zone in March 1946, to some degree thanks to the intervention of British intellectuals such as Bertrand Russell and Victor Gollancz.

Gollancz had published a polemic with the title *The Ethics of Starvation*[96] in the middle of 1946. As a Jew whose family had settled in Britain from Germany, Gollancz had no reason to love the Germans. What he objected to was the inhumane and unethical treatment of German civilians:

> I am a Jew: and sometimes I am asked why, as a Jew, I bother about people in whose name infamies have been committed against my race, the memory of which, I fear – though I would wish it otherwise – may never die. I am sometimes asked this, I regret to say, by fellow-Jews who have forgotten, if they ever knew, the teaching of the Prophets . . . It is indeed a fact that I feel called upon to help suffering Germans precisely because I am a Jew: but not at all for the reason imagined . . . It is a question . . . of plain, straight common sense, undeflected by that very sentimentality that deflects the judgement and corrupts the spirit of so many. To me three propositions seem self-evident. The first is that nothing can save the world but a general act of repentance in place of the present self-righteous insistence on the wickedness of others, for we have all sinned, and continue to sin most horribly. The second is that good treatment and not bad treatment makes them good. And the third is – to drop into the hideous collective language which is now much the mode – that unless you treat a man well when he has treated you ill you just get nowhere, or rather it will give further impetus to evil and head straight for human annihilation.[97]

Despite the great wrong perpetrated against his people, Gollancz could not sanction another crime: 'The plain fact is . . . we are starving the Germans.

And we are starving them, not deliberately in the sense that we definitely want them to die, but wilfully in the sense that we prefer their death to our own inconvenience.'[98] Over and over again in his letters to his wife, he is struck by the fact that these suffering infants might have been his own children.

From newspaper reports Gollancz prepared a chilling indictment: seven-tenths of people in the now British city of Hamburg had no bread for two weeks of every month. He quoted the UNRRA figure for daily subsistence – 2,650 calories. The minimum needed to sustain life was 2,000. In March 1946 the average for the British Zone had fluctuated between 1,050 and 1,591. This consisted of four and a half slices of dry bread, three middle-sized potatoes, three tablespoons of oatmeal, half a cup of skimmed milk, a scrap of meat and a tiny dollop of fat. At those levels you could survive in bed, but could not work. Then at the end of February the rations had been cut to 1,014 for those not doing heavy work, that is women. Infant mortality was now at ten times the rate of 1944. In Dortmund in February 1946 forty-six out of 257 children born that month perished.[99]

Politicians and soldiers – like Sir Bernard Montgomery – insisted that no food be sent from Britain. Starvation was punishment. Montgomery said that three-quarters of all Germans were still Nazis – although he did not reveal the source of his information. The Germans had only themselves to blame, and they should be last in the queue. The economist and chancellor of the Exchequer Hugh Dalton argued that the cost of the occupation was tantamount to paying reparations to the Germans.[100] Britain itself was recovering from the wartime dearth, however. The food minister John Strachey had proudly announced that meat consumption was at 98 per cent of pre-war levels, and that the British were eating 50 per cent more fish.[101] As Gollancz presciently wrote, Germany had been stripped of its bread basket cum milk-churn in the east, the pastures of Pomerania and East Prussia.[102] Meanwhile the British authorities in Germany were proposing to cut the rations back to 1,000 calories. The French were already at 950, while the Americans were not much more generous at 1,270. Gollancz pointed out that the inmates at Belsen had 800, which was not that much less.[103] In Baden-Baden, Alfred Döblin was suspicious: if they really had so little food they would be dead. He thought most of them were managing to supplement their diet from the black market.[104] That didn't necessarily help the old and infirm, however.

Gollancz followed *The Ethics of Starvation* with a further tract in January 1947. *In Darkest Germany* was the result of a six-week tour of the British

Zone which the publisher made in October and November 1946, just before the frost. It consists of eighteen letters and articles he had written to belabour the government. He regretted he had been unable to make it to Berlin. On the other hand he suggested that his performance was slightly superior to that of Hynd, who in the past year by his own admission had spent no more than twenty-eight days in Germany.[105]

Gollancz had gone to Germany with the 'attitude of a sceptic'. He nonetheless armed himself with a photographer, and to allay any scoffing at the veracity of his reports, he backed up everything he said with a picture. Most of the photographs include the figure of a benign elderly man in a dark coat and hat: standing behind naked boys suffering from malnutrition; holding up a particularly awful apology for a child's shoe; or comforting a crippled communist in his festering hovel. The point was to show that he had seen these things with his own eyes and taken nothing on trust.[106] Hunger oedema was not confined to the new Russian colony of East Prussia. Gollancz thought it affected up to 100,000 people. He saw some telling cases in the hospital, with the usual waterlogged legs. His photographer took a picture of a dying man. The death-rattle had already started. Another had a scrotum that stretched a third of the way down to the ground. On second thoughts Gollancz had this picture omitted from the finished text.[107] Tuberculosis was at four to five times its 1939 level. There was no penicillin available for the hospitals, because the Germans did not have the money to pay for it.[108] *The Third Man* said it all.

Gollancz was also interested in clothes. In *Darkest Germany* he reproduces a shocking collection of footwear ('shoes' is hardly the word). One child told him that he would not be able to come to school the next day because his father needed to use the shoes. When it rained there were appalling levels of absenteeism. In three schools he visited he inspected the feet of all the children. In one, the shoes of thirty-four out of fifty-eight children were kaput, in the next fifteen out of thirty-seven, and in the last thirty-four out of fifty-three. The problem was that even if there were Reichsmarks available these could not be used for clothing: you needed coupons or *Bezugmarke*. If you had the precious *Bezugmarke* the chances were that there were no shoes to buy. In Düsseldorf there were no nappies. Gelsenkirchen had 260,000 inhabitants. In June the following were available for *Bezugmarke*: fifty-six cardigans, forty-nine frocks, twenty-one pairs of knickers, four nappies, three babies' knickers, three rubber sheets, seven kilos of knitting wool and twenty-one small towels. There were 182 births that month.[109] There were other significant shortages: in Hamburg there were virtually no contraceptives, despite the dreadful levels of infant mortality.

The bombing of Hamburg had left the city with a hopeless lack of accommodation, forcing 77,000 people to inhabit bunkers and cellars. Of these Gollancz estimated that a quarter lived in conditions which resembled some of the more heart-wrenching pictures of Honoré Daumier. He went to Belsen to concentrate his mind, and wrote to his wife: 'I don't for a single second forget the other side of the picture.'[110] The bombing of the western Prussian town of Jülich had been the worst in Germany: 93 per cent of it had been flattened. Given the desolation around him, Gollancz was amazed to hear that 7,000 of the original 11,000 inhabitants were still living there. Their presence was indicated by the stove pipes peeping out of the ground and the tunnels that disappeared into the bases of the ruins. Still, 'in spite of everything', the town's mayor, an SPD man, continued to speak of 'liberation'.[111]

Leaving aside the humanitarian issue, the failure to feed the Germans, especially during the cruel winter of 1946–7, may have given rise to a deal of negative propaganda. Carl Zuckmayer reported conversations overheard in bread queues in the American Zone: 'Yes, Hitler was bad, our war was wrong, but now they are doing the same wrong to us, they are all the same, there is no difference, they want to enslave Germany in exactly the same way as Hitler wanted to enslave the Poles, now *we* are the Jews, the "inferior race", they are letting us starve intentionally, can't you see that is their plan, they take away all our sources of income and let us die slowly, the gas chambers worked quicker . . .'[112]

Gollancz had noticed this even before the frost set in. 'Youth is being poisoned and re-nazified: we have all but lost the peace . . .' he wrote to the editor of the liberal *News Chronicle*.[113] The problem had even broader implications: 'I should have liked to write about the general decline of public morality under the impact of growing despair and of the financial crisis in which the black and the grey sectors constantly encroach upon the legitimate one . . .' Gollancz thought German youth had no morality whatsoever, and the situation was not helped by the lackadaisical approach of the British authorities. There was just one monthly youth magazine published by the British, as opposed to nine in the US Zone; and most of those were fortnightly.[114]

Clay was profoundly concerned about the lack of subsistence. He noted that the people were receiving just 1,000 calories in the British Zone in February 1946, which would 'hardly maintain life'. Ernst Jünger, who seemed to receive regular gifts of food from his admirers, reported in March that the rations had sunk to half what they were. 'This is a death sentence for many who up to now have only been able to keep their heads above water with the greatest effort, above all children, old people and refugees.'[115] The US Zone had been up to 1,550, but by 18 March the figure had dropped to 1,313. Germans were better fed in the Soviet Zone. Even when spring returned, the American provision had only risen to 1,275. Without access to black-market supplies no one could live *and* work. Once again Clay reserved some of his bitterest comments for the French, who applied to him for wheat in January 1946. Without wheat the calorie count in their zone would drop from 1,380 to 1,145. Clay thought they had none because they had taken it all to France. Absence of wheat and the need to make bread had also obliged the French to close the breweries. In February that year Clay gave orders to reopen them in the American Zone.[116] On 26 May 1946 he spoke of a 'nutritional disaster'. Ever the propagandist, he thought it 'may seriously retard the recovery of Western Europe and probably disturb its political development'. German children under six were suffering from a high incidence of rickets, and children between six and eighteen were often stunted.[117]

Many Germans were prepared to see the Allies as liberating angels at first, but they were soon disappointed when they saw the all-too-human soldiers arrive filled with propaganda and hatred for the civilian population. The high-flown rhetoric of the Atlantic Charter now appeared to be every bit as pharisaic as the Fourteen Points of Woodrow Wilson had been.[118] The danger of hunger and famine was slow to abate. Gollancz had had faith in the idea of Anglo-American co-operation, but even with the creation of Bizonia the rations were pitifully low. As the cold weather began to set in, on 14 October 1946 the daily intake was only 1,550 calories.[119]

Stories abounded like those retailed in Paris during the Commune: dogs and cats were not safe from hungry Germans. Rats and frogs were eaten, together with snails – which made a filling soup. Horse was a relatively common dish, as the beasts often expired by the roadside and were then carved up by the locals with sharp knives. The Germans discovered the nutritious character of certain plants. Nettles were an obvious resource. Flour was made from shoots, rosehips and reed mace (cat's tail). Acorns, dandelion and lupine roots were ground to make coffee. In Austria to this day they will tell you that their fondness for elderflowers and elderberries dates from that time.[120] Wild mushrooms were a great boon in season: they stopped the stomach from rumbling but later tortured the consumer with their indigestibility. Even by the winter of 1948 the situation had not been remedied – the Germans had still to reckon with scanty rations. That winter the Americans brought in supplies of maize. As we have seen, the

Germans were not impressed: *Hühnerfutter* (chicken feed) one man called it; no jolly green giants for them.

The countryside should have had other uses. Germany was struck by a plague of wild boars after the war, which were in their way as frightening as the marauding gangs of eastern European DPs. The boars gobbled up potatoes and other crops. Farmers armed themselves with bows and arrows because they had been obliged to yield up their guns. Most of them had no way of killing the creatures, which then fell victim to Allied troops, who hunted them for sport, not out of hunger.[121]

The situation was made all the more acute by the failures of supply. The potatoes sent from Bavaria in the winter of 1946–7 arrived frozen. Those who had nothing to trade and no power to go out and scavenge fared the worst: of the 700 inmates of the lunatic asylum at Grafenberg bei Düsseldorf, 160 died. At the lowest point of that winter, the daily intake in British Nordrhein-Westfalen was 865 calories. Rumours spread: in Oldenburg the locals thought the Allies were hoarding food in preparation for a new war; or it was said that they were hoping that all the Germans would die, and save them the expense of feeding them. Special 'hamster' trains were organised to see if anything could be found out in the country – either by trading with the farmers or simply by scrumping. When rickets appeared in the British Zone, the authorities responded by issuing vigantol and vitimin D2. In Berlin, TB now accounted for one death in ten.[122]

Some relief was to be had from the Hoover Diet introduced in the summer of 1947: a 350-calorie meal for children. Former president Herbert Hoover had toured Germany and pronounced that its food situation was the worst in Europe and that its diet was providing the lowest number of calories for a century. He proposed sending over America's surplus potato production. Suddenly the school meal became the equivalent of a banquet. Germans learned to like peanuts and soya. At the beginning of 1948 there was a twenty-four-hour general strike in Bizonia in protest against the lack of food.[123]

On 17 June 1948 Carl Zuckmayer, now joined by his wife Alice, witnessed a full-scale demonstration from their Munich hotel room. The protesters were several thousand students in their twenties. From loudspeakers they chanted, 'We want no tyranny from hunger!' and 'We have not been colonised!' The demonstrators wore death's heads or white clothes painted with skeletons, and dragged coffins and gravestones along behind them. One had a bread-basket containing just a piece of crust; others carried symbols of misery, hunger and death. Other university cities witnessed similar protests that day: three years after the end of the war the people were still starving, and their intellectual hunger was also as yet unassuaged.

The Zuckmayers found it horribly reminiscent of other demonstrations they had witnessed in the city that had seen the birth of Nazism. In 1933 they had found themselves enmeshed in a pack of brutal Nazi students. They had been lucky to extricate themselves with their lives; and yet these students in 1948 were well brought up and highly intelligent. One of the organisers was a close relative of a member of the Scholl circle – the Weisse Rose. The Zuckmayers watched as armed MPs advanced at them from the Nazi Haus der Kunst, which was now an American officers' mess. Carl realised that the only way to make the Germans into decent people again was to treat them with kindness.[124]

Fringsen

It wasn't just the lack of food that killed, it was the extreme cold. In the winter of 1945–6 the coal ran out. Joseph Frings, archbishop of Cologne, addressed the 'people of the Rhineland' in his New Year's Eve homily: 'We live in times when we have to help ourselves to little things that are necessary to keep ourselves alive and to maintain our health, if we may not obtain them through our work or by requesting them . . . But I believe that in many cases it has gone much further than this, and when this happens there is only one solution: to immediately return any property you have no right to own, otherwise God will not forgive you.'[125] The people were only too ready to interpret the sermon: if you are going lose your lives by freezing to death, then help yourself to what you need! No one paid much heed to the second part of the paragraph, or indeed to the gist of the sermon. The story of the primate's condoning of theft spread like wildfire – the Church approved the stealing of coal. In February 1947 a train was stormed in Nuremberg, forcing the police to fire warning shots. On the 26th of that month it was reported that there had been 305 deaths from hypothermia in the Western zones, 1,155 cases had been admitted to hospital and 49,300 people treated for the effects of the cold.[126] By March 17,000 people had been arrested for stealing coal since the New Year.[127]

Frings had come into his own once the war ended. He was the one post-war churchman to originate a verb in German: *fringsen* – helping yourself (principally to Allied coal) when the troops weren't looking. It was similar to *zapp-zarapp* – helping yourself the Russian way. Frings was more a man of the people than the other high churchmen who had won their laurels objecting to Hitler's policies. He had suffered knocks with the best of them. In June 1943 a bomb had blown up the air-raid shelter he was in, killing two nuns and injuring five others. Frings rolled up his sleeves and helped to rescue the wounded. His own family house was destroyed, killing one of his sisters; a brother was killed during an air attack on Magdeburg; another died in a Russian camp.[128]

He had been appointed in May 1942 after his predecessor, Schulte, died in the course of another air-raid. The Nazis had already expressed their view of Frings when they attacked him in his parish, and Peter Winckelnkemper, the 'brown' mayor of Cologne, had thrown an ashtray at the priest, scarring his face. Perhaps because he had seen the suffering caused by both sides in the conflict, he was able to speak up for the victims. He stood up first to the Nazis, then to the Allies by rejecting 'collective guilt'. From his pulpit he called for justice and Christian love from the conquerors; he demanded the liberation of POWs, spoke out against famine and against the expulsions from the east and called for just proceedings in denazification. He also pleaded for the lives of those who had been condemned to death by the Allied courts.[129]

At Christmas 1945 he made this clear to his flock. The war was over, but the current situation was one of general suffering: 'I see it as my duty to relieve your pain as best I might . . . by speaking and writing. I have always made it plain that the whole nation is not guilty, and that many thousand children, old people and mothers are wholly innocent and it is they who now bear the brunt of the suffering in this general misery.'[130]

Frat

As already noted, there was to be no talking to the conquered Germans. 'Fraternising' was prohibited before the Western Allies arrived in Germany. The ban was first imposed after the First World War, but then the occupation of Germany had been limited to certain western districts. After the Second World War in some places it remained in force until October 1945, although it was perfectly ineffective.[131]

Soldiers were told not to be moved by the hunger of a 'yellow-haired German child . . . there lurked the Nazi'. In the American army paper *Stars and Stripes* servicemen were rehearsed in useful slogans: 'Soldiers wise don't fraternise.' A picture showed a comely German girl: 'Don't play Samson to her Delilah – She'd like to cut your hair off – at the neck.' Or quite simply: 'In heart, body and spirit every German is a Hitler!'[132] The British were almost as heartless. The order banning frat was introduced to British forces in March 1945. In his proclamation to the Germans Bernard Montgomery asked them to tell their children 'why it is the British soldier does not smile'. Very soon, however, Montgomery saw that the ban was unworkable with the children and exempted those under eight. On 12 June soldiers could address any child. The British scrapped the ban altogether in September, but until the following month Germans had to get out of the way of British soldiers on the pavement.[133]

In some quarters, the ban on frat was the source of acute frustration among Germans. Ursula von Kardorff heard about the prohibition on 11 June. Soldiers began to shout at the women: 'We would like to talk to you, but we are not allowed. Eisenhower said so.' Arthur Radley, a British officer serving in Austria, thought the whole thing ludicrous, but the ban had one unexpected advantage. His regiment had an RSM whom everyone disliked, but they could find no way of getting rid of him. Then, as they were marching into Styria, a girl asked him the time, and he replied. He was put before a court martial and broken to private. He was then transferred to another regiment. 'A lot of people could breathe again.'[134]

On 29 June Clay reported that the ban was 'extremely unpopular'. It was chiefly a 'boy–girl problem'. 'The only fraternisation that really interests the soldiers is going with the pretty German girl, who is very much in evidence.' He thought the whole thing made for bad propaganda: it should be the American soldier, not the German girl, who wins hearts and minds.[135] It was also wholly ineffectual: within a month of the Western Allies' arrival a German lover became the rule. What the soldiers did when they were alone was fratting. For George Clare, coining a mixed metaphor rather a long time after the event, British soldiers were 'cementing Anglo-German relations at the grass-roots'. His mess, a large, requisitioned Berlin flat, was 'liberty hall': you never went into any bedroom without knocking first. There was a chance there would be a 'Veronika' in there. Others went home to the family. One of Clare's friends shared a bedroom with a woman and her mother. The latter just turned over and went to sleep.[136]

Neither Allied soldiers nor German women were ready to co-operate with the ban. Part of the problem was a shortage of the opposite sex. Most German men aged between sixteen and sixty were absent; those who remained were often invalids or cripples. Women aged between twenty and forty outnumbered their men by 160 to 100. Margret Boveri reported four women mobbing a twenty-year-old German youth in Neukölln in

Berlin, and recalled the problems that had been caused for her generation by the loss of two million young men in the Great War. The conquerors, by contrast to the old men around, looked healthy and proud, which acted as an aphrodisiac of sorts. For the women themselves, their virtue had been compromised by two things – the experience of rape, often aggravated by violence, disease or pregnancy, and starvation. Clare's frat, 'Anita', was lucky to have been raped just once: she had tried to wriggle out of it by pointing to her groin and saying 'I sick!' The Russian was wise to that. 'I rubber!' he replied.[137] Very soon Clare learned that most if not all of his comrades in arms had adopted 'Fräuleins' and that certain nights when the men did not return to their billets were called 'Fräulein nights'.[138]

The way to the Berlin women's hearts appears to have been through their stomachs. From the Winston Club, British Other Ranks filled their haversacks with spam and cheese rolls, buns and cakes. A haversack filled with NAAFI food had the purchasing power of two cigarettes. You could feed a Fräulein and her family for four Gold Flakes or Players. British soldiers were rationed to 200 cigarettes a week, which made them the lords of the land with full seigniorial rights.[139] Morality was loose and prostitution rife. Both the Allies and the German authorities turned a blind eye to it. In Nuremberg one of James Stern's colleagues interviewed a prostitute. She said most of her customers were sad German soldiers looking for companionship, but there were American soldiers too, 'both white and coloured'. The AMG had not sought to interfere, but the prostitutes had to register and see a doctor once a week.[140]

It was generally not a formal business arrangement in that way. German women were prepared to have sex with Americans for reasons that stretched from companionship to the need for protection, cigarettes, food or stockings. There was a wood in Nuremberg that Stern called 'Conception Copse'. Between 6 p.m. and the curfew it was littered with GIs and German girls. As frat was still officially banned, they had to beware of MPs. There were, however, plenty of DPs acting as auxiliaries to the American forces who had no fear of the police – Germans, Hungarians, Czechs, Italians, Letts or Poles – and they too availed themselves of the German girls.[141]

13

Black Market

Old Reichsmark coins, which weren't valid any more because of their silver content – we weren't supposed to have them any more – and Party badges – all badges from Hitler's time, Hitler Youth badges – with those we went to the [American] barracks and in the barracks we got cigarettes. And the cigarettes we exchanged for food at the farmers.

> Quoted in Petra Goedde, *GIs and Germans*,
> New Haven and London 2003, 90

Cigarettes and CARE Packets

With a cigarette worth more than a hundred-mark note even the old nobles were happy to make a little money smuggling cigarettes across the green frontier. An American cigarette was worth a suburban railway ticket, and a packet counted as a major bribe. In October 1945, one cigarette was worth four ounces of bread. In a POW camp they could cost as much as 120 marks apiece.[1] The Germans who were best off were those who could still lay their hands on jewellery, watches or cameras. Franz Sayn-Wittgenstein remembered selling a badly damaged piece of Meissen porcelain to a black-marketeer for a considerable number of cigarettes. The piece was restored and sold to an American general's wife who kept it too close to the fire and the restored part promptly fell off.[2]

The importance of the cigarette trade is revealed in contemporary literature. Heinrich Böll's 'Kumpel mit den langen Haar' (My Long-Haired Mate) describes a raid on a black market. The central character sees jeeps drive up to a station filled with redcaps who then cordon off the area and begin their search. 'It went incredibly quickly. I stood just outside the cordon and lit a cigarette. Everything happened so quietly. Lots of cigarettes landed on the ground. Pity . . . I thought and I made an involuntary calculation as to how much money was now lying in the dirt. The Black Maria quickly filled up with its quarry . . .' The man wisely avoids going to his digs. He goes into the station and walks to the buffet where he hands over 200 cigarettes to Fritz the waiter and sticks the money into his back pocket. 'Now I was completely without wares, just a packet for myself.' He orders a bowl of meat stock and a piece of bread. He is joined by little Mausbach, quite out of breath. "You," he stammered. "You need to beat it . . . they have searched your room and found the coke . . . Christ!" He was almost choking. I patted him reassuringly on the shoulder and gave him twenty marks . . . Pity, I thought again . . . eight thousand marks gone up in smoke . . . You are safe nowhere.'[3]

One way of surviving was smuggling from the Russian Zone to the West. Libussa von Krockow traded American cigarettes in the Russian Zone and procured nylons in Chemnitz that she then bartered with a shoemaker in Holstein for a pair of shoes. She suspended the smuggling in 1946, with the onset of the killing winter.[4] In the spring of 1947 Clay made a move to stop the use of cigarettes as currency by banning their importation. He considered bringing in tobacco instead, thereby leading to a fall in prices as supply increased. Clay had to admit it was unlikely to remove the value of Lucky Strikes, as there had been a black market for American cigarettes before the war.[5] Rumours of currency reform were rife six months before the Allies made their move. Until that happened barter was still the means by which people normally lived. A woman wanting to have her hair washed, for example, had to bring with her the soap, a towel and five pieces of wood. Wood was an important commodity, especially in winter, and Ruth Friedrich was appalled to see that her lover's grave had been plundered of the pine fronds she had laid on it – an ancient and probably heathen Prussian tradition.[6]

For the Allies working in Germany shopping was done in 'Occupation Marks' – 'a currency with an appearance even more spurious than that of the million- and milliard-mark bills of the inflation period after the First War'.[7] Cigarettes were one means the Allies had of getting their way in Germany; another was chewing gum. A generation of Germans became addicted to gum as a result of GIs handing it out to children, so much so that even now chewing gum is nowhere in Europe so respectable as it is in Germany. Even the Old Etonian Stern was not averse to using gum as a way to the hearts of children.[8] Another important commodity was soap. Prisoners released from American camps hoarded soap, which they could sell for food or cigarettes. Former POWs from British camps had no such currency. A bar of soap had a monetary value of between fifty and eighty marks. The most highly prized was Palmolive.

In the winter of 1946–7, as many as 60,000 chiefly elderly Germans died of cold and hunger. CRALOG (Council of Relief Agencies Licensed to Operate in Germany) was a manifestation of the Allies' change of attitude to the Germans. By the beginning of 1947 it had distributed 30,000 tons of food. In April 1946 CARE (Co-operative of American Remittances to Europe) joined in. This was the beginning of the famous CARE packets: 1.9 million of them were handed out in 1946 alone. After the winter Clay called for relief from Washington. He expressed the view that there was no hope of introducing democracy to a starving population.[9]

In a Germany where there were 'calories but no food'[10] something always needed to be found to supplement the scanty commons provided by the Allies – and that meant the black market. 'Whoever wanted to live needed to find connections to the black market as a seller or a buyer.'[11] There was nothing new about black markets, which will emerge wherever there is rationing. The black market flourished during the Third Reich despite some draconian punishments, from the Junker who was made an example of and given four months for failing to deliver his milk to the co-operative, to the 5,142 black-marketeers who were executed for illicit trading.[12]

The black market was often based in the main railway station. In a remarkable number of instances, it was the only largely undamaged structure in the city centre. The atmosphere in these stations appears in Böll's early stories. Another man with an eye for detail was Zuckmayer – although with an important proviso. Zuckmayer points out that recording the man in the street often gives a false idea of how a country thinks because the stupidest have the loudest mouths, and more intelligent people either reflect more before they speak or hold their tongues.[13] The station was the point of arrival and departure and a transit point: 'In Germany there is . . . a ceaseless creeping, crawling and groping; an enraged ant-heap, the constant buzzing of swarms of wild bees; an eternal coming and going, tramping, running and criss-crossing; a scraping and creaking of millions of unquiet soles. This is the spirit of the "Black Market" or the "Green Border" [the unpatrolled frontier]; the world and the march of the homeless, the expellees, the masses torn asunder, the furtive traveller, the marauding youth.'

Railway stations were the centres of their universe, open all day and all night. 'Stations are not just miserable waiting rooms for overtired, exhausted travellers; they are homes for the homeless.'[14] On the north side of Frankfurt Station there was a hut operated by the Red Cross that served as a room for travelling mothers, where they could change their infants and receive a little nourishment in the form of porridge, gruel, skimmed milk or hot soup. There was no need of coupons. Despairing mothers often left their children in the hut, knowing that the Red Cross could hardly toss them out into the cold. On the far side of the Rhine, in the French Zone, there was rumoured to be a market for babies.[15]

Zuckmayer clearly enjoyed the curious parade of figures in every conceivable costume: a man wearing Tyrolean dress, his knees exposed to the freezing air and frozen blue scratching his wiry beard with the side of his zither case; another wrapped in a Yugoslavian sheepskin; men dressed in every form of military uniform and a lot of black jackets emblazoned with the fading legend 'PW' for prisoner of war. Women were also dressed in this motley fashion, from a worn-out silk cape to a pair of ski trousers that had seen better days.

To buy food or drink required prolonged queuing. If you were lucky you might obtain a glass of watery beer or a cup of beef broth on presentation of a ration coupon. Even then a cup or glass was only issued on payment of a ten-mark deposit. Most were there to trade, however. Zuckmayer compared it to Times Square on a Saturday night. If you moved among the mass you could hear the offers of butter, dripping, flour, cigarettes – Chesterfields or Luckies were the best – or gems, coffee, chocolate or soap. Papers were also traded, often on particular specialised platforms within the station. New names could be issued with the passport. Most people went for quite banal things they felt they needed, like tobacco. For a box brownie you might have received a carton of washing powder crammed with desiccated tobacco or crumbled cigarettes made up from fag ends called *Besen* or brooms. An opera glass yielded a kilo of dried peas and a bacon rind. On another occasion a camera was hocked for a goose.[16]

There were periodic *Razzien* or raids, when the traders scattered before the police – these were either 'minor' or 'major' raids. The former were carried out by the German police, who took their work seriously. They concentrated on rounding up prostitutes and taking them off to a clinic for examination. They were released with a 'hunting certificate' – or a clean bill of health – and went directly back to the station. The major *Razzia* was performed by foreign MPs. Those who were arrested spent a night in the cells. In Berlin that meant the police station on the 'Alex' or Alexanderplatz. It was not considered a disgrace to be caught and punished in this way, when so many Germans were in prison for innocent reasons.[17] Among those arrested was Ernst Jünger, who was in Tübingen to address students. One of his companions in the car was found to possess a suspicious number of cigarettes. He was put against a wall, and when the local Landrat intervened, the politician was made to join him.[18]

Some of the traders had already begun to cast themselves as 'business-men' by the winter of 1946–7. One young man called Dieter took Zuckmayer off for a drink at his favourite bar, which turned out to be close to Frankfurt Station. They had to walk though a gloomy and ruinous backyard. The bar had been decorated with fake flowers and a three-man ensemble played pseudo-swing music. An evil schnapps was available for monstrous prices, as were American cigarettes. There was a sign on the counter announcing that the under-aged were not allowed in, but Zuckmayer saw plenty of much younger boys and girls. Zuckmayer heard a boy pleading with a girl to sleep with him. He could not have been older than fifteen and still had a child's voice. The object of his attention was a powerful girl in a Manchester jacket and man's trousers: 'Will you not come with me tonight? You promised.'

'Leave me alone. I have already done it five times today.'

'But you promised!' the boy begged.

'Leave me alone. Do you think I do this for pleasure?'

'I've got a Hershey Bar.' The boy was almost in tears.

'Get on with you. I still need a carton of cigarettes. I need a new dress.'

Zuckmayer's 'businessman' did not relish the idea of this freebooting being brought to an end, but a money-based economy was bound to come. The other boys 'in business' looked well on it: they were strong and fit, although the girls, living mostly from their bodies, looked less so. There was chicanery there too. Some of the men who went into the ruins with the girls were promptly beaten up and relieved of their wallets.[19] Dieter lived with a girl who worked as a prostitute for the officers and men of the garrison. He was keen that Zuckmayer should not think ill of her for making her money that way. She was all right for all that, and Dieter thought that they could make it together, pull themselves out of the gutter. 'Who can navigate these times and remain wholly clean?'[20]

In Berlin the most famous black market was held around the ruined Reichstag building, stretching as far as the Brandenburg Gate – though this may have been a separate division. The main business was in cigar-ettes, and there were the usual police raids. One effect of the new currency was to increase the price of metal, and Paul Wallot's building was stripped of all its metallic features for cash. This rang the knell for a number of statues that were torn down and sold for scrap.[21] The legendary

Munich black market was in the Möhlstrasse in Bogenhausen. Here you could obtain anything, provided you had money, cigarettes or something to swap: 'flour and carpets, French cognac [sic], Spanish oranges, silver pots and cigarettes, English cloth and German cameras'. The traders were eastern Jews, Greeks, Hungarians, Czechs and Poles. There were also deals in the main Viktualienmarkt in the centre of the city, where business centred on the Stadt Kempten pub. Even the Hofbräuhaus was a black market in its day. Traders used ingenious devices to run cigarettes. There were James-Bond-style cars with false floors which could be lined with cartons.[22]

The situation in French-controlled south Baden gives an indication of values at the end of 1946: 1,200 litres of fermenting wine must plus 200 litres sweet must plus old wine barrels were exchanged for seven rubber tyres; 6,000 kilos of potatoes for twelve pairs of working trousers and four aprons; three flints for five eggs; six bottles of schnapps for three men's shirts; a watch for two kilos of butter; thirty litres of wine for eighty horseradish roots; two pairs of ladies' trousers for two calf pelts; a cuckoo clock with a ceramic plate for a thousand cigarettes; a 500-kilo pig for 200 litres of wine; two pairs of ladies' socks for a pound and half of butter.[23]

There were plenty of rhymes:

> Der Schmuck hat man als Butter aufgegessen,
> die Meissner Tassen trägt man jetzt als Schuh.
> So wächst dem Eigner, was er einst besessen
> Von Grund auf umgewandelt wieder zu . . .*

Here at last was 'zero hour'; the *tabula rasa*. Those family treasures that had not been destroyed by bombs, stolen or broken by Russians were now eaten up. That the black market had its positive side was pointed out by the Frankfurt city physician Dr Strüder: it offered an opportunity to supplement rations. Another – also illegal – solution was *hamstern*. Special trains took town and city folk out to country areas to trade with farmers and smallholders. If no one was to hand, the 'hamsters' helped themselves. The farmers did not trust money, so exchanges were in useful goods or objects. Another country activity of note was illegal distillation. A bottle of schnapps was a tradable commodity and a good way of turning a few apple trees into a money-making enterprise. Growers in Lower Austria

---

* The jewellery has been consumed as butter,
The Meissen cups are worn as shoes.
Behold the new man step out the gutter,
Ancient heirlooms put to better use.

fought shy of bringing their wine into Vienna, as they were often robbed by Russian soldiers. They preferred potential clients to come to them, at their own risk.[24]

Of course the black market bred crime as well. The buyer needed to beware of counterfeit foods. Tins were filled with filth, and the unwary could return to find everything they had acquired was rotten. Many of the Germans working at the black market were KZler – 'greens' or habitual criminals – and these were prone to show off their wealth in one or two prominent bars, such as the Queen in Cologne, by drinking real coffee and eating coupon-free menus. The fortunes of several West German businessmen were founded in the post-war black market.

The black market was also a stomping ground for DPs. While they waited to be repatriated many turned to crime. Western European DPs received a good press on the whole, but others were feared by the Germans. James Stern witnessed an ugly scene in Darmstadt, when the car he was in collided with a German cyclist with a wooden leg. A crowd of Polish DPs gathered around the injured man, evidently hoping that the Americans would beat him up – or worse. They were disappointed when they drove the man home instead. Wild bands of lawless DPs had become the new brigands of post-war Germany. Another man Stern interviewed, a lawyer, was obsessed with the risk of robbery by bands of Polish DPs. So far they had stolen three bicycles from him in a Munich suburb and a Pole had shot at him in the city centre. Russian DPs had attacked his neighbours and killed the wife, before stealing the couple's bicycles.

As Jünger had observed in his village near Celle, the DPs were at their worst around Hanover. The writer and journalist Leonard Mosely admitted that most of the cars had been stolen by the Allies themselves, but it was DPs who first led a reign of terror in Herford 'loaded with loot and drinks'. In Hanover they were out of control for several days.[25] Touring Hessen in the winter of 1945, John Dos Passos was told of a German killed and stripped by DPs the night before. The DPs formed robber bands that were responsible for a number of atrocious acts in both Germany and Austria. Near Stuttgart there were nightly attacks on isolated farmhouses. On 10 November 1945 at Spitalmühle near Margröningen a miller and his family fled to the cellar for safety, but all six were shot in the head by the intruders.[26] The American army was called in to deal with a gang of Polish DPs, and eventually had to use tanks in the course of a twelve-hour *Razzia* at Wildflecken near Fulda.[27]

For the time being no one seemed to have a policy for what to do with the foreign workers. They were to be found on the roads leading from the main cities, trying to find a way home. The exceptions were the Russians, most of whom would have done anything to remain in Germany, or travel on to America or Australia. Elena Skrjabina was appointed to visit some of the Russian camps. She reported that all the Russian inmates were 'driven by one feeling – to get as far away as possible from the Soviet Union'.[28]

Russian soldiers sold off some of their surplus watches and traded German marks for dollars, while the Americans bought Meissen porcelain with their PX rations.[29] A Russian soldier remembered encountering a black American who tried to sell him first a Colt pistol, then a jeep. Elsewhere blacks sold cigarettes, chocolates and soap.[30] Smuggling cars back to the Soviet Union ended when the Russian authorities imposed huge tariffs in 1946. The Americans used the Interzone train that ran from Osnabrück to Berlin and was called the 'the silk-stocking express' for that reason.[31] The British received fifty cigarettes free per week and could buy another 200 at duty-free prices. These were sold for marks and then changed back into sterling at RM40 to the pound. Anything could be obtained on the black market to improve the quality of life. There were drugs such as cocaine, morphine and opium; for VD sufferers there was penicillin, and quinine to provoke abortions. There were also contraceptives.[32]

One striking case of criminality that had its origins in the black market was that of Werner Gladow, the 'Al Capone of the Alexanderplatz'. Gladow was born in May 1931, the son of a butcher. He was too young to have experienced the war as a soldier, merely the chaos and depravity occasioned by the Allied bombing. At sixteen he made a modest start as a criminal on the Berlin black market. He was rounded up and imprisoned twice. In April 1948 he graduated from petty marketeering to proper crime when he smashed the window of a camera shop in the Rankestrasse and stole what he thought was a camera. The proprietor gave chase, but Gladow shot him in the leg. He and his gang stole a car and headed for the Soviet Sector. When East Berlin Volkspolizei or 'Vopos' surrounded the car, Gladow fired at them and the gang escaped.

Gladow formed his friends into a proper gang expanding to twenty-seven at its apogee. All the members had nicknames. Gladow was 'Doktorchen', or 'Little Doc'. He acted on tip-offs from Gustav Völpel, an executioner on both sides of Berlin between 1946 and 1948. The gang's first proper haul occurred when they held up the cashier of a funfair on the Prenzlauer Berg. Gladow was convinced that the way to succeed was superior firepower. To this end he held up a detachment of seven Vopos and stole their guns. These came in useful for the robbery of a number of jewellers' shops and a hold-up at a Tauschzentral* in the Frankfurter Allee. As the director of the Tauschzentral would not reveal where he had hidden the day's takings Gladow tortured him until he handed over RM6,000. Meanwhile the gang had run out of ammunition. The solution was to hold up another eight Vopos in January 1949 and rob them of their guns. The Gladow gang's attacks became ever more violent. During a robbery of a jeweller's they shot a man several times. A shocked general public pelted them with stones. They still managed to escape and the police found no trace of them. One reason why they were so difficult to track down was the position of Berlin and its sectors. As in *The Third Man* in Vienna, there was no co-operation between the police in the East and West. Berlin was a paradise for gangsters like Gladow.

In May 1949 the gang shot and killed the driver of a BMW and stole his car. Now the police finally uncovered the tracks of the gang and went to arrest Gladow in Friedrichshain in the Soviet Sector. After a gun battle in which Gladow was wounded twice, he was taken into custody and charged with 352 offences, including two murders and fifteen attempted murders. In the dock he was undiminished in his cockiness. Attempts to reduce the sentence on the grounds of age were rejected, and Gladow was beheaded in Frankfurt-an-der-Oder on 5 December 1950.[33]

---

* The Tauschzentral was a sort of pawn shop where goods were exchanged for money or food, an official version of the black market, established in all four zones. It was hoped that its presence would gradually eliminate the latter. Unfortunately, however, the Tauschzentral would neither sell food nor accept it in payment for goods.

14

Light Fingers

Naturally I nicked things sometimes, coal and that sort of thing.
Wood too. Just recently I even stole a loaf of bread from a baker's shop.
It was really quick and simple. I just snatched the bread and walked
out. I went out calmly, only when I got to the corner did I start to
run. You just don't have the nerves any more.

Heinrich Böll, 'Geschäft ist Geschäft', in *Wanderer kommst
du nach Spal – Erzählungen*, Munich 1997, 171

Theft was not confined to petty larceny among the *soldateska*, DPs or
starving Germans. Whole governments were involved in robbing
Germany of anything that took their fancy. It could have been just about
anything, such as Göring's yacht, the *Karin II*, which ended up in the hands
of the British royal family. One Soviet priority was the seizure of any
important works of art found in the capital. This was a fully planned operation, and no particular novelty. The greatest art thief of all time was
probably Napoleon Bonaparte, and French provincial museums are still
filled with paintings acquired on his campaigns. The Nazis too plundered
art wherever they went, but they proved themselves amateurs beside the
Red Army. The art works stolen by Soviet troops were originally planned
to be exhibited in a huge museum of war trophies – the equivalent of
Hitler's museum in Linz. As the tide of opinion changed, however, the
Russians chose to conceal the art works in special closed galleries throughout the Soviet Union. Many of them remain hidden to this day.*

In true Soviet style many of these works of art were destroyed in the
fighting and more were to be eradicated by negligence during the first days
of the occupation. The pillage was by no means limited to Berlin, and
within their zone and in the former German areas that were ceded to

---

* In 1999 an assistant director of the Hermitage in St Petersburg told the author that the pictures were still there, and that they had been in the museum from the day they were
removed from Germany. It was not Russian policy to give them back.

Russia and Poland the Soviets were able to make off with some two and a half million *objets d'art* including 800,000 paintings. Some of these had been stolen by the Nazis.

Art boffins travelled with the Red Army as they conquered Germany, grabbing anything of value. This was not always so easy, as the squaddies were often more likely to destroy works of art than to preserve them. Fyodor Chotinsky, for example, chanced upon his first haul when he entered one of the houses of a Graf Pourtalès on 10 March 1945. His excitement was mitigated, however, when over the next few days troops shattered the larger part of the porcelain, knocked over statuary, and poked out the eyes of portraits in the style of Rembrandt and Greuze. Even when troops were posted to watch over a collection, the boffins returned to find that the guards had slept in the tapestries and used the porcelain to cook in.[1]

The nemesis of this Russian pursuit of trophies was the MFAA (Monuments, Fine Arts and Archives) department of the US army. They too took art works into 'custody', including some 200 canvases found in Berlin. The Americans originally planned to ship a large percentage of Germany's art treasures home with them. This was a policy warmly supported by Clay, who wanted to 'hold them in trust for the German people'. There was a little more to it than that, however. Clay's concern for the art works encompassed an element of 'trophying': the 'American public is entitled to see these art objects'. He opposed the return of works from the Kaiser Friedrich Museum* in Berlin before a place could be found to exhibit them. Eventually President Truman stepped in and promised to send them back.[2]

This was in part due to Captain Walter Farmer, the author of the 'Wiesbaden Manifesto', who encouraged ministers, senators and museum curators to protest against official policy. Those works of art that had already been removed to America were brought back to Germany after their return had been officially sanctioned by Clay in March 1948. The Prussian Collections were given to Hessen, as the state of Prussia would shortly be abolished by the notorious Control Council Law No. 46 of February 1947. The former Prussian Collection from the Kaiser Friedrich Museum had found a temporary home in Wiesbaden. They included the famous bust of Queen Nefertiti. Much of Berlin's treasure was housed in the castellated flak towers that were National Socialism's most striking gift to the capital. In one of them, the Zoo Tower, Soviet art historians in

---

* Now the Bode Museum. It was in the Soviet Sector.

uniform discovered Heinrich Schliemann's gold: the treasures of Troy protected day and night by the director of the Museum for Antiquities, Dr Wilhelm Unverzagt. Unverzagt had managed to prevent the soldiers from finding the gold until 1 May, when a superior officer appeared. Then he revealed the contents of the cases. The officer posted sentries. A few days later General Bersarin made a visit to the tower and assured Unverzagt that the treasures would be taken to a safe place. At the end of the month Schliemann's gold was carried off on an army lorry. Its ultimate destination was Leningrad.

Unverzagt had one last job to perform: he had to supervise the inventory as the boxes were filled with other treasures as they were removed from the tower. The first convoy set out on 13 May. By the 19th the work was all but finished. On the 21st he learned that the lorries were heading for the Soviet army HQ at Karlshorst. Speed was vital: the Western Allies were due in Berlin at any moment and the Soviet authorities did not want the British or the Americans calling them to order. The Zoo Tower was going to be in the British Sector after all. The art historians had to convince the generals of the importance of what they were doing. Many of these senior officers were *demontageniki* – keener on using their lorries and railway trucks to ship out whole factories together with any heavy machines to rebuild the Soviet economy.[3] And there was still a problem: the flak tower was under Smersh – Military Intelligence – control, and the culture boffins had no right to remove the objects from it. They had to win over Marshal Zhukov. This was done by sending Andrei Belokopitov, in civilian life the director of the Artists' Theatre in Moscow, to see the marshal. Zhukov thought the visit was to do with the theatre and received Belokopitov cordially. When he learned that it was to do with the treasure in the flak tower, he became angry. Belokopitov told the marshal, however, 'If this collection falls into the hands of the Americans, you will regret this mistake.'

Zhukov summoned his adjutant, Antipenko. They would override Smersh: the culture boffins had twenty-four hours to empty the Zoo Tower. Belokopitov broke into the conversation: twenty-four hours were too few, because the objects were very large. Zhukov awarded the boffins forty-eight and dismissed them. They enlisted a detachment of some 300 experienced pioneers who set about dismantling the Pergamon Altar. They also loaded 7,000 Greek vases, 1,800 statues, 9,000 antique gems, 6,500 terracotta figures and thousands of objects of lesser value. The bigger job was finished by the beginning of June. When the Americans arrived they were told that the altar had been removed undamaged, but that some

Egyptian reliefs and Roman statuary had been smashed, and that a Chinese bronze gong had rolled away down the stone steps.[4] The largest piece of booty transported to Russia were the friezes from the Pergamon Altarpiece, which had been a present to Kaiser William II from the Ottoman emperor to thank Germany for its help in excavating the site. The Pergamon Museum had been built up around it.

The greatest tragedy of the sack of Berlin was the fire that took place in the Control Tower in the Park at Friedrichshain. The huge concrete tower was abandoned by its defenders on 2 May. Over the next three days it was picked over by various foreign workers who were chiefly looking for food. The tower was, however, the temporary repository of the classical antiquities from the Berlin museums together with the paintings from the picture gallery. There were 8,500 objects from the classical collections, as well as 1,500 in glass. Of the 411 canvases, 160 were Italian masters, a quarter of the total collection, and including works by Fra Angelico and Luca Signorelli. Italian sculpture was represented by Donatello's *Madonna and Child*. There were large works by Rubens, as well as pictures by Chardin, Zurbarán, Murillo and Reynolds. Of the German works one of the most famous was Menzel's *Tafelrunde*.

In the night of the 5–6 May the Control Tower burst into flames, destroying at least some of the art works housed on the first floor. It was thought that the fire had been started by Germans looking for food. Someone had the wilder theory that Werewolves had set the tower alight. Still it was impossible to convince the Russians to guard the tower, and some time between the 7th and the 15th another fire broke out that destroyed all that remained. The second fire may have been started by thieves trying to find valuable works of art, as some artefacts and at least one picture later materialised on the market. As there was no light in the tower it was supposed they had lit newspapers in order to see better. When art historians visited the site a few days later they found that the forced labourers had already scoured the remains, taking with them fragments of antique glass and pots. On contact with the air the marble disintegrated in the hands of the despairing experts.[5]

At the beginning of July the Russians took another look at the Control Tower in Friedrichshain. It was decided to sift through the ruins to see if there was anything worth retrieving. They filled fifteen chests with broken antiquities. One of the archaeologists was excited about a strangely shaped vase he found buried in the ashes. When he had dusted it down he found that he was holding a Russian bazooka shell that had failed to explode. The Russian experts knew that it was important to remove anything salvageable from the Control Tower before the autumn as the damp air would destroy the remaining artefacts. The military governor of Berlin, Colonel General Gorbatov, wrote to Zhukov to this effect, but work did not begin until December. By March 1946 around 10,000 objects had been dug out. Even the Americans from the MFAA were able to retrieve a few objects. There seems to have been little or no security at the tower.[6] More antiquities were taken from the cellars of the New Mint where they had lain around in pools of water, in many cases badly damaged. From the Museum Island the Russians selected fifty-four canvases from the cellars. Among others there was Goya's *May Pole*, and Ghirlandaio's *Christ on the Cross*. All the looted treasure was taken to Schloss Tresckow in Friedrichsfelde or the former abattoir for shipment back to Russia.

The fate of Hitler continued to trouble the Russians for many months: was he actually dead? The British too had launched an investigation, with the historian Hugh Trevor-Roper piecing his last days together. The Russians had the advantage of possessing the Chancellery, the bunker and – although they were confused at first – his bones. Trevor-Roper did not have those, although the picture he drew was substantially correct.[7]

Meanwhile the Soviet authorities were falling out over the bones. Stalin had been informed by Zhukov that Hitler had committed suicide on 30 April. His body and that of his new wife Eva Braun had been dug up in the garden, in the spot designated by Admiral Voss. As the Smersh soldiers were not certain that they had the right bodies, they reburied them, only finally exhuming them on 5 May, when together with the bodies of the Goebbels children, the chief of staff General Krebs and a couple of dogs, they were sent to their HQ at Berlin-Buch as important trophies. The autopsies were performed the next day. Contradictory evidence made the officers concerned reluctant to send in a final report on the cause of Hitler's death. The Soviet authorities preferred the version that had him taking poison – a cowardly way out. Shooting oneself was a braver, more soldierly death.

When the Soviets' Operation Myth was launched in 1946 to establish the real sequence of events leading to Hitler's death, some of Hitler's personal staff were brought back to Berlin and the bunker, in order to point out the precise details of the suicide and subsequent burning in the garden. The bones, for the time being, were stored in Magdeburg.[8] Of particular importance were the objects in Hitler's personal collection. For them an aircraft was laid on as Stalin wanted his bones examined by his foremost experts. The Führer's skull was eventually put into a paper bag and deposited in the State Archives. The paintings in his private collection were taken to the abattoir.[9] The area around the Chancellery remained out of bounds to Berliners. When Ruth Friedrich poked her nose into the *cour d'honneur* of the Chancellery in May she saw a Soviet squaddie comfortably ensconced in an armchair with a machine gun across his knees.[10]

At Schloss Sophienhof near Berlin, Russian soldiers destroyed the complete archive of Wilhelm von Humboldt. Part of the medieval-weapon collection housed in the Berlin Arsenal was destroyed on orders issued by the Soviet military authorities. At Karinhall, the house Göring had built for himself on the site of the the Kaiser's hunting lodge on the Schorfheide, the Russians indulged in an orgy of destruction, demolishing statues by Pigalle, Houdon and Boizo by using them for target practice. The hidden pictures by Emil Nolde (the Nazis had forbidden Nolde to paint) in Teupitz Hospital were burned.[11]

Not everything was rubbished. In Silesia delighted Russian officials seized immense numbers of wireless sets. In the villas of prosperous Silesians well-stocked libraries were found, and 40,000 art books were collected and despatched back to the Pushkin Museum. In Gleiwitz there was excitement when a horde of Stradivari and Amati violins was seized, until it turned out that they were fakes. Silesia, however, was not as rich in artefacts as its soil was fertile. A Kolbe figure was located and appropriated. As they searched for booty on one estate Soviet art experts found a group of soldiers about to hang a monkey. The creature was accused of having lifted its paw in salute when they had shouted 'Heil Hitler!' as a joke. The irony of the monkey's response had been lost on them. The art historians rescued the beast and made it their companion.[12]

Soviet officers – particularly Lieutenant Yevgeny Ludshuveit – were credited with saving the Schlosser of Sanssouci (the town palace was destroyed by British bombs in April). Frederick the Great's art collection, however, went east, and a Russian officer is thought to have slashed Philip de László's portrait of William II with a sabre.[13] Most of the Russian energy went into removing the best parts of the collections they found. In the old Cistercian monastery at Lehnin they found some stored works of art and organised their shipment. Frederick the Great's first palace, Schloss Rheinsberg, was stripped of its last contents, right down to the painted over-doors. Viktor Lazarev, however, a professor of art history at Moscow University, was one who respected the architectural ensemble where possible. In Potsdam he advocated leaving paintings, sculpture, chandeliers and tapestries *in situ*, when they were conceived as part of the *Gesamtkunstwerk*. As many as 60,000 POWs were used in the evacuation of these works of art, loading them on to 90,000 railway trucks.[14]

Berlin was not the only place rich in art treasure. The Russians had the run of Saxony and much of Thuringia, not to mention Pomerania and the prosperous port of Danzig. The electors and kings of Saxony had been great collectors, and the Dresden Gallery was one of the world's foremost art museums. Part of the collection had been stored in a quarry at Grosscotta near Pirna. Among the paintings there was the *Sistine Madonna* by Raphael. The art historian Natalia Sokolova was the first to see the pictures when a German unlocked the door to the store room.

> A simple goods wagon stood in the tunnel. The German handed me the candle. [Leonid] Rabinovitch turned on an electric lamp. In this twilight were glimpsed the gold frames of the pictures, that were tightly packed together. We turned our lights towards them and I felt I had gone deathly pale. Before me I could see the broad span of the eagle that bore off Rembrandt's *Ganymede* in its claws. Rabinovitch carefully moved the painting to the right, and another appeared.
>
> 'Do you see?' he whispered. 'Wonderful,' said the German . . . what lay before me was the *Sleeping Venus* of Giorgione . . . After that came the *Self-Portrait with Saskia* by Rembrandt and a small, silvery landscape by Watteau, a view of *Dresden* by Canaletto, Titian's *Portrait of a Woman in White* . . .

The conditions in the quarry were terrible: it was cold and damp: 'The Germans had lost any moral claim to [the pictures]. Now they belonged to the Red Army.' There was a fear that they might have to fight the Americans for them if they did not get them to their collection point at Schloss Pillnitz as quickly as possible. Marshal Koniev came to inspect the haul. He was also impressed and telegraphed Stalin to tell him that the treasure had been found.[15]

There was more booty in Schloss Weesenstein. Here the Russians found the Koenig Collection that had been bought by Prince John George of Saxony, and forty-five Rembrandt etchings that had belonged to the industrialist and banker Rudolf Gutmann of Vienna and had since been earmarked for the Führer's Museum in Linz. Only one of the etchings had been detached from the collection: *The Jewish Bride* was thought to portray too sensitive a subject.[16]

More paintings from the Dresden Gallery were found at Pockau-Lengefeld by the Czech border in the fortress at Königstein and some modern masters in a house in Barnitz. In Meissen orders were given to restart production of the famous porcelain. This was not possible, however, as the *demontagniki* had made off with the equipment. The contents of the Porcelain Museum as well as some valuable paintings were stored in the old castle at the top of the hill. Also in Saxony, Leipzig's most valuable collections had been placed in the strongrooms of banks. Nearly a hundred were found in a vault on the Friedrich-Tröndlin-Ring in October. Thirty more were found in a bank in the Otto-Schill-Strasse. The Russians took only 10 per cent of their find home, but that still amounted to over a hundred paintings. Another fifty-two came from the Coburgs' Jagdschloss Reinhardsbrunn and the palace in Dessau. Added to the pictures were whole libraries from Friedenstein, Gotha and Leipzig. These were taken to the Academy of Sciences in Moscow, together with the university libraries from Leipzig and Halle.[17]

At the beginning of May a search had been made for the vanished treasures of Danzig after the Russian shelling of the old city. The hunt began in the Arsenal, where the Trophy Brigade had to brave the stench of decomposing corpses to locate their quarry. After two days they found the hiding place and unearthed treasures from the town hall and the museum. The best bits went to Russia. A few odds and ends were given to the new Polish director of the museum. In the ruins of the famous Artushof, they looked in vain for the fifteenth-century wooden relief of St George. It had been destroyed in the fire following the shelling. In the wreckage of a bank, however, they unearthed the coin collection from Marienburg, the fortress of the Teutonic Knights.[18]

The Soviet forces perpetrated all sorts of theft. The most common was the pillaging which accompanied their arrival and which has never been accurately assessed. When it is considered that virtually every sewing machine, every gramophone and every wireless set went east, it can only be described as looting on a staggering scale. The trophy battalions followed on the heels of the soldiers who pinched anything that took their fancy. By 2 August 1945 these had seized 1,280,000 tons of material and 3,600,000 tons of equipment. This way they hoped to make good the losses they had incurred in the war. Officially they claimed the Germans had destroyed $168 milliard's worth of equipment, but that figure must also have included items they destroyed themselves in their retreat.[19]

It was not always the Russians who arrived first. The art historian Paul Ortwin Rave guided the MFAA to Ransbach where the Berlin State Theatre and the Opera House had stored their costumes. They found the remains of an orgy that had been enjoyed by Russian and Polish workers and prisoners together. Once their German guards had run off they had broken into the cases and dressed themselves up in costumes from *Aïda* and *Lohengrin*. They had also found a hidden fund of champagne and cognac. In their drunken state they had broken into cases containing Dürers and Holbeins, but at the sight of the saints they had fled in holy terror. The

Americans took the prize to Frankfurt in their zone. It was they who located the treasure in Altaussee, as well as parts of Göring's collection, including the sixteen cases which the Reichsmarshall had grabbed from among the pictures stored in the Benedictine monastery of Monte Cassino and which the Germans had taken into safe keeping before the British destroyed the building.[20]

Franz Sayn-Wittgenstein recalled examples of the Americans' cupidity in their zone. He was staying in his wife's family mansion, Budingen, when the US governor of Hessen, Newman, sent word to requisition silver and furniture for his palace. They fobbed him off with tableware, which was later returned. In June 1946 Clay rebutted a charge of looting made against some of his soldiers who were accused of stealing six paintings.[21] Easier to verify was the theft of the Quedlinburg Bibles by American soldiers in Thuringia.[22] The American commander in Budingen was a Captain Robinson, who swiped five pictures from the Städel Gallery in Frankfurt. 'Robinson revealed himself as nothing more than a common thief.' They were traced as far as Holland, whence they were in all probability shipped to the United States. They were put up for sale many years later, and the Städel was able to buy them back.[23] Most American cases were restricted to petty larceny out of a desire for souvenirs, though occasionally a shop was looted for objects like cameras. GIs had a passion for Nazi artefacts only equalled by the Soviet *soldateska* – as they advanced through Germany they trashed each SS barracks in the pursuit of flags and swastikas. There was also a celebrated case when two officers of the Women's Army Corps were tried for stealing $1,500,000 worth of jewellery from Princess Mary of Hesse, a fantastic sum then.[24]

Captain Frank M. Dunbaugh took the 50,000 tin and lead soldiers that were the pride of the Hirtenmuseum in Hersbruck in Franconia. They represented the armies that went to war in 1914. In an effort to relocate the soldiers the town contacted President Eisenhower, who promised his support. Some 500 of the figures were tracked down in Texas. When Dunbaugh was asked his excuse for 'liberating' them he replied that it was to 'deglamorize the Hitler war machine in every way possible'. Theft was therefore justified by JCS 1067. In 1958 another 20,000 of the soldiers were located and eventually shipped back to Hersbruck. An attempt to force the Americans to compensate the museum for the rest fell on deaf ears.[25]

The Americans were not all thieves. In Wiesbaden they organised a Central Collecting Point for Jewish paintings and books stolen by the Nazis. It was run by Theodor 'Ted' Heinrich, later professor of art history at the University of Toronto. Surviving Jews could apply to retrieve their belongings there. The Americans also located a favourite grey that had belonged to Queen Wilhelmina of Holland and which had been seized by the Germans during the occupation of her country. In the confusion at the end of the war, the horse had been given to a circus. The Americans returned the animal to its mistress who had it saddled in order to form part of a parade. When the music struck up, the horse got up on its hind legs and began to dance, a trick it had learned in the circus. Her majesty was not amused and the horse was put out to grass.[26] Queen Wilhelmina might have been more grateful that the horse had not been eaten by hungry Germans or DPs. In Munich Carl Zuckmayer reported that Poles had stolen the world's sole porcine tightrope walker, once the pride of Althof's travelling circus – they had then slaughtered it and had it for dinner. When the owner tried to prevent the Poles from killing his beloved pig he nearly lost his own life as well. Althof had had the hog insured abroad and apparently received no compensation for his loss.[27]

There were acts of common theft perpetrated by the British too. At the Krupp residence, Villa Hügel in Essen, an inquiry carried out in 1952 revealed that property valued at two million marks had been purloined during the occupation. Much of it was later found in Holland, where it was waiting to cross the Channel. The greatest scandal surrounding the British Zone was the use of Schloss Bückeburg, home of the Schaumburg-Lippe family, by the RAF. The process was begun by Air Marshal Sir Arthur Coningham, whom the art historian Ellis Waterhouse compared to Göring in his acquisitiveness. Coningham removed and distributed enormous quantities of valuable silver, furnishings and *objets d'art* from the Schloss, and much of it later remained unaccounted for. The affair led to the resignation of the military governor, Marshal of the RAF Sir Sholto Douglas.[28]

The British lagged behind the Russians and the Americans in purloining art works, but they had their own brand of organised theft in T-Force, which sought to glean any industrial wizardry hatched under the Nazis and bring it home to Britain. The Russians and the Americans were equally guilty on this score, but, as George Clare puts it, they 'preferred the inventors to the inventions', while the British were too hard up to feed their boffins. In Cuxhaven, however, they learned what they could about the workings of the V2, and they made off with all the German naval equipment they could find. One of the things that Clare saw at the Askanier Works when he was interpreting there was a prototype tape recorder.[29] In January 1947 the British launched Operation Matchbox designed to lure German scientists to their zone, but they were even less efficient than the

French; and the Americans had the pick of them.[30] As one American put it, 'The British and the Russians have got hold of a few German scientists . . . but there can be no doubt that we have captured the best.'[31]

The Allies stole men and women who for one reason or another were useful for their projects. Under the pretext of accusing them of seeking to develop an atomic bomb, bacterial warfare, space travel and guided missiles, the British and Americans arrested a number of nuclear physicists and had them brought to England in what was meant to be a species of joint enterprise.[32] These included Carl Friedrich von Weizsäcker, Otto Hahn, Werner Heisenberg and Max von Laue. With the exception of Heisenberg, the men were found in Hechingen in Württemberg, where they had been working on their uranium piles, drawn from the mines of Joachimsthal in the Sudetenland. Heisenberg was discovered in his family skiing chalet in Upper Bavaria. Others, such as Richard Kuhn and Wolfgang Gertner, were apprehended in Heidelberg. Some of the smaller fry were taken by the British in Hamburg.

Once the team had been assembled they were brought first to France, initially to Rheims and Versailles, before being lodged in a villa in the Paris suburb of Le Vésinet. They were eventually delivered to Farm Hall near Cambridge, where they were perceived to have nothing in common bar the title *Herr Doktor* 'by which they punctiliously addressed one another'.[33] Once the Anglo-Americans had learned everything they could about the Nazi atom-bomb programme they were released in Hamburg and Göttingen, but told not to stray into the Soviet Zone. That was also for their own safety. The Russians were keen to abduct or simply tempt away scientists and technicians who might have been useful to them. The Nobel Prize-winning physicist Gustav Hertz was taken to Russia to help them develop nuclear weapons. On 21 October 1945 a large number of skilled workers, technicians and scientists were freighted out by train. The Western powers made a weak protest, which the Russians simply ignored.[34]

15

Where are our Men?

The only thing I know for certain is that the prisoners-of-war are
dying of hunger and that the field in which they have to sleep is hell-
ish damp.

Ernst von Salomon, *The Answers*, London 1954, 423

The Status of German POWs

The history of the German POWs is murky, largely because the West,
by acting in an inhumane manner, lost the moral high ground they
had achieved by fighting a moral crusade against the Nazis, but also because
the German Federal Republic has allowed it to remain shrouded in darkness.

Around eight million German soldiers were captured at the end of the
war – making a total, if you add those taken before May 1945, of around
eleven million. This meant that every household in Germany was affected
in some way; and the women were asking, 'Where are our men?'[1] The
Western Allies captured some 7.6 million, while the rest fell into the hands
of the Red Army. About five of the eleven million were released within a
year. A million and a half, however, never came home, giving rise to a
number of stories of how they met their end. Some writers have averred
that they were all killed in captivity, and that it was a deliberate policy on
the part of the Allies. The only figures that exist refer to the 'missing'. The
Red Cross gives their number as 1,086,000. A more reliable tally would be
1.3 million in the east (including Yugoslavia, Czechoslovakia and Poland)
and around 100,000 in the west.[2]

Until 8 May 1945, the Swiss had been responsible for German prisoners of war. On that day they packed their bags – the Allies had decided that
the German Empire had ceased to exist. The German army had 'unconditionally surrendered' and the new prisoners were now at the mercy of

their captors, without recourse to protection by a neutral state. Two new terms – strange to the Geneva Convention – were created to describe the newly captured soldiers: they were 'Surrendered Enemy Persons' and 'Disarmed Enemy Persons'. POW status, as regulated by the Geneva and Hague Conventions, accounted for 4.2 million men who had been caught in the net earlier. The other 3.4 million in the West were SEPs or DEPs and were not entitled to the same levels of shelter and subsistence.[3] The Soviet Union had never signed the Geneva Convention, so the Red Cross never had any jurisdiction there; they were not POWs, or anything else for that matter. Their fate was often a matter of complete indifference to the Soviet authorities. The change in terminology is significant. The men had been robbed of their status as combatants, which left them open to prosecution, an outcome excluded by the Geneva and Hague Conventions. It presaged new uses for the men, who were to be put to work. With the exception of the Americans, the Allies all envisaged a prolonged use of German slave labour. While the International Red Cross had a right to inspect POW camps, the barbed wire surrounding SEPs or DEPs was impenetrable.[4]

The idea of using the POWs as slaves was aired at Moscow in 1943. The originators of the proposal were the British. At Yalta it was decided that the men could be made to repair the damage Germany had caused to the Allies. They were to be a 'work force' and were to be retained for an indefinite period. It was at that moment that it became clear that their status would have to be changed to get round the Geneva Convention. Once again it was the British who were most keen – the proposal was put forward before the full horror of the concentration camps was known. It was to have another advantage – the British could evade another of the Convention's stipulations, the requirement that they provide 2,000 to 3,000 calories a day. From the first day of peace the British would have had immense problems supplying that amount, and for most of the time levels fell below 1,500 calories. The more prosperous Americans were for rapid demobilisation and for adherence to the Convention.[5] There was no precedent either for the rough treatment of high-ranking officers. In the view of the Allies, German generals were complicit in war crimes and thereby lost their usual privileges. This was decided before any crime had been proven. There were generals' camps in South Wales and Russia, and there was rumoured to be a third near Nuremberg,* in close proximity to the courthouse.[6] They were not treated as badly as the hoi polloi, however. In

---

* Almost certainly Langwasser. See below p. 403.

Wales the German general officers had a small number of privileges, and in Soviet Russia they were exempted from work.

That the Allies should conspire to rob prisoners of their status was outrageous; to treat them with so little care that a million and a half died was scandalous. The Russian attitude is understandable, though not forgivable: the Germans had systematically killed three million of their Russian prisoners.* But this could not be claimed for Western POWs. Indeed the Malmédy trial of those accused of massacring American soldiers during the Battle of the Bulge and the quest for the killers of the fifty British airmen who had taken part in the Great Escape from a Silesian POW camp show quite clearly how rare it was that the Germans ill-treated American and British POWs. That the Americans should have pursued the perpetrators of the killing of a hundred or so soldiers with such ruthlessness while at the same time allowing anything up to 40,000 German soldiers to die from hunger and neglect in the muddy flats of the Rhine was an act of mind-boggling hypocrisy.

In parts of Europe the sight of a German POW became an everyday occurrence. In Britain these dishevelled figures often prompted acts of generosity, despite the fact that only a few months before British towns and cities were being wrecked by German bombs. In France and elsewhere German slave-labourers sometimes had a quite different effect. It was not money the local people threw at them but bricks, stones and – in at least one instance – grenades. The horrors of the war were fresh in the minds of the people. Many had been wounded themselves, physically or emotionally. 'What did the hunger, misery, sickness or death of a German POW matter?' In Russia that feeling would have been particularly widespread.[7]

Another novelty was the leasing of prisoners to other powers. The Anglo-Americans handed over around a million German soldiers to the French to help rebuild their country. The Belgians were given 30,000 by the Americans and another 34,000 by the British, the Dutch had 10,000 and the Luxembourgeois 5,000.[8] The Soviet Union gave about 80,000 Germans to the Poles, who hung on to some of them until as late as 1953. Germans worked Europe's mines and sawmills and factories; they laid roads and did menial chores in France, Poland and Yugoslavia. In Britain they harvested potatoes and turnips. German soldiers were imprisoned in some twenty countries around the world.

Those left on German soil after the summer of 1945 were only a small

---

* The Russians were quite capable of doing this too: at Katyn they murdered a large percentage of the Polish officer corps.

fraction of the total number of POWs. The Americans, for example, used their German camps for political prisoners and those awaiting trial or denazification. Like the British and the Russians, they tended to use the old concentration camps to house prisoners. Usually there was decent accommodation for the GIs in the neighbouring SS barracks. Any attempt to feed the prisoners by the German civilian population was punishable by death. It is not clear how many German soldiers died of starvation. Very soon people were comparing the conditions in American and French camps with those in the Nazi concentration camps. The psychoanalyst Alexander Mitscherlich, who examined former POWs, learned that they were prone to compare themselves to Hitler's victims, and to accuse the Allies of hypocrisy in their stories of German atrocities.[9]

On 10 December 1946, the industrious Cardinal Frings (he had received his red hat earlier that year) delivered a petition to the Control Council in Berlin. Ten million people had demanded the release of the POWs or *Kriegsgefangener*. At the Moscow Conference in 1947 it was decided that the Allies would send all prisoners home by the end of 1948. At that point the Soviets admitted to holding 890,532 (although the real figure might have been nearer to three million), the French 631,483; there were 435,295 in British hands, 300,000 in the Balkans, 54,000 in Belgium, 30,976 in American custody and 10,000 in Holland.[10] In the middle of 1948 the number of POWs yet to come home stood at one million. The return was agreed by the Western Allies, the Czechs and the Yugoslavs (who subsequently reneged on the deal), but not by the Russians and the Poles. That Christmas 1948 date decided the category of prisoner in the minds of the German public: a *Spätheimkehrer* (late homecomer) was released between 1949 and 1950. A *Spätestheimkehrer* (latest homecomer) returned between 1950 and 1956.[11] In 1979 there were believed to be 72,000 prisoners still alive in – chiefly Russian – custody.[12]

It was Adenauer who was the first German politician openly to raise the problem in 1950. Addressing the Bundestag, he called for an end to France's cruel treatment of its German POWs – who had, in fact, all gone home. The Yugoslavs were also singled out, and the German chancellor added that it was horrifying that several hundred thousand German men, women and children were still in Russia and Poland five and a half years after the end of the fighting. He could think of no parallel in history for such 'cold heartlessness'. Even such strong words failed to deliver all the goods. It was Adenauer's visit to Moscow that finally brought home almost all the last survivors, at the end of 1956.[13]

Adenauer's successors were more faint-hearted. In 1957 a wide-ranging academic study of the treatment of the German POWs was commissioned by the Federal Republic. The project allowed for fifteen separate studies in twenty-two volumes. The work was ready by the mid-1970s. In the meantime, however, Bonn had had a change of heart. It was the time of Willy Brandt's *Ostpolitik* – an attempt to link hands through the Iron Curtain; the Oder–Neisse Line was recognised in the West for the first time. The publication of a work of this sort would, they feared, upset relations with Russia and Poland. No names were mentioned in the texts, and much of the material was returned to the archives. The book was quietly issued, but only for 'official use'. Just 431 copies were printed: 391 for the Federal Republic, and 40 for abroad. The FRG made it clear to all the recipients that access was to be made difficult.[14]*

This coyness on the part of the Bonn government added fuel to the fire. In 1989 the Canadian journalist James Bacque published *Other Losses* in which he claimed the French and the Americans had killed a million POWs. It was called a work of 'monstrous speculation'[15] and was dismissed by an American historian as an 'absurd thesis'.[16] Bacque's book printed some evocative drawings made of the Rheinwiesenlager, and asserted, as was probably true, that thirty to forty Germans died every day in Rheinberg.[17]† Part of the problem was the little care taken by the Western Allies in registering the prisoners and the destruction of Wehrmacht records. The transfer of POWs from one nation to another often meant they were counted twice. The final number of deaths will never be known, but it has since been proved that Bacque misinterpreted the words 'other losses' on Allied charts to mean 'deaths', when it was in fact an oblique reference to prisoners who, for one reason or another, were no longer of interest to the statisticians: deaths, yes, but also deserters, Volksturm and other categories who were released without receiving a formal discharge.[18]

Bacque's red herring had a positive result, however, in that it pointed out that it was not just the Russians who killed prisoners of war. The Russians were still the worst, but who was the second worst? The Yugoslavs killed as many as 80,000 prisoners of war, which, given the numbers they started with, must put them in second place. About 2.5 per cent of all the Germans in French custody died, a figure that is proportionally far higher than the American tally.

---

* In the British Library, for example, the books are stored under the 'Cup' shelfmark, normally reserved for pornography, and users of the books are required to sit at a special table where they can be monitored more closely.

† For Rheinwiesenlager and Rheinberg, see below pp. 398–400.

The American Camps

The Americans honoured their promise to release prisoners early. The idea of slave labour was not popular with their trade unions. Men and women over fifty were let go in June and they made a great flourish by releasing two million prisoners at the end of July 1945. Some came home in triumph like the 12,000 prisoners returned to Austria.[19] The reality for a further 1.5 million men was anything but liberty, however: they were promptly 'loaned' to other powers – France and the United Kingdom.[20] The Americans even offered some men to the Russians. They refused, as they had enough already.[21] Also many SS men were retained to help with further inquiries. Later the 'grey' or Waffen-SS were allowed to go home, while the 'black' or Totenkopf units were put on trial. Deaths on the American continent were low: 491, with seventy-two suicides, seven murders, fourteen men executed and seventy fatal accidents.[22]

The first *Kriegsgefangener* had been shipped back to America during the war. One of these was Kurt Glaser, who was in a large camp in Texas. The inmates worked in nearby factories, where their status was similar to that of the local blacks. The food was decent, and, it being America, there were frequent film shows. Not long after the end of the war a man speaking German with a Frankfurt accent came to interrogate Glaser. He asked him how it had been for him under National Socialism. Glaser replied, 'Nicht schlecht' (Not bad). He then saw his interrogator circle the word 'Nazi' on his questionnaire. For inveterate Nazis like Glaser there was a new diet of propaganda. He had to watch a film entitled *Deutschland erwache!* (Germany awake! – the title of an early Nazi song). It was about Belsen and Buchenwald. In July 1946 he was shipped to Britain.[23]

Another account tells a similar tale of a more literary prisoner in an American camp. The news that reached him on 6 May 1945 led him to quote some lines from Thomas Mann: 'The fate of the most repulsive monster of our time, National Socialism, has been fulfilled. Had its death struggle been confined to its person, and not at the same time to a great and unfortunate nation, which now does penance for its bewitchment, we might be able to observe the catastrophe with cold satisfaction, for the sake of law and necessity.'[24]

When he was not working alongside southern blacks, the prisoner lived on a diet of films. On 9 May he could watch the celebrations marking the end of the war while his stomach rumbled. The inmates had just 2,000 calories a day, although the work details had 3,500 to 4,000. In a few months he would have learned to appreciate what he had. Instead of the usual cinematographic diet of Hollywood oaters, the prisoner now had to watch more and more propaganda. He learned new names besides Dachau – Buchenwald was unknown to him. He concluded that it was 'a *Kulturschande* of the first water, but what can I do about it? I am a German and I share in the guilt.' He was obliged to go and look at the pictures of 'his' victims. A guard with a truncheon stood over him. He felt he needed to wear a 'consciousness of guilt' expression as he leafed through the evidence of German crime. Then he signed a list stating that he had been aware of Buchenwald after all[25]* – anything to get them off his back.

The most notorious American POW camps were the so-called Rheinwiesenlager. When these were closed some of the prisoners were transferred to the camp at Mons in Belgium and were able to tell their fellow countrymen about the conditions they had experienced. They had been pushed into large, open areas by the banks of the Rhine, described as 'concentration areas' or PWTE – 'Prisoner of War Temporary Enclosures'.[26] The Americans had burned their kit, so they had nothing to protect them from the elements. April and May 1945 were particularly cold and wet, and there was plenty of snow. The soldiers were forced to endure this in open fields without tents; 'many dug holes in the earth with a spoon or a tin can or whatever was to hand, but with the constant rain the ground was soft and every night the holes collapsed and the people who had sought protection from them were buried. There was no night that passed that did not see the deaths of several men on the meadows.'[27]

The prisoners in Mons learned of the two most infamous camps, Rheinberg and Büderich. At its height the first contained 90,000 men. Büderich was slightly smaller with 77,000. If all twelve camps established by the Rhine and Nahe between May and July 1945 are taken together, the number of inmates was around a million men. They stretched from Düsseldorf in the north to Mannheim in the south, with the main concentration between Koblenz and Mainz. At Bad Kreuznach on the Nahe, the site of the camp was occasionally given as the 'Galgenberg' or 'Gallows Hill', although it is more likely that it was laid out between the railway line and the river. The camp at Remagen was arranged along a five-by-two-kilometre stretch of the river. Between the two camps at Remagen and Sinzig there were 400,000 prisoners. The Americans abandoned the camps in July. Britain was given Rheinberg, Büderich and Wickramberg, and the

---

* Incidentally a very National Socialist method of preventing anyone from opting out of difficult decisions.

French Bad Kreuznach-Bretzenheim, Sinzig, Andernach and Koblenz. The others were in the American Zone anyhow.[28]

In order to receive their rations the men had to walk along a slippery, muddy passage. Two tins were then tossed to them. Those who fell while trying to catch them were beaten with truncheons. Anyone caught stealing food had to eat himself sick. In another instance the thief was forced to eat all he had stolen covered with sugar. The prisoners discussed the merits of the different Allies: 'In general it was best to be with the English.' That guaranteed 'decent treatment'.[29]

The Rhine Meadow camps operated from February to July, with the worst outrages ending with the war, in May. Those hard-won tins were not enough – for the prisoners they were 'hunger camps'. The writer John Dos Passos, who was shown round the camps, came to the conclusion that the Germans were being deliberately starved. They were also systematically robbed of their wristwatches, cameras and any Nazi souvenirs the guards fancied. The men were deprived of anything they had on them when they arrived. In the circumstances prisoners showed they could be resourceful. Writing letters was prohibited to DEPs – as they were called here – but a postal service grew up for all that. A prisoner cut through the wire and escaped with the post. He would pick up supplies and slip back through the wires.[30]

It has been difficult to come to a reliable estimate of the number of Germans who died in the Rhine mud. The American figures do not even tally with the graves in the local cemeteries. The Americans admit to 2,310 by the end of May and 5,912 to July. The German tally is 32,000. Graves indicate nearly 2,000 prisoners died in the shadow of the vineyards in Bad Kreuznach; the Americans admit to just over half that number. In Rheinberg, where 140,000 Germans were crammed into 1,000 hectares of mud during the months it was open, the official figures account for 438 deaths. The real number might be between two and three thousand now that mass graves have been found within the camp. The total number of deaths in the Rhine Meadows is now thought to be as high as 40,000.[31]

The picture is complicated by the fact that the Americans may well have released all their Wehrmacht prisoners early – or lent them to others – but that rule did not apply to SS men and political prisoners. They came under the category of 'Automatic Arrests' or AAs. A POW or DEP could be released from custody and automatically rearrested on suspicion of being a Nazi or a member of the SS. The Americans maintained camps for up to 1.5 million of these.[32] As well as the AAs there were STs (Security Threats) from the Gestapo and the Sicherheitsdienst, BLs (Black-Listed men) and WCs (war criminals).[33] At Ebensee in Austria there were 44,000 SS men behind barbed wire, watched over by Polish KZler in one of Mauthausen's most gruesome former dependencies.[34]

The Americans believed they had a case against the writer Ernst von Salomon, and he tells us what it was like to be at the receiving end. They came for him at 6.00 a.m. at his home in Siegsdorf near Salzburg where he lived with his mistress, Ille Gotthelft. Two men called Murphy and Sullivan told him that he was to be interrogated across the border in Kitzbühel. They told Salomon it was because he was 'a big Nazi'. When Ille protested that she was Jewish, they took her as well. Even if the two men had no knowledge of who Salomon was on their arrival, they could have gleaned it as they went through the books in his workroom. It was clear that they assumed that only a Nazi would have been involved in the killing of the Jewish foreign minister Walther Rathenau in 1922. His mistress's protests must have been seen as at best irrelevant, at worst a lie. She suffered for her temerity, and was only released when she came close to death though sickness.

When they arrived in Kitzbühel they were put in the town lock-up. Salomon was philosophical. In his salad days he had seen the inside of several prisons, but he worried about his mistress, who had managed to live through the Third Reich without incarceration, and was now being subjected to that indignity by the Americans. Kitzbühel prison was filled with Party officials who were routinely beaten black and blue during interrogation. If Salomon was right it was policy to give them all a 'work-over' before returning them to their cells. Salomon was not interrogated in the prison, but taken to the US army HQ in the town, 'which I now discovered to be an American Gestapo-type operation'.[35] He was questioned by a German-speaker who revealed that his parents were artists in Dresden, and Party members. He did not want to believe that Salomon had not been a member. He knew all about the Rathenau murder: 'lucky for you you did not try to conceal it!' 'My dear sir, I've written books about it *this* thick.'[36]

Salomon's answers were not good enough. He and Ille were put in a lorry and driven to an internment camp he calls 'Natternberg' in Lower Bavaria. On the way they picked up other 'big Nazis' like a Herr Allin who had been arrested because he had averred in a private conversation with a friend in a café in Kufstein that Poland had started the war.[37] When they reached the camp they were driven through the gates with cries of 'Mak snell!' (*sic*) and made to line up. When their names were called out they were chased one by one into a hut, beaten with rifle butts, stripped, kicked and punched in the groin while American soldiers fought for space at the windows outside. The internationally acclaimed author was treated no better. Lieutenant 'Baybee', the officer sitting at the desk, shouted at him: 'You are a Nazi!' Once again Salomon denied it. He was beaten up, losing several teeth.[38]

His mistress was called to the hut. From where he stood he could see soldiers jostling for places at the window. She had been forced to strip and subjected to an intimate examination to make sure she was concealing nothing about her person. The 'work-over' was the prelude to an ordeal that lasted for months, and in some cases years. There were no exceptions – not even generals were immune, although one SS-Standartenführer who had 'solved the Jewish question' in Hungary with singular efficiency was treated with awe and absolved from the usual beating. As it transpired, once a prisoner was officially marked down as a 'war criminal', the physical abuse ceased. The higher judicial authority would certainly have learned of any beatings. This sort of rough handling was reserved for those the Americans deemed obscure or defenceless, not for Göring or Ribbentrop. There were too many journalists buzzing around the courthouse in Nuremberg.

For the mere soldiers the treatment was less brutal, but could be just as deadly. Hans Johnert was taken prisoner by a GI on 9 April 1945. The soldier snatched his watch and threw away his mess tin: 'Kriegst du alles neu!' (You'll get new ones!). He was taken to the Bavarian spa town of Bad Kissingen and given a tin of beans with bits of meat in it. Then he was transferred to the Pioneers' Barracks in Worms, where the gloves came off. There were 30,000–40,000 prisoners sitting in the courtyard, jostling for space. With no protection against the rain they froze. They went from Worms to France. As their convoy arrived on French soil, French civilians threw stones and lumps of coal at them. A black guard had to fire his weapon to keep them at bay.[39]

Behind bars back at Natternberg the violence slackened off, but did not die out. One memorable day the prisoners had to run the gauntlet – a punishment that had made the Prussians infamous in their time. The prisoners were called out in alphabetical order. The Americans formed two lines and the men ran between them while they rained down blows with rubber truncheons. Salomon noted that the elderly were the hardest hit, because they moved most slowly. Once again it was a Polish sergeant who was most feared for his brutality. He was in the middle of one of the rows. When L was called out it was the turn of Hanns Ludin, Hitler's ambassador to Slovakia. Ludin was determined to drink his cup down to the dregs. He walked slowly through the ranks. 'When he reached the Polish sergeant he lost one of his wooden shoes. He turned about and with his bare foot fished for the shoe he had lost. The sergeant ran after him, striking him, and dropped his rubber truncheon. Ludin leaned down, picked it up and handed it back to him.[40] The physical maltreatment of the inmates came to an end only when General Patton sent up a colonel to inspect the camp. After that the prisoners received proper rations and medical treatment. The earlier violence was attributable to JCS 1067, and ultimately to Morgenthau.[41]

The writer records plenty of cases of theft, the Americans being especially keen to steal porcelain. 'Baybee' had the women brought to his hut at night and bribed them with food, drink and cigarettes to sleep with him. There was a lighter side of camp-life that developed with time – cabarets, concerts, operatic performances, abstruse lectures, even theatre. It was Salomon who directed the plays. The most senior prisoner was Graf Lutz von Schwerin von Krosigk. He had been transferred from Hersbruck. Schwerin von Krosigk had had a deal of incarceration since he left Flensburg, and it was not going to stop for a while yet.

From Mondorf les Bains he had been transferred to Oberursel, which the prisoners called 'Alaska' because it was so cold and uninviting. He had met the pilot Hanna Reitsch there, and Percy Schramm, the military historian. The inmates were known as 'Gandhis' because they were so emaciated. During his first stay in Langwasser in Nuremberg, he was friends with the Austrian general Glaise von Horstenau, until he committed suicide. Then he reached Plattling, where Salomon now was, and he was able to fill Salomon in on the treatment he had received from the British at Flensburg.[42] Salomon obviously admired Schwerin von Krosigk, as many others did. The ex-minister became the apologist for the regime in a series of lectures delivered to the other prisoners: 'He spoke like a professor of history, in a calm, agreeable, careful, highly educated voice, each sentence well-rounded and deliberate. He covered the whole wretched story, from the day he entered Brüning's cabinet* as a minister to the atrocious end.'[43]

From Plattling, Schwerin von Krosigk was transferred to Ludwigsburg, where he was reacquainted with his cousin, Bodo von Alvensleben, the former president of the Herrenklub in Berlin. The Herrenklub was the city's most aristocratic club, and Franz von Papen was a member. It was at

---

* Schwerin von Krosigk was a ministerial director – or under-secretary of state – in Brüning's government. He entered the cabinet under Papen.

the Herrenklub that it was decided to allow Hitler to become chancellor – the distinguished gentlemen thought they could control him. Alvensleben joked that the reason he was in Ludwigsburg was that he was Hitler's grandmother: he had admitted Papen, who had admitted Hitler. The next stop for Schwerin von Krosigk was Dachau, before he was returned to Alaska. While he was in Dachau he learned that the Poles were demanding his extradition, because as minister of finance he had introduced Reich taxes into Poland.[44] After that the Americans transferred him to Nuremberg for his trial.

Another distinguished German who languished in a POW camp was Carl Schmitt (not to be confused with the post-war conservative politician Carlo Schmid), who was at one time known as the 'crown jurist of the Third Reich', although he fell foul of the regime before the war, and before the Final Solution was put into effect. The Americans had him locked up, and were anxious to have him put on trial at Nuremberg. Schmitt was interrogated, and not let go until 1947.[45]

The end of Salomon's ordeal was Langwasser, which was set up in the incomplete buildings of the Nazi Party Conference in Nuremberg. The prisoners were beaten and harried from Plattling to the train. Salomon protected himself with a bundle of blankets, but another was not so lucky:

> In front of me an old man fell, his cap was snatched from his head, and I recognized the elderly, white-haired conductor of the Bayreuth orchestra, Professor Reinhardt. The Americans were beating him, but two other American soldiers sprang forward and helped him to his feet. 'So there are decent individuals among them,' I thought to myself. Then I saw the two warm-hearted GIs cut the string with which the professor had tied his violin to the top of his pack. The road was several miles long.[46]

Another Langwasser inmate was Franz von Papen. After being sentenced to eight years' hard labour he had gone straight from the court to a hospital in Fürth. When that closed he was packed off to Garmisch-Partenkirchen and then Regensburg. While he was in Regensburg he was set upon by an SS man in the washhouse who beat him bloody, fracturing his nose and cheekbone and splitting his lips and eyelids. He was sewn up by another prisoner, a surgeon. Papen says he was singled out for special treatment. Meanwhile he was convinced that the right way to get out was to appeal for a shorter sentence rather than a retrial, which might have taken years to bring about.[47]

Once in Langwasser the prisoners were starved once more. There was an army kitchen near by, and when the wind blew in the right direction there was a delicate aroma of dried fruit. Every now and then they were slipped something by the cooks, 'negro soldiers, good-natured boys with whom the SS got on very well. "You second-class, me second-class," they would say, and they would give us food whenever they dared.' Albert Speer attested to the particular kindness of black American guards at Nuremberg.[48] Langwasser had gathered up all the senior Nazis and generals who were awaiting trail at Nuremberg. They signed a 'golden book' from the Langwasser Theatre. Salomon noticed some of the other names: Schwerin von Krosigk, who had written something in Latin or Greek, Field Marshals von Manstein ('For us the Reich must endure . . .') and von Brauchitsch ('Keep the sunshine in your heart, whether it snow or hail . . .'). It was the signal for Salomon's release. The order sheet was headed 'Subject: Release of erroneous arrestees'.[49]

The camps described by Salomon were not a figment of his imagination. In the spring of 1946 the former concentration camp dependency of Plattling contained 2,786 inmates and 1,464 foreigners of eleven nationalities; Langwasser was much bigger with 11,761 Germans and 1,389 foreigners from the same number of countries. For some reason Salomon chose to disguise the name of his first camp. This was almost certainly Auerbach on the far side of Deggendorf, which had 10,488 prisoners and 238 foreigners, as well as a women's section.[50] Another notorious camp was Zuffenhausen near Ludwigsburg in Württemberg. Otto Kumm, the last commander of the Leibstandarte Adolf Hitler, recalled the conditions: no food to speak of, wooden planks for beds, 'some of us were so under-nourished that we could hardly get up'. For months lunch was turnip soup, with half a potato for dinner. 'Deliberately they collected heaps of food outside the fence, which was burnt once a month in front of our eyes.'[51]

The long arm of American retribution spared no one; not even the princes. One of those whose spirit was broken in an American compound was the Kaiser's Nazi son Augustus William, or 'Auwi'. He was taken prisoner at the retirement home of his grandmother Empress 'Vicky' of Great Britain – Kronberg near Frankfurt-am-Main. He was in a pitiful state, but there were no medicaments to treat him. The Americans dragged him through thirty-three camps and prisons, where he slept on the ground, and denied him even the Bible to read. His sister Princess Victoria visited him in a camp near Stuttgart. She found him sitting outside a hut looking very thin. She was able to visit him again as a result of a theft at Kronberg, when some of the booty had been traced to America. Auwi was required to make a statement about the missing objects. He spent a short time after his release in Langenburg, in one of the castles of the Hohenlohes, and, for want of anywhere else to bury a Prussian prince, he was interred in the Hohenlohe family mausoleum there.[52]

Another prominent American prisoner was Prince Philip of Hesse. Philip had already suffered a good deal. He had been arrested on Hitler's orders following Mussolini's fall in 1943 and incarcerated in Flossenbürg in the Upper Palatinate. His wife Mafalda, daughter of the Italian king, was sent to Buchenwald, where she died from injuries sustained in an Allied air-raid. He was liberated in the South Tyrol with other prominent prisoners in April 1945, but the Americans had not finished with him. Philip had been an early member of the Nazi Party and the SA and the Nazi president of Hesse-Nassau. They hauled him through twenty more camps and prisons before he was released on New Year's Day 1948. He died in Rome in 1980.[53]

The art historian Prince Franz zu Sayn-Wittgenstein took refuge at the Schloss of his brother-in-law Prince Ysenburg at Budingen in Hesse. He had been a simple soldier, possibly because his mother had remarried the Jewish banker Richard Merton. He had deserted at the end and discarded his uniform. Prince Ysenburg had been a Pg, and was imprisoned in the schoolhouse from where he was initially sent out to sweep the streets. The Americans began to look for a tougher approach and locked him up in the prison in Butzbach, then in a camp at Schwarzenborn near Kassel. Sayn-Wittgenstein was also incarcerated in a former Polish camp near Hirzenhain. There were men and women there. The men were obliged to camp outside, while the women inhabited the cells. He was allowed to visit his wife, who was there with him. There was no question of sleep, and the place was crawling with insects. From there he was transferred to a POW camp near Giessen. The 2,000 soldiers there were discharged only to work as slave labour in France, while their numbers grew to around 8,000. Sayn-Wittgenstein had Prince Hubert of Prussia for companionship, but mainly remembered the boredom of his prison time. He was set free on the orders of an American officer who had fallen in love with his sister-in-law and who was broad-minded enough to arrange for Prince Ysenburg's release as well.[54]

Dachau was generally used for members of the SS, but not exclusively. It was also the main depot and transit camp for American prisoners. One of the oddest inmates was Paul Schmidt, Hitler's interpreter. He had originally been taken to Augsburg, but he was such a valuable witness to events between 1933 and 1945 that he was constantly being released to appear in trials. He was taken to Paris for Philippe Pétain's hearings, and was able to enjoy the cafés on the Champs Elysées and a meal at Fouquets, before being returned to a cell in Mannheim. He was naturally a key witness at the Nuremberg trials, and interpreted for the American psychoanalysts who were trying to assess the personalities of the war criminals. He was close enough to the gallows to hear the 'dull blows' of the men setting it up. Schmidt was released in 1948 at a time of a general amnesty for lesser internees who had served two years.[55]

Some tough nuts suspected of major war crimes were kept in the old penitentiary in the pretty town of Schwäbisch Hall near Stuttgart. Here prisoners were subjected to some particularly nasty forms of interrogation. Old boys included SS commanders Sepp Dietrich, Fritz Kraemer and Hermann Priess, all of whom denied issuing orders to shoot prisoners of war. Seventy-four SS men were finally arraigned for the massacre of American servicemen at Malmédy, but many of their confessions were subsequently withdrawn because they said they had been extracted under torture.[56] One of the last to break was the cigar-chewing SS officer Jochen Peiper, who was suspected of being chiefly responsible for the massacre. The Americans had used methods similar to those employed by the SS in Dachau. One of these was keeping the prisoner for long periods in solitary confinement. At Oberursel Peiper had been alone for seven weeks while his guards had subjected him to extremes of heat and cold. At Zuffenhausen he had been kept in a dark cellar for another five weeks. The prisoners were subjected to mock trials that resembled sessions of the Klu Klux Klan. Worse still were the mock executions, where the men were led off in hoods, while their guards told them they were approaching the gallows. Prisoners were actually lifted bodily off the ground to convince them they were about to swing.

More conventional methods of torture included kicks to the groin, deprivation of sleep and food, and savage beatings. When the Americans set up a commission of inquiry into the methods used by their investigators, they found that, of the 139 cases they examined, 137 had 'had their testicles permanently destroyed by kicks received from the American War Crimes Investigation team'. It was an indication of what happened if you failed to say what the investigators wanted.[57] The screams of the prisoners in Schwäbisch Hall could be heard throughout the little country town. The torturers were not all American: they included vengeful Polish guards like those mentioned by Salomon. The archbishop of Cologne, Cardinal Joseph Frings, kept a tally of reports of American brutality.[58]

The viciousness of the interrogators at Schwäbisch Hall was eventually brought to Clay's attention. The men charged were Harry Thon, Bruno

Jacobs, Frank Steiner and Joseph Kirschbaum – all German or German Jewish names. Most probably they all spoke fluent German – they would have needed it to be efficient interrogators. The man in charge was William Perl, a Czech psychologist trained in Vienna. It was Perl who organised the mock trials. Thon was a German refugee, 'excitable and untrained'.[59] Clay pronounced a muted apology that was tantamount to an admission: 'Unfortunately, in the heat of the aftermath of war, we did use measures to obtain evidence that we would not have employed later when initial heat was expended.' On the other hand he thought that the accusation of 'unbelievable cruelty' from Sergeant Bersin, one of the SS men, gave a distorted picture. He dismissed the appeals of the Malmédy prisoners, finding no evidence of maltreatment.[60]

British Camps

In May 1945 the British admitted to having 2.5 million prisoners as well as half a million wounded and a growing number of refugees from the east. Captivity was an easygoing thing in those days. An officer in the Welsh Guards, Andrew Gibson-Watt, recounts scenes of bacchic camaraderie in the South Tyrol at the end of the war, when guardsmen and German paratroopers had an all-night party with wine, exchanging cigarettes and family snapshots.[61] Fleeing from Mecklenburg, Charlotte von der Schulenburg and her children found themselves in the middle of a huge POW camp in eastern Holstein. The prisoners were living in barns and stables and receiving very short commons from their captors. She recalled the monotonous noise of soldiers crushing grain with stones to make gruel which was at least some sort of nourishment. The camp was known as the 'Kraal'. She recalled the extraordinary cultural activity of the place. Among the thousands of prisoners were actors, musicians, poets and theatre directors. Chamber music was performed, plays produced in barns. A poet read his works to hundreds of captured soldiers, sometimes under a widespreading tree, sometimes standing on the dung heap in the middle of the courtyard.[62]

The prisoners mixed freely with the refugees and helped one another. They organised their lives together, finding oats and shoes for the horses, chopping wood for heating and making schnapps on the sly. One night Charlotte von der Schulenburg recalled their slaughtering a cow. The animal was cut up and distributed and then all trace of the act was cleared away, so that when the gendarmes came looking for the culprits the next day they found nothing. For Charlotte the worry about feeding her six children was salutary: it prevented her from being overwhelmed by grief after the death of her husband.[63]

Some soldiers with homes to go to were gradually released. There remained the East Prussians, Pomeranians and Mecklenburger who had no way of knowing what had happened to their nearest and dearest. There were rumours that the senior officers were to be shipped to a camp in Belgium.* As the countess had learned to read cards, generals would bring her provisions from their scanty stores in order to learn a little more of their fate.[64] Not all the East Elbians were content to wait for news. One day Charlotte concealed herself in some straw in the back of a lorry travelling towards the Schulenburg mansion at Tressow in Mecklenburg. She wanted to fetch some provisions for the children, and the British were still in control of the western sector of the old Grand Duchy, as far as Lake Schwerin. After a while she realised she was not alone. She heard a rustling in the straw and turned round to see a man emerge looking like a cattle dealer. He was a von Wedel – like the Schulenburgs, of ancient Prussian lineage. He was escaping from the camp because he wanted to locate his family in the east.[65]

The Allies' attitude hardened, however, partly because they had witnessed or had been made to witness the barbarities committed by the Germans, and partly because they saw a use for the men as slave-labourers. At Bergen-Belsen they fed the SS men on starvation rations and made them carry the dead without gloves. The idea was to 'work them to death'. They achieved this in twenty out of fifty cases, but then a higher authority intervened. The SS were taken away and ordinary German POWs were made to do the work.[66] The British disposed of a great many camps in Britain itself. In 1944 there were already 250,000 German POWs in Britain and Northern Ireland. There were also camps filled with Russians who had been fighting alongside the Germans – at Malton in Yorkshire, for example, where they sought solace in drinking methylated spirits. The peak figure was achieved in the third quarter of 1946, when there were 391,880 working prisoners in Britain.[67] In 1948, a year before they were disbanded, there were 600 camps. The regime was not so hard, and in terms of percentages the number of men who died in British custody is strikingly low compared to the other Allies: 1,254.[68] Prisoners were taken first to the 'cages' that were set up on racetracks or football grounds to be interrogated by the PWIS or Prisoner of War Interrogation Section. These

---

* See below p. 413.

had the job of questioning the prisoners in the camp and awarding them grades A, B or C. A was 'white', or free from Nazism; B was grey, or mildly tainted; C was black, Nazi. Then they were allocated to camps that might have been just a collection of tents or Nissen huts, or, if they were lucky, a ramshackle stately home.

Country houses such as Crewe Hall in Cheshire, Grizedale Hall in Lancashire, Sudeley Castle in Gloucestershire and the Duke of Roxburghe's Sunlaws in the Borders were filled with prisoners. Colonel Wedgwood complained in the House of Commons about the use of this sort of luxury accommodation and asked facetiously why they had not considered the Ritz Hotel. Not all German POWs had been treated so well, and Wormwood Scrubs Prison in London was also used to house them. Jewish Pioneer Corps soldiers were given the job of guarding them at Bourton-on-the-Hill, Watton in Caithness, Moreton-in-Marsh, Cattistock, Tiveton, Cheltenham and Kempton Park.

The leading fliers were housed in a camp outside London. In order to prepare the cases for the prosecution in the Nuremberg trials, microphones were concealed to listen to the conversations between Milch, Bodenschatz, Koller and Galland. The British wanted to know about Göring, and to do so they planted listening devices like the Reichsmarschall's Forschungsamt (Research Office) or Stalin's NKVD. That way the British learned that Göring's generals did not hold their master in high regard. He was 'ungrateful' and he painted his fingernails mauve. Galland, however, corrected his comrades: it was transparent varnish, not paint. An American Major Emery was sent in as an *agent provocateur* on 5 June 1945 and told the generals that Göring had been blackening their names in his prison in Luxembourg. The men fell for it, and began retailing stories about how corrupt Göring had been.[69]

In Scotland Camp 21 at Comrie was used to house 4,000 hard-bitten Nazis – U-boat crews and Waffen-SS men who gruesomely lynched Sergeant Wolfgang Rosterg. He had expressed doubt at Germany's final victory and threatened to uncover a plot to rise up against the guards. He was hung up in the latrines. They also chased and beat Gerhard Rettig to death. Five of the murderers were hanged in Pentonville Prison in London on 6 October 1946, and another two were executed the following month. It took a tough former Prussian officer, and holder of the Iron Cross, Herbert Sulzbach to show them the error of their ways. He had written a respected book on trench warfare, but when the Nazis came to power they put him in a concentration camp as a Jew. Once more England's gain was Germany's loss. After leaving Comrie, Sulzbach went to Haltwhistle. This was a progressive camp with its own newspaper, orchestra, theatre and university which laid on exhibitions of prisoners' art. Sulzbach struck up friendly relations with many prisoners that continued after their release. He was considered the apostle of democratic ideas and a political confessor.[70] The youth camp at Cambridge possessed a similar figure in the pioneer Captain Starbroke who looked like a 'caricature from [the antisemitic paper] *Der Stürmer*', but was so respected by the prisoners that he was treated as if he had been made of porcelain.[71]

The former army commander in chief Walther von Brauchitsch was housed in No. 11 (Special) POW Camp, Island Farm, Bridgend – the so-called German Generals' Camp in South Wales. In his various court appearances he had been economical with the truth and denied having received a cash payment from Hitler at the time of his divorce and remarriage to a Nazi woman. He also claimed to have had no knowledge of the planning of aggressive war and to have been ignorant of the murderous 'Commissar Order' that required the shooting of Soviet political officers. From Bridgend he was transferred to the grim Münsterlager to attend trial before a British court, but died before his case came up.[72] At one time there were no fewer than 186 German generals or equivalent in the camp. One of them was Lieutenant-General Hans von Ravenstein, who had been taken prisoner at Tobruk. In the spring of 1946 he was transferred to Bridgend from a prison camp in Canada. He was to spend over two years in the camp before he was set free. No one had anything bad to say about him. He disliked Bridgend: the holder of the Pour le Mérite from the Great War looked down on a number of Hitler appointees who were not as well mannered as he might have hoped.[73]

The generals at Bridgend were housed in bed-sitting rooms big enough to accommodate a six-foot bed. Only field marshals were allowed separate sitting rooms. Ravenstein was befriended by a family of Plymouth Brethren who took him out for picnics, but he was not allowed to carry money. Field Marshal Gerd von Rundstedt was one of those at Bridgend with a set of rooms. Ravenstein admired him, but he was wont to hide behind superior orders when called upon to justify his errors and omissions.[74] The tank general Hans-Jürgen von Arnim had also been in British captivity since May 1943. At the time he was the second most important prisoner in England after Rudolf Hess. He was kept at a 'beautiful' mansion in Hampshire and allowed certain privileges concomitant with his seniority. He was not released until 1947. By then his estates had been mopped up by land reform in the Soviet east. He died in genteel penury in 1962.[75]

Some of the German POWs in Britain had been transferred from camps in the United States, and were officially 'on loan'. These were called *Amerikafahrer* (American travellers). There were 123,000 of them in all.[76] They made up work details, and one of their first jobs was to build a camp for the victory parade on VE Day.[77] One *Amerikafahrer* was Kurt Glaser, whose transport arrived in Liverpool in July 1946. He went first to Wollaton Park near Nottingham, where he lived in a hut with fifty other men in the shadow of the 'Schloss'. An officer came to see him and asked him six questions about National Socialism, similar to those asked in Texas which had branded him a Nazi. He worked for a farmer in Nottinghamshire, and harvested turnips and potatoes. He was later transferred to Revesby in Lincolnshire where once again he worked on the land. A British intelligence officer informed him that he was working to feed his fellow Germans, as there was not enough food in the zone to nourish them. In September he heard James Byrnes's Stuttgart speech. When he learned that America had released all its POWs, Glaser could not believe his ears. There were still 355,000 German prisoners in Britain. In the main they were treated with much kindness, however, and when Glaser went for a walk in the manicured grounds of Nottingham Castle an old man came up to him and gave him a florin. Shortly after that, like all the *Amerikafahrer*, he was sent back to Dachau in Germany to be released.[78]

The literary prisoner who had found himself hungry on the 2,000 calories he had received in America began to understand the real meaning of the word when he arrived in Sudbury Camp near Derby. As usual he was shunted through a number of different camps – Pendleford Hall, Wolverhampton; Halfpenny Green, Staffordshire – presumably according to the demands of local agriculture. Meanwhile his stomach rumbled.[79] Intellectual nourishment was provided by a Dr R, a 'naturalised emigrant' who talked to the prisoners about the Nuremberg trials. On 1 October they learned of the executions after the International Military Tribunal (IMT) verdicts.[80] Meanwhile they were being graded for their levels of political reliability. The uncertainty about their future had consequences: 219 of them committed suicide.[81]

The prisoners began to receive a little money for their work – two shillings a day. The British people were strikingly generous towards their former enemies. A woman gave the man two oranges and an apple, although fruit cannot have been that easy to obtain. Soon the prisoners were allowed to walk out of their camps if they remained within five miles. The prisoner admired English Gothic architecture and enjoyed visiting the village churches. Pubs were out of bounds, but he chanced it. 'From all sides' he was 'cheerfully and amicably greeted'. He came out richer than when he went in. The men had bought him drinks and there had been a whip-round. He had been given five shillings.[82]

The prisoner was back in Germany in the cruel winter of 1947. He saw some prisoners who had been released from the Soviet Union dressed in rags: 'We are ashamed that we have warm winter clothes.' The treatment of German prisoners of war was still nagging Frings, who used a trip to Rome in February 1946 to pick up his cardinal's hat as a pretext to rally German soldiers incarcerated in Italy, together with Cardinals Innitzer of Vienna and Faulhaber of Munich. He visited Britain in September that year and went to no fewer than twelve camps containing a total of 20,000 men. Later he addressed a congregation of 3,000 British Catholics in Westminster Cathedral calling for the men's release. In 1947 he performed a similar mission to Canada to try to secure the liberation of Germans in Canadian camps.[83]

The big fry might visit London from time to time to be interrogated in the London District Prisoner of War Cage of the Combined Services Detailed Interrogation Centre (or CSDIC) in the plush surroundings of Kensington Palace Gardens.* It was here that Lieutenant-Colonel Alexander Paterson Scotland led a team of German-speaking officers and NCOs whose job was to compile the dossiers to be handed over to the war crimes tribunals. Their principal concern was the crimes committed against British nationals and above all POWs. The Great Escape loomed large, specifically the killing of fifty of the airmen who had escaped from the Stalag Luft III in Sagan in Silesia. Thirteen Gestapo men were eventually brought to justice and hanged in Hamelin Gaol in 1948. The case was not actually closed until 1964.[84]

The investigators based in Kensington Palace Gardens were also exercised by the several atrocious massacres that had been carried out by SS units in France. One was the killing of ninety-seven soldiers from the 2nd Battalion of the Royal Norfolk Regiment at the strikingly inappropriately named village of Le Paradis on 27 May 1940. Responsibility for the crime was pinned on a company commander in the SS-Totenkopf Division, Fritz Knoechlein, who had learned to hate all non-Nazi forms of humanity in the hard school of Dachau: to be a guard at Dachau or any of the other camps required proof of a man's contempt for his fellows. Knoechlein had absorbed his lessons well. He was hanged.[85]

Germans complained of their treatment at the hands of Scotland and his

---

* MI5 had another interrogation centre at Latchmere House in the London suburbs – Camp 020. This was commanded by Colonel Robin Stephens until his transfer to Bad Nenndorf.

team, but the work-over seems to have been gentle compared to those carried out by the Americans. The SS officer Otto Baum said he had been slapped and threatened with extradition to the Soviet Union. Scotland vigorously denied the charges, which could have been brought before the courts in an attempt to prove that a confession had been extracted by force. The prisoners naturally had a number of ruses up their sleeves, accusations of torture being just one of them. Another was to blame everything on a man who was dead, or in Soviet captivity – where there was no chance of corroborating the story, and a fair chance that he would eventually perish anyhow if he hadn't done so already. That Scotland beat and abused prisoners, however, seems beyond doubt. He even admitted as much in his autobiography, although the relevant passages were cut at the request of MI5.[86]

Scotland's men were investigating a full-scale massacre of British soldiers that took place at the time of the evacuation of the British Expeditionary Force at Dunkirk. The command to kill a hundred or so men mostly from the Royal Warwicks was probably issued by the later SS-Brigadeführer Wilhelm Mohnke, after his men had taken a pasting from the British during the rearguard action. In connection with the inquiry the Scotland team were able to bring in Sepp Dietrich, the commander of the Leibstandarte Adolf Hitler, who was in American custody. Scotland was surprised to find that the former coachman who had become Hitler's darling was a broken man. He was squat and balding, 'rough in manners and crude in speech'.[87] Scotland had evidently believed what he had heard about the SS superman. He failed to get a confession from Dietrich, or from any other SS man, and concluded that they took their oath of loyalty very seriously.

The British also had their prisons in Germany and Belgium. The Belgian camp was meant to be particularly gruelling, and conditions for the 130,000 prisoners were reported to be "not much better than Belsen".[88] Those awaiting trial for war crimes were housed in the former Prussian town of Minden or in Münsterlager. Conditions here were scandalously bad. When the camp was inspected in April 1947 there were found to be just four functioning lightbulbs in the whole place. There was no fuel, no straw mattresses and no food apart from 'water soup'. The camp was chiefly guarded by ex-Nazi POWs. The inmates saw no British officers, and even the sighting of an NCO was a rarity. Hygiene was equally nightmarish: there were two washhouses for every 500 men, no soap and no towels.[89]

British civil servants showed scant concern for the idea that Germans were dying in British camps. Con O'Neill at the Foreign Office minuted a paper written by Hynd in July 1946 to say that a few more deaths might be a good thing, as no one needed more Germans. A suggestion was mooted that the prisoners should be made over to the Russians, as they would know how to deal with them. The Russians would have no foolish sentimentality and would kill them off.[90]

The British also ran their Civilian Internment Camps or CICs for political prisoners, who had not all been screened or charged, and which contained prisoners as young as sixteen. When questions were asked about the camps in the House of Commons Wing Commander Norman Hulbert called them 'concentration camps', the 'only right and proper description'. This was where the British haphazard denazification took place. Anyone could have ended up there: *Junkertum*, being a member of the east Elbian or Prussian nobility, called for 'discretionary arrest'. Anyone with 'von' before their names had to watch out. The British decided that it might be better to place the civil prisoners offshore; perhaps that way fewer people would see them. The proposal was to create an 'Alcatraz' for up to 10,000 prisoners, but this never happened as the RAF was using the available islands for bombing practice. When the new camp Adelheide was opened there were only 473 prisoners, but thirteen of them were over sixty and another 136 over fifty.[91]

Once convicted of war crimes the Germans might have ended up at Werl near Dortmund. Death row was in the Pied Piper town of Hamelin. Execution exerted severe demands on the British hangman, Albert Pierrepoint, who could not be in all places at once. It took him seven hours to hang six prisoners in pairs. At one point the British were handing out between thirty and fifty death sentences a month, although a third of them were quashed on appeal.[92] There was a suggestion that the British might turn to the guillotine, as it was quicker. Soldiers had made it clear that they did not like carrying out firing squads.[93] At Bad Nenndorf near Hanover, CSDIC 74 also possessed an interrogation centre where men were tortured. The centre of the town was sealed off with barbed wire. The torture-chamber was the old pumproom. Here they were beaten, deprived of sleep, threatened with execution or unnecessary surgery. As many as 372 men and 44 women passed through Bad Nenndorf before it closed in July 1947.

Initially they were SS men and Pgs, as well as industrialists and 'plutocrats' who had done well in the Third Reich. The British were also frightened of Werewolves, and brought in several Hitler Youth leaders for interrogation. Later many of them were Germans who had been 'turned' by the Soviets, and were spying on the British Zone. The camp commander was Colonel Robin Stephens, an MI5 officer. His staff consisted of twelve British – including civilian linguists – a Pole, a Dutchman and six German Jews. They were helped by young soldiers. Some of these had been present at the liberation of Belsen and felt no goodwill towards the Germans. Others had committed minor offences of discipline, assault or desertion and were being punished.

The activities in Bad Nenndorf eventually reached the ears of the prime minister, and Sir Sholto Douglas launched an investigation into the abuse of POWs. A court martial opened in Hamburg on 8 June 1948 at which Stephens was tried together with a German-born Jew, Lieutenant Richard Langham. It was transferred to London and heard *in camera*. The officers were acquitted. There was alarm in government circles that the public should learn that the British were running a number of branches of CSDIC in Germany, and that 'Bad Nenndorf' should become a rallying cry. Lord Pakenham expressed his concern about the accusation that the British were treating prisoners in a manner 'reminiscent of the German concentration camps'. Following the court martial Bad Nenndorf was closed down, but interrogations went on in the British base in Gütersloh. When Pakenham heard of this he complained to Robertson. The military commander apparently took no notice.[94]

Almost all the men who were not suspected of any great crimes, however, were sent home for Christmas 1948 – that is, if they still had a home to go to, or knew how to locate their families.

The Treatment of the Cossacks and Russian Civilians in Germany

Marshal Zhukov raised the question of the return of Russian POWs as early as 5 June 1945 when the Allied commanders met in Berlin. It had been agreed that these soldiers would be handed over to the Russians. Most of the men were Cossacks and Ukrainians who had fought in German units, chiefly SS. Some of them were also labour conscripts and white Russians who had been caught up in the war zone.[95] They did not have to be Russian, as the Russians acted for their clients too. The character of Anna Schmidt in *The Third Man* is one of these. She is from Czechoslovakia. Her lover Harry Lime has had papers made for her. The Soviet authorities allow Lime to carry on hiding in their sector as long as he continues to inform them of cases like hers.

In the film Major Calloway is reluctant to hand Anna over to Brodsky, considering her an insignificant case. In Austria the British co-operated with the NKVD over Russians who had fought in SS units, although they had no doubts that they were leading the prisoners to certain death.[*] The Anglo-Americans had 150,000 Russian prisoners. Over of a fifth of these were returned to the Soviets and presumably slaughtered. The Russians were furious not to receive the full tally. One of the most tragic incidents was the handing over of part of Vlasov's Russian Legion to the Soviets across the border on 24 February 1946. The Russians were housed at Plattling. Guessing their fate, they mutinied one night and the men at nearby 'Natternberg' could hear the sound of shooting. They were rounded up and taken to the Czech border. After the Russians were liquidated, Salomon and the other men from Natternberg were transferred to Plattling, along with the Hersbruck camp and the Nuremberg witness camp and the SS men who had been held in Dachau.[96]

Salomon later learned the whole story. One day a Soviet official had arrived at Plattling and demanded the files on the prisoners. When the Russian POWs got wind of what was going to happen, they mutinied. A senior American officer had placated them by telling them that they would not be handed over, and that they would be resettled[†] in southern Europe – the same lie the Welsh Guards used in Carinthia. Then the tanks rolled in. The American guards had been issued with rubber truncheons and went to the Russian huts in the middle of the night, beating them out of their bunks – 'Mak snell, mak snell' – and into waiting lorries. They were taken to Zwiesel near the border. American guards reported that corpses could be seen hanging from trees behind the Russian lines. The precise number of Russian soldiers killed is not known. Estimates range from 300 to 3,000.[97]

The French Camps

A total of 1,065,000 German POWs were attributed to the French. Of these about a quarter – 237,000 – had been captured in France. The rest were an American 'loan'. Their treatment was particularly brutal,[98] probably because the memory of internment in Germany was still fresh in the minds of many French civilians, who had not recovered from the humiliation of occupation either. At the beginning of November 1944, there had

[*] See above pp. 305–7.
[†] The verb to 'resettle' had a particularly lethal significance when the Nazis applied it to the Jews.

been 920,000 *poilus* in German POW camps.[99] Here was the chance for revenge. Very soon after the end of the war the Red Cross reported that there were 200,000 prisoners on the brink of famine in France. The United States treated this report with some scepticism, but it stopped the transports and brought 130,000 of the worst cases back to the US in 1946 because they were in such poor condition that they could no longer work. The Americans compensated the French with another 100,000 *Amerikafahrer* but were careful to deliver food so that the same thing did not happen again. The French received the prisoners only once they had agreed to abide by the Geneva Convention. The good behaviour did not last long.[100] When the Americans put pressure on the French to release their prisoners, the latter complained that neither the Americans nor the British had lost as many labourers in the war and that the German slaves were 'indispensable for the rebuilding of their country'. France hung on to the men until the end of 1948, when the last 23,609 went home. An attempt to make the work voluntary was unsuccessful.[101] Neglect and brutality took their toll: officially 21,886 German POWs died in France, or 24,178 men from the Axis powers.[102]

Salomon cites one case of an elderly Alsatian German historian who starved to death in a French 'dungeon'.[103] In another camp in the Sarthe, prisoners had to survive on 900 calories a day. In the prison hospital an average of twelve POWs died daily. Camp 404 at Septèmes near Marseilles was originally set up by the Americans and was partly run by vicious 'Jabos' or Yugoslav guards. It was a gigantic place with twenty-five separate 'cages' filled with tents. Solid structures came later. In February 1946, however, Septèmes was handed over to the French as part of the Western Allied loan policy. The Germans felt they had been betrayed. There were 'indescribable scenes' of panic and several suicides and self-inflicted injuries. More, there was the nightmare* – as far as the Germans were concerned – of finding that their new captors were colonial troops.[104]

The march of German captives through France provided the French public with the chance to tell the *Landser* (privates and NCOs) what they thought of them. One woman who disregarded an order to stop pelting the prisoners with stones was shot by a black American soldier. 'She lay there in the street. No one took any notice of her . . .'[105] Another prisoner who was taken to a camp near Annecy to work in the quarries was told that the French were receiving one mark for every prisoner they took off the

---

* This went back to the First World War. There was generally a certain empathy between Germans and black American troops. See above pp. 241–2.

Americans. As they were marched through France a French soldier showed off to little girls at the roadside by kicking him in the backside. Watch-stealing was almost as common in the west as it was with the Red Army.[106] One German describes a sergeant-major who showed him his watch, only to lose it soon afterwards. The prisoner was not so badly treated for all that. After the quarries he was able to work on the land and the local farmers fed him well – all but one, that is, who cooked 'roast cat' in a cream sauce that Christmas. He ate some of the sauce, but spurned the cat.[107]

On 22 July 1946 Hans Johnert learned that America no longer possessed prisoners of war. They had all been put out on loan. Soon after his 'repatriation' he was moved to Pont d'Ain, near Bourg-en-Bresse. The Germans were used to provide labour for the local community. They worked on the farms and in the quarries. They served different masters, some of whom were kind, some not. On 9 December Frenchmen dressed as Germans threw grenades at the POWs, killing two of them and injuring many more. Johnert was sent home in the spring of 1947.[108] Another, anonymous prisoner also found himself handed over to the French by the Americans. He was originally taken to a tent camp outside the Breton city of Rennes where the prisoners slept on the wet earth. The Americans were particularly trigger-happy and one man was killed simply for running to pick up a cigarette butt thrown down by a guard. Any prisoner found guilty of theft was buried up to his neck in a hole in the ground. Those who tried to run were confined for thirty days. 'Vae victis,' concludes the prisoner – 'woe to the vanquished'.[109]

On 24 June 1945 the prisoner in Rennes learned that the French were due to take over the camp. Despite the rough way they had been handled by the Americans it was not a pleasant thought – 'the modern slave-trade' he called it. If anything, the French were even quicker on the draw than the Americans. Soon after they took control of the camp they shot three Germans, two in the head: 'Buy combs, you lot, there are lousy times ahead!' Shooting continued to be a frequent occurrence at night. Poor provision meant that people died of hunger too. Two men starved to death in the huts, but the prisoner added that about twenty died daily in the camp sickbay. 'Die. Who would ever learn about it – who would believe it? The dead tell no tales.' This death rate would tally with the known figures for France in 1945.[110]

One evening a drunken guard fired into a group of prisoners. He missed the Germans but hit a black American guard outside the perimeter, killing him outright. Red wine was responsible for the guards hurling salvoes of stones at the prisoners to shouts of 'Vive la France!', 'Vive de Gaulle!' and 'boches!' At least one of the guards was from Alsace. The Germans inflicted revenge on him by using the insulting word *Wackes* behind his back.* On 8 August another eight men died of hunger in the sickbay. On the other hand most of the starving men were in the huts, not in the sickbay. When the Red Cross parcels arrived that August the men were as happy as children. The arrival of food, however, failed to prevent ten more men dying on the 22nd. One of the prisoner's friends cut his wrists when the guard discovered the tell-tale blood-group tattoo in his armpit. Meanwhile, the scandal of the camps had reached the French press: reporters were comparing them to Buchenwald. In the *Figaro* a writer acknowledged that the Germans had committed terrible crimes but 'these horrors should not become the theme of a sports competition in which we endeavour to outdo the Nazis . . . We have to judge the enemy, but we have a duty not to resemble him.'[111]

The prisoner volunteered for a work detail that took him off to defuse mines around the Breton coast – in blatant violation of the Geneva Convention – but he was happy to do anything to escape from the misery of the camp, and possibly get something better to eat. As he was signed up there was a new spate of robbery, this time by both guards and civilians. The men were beaten and kicked and they lost their watches, rings, shoes, even their trousers.[112]

Belgium

Britain and America donated over 60,000 of their POWs to the Belgians. One German soldier who ended up in a camp near Mons in the south of the country had been captured in the South Tyrol. At the airport he was robbed by an American soldier. Travelling through Germany he was able to toss out a letter on Günzburg Station. A nod from the station master told him that he would deal with it. In Mannheim they came across some soldiers who had been shipped up from Lake Constance. 'They reported that the *Franzmann* [army slang for a Frenchman] was taking everything away.'[113]

The Americans left them in Erbisoeuil camp with 30,000 others. Before they quit their charges, the GIs robbed them of their wristwatches. What they failed to take, the Belgians grabbed, adding that they would have it back on their release: 'These people were the worst we had met up to now.'

---

* The word *Wackes*, meaning an imbecile, was responsible for the so-called Zabern Incident in 1913, when the German army's treatment of the Alsatian locals led to mass demonstrations, and there was a vote of no-confidence in the German chancellor in the Reichstag.

The prisoners were registered. When they produced their pay-books, the Belgians were astonished to learn that they were not SS men, but that did not prevent them from stealing the prisoner's pen, money and clothes. Once the Germans were admitted to the camp it became clear that the guards wanted to see them as the perpetrators of brutal acts in concentration camps: 'You did this too in concentration camps . . .' they said. When the men tried to leave their huts to urinate or defecate, the guards shouted at them, 'You German pigs, do it inside, that's how it was in the KZ!' When one of them chanced it, he was shot at. They got round the problem by urinating through the window.[114] The prisoner could not understand why they had been sent to the camp: 'The Belgian people don't want us at all, and they are frightened of unemployment and are threatening to go on strike.'[115]

The prisoner was put to work in the mines. The work was only for the *Landser* – the officers were exempted. The Belgian prime minister, Achille van Acher, had given him some hope by affirming that the men would be sent home in the spring of 1947. It was not just the work which was gruelling, it was the occasional letters from home which painted a disturbing picture of the life of their dear ones. They heard about the rapes in the Russian Zone, the theft of all their belongings and the penury of their families, and the desperation to get home meant there were frequent attempts to escape. There were, however, advantages to living in the British or Soviet Zones. It is not hard to see that the experience with the Americans had made the prisoner bitter: 'In the English [*sic*] or Russian Zones the women receive a little support at least, but with the Yanks and their complete democracy, everyone has to get on with their life as best they can.'[116]

The official statistics for deaths in custody in the Benelux lands are 450 in Belgium, 210 in Holland and 15 in Luxembourg.[117]

The Russian Camps.

The Russians seemingly made no distinction between a POW and a civilian, and both were liable to arrest and to be shipped to the Soviet Union to work, or to rot in camps. On 29 June 1945 the Soviet Union was said to have between four and five million Germans within its borders, helping rebuild its cities.[118] The imprisonment of German and other Axis POWs in Russia was marked by an element of callous chaos. Huge numbers of Germans went east – not just soldiers, but non-military men aged between sixteen and sixty, including scientists and technicians. Records attesting to their identity were inadequate, and whether they lived or died was clearly a matter of supreme indifference to the Soviet authorities. As it happened, 1,094,250 soldiers perished, half of them before April 1945.[119] Sometimes it was the vast majority: of the 90,000 soldiers taken prisoner at Stalingrad, only 5,000 returned home. By 1950 numbers had considerably decreased. At the beginning of that year there were still 46,841 POWs in Russia; by its end the number had sunk to 28,711.[120] It was roughly the same figure as those who had been put on trial for war crimes. They had all received twenty-five years.

On 31 May 1945, Margret Boveri made a list of her journalist colleagues whom she knew to have been arrested by the Russians: Molkenthin, who was not a Party member but had joined the SS to protect his back, and was a harmless reporter; Scharp, who had been forced to join the Party in Prague in 1939; Sprang, a real Nazi; Wirths, a known anti-Nazi, but the Russians refused to believe him because he was assistant editor of *Das Reich*; John Brech, economics editor of the same paper, an anti-Nazi, but who had been forced to join the Party in 1938; a lot of people from the DNB (Deutsche Nachrichten Büro, the official press agency), including anti-Nazis; Seibert from the *Völkische Beobachter*. All the others fled in good time. The ones who were really important had naturally vanished without trace, but the Russians were too foolish to know that. The treatment of the smaller fry was not too bad. The food was decent, and the interrogations polite; only the living conditions were bad. The bankers she knew came out after two or three weeks. Three girls from the Foreign Office were locked up for three days, during which they were beaten and had their hair pulled. They could not tell the Russians where the bigwigs were. Then they were dismissed. Even men and women who had been involved in the July Plot were arrested and interrogated in this way.

Things got worse when the prisoners were marched off into captivity. Some managed to escape. The Russians reacted by arresting the same number in the next village so that they delivered the correct number of internees as listed on the paperwork. Their flats and furniture were requisitioned. Unimportant prisoners taken in Poland might eventually turn up in the Russian Zone. Libussa von Krockow's stepfather Jesko von Puttkamer, who had done no more than lead the local Volkssturm in the Second World War, had last been heard of in prison in Danzig. In the spring of 1947 his family received a message that he was in a POW camp in Leipzig. Libussa knew the way over the green border and made her way to Leipzig. She found the camp in a suburb of the city, and spoke to a prisoner through the barbed wire. She went back later that evening with a crowbar. By dawn he was free.[121]

The Soviet authorities were as wont to arrest monarchists as Nazis. Hermine of Reuss, the Kaiser's second wife, might have been described as both. She had flirted with the Nazis before the Second World War and damaged the reputation of her husband's family in the process. After the Kaiser's death in 1941 she had withdrawn to her Schloss Saabor in Thuringia. At the end of the war she had sought refuge near by with her sister, Princess Ida zu Stolberg-Rossla. The Duke of Brunswick, who was married to the Kaiser's daughter, Victoria Louise, went to Thuringia to warn her about the Russians. She replied that Thuringia was under American occupation and that she had no reason to move. She remained obstinate when the duke told her, 'Just think who you are; you must not fall into Russian hands.' She replied, 'I have no reason to reproach myself. I shall stay here.' She was not warned of the American withdrawal in July, and soon the Russians arrived to take her into custody. After a long period in which there was no news, she re-emerged in Frankfurt-an-der-Oder, where she remained under house arrest in a building on the edge of the town. She died in August 1947 of a heart attack brought on by 'uncertainty and profound mental suffering'.[122]

The Russians were keen to get their hands on all the leading army commanders who had operated in their territory, whether they had been party to the atrocities or not. One who is credited with having been a humane general was Field Marshal Ewald von Kleist. He had been dismissed from his command by Hitler at the same time as Erich von Manstein. They were clever officers, but not National Socialists.[123] Kleist retired to his Silesian estate, moving to Bavaria at the approach of the Red Army. There he was arrested by the Americans, who handed him over to the Yugoslavs in 1946 – Kleist had performed an important role in the invasion of Yugoslavia in 1941. The former army commander was incarcerated in no fewer than twenty seven prisons in nine years. The Yugoslavs tried him and sentenced him to fifteen years as a war criminal. After two years he was extradited to Russia, where he was charged – with heavy irony – with having 'alienated through mildness and kindness the population of the Soviet Union'. In March 1954 he reached the end of his Calvary at Vladimir camp, where he was finally allowed to make contact with his family. He died in October that year of 'general arteriosclerosis and hypertension'.[124]

Field Marshal Friedrich Paulus, defeated at Stalingrad, had the doubtful honour of being among the 5,000 or so of his troops to return to Germany, but that did not occur until November 1954, when he had already served eleven years. His treatment was not bad. He was kept under house arrest in Moscow, and once he began to co-operate with the Soviet authorities after 20 July 1944 he was accorded some privileges. He gave evidence for the prosecution at Nuremberg, but even on his release he was not allowed to join his family in the West and died of motor-neuron disease in Dresden in 1957.

If life was tough for German POWs in Russian camps, one or two of them could claim that the Soviet authorities preserved their lives. SS-Brigadeführer Wilhelm Mohnke, who led the defence of the government quarter in Berlin in April 1945 and was taken prisoner on 2 May, was wanted by the Western Allies for ordering the execution of unarmed POWs. Had he fallen into British or American hands he would almost certainly have been hanged. As it was he was released from Soviet custody in 1955, when the Anglo-Americans were no longer interested in pursuing German war criminals, and died in his bed forty-six years later.[125]

Mohnke's ten years in captivity were a curate's egg. They began with a remarkable meal in the Belle Alliance Strasse of Berlin. After they surrendered, he and twelve other SS officers were taken to a four-storey building and invited to a proper Russian feast complete with caviar and vodka. The Germans failed to tuck in with a gusto equal to the Russians. At 10.30 p.m. the dinner came to an end and the Germans were locked up. The next day Mohnke and Rattenhuber of the SD, Hitler's pilot Baur and his chief bodyguard Günsche were taken to a transit camp for high-ranking German officers in Strausberg. On 9 May they were moved again – this time to Russia.[126]

The Soviet authorities refused to extradite Mohnke or to give any information on his whereabouts. With time any pretence at co-operation in these matters broke down. One of the reasons the British tried Manstein, it is said, is because they did not wish to hand him over to the Soviets. Mohnke was taken to the Budirka Prison and finally to the Lubyanka, where he walked the gangways with Admiral Erich Raeder and Field Marshal Ferdinand Schörner. In the meantime he was beaten and tortured by Soviet secret agents. Interrogations by the NKVD were no gentler than those carried out by the Americans. Baur, for example, was deprived of sleep for twenty-one nights in succession.

These were important Nazis, but there were plenty of men in Russian camps who had no particular affiliation to the regime. Heinz Pust was a typical German POW in Soviet captivity. He was taken prisoner in Czechoslovakia, as a soldier in Schörner's vast army. On 9 May 1945 he had heard the Soviet soldiers shooting into the air. It was the first he was even aware that the Germans were losing the war, let alone surrendering. He was given papers that released him home, but he was caught hiding in the woods by partisans and locked up in a school house. He was decently treated after a local policeman decided to give the partisans a lecture on the laws of war. On 16 May he was handed over to the Red Army.

He was taken to Georgievsk in Russia with a number of Hungarian soldiers. Discipline tended to be relaxed in the camp. Sometimes you could come and go as you pleased. The food was poor and the men were always hungry. Two or three times a day there was *kasha*: gruel. They had seventeen grams of sugar and five grams of tobacco which they made up into cigarettes with old newspapers. To supplement this there was a daily ration of 300–600 grams of soggy bread and seventeen grams of fat or meat. Sometimes there was a soup made from rotten vegetables. The prisoners would strew the sugar on the bread to give themselves the illusion of eating cake. Pust's first packet from home came in 1950 or 1951.[127]

Molotov stated at the Moscow Conference in March 1947 that there were 890,532 German prisoners in Russian captivity. It was a moment of terrible disappointment: only a third of Germany's missing men were alive.[128] The news broke through to Pust that all POWs would be released by the end of 1948, 'but the year 1948 came and went without anyone in our camp noticing any acceleration'.[129] Clay can't have believed the Russians, but he could see a stick to beat the enemy with when he called for a tough stance: 'tell the truth about Moscow' – they have two million POWs. As he told Senator Kenneth Keating, 'Don't let's be the first to get nervous in this war of nerves.'[130]

There were no Russian trials until 1949. Most of the important prisoners received the same tariff of twenty-five years' hard labour. On 6 December 1949 Pust was indicted for war crimes. In Moscow he was placed in 'investigative custody'. The men were tried in batches. It took all of fifteen to twenty minutes. They each received twenty-five years, even – it seemed – a Berlin bus driver whose main crime was to have been found wearing his uniform. Now Pust's imprisonment took on an official status for the first time. At Rostov on the Don his head was shaved, and his picture taken along with his fingerprints.[131]

The generals and staff officers were exempted from work, but that did not always mean that their lives were any more pleasant and many volunteered simply in order to have something to do. They were sent to the generals' camp at Voikova, which contained 186 senior German commanders, where they peeled potatoes, tended the garden, fed rabbits and brought in the harvest. Although officers could lead a lazy life, there was little chance of getting out. The higher the rank the less the possibility of reprieve: in 1947 officers represented 7 per cent of prisoners held; by 1949 the percentage had risen to 36.[132] There was no hope of reprieve before Stalin's death in 1953. After Chancellor Adenauer's visit in 1955 three Russian generals appeared in the camp to break the news that the men were free. Mohnke and his comrades then had a second feast from their Soviet captors.

Pust was one of the 27,000 POWs who learned that he would not be released until 1974, but despite that cruel verdict prisoners began to be freed in more regular batches. The first to leave were the Hungarians and the Romanians, probably because their countries had now become Soviet satellites. Books became vital. A comrade in arms had given Pust a copy of *Faust Part One*, much of which he now knew by heart. Some books published by the Aufbau Verlag* appeared in the camp: German translations of Gorki and Tolstoy as well as suitable German literature: Plivier, Heinrich Mann and Arnold Zweig. The regime lasted as long as Stalin, then Pust went home.

Otto Engelbert had a different experience to Pust. He volunteered to attend the 'Antifa' school in Talizy – freedom at the price of ideological indoctrination. He went in November 1945. Talizy had been built as a penal colony during the First World War. The area was rich in peat, which was used to fuel the local power stations. The prisoners were assessed on their arrival, by being questioned on their positions regarding East Prussia and Silesia and what they thought about the Oder–Neisse Line. Then they went on to the next stage: history according to the Marxist dialectic. They were given courses on the reasons for Hitler's defeat; the sources of the USSR's victorious power; the main stages of Germany's development to industrial capitalism (1500–1815); the foundations of capitalism; the Revolution of 1848; the creation of Prussia-Germany; reactionary Prussia and Prussian militarism; imperialism; the growth of the workers' movement; the November Revolution etc, etc.[133] When Engelbert finished his course he swore an oath to fight Hitlerism. The reward was a proper feast. A pig was slain; there was hot food, cake and tea, wine and schnapps. The intellectuals, however, were not released. Engelbert was sent back to Germany to spread the word.[134]

---

* See above p. 224.

Prisons in Czechoslovakia, Poland and Yugoslavia

Poland was well and truly a Soviet client and retained tens of thousands of German soldiers. In the summer of 1948 Clay was concerned about this: 'I always pushed for the return of German prisoners of war.' His reports told him there were still 40,000 of them, more than three years after the cessation of hostilities. A paltry twenty-one had reached the American Zone that year. The German agencies involved in tracking them had informed the American commander that 'they also believe the POWS to be receiving very bad treatment'.[135] In the Neuhammer mines in Silesia, the mortality rate was 15 per cent: 5,400 dead. The Jaworzno camp claimed 1,817 military and civilian lives. The total number of deaths in the camps is given at 4,500, but the figure seems suspiciously low.[136] In Warsaw the Germans rebuilt the historic centre, putting back the buildings destroyed in the Blitzkrieg of 1939 and the wide-ranging destruction of the historic heart of the city which was effected after the Warsaw Uprising. There were still 4,240 German POWs left in Poland in 1950.[137] One who never returned was Gauleiter Koch, who lived to a remarkably ripe old age in a Polish prison.

There were still 600 Germans toiling in the uranium mines of the Joachimstal of Czechoslovakia in 1950 to feed the Russian A-bomb programme.[138] The Czechs claimed that 1,250 POWs were killed of the 25,000 prisoners they had.[139] The Yugoslavs were among the most draconian. The official figure for deaths of POWs in their custody stands at 6,215, but that number is considered 'too low by far'. Around 80,000 would be closer to the truth.[140] One of the lighter duties these prisoners had to perform was the construction and decoration of Tito's new summer palace and later guest house on Lake Bled. A painter was called in to decorate a double-cube room on the first floor with blood-curdling scenes depicting the battles between Tito and Hitler's forces. The German POWs played all the roles, from the slain who littered the field of battle to the Yugoslav warriors who pierced them with their bayonets.[141] The final batch of 1,300 Germans was sent home in 1949.[142]

The Return of the Warrior

Once the POW was released, the homecoming could be bitter-sweet. Ruth Friedrich was horrified by the sight of returning German warriors in the American Sector of Berlin. 'Oh, great God! How bad misery can be!'

The rags of the Germans contrasted with the smart uniforms of the Americans as they walked through Steglitz on 30 July 1945. Some lacked arms, others legs, they showed signs of illness and plague, they were abandoned and lost.[143] The experience of returning soldiers forms the background to some of the early stories of the Nobel Prize-winning novelist Heinrich Böll, and provided the theme for the play *Draussen vor der Tür* (Outside the Door) by the writer Wolfgang Borchert.

Borchert and Böll both lived through those times and spoke from experience. Borchert, an aspiring actor who had been on the Eastern Front, had been wounded and shipped home but was then obliged to return to the colours before he was truly mended. The illness he incurred from poor hospital treatment was to kill him at the age of twenty-six. *Draussen vor der Tür* was first performed on 21 November 1947, the day after his death. It was later filmed as *Liebe 1947*.

In the play, the NCO Beckmann returns from Siberia to find his wife in bed with another man. He tries to drown himself in the Elbe but the river rejects him. He becomes part of the mass of alienated German men, whose defeat and complicity in crime had rendered them rebarbative even to their own women: 'your Germany is outside, in the rainy night, on the street'.[144] Beckmann carries the responsibility for a minor massacre of his own men. He wants to rid himself of it. He goes to see his colonel, in the hope of passing the responsibility on to him. The colonel is prosperous and doesn't want to know. Beckmann looks for his parents. They are dead. They had been Nazis and had been thrown out on the streets at the end of the war – they also are 'outside the door'. They had preferred death to denazification. Early on he meets a lugubrious God, but he fails to find him again: 'Where is he then, the old man who calls himself God?' Doors are slammed in his face as he looks for work, women and humanity: 'That is life! There is a man, and the man comes to Germany and the man freezes. He starves and he limps! He comes to Germany! He comes home, and there is his bed, occupied. A door slams, and he is left outside.'[145]

It is a theme Böll returns to time and again. In *Die Botschaft* (Breaking the News) a soldier takes the effects of a dead warrior back to his widow. When he arrives she is laughing with another man. He puts down the soldier's wedding ring, watch and pay-book, and a few well-thumbed photographs. The woman has to sit down, 'and I realised that the war would never be over so long as there was still someone bleeding from an injury it had caused'. She wants to know whether her husband died in the east. No, says the man who brings the news. "No . . . in the west, in a POW camp, there were more than a hundred thousand . . ."

"And when . . ."

"In July 1945," I said softly.'

One difference between prisoners in British camps and those in American captivity was that the British allowed the Germans to sport insignia of rank and the Americans did not. In Böll's story, 'When the War Was Over', the little literary type is busy sewing his braid back on his uniform as the soldiers head for Bonn and discharge in October 1945. The narrator recounts his treatment at the hands of the British and the Americans. He has been captured by the latter in April. The corporal asks him, 'Hitler Youth, SA or Party?', to which he answers, 'No.' The American then bawls at him and accuses his grandmother of various sexual practices that he can't properly work out as his English isn't good enough.

When later an English corporal asks him for papers he says he has none. He has sold his pay-book for a couple of cigarettes. The Englishman searches him and finds a diary he has kept in captivity: a hundred closely written pages made out of paper bags stapled together. In fury the corporal tosses it into the latrine. No one is supposed to know what has been going on.

16

The Trials

We had gambled, all of us, and lost: lost Germany, our country's good repute, and a considerable measure of our own personal integrity. Here was a chance to demonstrate a little dignity, a little manliness or courage, and to make plain that after all we were charged with, we at least were not also cowards.

Albert Speer, *Spandau: The Secret Diaries*, London 1976, 14

The Allies' decision to indict the Nazi leaders had a precedent. Article 227 of the 1919 Treaty of Versailles called for a trial of major German 'war criminals', with the Kaiser at the top of the list – who, Lloyd George proclaimed, should be hanged. It demanded the extradition of up to a thousand Germans but proved a soggy squib: neither Holland – where William II had been granted asylum – nor a largely unoccupied Germany would agree to hand over the defendants. To show willing, the Germans themselves put on a trial in Leipzig. Thirteen men were convicted, but as they were perceived as heroes in Germany they all managed to escape.[1]

At their various meetings, the Second World War Allies agreed on the need to liquidate the top Nazis. The question was how? Should they suffer summary execution, a drumhead court martial, or should the victors risk a trial?[2] When the fate of the 'war criminals' was discussed in Moscow in October 1943, the American secretary of state, Cordell Hull, was in favour of a drumhead court martial. The Soviet delegation could not have approved more strongly. As their Nuremberg judge, General Iona Nikitchenko, put it: the accused were 'war criminals . . . who have already been convicted'. It was the British and Anthony Eden who reminded the conference of 'legal forms'. Legal form was clearly important, but they all knew whom they wanted to eliminate. The British prosecutor, attorney-general Sir David Maxwell Fyfe, put it in a nutshell: 'Our work . . . is to see the top-notch Nazis tried, condemned, and many of them executed.' Hull's master, Roosevelt, was in favour of shooting them, and appointed a judge to look into the possibility. His advisers, however, told the president that it would be illegal. America switched course and called for a trial, and Soviet Russia joined in. By this time the British had changed their minds and favoured summary execution![3]

If there were to be trials, there had to be a law to try them by – the old maxim runs *nulla poena sine lege* (there is no crime without laws, sometimes rendered as *nullum crimen sine lege*). The Allies had to invent a body of law that would criminalise Nazi offences and backdate it to cover the period in question. It would be a code based on merging two conventions: the Hague Convention on Land Warfare of 1907 and the Geneva Convention of 1928, to which Germany (and not Soviet Russia) had been a party. It had been argued that the Hague Convention had merely framed laws and usages that had existed for centuries, but it had been assembled at a time when, for example, aerial warfare was unknown and when guerrilla armies were not taken into consideration. Some things emerged with crystal clarity: Article 23 of the Geneva Convention stated that it was an illegal act to kill or wound a soldier who had laid down his arms. It was also illegal to deny quarter. German soldiers had the Ten Commandments printed in their pay-books. It was correctly assumed that those who slaughtered POWs knew they had done wrong, and there were instances when their comrades in arms shunned them as pariahs as a result.

The result of the fusion was 'Nuremberg Law'. Nuremberg Law was the basis of the Royal Warrant of 18 June 1945 used in the military courts in the British Zone. The British defined the 'war crime' as a violation of the laws and usages of war. Stalin threw everything he could at the invading German armies; and he did not play by the book. German soldiers were rightly terrified of falling into enemy hands alive. Savage reprisals were directed towards the civilian populations of the Soviet Union when German troops were slaughtered behind the lines. It was a policy that had been losing German armies friends since the time of the Franco-Prussian War, but it was an accepted 'usage' allowed by Article 453 of the British Manual of Military Law. As the Labour MP and KC Reginald Paget put it, 'It was really unreasonable to expect the Germans to fight these all-in wrestlers in accordance with the Queensberry rules.'[4] The Americans were even more ruthless: 'one shot merited the destruction of a village. You will see the result in some heaps of rubble in Bavaria and Franconia. As they advanced, if a shot was fired from a village, they either stopped, or evacuated, and whistled up the air force. The isolated heaps of rubble in this relatively undamaged countryside are very striking. The result was that the Americans had very few casualties.'[5]

The Germans were to be judged for their behaviour in foreign territory. This was inserted at the behest of the Russians and the French. It involved the treatment of civilians: murder, abuse, deportation, slave labour; the murder of prisoners of war, killing hostages, plunder of public or private property, 'the wanton destruction of cities, towns or villages, or devastation not justified by military necessity'.[6] 'Genocide' was a new word for a relatively new crime. The destruction of the European Jews figured as only a small part of the case against the Germans in the early trials. The killing of German and Austrian Jews on the territory of the Greater German Reich was not automatically covered as it was theoretically the legal right of a sovereign state to dispose of its citizens as it pleased. On the other hand there was agreement that Julius Streicher should be done to death, so legal nicety had to be bent a little as he was not really guilty of any other crime that had been brought to the Allies' attention.[7] The persecution of German and Austrian Jews at home was therefore vaguely included under the aegis of 'aggression and the preparation for unjust war'.

For the Russians the massacre of Jews was hardly of interest, although half a million of their Jewish citizens were slaughtered by the Nazis. The reason for this was the rampant antisemitism they themselves experienced after the war in reaction against the upsurge in Zionism. On the other hand the prosecution found the Final Solution increasingly useful when it came to breaking down the defendants. Films of the concentration camps had a sobering effect even on such seasoned performers as Göring and Hess. By the time the trials were under way no German was an antisemite any more. As one later commentator glibly put it, 'there was hardly a defendant who could not produce evidence that he had helped some half-Jewish physics professor, or that he had used his influence to permit a Jewish symphony conductor to conduct a little longer, or that he had intervened on behalf of some couple in a mixed marriage in connection with an apartment'.[8]

There was very little call for retribution from Jewish groups at first. Henry Morgenthau remained a voice in the wilderness, and Truman for one wanted to keep him there. He later resigned in a huff. Zalman Grinberg, president of the liberated Jews in the American Zone, accused the Allies of a lack of concern, and wondered whether this would have been the case if another race had been the victim of a similar purge. Morgenthau continued to thunder, as did the presidential adviser Bernard Baruch and the columnist Walter Winchell, but they were not greatly heeded. On the other hand the enormity of the crimes committed by Germans did provoke Americans to calls for the severest punishments in the spring of 1945. Joseph Pulitzer of the *St Louis Post-Despatch* thought 150,000 Nazis should be shot. Congressman Dewey Short of Missouri advocated mass executions of SS and OKW men.[9]

The hypocrisy of Nuremberg Law alarmed many people. One was the Indian jurist Rahabinode Pal, a judge in the Tokyo trials, who dissented from the judgments, seeing the sentences meted out as retrogressive, 'a sham employment of legal process for the satisfaction of a thirst for revenge'. Field Marshal Lord Montgomery also disapproved of the tenor of the trials that 'have made the waging of unsuccessful war a crime, for which the generals of the defeated side would be tried and then hanged'. He understood that if the Germans had won the war, he might have been put on trial himself.* Shortly after a British Military Court in Hamburg sitting in the aptly named Curio-Haus had condemned Field Marshal Erich von Manstein to eighteen years in prison, the Korean War broke out, and the German press was happy to report that the American army was accused of precisely the same atrocities as the field marshal.[10]

Many contemporary observers agreed with Pal and believed the scores of trials that took place after the end of the war were simply a case of victors' justice. These dissenters included soldiers, jurists and judges. The Soviets, who provided a general as their prosecutor in the main trials in Nuremberg (he had been involved in fake trials in the 1930s and later became the director of Sachsenhausen concentration camp in its first years under Soviet management) and a more junior officer as a judge, constantly reminded the Western Allies that the purpose of the tribunals was to punish the defeated enemy. Yet the Soviet attitude was in some senses the most lenient, because they of all the nations that had defeated Nazi Germany were the most likely to have committed atrocities on a similar scale.

Reginald Paget KC was one of the most stentorian voices raised against the trials. He agreed to lead Field Marshal von Manstein's defence team gratis, describing the Royal Warrant as 'simply an exercise of the power of the victor over the vanquished'. As far as he was concerned, none of the convictions would have been secure in an English court, and they would all have been quashed by the Court of Appeal. For Paget the conqueror had no right to impose a form of trial which he 'would consider inadequate for his own citizens'.[11]

And yet something needed to be done. The Germans had performed terrible acts. To claim that what they had done was in no way illegal

---

* Sir Bernard Freyberg's bombing of the Benedictine abbey of Monte Cassino killed around 400 Italian civilians who had taken refuge there, and not one German.

because they were obeying higher commands or putting through the secret policies of the state was simply not good enough: not all Germans had sat around waiting for homicidal orders; many had acted on their own initiatives. Trials would also have the further advantage of recording the acts of the Nazi regime, providing a huge quantity of sworn evidence about the workings of the state. They would also have the effect of laying the blame. The American prosecutor Justice Robert H. Jackson made it clear: they were not trying the German people, just the men in the dock. Although many condemned the trials at the time, a precedent was set for war crimes and crimes against humanity and there is little protest against global jurisdictions today. Clay realised that the courts were establishing something. Writing to Jackson's successor Colonel Telford Taylor on 17 October 1947, he said, 'At Nuremberg we are establishing procedure for [the] future and not aiming at any specific individuals. History will make no distinction between a von Rundstedt and a von Leeb.'[12]

Under Nuremberg Law, the implication was that any officer who received what was *later* liable to be interpreted as a criminal command must refuse to carry it out, although – as Paget pointed out – both the British and American Manuals allowed superior orders to be used as a defence for 'criminal' actions.[13] In reality that meant an officer had to resign his commission. In Nazi Germany the response would have been a court martial and a firing squad. Colonel General Beck *did* resign his command in 1938, and encouraged other generals to follow his example (none did), but that was not in wartime. He was one of the movers and shakers behind the various military and civil plots to remove or kill Hitler between 1938 and 20 July 1944, when finally he did indeed pay with his life.

Suggesting that generals had absolute authority within their areas of command was also to misunderstand the nature of Hitler's regime. Like Stalin, the Führer was a great believer in *impera et divida*. He alone had enjoyed unrestricted power; the underlings had to jostle for position beneath him. On the battlefield this became a struggle for control between the SS and the Wehrmacht. The SS reported to Himmler, who answered to Hitler. The Waffen-SS had the advantage of better equipment, while the traditional army tended to lead the campaign under experienced generals, the majority of whom hailed from the traditional, Prussian officer corps. The SD was responsible for the dirty work behind the lines. It, too, answered to Himmler, but its actions within the Wehrmacht domains were agreed by the general commanding, which – as so often in Hitler's state – involved making the traditional general *complicit* in the actions of the SD either by co-operating with it or by agreeing to take over its functions by rounding up commissars, partisans or Jews. It was not Hitler's or Himmler's intention that anyone should emerge from the conflict with clean hands. Even diplomats were obliged to sign memos that said they agreed with the policy of deporting the Jews.

Paget pointed out that 'usages' were not considered binding in the British Manuel of Military Law and 'could be disregarded by belligerents'. There were other fishy aspects to the Royal Warrant that had been taken from Nuremberg Law: the accused was not allowed to know the charges nor what evidence was adduced against him; he could not challenge the authority or jurisdiction of the court; he could not insist on being tried by his peers – and was generally subjected to the judgments of those holding inferior rank and therefore diminished responsibility. The Royal Warrant disregarded the long-established rules of evidence and admitted hearsay. The statements of hearsay witnesses were not only given credence, the witnesses were not summoned and could not be cross-examined. There was no right of appeal.[14]

Paget also made it clear that the defendants remained prisoners of war, because Britain had not brought hostilities to an end. As POWs they could demand particular treatment. POWs had rights in international law: the captor had to treat them as well as he did his own troops and subject them to the same law as he would apply towards his own men.[15]

Interrogations

Before the German war criminals could be put on trial they needed to be apprehended and interrogated. The British, for example, possessed a remarkable collection of Nazi-hunters. They included men who later achieved fame in other spheres, such as Robert Maxwell[16] and the historian Hugh Trevor-Roper. The interrogations and the accumulated details of Nazi crimes had another role – they could be used against the German population. Trevor-Roper was compiling his report for British intelligence at the time. It was published as *The Last Days of Hitler* and was considered to be excellent propaganda for the Allied cause. Trevor-Roper hardly needed to be encouraged to belittle the Nazi leadership and show the Germans how foolish they had been to follow them.*

* Information from Blair Worden, August 2004: Worden is Lord Dacre's literary executer. *The Last Days of Hitler* was not intended for publication and Trevor-Roper was surprised when British intelligence consented. Any interrogations he carried out were concerned with the report. They had nothing to do with collecting evidence for Nuremberg or other trials.

Maxwell was a Czech Jew and many of those employed to find the Nazis were Jews from Germany and Austria. They had the ability to interrogate Germans in their own language, and in many instances they felt a real sense of motivation in their work. These included Peter A. Alexander, a former bank clerk from Vienna. Major Frederick Warner (formerly Manfred Werner from Hamburg) and Lieutenant-Colonel Bryant (Breuer) formed part of an eighty-man team that arrested, among many others, the chief of Bremen's Gestapo Dr Schweder. They left him in the hands of a group of RAF officers, who he thought would treat him relatively kindly. They did not, and staged a mock trial in the best Gestapo tradition, so that Schweder thought his last hour had come. When Warner returned Schweder was overjoyed to see him.[17]

Peter Jackson (formerly Jacobus) was responsible for arresting the Auschwitz commandant Rudolf Höss, having tracked him down to a farmhouse kitchen where he was hiding. His superior officers were aware that Jackson's mother had been killed in Auschwitz, but they still believed he was the only man for the job of interrogating the prisoner. The revulsion Jackson felt towards Höss could be overcome only by drinking large quantities of whisky. He was allegedly drunk for a week.[18]

Former Pioneer Anton Freud was the man who captured Dr Tesch, who had produced the gas for the 'showers' at Auschwitz. Freud's team also apprehended Himmler's deputy, Oswald Pohl, who was delivered to Nuremberg and condemned to death. Fred Pelican (born Friedrich Pelikan in Poland) was the man who caught Hans Esser, the Nazi leader in Neuss in Silesia. Flight Sergeant Wieselmann was involved in the search for the killers of the fifty British airmen who were shot after the Great Escape. A Sergeant Portman worked on the dossier concerning the deaths of 7,000 Jews who had died while being transferred from one concentration camp to another.

One Nazi who particularly interested the British was William Joyce, the American-born, half-Irish fascist who was known to all and sundry as Lord Haw Haw. He had fled from Hamburg and was living in an inn near the Danish border with his wife. On 28 May 1945 two British officers were searching for kindling in the local wood. Joyce, who was doing much the same, couldn't resist giving them a hand, and shouted to them in French, telling them where they might find some pieces of wood. He then repeated himself in English: 'There are a few more pieces here.' His voice was instantly recognised. 'You wouldn't happen to be William Joyce, would you?' Joyce put his hand in his pocket. The officer thought he was going to draw a gun and shot him in the leg. Joyce groaned that his name was

Fritz Hansen (his forged German papers said his name was *Wilhelm* *Hansen*), but he was still carrying his military passport, which had him down as William Joyce. He was taken back to Britain, where with doubtful legality he was tried for treason and hanged in Wandsworth Prison.[19]

Despite the huge dragnet and the large forces at the Allies' disposal, very few of the top Nazis were executed. Many of the most important ones like Hitler and Goebbels killed themselves before capture. Others managed to commit suicide in captivity. A surprisingly large number of leading Nazis were able to take poison behind bars, posing the question whether the Allies turned a blind eye to such things. In his memoirs, Franz von Papen claims that he was offered means to take his own life on two occasions, both times by American guards.[20]

Himmler, the most important war criminal after Adolf Hitler, never reached the courts. He had been spurned by Dönitz and issued instructions to the leading SS men around him to disappear while he lay low in Flensburg with his mistress and their children. The leading lights of the SS were provided with false papers and cyanide capsules. Himmler himself assumed the identity of Sergeant Heinrich Hitzinger of the Field Service Police, a man whom he had had executed for defeatism. He shaved off his moustache and, putting a patch over one eye, set out to join the Werewolves in Bavaria. Unfortunately for Himmler the Allies had outlawed the Field Service Police, and on 21 May the British picked him up halfway between Hamburg and Bremen.

The British failed to recognise him. Eventually Himmler revealed his identity himself. He still thought he had something to offer the Western Allies, and asked for a meeting with Montgomery or Churchill. At Second Army HQ at Barfeld he was strip-searched. A Captain Selvester found two brass tubes on him. It is not altogether clear why they did not search his mouth. Selvester alerted Montgomery's intelligence chief Colonel Michael Murphy. Murphy decreed that the formal interrogation should not begin before he arrived. Selvester ordered some thick cheese sandwiches for the prisoner and watched him as he ate. An intelligence officer could not resist taunting Himmler with some photographs of corpses taken at Buchenwald. Himmler shrugged him off: 'Am I responsible for the excesses committed by my subordinates?'[21] It was an extraordinary response: of course he was.

Himmler was brought a change of clothes, but he refused to don a British army uniform, preferring to wrap himself in a blanket. He was still insisting he wanted to see Montgomery or Churchill. Colonel Murphy arrived at eight and had Himmler bundled into his car. Murphy handled him roughly and called him a 'bastard'. He was driven to a villa outside Lüneburg and ordered to strip again by a Sergeant-Major Austin. Himmler responded by saying, 'He does not know who I am.' Austin replied, 'Oh yes I do: you're Himmler. *Ausziehen!*' Himmler was then examined by Dr C. J. L. Wells, who noticed the phial in his mouth. Himmler was too quick for them, however, and was able to flick the phial out with his tongue and crack it. There were attempts to save him, but the effect of the poison was immediate. Himmler died just after 11.00 p.m. on 23 May. He was buried in an unmarked grave on the Heath two days later.[22]

Göring took a long time to realise that the Allies were not going to treat him, or anyone else for that matter, according to the rules that had governed VIP prisoners in previous wars. On 7 May 1945 US forces commanded by Brigadier Robert Stack were searching for him around Mauterndorf[*] in Austria, where he possessed one of many mansions. The Görings were still half convinced that they were going to be shot after Hermann had tried to wrest authority from the Führer in the bunker. There was a large SS guard with them. The Americans and Göring were converging on Fischhorn Castle near Zell-am-See, which had been requisitioned for the latter's use.[†] Here Göring was hoping to negotiate with Eisenhower. When the Americans arrived, Göring was still bogged down in traffic in a car laden with his monogrammed pigskin suitcases.

He had been out of touch with reality of late. He had badly overplayed his hand with Hitler, and persisted in believing that Eisenhower would deal with him directly. The Americans were generally courteous for the time being, and Göring posed for photographers in Kitzbühl the next day. Some said he had been seen talking to American officers on the balcony of the Grand Hotel with a champagne glass in his hand.[23] He was encouraged to blab about other Nazi leaders at informal gatherings. This was part of the process of softening up the prisoner. He was still cross with Hitler for ordering his arrest and described him as narrow-minded and ignorant. Ribbentrop – never his favourite – was a scoundrel, and Hess an eccentric. It was not until the 10th that he came face to face with General Spaatz, the commander of the US air force. Then the Americans took him into the

---

[*] Göring had been left the medieval castle by Hermann von Epenstein, the Jewish doctor who was his mother's lover and Hermann's godfather. Hermann's Christian name was most probably in homage to the doctor and freshly minted nobleman. David Irving, *Göring: A Biography*, London 1989, 26–7.

[†] The castle was owned by Hermann Fegelein's brother Waldemar. Hitler's brother-in-law Hermann Fegelein had been executed in the Chancellery garden a few days before. The castle was teeming with further SS men, something calculated to make Göring no more comfortable.

kitchen and stripped him of his medals and insignia, leaving him only his epaulettes. He was housed in a prison compound for high-ranking Nazis, with a tall black soldier posted outside his door.

He discovered Robert Kempner among the American officers. Kempner had been in Police Department 1a, the political police that had sired the Gestapo. He had been sacked by Rudolf Diels in January 1933, and as a Jew he then thought it prudent to leave. Göring must have realised that Kempner would be a powerful adversary. The Americans asked him about the concentration camps. The man who had nominally hosted the Wannsee Conference denied all knowledge. He pointed out that Hitler had been deranged at the end of his life. He later denied that he had ever signed a death warrant or sent anyone to a concentration camp.* Shown pictures of Dachau he blamed Himmler.[24]

The robber-in-chief now had the disagreeable experience of being robbed himself. US army engineers discovered his picture collection in Berchtesgaden: works by Rembrandt, Rubens, Van Dyck, Boucher and Botticelli were all hauled out. One Rembrandt bought in Paris in 1940 turned out to be a fake. French Moroccan soldiers had already pilfered some of his jewellery; a GI stole his field marshal's baton, which was intercepted at customs and eventually found its way into the collection at West Point; his 1935 wedding sword was stolen by a platoon sergeant who placed it in a bank vault in Indiana. Later his wife Emmy was defrauded of an emerald ring by a sergeant who came to tell her that Göring was about to be released.[25]

Prison Walls

On 20 May 1945 Göring was flown to Mondorf-les-Bains in Luxembourg to join fifty-two other Nazi big fish in 'Ashcan', Allied Supreme Headquarters Centre for Axis Nationals. The gloves were off: Göring was treated with scant respect when the aircraft landed. He was struck by the monotonous movements of the GIs' jaws churning up their chewing gum.[26] The prisoners were strip-searched for poison and weapons, and anything of value to them was taken away. The first to arrive had been Arthur Seyss-Inquart, who had succeeded Kurt von Schuschnigg as chancellor at the

---

* In June 1940, Göring told Hitler he had had two Catholic priests sent to a concentration camp because they had failed to rise when he entered a Rhineland inn. He gave orders that they should have to give the Nazi salute to one of his old caps every day. Henrik Eberle and Matthias Uhl, eds, *Das Buch Hitler*, Bergisch Gladbach 2004, 123.

Anschluss, and had later been Reich commissioner of Holland. He had been responsible for throwing all the leading Austrian non-Nazis – including a sizeable number of government ministers – into Dachau and beginning the persecution of the Jews.* In Holland he bore responsibility for the deportation of most of the Jews. Hans Frank was next, much the worse for wear after slashing his wrists. He had been the governor general of Poland who proclaimed his mission to be ridding 'Poland of lice and Jews'.[27] Göring was reunited with Frank, Bohle, Brandt, Daluege, Darré, Frick, Funk, Jodl, Keitel, Ley, Ribbentrop, Rosenberg and Streicher. The Americans dubbed him 'fat stuff'. Three days later there was a fresh delivery: Admiral Dönitz arrived together with Speer. Speer did not stay long. He was flown to Eisenhower's HQ at Versailles and then to the British-run interrogation centre named 'Dustbin' in the medieval castle of Burg Kransberg in the Taunus. Here he received a visit from Hugh Trevor-Roper, who was then researching his *Last Days of Hitler*. They seem to have got on: in the summer of 1947 Trevor-Roper sent a copy of the book to Speer for his comments.[28]

Franz von Papen was delivered to Mondorf in May 1945, but he was not considered important enough for the Grand Hotel, where the leading Nazis were lodged, and went to a smaller establishment next door instead. He had been pushed further and further out of the nest, as ambassador to Austria before the Anschluss and then as ambassador to Turkey. He was still claiming to be surprised that he had been arrested at all. He had been housed in some comfort in a château near Spa in Belgium where he had the Hungarian regent Admiral Horthy for a cellmate.[†] Horthy also accompanied him to Mondorf.[29] Papen and Horthy's regime was Spartan, and the elderly regent's health began to suffer. Papen claims in his autobiography that he tore the notorious American gaoler Colonel Andrus off a strip for maltreating a head of state. Papen's prison was beginning to establish itself as the place for the B-stream Nazis. Soon they were joined by Schwerin von Krosigk and the Freiherr von Steengracht from the German Foreign Office. There were now six to a room. Papen tried to pin Andrus down on the subject of the Hague Convention governing prisoners of war. Andrus shook him off, but permis-

---

* Those who had enforced the ban on the NSDAP were singled out for particularly harsh treatment: politicians, judges and the guards at the Corporate State's own concentration camp at Wöllersdorf in Lower Austria. The hangman who had executed the Nazi participants in the assassination of chancellor Dolfuss in 1934 did not survive the first night in Dachau. See Bruno Heilig, *Men Crucified*, London 1941.

† Horthy had been Hitler's ally, but Hitler had had him deposed after he started negotiating with the Allies. One reason why the two fell out was Horthy's refusal to 'deport' Hungary's large Jewish population. Hitler had him interned in 1944. He did not return to Hungary and died in Estoril, Portugal in 1957.

sion was swiftly granted to write letters. On 15 June Joachim von Ribbentrop was brought in. He had been tracked down in a bed and breakfast in Hamburg, having spent six weeks on the run, during which he had composed a letter to the British government. He was arrested after a tip-off on the 14th. A British lieutenant found him in bed, dressed in pink and white pyjamas.

The old rivalries and hatreds persisted. There was a ridiculous adherence to correct forms of address. Even after the sentences were pronounced, Speer would ask the former deputy Party leader, 'What did you get, *Herr* Hess?'[30] Göring could not abide Ribbentrop, Speer or Dönitz. With Dönitz the feeling was clearly mutual. Once when Göring was complaining that his lot was the worst, because he had more to lose, Dönitz acidly remarked, 'Yes, and all of it stolen!' Göring was interrogated by Major Hiram Gans and Lieutenant Herbert Dubois. Dubois asked him if he were ashamed of the milliard-mark fine imposed on the Jews in 1938. Göring expressed his muted regrets: 'You have to take the times into account.' He soon got the hang of how to deal with the interrogations. When a Russian team arrived to prepare their case he had them roaring with laughter.[31]

The Trials

The Allies were now finalising the procedure for the war-crimes trials that were to be held in Nuremberg. On 8 August the 'London Statute' was drawn up and signed by Justice Jackson from the United States, the future Lord Chancellor Sir David Maxwell Fyfe from Britain, Professor Gros from France and General Nikitchenko from the Soviet Union. (Nikitchenko started out as prosecutor and later served as a hanging judge.) It was hardly difficult to tear holes in the text: there were four different powers with four different ideas of law. One of the nations prosecuting was as totalitarian as Nazi Germany had been. There was little hope for the defendants: the prosecution had all the advantages, the defence all the disadvantages; and there was to be no questioning of the competence of the tribunal. Article 6 contained the meat – the court had the right to condemn persons, either as individuals or as members of organisations, for crimes against peace and conspiracy to wage war, war crimes and crimes against humanity. These had not, of course, been crimes when they were committed, nor were any of the prosecuting powers immune from accusations of this sort – particularly Soviet Russia. When the defendants brought this up the response of the court's president Lord Justice Lawrence was to say, 'We are not interested in what the Allies may have done.'[32]

Article 9 ruled that carrying out orders was not an excuse; evidence of atrocity by a member of an organisation would be taken as evidence of the criminal nature of the organisation. The defendants at Nuremberg were mostly intelligent men, and there was a fair smattering of jurists among them. Naturally they protested, but it was cogently impressed upon them that they might just as easily have been put up against a wall.

Although the Allies had plenty of time to prepare their cases, a lot of their accusations proved groundless, or they were obliged to let a major criminal go free for want of evidence. Papen was still falsely accused of being a member of the Party even when the Americans were in possession of the full Nazi Party membership archive. The case against him was that he had conspired to wage aggressive war, which was a difficult one to prove given that he was nowhere near the inner circle of the regime, and came within inches of losing his life during the 1934 Röhm Putsch, the so-called Night of the Long Knives. His real crime was folly – believing that Hitler could be contained. He was by no means alone in this.

Papen and his friend Horthy had not yet understood the new post-war world. Horthy composed a letter to Churchill pleading for the maintenance of a 'big' Hungary with access to the sea as a bulwark against Bolshevism. There was no reply. In August the inhabitants of the annexe were transferred to a wing of the Grand Hotel. Horthy was sent away. Papen now found himself together with the major Nazis, and reflected on how different they looked in their shabby beltless uniforms and worn-out laceless shoes to the last time he had seen them all strutting about at a rally in Nuremberg in 1937. Nuremberg was also where they were now heading. The party was taken to Luxembourg aerodrome.

Göring was housed in a proper prison cell in the courthouse now, as opposed to a maid's room in Mondorf. He was watched at all hours of the day. Humiliations were arranged for him, such as a formal discharge from the German armed forces (arranged by the Americans), which had the effect of bringing on a minor heart attack. The Allies turned up the heat during the interrogations, but Göring was given a defence lawyer in Otto Stahmer from a short list of jurists who had managed to keep their noses relatively clean during the Third Reich. It should be added that few of them were entirely clean: the list contained 206 names, of whom 136 had been Pgs and 10 were former members of the SS. One, Rudolf Dix, had been president of the Nazi bar association; another, Ernst Aschenbach, had been an expert in deportation attached to the Paris embassy.[33] Stahmer was a patent lawyer. Papen chose a Breslau lawyer called Kubuschok, with Papen's own son acting as his junior. Speer made a wise choice in Hans

Flächsner, a diminutive Berliner who gave him useful advice, telling him not to over-dramatise his role in the Third Reich and pointing out that the Allies had already decided he was only a minor criminal and that he was not to put on the airs of a major one. Speer was probably right in believing he owed a deal of his salvation to Flächsner. Being contrite, or undergoing religious conversion, availed the prisoners little. Both Frank and Seyss-Inquart showed contrition. Both were hanged.[34]

To Papen's horror he chanced upon Horthy again on one of his weekly trips to the showers. Papen was beginning to learn something of the charges against him: he had instituted the terrible People's Courts, which had been set up after the acquittal of the Bulgarian communist Dimitrov. It was not a charge that was likely to stick. The Americans were understandably baffled that Papen had continued to serve the Nazis after the Röhm Putsch, when his speechwriters were murdered for writing an anti-Nazi speech for him.[35] Another who claimed that he had no idea why he was there was Dönitz. Hitler's successor stressed that it was not for generals to take decisions to go to war, and had he refused to carry out his orders 'he would have received the heaviest punishment'. He was also charged with using concentration-camp inmates as workers in his dockyards.[36] The charge was pretty pharisaic, given that the Allies had millions of POWs working as slaves for them at the time of the trial.

John Dos Passos arrived in Nuremberg on 19 November 1945 to cover the trials. The arrangements in the courthouse were compact. For the spectators and journalists the facilities were good, and they had their own post office and a smart snack bar.[37] The chief defendants were housed in the basement and brought up in a lift. Then it was just a few steps down the corridor to the courtroom.[38] There was a consolation for Göring, at last: at Nuremberg he regained his supremacy. He was number one on the list, meaning that he was the first into the dock with a seat on the front bench at the extreme right facing the judges. The hated Bormann – tried *in absentia* – was down at number nineteen and Speer at twenty-two. Dönitz had been positioned at a measly fourteen.

His neighbour in the dock was Rudolf Hess, who was flown from England to Nuremberg on 8 October. After his mysterious flight in May 1941, Hess had been incarcerated in Britain. He was now brought home for the gathering of the clans. The frugality of prison life in Nuremberg came as a shock to him after the relative comfort of his confinement in Britain. He was pretending to have lost his memory and stared stonily at everyone who tried to remind him of details of his distinguished past. He later announced that he had been acting all along: 'Good wasn't I? I really surprised everyone, don't you think?' he asked his fellow inmates. Despite being officially *compos mentis* Hess still paid no attention to the court. He would not wear the headphones, but read books and chatted throughout the proceedings.[39]

As Hess could not be indicted for most of the juicier atrocities committed by the regime (which had taken place while he was in British captivity), he was given the Streicher treatment and tried for conspiracy against peace and humanity – a charge concocted for Nazi leaders who were earmarked for long detention or execution, and who had been essentially condemned before they entered the dock. His crimes were not great by comparison to some: he was tangentially involved in the drafting of the antisemitic Nuremberg Laws and with the invasion of Poland. Göring laughed off many of the Allied accusations. He swiftly dealt with an attempt to foist responsibility for the Reichstag Fire on him, and the interrogator, Kempner, did not raise the matter again. Göring might well have begun to waver when he learned that the Americans had arrested his wife Emmy in October and put his daughter Edda in an orphanage (although she was later allowed to join her mother in Straubing Prison). Emmy was not a political figure. She and Edda were eventually released when the Americans realised that this sort of *Sippenhaft* – a method favoured by the Nazis – would not make it easier to justify their cases before the courts.

Göring stood his ground, however. He had a positive attitude towards life and for the time being was not tempted to follow the examples of some others: Ley managed to strangle himself with the hem of a wet towel attached to a lavatory cistern, and the mass-murderer Dr Leonardo Conti also killed himself, leaving a note saying he had lied under oath to cover up his knowledge of medical experiments.[40] Field Marshal Werner von Blomberg died of a heart attack in March 1946.* In 1948, General Johannes Blaskowitz committed suicide by jumping from the third storey of the prison block.†

In all this gloom Göring might have taken heart at the news that his IQ

---

* Blomberg had been out of the picture since January 1938, and had not even played a role in the Anschluss. Hitler managed to push him out of the way when it was discovered that he had married a former prostitute. His conscience cannot have been said to be clear, however, as it was he who brought the army in behind Hitler, in recompense for the murder of Röhm and the others who would have had the SA take over from the traditional Wehrmacht. The Night of the Long Knives had seen the killing of army officers as well, but Blomberg was happy to celebrate its success with a slap-up meal with Göring at Horcher's restaurant in Berlin.

† Blaskowitz's suicide is odd for the fact that he was one of the few generals to file a formal complaint about the activities of the SS, in this case after the invasion of Poland. There was a rumour that he did not take his life at all, but was murdered by SS men.

was placed third among the remaining Nazi prisoners, exceeded only by Schacht and Seyss-Inquart.[41]* The time of surveys ceased, however, when on 19 October 1945 Göring and the others were served their indictments by none other than Major Airey Neave, a British intelligence officer who had successfully escaped from Colditz and who would later become a member of Mrs Thatcher's shadow cabinet.[†] German civilians took a muted interest in the show trials. Göring may have impressed the court, but little of this seeped out to the German population. Such reports as there were of the trials were heavily censored. The radio broadcasts delivered by a Gaston Oulman every night were confined to the more sensational aspects of the prosecution's case.[42] In Berlin, Ruth Friedrich thought the indictments had little relevance to 'good Germans' but she approved, as it gave heart to the Allies. 'Not so much for us, but for the farmer in Oklahoma, who wants to make sense of his son's missing leg.'[43]

Papen had finally learned that he was charged with conspiracy to wage war. Dos Passos, who arrived on the day before the trials were to start, heard an address from Colonel Andrus, in which he regretted to inform the press that the former SD chief Kaltenbrunner was ill and would miss the first day. He seemed disappointed that he had not managed to keep all of them fighting fit for the première. Frick was paralysed in his left wrist after a suicide attempt, but Göring was in better health than he'd been in twenty years, having lost weight and been weaned off drug addiction.[44] The trial of the major war criminals began at 10 a.m. on 20 November. The president of the court Lord Justice Lawrence was assisted by Francis Biddle from the US, and his deputy John J. Parker. From France came Professor Henri Donnedieu de Vabres, who scribbled away silently throughout the trial without ever uttering a word. The Germans had a particular contempt for General Nikitchenko, the one judge who disdained the use of the gown, and wore his military uniform through-out: 'We knew what his verdict would be, with or without a trial.'[45]

Dos Passos sized up the prisoners in the dock: Göring looked like a 'leaky balloon', 'a fat man who has lost a good deal of weight'. Ribbentrop was a 'defaulting bank cashier', Schacht, 'an angry walrus'. The former head of the Luftwaffe was still 'the master of ceremonies . . . Nero must have had a face like that'; while Hess paid 'no attention to anything'.[46]

---

* Papen remembered things differently: *he* was third, after Schacht and Speer. Streicher came last, 'a position which could have been occupied by almost any of the other Gauleiters'. (Franz von Papen, *Memoirs*, London 1952, 547.) Speer, on the other hand, recalled that it was Seyss who had won the intelligence competition. He modestly concealed his own place in the line-up. (Albert Speer, *Spandau: The Secret Diaries*, London 1976, 9.)

† He was murdered by the IRA in 1979.

The charges were read out and Jackson made a speech in which he offered the estimate that 5.7 million Jews had lost their lives as a result of Nazi orders. Most of the defendants claimed they knew nothing of this. Schacht advanced the ingenious argument that he had been helping the Jews to emigrate by framing legislation that would rob them; Streicher claimed to be a Zionist, which, in a way, he was.[47] During the recess Göring was asked who had issued those orders. Göring replied, 'Himmler, I suppose.'[48] The camps came back to haunt them: films were shown of their victims. The psychiatrists Kelly and Gilbert took notes as the defendants watched scenes of civilians being burned in a barn. Hess was captivated, others tried to look away; Frank choked back tears; Funk actually shed some at the sight of the crematorium ovens. When Hess muttered disbelief, Göring told him to shut up.[49]

Göring indulged in a few jokes. There was a strong Jewish presence at Nuremberg in the form of jurists attached to the army, translators and interpreters. At one stage he spotted a group of Jews in the public gallery and whispered: 'Look at them, nobody can say we have exterminated them all!'[50] He was outraged by the testimony of Lahousen, the Austrian Abwehr chief, who spoke on 30 November, giving details of the plans to kill Hitler. Göring blurted out, 'That's one we have forgotten to knock off after 20 July 1944.'[51] The leading Nazis could not shake off the accusations levelled against them for the very reason that they had been slack about destroying the evidence – too many papers had lain around at the end of the Thousand-Year Reich. The other problem was the officials and SS men who were prepared to give evidence against them. Turning 'king's evidence' for the prosecution was a way of saving your life for the time being. Some of the worst criminals even stayed out of prison while they made themselves available to the courts.[52]

The apparently honest statements of the state secretaries Bühler and Steengracht were particularly damning, as well as those of the SS men Ohlendorf, Wisliceny, Höttl, Höss and Pohl. One man who outraged all the main defendants was Erich von dem Bach-Zelewski, possibly the most brutal of the police generals, and one who was perfectly aware of the crimes he was committing.[53] He may have just been buying a sort of freedom (he died in a prison hospital in Munich in 1972). Before 1949 he appeared as a prosecution witness no fewer than twenty times, earning Göring's loud condemnation as a 'Schweinehund!'

That opening day was also notable for the surprise announcement from Hess that he wished to take responsibility for his actions, and that he had never lost his memory, he had been pretending all along. Hess was a puzzle even to his own colleagues. Papen confessed that he didn't know if he were sane or not. He thought he had been *compos mentis* at the time of the flight to Britain. During the trial he read novels by the Bavarian writer Ganghofer. Göring, with support from his old enemy Ribbentrop and from Rosenberg, persisted in his claim that the court had no authority and that the British and Americans were equally guilty of infringing international law. He was occasionally seen plotting with Hess. Like the other prisoners, he gave Streicher a wide berth. He was contemptuous of Hans Frank, who had been smitten with religion since his incarceration and was much given to tears – he had been behind the brutal treatment of the Poles. Göring claimed to be shocked by what he now learned of the camps, and declared that the story was incredible. But we also know that he tried to save people from the camps, so it was pretty clear he knew that something nasty went on there.[54]

Göring could not claim so easily that he had had no knowledge of the killings that took place on the Night of the Long Knives in 1934. It had been chiefly his party. He dismissed Röhm, however, as a 'dirty homosexual swine' and justified himself by saying it was them or him. As Speer and others sought to atone for their roles in the mass murders, or claimed a dubious role in opposition, or – like Paulus – chose to implicate Hitler and his gang in monstrous crimes, Göring started to talk about honour. He didn't care whether he lived or died, but he was not going to grovel before the court. He urged the generals to be equally resolute. He said they were all going to be treated as martyrs before too long, and their bodies set up in mausolea like Napoleon's.

When the defendants were shown a Soviet film of German atrocities, Göring yawned and scoffed. With a little justification he pointed out that the Russians did not necessarily occupy the moral high ground. As it turns out, he was right to be scornful: the Soviet film showed images of Katyn, and the mortal remains of a large element of the Polish officer corps, murdered not by the Germans but by the NKVD. (The massacre was part of the Soviet indictment.) He was, nonetheless, appalled by the images he had seen.[55]

The defendants all took the trial very differently. Jodl was calm and soldierly, and awaited his fate. Seyss-Inquart thought he would be acquitted, and told Viennese stories. The one thing that disturbed him was the knowledge that Hitler had appointed him in his will to replace Ribbentrop. Frank admitted his guilt and spent his time in meditation. He, Papen, Seyss-Inquart and Kaltenbrunner were regular in their attendance at Mass. Ribbentrop continued to write long letters in self-justification; Rosenberg made pencil-sketches of the witnesses; Streicher let out cries and screams during the night. To the end he maintained that the trial was the triumph of world Jewry.[56] Of the service chiefs Keitel remained his pompous self, pleading not guilty to the indictment, but Dönitz and Raeder – who had been turned over by the Soviet authorities in a rare gesture of co-operation – conducted themselves with dignity, as did Neurath.[57]

The prosecution opened its case against Hess on 7 February 1946. Göring took the stand at last on 13 March, and remained in the dock until the 22nd. He had waited five months for his moment. He put on a fine performance and refused either to grovel before the court or to deny his role in the 'movement'. He gaily quoted Winston Churchill's line, 'In the struggle for life and death there is, in the end, no legality.'[58] He took responsibility for everything he could, thereby removing much of the case against Papen, for example, when he claimed that the Anschluss had been his show.[59] Asked about some aspect of mobilisation, Göring answered that the Americans had so far kept quiet about their own strategic plans. The Americans now began to doubt the wisdom of this sort of public trial. Göring was in danger of becoming a hero again. Even the American press reported. 'Göring wins first round.'[60]

There was a reluctance among the Allies to produce witnesses for the defence, and it took them a while to locate Göring's chief of staff, Koller, even though he was in British captivity.[61] The British proved more successful at badgering Göring than the Americans had been. Under Sir David Maxwell Fyfe's cross-examination he began to sweat. The British case hinged on the shooting of the fifty airmen after the so-called Great Escape – a terrible crime and a contravention of the Geneva Convention, but one that looks peripheral now compared to others perpetrated by the Nazis. They had been shot on Emmy's birthday. Göring may well have known nothing about it, but that hardly absolved the Luftwaffe chief of the ultimate responsibility for the crime.[62]

One of the Nazis who dramatically turned his coat at Nuremberg was Frank, the governor of the Polish General Gouvernement. Many of the most repulsive acts of grisly murder and cruelty had occurred on his beat, even if it was not necessarily true that the murderers were in any way responsible to him. When asked if he had participated, however, he replied with a clear 'Yes'. It had been the testimony of Höss, he said, that had made him want to take the responsibility on to himself: 'My conscience does not allow me to throw the responsibility solely on these minor people. I myself have never installed a concentration camp for Jews, or promoted the existence of such camps; but if Adolf Hitler personally laid that dreadful responsibility on his people, then it is mine too, for we have fought Jewry for years; and we have indulged the most terrible utterances – my own diary bears witness against me . . . A thousand years will pass and still this guilt of Germany will not have been erased.'[63]

The atrocities in the concentration camps nettled even the most obstinate Nazis. After the camp commandant Rudolf Höss had given his testimony Göring turned to Raeder and Jodl and said, 'If only there weren't this damned Auschwitz! Himmler got us into that mess. If it weren't for Auschwitz we could put up a proper defence. The way it is our chances are blocked. Whenever our names are mentioned, everybody thinks of nothing but Auschwitz or Treblinka. It's like a reflex.'[64]

Some of Göring's greatest crimes were not even mentioned in the indictment. Nowhere did the Allies make mention of the bombing of Warsaw, Rotterdam, London or Coventry. The Soviets, who had not possessed the capacity to bomb Germany with the same ferocity as the Anglo-Americans, had wanted to bring the matter up, but it was vetoed by the West. For good reason, thought Speer: 'The ruins around the courthouse demonstrate all too plainly how cruelly and effectively the Western Allies on their part extended the war to non-combatants.'[65]

Göring addressed the court for the last time on 31 August 1946. He reiterated the precept of *nulla poena sine lege* and declared that the German people were ignorant of crime and 'free from blame'. He would expiate their guilt with his martyrdom.[66] Less dramatically perhaps, he reminded the court of his efforts to negotiate a peace in 1939 – behind Hitler's back. More and more was leaking out from the courts. It was not just the Germans who were shocked. In Bendorf in the Rhineland, Elena Skrjabina thought the whole process hypocritical, and the bench's impartiality compromised by the judges from her own land. On 1 September she wrote:

> Recently the Nuremberg trials have been creating great interest. Now they are over. The accused have been most severely punished and rightly so. However, who were the judges? When I think that the most savage measures of punishment were being demanded by the representatives of the Soviet Union, I cannot help but feel oppressed by the injustice of it all. Indeed, the Soviet Authorities have destroyed and are right now destroying millions of their own people for nothing whatsoever. No other country in the world has so many jails and camps.[67]

The French academic Robert d'Harcourt had no reason to love the Germans, having had two sons pass through Buchenwald. He was even harder hitting in his accusation of hypocrisy: the Germans 'are not angry with the fliers who destroyed their towns today, it is the judges. By their attempts to forcibly convert them the Allies have lost most of the moral high ground that they had obtained through victory. To take on the role of Solomon presupposes a moral qualification. It is this moral authority that the vanquished no longer recognise in the victors.'[68]

The summing up began on 30 September. The judges rehearsed the entire history of the Third Reich, giving the impression that the trial was entirely political. It was Lord Justice Lawrence who read out the sentences: his speech lasted a day and a half. The defendants slept ill that night. Lawrence began with Göring, who was found guilty on all four counts and sentenced to death on 1 October. Apart from Hess – who was given life – similar sentences were meted out to those seated on the front bench until the judge reached Schacht. Göring flinched when Schacht was acquitted, then slammed down the earphones in disgust. Hess was not wearing his earphones and later told Speer that he had assumed he had been awarded the death penalty, but he had not bothered to listen.[69] In the back row there were custodial sentences for Dönitz and Raeder, then came Papen, who was also acquitted. In Berlin 25,000 workers downed tools in protest when they heard the news about Papen.[70] The Russians still insisted he was an important Nazi.

Göring's counsel entered a plea in mitigation, again mentioning his efforts to maintain peace in 1939 – moves that must have been known to the British government at least. The British had no desire to modify the sentence, and the government issued an instruction to Sir Sholto Douglas in Berlin that such a thing would not be politically expedient. As it was, the Soviet judge, Nikitchenko, had called for the three acquitted men, Schacht, Papen and Goebbel's deputy propaganda chief Hans Fritzsche, to be convicted, and wanted the death sentence for Hess.[71] Schacht had been liberated because his role in the expropriation of the Jews was a pre-war internal matter, but Streicher had been sacked as Gauleiter of Franconia in 1940 and banned from public speaking two years before. Fritzsche believed he had been tried because Goebbels was not around to take the rap.

After the sentences those on 'death row' were creamed off – Göring, Ribbentrop, Keitel, Jodl, Streicher, Sauckel, Frick, Rosenberg, Seyss-Inquart, Frank and Kaltenbrunner. The cellar of the courthouse emptied, leaving the condemned men to themselves. The seven men who were eventually to be transferred to Spandau Prison in the British Sector of Berlin were provided with new cells upstairs: Hess, the economics minister and Reichsbank chief Walter Funk, the Grand Admirals Dönitz and Raeder, the Hitler Youth leader Baldur von Schirach, the former foreign minister and 'protector' of Bohemia and Moravia Constantin von Neurath and Speer. They had been given sentences ranging from ten years to life.

Göring cheated the executioners by taking cyanide from a phial he had managed to conceal from his guards. One of the reasons he gave for his choice of end in the note he left in his cell was the Allied decision to film the deaths of their prisoners. The gallows equipment arrived at Nuremberg on the night of 13 October. The next day hammering could be heard from the gymnasium, and the slave-driver Fritz Sauckel had begun to scream. In the absence of Göring, the other Nazis went to their deaths at the appointed hour on the 16th. Ribbentrop was now the leader. The hang-man botched the execution and the rope throttled the former foreign minister for twenty minutes before he expired. The others died as planned.* Speer could hear them being collected from their cells: 'scraps of phrases, scraping of boots, and reverberating footsteps slowly fading away'. When Streicher's name was called, someone cried, 'Bravo, Streicher!' Speer thought it was Hess. As they went to their deaths, the others shouted words of defiance. Keitel's last utterance was 'Alles für Deutschland. Deutschland über alles' (All for Germany, Germany above all else). Ribbentrop, Jodl and Seyss-Inquart said something similar. Streicher chanted, 'Heil Hitler! This is the Purim Festival† of 1946!'[72] The bodies were photographed. On 16 October they were taken to a house at 25 Heimannstrasse in Munich-Solln which the Americans had been using as a mortuary. They were inspected by Allied teams before they were cre-mated. The ashes were scattered into the Conwentzbach seventy-five metres downhill from the house – a muddy, Bavarian ditch. The cremated were entered in the books under false names: Hermann Göring was Georg Munger, and the scourge of the Jews, Julius Streicher, received the name of Abraham Goldberg.[73]

The next morning the seven men they left behind to serve out their sentences were called to clean out the cells. Speer observed the remains of the last meal in their mess tins. Papers and blankets were strewn about. Only in Jodl's cell was everything in apple-pie order, the blankets neatly folded. On Seyss's wall he noted that the former Austrian chancellor had put a cross on the calendar for the 16th, the day of his death. In the after-noon Speer, Schirach and Hess were handed brooms and mops and sent into the gym where the men had been hanged. The scaffold had already been taken down, but – spotting a mark on the floor he took to be a bloodstain – Hess stood to attention and raised his arm in a Nazi salute.[74]

---

* The *Berliner Zeitung* reported that it had taken Ribbentrop 14 minutes 45 seconds to die, and Jodl a little longer. Ruth Andreas Friedrich, *Schauplatz Berlin*, Frankfurt/Main 1985, 148.
† A spring festival to commemorate a plot to massacre the Jews.

17

The Little Fish

A Prosecutor cannot also be a judge . . .
    Justice is by its nature light, which also renders the shadows starker.
The less passion is reflected in its source, the clearer the crime emerges
in its hideousness.

Ernst Jünger, *Der Friede*, Vienna 1949, 50, 51

Lesser Nuremberg Trials

The Allies put a brave face on it, but the International Military Tribunal had not been deemed a success and it was put in mothballs. Robert Jackson was 'thoroughly disenchanted' with the trials. He had particularly disliked the methods of the Soviets. The Allies had in fact taken stock of the criticisms levelled at the trials. The presence of a Russian judge on the bench (and a general rather than a jurist) had been an embarrassment. It was decided that the Allies should try their own Nazis in their own zones. That way the ideological differences between the Allies would be less immediately obvious. Jackson had recommended to Truman that any more international trials of this nature would have to be held in Berlin. This never happened, of course.[1] Nuremberg would go on, but as a solely American jurisdiction. After the first eleven victims had been despatched, the cells filled up with new inmates who were to pass before the tribunal.

On 8 September 1947, while the Krupp and 'Stormtrooper' trials were in full swing, Clay tried to whittle down the number of cases before the Nuremberg court. He planned just six more: the big six banks; the Press and Propaganda Office; the Foreign Office; those members of the military leadership who had violated the rules of international warfare; the military leaders responsible for the POWs; and the directors of the Hermann-Göring-Werke. He could see no possibility of having them all and thought about running some of them together. He was inclined to drop the

Hermann-Göring-Werke case, possibly the Press and Propaganda trial as well.[2]

When the final decisions were made, 185 men were arraigned before a dozen tribunals. First was the trial of the medical doctors, which resulted in seven death sentences; next that of Field Marshal Milch, who was tried in solitary splendour for directing slave labour and sent down for fifteen years. The third trial judged the Nazi judiciary; the fourth Oswald Pohl and the concentration-camp hierarchy. Pohl swung, but two other death sentences were commuted. Next in line were the industrialists from the Flick Group, followed by trial six: the senior administration of IG Farben. The next in the dock were the generals who had fought the battles in the south-east. Field Marshal List received a life tariff. The RuSHA (Race and Resettlement Office) were trial eight. No death sentences were handed out, but RuSHA chief Richard Hildebrandt was shipped over to the Poles. Ohlendorf and the other Einsatzgruppen (death squad) leaders were trial nine. Five men were executed, one by the Belgians. Nine death sentences were commuted. The tenth arraigned the twenty-three directors of Krupps. Alfried Krupp received twelve years. The eleventh judged members of the German Foreign Office and other officials – the Wilhelmstrasse case. The sentences were quite haywire, with Ernst von Weizsäcker receiving a seven-year tariff (later reduced to five) and a man who condemned thousands to death in Auschwitz, like Edmund Veesenmayer, receiving twenty years (reduced to ten). The last trial was for the generals who had invaded Russia. There were no spectacular sentences, nor were they handed over to the Russians.[3]

Speer and the rest of the seven were still carrying out their menial duties in Nuremberg. The architect was able to offer a smile to Alfried Krupp one day, and on another occasion he saw the Alsatian surgeon Karl Brandt. He had interceded on Brandt's behalf when Hitler had had him condemned to death for sending his wife and child out of Berlin. Brandt gave Speer a sad wave. Speer claimed that he had not known that Brandt had been in charge of the Euthanasia Programme and had initiated the experiments on human beings in the concentration camps.[4] When the SS leadership arrived, Speer observed, 'These are all candidates for death row.'[5]

Like many other prisoners, Speer was called upon to give evidence at the trials of his former colleagues. Field Marshal Milch had been in charge of armaments for the Luftwaffe, and had been closely allied to Speer. He had requested labour from Speer, including concentration-camp inmates. Speer's use of slaves had been an important part of the indictment against him. He permitted himself a philosophic reflection in the secret journals he was penning at the time: 'Of course all these trials are judgements by the victors on the defeated. In various ways I keep hearing that German prisoners of war, contrary to law, are also being put to forced labour in armaments and supply bases. Who here is the judge?'[6]

The Americans were insistent on the trial of the industrialists. The old paterfamilias, Gustav von Bohlen und Halbach, had bequeathed his firm to his son Alfried in November 1943 and gone into retirement. Before he did so, he had Hitler enact a 'Lex Krupp' imposing primogeniture in violation of the laws of Weimar, which were still in force in Hitler's Germany.[7] As it was eventually decided that Gustav was too ill too stand trial, the major charges were heaped on Alfried, who had been taken prisoner when the Americans went into Essen on 10 April 1945. Alfried suffered the usual series of camps before being taken to the Nuremberg courthouse. After his arrest American soldiers helped themselves to souvenirs at the Villa Hügel – typewriters, a portrait of Hitler, and a model cannon.[8] When the British replaced the Americans in Essen they set about arresting the other directors: they wanted to make an example of Krupps along with Flick and IG Farben as 'Samson's hair' – the symbol of Germany's industrial might.[9] The idea of making Alfried responsible for his father's crimes came from the French. The Americans got cold feet about this and Gustav received a seat in the dock at the main trial, which he was never to occupy. He died in 1951.

The trial of the generals who had led the campaign in the Balkans was considered a watershed. For the first time the second tier, the generals who had acted on Hitler's orders, became responsible for massacres. The German advocates made a brave effort to prove that the taking and shooting of hostages as reprisals for acts committed by partisans or guerrillas was permitted in the British, American and French military manuals; and they pointed out that a similar charge had been controversial in the Kesselring trial, which the British held in Venice, and that the *Manchester Guardian* had thundered, 'This is not justice as we know it.'* They accused the British military of sentencing a man to death for being a figurehead.[10] Cross-examined, List pleaded a hard fight against non-regular forces. It was a Balkan war, 'harsh measures' needed to be taken against partisans who obeyed no laws, who fought 'Balkan-style, treacherous and atrocious . . .' It did List no good.[11] Tito had been on the Allies' side.

The US Supreme Court had refused to grant leave of absence to its

---

* Kesselring's sentence was commuted to life. Both he and List were released in 1952.

members to serve in Germany, and the three judges in the Krupp case were a member of the Tennessee Appeal Court, a member of the Supreme Court of Connecticut, and another from the Supreme Court in Seattle. This was a reasonable showing. There was resistance to using elected judges, particularly from Clay. Non-professional jurists would lead to further criticism of the trials. Clay also resisted the idea of sending out a number of black attorneys to work at Nuremberg – not because he objected to them *per se*, but because Germany did not have a black population.[12]

Alfried Krupp von Bohlen und Halbach had already suffered eighteen months of detention before the trial began, and he maintained a dignified silence throughout. An empty chair had represented his senile father at the international trial. Now it was his turn to be judged – *in loco parentis*. Thirty German lawyers had been engaged to defend the directors during the eleven months of the trial. More than 200 witnesses were called. The minutes run to 13,454 pages.[13] The directors were indicted for crimes against humanity, pillage, appropriation, spoliation and exploitation. They were also accused of participating in atrocities and being complicit in deportation, imprisonment, and racial and religious persecution. A further charge laid against them was planning aggressive war, despite the fact that only two of them – Alfried and Ewald Loeser – had been on their boards at the time. Evidence that would have been inadmissible in an American court was accepted at Nuremberg. Some of it had as little value as common gossip. The directors answered for any act performed by any one of a quarter of a million employees.

Of course Krupps was up to its neck in the activities of the state. It profited from German expansion in all directions and took over the running of sequestered firms in France and Holland. It used armies of slave-labourers who were treated with sickening cruelty. For this reason the sentences were severe: Alfried was sent down for twelve years, to be spent in Landsberg Prison. The other directors received similar tariffs. In addition to this Alfried was relieved of *all* his personal property. He was the only man tried at Nuremberg to receive this punishment. The president of the court thought the decision ran counter to the law and dissented.[14] The Krupp case showed up many of the weaknesses of the Allied jurisdiction: Alfried had wanted to use an American lawyer, but that was not permitted. He had then decided not to defend himself, but that was also not allowed. The German lawyers demanded a conference room, but this was not granted either. When they left the court in protest, they were brought back by force and six of them were arrested for contempt.[15]

The jurists' trial opened in March 1947. Some of the worst Nazi lawyers had been spared by premature death. Among them was the president of the People's Court, Roland Freisler, who had been crushed under a wooden beam during an Allied raid on Berlin in February 1945. Hans Frank had been executed by the Poles. A large number of jurists had killed themselves as they saw the regime fall. One of these was the minister of justice, Otto-Georg Thierack. In all, sixteen defendants stood trial; including the three state secretaries Franz Schlegelberger, Curt Rothenberger and Herbert Klemm. The others were officials from the People's Court. The judges examined 2,093 exhibits and questioned 138 witnesses. They reached their verdict in December 1947. They have been praised for their impartial and balanced approach: 'If anything, the judgment erred on the side of caution.'[16] Some of the German jurists were exonerated. Four life sentences were handed down.

The Wilhelmstrasse trial arraigned twenty-one senior civil servants. There was a slight modification of the London Statute and of Control Council Law 10 of 20 December 1945, in that the court finally recognised the principal of *nullum crimen sine lege*, if only in *international* law, which was a fairly nebulous jurisdiction.[17] The names included Ernst von Weizsäcker, Wilhelm Keppler, Ernst Bohle, Ernst Woermann, Karl Ritter, Otto von Erdmannsdorff, Edmund Veesenmayer, Hans Lammers, Wilhelm Stuckart, Walter Darré, Otto Meissner, Otto Dietrich, Gottlob Berger, Walther Schellenberg, Gustav Adolf Steengracht von Moyland, Schwerin von Krosigk, Paul Körner and Paul Pleiger. It was a hotchpotch of Nazi and non-Nazi diplomats and civil servants which included some who had acted counter to the interests of the regime, some who had simply toed the line – like Schwerin von Krosigk – and murderers like Veesenmayer. Veesenmayer had been allowed to continue at liberty while he gave evidence against his former colleagues. He had freely surrendered to the Allies, but he continued to see them as his enemies: 'I am a criminal who must be exterminated.' But he was not executed, despite his role in the deportation of Hungary's Jews. He was released from Landsberg Prison in 1951.

In the case against the diplomats, four old-school examples (Weizsäcker, Woermann, Erdmannsdorff and Ritter) were flanked by the same number of Nazi outsiders (Steengracht, Keppler, Bohle and Veesenmayer). As Margret Boveri knew, it was not always possible to see them as wholly black or wholly white. Weizsäcker stuck his neck out for a few Jews here and there; Steengracht, his pure Nazi successor, managed (by adding a zero to the figure of 400 Hungarian Jews who had been given permission to travel to Sweden) to save a further 3,600.[18]

The case for the prosecution ran to 39,000 pages of which the British evidence alone amounted to 28,000 pages. The bundle was made up of 3,400 documents. The main arguments against the defendants dealt with crimes against humanity, the deportation of the Jews and their murder in concentration and annihilation camps.[19] Ernst von Weizsäcker is now acknowledged to have been one of the first and most important opponents to the regime operating in the German Foreign Office, but as state secretary he had been singularly powerless to prevent or alleviate the tragedy of those years. His own son Richard is clear on this: 'from documents and spoken report he knew more than enough to reach his own decisions'.[20] The state secretary saw it as his role, to the extent of his powers, to prevent the outbreak of the war, and, once he had failed there, to limit its effect by averting the war against the Soviet Union. We now know much more about this than we knew then. We know, for example, that Weizsäcker was a party to the despatch of Adam von Trott first to Britain and later to the United States, to explain the position of the German opposition. Indeed Ribbentrop himself had said that the only reason that Weizsäcker was not arraigned before Roland Freisler and the People's Court was that on 20 July 1944 he was already safe behind Allied lines, as ambassador to the Vatican.

Once in the Vatican, Weizsäcker had been free to protect Jews from the maniacal purge that was put into action after Italy went over to the Allies. The prioress of the nunnery of Our Lady in Sion attested to the fact that he had directed 185 Jews to her door and issued her with a letter that forbade the SS from searching the premises.[21] The question arose whether Weizsäcker was actually a traitor, in that he had warned the British ambassador, Nevile Henderson, that Germany was about to sign a pact with Russia in August 1939. Was he thereby willing defeat on his own country and the death of his country's own soldiers? Weizsäcker was categorical: 'I wanted peace without Hitler, but not a defeat that would lead to Hitler's ejection.'[22]

The indictment, however, accused Weizsäcker of supporting Hitler's war policy and making it possible, which his son describes as the 'absolute and grotesque opposite of the truth'. On the other hand the defence case was not easy, as the witnesses were foreign statesmen, who were not always easy to subpoena. The British did much to sabotage his case by putting pressure on diplomats and former ministers to stay clear and reveal nothing of Weizsäcker's role in the various plots of 1938 and 1939. One exception, however, was Lord Halifax, who gave a 'helpful and honest testimony' for the state secretary.[23] Among the more damning accusations brought to bear in the case was the contention that Weizsäcker had allowed himself to utter the Nazi slogan 'Deutschland erwache!' (Germany awake!) at the funeral in Paris of Ernst vom Rath, the German diplomat murdered in 1938 by the Jew Herschel Grynspann. Vom Rath's death was used as a pretext to launch the Reichskristallnacht on 9 November that year. Eyewitnesses maintained he had done no such thing. As the coffin was despatched to Germany Weizsäcker had actually said 'Deutschland erwartet Dich!' (Germany is waiting for you!), which was nothing less than the truth.[24]

Richard von Weizsäcker managed to have himself attached to the defence team, despite the fact that he had yet to be called to the bar. The greatest difficulty he had with the Allied jurists in Nuremberg was that they were still infected with 'Vansittartism' and had yet to learn the real nature of the Third Reich. Americans also had a particular problem with diplomatic language, and the double meanings with which men such as Weizsäcker sought to conceal the real sense from the Party authorities, as their internal memoranda show.[25]

The American prosecutor was the former Prussian civil servant Robert Kempner. He had worked closely with Carl Schmitt, who was also held as a prisoner in Nuremberg. On Kempner's authority Schmitt was released in May 1947. Others were also released from their more severe punishments once they had come to an understanding with Kempner.[26] Such methods did not work with Weizsäcker. He shunned the *quid pro quo* and relapsed into an injured silence. The case lasted eight months. On 13 April 1949 Weizsäcker was sentenced to seven years' imprisonment, which was later commuted to five as already noted. One of the three judges dissented and said he should be freed. John McCloy thought so too. In the autumn of the following year he released the former state secretary as his first response to the Nuremberg judgments

Even after three of the Einsatzgruppe commanders had been condemned to death at Nuremberg in 1947, they managed to stave off execution by giving evidence at the trials of their peers. Writing after his unsuccessful attempt to defend Field Marshal von Manstein, Reginald Paget wondered whether Otto Ohlendorf had actually been telling the truth to Himmler. How had he managed to kill so many Jews with such limited resources? Ohlendorf was credited (in a Nazi sense) with having wiped out up to 90,000 Jews during his four-and-a-half-month tenure of Einsatzgruppe D. The strength of his unit lay at around 500 men divided into five companies; of these, 200 men served as clerks. Each company had just ten vehicles.

Otto Ohlendorf is a puzzling case. He was a Nazi humanist who, while he was murdering Jews in huge numbers, was rebuilding schools and hospitals for the Volga Germans. Ohlendorf described his methods at his trial. Jews were required to register before 'resettlement'. This was the pretext for taking them to their deaths. Then they were ferried to a ditch some ten kilometres outside the town and shot where as few people as possible would witness the killings. During this time the SD were also fighting partisans, who were active in their sectors. Paget found it incredible that single companies of SD were able to claim that they were killing between 10,000 and 12,000 Jews in two or three days. The maximum number of Jews that could have been accommodated in a lorry was twenty to thirty and each ten-kilometre journey would have taken near on two hours to load, unload, assemble, kill and return to the town or village to fill up again. It was claimed that the SD had killed 10,000 Jews in Simferopol, but by Paget's calculations the number could not have exceeded 300.

Ohlendorf claimed that he had rid the whole Crimea of its Jewish population: 'He was clearly a man who was prepared to say anything that would please his employers. The Americans had found him a perfect witness.'[27] Paget thought he was lying to save his skin, telling Himmler what he wanted to hear. In which case why did he not try to save himself at Nuremberg? If mass slaughter was not a big element in Ohlendorf's curriculum vitae after all, if – as Paget suggests – the figure of 90,000 needs to be shortened by a nought or two, it hardly exonerates him from the charge of mass murder, nor did he ever try to deny it himself. Indeed, he was chillingly factual about the killing of children. Once again he took pains to point out that the Allies had not been particularly scrupulous about it either.[28]

The final trial of the Nuremberg twelve took place in 1948. This show was reserved for the General Staff and the OKW. One of those indicted was General Walther Warlimont, a mere pen-pusher who had been responsible for operations and whose sin was an unquestioning loyalty to the regime. He was accused of war crimes and crimes against humanity and sent down for life. The case hinged on the two orders that infringed the laws of war: the Commando and the Commissar Orders. Warlimont was punished harshly because he was perceived as one of the planners, whereas Gerd von Rundstedt ('My Führer, whatever you order, I shall do to my last breath')[29] was able to settle in West Germany after four years in a POW camp. In 1951 Warlimont's sentence was reduced to eighteen years. He was released six years later.

Elsewhere

The British made a first stab at administering justice by dealing with the culprits at Belsen. They were put on trial in the nearby town of Lüneburg. Josef Kramer, the camp commandant, stood in the dock with forty-four others on 17 September 1945 in a converted gymnasium at 30 Lindenstrasse. This was the first of the trials, a dress rehearsal for those that came later where international, rather than German law would be invoked. The defendants were accused of war crimes. It was hard to prove that they had done more than callously neglect their charges, as there were no gas chambers at Belsen and the prisoners had been given food, though not nearly enough. The cases against Kramer and Dr Fritz Klein were easier to prove, in that both had worked at Auschwitz, where they had been cogs in the killing machine. It is interesting to record now that the indictment said nothing about Nazi genocide nor about its specifically antisemitic character.

In the dock along with Kramer, Klein and the 'Blonde Beastess' Irma Grese were a number of Polish kapos, former prisoners whose improved status had allowed them to wallow in acts of brutality. Various lawyers in khaki were roped in to defend the SS men and women, and did it as diligently as they could, even describing Kramer as a scapegoat. The legal formula of *nulla poena sine lege* was of course ignored, prompting comparisons with the Nazis themselves: those indicted had not broken any German laws as they went about their business at Belsen. Reading an account of the trial now, it is striking how many inaccuracies were allowed to pass and how little the British knew about the workings of the camps.

As far as Irma Grese was concerned, there was an indecent amount of prurience expressed in the British press about her fate. She was blonde and good looking. She had also been involved in the selections at Auschwitz, where she had a reputation for brutality without parallel among the female guards. The court adjourned on 16 November and delivered its verdicts after six hours and eight minutes: eleven people, including Kramer, Klein and Irma Grese, were condemned to death. Kramer submitted an appeal to Montgomery, but it fell on deaf ears. Klein refused to appeal, saying that his part in the Final Solution 'was such that he was not fit to live'. Britain flew in Albert Pierrepoint to carry out the executions. They died on 12 December.[30]

The concentration-camp trials were to continue for twenty years. The Belsen trial was a warm-up for Nuremberg. The staff at Stutthof camp near

Danzig were also arraigned. Seventeen SS guards and five block supervisors were executed and fifty-eight others given sentences of up to fifteen years. The British hanged Sturmbannführer Max Pauly, second in command, but after the Allies ceased to be responsible for the nemesis the West German courts were often disgracefully lenient. Pauly's successor, Paul Werner Hoppe, was given a nine-year sentence. One sadistic guard received two years from a Hamburg court, and Otto Knott, who fed the gas chamber, was set free by a court in Tübingen.[31]

One of the more controversial sentences was that meted out to Field Marshal Erich von Manstein, who had always received a good press, particularly in Britain. Manstein, however, was in his way every bit as blinkered as Warlimont, and would not have been described as a general with a 'heart'. In one of his more ridiculous moments he had stood up before Hitler and exclaimed 'Führer befehl! Wir folgen!' (Führer command! We shall obey!). Hitler had thought he was mocking him, and Manstein later received a hefty reprimand behind closed doors, leaving Hitler's bunker like an admonished schoolboy. The source for the story was the SS man Otto Günsche, who would not have been sympathetic to the stock-Prussian general, but Manstein's unappetising coldness and stiffness is well attested, and his response to an overture to co-operate with the military opposition ('Prussian generals do not mutiny') was as telling as it was untrue.[32]

It was the British who subsequently tried Manstein. They awarded him a heavy sentence, but he was released after only four years and at the end of his life was an adviser to Adenauer's government on military matters – an indication of how seriously the war crimes tribunals were taken by West German conservatives. The probable reason for the harshness of his punishment was the clamour from the Soviet Union. Manstein's charm worked little on the Soviets, who would almost certainly have killed him. Reginald Paget, on the other hand, thought Manstein a perfect gentle knight, the 'Hector' of the Wehrmacht, and the longer he represented him, it seems, the more he grew to like him. Paget formed a team with Sam Silkin (who being Jewish was making a statement by taking on the case) and two German lawyers, Drs Laternser and Leverkühn. The former had already defended Field Marshal von Leeb before an American court and Kesselring before a British one; the latter had worked in Canaris's Abwehr, and had come under suspicion himself when Canaris and his team were arrested by the Nazis.

Once again Paget learned that you would get nowhere by citing cases of similar atrocities carried out by Allied armies: the Allies were above reproach. But there was a great deal more readiness on the part of the British to socialise with the German defence team. The Americans had treated them as pariahs.[33] Once the trial began Paget was to note more features that contributed to the miscarriage of justice. One of these was the right to bring in photographers to snap the defendant over an extended period at the beginning of the trial, which made it resemble Nazi justice, and the journalists present filed stories that would have been *sub judice* in an English court. As it was not a 'real' trial they were immune from accusations of contempt. Another rub was the simultaneous translation. The defendant could listen to a translation of the case as it proceeded, but the interpreters were often not up to the task.[34]

Manstein was not the only important general to be omitted from the lineup at Nuremberg. As we have seen, Field Marshal Albert Kesselring was tried by the British in Venice for atrocities carried out under his command there. These included the massacre of 335 Italians in the Ardeatine Caves and another 1,087 people killed in reprisals after attacks by partisans. Kesselring mounted an impressive defence, showing that the SD and not he had responsibility for security. He was nonetheless sentenced to death. The verdict was controversial enough for Churchill to intervene with his successor, and Kesselring's sentence was commuted to life imprisonment. In 1952 he was released after a serious head injury.[35]

The IMT dry-run for the Americans was the Dachau trial in November 1945. In the dock were the commandant Martin Weiss, four SS doctors and the seventy-four-year-old Professor Klaus Schilling, the malaria expert who had been trying out his theories on the prisoners. There were forty people indicted in all and the court handed down thirty-six death sentences. General Lucien Truscott, presiding, later commuted four of these, but not Schilling's.[36] Sepp Dietrich was the most distinguished SS general of the war. Troops under his command were responsible for a vast number of atrocities, particularly in the Soviet Union. At the end of the war he surrendered his army to Patton at Krems, and was kept in a number of camps ending up with his trial at Dachau. It was one of sixty-seven trials held in the former flagship concentration camp which were to mete out death sentences. The main case against him was the slaughter of between 300 and 600 American troops and 111 Belgian civilians at Malmédy, which was carried out under orders from Jochen Peiper. The court dismissed claims that the SS men's confessions were extracted under torture. Peiper behaved with dignity in the dock, and recounted some of the ways in which the interrogators had behaved – pretending that they already had signed confessions from the others, that his death sentence was assured, that he would be better off saving his comrades, and so on. Peiper's plea that international law allowed a certain leeway with

POWs in the heat of battle if that meant that victory could be ensured was not entertained by the court.[37]

On 16 July 1946 the defendants in the Malmédy trial learned of their fates. Forty-three men were sentenced to death by hanging, including Peiper; twenty-two more received life sentences, including Sepp Dietrich. The prisoners were then transferred to Landsberg Prison, the very place where their former master Adolf Hitler had penned *Mein Kampf.* Dietrich's sentence was commuted to twenty-five years in 1951, and he was released four years later. Many of the men on death row survived. There was a discomfort felt by many of the Americans who had been involved in the case. The presence of so many Jews in the court, the way that the confessions had been extracted and the fact that many of the Americans could recall their troops carrying out similar illegal acts contrived to raise doubts about the security of the convictions. A year later the sentences were reviewed, with a number of the death sentences being commuted. In the middle of 1948 there were still 150 men in Dachau on death row. Clay still wanted to execute them. Most of them wriggled off the hook in the end. A few months later there were ten cases on his desk from the condemned men of Dachau: six writs of habeas corpus and four who had been granted leave to appeal. Another ninety-five were still supposed to be hanged. On 4 March 1949 Clay was anxious to dispose of ten of the Malmédy murderers; twelve more were still on appeal.

He did not think much of their claims to have been tortured. On 12 March he examined the appeal of Sergeant Tank Commander Bersin of the 1st SS-Panzer Regiment: 'He was forced to spend two months on a prison floor, beaten and kicked by the guards to the extent of losing several teeth, carried to the dental clinic and to interrogations with a hood over his head and grossly mistreated in an interrogation of March 20 1946 by Mr Kirschbaum in the presence of Mr Ellowitz.' Clay had no doubts about Bersin's guilt. The supposed torturers denied the charges against them.[38] Whatever Clay felt, the methods used to extract confessions had discredited the trial.[39]

On top of these he had nineteen death sentences from the Buchenwald trial to ratify, including Ilse Koch – the 'Bitch of Buchenwald' – who had managed to get herself pregnant.[40] She was the wife of Karl Koch, the camp commandant, and was renowned not only for her collection of lampshades but also for her fondness for riding through the camp on a horse and lashing out at the prisoners. Her case presented particular difficulties. She had left Buchenwald in August 1943 and no one seemed to know what she had done after that. Clay commuted her sentence, but by doing so he aroused a storm of protest. He found a way out of 'double jeopardy': she could be transferred to the German courts because there were German nationals in Buchenwald. This stratagem worked, and she was sentenced to life imprisonment. She committed suicide in prison in 1967.[41]

Dietrich's life sentence was severely criticised, as no link could be found between him and the murderous command. Unfortunately for him, Clay was not prepared to revise the decision. On the other hand now only twelve men remained on death row. Clay later halved that number again. The last six were let off in 1951, at the same time as the revision of Dietrich's life ticket.[42]

Germans accused of atrocities conjured up some ingenious arguments in their defence, but as the courts had been able to impose their own rules they stood little chance of success. So it was that the SS man Fritz Knoechlein, accused of killing ninety-seven British POWs in cold blood, claimed that there had been a *Standgericht* – or drumhead court – before the massacre, something that was permitted by the rule book. On the other hand the court was told that such a tribunal could not be set up once soldiers had laid down their arms. POWs are entitled to protection by the opposing army.[43]

The SS regimental commander Kurt Meyer was tried by a Canadian court for ordering the killing of forty Canadian POWs. Meyer was effectively being tried for atrocities committed by his regiment, as no evidence could be produced to show that he had issued the fatal orders. Allied commanders were mercifully spared this 'chain of command' principal. In general Meyer impressed the court by his dignity at the trial. He was convicted, however, of responsibility for the deaths of eighteen soldiers and sentenced to death by firing squad. This was later commuted to life imprisonment by the general commanding Canadian forces in Germany whose conscience, it is alleged, was not entirely clean when it came to the actions of his own men in dealing with German and Italian POWs. Meyer was imprisoned in New Brunswick before being transferred to the British high-security prison at Werl near Dortmund, where he had Kesselring for a cellmate. He was released in 1954.[44]

The Canadians lost heart after that, and allowed the British to look into atrocities perpetrated against their men after D-Day when widely circulated rumours that Canadian and British troops were not taking prisoners led to some scenes of savagery on the part of the SS.* Once again the orders to

* There must have been some truth in these allegations. When the author was living in France in the early 1980s he met two people who had witnessed massacres carried out by Allied troops: a man who had been eighteen at the time, and a woman who had been a child of six. She had run out of the house to find British paratroops bayoneting German POWs in her garden. A British friend of the author's who had studied at Heidelberg before the war and was intelligence officer to his regiment, told him that he was unable to interrogate a single prisoner after the massacre at Oradour-sur-Glane, because the British soldiers had killed the lot.

refuse quarter appear to have come from Wilhelm Mohnke. The killings at a first-aid post were carried out by an SS man called Wilhelm Schnabel. His superior officer, Bernhard Siebken, actively resisted implementing the orders and was not present when the shootings took place. The trial began in Hamburg on 28 August 1948. When Siebken was sentenced to death, a plea was entered in mitigation, but the deputy judge advocate, Lord Russell of Liverpool, decided that the court had pronounced the correct verdict. Both men were hanged in Hameln by Pierrepoint on 20 January 1949. It was a classic case of *vis victis*, or victor's justice.[45]

Another Nazi who was imprisoned in Dachau was the former Gauleiter of Mecklenburg. Tisa von der Schulenburg travelled to Dachau to see Friedrich Hildebrandt, who was implicated in the shooting of two American airmen. She was told that she could not save him, even though he had protected her and her sister-in-law after 20 July 1944. She tried to understand why Hildebrandt, a 'harmless' man, would have ordered the shooting of the fliers, and she remembered that it was in response to the strafing of a train, in which a hundred people, chiefly women and children, had been killed. Hildebrandt had decided that the next 'terror-bombers' that fell to earth alive would suffer accordingly.

The Germans Begin to Prosecute Nazis

Those who were liquidated first tended to be those who had committed atrocities against Allied citizens. Hence the Russians wanted the heads of the generals responsible for invading the Soviet Union; the Yugoslavs and the Poles those who had performed that role in their lands; the Czechs those who had administered their country. The Russians killed the SS chief Friedrich Jecklen in 1946; the Yugoslavs the minister Siegfried Lasche and the general Alexander Löhr; the Poles executed Josef Bühler, Jürgen Stroop and Rudolf Höss, and the more prominent Nazis in Danzig were also passed though the Polish courts: the Gauleiter, Albert Forster, was caught by the British and handed over to the authorities in Warsaw. He and Richard Hildebrandt, head of the RuSHA, were executed. Before his despatch, Greisser, the head of the Danzig Senate and Gauleiter of Posen, was paraded in an iron cage through the streets of the city that had reverted to its Polish name of Poznań.[46] The Czechs killed Karl-Hermann Frank, Hanns Ludin and Dieter Wisliceny.

Officers who had ordered the killing of Allied POWs could expect death sentences. Many who had ordered the killing of thousands of their own citizens escaped scot free: Mengele, Gestapo Müller, Alois 'Jupo' Brunner and others managed to elude the Allies, and some say that the Allies connived at their disappearance. The Allies' fury was quickly spent. In the main Nuremberg trials sentences became lighter with the passage of time; and even those given capital sentences or life often had the tariff commuted or reduced. As the trials edged towards the end of the 1940s, the fear developed among the judges that the Soviets were about to invade western Germany and wind the proceedings up.

There was a large element of hypocrisy. Since that time many Allied atrocities have come to light, particularly the killing of POWs at Biscari, on orders from General Patton. The sinking of the French fleet at Oran by the British, with the loss of some 1,500 French lives was no secret. It was a continuation of a British naval tradition that originated at Copenhagen in 1805. The last German Kaiser had feared that it would happen to his fledgling fleet. It was possibly a 'usage', but it can hardly be called any more legal than the German Blitzkrieg.

The British made the decision to stop the trials in April, and in September they handed the business over to the Germans. They passed Nazi Party members before the Spruchkammer according to the American Law for Liberation issued on 5 March 1946. Nazis were now being judged by Germans, essentially their former political enemies in the SPD or the KPD. The biggest calls for retribution came from the American Zone, as a response to pressure from OMGUS, the American military government. One of those arraigned before the courts was Winifred Wagner, who was reduced to penury, cycling up to seventy kilometres a day to forage for kindling. In between foraging for wood, she put together a sixty-four-page document on her relations with Adolf Hitler, appending copies of documents showing how she had gone out of her way to help the oppressed of the Third Reich. She also quite rightly pointed out that she had not broken the law by joining the NSDAP at the time.[47]

In her deposition, Winifred claimed to have only the vaguest knowledge of the concentration camps, though other documents showed that she had been involved with trying to get someone out of Auschwitz. She had probably been given poor advice, but by that time she had seen how savage the courts had been with some of her friends, who had been guilty of little more than Party membership. Particularly galling had been the treatment accorded to her doctor Helmut Treuter, who was dispossessed and imprisoned, largely as a result of denunciation by a rival. It was not until November 1949 that he was able to practise again. Winifred feared the worst.[48]

She had no problem understanding the methods of her interrogators. They were similar to those employed by the Gestapo, ranging from threats to normal chit-chat. She learned that she had been indicted because she had made Hitler 'socially acceptable'. Meanwhile her daughter Friedelind – an American citizen – was telling the world that Winifred's former lover, Heinz Tietjen, had been used to interrogate British spies. It transpired that she meant Hermann Göring (or 'Teddie', as he was known in the Wagner household). Indeed, the case against Winifred relied substantially on the account of the family's history provided by her daughter's book.[49]

Winifred Wagner's trial took place in Bayreuth. The principle was *sauve qui peut*. Heinz Tietjen, who had directed the festival after Siegfried Wagner's death, cried off. His own denazification trial was coming up, and he preferred not to venture out. Winifred was again scrupulously honest about her belief in Hitler, which had seized her as early as 1923. Hitler's love of Wagner and Wagner's hatred of the Jews were also aired at the trial, though neither could have been said to have had any bearing on the case against Winifred. The Spruchkammer showed an unfortunate bias towards conviction that must have reminded many Germans of the proceedings of the infamous People's Court it had to some extent replaced. When one witness said that she saw things 'from a different point of view', the prosecutor rejoined, 'Your different point of view is of no interest to us here.' It might have been Roland Freisler himself.[50]

The prosecution called for Winifred to be classed grade one. If she had provided help to victims of the regime, it had not been from sentiments of opposition. They called for a sentence of six years in a labour camp and the confiscation of her assets. As it was, Winifred was condemned grade two. She had to do 350 days' community service and yield up 60 per cent of her assets. She was later reclassified as a 'lesser offender' on appeal. The initial sentence proved controversial. Some Germans howled about the leniency of the court. Foreigners sent her food parcels. As one Jewish friend conceded, her chief crime was succumbing to the widespread delusion that Hitler had not been responsible for the crimes committed in his name. It was a view she was later to express to a like-minded person, the historian David Irving. To the end of her days Hitler was 'USA' – 'Unser selige Adolf' (Our blessed Adolf).

The Western Allies started out well. In the summer of 1945, for example, they sacked 90 per cent of legal officials in their zones, but they soon realised that by doing so they were greatly adding to their own workload, and that they would have problems rebuilding the German legal system. Many of the German lawyers were able to receive testimonials from colleagues attesting to their 'inner' rejection of the system. Once these had been approved, a *Persilschein* was issued: named after the soap powder, it 'washed white' the former Nazi. Similarly, prison officials who had been responsible for myriad murders and who had carried out a policy of un-rivalled brutality were absolved for the simple reason that the prison service was short staffed. In the new state of Baden-Württemberg the proportion retained was an astonishing 96 per cent.[51]

Once washed clean, the jurists returned to the bench or ministry. About 80 per cent of Nazi jurists went back to work in the Federal Republic, including seventy-two former judges and prosecutors from the notorious People's Court. Some of these continued to serve as late as the 1970s. The German courts proved incapable of sentencing any former Nazi judge or prosecutor. Their excuse was that they were applying the law as it existed at the time.[52] In the East the situation was different. After the initial teething problems, when a lot of very dodgy men were elevated to the bench, of 1,000 GDR judges in 1950, only one had been a member of the NSDAP. To deal with the shortage of skilled jurists, judges were given crash-courses. These judges however, would not have been impartial. The prison service was similarly purged, but again this hardly made the prisons of the GDR preferable to those administered by ex-Nazis in the West.[53]

The Americans pulled the plug on denazification on 8 May 1948. By then US, British and French courts had tried over 8,000 cases and sen-tenced a tenth of the accused – 806 – to death. Fewer than half of those were commuted, and 486 went to the gallows. The Americans tried 1,672 people for war crimes. Of the 255 they executed at Landsberg-am-Lech, 102 were skilled workers, thirty-seven civil servants, with a few academic titles here and there, twenty-three were academics, twenty-two workers, eleven soldiers, and the rest were made up of the professions, Nazi func-tionaries and schoolboys. The oldest was Dr Schilling at seventy-four. (Twenty more died from naural causes.) All the lifers were eventually released, with one exception – Hess.[54] German courts reopened in the summer of 1945, and they too passed judgment on former Nazis. Between 1945 and 1950 the courts sentenced only 5,228 defendants for Nazi crimes. Sentences were either short or the criminals were swiftly pardoned. In the years from 1951 to 1955 there were only 638 convictions. It is now clear that many of the worst culprits, the operatives who sent thousands to their deaths, were not punished at all.[55]

PART IV

The Road to Freedom

18

Peacemaking in Potsdam

18 July 1945
Now it will be decided whether we can carry on living in Europe or if we must try to live our lives as a refugee God knows where. A year has elapsed since the [assassination] attempt of 20 July. A year filled with blood and misery which might perhaps have been avoided. But our people had to drink the cup down to the dregs, and in the end, it was all for the good.

Ursula von Kardoff, *Berliner Aufzeichnungen, 1942–1945*,
Munich 1994, 337

The wartime conferences had calmly discussed the Germans' fate, but at the Potsdam Conference the Allies finally realised that 'Uncle Joe' had stolen a march on them. He would call the shots. The Allies met from 17 July to 2 August 1945 at the palace of Crown Prince 'Little Willi', the Cecilienhof in Potsdam. The Western Allies were able to see their handiwork for the first time. In a fifteen-minute raid on 14 April they had flattened the centre of Frederick the Great's *Residenz*.[1] The town centre had lost '*everything* that was historic, a memorial or artistically important', according to Hanna Grisebach.[2] There were consolations: 'The voices that we have had to listen to for over twelve years have been silenced.'[3]

Hanna Grisebach was a Jewish convert to Protestantism married to a Heidelberg colleague of Karl Jaspers. For many of the same reasons as the philosopher, her husband was forced into retirement in 1937. The couple moved to the so-called 'von-Viertel', the aristocratic quarter, of Potsdam. Frau Grisebach was taken into the circle of the largely royalist nobles like the Wedels, Schulenburgs, Buddenbrocks and an old Princess Trubetzkoy who lived in Potsdam, many of whom subscribed to the 'confessing Church' and were wholly opposed to Hitler's regime. Like Gertrud Jaspers, Hanna Grisebach spent the last few days of the Third Reich in hiding.[4]

On 24 April Hanna noted 'the first Russian in our house'. Their Polish maid Marja was able to interpret and shoo the Russian away, saving the life of her young son. Her teenage daughter she now dressed as a boy, cutting off her long plaits to save her from being raped. By now the Germans had retreated, leaving a sorry spectacle of destruction: 'battered vehicles, shattered cars, discarded pieces of uniform and weapons of every kind lie scattered around . . .'[5]

The Russians showed more respect for Potsdam's cultural monuments than the Anglo-Americans. During the battle for Potsdam the business of safeguarding the palaces in the park of Sanssouci was given to Yevgeny Ludshuveit, an art historian. He sent a radio message to German High Command to ask them to cease shelling the park: 'I was very worried about the treasures, and wanted them to be preserved.'[6] The Glienecke Bridge, which connected Potsdam with Greater Berlin to the north, was another victim of the bombardment. You might still cross to the Wannsee side, but only by means of a 'hair-raising climb' over the pylons that had previously held up the suspension bridge. In their destructive rage the SS had set fire to all the fine boats belonging to the Imperial Yacht Club moored on the Havel.[7]

The care taken over the remaining monuments was not extended to the private property of Potsdam's townsfolk. There was the usual hunt for watches and bicycles. The Grisebachs lost eight watches, as well as all their bicycles. Hanna's son managed to buy another of the latter with a gold watch, but that was also later stolen. Surviving meant helping yourself to what you could. Hanna Grisebach brought back part of a horse and marinated it in vinegar and spices. The dish brought forth whoops of joy. She also received her share of a cow that had trodden on a mine. Possibly the greatest discovery of all was the contents of the cellar of a villa which the owner had thrown into the waters of the Hasengraben, in order to prevent the Russians from drinking it. Hanna's daughter, together with a friend, had located the booty and they were prepared to wade out to their hips to bring up the precious bottles: 'top wines from famous sites'. The Grisebachs drank them with relish, while the one who had donated them lay in bed with a cold. The wine put the food to shame. Anything they didn't want, such as a bottle of Malaga, could be traded with the Russians for bread and bacon.[8]

On 5 May Hanna heard a rumour that the Americans were coming to Potsdam. Stories of this sort were rife at the time – there was no connection with the Potsdam Conference in July. The first Russian wave was moving on. A baggage train set off, creating a 'picturesque scene' reminiscent of Tolstoy's *The Cossacks* or similar episodes from *War and Peace*. Boys spent their time shooting ducks and riding horses around, while abandoned boats bobbed on the water. The Americans didn't come, however, and from mid-May there was very little food. Supplies of meat and fat dried up and the Grisebachs lived on potato flakes and whatever fruit and vegetables they could scrump from abandoned gardens. Added to this they caught fish in the Havel or the lake, sometimes picking up a few after the Russians had tossed a grenade into the water – their usual form of angling.

In their hunger they were pleased to hear that professors were equated with manual workers in the handing out of ration cards: they were eligible for the card I. When a field full of potatoes was located twenty kilometres away in Buckow, Hanna and others set off on replacement bicycles they had unearthed. They had to dodge Russian fire to get at the tubers, as the soldiers wanted to distil them. Still, despite several setbacks, Hanna was able to get away with thirty-five kilos.[9]

First Contacts between East and West

One pretext for the Allied conference was to enforce the zones decreed at Yalta. The Allies had all ended up in the wrong places: the French had been in Stuttgart; the Americans were in Thuringia and had advanced to Halle in Saxony; the British had occupied the western half of Mecklenburg, while other American units had crossed the Harz Mountains to reach Magdeburg on the Elbe. This so-called Magdeburg Pocket was due to the Soviets. The Allied zones remained fluid until just before Potsdam, and there was a good deal of idle speculation about who would fall to whom. Even at the beginning of September it was still not clear to Berliners who was where. It was said that the Russians were to evacuate Eisenach and Jena and that the British had control of the airport in Erfurt (all three were in the Russian Zone). The British were to receive Thuringia, they heard, and the Russians would be compensated in East Asia. The Western Allies were forced to retreat to positions previously agreed by the politicians at Yalta behind the Elbe and the Harz. The generals grumbled. In their enthusiasm to take back their rightful territory, the Russians also attempted to grab Coburg in Franconia, probably because they thought the town was in Thuringia. This led to a stand-off with the Americans.

On 11 July 1945, Margret Boveri reported a fresh wave of arrests connected with the conference. The neighbouring communes were being cleared of Germans to make room for the delegates. Babelsberg was already purged, now it was the turn of Wannsee. Intellectuals were the main targets, Pgs or non-Pgs. *Pace* Hanna Grisebach, there were disadvantages to their academic status.

The conference proved a chance to survey the behaviour in the Allied camps. There was bad blood on both sides. The Soviets still believed that they had done the lion's share of the fighting and borne the brunt of the losses. The East did not trust the West, and vice versa. The Russians believed that the Western Allies were merely taking a breather before they attacked the Soviet Union and that they had kept their options open throughout the war by conducting secret negotiations with the Germans. That channels were open is undoubtedly true, and the Soviet authorities had been informed of the fact by the British intelligence officer Kim Philby and others. The Russians said they were not allowed to interview all the prisoners held by the West. But they were allowed to talk to a number of them and 'the records of the interrogations confirmed that there had been some backstage negotiations between the Nazis and the US and British Intelligence about the possibility of a separate peace.'[10] The Russians had also held talks with the Germans.[11]

There were advocates for war against the Soviet Union in both the British and American camps, but how far up they went was concealed during the Cold War. The *Hitler Book*, prepared for Stalin from interrogations with high-ranking German POWs in 1948, abounds with accusations of Western Allied perfidy.[12] Some British generals, notably Montgomery, were anxious to push on against the Russians. This had been supported by Churchill, but the plans would have been leaked to the Russians by Donald Maclean of the British Foreign Office, adding to the feeling of distrust that existed among the Big Three. In 1945 the Russians believed the British were holding back a substantial German army for use in the next campaign and for that reason had omitted to disarm German forces in their zone. At Potsdam Zhukov made a formal protest, claiming the British were keeping the 200,000-man Army Group North in readiness and that a million men in Schleswig-Holstein* had not been given POW status.[13] The Americans were rounding up scientists and taking them back to the United States to use in – among other things – their atom-bomb programme.[14] That the Russians were hardly averse to this themselves does not figure in Zhukov's memoirs. The Russians believed that the Anglo-Americans had intentionally failed to bomb targets that would be of use to them later. One example of this was the headquarters of IG Farben in Frankfurt, which was

---

* See above p. 70.

virtually intact – so much so, in fact, that the Americans took it over as their own HQ.[15]

Truman had no desire to continue the war against the Soviet Union and agreed to fall back to the lines agreed by the Big Three at Yalta. Churchill now expressed 'profound misgivings' in a cable to the president.[16] These pieces of territory might have been used for bargaining, for example, on the Oder and Neisse rivers. There was a little warm-up for Potsdam in Berlin on 5 June when Montgomery and William Strang from Britain, Eisenhower, Clay and Robert Murphy from the United States, and the French commander de Lattre de Tassigny were invited to settle the government of the city at Zhukov's HQ in Karlshorst. The Anglo-American generals were then invested with the Order of Victory, while de Lattre de Tassigny had to make do with the Order of Suvorov First Class.[17] Clay gave Zhukov the Legion of Merit.[18]

The inferior decoration handed out to de Lattre was emblematic of the status of the fourth ally: France was not invited to Potsdam.* It was 'a bitter blow to French pride'.[19] Truman had given the French assurances that their wishes would be noted and their arguments put forward, but they had not endeared themselves to the Americans through their behaviour: they had occupied Stuttgart and the Italian Val d'Aosta and they had indulged in colonial rivalry with the British in the Levant. The French had forgotten nothing, and learned nothing. In 1919 they had taken 50 per cent of Germany's reparations; now they demanded machines, coal and labour, as well as the restitution of all that the Germans had taken from them. The French were desperately angling for the Ruhr with its natural resources and heavy industry, but the incoming foreign secretary Bevin and the British in general did not want to give an inch, fearing that the Russians would also claim their pound of flesh.[20]

At the Berlin meeting Germany formally ceased to exist as an independent nation. The Allies signed the Declaration of Defeat and Assumption of Sovereignty. The four powers also agreed the form of the Allied Control Council that was to rule Germany, but the Russians made it clear that the Western Allies would not be allowed to take up their sectors in the capital until they had complied with Yalta: they had to fall back behind the River Elbe and the Harz Mountains. Western politicians wanted this decision to be taken by the Control Council, but Eisenhower (who was impressed by Zhukov) was in favour of giving in to the Russians, and Truman's emissary

---

* Eisenhower's secretary – and mistress – Kay Summersby says the medals were handed to the Western Allies in Frankfurt, when Zhukov returned their visit.

Harry Hopkins had discussed this *quid pro quo* in Moscow.[21] Zhukov believed that the Western Allies were prepared to accept this loss of territory because they were still anxious for the Russians to play a military role in the war in the Far East.[22] Ursula von Kardorff already had a fair idea of the future Russian Zone on 11 June – Weimar, Leipzig, Dresden – and doubted Stalin's credentials as a 'benefactor of mankind'. The zones were ratified on 26 July.[23]

Zhukov also had a meeting with Hopkins the next day, 12 June. Hopkins had flown in from two weeks in Moscow, where he had had six meetings with Stalin to discuss the UN Charter among other things and the chance of fitting in a few non-communists in the government of the Lublin Poles. Otherwise his task had been to reassure the Russian leader that the United States had no foreign political ambitions in Europe, thereby leaving him a free hand in Poland and Austria. Hopkins had not consulted Churchill, whom Truman was holding at arm's length, while he refused to speed up the scheduled talks. Members of Truman's entourage, however, took a completely different view, arguing for a showdown with Russia. These included Harriman, Forrestal and Leahy.[24]

Stalin and Molotov backed four or five of Hopkins's Poles, who later had to flee for their lives. On the way out Hopkins's aircraft had flown over Berlin. Seeing the ruins he remarked, 'It's another Carthage.'[25] He was sympathetic towards the Russians, and regretted the former president's sudden death. He had no close relationship with Truman: 'It is a pity President Roosevelt didn't live to see these days. It was easier with him.'[26] Hopkins told Zhukov that the Americans would not be ready for 15 June and that they would need to postpone the leaders' conference for another month, until 15 July. Zhukov proposed Potsdam because there was no suitable building in Berlin in a good enough state of repair. The only place in Potsdam was the crown prince's palace, but there was the advantage of Babelsberg, a largely undamaged area of villas that had been inhabited by film-folk and politicians in Weimar times.[27]

The themes on the agenda were the political and economic future of Germany, denazification, demilitarisation and decentralisation, Germany's eastern border, the status of Königsberg and East Prussia. Austria was also on the agenda, as well as all the other former belligerent powers. Zhukov took Hopkins and his assistant Charles 'Chip' Bohlen on a tour of the ruined city and afterwards there was a buffet lunch that was 'light on food, heavy on vodka'.[28]

Hopkins had been present at Yalta, and knew his old master's mind. He had been sent to deal with de Gaulle, which he clearly found an onerous duty. When Roosevelt's interpreter at the conference, Chip Bohlen, had said, 'We can all admit that de Gaulle is one of the biggest sons of bitches who ever straddled a pot,'[29] the late president had laughed. Roosevelt was insistent that de Gaulle should not receive a place at the top table. Churchill had to present the French case and obtain an occupation zone in Germany. Stalin only agreed as long as it took nothing away from his portion. What is striking is how little fight the Western Allies put up against the Russian leader even at Yalta. Hopkins had advised Roosevelt to accept Stalin's huge reparations demands,[30] and when America and Britain gave way on Poland's western borders, it is not clear they knew exactly what was involved.

Churchill had tried to settle the Polish issue before the Red Army arrived, but Russia's might had won the day. He had had a change of heart. On 15 December 1944 he had been quite open about the complete expulsion of Germans from the eastern territories, but he was worried about numbers. It appeared that he thought six million was the upper limit, and now he learned that the figure would be eight or nine, which was completely impossible to effect.[31] Churchill clung to his Wismar pocket as a bargaining counter, and on 9 June 1945 he cabled Truman to advise him to do the same and hold on to American positions in Thuringia and Saxony. He might have hoped for a better rapport with Truman, as his relations with Roosevelt had been strained at the end of the late president's life. He told Truman not to consider withdrawing until the Austrian question had been properly settled. On 14 June Truman cabled Stalin, however, and agreed to move his troops back to the Elbe. Churchill had no alternative now but to comply with his ally's decision. He now informed Stalin that the British would be gone by the 15th. Stalin then played for more time. He requested that the Allies wait until 1 July before taking up their lines in Berlin. There were mines to be cleared, and other chores to be effected first.[32]

They should have known what they were in for by now – Stalin had already shown his hand in eastern Europe. Czechoslovakia was a case in point. The government in exile had taken leave of King George VI on 15 February and left England on 12 March. On 19 March Beneš and Masaryk were in Moscow. On 6 April they arrived in Prague to be welcomed with bread and salt. On 9 April an interim government was set up under Zdenek Fierlinger with representatives of the four parties and four non-party members. The highest goal was co-operation with Moscow.

The Poles had been obliged to accept the Curzon Line in the east, but on 21 July 1944 Stalin was able to placate the Lublin government by dangling compensation in front of their eyes, in the form of German territory in the west. Churchill and Roosevelt had raised no objection to the Oder–Neisse Line at Yalta, although there had been misgivings about giving the Poles such a large amount of German territory and it was left that land would be found for them in the west and north. The Poles were well aware of what they wanted from the Potsdam conference. The Lublin regime had formally stated that they wanted the Oder–Neisse on 5 February 1945. As Władisław Gomułka put it, 'we must expel all the Germans because countries are built on national lines and not on multinational ones'.[33]

The issue was scheduled for review at Potsdam. The reason why the Russians had stood by and watched the Warsaw Uprising from the other side of the Vistula was that they wanted those elements out of the way that were not in favour of a communist or pro-Moscow Poland. The Western Allies continued to support the regime in exile in London. The sixteen London government emissaries who went to Moscow to enquire about possible collaboration were arrested. Meanwhile the Lublin men trotted along behind the Red Army. In March 1945 they created five new Polish *woiwode*: Masuria, Pomerania, Upper Silesia, Lower Silesia and Danzig. They were already referring to the areas as the 'Recovered Territories'. The move resulted in protests from Washington: there had to be peace talks first![34]

In their policy of demontage and cultural pillage, the Russians showed no desire to co-operate with the West. Some of the Soviet generals, such as Bulganin, thought like Montgomery – they had won a battle, not the war. Fascism had to be defeated, particularly in America. 'America is now the arch-enemy!' said Bulganin on the eve of the storming of Berlin. 'We have destroyed the foundations of fascism, now we must destroy the foundations of capitalism – America.' In cultural terms this was expressed by the Russian officer Vladimir Yurasov prior to the Western Allies' arrival in Berlin: 'Take everything out of the Western Sector of Berlin. Do you understand? All of it! What you can't take, destroy. Only leave nothing for the [Western] Allies: no machine, not even a single bed; not even a chamber pot!'[35] Berlin and its industrial satellites were being stripped bare: the hardware of companies such as Osram and Siemens, of the telephone exchanges, of the S-Bahn and so on, right down to their typewriters, was being loaded up and shipped back to Russia.

The Russian leader was also wary of American and British attempts to promote capitalism. The American minister responsible for Germany was John McCloy, who was a banker in normal life. He had some sympathy for the defeated Germans in that his wife had been born in Germany. In opposition to the Morgenthau view (which was essentially behind demontage) McCloy encouraged the rebuilding of Germany. Morgenthau had not abandoned his famous plan. In 1945 he published *Germany is our Problem*. Truman had been opposed to the plan even as a senator, so he was happy to listen to McCloy. Another opponent of Morgenthau was the secretary of war Henry Stimson, who thought the secretary for the Treasury 'biased in his semitic grievances'. The day before his departure for Potsdam, Truman accepted Morgenthau's resignation, commenting, 'That was the end of the conversation and the end of the Morgenthau Plan.' On the other hand the plan was still present in the minds of many of the soldiers, and their desire to lay waste to Germany had been sharpened by what they had seen in the concentration camps.[36]

In their recorded statements the Russians showed themselves more sympathetic to the conquered Germans. Anastas Mikoyan, then vice-president of the Council of People's Commissars, expressed the view in an interview with *Pravda*, which found its way into *The Times*: 'We have crushed Hitler's armies in fierce combat and taken Berlin, but our moral sense and our traditions do not allow us to ignore the suffering and privations of the German civilian population.' It was a far cry from the realities of life under Soviet dominion. Germans also clung to the comforting line of Stalin's – 'Hitlers come and go, but the German people remain.'[37]

It was also becoming clear how little the Anglo-Americans could trust Stalin. The Russians had occupied the Danish island of Bornholm, which, they said, lay to the east of the line of their own sphere of influence. The truce in Hungary was signed without any participation of the Western Allies, and at the time of Potsdam the west had yet to be allowed into Vienna. Just how much Stalin was lying at Potsdam is clear from an exchange between Clay and Zhukov on 7 July, just ten days before the meeting of the Big Three. Zhukov informed the American general that Silesia had already been turned over to the Poles; 'the Germans had moved out of the area in such huge numbers that there is little agriculture remaining for this area'. The Russians did not even have access to the coal, said Zhukov. They had to pay for it like everyone else. The British and the Americans were having to supply the Germans with 20,000 tons of food every month. The loss of Silesia was therefore highly significant. The United States had already protested about the handing over of Silesia to the Poles.[38]

At the Cecilienhof – the palace of the Prussian crown prince and the venue for the Potsdam Conference – the Russians planted a great red star of geraniums, pink roses and hortensias in the flower bed at the entrance.[39] Inside the house there were frantic preparations for the arrival of the Big Three.[40] The different quarters were to be colour-coded: blue for the Americans, white for the Russians and pink for the British. The conference table had been specially made in the Lux Factory in Moscow.[41] The Russians and the Americans were already observing one another from either side of the Glienecke Bridge, as they were to do until the end of the Cold War.

In Potsdam itself Hanna Grisebach and her family were made aware of the coming of the Big Three by increased security around the Neue Garten and the Cecilienhof. They were lucky enough to be on the far side of the Heiligensee. All the streets leading directly to the palace had to be evacuated. GPU carried out a wave of arrests and a sentry was posted in their garden. There were one or two advantages: the Russians quickly laid out a new street and a bridge was thrown across the Havel to Babelsberg where the leaders were staying. A pontoon bridge was also put up to allow access to Sacrow and the airport at Gatow. Russian soldiers rode bareback and naked into the waters of the lakes, reminding Hanna of centaurs, but she was less pleased to find herself under house arrest from 16 July, living in a state of impotent rage while she observed the Red Army guard knocking twenty-five kilos of unripe apricots off their tree in the garden. Any attempt to go out was greeted by cries of 'Dvai–Dvai! Zuhrick nah Haus!' (Quick, quick! Back in the house!). When an aircraft flew low over their street she hoped it was the British and American leaders going home.[42]

Stalin arrived by train on 16 July. He wanted no special arrangements, no regimental bands. He told Zhukov to meet him, and to bring along anyone he thought necessary. Zhukov sat beside him in the car and they drove to a luxurious villa. Stalin wanted to know who had lived there. He was told it had belonged to General Ludendorff.[43] The British and Americans arrived the same day. Truman and Churchill were in frequent contact in the run-up to the conference. Churchill had wanted King George VI to attend, and also to review the British forces in Berlin, but that idea was dropped in June.[44] The British had had a general election on 5 July, but because British servicemen were scattered throughout the world, the results would not be in for three weeks. Churchill informed Truman that, whatever the results of the election, the conference should not be hurried.[45]

Truman came via Amsterdam. He was very much an innocent abroad and relied on his secretary of state, James Byrnes. He had no strong feelings of his own. He had inherited from Roosevelt the idea that America and the Soviet Union could happily coexist. Kennan, for one, thought this an illusion.[46] Truman and Byrnes flew in separate aircraft, Byrnes himself piloting the plane between Cassel and Magdeburg. Truman looked at both cities from the window. He could see not one single undamaged building. He landed on the 'British' airfield at Gatow, which was conveniently close to Potsdam. They drove to their quarters in Neubabelsberg. British and American soldiers lined the route until they reached the Soviet Zone.

The Americans had already decided they wanted to undermine communism in Germany. To that end they desired to see the creation of some centralised agencies that might squeeze out Soviet influence. It was one of the first rumbles that presaged the Cold War. Neither Truman nor Byrnes thought Germany was a danger any more: it had been destroyed, and the atom bomb was there should it ever seek to menace world security again. Byrnes was also firmly in agreement with the British in wanting to keep the Ruhr free from the Russians. Besides, the cession of the Ruhr would upset the struggling German economy and make the occupation even more expensive for the Anglo-Americans.

Truman was lodged in a three-storey villa at 2 Kaiserstrasse on the Gribnitzsee, which had been the home of 'the head of the movie colony' who had been sent 'back' to Russia – 'for what purpose I do not know', Truman wrote to his mother and sister. It was evidence of a certain naivety as far as Russia was concerned, and did not augur well. The house had been newly painted, and received the ironic title of the 'Little White House', 'although it was painted yellow'.[47] Churchill had a house of the same size, two blocks away at 23 Ringstrasse. Truman went to bed early to prepare himself for what was likely to be a tough day on the 17th. He met Churchill in person for the first time the next morning, but felt he was no stranger.[48]

Churchill was accompanied by his daughter Mary, Sir Anthony Eden, the head of the Foreign Office Sir Alexander Cadogan and his naval adjutant, Commodore C. R. Thompson. Truman told Churchill he wanted to suggest an agenda, and asked him if he had brought one himself. 'No,' he said. 'I don't need one.'[49] In fact both the British and the Americans had decided to toughen their stance over the Oder–Neisse, to the degree that they were prepared to go back on what they had indicated they would accept at Yalta. Stalin had made it clear at Yalta that he meant the Western, not the Eastern Neisse.* Now the diplomats arriving in Potsdam were to

---

* In German they are called the Lausitzer or Görlitzer Neisse and the Glatzer Neisse. The Glatzer Neisse joins the Oder at Schurgast in Upper Silesia, the Polish Skorogoszcz. In Polish the river is called the Kłodzka.

play innocent and carried instructions *not* to permit an extension of Poland to the Western Neisse. The Americans also wanted to prevent the subtraction of most of Pomerania. Poland was to receive the southern half of East Prussia, Danzig, Upper Silesia and *part* of Pomerania, but that part would be *far* east of Stettin.[50]

The Americans were ready to dig their heels in, though the British were more concessionary, as they had been at Yalta. The sticking point was the Eastern Neisse. The British wanted the border drawn there, which would leave a substantial part of Lower Silesia in German hands, together with three million Germans. The negotiations would hinge on reparations: the Russians would not receive a brass farthing from the Western zones of Germany if they insisted on advancing the Polish border to the Western Neisse. What the Western Allies had not reckoned with was the obduracy of Stalin. He was not prepared to budge on this issue, and their opposition simply caved in.[51]

Truman allowed himself a little excursion to the capital. He saw the remains of the Reich Chancellery, 'where Hitler had conducted his rule of terror'. He looked at the mess and was thankful that his own country had been spared such 'unimaginable destruction'. 'That's what happens . . . when one overreaches oneself,' he added sententiously.[52] The news of the statesman's Berlin walkabout reached the ears of Ruth Friedrich: 'They are having a very discreet meeting in Potsdam, no noise penetrates the kilometre-thick cordon. As a result it is exciting to learn that the foreign heads of government have visited the inner city and the Tiergarten district and seen over the ruined buildings of Hitler's Reich Chancellery and the air-raid cellar.'[53] She would not have been so impressed had she known how profoundly Truman had understood the plight of the German people. On the second day of the conference the American leader characterised the Soviets as the sort of people who stole rare old grandfather clocks and damaged them in the process.[54]

Stalin visited Truman in the Little White House shortly after his arrival in Potsdam. He came with Molotov and Pavlov the interpreter and insisted on being called 'generalissimo' and not 'marshal', in tribute to his great victories in the field.[55] Truman wanted him to stay for lunch. Stalin tried to fight him off, but he stayed in the end. Truman congratulated himself, and felt that he could do some good for the world as a result of this small domestic triumph.

The conference began at 5.10 p.m. on the 17th. Stalin proposed that Truman should preside, and Churchill seconded him. Truman's first move was to propose a quarterly conference of foreign ministers as a means of avoiding the pitfalls that had followed the First World War. This had been foreseen at Yalta in February. The Allied Control Council was to start work at once. Truman made his demands: he wanted complete disarmament for Germany, and Allied control of all industry that might be used to produce arms. 'The German people should be made to feel that they had suffered a total military defeat and that they could not escape responsibility for what they had brought upon themselves.' The Nazi Party was to be destroyed, its officials removed from office. The country was to be reconstructed on democratic lines prior to its eventual peaceful participation in international life. Nazi laws were to be rescinded and there were to be trials for war crimes. On the other hand the seeds were to be sown for reconstruction: Germany was to be seen as *one* economic unit.[56]

Now it was Stalin's turn. As far as Germany was concerned he wanted his share of the German merchant fleet and navy, and reparations and trusteeships due to him under the UN Charter. He made demands relating to other countries before finishing with Poland's western borders and the liquidation of the London-based government in exile. Churchill was not happy about giving Stalin the German fleet. He told the dictator that 'weapons of war are terrible things and that the captured vessels should be sunk'. The wily Georgian had an answer to that: 'Let us divide it . . . If Mr Churchill wishes he can sink his share.'[57] That concluded the first day.

There was music playing all over Potsdam that July, or so it seemed. Hanna Grisebach was a violinist and played Mozart with a local doctor and a Frau von Kameke. The Russians came to the house of the latter and loudly applauded. This led to one of her strangest engagements: to play before the NKVD. She was very pleased to oblige, as it meant a hot meal. Her elderly husband, however, remained at home in profound anxiety. It was only when he heard the valedictory word 'Dosvidania' on the doorstep that he calmed down.[58] On 18 July Ursula von Kardorff noted that the Big Three were sitting in Potsdam 'like the Norns' in Wagner's *Götterdämmerung* who spin the golden rope of world knowledge that binds past, present and future. In the opera the rope snaps.[59]

The second day continued the discussions about the Conference of Foreign Ministers before the Big Three came to the subject of defining Germany. Churchill was vague. He said Germany was what it had been before the war. Stalin countered by asking whether Austria and the Sudetenland were part of Germany. For him Germany was 'what she has become after the war. Austria is not part of Germany.' Truman proposed the 1937 frontiers, before Germany began to expand. Stalin would accept that, 'minus what she lost in 1945'. Truman was evidently perplexed: 'Germany lost all in 1945.'[60]

Stalin was impatient to broach the Polish issue. He had obviously made promises to the Lublin Poles. The Western Allies were content to leave this issue for the proposed peace conference. Truman did not think they had adequately defined Germany. Stalin's answer was evasive. Germany had no government, no definable borders, no frontier guards and no troops. The country was divided up into four zones of occupation. Truman insisted on the 1937 borders and Churchill agreed.[61]

Stalin returned to the ownership of the German fleet on the 19th. He made it crystal clear that he saw war material as plain, old-fashioned booty. Indeed, his view throughout – and indeed that of the Red Army – was the traditional one – the victor has the right to live off the conquered, take his chattels, eat his food and help himself to his women; and it is for the conqueror to decide whether he should preserve the life of the vanquished. Stalin had his grievances. On this day it was Franco and the Blue Division which had fought in the USSR; on another it was the Italians who had done the same. When there was mention of the Yugoslavs, who were embarrassing the West by demanding large-scale repatriations of their citizens from Austria, Stalin said he would not discuss the matter, as the Yugoslavs were not present. Eden reminded him that they had discussed the matter at Yalta, and the Yugoslavs had not been there either.[62]

Truman assured the Soviet leader that he would carry out the Yalta Agreement to the letter. He was getting bored, and perhaps just a little worried about what he had let himself in for.* He threatened to leave. Stalin laughed and rejoined that he would like to go home too. Truman gave a state banquet in the Little White House. The young American pianist Eugene List, a sergeant in the US army, played Chopin's Opus 42. Appropriately for a man who had belatedly set himself up as the patron of the Poles, Stalin was a Chopin fan. He was impressed and drank a toast to the pianist. Stalin liked the wine and asked where it came from. It was Californian. Truman also played the 'Missouri Waltz' for his guests. Only Churchill failed to see the charm of it all: 'he did not care much for that kind of music.'[63]

The following day Truman inspected American troops in Berlin. The session that afternoon raised the question of Vienna. Churchill complained that his soldiers had not been allowed to take possession of their sector. Stalin said the zones were now settled, and he could bring his army in now. The Polish issue had been handed over to the foreign ministers to solve.

* The part of the Yalta Agreement would result in the deaths of thousands of Russians and Yugoslavs.

They reported back on the next day, the 21st. The Lublin Polish leader Bolesław Bierut had told Byrnes that the Poles would still be at a disadvantage despite the huge amounts of German territory they were to swallow. Poland would still be smaller than it was before the war, because it had lost 180,000 square kilometres to the Russians. On the other hand he conceded darkly that it would be a more homogeneous state.* Yalta had decided that it was for the peace conference to give Poland its shape, but that the Allies would consider the Poles favourably. Truman continued to insist on the 1937 German borders, but he was beginning to realise that Stalin had presented him with a *fait accompli*. 'It now appeared . . . as if another occupying government was being assigned a zone in Germany. This was being done without consultation . . .'[64]

Stalin reiterated the position as seen at Yalta – the eastern borders would follow the Curzon Line. That meant he would hang on to what he had gained from his deal with Ribbentrop in 1939. 'It had been decided at Yalta that Poland should receive cession of territory in the north and west.' Truman agreed, 'but insisted that it was not correct to assign a zone of occupation to the Poles'. Stalin then uttered two monstrous lies: 'What had happened . . . was that the German population in these areas had followed the German Army to the west, and the Poles had remained.' The Germans were not only still there, but, with the exception of some parts of Upper Silesia, there were *no* native Poles.[†] Stalin went on to say that 'he was unable to see what harm had been done by the establishment of a Polish administration where only Poles remained'.[65] He then added, 'The western frontier question was open, and the Soviet Union was not bound [by Yalta].' 'You are not?' Truman asked. 'No,' said Stalin. According to Truman Churchill had a good deal to say but gathered that it was not the time to say it. Truman reiterated that it was a matter for the peace conference.[66] In the meantime the brutal torture and expulsion of the civilian populations of the region continued unabated. Even if the peace conference had been held in Paris in the summer of 1946, by then there would have been only a small minority of them left.

Stalin mentioned East Prussia, adding that 'it would be very difficult to restore a German administration' there. In his view, 'an army fights in war and cares only for its efforts to win the war. To enable an army to win and

---

* The population east of the Bug was mixed, and the Poles were not intending to permit any Germans to remain east of the Oder–Neisse. This way the problem of racial minorities was solved.

† Any areas where there had been substantial minorities of Poles were awarded to Poland at Versailles.

advance, it must have a quiet rear. It fights well if the rear is quiet and better if the rear is friendly . . .' This was the prologue to the revelation that the East Prussian Germans had all packed their bags and left as well – an act of great consideration towards the advancing Russians, as they had realised that the Red Army would want to know they had a quiet rear. 'Even if the Germans had not fled . . . it would have been very difficult to set up a German administration in this area because the majority of the population was Polish . . .' Truman and Churchill were fobbed off with more lies. Stalin 'insisted there was no other way out'.[67]

The matter was then placed in hock for the peace conference. Churchill continued to worry about British interests. He didn't want to have to foot the bill for feeding the Germans. The regions the Russians had *de facto* ceded to Poland represented a quarter of Germany's arable land. Truman expressed either terrible weakness or the hopelessness of the Western Allies when he said he 'did not think there was great disagreement on Polish frontiers'. This was probably yet another attempt to delay the decision, but until a time when Stalin's contention that there were no Germans had become reality. When he repeated that 'there was no German population' because they had 'all fled westward' and so 'there the [area] falls to Poland', Truman countered that 'nine million Germans seemed like a lot to me'. Churchill enquired, 'who is to feed them?' He was reluctant to take on this role without having the means at his disposal. It was a repeat of his concerns over provisions for the British Sector in Vienna.[68] The needle had stuck in Stalin's gramophone: the population had disappeared before the Red Army arrived – 'he emphasized that no single German remained in the territory to be given to Poland'.[69]*

It was at that moment that the president's aide Admiral Leahy whispered his famous interjection: 'Of course not . . . The Bolshies have killed all of them.' In his memoirs Truman took a tough stance: 'Of course I knew that Stalin was misinterpreting the facts. The Soviets had taken the Polish territory east of the Curzon Line, and they were trying to compensate Poland at the expense of the other three occupying powers. I would not stand for it, nor would Churchill. I was of the opinion that the Russians had killed the German population or had chased them into our zones.'[70] Churchill later claimed that had he returned to Potsdam he would have prevented the

---

* At the beginning of June there were 800,000 Germans left in East Prussia and 65 per cent of the Germans were still in Silesia. Half the Germans in Pomerania had moved out, but only 30 per cent of those in Brandenburg. In the Sudetenland only 3 per cent had left so far. (Gerhard Ziemer, *Deutsche Exodus: Vertreibung und Eingliederung von 15 Millionen Ostdeutsche*, Stuttgart 1973, 87–8).

Soviets from making off with so much of Silesia, but his contention was never put to the test.[71] It was a pity he did nothing at the time, beyond repeating that it was a matter for the peace conference. No monitors were despatched east, no enquiries were made among the incoming treks or among the miserable trainloads of refugees that discharged their cargoes in the Western zones. They did not want to know.

Churchill *was* concerned for the beleaguered British economy. Silesia's coalmines had been awarded to Poland, so that coal was not available for Germans. The West would have to foot the bill again. He was concerned that Germany needed to be built up again to avoid becoming a burden on the West. Reparations therefore had to take second place.[72] Stalin came up with his most ingenious argument to date at this point: 'the less industry there was in Germany, the greater would be the market for American and British goods'. Churchill reiterated, 'We do not wish to be confronted by a mass of starving people.' Stalin replied, 'There will be none,' and added, 'Are we through?'[73] That night Stalin gave his banquet. For occasions of this sort there was no shortage of provisions. On the contrary, it was quite a thing, with vodka and caviar at the beginning and melon and champagne at the end. There were at least twenty-five toasts. Truman took care to eat little and drink less. Stalin was not to be outdone by Eugene List, and had two great pianists and violinists perform. Truman was interested in what Stalin was drinking in his tiny glass. He presumed it was vodka, but the Russian leader was employing the same ruse as his marshal Koniev. Stalin finally told him with a smile that it was French wine – since a recent heart attack he could not drink as much.[74]

The next day, 22 July, was a Sunday. Truman studied the Yalta Declaration to see what it said about Poland's western borders. The Big Three had accepted the Curzon Line then, but had left the western border open. They had not expected problems on this issue. Truman concluded that there was no case for the Poles receiving a zone. He did not really object, but he didn't like the manner in which it had been done. Stalin thought that the Western Allies should listen to the Poles on this subject. Meanwhile the Soviet leader was romping home. He pointed out that the leaders at Yalta (Churchill was still at the conference at this point) had not meant the Eastern Neisse, but the Western Neisse. There were indeed two rivers of that name in Silesia, as we have seen – one which ran into the Oder below Breslau and one that joined it below Guben. This meant that the line demarcating Poland's western borders would run to the left of the town of Stettin, and more than a hundred kilometres to the left of Breslau, and would encompass all that part of German Lower Silesia that ran between the two rivers. To make it clear to the Western leaders, Stalin rose and showed them the area on a map.[75]

This cunning confusion over the two Neisse rivers added greatly to the Polish cull. Not only were the Poles to be richly rewarded with their half of East Prussia, Danzig, all of Hinter Pomerania and a large chunk of Brandenburg east of the Oder and the so-called 'border area', they were now to receive such stock German towns as Brieg, Bunzlau, Frankenstein, Glatz, Glogau, Goldberg, Grünberg, Hirschberg, Landeshut, Liegnitz, Ohlau, Sagan, Waldenburg and Warmbrunn, containing altogether some 2.8 million Germans.[76] In all they would be awarded 21 per cent of Germany's pre-1937 territory, while the Russians made off with 3,500 square miles of East Prussia. All in all Germany would lose a quarter of its extent, and a large part of the arable land that had fed it in the past. In return the Poles were meant to shut up about Poland east of the Bug, and accept their place in Stalin's world.

Truman and Churchill were giving way at every point. Stalin talked of Königsberg as a conquest next. This was booty – not in keeping with Churchill's and Roosevelt's high-minded utterances in Newfoundland in 1941 – but Byrnes thought Churchill understood Stalin's desire to grab a colony or two. The status of the city had been discussed at Teheran. The Soviet Union 'should have an ice-free port at the expense of Germany'. Stalin added that the Russians had suffered so much at the hands of Germany that they were anxious to have some piece of German territory as some small satisfaction to tens of millions of Soviet citizens. Besides, Roosevelt and Churchill had already agreed. Churchill made a weak attempt to backtrack. He said it would be difficult to admit that East Prussia did not exist and that Königsberg would not come under the authority of the Allied Control Council. Once more, the region's ultimate status would be left for the peace conference that was never to be.[77]

The conference then heard a report from Field Marshal Alexander about the British Sector of Vienna. The area contained 500,000 people, but the British had no means of feeding them, their zone being hundreds of miles to the south and west of the city. Stalin promised to look into the matter with Renner. On the 24 July he generously agreed to feed the British charges for the time being.

The conference returned to the thorny matter of the Polish border on the 25th. Churchill and Eden had met the Polish delegates, headed by Bierut, the previous day. Bierut was a Soviet pawn who simply lied to and stonewalled the British leader, but all the same he provided a rather more generous estimate of the number of Germans remaining beyond the Oder.

He believed there were a million and half of them. At the next session Churchill said that the question of the transfer of populations from Germany, Czechoslovakia and Poland should be discussed: 'This area was part of the Russian Zone and the Poles are driving the Germans out. He felt this ought not to be done without consideration being given to the question of food supply, reparation and other matters which had not yet been decided'. In his reply, Stalin came close to being frank. The Poles, he said, 'were taking their revenge upon the Germans . . . for the injuries the Germans had caused them in the course of the centuries'. Churchill expressed a material consideration once more – that revenge took the form of throwing the Germans into the American and British Zones to be fed.[78]

Truman reminded Stalin that the Poles were his responsibility too, and that he was also at the mercy of the Senate; and that they might easily refuse to ratify any proposed treaty. Stalin brought up another bargaining counter, one that was not in his hands: the Ruhr. This was in the British Zone, and the British were having a hard time keeping the French out. Churchill announced that he was leaving for Britain. 'What a pity!' said Stalin. 'I hope to be back,' replied the British premier. Stalin suggested that, judging from his rival's face, 'he did not think Mr Attlee was looking forward to taking over Churchill's authority', apparently adding, 'He does not look like a greedy man.' The British left Alexander Cadogan to mind the fort.[79]

There was no meeting on 26 July, as the British were absent. Truman flew to Frankfurt-am-Main to visit Eisenhower. On the way to Schloss Berckheim, General Bolling's palatial headquarters in Weinheim, he drove through unscathed villages, and saw healthy-looking Germans. Eisenhower was based in the big IG Farben building in Frankfurt, which reminded Truman of the Pentagon. The British delegation had still not returned on 27 July and Truman relaxed with Eugene List's piano-playing. He wrote to his mother and sister of this 'Godforsaken country'. 'To think that millions of Russians, Poles, English and Americans were slaughtered all for the folly of one crazy egotist by the name of Hitler. I hope it won't happen again.'[80] The day before he had met a Lieutenant Hitler, who came from the solidly German town of St Louis.

Churchill had very much expected to be back, but Attlee won by a landslide and became prime minister on the 26th. On the 27th he unexpectedly named the former docker Ernest Bevin as foreign secretary. Bevin himself thought he was destined for the Treasury, and that Hugh Dalton would get the Foreign Office. Attlee had even told Dalton as much when he saw him that morning. The Foreign Office, however, was not happy with Dalton, possibly fearing that the Old Etonian economist would be 'too soft' on the Russians. The permanent under-secretary, Cadogan, thought Bevin 'the heavyweight of the cabinet'. A further deciding factor was the king's antipathy towards Dalton. He too preferred Bevin.[81]

Bevin had no problem thinking himself into the role of chief diplomat. As he told his private secretary Nicholas Henderson, he knew all about 'foreigners'. He had had plenty of experience of ships' captains. 'Oh yes, I can handle them,' he said. As it was, he was devoted to the old guard at the Foreign Office and the Foreign Office liked him too, because he did not prevent them from shaping government policy. Bevin was strongly anti-Soviet and had become fed up with Churchill's softness towards them. He thought the Conservatives had thrown too many 'baubles at the Soviets'. On 28 July, badly overweight and heavily dependent on drink and cigarettes, Bevin went to Brize Norton to take his first flight.[82]

Truman was introduced to Ernest Bevin. Both he and Byrnes were rather shocked by his aggressiveness towards the Soviets. When he got to his digs, Bevin told General Sir Hastings Ismay that he was 'not going to have Britain barged about'.[83] His passion for the British Empire would not have been popular with the Americans or the Russians. Britain, however, had far less might than the other two. Economically it was on its back: six years of war had cost a quarter of the country's pre-war wealth; its income was reduced by half; exports were just a third of what they had been, and its merchant fleet was down by 30 per cent. It had also lost 40 per cent of its markets – chiefly to the Americans. Together with these problems, the colonies were crawling with nationalists who were looked on with sympathy by the other two powers round the Russian table in Potsdam.[84] Despite the limited affections of the Americans, Britain had only one way to turn. The Americans were avowed enemies of colonialism and the sterling bloc, which they saw as a threat to the open world economy.[85]

Naturally Stalin knew Attlee well. The later arrival of the British meant that the conference did not kick off until 10.15 p.m. on the 28th. Bevin was seeing the Russian leader for the first time. He decided he was like a 'renaissance despot' – it was always yes or no, 'though you could only count on him if it was no'. Bevin immediately protested about the Oder–Neisse Line.[86] For the time being, however, the conference continued to discuss booty. Stalin agreed that he would not seek reparations from Austria (he was insisting on payments from Italy). He would find another way of making off with the booty he desired – by sequestering 'German' assets. Truman was growing impatient with the reparations issue.

He realised all too well that when these countries were bankrupted by reparations they would need bailing out by the United States. It was after midnight when the meeting broke up.[87]

The 29th was the second Sunday of the conference. Truman attended a church service in Babelsberg. Stalin had caught a cold and had stayed in bed, thereby postponing the end. Truman thought he was faking the illness, and that he was merely disappointed that Churchill had been replaced by Attlee. Molotov took his place at the table. Zhukov remarked that Attlee was rather more reserved than Churchill, but that he continued Churchill's line of argument.[88] Truman's original suppositions about Stalin had been revised – he had never met such stubborn characters before and hoped he would never do so again.[89]

The American secretary of state James Byrnes read out a statement offering a definition of Poland's western borders that would prevail until the matter could be decided by the peace conference. The area was to be administered by the Poles 'until Poland's final western border was fixed' by the peace conference.[90] Byrnes drew a line starting at Swinemünde, west of Stettin, and proceeding down the Oder to the Neisse before following the *Eastern* Neisse to the Czech frontier. The Poles would also administer Danzig and the lower half of East Prussia. It would not be considered a part of the Soviet Zone.[91]

Molotov immediately objected: he wanted the border fixed at the Görlitzer or *Western* Neisse. Truman thought he 'requested a very large concession on our part'. That was a considerable understatement. Truman was already annoyed by the Russian–Polish *fait accompli*. The Russians had warned their clients in Poland and Czechoslovakia to put a temporary stop to their expulsions, at least until such time as the Allies could find places for them within the shrunken Germany. The miserable German population in Silesia were hoping vainly for justice from Potsdam. The Polish authorities had now declared them to be 'outside the law, without possessions or honour'.[92] The final decision was pure whitewash.* Molotov returned to the Ruhr. It was the bit of western Germany the Russians wanted and had failed to occupy. Now he demanded two milliard dollars

---

* Polish–East German agreement was not made until 1951 when an accord was signed in a villa in Frankfurt-an-der-Oder. The place later became the House of German–Soviet Friendship and a plaque was set up to mark the spot. It was one of the few restaurants in Frankfurt when the author ate there on 17 August 1991, the day of the Moscow Coup. Bewildered Soviet soldiers wandered around the garrison. *Soljankasuppe* seemed appropriate: it was the one culinary contribution made by the Russians in the long years of occupation.

or its equivalent – five to six million tons of machinery. Russian reparations had already been fixed at Yalta. They were to receive a quarter of the equipment in the Ruhr. There were other little points of that nature to clear up. The naval issue was settled by a three-part division.[93]

Stalin continued indisposed. Truman wrote to his mother and sister. He was not convinced that Stalin was ill. Perhaps the generalissimo genuinely missed Churchill, for it was certain that Attlee would make just as many concessions, if not more. Stalin did not please the American leader: 'You never saw a more pig-headed people as the Russians. I hope I never have to hold another conference with them.'[94]

The end drew near. The eleventh and penultimate meeting took place on the 31st. The Ruhr was British, and Bevin fixed the Russian share at 10 to 15 per cent. That meant 15 per cent in commodities or 10 in reparations. Bevin also held out for the Eastern Neisse, but Byrnes was ready to concede and grant the Russians the plum they longed for. Truman added forlornly that it was only a temporary measure. Bevin was still insisting on the 1937 borders and hoping for a deal of some sort before he would concede. The Americans pulled the carpet out from under his feet. He wanted to know if the British could also give away parts of their zone to other countries.* Truman added in what was no doubt a resigned tone: 'we all agreed on the Polish question'. Stalin said, 'Stettin is in Polish territory.' Bevin added, 'Yes, we should inform the French.' And they decided to tell the French. The French had wanted it thus all along.[95]

The Anglo-Americans had lain prostrate while the Russians had walked all over them. Truman thought the Polish compromise was 'the best we were able to get'.[96] It begs a number of questions: had Stalin placed the border at Berlin and the Spree, would the Allies have consented? Berlin had a Slavic history too, as indeed did Magdeburg. Why not fix Poland's border at the Elbe? For the Germans on the right bank of the Oder, however, Potsdam gave an ambiguous verdict, leaving the Oder–Neisse issue open until 1974 and later. The final decision was to be left until a peace treaty was agreed. This never happened. The Oder–Neisse Line therefore became a temporary frontier until a permanent one was fixed at a later conference. In the meantime the Poles resumed their expulsions from the areas allotted to them by the Soviets. The cities of Breslau and Stettin felt this decision acutely. The Anglo-Americans had not intended to leave them in Poland, either permanently or temporarily. They had planned to divide Breslau,

---

* The Anglo-Americans had taken the decision to award part of their zones to the French. The Soviets were indifferent.

leaving the bulk of the city in German hands, and the right-bank suburbs were to go to Poland. At Yalta Churchill had said, 'It would be a great pity to stuff the Polish goose so full of German food that it died of indigestion.'[97] Zhukov claimed that the Oder–Neisse Line had been settled at Yalta, and that Churchill was backtracking.[98] Without Churchill's at best limp resistance, Truman agreed to the Oder–Neisse Line including the Eastern Neisse and Breslau.[99]

At the next meeting Stalin was after booty again. He wanted a line drawn from the Baltic to the Adriatic, and the opportunity to appropriate any German property to the east of that marker. They discussed war criminals: the Russians wanted the Krupps indicted. Krupps had made possibly the greatest demands on the Nazi government for Russian slave labour and raw materials. The Russians complained that Rudolf Hess was living comfortably in England. Bevin replied that the British would send the Allies a bill for his upkeep.[100] Attlee thought the Russians had Goebbels. Stalin was evasive. He wanted to have a list of war criminals who might be in the Soviet Union, but the Americans opposed this. Stalin asked for just three names, at which Attlee suggested Hitler: 'Stalin replied that we do not have Hitler at our disposition but that he had no objection to naming him.'[101]

Stalin reverted to the western Polish border at the last meeting, which began at 10.40 p.m. on 1 August. Molotov had amended the line on the map. Stalin said that he wanted it fixed immediately west of Swinemünde, but that the precise location would be decided by the Poles and Russians. Bevin objected. 'No,' he said, 'the British could not cut themselves out of this . . . The line must be recognised by the United Nations.' The delegates continued to bicker about Swinemünde and how many other German villages to the west of the coastal town would fall to Poland. The session broke up at 3 a.m.[102]

The Potsdam Conference laid down the guidelines for the transfer of populations. An estimated 3.5 million Germans were to be brought out of the new Poland and settled in the British and Soviet Zones in an orderly and humane manner as enshrined in Article 13. A schedule was drawn up which foresaw the entire number crossing the frontier before August 1946.[103]

The Big Three agreed to create a number of 'central agencies' that would be law in all four zones. The French smelled a rat: central agencies smacked of the 'Reich'. 'There is thus a German state,' complained de Gaulle; that was 'inadmissible'.[104] It was not only the French who were unhappy. Potsdam ended in recrimination. The path to the Cold War was open. From now on decisions would be taken at the regular meetings of the Allied foreign ministers. The Russians had the dropping of the US atom bombs on Japan to concentrate their minds. On 22 August Truman put an end to Lease–Lend while de Gaulle was on a visit to America. Franco-American relations were marked by mutual incomprehension. France, which had signed a treaty with Soviet Russia in December, was playing the communist card. It was easily done with the Communist Party the largest in the French Assembly.[105]

The Western Allies were shocked that they had made so many concessions to the Soviets. They had managed the conference badly. Soviet power was at its height, while the British were at the nadir of their fortunes. The death of Roosevelt in April had meant that the only delegation to have maintained the same *dramatis personae* at Teheran, Yalta and Potsdam had been the Soviets, and they had known how to invoke past agreements.[106] Although Truman had accepted Morgenthau's resignation, it was only at Potsdam that the politician's thinking really became a dead letter.[107] One of the most influential critics of Potsdam was the diplomat George Kennan, who was stationed in Moscow and knew the Soviet leaders well. He viewed the whole conference with 'unmitigated scepticism and despair'. 'I cannot recall any political document the reading of which filled me with a greater sense of depression than the communiqué to which President Truman set his name at the conclusion of these confused and unreal discussions.' Quadripartite control was, thought Kennan, 'Unreal and unworkable'.[108]

He believed that the agreement was wrong, point by point. War crimes needed to be settled by immediate execution, and there was no common ground to be found with the Soviets. 'In all fairness' the granting of Königsberg to the Soviet Union had been agreed by Churchill and Roosevelt, 'but the casualness and frivolity with which these decisions were made . . . the apparent indifference on the American side' appalled Kennan. He also showed how Truman and Byrnes had been hoodwinked. The Russians required an ice-free port, and felt they deserved one after the sacrifices made by the Soviet people. Kennan pointed out that they already had three – Ventspils, Libau (Liepaja) and Baltisky – and Königsberg was forty-nine kilometres from the sea. The result was a disaster 'without parallel' in modern times.

Not only were the East Prussian population subjected to the most ghastly fate imaginable (and in many cases it was unimaginable), but – as Kennan pointed out – it resulted in the most terrible squandering of the resources of a rich agricultural province. Gone were 1.4 million head of cattle, 1.85 million pigs, four million tons of wheat, fifteen million tons of rye and 40 million tons of potatoes in a yearly average.[109]

Some Germans, however, were relieved to hear the outcome of the Potsdam Conference. For Ruth Friedrich it was as if a 'stone had fallen from our hearts: so there is not to be a fresh war but they were going to rebuild and rule together'. The order was enshrined in Control Council Proclamation No. 1 of 5 June, which informed the German people that the four powers would jointly govern Germany.[110]

For the Potsdamer life returned to what they now called normality. Hanna Grisebach was free to scrump again, stealing potatoes from the crown prince's garden. She was caught red handed by a Russian: 'Zapp-zarapp kartoscha!' Her daughter pacified the soldier with a little school-book Russian. He dismissed them: 'Na Haus!'[111] The shadows lengthened and the cold set in. By February it was fifteen degrees below, and there was no glass in their windows. They slept in their coats and animal skins. The shortage of potatoes had been joined by a dearth of coal and wood. It was Karl Jaspers who finally helped them out by recalling August Grisebach to his chair in the newly reopened university. His wife and children had to remain behind in Potsdam until repeated visits to OMGUS, the American HQ in Berlin-Dahlem, yielded the necessary papers.

19

The Great Freeze

Whenever I think of the winter of 1946 to 1947 in Germany, I always recall the glitter on the walls and in the interiors of houses, that I must have seen a hundred times in German homes and which resembled the sparkly sheen on the unpolished side of a granite block. It was the glitter of a wafer-thin layer of white frost, an icy blast of damp; the frozen moisture in the atmosphere created by men, sweat, coughing and breathing; men whose clothing was sometimes soaked though with snow, and who dried out slowly when they got home.

Carl Zuckmayer, *Deutschlandbericht für das Kriegsministerium der Vereinigten Staaten von Amerika*, Göttingen 2004, 82

After Potsdam the stage was set for the Cold War, but it did not come for a while. One reason for this was that Stalin did not want a war, hot or cold; and it was the Western Allies, first Britain, and then America, who pushed him into it. He had no desire to reach the North Sea, the Rhine or the Atlantic. The Soviet Union was exhausted by war. If Stalin had considered resuming the march west, he knew that his country needed a good twenty years to recover first. When goaded to invade western Europe by one of his generals, he answered, 'But who would feed all its people?'[1] Similarly, he tried to restrain Tito's wilder ambitions – although this did not come out at the time – when he appeared to back his territorial claims. Stalin's system was about security, and his almost paranoiac sense that the Soviet Union was in danger. Poland was the lynchpin: he wanted a good, deep buffer. In Germany he saw something more akin to an ally. He sought to avoid division, although he allowed certain policies – such as agrarian reform – which could only have been intolerable to the West. The Cold War was the result of what Vojtech Mastny has called the 'Western perception of a Soviet threat'.[2] Stalin kept his options open.

There was friction at Potsdam, but the Allies went home in the belief that they were policing the globe together. They had instituted a regular conference of foreign ministers (CFM) to keep the world in check. The merry-go-round had taken the foreign ministers to London in September 1945. It was their first meeting since Postsdam. There was a predictable scrimmage over who was to receive what in the way of German resources. The French were still clamouring loudly for the Rhine and the Ruhr and 'justice', by which they meant coal, machinery, locomotives, consumer goods and men. They were pre-empted by the Soviets, who had awarded themselves 50 per cent of reparations, with 20 per cent each to Britain and America. France and the other claimants had to make do with 10. Bevin was still firm on the Ruhr. He was generally sympathetic to the French, but in this instance he realised that any internationalisation of the area would be tantamount to opening the door to the Russians.[3]

French behaviour upset Molotov and led to a chilling of relations between the two countries. On 7 October 1945 *Pravda* ran an article saying that the French had less right to discuss eastern Europe than the Yugoslavs, Czechs or Poles. Moscow complained that the French were not prepared to deport Russian POWs, by which it almost certainly meant those Russian citizens who were hiding under French skirts because France had not been party to Yalta. The Russians responded by saying they would not return French POWs, which meant Alsatians who had been recruited into the German army after 1940.[4] They would have to spend another winter in the Gulag.

The winter of 1945–6 was not abnormally cold, but the terrible lack of coal and food was felt acutely by the very large numbers of Germans without proper roofs over their heads. The ground was rock hard and the lakes froze. The Kommandatura authorised a *Holzaktion* in the Grunewald woods, allowing Berliners to cut down the venerable trees of the former royal hunting reserve. That winter 167 people committed suicide from despair, and the British authorities in Berlin decided to evacuate children aged between four and fourteen to their zone. This involved 50,000 children and 10,000 accompanying adults. Despite this precaution, 60,000 Berliners are believed to have died before March 1946. The following winter killed off an estimated 12,000 more when temperatures hovered around thirty degrees below.[5]

As noted in the previous chapter, the meetings between the Big Three had foreseen a peace conference, similar to that which met in Versailles in 1919, putting the final coat of varnish on the post-war settlement. There were endless discussions about this, and about just who was to be allowed a seat at the table. Byrnes was still courting Stalin. He sat next to him at dinner in Moscow at the CFM in December 1945 and raised a toast:

'Whom we hath [*sic*] joined together, let no peace put asunder.' By his own admission it went down like a lead brick. The brief American–Soviet rapprochement struck fear into Bevin, but on 9 February 1946 Stalin appeared to open the batting in the Cold War with his speech hailing the victory of the Soviet people. The war, he said, had been the result of monopoly capitalism.[6] It was very probably true, however, that the Soviet leader had not meant to frighten the Western Allies. Both he and Molotov were still keen on East–West co-operation. So, to some extent, was Byrnes; but his attempts to maintain the peace between East and West were undermined by Truman, who pronounced himself 'tired of babying the Soviets'. He would go so far, and no further.[7]

Churchill made his speech in Fulton, Missouri on 5 March in which he was supposed to have coined the phrase 'Iron Curtain'. The words had, in fact, been first used by Joseph Goebbels.[8] Churchill's views were loudly cheered by the Foreign Office, though they were very cautiously received in America at first, which was moving only slowly in that direction.[9] The idea persisted in some quarters that Soviet Russia and America could carve up the world. The notion had found favour with Roosevelt. It often had to do with a profound Anglophobia on the part of senior American army officers.[10] Now voices of dissent began to ring out.

The Soviets had no desire to see Germany break up – they had their eyes on the Ruhr with its industries, and on their 10 per cent share of German production. After the Berlin election of May 1946 that went by the board. The Russians were proceeding with their idea of setting up 'democratic' government in their zone. The political resolve of the Western Allies in Berlin had first been put to the test in March that year when the Soviets called for the merging of the SPD and the KPD. In April the socialists and communists of the SBZ held a conference in the Admiralspalast Theatre where the call for the new 'Socialist Unity Party' or SED was unanimous. Elections by secret ballot were held in the West but were banned in the Russian Sector. The Soviet ban was challenged in both Prenzlauerberg and Friedrichshain, but Russian troops broke up the polling station and carried off the ballot boxes. In the Western sectors the vote was a disaster for the Russian plans to introduce a one-party state: 29,610 Social Democrats voted against, with just 2,937 agreeing to the merger. It had been 'the first free and secret election on German soil since 1932'.[11] Russia's policy had blown up in its face, especially when free elections were allowed.

The New Ideologists

The East–West co-operation that had won the war was going out of intellectual fashion. A different set of men were wielding influence in the
Western corridors of power. George F. Kennan had served in the Moscow
embassy during the war. For him the Soviet Union posed a threat to the
American way of life.[12] He believed the Americans were deceiving themselves if they thought they could change events in the areas already under
Soviet hegemony; on the other hand he could see no reason for making
things easier for them. Germany was not going to work – a shared
Germany was a 'chimera'. In the summer of 1945 Kennan wrote his
famous 'long telegram': 'We have no choice but to lead our section of
Germany – the section of which we and the British have accepted responsibility – to a form of independence so prosperous, so secure, that the East
cannot threaten it.' Better a dismembered Germany than totalitarianism at
the North Sea.[13] Kennan's memorandum was echoed by three similar
telegrams from the British diplomat Frank Roberts, although he expressed
himself with more caution.

In retrospect Kennan probably went too far. It is highly unlikely that
Stalin wanted to cross the Elbe. It did not make a lot of sense to strive for
a communist Europe while the Americans and the British retained large
forces on the mainland. If that had been what he desired, it was better to
wait: the fruit might fall from the tree without any need to struggle.
Besides, America had the atomic bomb, and was to possess a monopoly in
nuclear weapons until 1949.[14] The Soviets were still keen to reform their
zone. The Soviet diplomat A. A. Sobelev told Murphy that the pan-
German central government laid down by Potsdam would need years of
preparation, as the spirit of Prussia had to be excised from the administration first.[15] The changes of attitude were in the West, where the Americans
feared an attack on the open economy and the British an attack on their
interests in the Middle East and the Mediterranean.[16] Kennan was not
deceived by the Czechs. By 1945 the country was already under the sway
of Moscow. 'Personal acquaintance with the Czech ambassador in Moscow,
Zdenek Fierlinger, had given me the impression that we had to do in his
person not with the representative of a free and independent
Czechoslovakia but with one who was to all intents and purposes a Soviet
agent.'[17]

Views like Kennan's were becoming common currency in America.
General George Patton was a case in point: with time he preferred Nazis

to communists. A more analytical indictment of the policy that led to the Anglo-American rout at Potsdam appeared in Ralph Keeling's *Gruesome Harvest* of 1947. Keeling called it 'one of the most brutal and terrifying peace programmes ever inflicted on a defeated nation'. Germany was not a pawn in the battle between East and West, thought Keeling, 'she is the major prize'. Germany needed to be attracted over to the American side and kept there.[18] This was to become American policy before the year was out. Keeling echoed many of Victor Gollancz's views on the treatment of the Germans, but he was rare at the time in being prepared to bring up Allied wartime atrocities, such as the bombing of civilian targets and the firestorms where men, women and children were fried at temperatures of 1,000 degrees. The Oder–Neisse Line contradicted the Atlantic Charter, and – Keeling pointed out – even the draconian Morgenthau had limited his territorial demands for the Poles to the southern half of East Prussia and the mixed Germano-Polish area of Upper Silesia.[19]

In Britain, Roberts's views prevailed in the Foreign Office, which was calling for an all-out offensive against Russia's mission of 'dynamic and proselytising communism'. What Roberts feared was 'communism on the Rhine'. The British attitude was so aggressively anti-Soviet in Bevin's Foreign Office that some observers have suggested that the British were the prime movers in the Cold War.[20] There were still delusions of grandeur in Whitehall and Bevin was certainly all in favour of the hard line. He thought it might be necessary to abandon the idea of a united Germany but insisted that responsibility for the breakdown in relations between the wartime Allies should rest fairly and squarely with the Soviets. Though the Russians appeared peaceful in Europe, they were already moving troops into Iran, the move that was to prompt Churchill's Iron Curtain speech.[21] The Americans were the last to abandon their faith in a united Germany, but Byrnes was defeated in Paris, the location both of the farcical peace conference and of the Quai d'Orsay, which was most famously opposed to German unity. Byrnes could not believe a peace conference had any value now that so many countries had been absorbed into the Soviet bloc.[22]

Bevin was also worried about money, especially as Britain did not have much. Reputations die hard, but Britain's subaltern position was recognised by the permanent under-secretary, Cadogan, who referred to the leaders of the Allied coalition as 'the great two and a half'. In 1945 the economist Maynard Keynes was talking of a 'financial Dunkirk', and as the fuel crisis set in during the cruel winter of 1946–7 Britain's economic handicap was patently obvious.[23] In 1945–6 alone, Germany cost the British taxpayer

£74 million, while the British people had to put up with a continuation of wartime rationing.

Although Truman had recognised the Oder–Neisse Line on 9 August 1945, the Americans were ready to backtrack almost immediately. For the time being, however, the Control Council defined Germany as the land between the Line and the 'present western borders'. The French had made it clear as well that, although not party to Potsdam, they approved the cessions in the east. It was Byrnes who reopened the can of worms by raising the question of border revision and threatening Poland with a peace conference.[24]

That other Russo-sceptic, Clay, drew his inspiration from Byrnes. On 19 August he wrote to the secretary of state, 'You are carrying so much of the hope of the world on your shoulders against almost insurmountable odds that you should be free of all other worries. If you cannot win the fight for peace, no one can.'[25] The Berlin elections were coming up. Clay thought the Americans should support the democratic parties in the west – the CDU and the SPD represented the 'substantial majority of the population'. 'I am not unduly apprehensive of the election results in Berlin,' he wrote, as he did not trust them anyway. Berlin depended on Russia, which fed its people, and was subject therefore to Soviet economic pressure.[26] Indeed, there was a feeling that the Germans in the SBZ could not be trusted and that they would turn to communism under the blandishments of the occupiers. Even when there was plenty of evidence to the contrary – as in the Austrian elections – the Anglo-Americans still persisted in their view. The feeling that Germans in the east had been seduced by the Soviets strengthened their resolve to create a separate state in the west of the country. As early as May 1946 Bevin explained to the cabinet why he felt a divided Germany was desirable. The Russians presented a danger as great as, if not greater than, a revived Germany. The idea was to create a Germany 'that would be more amenable to our influence', whereas a united Germany would be more under Soviet hegemony.[27]

Byrnes was also the architect of Bizonia – the idea of merging the Western zones rapidly replaced Bevin's notion of a 'loose federation'. In April 1946 the four powers met to discuss the situation in Germany, and Russia was accused of reneging on the agreements made at Potsdam. The result was an economic amalgamation of the British and American zones. The conference affirmed the fact that the enemy had changed since the onset of the Cold War: the Germans had become allies in the new order. The British cabinet agreed in principle to Bizonia on 25 July 1946. Germany should become self-sufficient again by 1949.[28]

Byrnes made his statement of intent in Stuttgart on 6 September 1946. He had been attending the impotent Paris Peace Conference and had left for Berlin before flying on to the Württemberg capital. He met the German minister presidents and addressed an audience in the Opera House. The German politicians told him a new Hitler was an impossibility: were such a man to emerge, he would have to be a communist. Byrnes said it had been a mistake for America to lose interest in Europe after the First World War. 'The American people want to help the German people to win their way back to an honourable peace among the free and peace-loving nations of the world . . . What we want is lasting peace. We will oppose harsh and venge-ful measures which obstruct our attempts at peace. We will oppose soft measures which invite the breaking of the peace . . . We do not want Germany to become the satellite of any power or powers or to live under a dictatorship, foreign or domestic.' There were sideways swipes at the Poles for seizing land before they had been granted leave. Poland's borders, he warned, were not final; there had been no agreement. The French were also put in their place: America could not deny their right to the Saar, but it would not support any encroachment on the Ruhr or the Rhineland. The criticism of the French in Stuttgart, of all places, must have been especially piquant.[29]

Byrnes's hard stand was heartily approved by Clay. The British were also enthusiastic. Churchill cabled his congratulations. After some initial reti-cence, Bevin appeared pleased and made similar noises before the House of Commons in October.[30] Attlee was all for withdrawing from Germany, but Bevin, the Foreign Office and the chiefs of staff ganged up on him, claim-ing that it would be tantamount to another Munich. They wanted confrontation, not retreat. Above all Byrnes's speech went down well with the Germans. The *Wiesbaden Kurier* called it 'a ray of light at last'. Then again, in Wiesbaden, it was wise to praise anything the Americans did.[31] When Byrnes went, Clay continued the hard line. Washington interfered very little with American military commanders in Germany.[32] Not so enthralled by Byrnes's words were the Poles, who staged a protest outside the American embassy in Warsaw.[33]

John Dos Passos had the chance to interview Clay in Berlin at the end of 1945. Clay exerted his charm on the journalists, telling them 'with a smile that we weren't necessarily trying to produce an efficient Germany, we were trying to produce a democratic Germany'. He did not know if he would succeed in this. Nor could he say whether the Germany they pro-duced would be separate or unified: 'That decision couldn't seem to get past the [Control] Council.' Clay was referring to the French, who obstructed anything that exuded a whiff of unity.[34]

The French were up to their usual tricks and not playing ball with the Anglo-Americans. From the very beginning they sought to disable the Control Council and resist the implementation of the Potsdam Agreements as far as creating 'central agencies' was concerned. There was to be no recreation of the 'Reich'. Pierre Koenig wielded his veto like a bacon slicer. On 20 October 1945 he put paid to the idea of a unified trades union structure. The Americans were incensed. First Eisenhower threatened to scrap the Control Council, then the matter came within Clay's domain, and Clay was permanently furious with the French for their obstructions. The latter still had their hearts set on the dismemberment of Germany and looked approvingly to what had happened on the other side of the Oder–Neisse Line. As Bidault put it: if you can do it with Breslau, why not Mainz?[35]

The South Tyrol

One issue that was festering in the autumn of 1946 was what to do with the German-speaking South Tyrol. Hitler had been surprisingly pragmatic about ethnic Germans. Where 'Heim ins Reich' (home in the Reich) provided a pretext for annexation in most cases, for the German-speaking majority in the South Tyrol and Gottschee it meant 'come home to the Reich': Mussolini was to be allowed to continue Italianising this former Austrian territory north of the River Adige or Etsch.[*]

In 1919 the region had been 95 per cent German, but self-determination was nonetheless denied to its people. The Allies had promised the Italians the Brenner to lure them over to their side in 1915. Some vague noises had been made about autonomy, but once the Italian fascists came to power they were keen to consolidate the region by evicting the natives and replacing them with poor peasants from the south. Mussolini encouraged new industries in Bolzano (Bozen) and Merano (Meran), and brought in Sicilians to man them. The fanatical Ettore Tolomei from Trentino pursued a policy of promoting Italian institutions and banning the German language and place names. Many changed their family names to something more Italianate in order to retain their farms. The experience of persecution had been a bitter one for the South Tyroleans; and they had been only partly mollified in 1943 when the Germans had taken over from the Italians and

* Cf. the Deutschlandslied: 'Von der Etsch bis an der Memel' – Germany ran from the Adige to the Memel, on the Lithuanian border.

Mussolini's drive had abated. The Soviet Union might well have consented to hand over the territory had it not been for Marshal Badoglio's coup against Mussolini that year. Now Italy was on the winning side again, and would not be penalised in a post-war peace settlement. Similar sentiments were expressed by Churchill's foreign secretary Anthony Eden: there was more to be gained by sparing Italy further humiliation.[36]

From May 1945, the South Tyroleans naturally hoped that they would be allowed the chance to join their cousins in the north, and become part of an independent Austria. This was the aim of the SVP (South Tyrolean People's Party), founded on 8 May. Karl Gruber had been active in reclaiming the South Tyrol from the very moment the Allies arrived in Austria. He felt that Austria had proved its victim status, and could now reap the reward. In September 1945 there had been a demonstration on the streets of Innsbruck, and Figl expressed the view that 'The return of the South Tyrol to Austria is every Austrian's dream.'[37]

The Italian foreign minister Alcide De Gasperi was from Trent and was more prepared to see Trieste fall to the Yugoslavs, however, than the South Tyrol return to Austria. He tried to frighten the Anglo-Americans by conjuring up a vision of a communist Austrian state on the Brenner. This was calculated to have an effect on Truman. In general the Allies were split, with the American Austrian expert James Riddleberger siding with Austria, and the Italian authority Samuel Reber resisting. In Britain Lord Hood and Arnold Toynbee were in favour of Austria, while A. D. M Ross and the historian of the Habsburg Monarchy, A. J. P. Taylor, were against.[38]

Renner sent notes to the Allies on 6 and 16 September 1945 canvassing their views on a return of the region to Austria.[39] In January 1946 the Austrian government issued a note to the Allied Council with a request that it be forwarded to the member governments. The note requested the return of the province of Bolzano-Bozen – its agricultural production was vital to the Austrian economy. The request had support from some unusual circles. In the House of Lords Robert Vansittart spoke in favour of the cession of the South Tyrol to Austria, and the foreign secretary Bevin lent it a sympathetic ear.[40] The South Tyrol, however, was not what it had been in 1919. As a result of Mussolini's transfer of poor Italians from the south and Hitler's encouragement of the 'Heim ins Reich' programme to bring German-speakers to Germany, the Italian minority amounted to nearly 40 per cent of the population, and their presence was particularly strong in the bigger towns.

Gruber had assumed office as foreign minister with a desire to pursue a 'dynamic foreign policy' that was mostly thrust at the idea of getting the South Tyrol back.[41] A petition was signed by 158,628 South Tyroleans and handed to Figl in Innsbruck. On 1 May 1946 the Allies refused a South Tyrolean request for a plebiscite. The question was deferred to a putative Paris peace conference.

On 5 May 20,000 South Tyroleans gathered in the bailey of Schloss Sigmundskron wearing placards that read, 'Wir bitten die Siegermächte: schenkt uns unsere Heimat!' (We ask the victorious powers, give us our home!). Gruber now suggested that the South Tyrol be administered by the United Nations. When Austrian demands were rejected by the Italians, a general strike was organised in Innsbruck, Salzburg and Vienna. Gruber was invited to 'air his views' in Paris in August. By the end of the month his demands had been modified: South Tyroleans were to enjoy political liberty; the province of Bolzano was to have economic autonomy; there was to be a special customs policy between Austria and the South Tyrol.[42] The Italians agreed to a different statute for the region within the province of Trentino-Alto Adige. Trentino had also been a part of the Austro-Hungarian Empire, but its population was almost entirely Italian-speaking. As it was, the Allies made the decision to evacuate Italy at the Paris CFM on 24 June 1946. On the question of the South Tyrol, the foreign ministers were content to ask Italy for certain guarantees for the German-speaking population. They had eventually resolved to maintain frontiers, where possible, as they had been before the war. The French were more in favour: they had to put away a dream of extending their Austrian zone to the Adige. The decision to maintain the status quo was bitterly disappointing to the Austrians. Renner scrapped a banquet that was to be offered in 1946 to commemorate the victory over Germany.[43]

The injustice of the South Tyrolean position finally led to a meeting between the Austrian foreign minister and his Italian counterpart De Gasperi in Paris on 5 September 1946. They met to consider a South Tyrolean 'Magna Charta'.[44] The accord guaranteed the rights of the German-speakers. Once again they were to be entitled to German schools, and Germans might occupy a number of local-government positions. Place names could be written in German again. Exchanges between the north and the south of the Tyrol were encouraged with an automatic right for qualified students to study at Innsbruck University. In 1948, however, hopes of autonomy were dashed when the southern region was bound into the new area of Trentino, where Italians had a two-thirds majority.

The Paris Conference proved a humiliating experience for De Gasperi, but good news was on the horizon in the form of Trieste. The British had managed to keep the Yugoslavs out, and the following year the port, with its 80 per cent Italian population, reverted to Italy. 'Co-belligerency' with the Allies had once again saved the Italians from the worst punishment. Italy lost its African colonies, and had to cede Fiume and Istria to Yugoslavia and the Dodecanese to Greece. A few Alpine villages were transferred to France.[45]

The Russians Come into the Cold

Russian attempts to show the Germans they were soft and cuddly did not help when it came to Berlin's first free elections for fourteen years. The poll, which was held in October 1946, gave very different results to the local elections which the Russians had been able to run by themselves. The SED received a paltry 19.8 per cent, trailing behind the right-wing CDU, with 22.2 per cent, and with less than half the votes of the SDP, based in the Western sectors. For the SPD it was the best score they had achieved since 1925; Berliners perceived the SED as the 'Russian party'.[46] Some saw the behaviour of the Red Army as being partly to blame. A majority of female voters in Austria had certainly refused to support political parties that appeared to emanate from the same place as their rapists. The bourgeois parties in the SBZ had also been able to exploit the women's plight. The Russian journalist K. Gofman took the matter up with the Bulgarian ideologist Georgy Dimitrov in Moscow, condemning 'this evil which carries such a huge cost for our local prestige in Germany'.[47]

The news that the hated wartime coalition might be on the verge of collapse was rapturously greeted in the courthouse prison in Nuremberg. When Churchill began to criticise the Soviet Union, even Hess forgot that he had lost his memory and told the other major Nazis that he had always known it would be thus, that the trial would end, and that they would be restored to their high-sounding titles and dignities. Göring too slapped his thighs in glee and exclaimed, 'History will not be deceived! The Führer and I always prophesied it! The coalition will break up sooner or later.'[48]

The first calls from the Soviet Zone to create pan-German committees in keeping with the Potsdam Agreement came as early as 1945. They were issued by the LPD or Liberal Democrats. They suggested the creation of a 'general plenipotentiary' to act as a liaison man between the different centres of power, or the formation of a 'party control commission'. In 1946 the Liberal Democrats called for a German Zone Council, and the following year a committee made up of all German parties. That same year the CDU in the Soviet Zone demanded 'national representation'.[49]

The Russians were also changing their minds about their wartime partners. A *New York Times* reporter who interviewed a Soviet general in Dresden, heard him say that the destruction was 'your work and now it is our work to clear it up'.[50] A new froideur had set in with the Allies since the attempt by the Soviets to manipulate the elections. This was the beginning of the squeeze on West Berlin that was to culminate in the airlift and the failed attempt by the Russians to overrun the Western sectors. Berlin was to be 'a Danzig without a corridor'. What was more, the Western Allies were pathetically understaffed, particularly in Berlin, where the US had no more than two battalions of troops to face the Red Army.[51] The day after the poll the NKVD began rounding up over 400 scientists and technicians in the Russian Sector and shipping them back to the USSR. Three days later the British protested against a violation of human rights. In a rare moment of candour Colonel Frank Howley admitted that the Americans too had taken away German scientists. They were 'hardly in a strong position' if they chose to protest.[52]

The Great Freeze

The winter of 1946–7 was possibly the coldest in living memory. In Cologne there were sixty four days in the 121 from December to March when the temperature was below zero at 8.00 a.m. Near Frankfurt further to the south, deep snow lay on the ground until March.[53] The puny 'cannon oven' was the only source of warmth for most. It was capable of warming one side of the room, but its effect rarely extended to the other. The cannon oven gave off an intense heat, but only for a short period, as the rations of fuel were soon burned up. In the American Zone households were limited to six briquettes, and sometimes there were none at all.

The cannon oven was a way of locating life in the ruins. A makeshift chimney indicated a room under the rubble. The stench was appalling, reminding Zuckmayer of a working coalmine. The inhabitants of these smoky dens were happy for all that – at least they had some sort of roof over their heads. They were lucky, too, if they were not obliged to share a room with another family. Only in the relatively rubble-free western districts of Berlin where the Allies had requisitioned many of the houses could one find fresh air and the scent of pine trees, but even that was spiked with benzene. Fuel was short here, however, and living in an elegant villa meant little if it could not be heated. The privileged inhabitants of Zehlendorf or Dahlem froze with the rest.[54]

Everything was burned that winter. Germans might have regretted that they had been so quick to put their Nazi literature into the stove. A rumour went round that there were to be public burnings of Nazi books, but the truth was only that the Berlin public libraries threw out the now ideologically suspect material in September 1945, and the others naturally followed suit. Using Nazi paraphernalia as fuel had begun even before the Führer's death. The anonymous Woman in Berlin was cooking on National Socialist literature on 27 April 1945. Later she burned the Movement's sacred text to keep warm. 'I suspect . . . Adolf's *Mein Kampf* will one day become a collector's item.'[55] Christabel Bielenberg, taking refuge in the Black Forest, wondered where the big portrait of the Führer had gone that had previously adorned the walls of the Burgomaster's office: 'In the stove,' she was told.[56]

By 20 November 1946 the icy wind was causing alarm among Berliners, who were turning up their threadbare collars against the cold. On 6 December Ruth Andreas Friedrich and her friends were wondering if they could hold out. Ten days later it was minus twenty. The pipes were frozen. The women returned to fetching water from the pumps. On 21 December the ice had to be broken in the buckets to make morning coffee. In the American Sector the electricity was turned off for eight to ten hours a day, and the situation was worse in the British. As the lavatories were frozen over, the Berliners packed up their excrement and dumped it in the nearest ruin. Prices rocketed at Christmas. The Andreas Friedrichs were able to steal a tree in Teltow, but a goose at RM1,400 was more than a pair of shoes and much more than they had to spend. A pound of chocolate was RM500, a bar of soap RM40. The maximum monthly earnings were in the region of RM1,000.[57]

One of the sufferers that winter was the publisher Peter Suhrkamp, who was seriously ill as a result of his confinement in Ravensbrück. His wife was trying her best to treat an inflammation of his lungs by giving him access to fresh air, yet that meant freezing air. Suhrkamp literally risked life and limb every time he ventured to the lavatory. The cold had been so intense that it not only froze the water pipes, but also caused the pipe from the lavatory to explode, leaving the bathroom floor covered in frozen excrement. A hot-water pipe had been fed through the bathroom to afford some feeble warmth. This turned the sewage into a semi-liquid mass the colour of coffee ice-cream. The only way to rid the bathroom of this stinking mass was to scrub it with boiling water, but with the lack of combustible material and the terrible cold, it was not possible to get water that hot. It was weeks before a plumber could effect the necessary repairs; meanwhile the bathroom remained a serious health hazard.[58]

In the courthouse in Nuremberg the Seven survivors from the first IMT trial felt the cold like everyone else. Speer, who had been ruminating on how Air Marshal Harris had expressed himself when he spoke about the Germans – had he used words like 'extinction' or 'annihilation'? – suddenly began to shiver. On 22 December he sat in his cell wrapped in a blanket, watching his breath. He was wearing his spare underwear around his feet. On Christmas Eve the men buried the hatchet, or at least declared a truce: Funk gave Dönitz a sausage and Schirach handed Speer a piece of bacon as neither had received any provisions from home. Neurath also shared his Christmas biscuits with Speer, while the American chaplain gave them all cigars, cigarettes and chocolate.[59]

That Christmas the grim news leaked out that a second frozen train had arrived from Poland. Of the refugees, thirty-five had died, stripped of their clothes at the border, 182 were seriously affected by frostbite, and twenty-five more required amputations. Among the victims were thirty children. The Berliners' stomachs rumbled and they grumbled: under Hitler there had been potatoes. The political risk of letting them go hungry was becoming apparent.[60] This might have prompted the reforms in the SBZ. Ration Card VI was scrapped and demontage halted. Seventy-four Berlin industries were returned to the people. On 7 January 1947 the barometer had plunged once again in Nuremberg, this time to minus eighteen Fahrenheit. Speer learned that in Berlin people were burning their last sticks of furniture. The prisoners' shower had frozen.[61] The thermometer sank again on 31 January. The power in Berlin was cut for eight to ten hours a day again. The Berliners went out with their rucksacks to scour the Grunewald for kindling.[62]

The winter bit everywhere in Europe. Britain had to cut back on its commitment to the fight against communism, so Greece became an American sphere of influence. The Soviets made more mischief at the London Conference of Foreign Ministers of 16 January 1947. Stalin's advice appears so contradictory it is small wonder that the Western Allies could not get the measure of him. He told his delegation that if reparations obstructed German renewal they should drop their demands,[63] yet the Soviets backed the Yugoslav leader Joze Vilfan, who was demanding $150 million, 2,470 square miles of Carinthia (including the provincial capital Klagenfurt and part of the city of Villach), and 130 square kilometres of Styria (although to the Russians the Yugoslavs said they would be happy with sixty-three square kilometres on the Drau, and an important power station). These areas possessed large Slovenian populations. The Soviets added that they wanted a special statute to protect the Croats in Burgenland. Lord Pakenham dismissed the Yugoslav request, adding that it was not worth the paper it was written on.[64] The game came to an end the following year when Stalin and Tito fell out at the Villa Bled.

Business took Ruth Friedrich to Hamburg that winter. She noted a rise in the popularity of the Nazis. People had been scrawling '88' on walls. Someone explained that H was the eighth letter of the alphabet, and 88 stood for 'HH' or 'Heil Hitler'. The British were to blame. They were not sufficiently tough on the Nazis.[65] They had lodged many of the bombed-out citizens in Nissen huts, where they froze. The police were turning a blind eye to thefts of coal. They believed that protecting coal supplies was down to the conquerors. Ruth Friedrich was keen to compare prices with Berlin. A half-packet of soap powder cost five marks, a quarter pound of tea a hundred.[66] On her return she missed her connection to the military train in Hanover, and had to spend twenty-four hours there before she could catch the next. At first she found a sort of buffet in a bunker where the people smelled of fish and onions. She had to pay a ten-mark deposit for a beaker to drink some coffee. Later she ran across the black market where American soap was changing hands for fifty marks a bar. The hand of the woman who offered it to her was so dirty that she wanted to tell her to use it herself. She made her way to an official doss-house where she was put into the women's dormitory. There she met a woman who had been raped eight times trying to cross the 'green border'. She was bleeding badly and stank.[67]

Another smell permeated Berlin that winter: the carbide lamp that reeked like garlic. Filth, and washing, was a huge problem. Like Hitler's victims who languished in concentration camps, it became imperative to retain human dignity that winter. Zuckmayer spoke of the necessity of keeping fingernails clean and brushing teeth. Germans went to extra-ordinary lengths to polish their shoes, even though there was no bootblack. Despite the outside temperatures, some Germans – particularly refugees from the east – were virtually naked and concealed their shame behind ragged blankets. On their feet they wore bits of planking tied on with lengths of cloth.[68]

Vienna was no warmer. General Béthouart recalled the miserable figures stumbling past his Hütteldorf villa returning from the Vienna woods with faggots. The Viennese spoke of the 'blue hour' when gas was issued to the pipes to allow the citizens to cook their dinners on a low flame.[69] Food was

scarce and money no longer had any value. As in Germany, American cigarettes had the greatest worth. Josefine and Leopold Hawelka had managed
to reopen their café in the Dorotheergasse. Leopold went off each day to
the Vienna woods to find kindling to keep the stove alight and boil the
kettle for the coffee. Once Josefine forgot she had hidden some cartons of
cigarettes in the stove, and lit it. A great deal of money went up in flames.[70]

Bizonia

Clay was in favour of inter-zonal co-operation from the first. Once more
it was the French who stood in the way. He had put his hope in the provision for central agencies that had been decreed at Potsdam, but the
French didn't like the idea of resurrecting the 'Reich'. 'If these agencies
cannot be obtained and/or the boundaries of occupied Germany are to be
changed, the present concept of Potsdam becomes meaningless,' he wrote
in the spring of 1946. There was no exchange of commodities between the
zones. Clay thought it essential to have a common financial policy and
freedom to travel from one to the other. He was so angry with the French
by 16 June that he sued for permission to retire.[71]

In Paris on 11 July 1946, Byrnes offered to merge the American Zone
with anyone who was interested. The British took up the offer at the end
of the month and all the problems were ironed out by 9 August. The
joined zones would have a common standard of living, pooled resources
and a common export policy, and would fix imports necessary to supplement indigenous resources.[72] Heralded by General George Marshall's
Harvard speech that laid the keel of the famous 'plan' to relieve impoverished, war-torn Europe, Bizonia kicked off with an Economic Council in
Frankfurt in June 1947. For the first time in fourteen years the national tri-
colour was raised. When the Americans noticed, they objected, and it had
to be hauled down. In the course of the Council the Transitional Law was
passed that legalised federal authority over the provincial *Länder*. It was a
move towards the creation of a sovereign, federal state.

A Thaw in the Weather

In March 1947 milder weather set in, bringing fresh dangers. The hospitals
had filled up with cases of broken bones: people who had slipped on the
ice; and there was now a great stink to replace the great freeze.[73] It was

time for the Moscow Conference, which came hard on the heels of the announcement of the Truman Doctrine, which was designed to lure Europe away from communism by stick and carrot. Marshall, who had replaced Byrnes as secretary of state, would develop the policy into the Marshall Plan in his prize-giving speech at Harvard in June. General Mark Clark considered Moscow the most important planning meeting between the Allies since Potsdam. The idea of a peace treaty for Austria was brought up, and returned to the files. There were attempts to conclude peace with Germany as well, which had faltered at Paris and New York in December, and which made no progress in Moscow either.[74] Already the London Conference discussions just prior to Moscow had been bogged down by Yugoslav demands. Moscow was a trying time for Clark, who had already made up his mind to go home. During the night he was woken by calls from females asking if he needed anything, so that he had to wrap his telephone in a towel and put it in a drawer. The rooms at the hotel were bugged, and for privacy the American delegates spoke to each other as they walked around the Kremlin walls.[75]

Stalin was comparatively unmoved by the Truman Doctrine and still hoped to effect German unity. The French predictably blackballed it. In April that year French policy changed a little, as the French communists left the government which they had haunted since the liberation. It was the Marshall Plan that seemed to threaten Soviet security, in that it extended offers of assistance to countries within Stalinist eastern Europe. Molotov was instructed to break off talks with the West in Paris on 30 June when it became clear that the Anglo-American plans were directly aimed at the Soviet Union. The Soviet satellites were ordered to ignore the siren offers of aid.[76] The Soviet response was Cominform. It was intended to keep the Eastern bloc on the straight and narrow.

Bevin was more fearsome than Marshall in his belligerence towards the Soviet Union. There is a story about the London CFM in November 1947, when Bevin confronted the Russian foreign minister. 'What do you want?' he demanded to know. Molotov replied, 'I want a unified Germany.' Molotov came to the conclusion that it had been easier to work with the patrician Eden than with this man of the people. After the London meeting Soviet policy changed – the Russians were seeking confrontation. The Cold War had begun.[77]

The Carthaginian peace was aired for the last time in October 1947 when the British and Americans announced an unpopular scheme to dismantle all industries that had originally been constructed for the war effort. Adenauer protested, pointing out that industrial production was a third of pre-war levels. Lord Pakenham also had his doubts about the fairness of a policy which was reminiscent of the savage demontage in the Soviet east that had stripped industry down and bled the zone white.

Nacht und Nebel

By 1947 Austria was liberated, but still not free. At the 'peace conference' in Paris the previous autumn that settled matters with the 'satellite' states which had been allied to Hitler's Reich, Austria was not considered. Austria was a 'victim' when it suited the Allies but most of the time it did not, and the Russians had never really believed in Austrian innocence.[78] For the Austrians the situation was highly frustrating, especially as 71 per cent of them thought they bore no guilt for the war, and only 4 per cent were prepared to concede that Nazism had something to do with them; although at least 8 per cent had been members of the Party and a million or so had served in the Wehrmacht – and half of those in the savage war in the east where no one wore kid gloves.

Austria had also been properly turned over to war work. The Danube had been pressed into service, forty-two airfields and landing strips had been created and 50,000 Austrians had been involved in building warplanes. The Russians in particular were keen to show how many concealed weapons they had found in their zone – evidence that the Austrians were not trustworthy.[79] The Austrians countered that there had been 35,000 Austrian victims of National Socialism, and 65,000 Jews had lost their lives (the Jews were generally mentioned when it was deemed convenient). They talked of their resistance and published their *Rot-Weiss-Rot Buch* in which Austria's anti-Nazi stance was fully documented. Moscow poured cold water on it, and dubbed it a 'Viennese Masquerade' – an allusion to the farce at the heart of Strauss and Hofmannsthal's *Der Rosenkavalier*.[80]

The Cold War was now revving up and the Soviets were anxious to hang on to what they had. Attempts to control the police were finally checked by the Western Allies, but the West was not able to put a stop to Nazi-style *Nacht und Nebel* disappearances which claimed around 400 people over three years. An American report on Soviet kidnappings was submitted on 18 July 1947. The problem became acute that winter when the Russians were turning up the heat in Berlin. On 12 April 1948 Martin Herz wrote, 'Hardly a week passes in Austria without some person disappearing without trace . . . last seen being invited by uniformed Soviet personnel to enter a waiting vehicle'.[81]

The wave began with some Balkan subjects the Russians wanted to talk to. In May 1947 a woman was removed rolled up in a rug. In December Dr Paul Katscher, who worked in the Ministry of Transport, was kidnapped as he passed the statue of Goethe near the Hofburg. The next day he had been due to speak in Geneva about the number of Austrian railway carriages that had disappeared in the east. The Russian commander, Kurasov, refused to allow Figl to comment on Katscher's disappearance – he was suspected of being a British agent. Katscher is believed to have perished in a Soviet prison. Similar charges were levelled against Dr Rafael Spann and Gertaude Flögl, who were also kidnapped. Another woman, Ernestine Sunisch, was arrested on the busy Kärtnerring in broad daylight.

By the time the Russians kidnapped Anton Marek, a chief inspector of police and former Dachau inmate, on 11 June 1948, the Berlin blockade was in full swing. Marek had annoyed the Soviets by purging the police of its communist stooges. He was grabbed outside the Ministry of the Interior. In Russia he was sentenced to the standard twenty-five years, but was released after seven, at the conclusion of the State Treaty. The gendarmerie official Johann Kiridus suffered a similar fate. Another civil servant kidnapped in this way and also released in 1955 was Frau Ottillinger, head of economic planning. She was taken from the car of her minister, Peter Krauland. She was not in the Soviet Zone. In 1948 alone it is thought that around 300 Austrians were the victims of *Nacht und Nebel* kidnappings.[82]

A Solution in the East

The GDR was still not a foregone conclusion. There was limited room for manoeuvre at the beginning, and Stalin hung on for longer than the West before creating his puppet regime. The French sat in their corner and clamoured for the Ruhr. The Anglo-Americans had made the first moves when it came to dividing Germany.[83] That the Russians were still making concessions is clear from Stalin's meetings with the German Muscovites. At the end of January 1947 a delegation from the Soviet Zone had visited Moscow to report to Stalin and Molotov. It contained Pieck, Grotewohl, Ulbricht, Max Fechner and the interpreter Fred Oelssner. Stalin toyed with the idea of allowing the SPD back into the Soviet Zone. He was not impressed by Grotewohl's opposition to this, which he saw as a sign of weakness.[84]

Stalin wanted to know what the SED thought of a referendum on the future structure of Germany. Was it to become a united state, or a federal state? Grotewohl estimated a 60 per cent majority for a united state. Stalin did not think that was enough. He wanted to know if there were not more people to win over in the west who were prepared to accept a state that looked east. This idea was at the heart of the pan-German people's congress at the beginning of 1948 and led to the creation of the NDPD (the National Democratic Party of Germany) in the Soviet Zone. Stalin was still keen to see a structure for all Germany. The KPD was renamed the SED in the Western Zones, but the West refused to accept the change.

The falling out between the Allies was now plain to see. In Berlin the Western Allies felt particularly vulnerable, and they were surrounded by Soviet troops.[85] The Soviet plan to erect national German legal jurisdictions foundered at the Moscow Foreign Ministers' Conference. The abject failure of the conference fanned rumours of war. On 6 and 7 December 1947 the People's Congress for Unity and Just Peace met in East Berlin. Of the 2,215 delegates, 664 came from the Western zones. Their mandates were dodgy, in that they had been selected by parties rather than by a popular vote. The idea was to elect a delegation to go to London to put pressure on the foreign ministers' meeting there and call for national unity. A delegation was elected, but it did not receive permission to enter the United Kingdom.[86]

Before it broke up, the Congress had issued a manifesto calling for a central German administration, the nationalisation of industry in the Western zones and the formation of a united German government once a formal peace treaty had been signed. A standing committee was also chosen to prepare for a second congress in March 1948. Such moves were not rejected out of hand by the Liberal and Christian Democrat parties in the Western zones. The CDU already possessed a 'working community' with its Eastern sister and was equally keen to see the establishment of national representation. Even the SPD leadership was prepared to co-operate in principle. On the other hand they would not work with the SED as long as the SPD was banned in the Soviet Zone. It was therefore Grotewohl who stood in the way of progress in this matter, together with the Allied Control Council. The French once more smelled the unity-rat and were particularly adamantine in their refusal to allow cross-zonal political activities. Another negative voice was that of Jakob Kaiser, which prompted the Soviet authorities to banish him from their zone. The SED were left as the sole voice behind the 1948 Congress, which effectively destroyed its credibility.

As it was the Congress met on 17–18 March 1948 in East Berlin. There were 2,000 delegates, 500 of them from the West. The SED presence was naturally that much stronger, and the percentage of CDU delegates declined from a quarter to a fifth. The Congress created a German People's Council composed of 300 East German members and a hundred from the West. This was divided into committees, and discussions began on the form of a constitution for a united German Democratic Republic. There was a repeat too of Stalin's call for a plebiscite. There was an immediate negative response from both the Americans and the French, who refused to recognise the gathering in Berlin. The British tolerated the Congress but nonetheless described the suggestion as 'useless, unnecessary and uncalled for'. With the Western powers turning their backs on the call for unity, the take-up was almost completely limited to the Soviet Zone.

The West had already made its decision. A six-power conference meeting in London in February and March 1948 backed the Marshall Plan: American finance would help rebuild Western Europe. Germany had to play its role in this, and could not be plundered for ever. It became clear at the time that the West already had plans to create a separate German state in its zones.[87] The Russians were naturally angry that discussions were being held about Germany to which they were not party and called the entire Control Council into question. They saw the Marshall Plan as the embodiment of American imperialism. In February 1948 the bourgeois parties were eliminated from the Czech government, giving a clear signal that the Soviet Union was consolidating its power within its bloc. All over the east the Russians began to show their hand – in Romania, Poland, Hungary and Bulgaria. When a separate German state was mooted at the Second London Conference that took place between April and June 1948 and a new currency agreed on 18 June, Germany's split had been effectively achieved.

20

The Berlin Airlift and the Beginnings of Economic Recovery

24 June 1948
With a rattling din yesterday night an iron curtain fell between Helmstadt and Marienborn.

Ruth Andreas Friedrich, *Schauplatz Berlin*,
Frankfurt/Main 1985, 236

Three years after the end of the war, Germany was limbering up for economic recovery. Nineteen-forty-eight was to be the year of German rehabilitation, but there were political problems to face first. Heinrich Böll's early short stories describe the beginnings of business after the war. In 'Geschäft ist Geschäft' (Business is Business), a man spots an acquaintance, a former soldier like himself. After the war they had both been depressed: 'We had our old army caps pulled down over our brows, and when I had a little cash I'd go to him, and we'd have a chat; sometimes about hunger, sometimes war; and sometimes he gave me a fag, when I was broke; and I occasionally brought him bread coupons as I was clearing rubble for a baker at the time.' Now there he was in a brand-new, white-painted wooden shop with a corrugated-iron roof at a busy intersection. He was licensed to sell cigarettes and gobstoppers. He looked well fed. The man watched as he sent a little girl packing who didn't have enough pfennigs for a gobstopper.

The narrator had not done so well. He thought back to the various digs he had occupied since the end of the war, above all the cellar, which was not too bad when heated with stolen briquettes. Then the newspapers learned about it and took photographs and wrote an article on the tragedy of the returned soldier living in squalor. He had to move. He did occasional jobs, humping and carrying, or cleaning bricks. At other times he stole: coal, wood, a loaf of bread. During the war they stole constantly – somebody stole and the others reaped the reward. Now the same was true again. He alone was left waiting at the tram-stop, while the others were already on board heading for their destinations.

He stood watching the man in the booth. The other gave him no sign of recognition. He watched another man picking up fag-ends. In his POW camp he had seen colonels doing just that, 'but this one wasn't a colonel'. He was one of the unlucky ones like the narrator. For some people coming back from the war was like getting off the tram at their stop. The house was still there, if a bit dusty, there was jam in the cupboard and potatoes in the cellar. Life went back to normal; the old firm took them back. 'There was still medical insurance; you went through the paces of denazification – just like a man going to the barber to have an annoying beard shaved off'. On holidays and holy days they could chat about their medals and about acts of gallantry and come to the conclusion 'that we were really splendid fellows, in the end just doing what was required of us'.

In another story, 'Mein Onkel Fred' (My Uncle Fred), Böll's eponymous hero comes back from the war, possessing nothing but a tin can containing a few cigarette butts. He demands bread, sleep and tobacco; then he lies down on the sofa and, complaining it is too small for him, remains there, scarcely stirring, for months.

The fourteen-year-old narrator is the family breadwinner. His father has been killed in the war, and his mother has a small pension. The boy's job was to take unwanted possessions to the black market, swapping a Dresden cup for some semolina, three volumes of Gustav Freytag for two ounces of coffee or a pillow for some bread. Freytag's brand of German nationalism must have seemed highly dispensable just after the war. At other times he stole coal. His mother wept at the thought of this, but did nothing to stop him.

Meanwhile Uncle Fred snoozed on the sofa. One day his sister – the boy's mother – suggested gently that he might enquire whether there was a position going in his old firm, where he had kept the books. The boy was sent to find out. He discovered a pile of rubble about twenty feet high. Uncle Fred was clearly elated when the news was brought to him. He asked the boy to break open a crate containing his few effects. In it was his savings book, containing 1,200 marks and a few other objects of trifling worth and his diploma from the Chamber of Commerce. The boy was told to collect the cash and sell the rest. He managed to dispose of all but the diploma, as Uncle Fred's name had been inscribed with India ink. This provided enough food for weeks, a considerable relief as the schools had opened their doors again and the narrator was compelled to finish his studies.

Uncle Fred rose Lazarus-like from the sofa, shaved and called for clean underwear. He borrowed the boy's bicycle and set off for the city. He returned smelling strongly of wine and armed with a dozen buckets. He had decided to revive the flower trade in the town. He set up beside the tram stop and with a shout of 'Flowers, fresh flowers – no coupons required!' he began his new life. Within three weeks he had three dozen buckets and two branches, and a month later he was paying taxes. It was impossible for the boy to keep up with his uncle's progress: there were ever more buckets and branches, and soon he had colonised the entire town. The boy retired from his branch of the family business and concentrated on school. A few years later his uncle was a man of substance in a red car, and the boy was designated his heir – only he had to go to business school first.

In the spring of 1947 Alfred Döblin paid the first of two visits to the German capital. It was here he had achieved fame for *Berlin-Alexanderplatz*, the most famous novel of the Weimar Republic, and also the best-known fictionalised account of Berlin life. By his own account, Döblin entered though the back door. Like Renée Bédarida he landed in Frohnau in the French Sector. It was a soft introduction, but he had few illusions: 'Reality exceeds fantasy.' He went into the centre, arriving at the same Stettin Station that had received him and his family when they came from the Pomeranian port in 1888. He was immediately struck by the vision of an elegant restaurant with chandeliers and brightly painted shutters. Outside the signs were in Cyrillic. It was for Russians.[1]

He went west, arriving in an incongruously elegant flat in the Kurfürstendamm, in the British Sector. There was a publisher there (possibly Suhrkamp). 'I asked what do the people get up to here? I was told that many sold their possessions, if they still had any, and lived off the proceeds. One piece after another disappeared in this way. Many dealt on the black market, very many.'[2]

The terrible weather was over – it was a sunny day, and they went out to the Café Wien. There was no coffee to be had, and the 'cup' turned out to be no more than coloured mineral water. Döblin looked for the cinema that had given the première of the film of his novel *Berlin-Alexanderplatz*. It was no more. The fashionable literary café of the Weimar days, the Romanischen, was open – to the skies. The sheer enormity of the destruction at last dawned on Döblin. Here was the city he had so ably chronicled in his novels, and almost all of it was gone: the Wintergarten with its variety shows, the Viktoria Café. There were no buildings either side of the Brandenburg Gate. He watched with astonishment as a Russian soldier walked past the Kranzler Eck with his lover on his arm. A paper seller gave him what for: 'As things are going in Europe and the world, anything is possible, and who knows if, after ten or twenty years, a Russian soldier and his wife will be walking along the wrecked boulevards of some western city.'[3]

Döblin continued his voyage of discovery. On the Schlossbrücke (called the 'Dolls' Bridge' because of the statues of Prussian worthies) he had recollections of the various Kaisers. There was little more than the river. On Alexanderplatz he looked at the great department store Tietz: 'It looks like a man who has had his neck broken by a blow, and whose skull has been pushed down into his ribcage.' Döblin was bitter. He had converted to Catholicism, but he could not quite bring himself to bestow mercy on his former tormentors: "What am I actually doing here . . . They allowed themselves to be defiled . . . I feel like a man who has been betrayed.'[4] In the Königstrasse he noticed women pushing prams past the wreck of another Jewish department store, Wertheim – they were filled with wood. His goal was the Frankfurter Allee, where he had lived and practised: a popular quarter that provided him with models for his books. 'The sight was shocking. A terrible martial violence must have descended to knock these houses flat . . . Every now and then a façade reported for duty. There the house must have stood . . . It is no longer what I knew and where I lived.'[5]

Döblin returned to give a lecture the following year. Berlin made him uneasy: 'This was the principal theatre of the horror. This is where the crime took wings. The nation allowed itself to be deafened by singing youth and applauding bystanders.' He was hard on Berlin, a city that was no more enthusiastic about Hitler than many others. 'The judgment of history speaks in a terrible voice.' But Döblin's message is one of hope: 'A man finds it easier than a city to change. A man may transform himself where a city crumbles away.'[6]

Currency Reform

The currency had been chaotic since the end of the war. The Soviets had simply printed money when they needed it, and this had caused rampant inflation.[7] Nobody trusted cash. Farmers and shopkeepers were placed in a difficult position. The former avoided the market. The latter ruled over empty shops in the basements of ruined buildings. Germany's post-war planners therefore conceived of a system that would inject confidence into the currency and wind up the black market and the cigarette economy. They wanted to create a marketplace where shopkeepers and manufacturers were kept permanently short of working capital to create a powerful incentive for rapid turnover and all cash received would promptly be spent on new goods. The scheme was an instant success. The Germans were often literally 'drunk' with the opportunities it gave them, and the black market disappeared overnight.[8]

The first proposals for monetary reform were made in the autumn of 1946. The Reichsmark was pegged at ten to a dollar. Barter markets were created in order to undermine the illegal black markets where most Germans did their shopping. In January 1947 Clay believed the new money to replace the Reichsmark should be centrally printed in Berlin, but there were doubts about the Russians. As it was, the cigarette economy had its own ways of regulating itself. The price of a twenty-cent packet of cig-arettes was RM120, which remained the same for six months even in Berlin. French cigarettes were a third of that sum. A month's shopping amounted to only RM50. A dollar was worth 600 marks, so six marks bought you a cigarette. In the Rhineland Elena Skrjabina was able to buy a lorry with a suitcase filled with cigarettes.[9] With rumours that the old money was shortly to go, there was frenzied buying to get rid of potentially worthless currency. In May 1948 the price of a pound of strawberries had gone down to RM25 and cherries were now at 12. The pubs were filled with Berliners drinking away their reserves. Elena Skrjabina's Bendorf shop was doing a roaring trade.[10]

The problem was that the new money did not come, and the prices began to rise again. On 16 June a pound of coffee cost 2,400 marks. Two days later the word was out that the new currency was to be called the 'Deutsche Mark'. On 25 June 1948 currency reform was introduced in the Western zones. The old money would be exchanged at a rate of one-tenth of the new, though for a while the two currencies ran side by side. The SBZ had been excluded from monetary reform because the Russians could not have been trusted to print the right amounts.[11] By June 1948 Ludwig Erhard had made arrangements to print 500 tons of banknotes in the US and have them airlifted to Frankfurt. Virtually all rationing and price controls were abolished. Clay told him that his ad-visers had said that the move was a terrible mistake. Erhard replied: 'Herr General, pay no attention to them. My own advisers tell me the same thing.'[12]

The Soviet answer was immediate. That same day the Russian com-mander Sokolovsky required the SBZ to introduce 'immediate and necessary measures to protect the interests of the German population and the economy of the Soviet Zone'.[13] The Russians acted that night:

passenger trains were halted, and at the beginning of July they cut the city off completely from the West.*

In the meantime shops in the Western zones filled with goods; black markets disappeared; people ceased to 'hamster'; and production increased. The atmosphere changed too. Every man, woman and child received DM60 in two instalments, and they all set out on shopping sprees. Ruth Friedrich's friend Frank reported from Munich that the shops were crammed with food and that no one spoke of calories any more, because they all had enough to eat.[14] Clay wrote to his guru Byrnes to complain about the British and the French, who had dragged their feet over the currency reform. Clay could report the immediate benefits: 'Overnight hoarded goods appeared on the shelves as the stores had to sell to meet payrolls . . . even fruits and vegetables from the farm once more went on sale in the market place.' In one month productivity had risen by 10 per cent.

In Hehlen the Schulenburgs were now the proud possessers of DM280, but Charlotte still didn't know where the next tranche of money would come from. There was a knock at the door and her faithful cook and maid Klara came in wearing a white apron. Charlotte handed her DM40, and Klara said, 'I want to tell her ladyship something, I don't want any more money.' When Charlotte replied that she had none to give her for the time being, the maid said, 'I am doing this for his lordship's sake.' She meant: you don't have to thank me.[15]

Crisis in Berlin

Döblin's second visit marked the moment of change in Berlin. From June 1947 the city had a new mayor in Ernst Reuter, a former communist and intimate of Lenin's who had gone over to the socialists in the 1920s and had emigrated to Turkey on the arrival of the Nazis. He had returned to Germany in November 1946 and taken a British train from Hanover to Berlin at the end of the month. On 5 December he was elected to the council. It was a bad moment to start, just before the killer winter. The council worked just half the day, as the offices could not be heated.[16] The Russians vetoed his election as mayor, because, they said, Turkey was a fascist country. Louise Schroeder had to take his place meanwhile. Stalin was looking to find a way of preventing the Western Allies from creating their own Germany. It was the policy that Bob Murphy called 'irritate and

* See below pp. 527–8.

tire' – wear down the West.[17] Come what may, the Russians would force the Western Allies out. Molotov made it sound like 'them or us': 'If we are to lose in Germany we would have lost the war.'[18] Everything short of military force was to be used. The Russians were constantly probing and pushing, spreading rumours that the Western Allies were about to pack their bags. They invaded the railway offices in the US Zone, but the Americans resisted and they backed off. They made applications to the Americans for any of their citizens hiding in their sector.[19]

Currency reform was the pretext, but it wasn't really about that. The Soviets saw the chance of making the Western Allies abandon Berlin, thereby losing their attraction to the Germans, or forcing them to drop the London programme for a separate state, or obliging them to return to the grand alliance as embodied in the CFM mechanism.[20] There was fear in some quarters that the Russians would succeed.[21] Clay for one was looking for a showdown:

> I doubt very much if this action would imperil the quadripartite machinery. If it should, we still force the Russians to slam the door and even if they did slam the door, we should still continue in Berlin. However, we cannot continue successfully unless we establish a governmental machinery for western Germany. The resentment of the Germans against colonial administration is increasing daily and those democratic Germans who hate communism and would prefer to establish the types and kind of government which we desire will soon lose their positions of leadership with their own people.

He told the under-secretary of the army, William Draper, that 'two and a half years without government is much too long'. On 5 November 1947 he said that a provisional government would be established no later than 31 January 1948.[22]

The others were not so sure. General Robertson was for appeasement. The French even considered allowing the Russians the stake in the Ruhr they coveted so much.[23] Clay was right that the Russians were not actually looking for a fight. They wanted to humiliate the West by offering to provision all the Berliners. That way they would win their love. The Berliners certainly did march on their stomachs, and their stomachs were empty. The Russians were going to keep the air corridors open and avoid military confrontations. They made no preparations for a military emergency. Nor was the Western bluff that convincing: the bombers the Americans sent to Britain were not configured for atom bombs.[24]

From 23 February 1948 the London Conference was debating just this question. The Russians had jumped off the CFM carousel at the end of the previous year. They were not invited to London. In their absence and in the imposing setting of India House the foreign ministers of Britain, Belgium, France, Holland, Luxembourg and the United States were giving form to the state of West Germany. On 17 March the Brussels Pact was signed as the first step towards NATO. The terms were leaked to the Soviets by Donald Maclean on the same day the Prague coup took place. Most of the Western ministers were convinced that the time had come to split Germany in two, but the French held aloof for the time being. They thought the Russians would prevent it. They only reluctantly agreed to the idea of West Germany because of Prague and because Sokolovsky walked out of the Control Council on the 20th. Couve de Murville, the French foreign minister, began to panic and decided there would be a fresh war within three years.[25]

Howley had been made American commandant at the Kommandatura on 1 December 1947. He was looking forward to a scrap too. He called his British counterpart, General Herbert, 'shockingly defeatist'. When the Russians cut off the city in June, Herbert predicted that that would drive the Westerners out by October.[26] He might have been conscious of just how weak the West was. In a reply to Senator Henry Cabot Lodge dated 5 March 1948, Clay detailed the strength of the American forces in Berlin – there were fewer than 2,000 soldiers. 'It is obviously our desire to retain as small as garrison as possible.' The Americans also had some German police auxiliaries, as the Russian-backed Markgraf Police (run by Paul Markgraf) were not meant to function in the American Zone.[27]

On 18 March there was cause for a little celebration in Berlin. It was the centenary of the March Revolution of 1848 which had brought a brief triumph to the cause of the German middle classes, before they joined the more reactionary nobility and rallied behind Bismarck and the Empire. A crowd of 30,000 gathered at the ruined Reichstag. There were speeches from Franz Neumann of the SPD, Jakob Kaiser of the CDU and the mayor-elect, Ernst Reuter. Reuter alluded to the events in Prague. 'Who will be next?' he asked. Berlin would be next. 'If the world knows this we will not be abandoned by the world.'[28]

The situation was worsening with each month. There were no barriers between the sectors, and those fleeing the Russians could try to disappear in the west of the city in the hope of finding a way out to the West. On 25 March the journalist Dieter Friede disappeared in a *Nacht und Nebel* kidnapping. The Soviet authorities later justified their actions by claiming that he was a spy. The 'Mini Blockade' was next. It began on 31 March and lasted until 2 April. The SBZ's policy was improvised.[29] This time it was provoked by an Anglo-American refusal to allow the Russians to board their military trains.[30] One of these crossed the Soviet Zone daily. There were also several freight trains every week, thirty-two daily 'paths' – or crossings – to supply the garrison and the Germans and a daily passenger aircraft. It was a warning shot, a trial run. Three days later, on 2 April, the Allied Kommandatura was dissolved. More disappearances followed. Some 200,000 people were reported to have been forcibly taken to the USSR since the end of the war. The Berliners felt particularly vulnerable once again. The Russian-backed SED launched a propaganda campaign in the Western sectors.[31]

The Soviets had shown their hand in the communist takeover in Prague in February and Jan Masaryk's suspicious death the following month. They were now openly demonstrating what was in store for their bloc. Truman understood that Berlin needed to be held for propaganda purposes; it was also necessary to stop the flow of communism west. 'If we failed to maintain our position there, communism would gain great strength among the Germans.'[32] Like Clay he gave the Germans no credit for being able to make up their own minds.

Prague brought the French down to earth. It was timely that Robert Schuman was president of the council, and possessed the sort of wise head France needed at the time. In March Koenig met Clay and Robertson in Berlin for talks on the German constitution and the French merging with Bizonia to form Trizonia. Koenig became predictably uppity at the idea of a 'Reichstag'. On 6 April Couve de Murville flew to Germany to see Clay. He was concerned that Berlin might fall to the Russians. They also discussed currency reform. When the Russians did move to cut Berlin off from the west, the French foreign minister Bidault stressed that for the sake of Allied prestige there could be no backing down. Schuman, who had begun his political career in Germany, insisted that Berlin was a symbol that could not be abandoned. It was not thought politic that any French soldiers should *die* for Berlin, however, and the French air force was kept out of the operation, the excuse being that it was too weak – which was probably true.[33]

Airlift

Russian 'milk snatchers' formed the pretext for the airlift. The Russians were supposed to provide food for the entire population of Berlin, although the Western Allies donated the flour. To this end the Russians had 7,000 cows in suburban farms. In the early summer of 1948 they cut off the milk. Berliners were obliged to go to the east in lorries to collect it. The American medical officer reported to Howley: 'Unless we get fresh milk, six thousand babies in our sector will be dead by Monday.' Three years before, the Anglo-Americans had had fewer scruples about infant mortality. Howley saw Russian uncooperativeness as an attempt to intimidate the Americans and ordered in 200 tons of condensed milk and another 150 tons of powdered milk. Howley proudly reported that not one baby died in his sector.[34]

Clay thought he might keep his meagre garrison alive, but not the Germans. The Soviet attempt to prevent the Western Allies from reaching their sectors of the city provoked a discussion between Clay and Robertson on the legitimate response. The British decided they would not shoot if the Americans did not. 'I believe this [the Russian move] is bluff,' wrote Clay, 'but do not wish to bluff back as British may be doing unless we mean it [sic].'[35] The American secretary of the army, General Kenneth Royall, thought the president should send Stalin a note. He was not certain how serious the situation had become. Clay replied, 'I do not believe this means war but any failure to meet this squarely will cause great trouble.' He added that he would rather go to Siberia than abandon Berlin. The Soviets were now challenging the Western Allies' right to be in Berlin in the first place. Clay cited the EAC agreement made during the war, by which the German capital would be administered by the three powers. Added to this there was the oral agreement with Zhukov of 5 June 1945 and 'three years of application'. The right to provision the city and its Western garrisons was governed by mostly tacit or oral agreements.[36]

Clay was not prepared to put up with hair-splitting: 'Legalistic argument no longer has meaning . . . our reply will not be misunderstood by 42 million Germans and perhaps 200 million West Europeans. We must say, we think, as our letter does, "this far you may go and no further." There is no middle ground which is not appeasement.'[37] Clay continued to see the idea of the Russians inspecting trains as the thin end of the wedge: the 'integrity of our trains is a part of our sovereignty'. It was a 'symbol of our position in Germany and in Europe'. When the Anglo-Americans put the Russian 'bluff' to the test the Soviet authorities would not let them cross the SBZ without prior inspection. The managers of the trains all refused bar one American, who panicked and let the Russians on board. The decision was made to switch to aircraft.[38]

That was also not without difficulties at first. On 5 April a Soviet Yak fighter dived under a scheduled British BEA Vickers Viking aircraft as it came into land at Gatow. As it rose it took off the starboard wing of the

Viking. Both planes crashed, killing the fifteen British and American passengers and crew together with the pilot of the Yak. Robertson called for fighter protection for the transports and immediately went to see Sokolovsky in protest. The Russian commander was adamant that the pilot had had no orders from him to buzz the British plane. He would not direct the Soviet air force to molest flights in the corridor. Robertson was satisfied with his answer and called off the escort. Later the Russians showed a similar docility when there were complaints about the positioning of a barrage balloon. No one wanted to take responsibility for war.[39]

Clay was not going to budge. There was little or no freight for the time being, as it required permission from the Russians, 'which I will not request'. The British had their own aircraft, but the French had 'no air transport worthy of the name' even if, for the time being, they were happy to keep their small force in Berlin. Clay was still stubbornly determined: 'We are convinced that our remaining in Berlin is essential to our prestige in Germany and Europe. Whether for good or bad, it has become a symbol of American intent.'[40]

The balloon went up again when the Russians walked out of the Kommandatura on 17 June, Howley was relieved. They claimed that there was an urgent need to repair the roads near Magdeburg and the bridges over the Elbe, which therefore had to be closed. On 22 June the price of coffee had risen to RM3,000, bread was at 200 and a single Chesterfield was 65.[41] On the 24th the motorway was blocked between Berlin and Helmstedt.[42] Only military convoys were allowed to pass. They also cut off supplies of gas and electricity to the Western sectors of the city. Ruth Friedrich noted in her diary that an 'iron curtain' had abruptly fallen between Helmstadt and Marienborn.[43] 'We poor little Berlin mice!' They had spent all their money, and the Russians were doing their best to prevent the new currency from crossing their zone. 'In the end the entirety of Berlin had harmed their stomachs in the prospect of currency reform.'[44] The new currency was issued in the Western zones on 25 June at 7.00 a.m. That same day the Russians stopped the supply of brown coal to the city. From 7 July coal would also have to be brought in by air. 'I do not expect armed conflict,' wrote Clay; the 'principal danger is from Russian-planned communist groups out looking for trouble'. For such a propagandist, he was surprisingly worried about the behaviour of the Berliners: 'Perhaps the greatest danger comes from the amazing resistance of the Berlin population. This is driving the Soviet administration and the SED to further extreme measures.'[45]

'June 24 1948', wrote Howley grandiloquently, 'is one of the most infamous dates in the history of civilisation. The Russians tried to murder an entire city to gain a political advantage.'[46] There were 2,250,000 Germans in the Western sectors, and just 6,500 soldiers to protect them. The Russians had 18,000 men in their sector and another 300,000 stationed in their zone.[47] In order to stress the weakness of the Western powers the Russians began military manoeuvres. Bevin, who (as opposed to Attlee) was running the show in London, chipped in by inviting the Americans to station B-29 bombers in Britain. It was hoped that this gesture would concentrate the Russians' minds, even if there was no provision for their carrying nuclear weapons. Britain was rapidly becoming a client nation of the United States.[48]

The Berlin airlift began on 26 June. The idea came from the British. Air Commodore Reginald Waite proposed a scheme to supply the civilians as well as the garrisons. He and Robertson took the scheme to Clay, who up until then had preferred the idea of a convoy.[49] General John Cannon was responsible for the name 'Operation Vittles'. Ruth Friedrich noted the change: 'The skies are buzzing as they did during the Blitz. For the time being the American military authorities have increased air traffic to Berlin to a maximum.'[50] The density was to increase. At first the excuse was the need to provision the American and other Allied garrisons, then Clay made it clear that the Soviets would not be allowed to starve the Berliners in the Western sectors. For eleven months American C-47s ('Gooney Birds', which the Berliners called 'Rosinenbomber' or raisin bombers) and C-54s, as well as British cargo planes, under the command of the American Major-General Tunner and the Briton Air Marshal Williams flew in 4,000 tons of food daily. British Sunderland flying boats landed on the Havel, bringing much needed salt from Hamburg. At the height of Operation Vittles, 13,000 tons of food was delivered in twenty-four hours.

British planes left Frassberg for Gatow, while the Americans flew from Wiesbaden to Tempelhof. The Americans operated two-thirds of the flights, the British the rest. West Berlin was the prize won for the new, Allied-backed West German state.[51] Clay wanted to know if American service families should be flown to safety. Truman advised against it, saying that it would have a bad 'psychological effect'. Clay agreed to make 'emergency arrangements for essential supplies'.[52] The political nature of the blockade was swiftly understood by Truman. It was fully in keeping with his doctrine: this far but no further. He told Clay to make the blockade-busting formal. The humanitarian aspect was important, but so was access to the former capital. On 26 June Truman directed that the airlift be put on a full-scale organised basis. Every available aircraft was to be used.[53] The same day the Russians introduced Order 111 which created their own currency. This took the form of coupons attached to existing banknotes. The coupons were stuck on with glue made from the ubiquitous potato. On the fourth exchange it fell off. The Berliners were quick to dub them *Tapetenmark* or wallpaper money. The new notes were ready on 26 July.

The SBZ authorities were credited with saying they were going to 'Dry out the Western Sector as we would tie a tourniquet around a wart.'[54] On 26 June it was reported that the Americans could provision the city for another thirty days. News was transmitted by the RIAS (Radio in American Sector) van. Ruth Friedrich remarked on the 'frustration of being at the centre of the world stage and yet only [having] the chance to be informed of this between twelve midnight and two o'clock in the morning'. Meanwhile an aircraft flew over her head every eight minutes.[55]

On 28 June American soldiers arrested Sokolovsky – allegedly by mistake – for speeding in their sector. He identified himself, but they still held him for an hour. Sokolovsky told Robertson that the blockade was about the currency, and he could draw his own conclusions. The Russian was unconvinced by the game his countrymen were playing in Berlin. Rumours flew this way and that. Clay was later told that the Russians intended to put up barrage balloons to impede landing.[56] When the first proper banknotes were issued in the east, the SBZ further exacerbated the plight of the westerners by making them go deep into their sector to convert their old coupons. The dollar was now worth DM28, and a flight to the West cost $28. No one had DM784. Anyone who might be able to scrape together such a princely sum had left. Even Ruth Friedrich, who had endured the worst of it, now thought it was time to go.

Clay's airlift was as much a propaganda success as the Soviet blockade was an own goal. In West Berlin and Western Germany the wholly negative picture of Soviet aims never disappeared. The crisis also accelerated the polarisation of the two sides. Otto Grotewohl addressed the SED Central Committee on 30 June to affirm his clear commitment to an 'Eastern orientation', even if this did not change the Party's policy on unity.[57] Currency anarchy continued. The Eastern 'coupon mark' was now worth ten Reichsmarks. It could also be used in the Western sectors, but not for everything. A money market grew up around the Zoo Station. Certain currencies were used for different goods: matches were paid for with Western money; onions half and half; raisins Western; sugar Eastern. You bought a newspaper with Eastern money, but the printing had to be paid for with Western currency.[58]

The Western authorities prevented the new currency from reaching

Berlin, but the SBZ did not call off the blockade. 'Technical problems' had required the closing of land routes and waterways to Berlin. As Lucius Clay put it, 'the technical difficulties would last until the Western Powers buried their plans for a West German government'.[59] On 2 July the Russians cut off the water to the Western sectors, claiming the need to repair the locks. Howley pointed out that water was needed to make bread, although once again he was unclear about how much.[60]

A great disappointment to the Berliners was the craven behaviour of Wilhelm Furtwängler, who cancelled his appearance with the Berlin Philharmonic Orchestra on 7 July 1948. The conductor was due to direct the orchestra in Potsdam with American soloists. He evidently thought it would be too risky, even though the Americans had agreed to lay on the transport. The Berliners had to be satisfied with Leopold Ludwig.[61] As a result of the airlift, the Russian-occupied Radio Station could no longer be used. Eventually the Soviet authorities gave up their island in the British Sector and built themselves a new station in Adlershorst in their own fief. The next day the blockade claimed its first life when an American Dakota crashed. The second crash occurred two weeks later on the 25th when a C-47 ploughed into a house in Friedenau killing the crew.[62]

On 14 July the Russians dropped all pretence about 'technical difficulties'.[63] A week later a plane was landing every three minutes, but the situation was dire, and in November and December the operation was often hampered by fog, even if the weather miraculously improved when the food situation was at its worst. Radar allowed some planes to land. The lack of landing space had meant that the French airstrip at Tegel was being rapidly made ready for aircraft. As many as 17,000 men were working on the runway, on the promise of a hot meal every day. Berliners received at best a couple of hours' electricity at day, and often had to wait until the middle of the night to cook. The short-lived burst of electric light brought the same sort of euphoria as a glass of wine. The lucky ones lived in an Allied-occupied building. They had power and light.[64]

On 23 July Clay reported to Truman in the White House. It was not going to be a repeat of Potsdam. Truman was not to be bamboozled. He returned to the idea of supplying the city by armed convoys. Clay was not so keen, but he did not think the Russians were prepared to go to war.[65] In America voices were raised calling for a break with the Russians. 'These people did not understand that our choice was only between negotiations and war,' Truman said. 'There was no third way.'[66] The real reason for the blockade must have become obvious to all and sundry on 27 July when the Conference of Foreign Ministers in London decided that they had agreed on the creation of a West German state. All that was needed now was a 'basic law' to serve as a constitution. The basic law (*Grundgesetz*) would be ratified by the provincial assemblies or Landtage. There would be no vote in the east, as the ministers had decided the people were not free to express their opinions and might vote against. Clay concluded once again that the Germans needed the responsibility of self-government. Germany was to have its own administration *before* the peace treaty. This little bombshell made the Western Allies reconsider evacuating some Berliners who might otherwise have been abducted.[67]

The West had finally had enough of the Soviet-controlled Markgraf Police and on 26 July organised their own force under Johannes Stumm, Markgraf's former deputy. Three-quarters of the Markgraf Police promptly deserted to the Stumm. When on 29 July the Magistrat or town council tried to meet at the Red Rathaus they were met by SED members chanting, 'We want just one currency!' Members of the council were intimidated and beaten up, and Western policemen were carried off by SED thugs. One who was manhandled was Jeanette Wolff, a Jewess who had survived two concentration camps. She was called a 'Judensau' (Jewish pig) in the Rathaus carpark. 'I have only one life to lose, and this life belongs to freedom,' she exclaimed. The communist stooges stormed the council chamber. The future author of Berlin's constitution, Otto Suhr, refused to begin the session until they left. Louise Schröder, standing in for Reuter, told the communists to be reasonable, and to go home and listen to the session on the radio. The SED men withdrew. 'The storming of the Bastille' was over.[68]

Berlin was sealed off by road, rail and water. Contingency plans were made to withdraw the Allied armies to the Rhine. On 2 August Stalin said he would lift the blockade if both Eastern and Western marks were allowed to circulate freely throughout Berlin. It was also the 'insistent wish' of the Soviet government that the Allies 'postpone the next stages planned in the integration of the Western Zones'. The Russians admitted that the West was in Berlin 'on sufferance', but would not concede that it was 'there by right'.[69] The next day Clay said he was prepared to compromise on the currency issue. Molotov wanted more: on 10 August he demanded control of exports from the Western sectors. Clay told Washington to reject this request.[70] In the meantime the Markgraf police were being increasingly tough on people seeking Western currency. On the 12th they arrested 320 on the Potsdamer Platz. On the 24th Stalin changed his mind, and once again requested the withdrawal of the currency, but the West said no: it had been a success. That same day there was a mid-air collision between two C-47s. Both crews perished.[71]

The four military governors met on 1 September. Sokolovsky was concerned that the air transports might be used to flood Berlin with new Deutsche Marks. Three days later the Russian commander came clean: the restrictions were the result of the London Conference and were aimed at the splitting of eastern and west Germany'.[72] Berliners were getting by with dried potatoes and other vegetables and tinned meat. The suicide rate rose again. There were now around seven a day. Sokolovsky also announced that the Soviet Union would start air-force manoeuvres over Berlin on the 6th. This was, he said, normal practice for this time of the year. Clay noted in his report to Washington, 'This is amusing since in the four summers we have been in Berlin we have never heard of these manoeuvres previously.' Robertson expressed the hope that the Soviet manoeuvres would not interfere with the air corridor. Sokolovsky replied, 'Certainly.' Clay was not certain whether that meant 'Certainly yes' or 'Certainly no'.[73]

On 6 September there was an attempted *coup d'état* at the Stadthaus. Clay naturally had a report of the new outrage:

> Meanwhile their [that is, the Soviets'] tactics in Berlin are getting rough. Yesterday a communist mob prevented City Assembly from meeting. It manhandled three American reporters at the scene. Today a well-organised mob was on hand again. The deputy mayor foolishly took forty-odd plain clothes men from western sectors to keep order. Uniformed police of the Soviet sector under direct orders of Soviet officer started to arrest them. They rushed into offices of three western liaison representatives where some are still at siege. However, Soviet sector police broke into our office and led about twenty of the poor devils off to death or worse.
>
> Pride is a cheap commodity, thank God, or I could never hold my head up. We are being pushed around here like we were a fourth class nation. My impulse was to send our military police in to restore order as Americans were being pushed around by Germans.

Clay thought there would be more 'inspired rioting in western sectors'. Robertson was optimistic. Clay was not.[74]

The meeting was the last one held in the Red Rathaus. As the Western delegates were unable to make it through the Soviet Sector they met in the Taberna Academica on the Steinplatz in the British Sector instead. The Russians responded by kidnapping some of Stumm's men, and the intimidation did not stop there: even Howley suffered from anonymous nocturnal telephone calls.

In Washington General Draper expressed concern. Clay thought there would be more of these Goebbels-style 'spontaneous demonstrations'. 'I think mob-violence is prelude to Soviet-picked city government taking over the city; then spreading mob-violence into western sectors.' When Clay protested to Sokolovsky's deputy Kotikov on 8 September the Russian said the 'mob' were workers proceeding legitimately to the town hall. The Western police had attempted to stop them. He accused the American MPs of being drunk and disorderly.[75] In fact Sokolovsky was innocent of the outrage, which had been organised by Tulpanov and Ulbricht off their own bats.[76]

The Westerners responded with a massive demonstration of support for democracy before the Reichstag on 9 September. 'On Thursday hundreds of thousands of Berliners demonstrated on the Platz der Republik for democratic freedom and against the shocking events at the Stadthaus ... women deserted their cookers, hairdressers left their clients in the lurch under their wave machines and the newspaper-sellers closed up shop. All of them ran thinking I must demonstrate; we belong to the West. We must prove it.'[77]

The response had been impressive: 300,000 Germans staged an anti-communist rally. The Berliners were rallied by their mayor, Reuter. Before the ruined Reichstag he told them, 'Look at this city and admit that you cannot abandon it!' The city under siege became the symbol of moral re-naissance and contributed greatly to German rehabilitation.[78] The red flag was torn down. Fifteen-year-old Wolfgang Scheunemann was killed and 222 people injured when the Russians fired into the crowd. The volleys ceased, however, when the British deputy provost calmly walked over to the Russians and pushed them away with his swagger-stick.[79] The Russians took it out on five men they had arrested at the scene. On 9 September these unfortunates were sentenced to twenty-five years' hard labour.[80]

Clay was slow to see the significance of the Reichstag demonstration. He noted that a communist counter-demonstration was planned for the Soviet sector. He seemed doubtful of the wisdom of the British in issuing a permit for the rally. 'The huge attendance was I am sure a great surprise even to the Germans and led the German political leaders to inflammatory speeches.' Clay thought they were 'playing with dynamite'. He saw a risk of the whole business blowing up in their faces – such demonstrations 'could turn into mass-meetings against the occupying powers and could develop into the type of mob government which Hitler played so well to get into power'. He concluded that it had set 'a dangerous, habit-forming precedent'.[81]

Accidents continued to occur. The British crashed an Avro York on 20 September killing five, and a month later a C-54 went down in Frankfurt.

But the situation had now become static. The Allies needed to bring in a minimum of 4,500 tons a day, though 5,500 were ideal. As it was there were days when the tonnage reached 8,000. It was now a question of who would back down first. 'The airlift has been a magnificent success and can keep us in Berlin through the winter. As long as we pursue diplomatic means to gain a settlement the airlift adds to our prestige.' Clay still had acute reservations about the French and apparently had problems with the Labour government in Britain: 'Our difficulties with the French continue. Neither is being in partnership with the British a bed of roses.'[82]

While the blockade was in force neither Bevin nor Marshall would communicate with the Soviets. The Soviet foreign minister had stayed away from the meeting of the Brussels Treaty Organisation in September. The Western powers decided that the case would be referred to the United Nations.[83] Soviet deputy foreign minister Andrei Vyshinsky in New York denied the existence of a blockade or any threat to peace. Meanwhile the Soviets were also trying their hand at propaganda by broadcasting their own peace plans from Moscow. They offered an all-German government, a formal peace treaty, a united Germany west of the Oder–Neisse Line, four-power control of the Ruhr, higher industrial output and, most important of all, higher rations.[84] The Americans, however, had a new trick up their sleeves. They were going to win over the children: Harry King, the president of the confectioners Huylers, had obtained ten tons of sweets and some parachutes, and on 26 October Clay saw the chance for some excellent propaganda. The 'morale value would be real if candy could be flown out'.[85] This was the cue for Operation Little Vittles when airman Lieutenant Gail Halvorsen's 'Candy Bombers' dropped packets of sweets for the children by parachute into Berlin. Some even fell in the Eastern Sector.

The new airfield at Tegel opened on 5 November when the top brass flew in. The French commander General Jean Ganeval thanked his workers for their 'almost Egyptian labour'.[86] The city was suffering from TB, with 84,000 recorded cases. By November the Magistrat was divided in two with the Soviet Sector meeting in the Red Rathaus and the Western sectors meeting in the town hall in Schönefeld. The situation was formalised on 1 December. Clay predicted that the Berlin elections that were due to take place on 5 December 'will almost certainly result in a split city'. It was a chance to take back the promise of abiding by the Soviet-inspired Eastern mark. This would 'necessitate immediate issue of western currency'. Clay's prediction came true that time.[87] As Germany polarised, so did Berlin. In the East they elected a mayor to be the counterpart of

Reuter in the West. It was Friedrich Ebert, 'a fat, repulsive man' according to Howley,[88] who was to remain in the post for twenty years.

The process of making two Berlins was accelerated by the establishment of a 'Free University' in the buildings of the old Kaiser Wilhelms Gesellschaft in Dahlem, with General Clay's blessing. The pretext was provided when the Soviet-backed authorities at the Humboldt University in the Linden had expelled three students, Otto Hess, Joachim Schwarz and Otto Stolz, although all three were wholly above board, and Hess had the added advantage of Jewish blood. Clay wanted the new university to open its doors by the autumn.[89] The Allies distributed coal that December. Each household received 18 kilos, and those with children were allocated four times that amount. In the woods 120,000 cubic metres of trees were felled to provide fuel. Even this largesse was hardly able to stave off the cold of Yuletide in Berlin, and as many as 2,000 Berliners died of cold and hunger that winter. It was second only to the winter of 1946–7.

General Ganeval brought the French glory in the long run. The antennas of the Soviet-controlled Radio Berlin posed a danger on landing and take-off at Tegel. Ganeval decided to seize the initiative. He requested that the directors of the radio remove the masts as being a danger to planes. When they did nothing, Ganeval coolly blew them up at 10.45 on the morning of 16 December. The Russian General Kotikov was furious, and demanded to know how he could have done such a thing. The Frenchman replied, 'With the help of dynamite and French sappers.'[90] The Russians exacted their revenge by making off with the outlying village of Stolpe, which up to then had lain in the French Sector.[91]

At Christmas the SED leadership was summoned to Moscow. On his return Pieck announced that the East was not ready to embrace popular democracy. There were no immediate plans to create an East German state. Stalin made it clear that it was not just the Western orientation that needed to be fought in Germany, he wanted the Americans out.[92] In West Berlin they had a treat in the form of a visit by Bob Hope and the aptly named Irving Berlin. The stars performed at the Titania Palast in Steglitz. At the end of the year electricity was pumped out between 11 p.m. and 0.30 a.m. to allow the Berliners to welcome the New Year.[93]

It was in January 1949 that the diarist Speer alluded to the airlift for the first time. He noted that the Alliance had broken down and that had led to the blockading of the roads to Berlin: 'day and night transport planes roar over our building'. They were on their way to the British airfield at Gatow near by. As they toiled in the garden, the Spandau Seven wondered what the events meant for them. They came to the conclusion that they would be handed back to the countries that captured them. Speer was comforted by the idea he would be returned to the British.[94] It meant no such thing: the only real effect it had on the men was that their wives were unable to pay them visits because they could not reach Berlin.[95]

The battle for Berlin had descended into mud-slinging. The Russians condemned the Anglo-Americans for the barbaric bombing of Dresden. Clay again saw the possibility of propaganda: he seemed to recall that the bombing had been carried out 'at the specific request of Red Army'. He wanted to know if there were any written communications along those lines that might be leaked.[96] On 30 March, Moscow decided that Sokolovsky had failed and had him replaced by Vassily Chuikov. The Western Allies had no more problems dealing with the emergency:[97] the Russians might as well let the trains run unmolested.

George Kennan visited Berlin on 12 March that year. He went to stay at Harnack House in Dahlem, once part of the Kaiser Wilhelms Gesellschaft; the Americans had taken it over as a social club that mirrored Marlborough House in the British Sector. The city was not a pretty sight. Not only was it still ruinous, but it was dead – 'a ghost of its former self'. Harnack House was one of the few places that was still alive. It was 'like a garish honkey-tonkey that has stayed open too late in a sleepy provincial town. It was Saturday night . . . A German band was faithfully whacking out American dance tunes which they knew by heart. The faces of the musicians were drawn and worn . . .' Kennan observed a major studying the bill of fare: 'Look what's on de menu. Tuna fish. Tuna fish, for God's sake. We been feedin' it to our dog. He don't even like it any more. He jes' looks at me and says: jeez, tuna fish again.'[98]

He went to see the mayor. Reuter told him, 'this is the hardest time of the year. Fresh food is at its lowest. The grippe season was upon them. But morale could be maintained as long as we Americans evidenced determination to remain.' Kennan learned that, contrary to all appearances, the housing situation in Berlin was far from being the worst in Germany. Berlin had lost 40 per cent of its accommodation, but it had also seen a 25 per cent drop in its population. When the airlift reached a consistent 8,000 tons a day the Russians would have to concede. That night there was a colonial-style dinner party. The conversation addressed 'the price of antiques, the inadequacies of servants, and the availability of cosmetics at the PX'.[99]

During the eleven months of the airlift, Berlin had returned to wartime conditions. There was an evening curfew, and lack of gas and electricity obliged its inhabitants to live by candlelight and eat the dehydrated food provided by the Western Allies. The city was deserted in the evenings and there was no street lighting. There was no work. The Russians decided to drop their demands for the scrapping of the new Deutsche Mark, but they still insisted that the West cease its attempts to create a West German state. The Russian blockade failed. The Soviet operation had been both a waste of time and a loss of face. One recent historian has called it 'a harvest of blunders'.[100] On the night of 11–12 May 1949 road traffic was resumed. 'Hurrah, we're still alive!' shouted the grateful Berliners, who were driven into the arms of the West in gratitude. One of the main streets of Berlin-Zehlendorf was renamed in Clay's honour. The Anglo-Americans could now congratulate themselves that they were winning the propaganda battle for Berlin. The citizens of the former capital were turning against communism. Even the slowest Germans now began to understand that they were best off with the Western Allies. Not all West Berliners, however, supported the American and British action, and 120,000 of them registered for food rations in the East. Howley dismissed them as 'spineless backsliders'.

The Americans celebrated in Hollywood too, where three films had been made by December 1948. The most popular of these was *The Big Lift* with Montgomery Clift. In the Berlin streets the urchins played a new game: Airlift.

Austria

The airlift had its echoes in Austria.[101] Methods were used that were once again reminiscent of the Berlin blockade. In April 1946, the Soviet acting commander, L. V. Kurasov, demanded the removal of the radio-control tower at Tulln. The main road to the airport was often closed. The Russians caused difficulties for the British in Semmering and at the airport in Schwechat that they shared with the French. They tried to board the Mozart Express which linked the American Zone with the US sector in Vienna, and which was run for the exclusive use of American personnel. This led to an incident in the winter of 1946 when two Russian officers boarded the train and pulled a gun on Specialist Sergeant Shirley Dixon; Dixon replied by drawing his own gun, shooting one of the men dead and injuring the other. The Russians were naturally furious, and demanded that the Americans hand Dixon over for trial. The Americans refused. They tried Dixon themselves and acquitted him. The Russians demanded a fresh trial, but by that time Dixon was out of harm's way. The Russians then began to cut up the air traffic arriving and leaving Tulln, going so far as to fire on the aircraft. General Mark Clark responded by arming the planes coming into Tulln and informing the outgoing Soviet commander Koniev that he had done so. Clark says there were no more incidents.[102]

Contingency plans were drawn up to withdraw the Western Allied forces to a line along the River Enns,[103] and the Western Allies considered transferring their administrations to Salzburg. As the Cold War dawned, Béthouart was conscious of his inferior strength when it came to resisting the Russians. From the autumn of 1945 he possessed no more than a weak division of mountain troops.[104] The situation was similar for the other Western powers: for Soviet divisions you read Western battalions. Washington and London were sceptical of the need to reinforce the armies in Austria. London refused to countenance the idea of a Russian attack and Washington believed the likelihood to be remote.[105] That changed once the Soviet Union began to topple the post-war regimes in Budapest and Prague and flex its muscles in Berlin. Béthouart was summoned to a meeting at the Hôtel Matignon in Paris, attended by General Revers, chief of the general staff, and Koenig, Béthouart's opposite number in Berlin. The government wanted to know how the French Zone could protect itself. As a result mines were provided to blow up the roads in the event of a Russian advance; there were parachute exercises in the mountains and stocks of weapons and food were built up for use by Austrian resisters.

The Americans were also ready to fight any Soviet aggression, but the British, who were defending the port of Trieste, were much more reluctant. On 5 August 1948 General de Lattre de Tassigy organised a conference of the Western powers in Strasbourg, where the possibility of rearming the Germans was voiced for the first time.[106] It was the first step towards bringing West Germany into NATO.

There was much bandying about of accusations. Like Zhukov north of the Inn, Koniev indicted the British for keeping the Germans under arms. The political commissar, Colonel-General A. S. Zheltov, half in jest, focused on factories capable of making buttons for military uniforms. The Soviet Union could not be satisfied until Austria's ability to make such buttons was eliminated. The Western Allies were also dragging their feet over denazification. In the circumstances Austria would have to wait for freedom.[107]

The Russians pointed to cases of rape and theft by American servicemen in Vienna in October. Over a number of days the Soviet-backed *Österreichische Zeitung* reported beatings of black American troops by their white comrades, robberies, hold-ups and sex crimes. On 16 September Americans were alleged to have raided a nightclub shouting 'Niggers out!'

The US minister, John Erhardt, neither accepted nor denied the stories. The British were not well regarded in the East either – they were accused of collusion with anti-Tito partisans who had been engaged in armed activity and shoot-outs on the border with Carinthia.[108] There was some fear that Vienna would become the victim of a full-scale blockade, but the Americans comforted themselves with the reflection that the operation in Germany had not been a shining success. Feeding the Viennese was also the responsibility of the Austrian government even if there were no airfields suitable for the use of the Western Allies within Vienna. The ructions were many and annoying, but the situation never came close to war as it did in Germany, and the co-operation between the four powers continued.[109]

Chaos reigned too when it came to currency, with German Reichsmarks, Occupation Schillings and Austrian National Schillings all in circulation. None had any real purchasing power – for that you needed cig-arettes. The Schilling had been re-established in 1945, but its value plummeted and in December 1947 a 'new Schilling' replaced it, at a value of three old ones. Meanwhile the Allies continued to bleed the stricken state. In 1945 the Allied armies of occupation absorbed 35 per cent of the Austrian budget. With difficulty this was reduced to 15 in 1947. That year the Americans dispensed with their share, but it was not until 1953 that the other powers decided they could pay their own way.[110]

The Federal Republic

On 7 April 1948 General Robertson told the members of the Nordrein-Westfalen Landtag that they were to make the best of the western part of Germany for the time being; 'the rest will come in time. We offer you our good will and co-operation.' The effect of the speech was to hearten the Germans.[111] Adenauer was in on the European movement from the start. In May 1948 he was one of 800 delegates at the United Europe Congress in The Hague. His adviser Herbert Blankenhorn would have carried with him some of the ideas current at meetings of the Kreisau Circle during the war, when the notion of removing borders was seen as a means of pre-venting future wars. Sovereignty was also to be played down – as Adenauer himself put it, 'to secure common political and economic action'.[112] Churchill delivered a speech at the conference and received Adenauer per-sonally. Adenauer had sent a message to Churchill via Frank Pakenham: 'We were Hitler's prisoners and but for Mr Churchill we would not be alive today.' He was playing the victim card again.[113]

The London Conference of the Western Allies published the London Agreements on 7 June. It proposed the setting up of a constituent assembly, the defining of an Occupation Statute for the Allied armies and the creation of a Ruhr authority to allocate coal and steel production. It was typical of Adenauer that he was unconcerned about events in Berlin. The man of the moment was Reuter. Adenauer was chiefly concerned with the Ruhr authority, which he interpreted as an affront to German dignity. The Versailles Treaty was 'a bed of roses by comparison'.[114] As a recent biographer has written, given the situation in Berlin, Adenauer's protestations sounded like 'complaints about the functioning of the parish pump'.[115] More important were the meetings to decide the form of the future constitution. Documents were issued to the minister presidents of the three Western zones. The Länder called a conference in Koblenz on 8 July which was followed by another at Frankfurt that began on 20 July. On 10 August they met again on the Herreninsel in Lake Chiemsee. There was little agreement between the CDU and the Bavarian CSU, and Adenauer disliked the Bavarian party chairman, Josef 'Ochsensepp' Müller.

On 26 July the minister presidents agreed to summon a constituent assembly to be called the Parliamentary Council in Bonn on 1 September. It was to be a conference of party officials, arranged proportionate to seats in the three Landtags. Bonn was not Adenauer's idea. He would have preferred Koblenz, which was in the French Zone.[116] It was in Bonn that one of the architects of the *Grundgesetz* or basic law came to the fore – Dr Carlo Schmid. Schmid was the SPD's constitutional expert and it was the job of his committee to produce the legal foundations for post-war Germany. The SPD scored a small victory over Adenauer, who was anxious to prevent them from constituting a majority in the new Bundesrat, or upper house (the lower house was to be the Bundestag). He was trying to exclude Berlin from the body, both because of his animus against the city and because its inclusion would mean that the SPD carried the day. The SPD, however, succeeded in establishing that the size of the Land's population would decide how many delegates would go to the Bundesrat.

It was at this time that Blankenhorn entered the stage. He had been a colleague and friend of Adam von Trott's in the German Foreign Office, and was well aware of the aims and ideologies of the Kreisauer. He was an Anglophile, and fell out with Adenauer only when the latter opposed British membership of the Common Market. Blankenhorn could do what Adenauer could not: he could charm Allied generals and talk to journalists. Adenauer was too much of a stuffed shirt to appeal to them.

The French were distressed to see the progress being made towards a

German government under the lead of Adenauer. Work was proceeding at such a lick that the minister presidents of the Länder were worried about taking the responsibility of splitting Germany in two. Not so Adenauer. He thought Germany's future lay in the west in the defence of Romano-Christian culture. He knew that his bread was buttered in Paris. The French nonetheless wanted him to slow down, and confine his attentions to the basic law. When Clay and Robertson issued Bizonia Law 75 giving the Germans the cue to decide the future of the Ruhr, the French uttered a last gasp of fury embodied in a formal complaint from Schuman.[117]

Despite this, Adenauer was still flirting with the French. One of the contacts he made at the time was with Schuman. They met first in October 1948 at Bassenheim in the French-administered Pfalz, in the residence of the governor, Hettier de Boislambert. Adenauer had no desire to let the Anglo-Americans know of his talks and travelled to the meeting wrapped in a blanket with his Homburg pulled down over his eyes. The Ruhr was still a sticking point. Schuman had to go carefully. Even after 1949 the Saar was the cause of frequent friction between the French and Adenauer.[118]

The parliamentary capital had yet to be decided. Berlin was out, not just because of Adenauer's loathing of Prussia, but because it was behind Russian lines and increasingly prone to Soviet intimidation. The natural capital was Frankfurt, in that it had been a semi-independent imperial, coronation city before 1806, and it was also the scene of the abortive German parliament of 1848. After 1848, German liberals believed the country had taken the wrong path – the path that led to the First World War and the Second. It was also famously the birthplace of Goethe. Frankfurt was the choice of the SPD. The CDU was for Bonn, a small city associated with the archbishop of Cologne, and with the Prussian university founded there in 1815. Bonn was the birthplace of Beethoven. The British decided in Bonn's favour by offering to make it autonomous and free from their control. Frankfurt was administratively too important for the Americans to relinquish it. The Germans could finally be masters in their small house.

Conclusion

The policy of constraint applied by the victors brings only fragile and misleading solutions . . . For as long as there is reason for revenge, there will be a renewed risk of war.

Germany was never as dangerous as when she was isolated.

Robert Schuman, *Pour l'Europe*, 2nd edn, Paris 1964, 107, 110

That means the old borders must fall and be replaced by new alliances, and a new, bigger empire must unite the nations . . . That is the only way to end the feud properly to everybody's advantage.

Ernst Jünger, *Der Friede*, Vienna 1949, 31

The Soviets had failed. They had failed twice: they had neither pushed the Western Allies out of Berlin nor forestalled the creation of a Western German state. The stage was now set for the division of Germany into two camps, each with its own ideologically orientated government. On 8 April 1949 the Allies in Washington decided to transform their Military Government into an Allied High Commission, and the French agreed to join Bizonia, briefly to be called Trizonia. On 23 May 1949 the basic law or *Grundgesetz* was signed in the presence of the three Western Allied governors. The Federal Republic was waiting in the wings. Adenauer claimed that the *Grundgesetz* constituted 'a major contribution to the reunification of the German people'.[1] This was clearly untrue, and it is interesting to speculate today how much Adenauer ever genuinely desired to see the family reunited. Some maintain that Adenauer was biding his time, waiting for the East to fall into his hands. For the time being, however, Germany east of the Elbe was cast adrift and would not come back into harbour until 1989, twenty-two years after Adenauer's death.

Some would argue that Adenauer – indeed the West – was powerless to alleviate the plight of those Germans caught behind the Iron Curtain, but this is only true up to a point. There was another way: it was the solution which, after 250 days of negotiation, resulted in the Austrian State Treaty in 1955. The Allies then packed their bags and went home. That solution was presented to Germany too. On 10 March 1952 Stalin made Adenauer an offer of an armed and unified Germany. The only condition he sought to impose was that Germany – like Austria after 1955 – should not belong to any military alliance. Stalin was still worried about security. Adenauer pocketed the note. He said it contained nothing new. He thought it more important to integrate his West German state with the West than to unite with his brothers across the Elbe.[2]

The rest may be summarised. Elections in West Germany were set for 14 August 1949. Adenauer went into the lists claiming that the British were funding the socialists, which made him more sour than ever, even if he didn't actually believe a word of it. The result was a hung parliament, with the CDU/CSU winning 31 per cent of the vote and the SPD 29.2 per cent. A coalition was inevitable. On 21 August Adenauer held a CDU coffee party at his home in Rhöndorf. The leader of the FDP, or Free Democrats, Theodor Heuss, was to be fobbed off with the ceremonial presidency. Adenauer pushed the CSU aside to clasp the chancellor's role for himself. On 15 September it was put to a vote among the members of the Bundestag. Adenauer secured the Chancellery by one vote – his own. Kurt Schumacher dubbed him 'the Allies' Chancellor'.[3] The new Germany could now start work. The adoption of the basic law that month ended the military occupation of Germany.

Adenauer's election prompted an equal and opposite move in the East. On 16 September a SED delegation arrived in Moscow to receive instructions from the Politburo on how to cope with the creation of a 'West German imperialist state' and to plan the creation of the German Democratic Republic. It was much the same crew: Pieck, Grotewohl, Ulbricht and Fred Oelssner on the German side, and Malenkov, Molotov, Mikoyan and Kaganovitch on the Soviet. America was cast in the light of a colonising power. The West German regime was to be unmasked as the organ of the Western powers.[4]

The GDR was created on 7 October not only as a response to the FRG, but also as a result of East Germany's abandonment by West. At the end of 1949 the Soviet regime made promises that it did not keep, among which was an agreement to release all German POWs, and to close the camps in Germany. At the outset there had been eleven such establishments, but this number was now reduced to just three. At their peak the camps had contained 158,000 Germans. There were still 16,000 as 1949 turned into 1950, and the camps did not finally close until after Stalin's death. As a special treat the German delegation had asked for some translations of Stalin's speeches. The incentive was to be rid of the SBZ, which with time the East Germans were, although no one can argue that Moscow failed to keep them on a tight leash.

Adenauer's courting of the French not only ensured their eventual support, it had one lasting benefit: it laid the foundations for the Common Market, or European Union as it has now become. The idea has its precursors. Emperor William II of Germany made frequent references to the subject and voiced a hope that it would come to fruition. It apparently derived from his chancellor Caprivi.[5] Aristide Briand had proposed a European Federation in 1929–30 as a means of matching the might of the United States after 1918, but the suggestion was put aside by the slump that followed the Wall Street Crash. Robert Schuman became interested at that time as a deputy for Lorraine in the French Assembly.[6] During the war the notion of European unity surfaced on both sides of the Rhine. In Germany it tended to be the left who took it up, especially some of the intellectuals in the Kreisau Circle. Adam von Trott, for example, was keen to revive a 'Carolingian' Europe and it was a conception that found echoes in the Quai d'Orsay at the end of the war.[7]

In France a union of Europe was more popular with the right, often as an unlikely benefit that had accrued with defeat. Ernst Jünger, who must have encountered its champions on both sides of the Rhine, thought it a lost opportunity that the French and Germans were not brought together on an equal footing after the Fall of France. Writing in the middle of the war, he saw the forging of a new 'empire' to be a task for the peace: 'Can someone like an Alsatian live as a German or a Frenchman without being forced to turn from one to the other?' Jünger was also swayed by the Carolingian idea – to build a new empire that would be as strong as its rivals.[8] His thoughts were not far from those of Schuman.

De Gaulle too took up the banner in September 1943, when he spoke of Europe's 'common identity'. The first task was to remove customs barriers. The plans were more elaborately worked out by the French radical politician René Mayer in a memorandum of 30 September 1943. He called for an 'economic federation' centred on France and taking in Benelux and 'Rhenania' (the German territories bordering the Rhine), and possibly Italy and Spain too.[9] Jean Monnet, the head of the French General Planning Committee, put forward a line of argument similar to that of Helmuth James von Moltke: there would be 'no peace in Europe if states re-establish them-selves on the basis of national sovereignty . . . To enjoy . . . prosperity and social progress . . . the states of Europe must form . . . a "European Entity", which will make them a single European unit.'[10] For Schuman, a fragmentary Europe was anachronistic. The resources of individual states were not enough, as France discovered after the war: they needed German coal. The solidarity of nations should be greater than 'outworn nationalism'.[11]

The European idea even found a few champions in Britain. Victor Gollancz warned of the dangers of an isolated, dismembered Germany: 'A federal Europe, a hundred times yes; an atomized Germany in an un-federalised Europe, danger and folly.'[12] Sir Robert Birley, headmaster of Eton, and the man who had been chosen to shape education policy in the British Zone, looked forward to European Union in his 1949 Reith Lectures, and for much the same reason – sovereignty needed to be sacrificed to collective security.[13] And Britain was present as the first steps were taken towards union. It was one of the signatories of the Western European Union on 17 March 1948 and of the Atlantic Pact a year later, even if it fell by the wayside before the Treaty of Rome established the Common Market in March 1957.

De Gaulle found the notion of embracing the whole of German territory in French plans too ambitious. He focused his attention on westward-looking 'Rhenania', and Adenauer was cunning enough to sell him a Germany that was just that.[14] Indeed, Adenauer was also keen to play the Carolingian card, based on France and Germany's common Frankish inheritance. The new Germany based in Bonn would defend Romano-Christian culture from – guess who? The Slavs.[15]

Germany's experience of post-war bloodletting was not an isolated one. In the wake of the Second World War there was imprisonment, trial and retribution – *des rendements de comptes* – all over the world. In 1956 Margret Boveri estimated that as many as half a million French people had been arrested after the war, resulting in 160,000 trials. In Belgium the number of investigations was as high was 600,000, in Holland 130,000. Even in America, 570 federal officials were dismissed and 2,748 resigned during Truman's term; another 8,000 were sacked by Eisenhower. In England they hanged Lord Haw Haw and John Amery, and branded up to 10,000 people with 'legitimate doubt'.[16]

The question arises whether the Allies achieved what they desired. The war horses on the American side had their doubts. The Cold War showed them that they had not defeated the enemy – Germany was not the enemy any more. That was the Soviet Union. For Patton or Mark Clark it had been a botched job. Clark wrote: 'We had not won the war. We had stopped too soon. We had been too eager to go home. We welcomed the peace, but after more years of effort and expenditure we found that we had won no peace.'[17] America had succeeded elsewhere, however. It was able to shove the ailing Great Britain aside and assume the leadership of the Western world. The days of the Raj and the rest of the British Empire were numbered. British India was over even before the signing of the *Grundgesetz*. Britain would be encouraged to drop its pretensions to power and follow at the American heel.

The Russians had been checked at the Elbe, but they had the security Stalin craved, and it was thirty-five years after Stalin's death before their European empire finally tottered and fell. The most surprising victors of the peace were the French, who started right at the back yet finished by realising all their war aims. For the Poles and the Czechs it proved bitter-sweet: they had their national states without the dangers presented by racial minorities, but they had communism, and Soviet Russia squatting on their national aspirations.

And what did the Germans gain from the peace? The Allies had helped them 'throw the baby out with the bathwater' in what was an often misguided desire to dig out the roots of the evil. They promoted an idea of Germany's past as 'another country' which became enshrined in Jurgen Habermas's dictum that 'history begins at Auschwitz'. They were well rid of Adolf Hitler and his cronies, who had led them to ruin and besmirched their name for all time. They gained stability created by a monetary reform which ushered in a new era of prosperity.

The Germans didn't want to know their sullied history. Weary of the past they began to take pleasure in the destruction of their towns. Those few towns and villages in Germany and Austria that had emerged unscathed were ripped down all the same in the 1950s and 1960s: the past had to go, to be replaced by an anodyne notion of comfort and prosperity. The myth of zero hour was taken to all their hearts. The perceptive writer Alfred Döblin noticed this tendency as early as 1946. For the time being there was little construction going on. Commerce thrived in the ruins. The people made no bones about the state of Germany: 'They are not depressed by the destruction; they see it rather as an intense spur to work. I am convinced that, if they had the means they lack, they would rejoice tomorrow that all their outmoded, badly laid-out conurbations had been knocked flat giving them the opportunity now to build something first class and wholly contemporary.'[18]

The west was patched up quickly; buildings went up here there and everywhere to replace those destroyed in the war. A vast ugliness replaced the ruins. If they were allowed to, they could finally forget the blood they had spilled, and concentrate on the birth of the new Germany, which they had watered with their own.

Notes

PREFACE

1 A. J. Nicholls, *Weimar and the Rise of Hitler*, 3rd edn. London 1991, 136–7.
2 Quoted in Ernst Jünger, *Jahre der Okkupation*, Stuttgart 1958, 130.

INTRODUCTION

1 Gerhard Ziemer, *Deutsche Exodus: Vertreibung und Eingliederung von 15 Millionen Ostdeutsche*, Stuttgart 1973, 94. Ziemer's figures are based on those published by the Statischen Bundesamt in Wiesbaden in 1958.
2 See also Manfred Rauchensteiner, 'Das Jahrzehnt der Besatzung als Epoche in der Österreichischer Geschichte', in Alfred Ableitinger, Siegfried Beer and Eduard G. Staudinger, eds, *Österreich unter alliieter Besatzung – 1945–1955*, Vienna, Cologne and Graz 1998, 18–19.
3 Alfred Döblin, *Schicksalsreise, Bericht und Bekenntnisse*, Frankfurt/Main 1949, 420–2.
4 Heinrich Böll, *Kreuz ohne Liebe*, Cologne 2003, 285–6.
5 Robert Jan van Pelt and Deborah Dwork, *Auschwitz, 1270 to the Present*, New Haven and London 1996, 10.
6 Anonymous, *A Woman in Berlin*, introduced by C. W. Ceram and translated by James Stern, London 1965, 139.
7 Raul Hilberg, *The Destruction of the European Jews*, 3rd edn, London and New Haven 2003, III, 1138.
8 David Blackbourn's *The Conquest of Nature*, London 2005, sees early Nazi tendencies in the desire to control Germany's waterways.
9 Michael Balfour and John Mair, *Four Power Control in Germany and Austria 1945–1946*, Oxford 1956, 28.
10 Ibid., 15.
11 Eugene Davidson, *The Death and Life of Germany – An Account of the American Occupation*, 2nd edn, Columbia, Miss. 1999, 6–7. Davidson possibly means Adam von Trott, who arrived in America in September 1939 – see Giles MacDonogh, *A Good German: Adam von Trott zu Solz*, revised edn, London 1994, 307–19. It was Roosevelt who told J. Edgar Hoover to have him closely followed: the president considered Trott a threat to national security.
12 Curtis F. Morgan, Jnr, *James F. Byrnes, Lucius Clay, and American Policy in Germany, 1945–1947*, Lewiston, Queenston and Lampeter 2002, 2, 5.
13 Henric Wuermeling, *Doppelspiel: Adam von Trott zu Solz im Widerstand gegen Hitler*, Munich 2004, 142–4.
14 Davidson, *Death and Life*, 5; Balfour and Mair, *Four Power Control*, 34.
15 Balfour and Mair, *Four Power Control*, 30–1, 36.
16 Ibid., 34; Paul W. Gulgowski, 'The American Military Government of

United States Occupied Zones of Post World War II Germany in Relation to Policies Expressed by its Civilian Governmental Authorities at Home, During the Course of 1944/1945 through 1949' (doctoral dissertation, Frankfurt University) Frankfurt/Main 1983, 22.

17 Balfour and Mair, *Four Power Control*, 18.

18 Morgan, *Byrnes, Clay*, 8–9.

19 Ibid., 7.

20 Ibid., 15.

21 Hermann Graml, *Die Alliierten und die Teilung Deutschlands. Konflikte und Entscheidungen 1941–1948*, Frankfurt/Main 1985, 27, 60.

22 Morgan, *Byrnes, Clay*, 41; Graml, *Teilung Deutschlands*, 53, 56.

23 Norman M. Naimark, *The Russians in Germany – A History of the Soviet Zone of Occupation, 1945–1949*, Cambridge, Mass. and London 1995, 9; Morgan, *Byrnes, Clay*, 52–3.

24 Naimark, *Russians in Germany*, 76.

25 John W. Young, *France, the Cold War and the Western Alliance, 1944–49: French Foreign Policy and Post-War Europe*, Leicester and London 1990, 9.

26 Vojtech Mastny, *The Cold War and Soviet Insecurity*, New York and Oxford 1996, 17.

27 Ibid., 19.

28 Oliver Rathkolb, 'Historische Fragmente in die "unendliche Geschichte" von den Sowjetische Absichte in Österreich', in Ableitinger et al., *Österreich unter alliierter Besatzung*, 139–42, passim.

29 Jean-Pierre Rioux, 'France 1945: L'Ambition allemande et ses moyens', in Klaus Manfrass and Jean-Pierre Rioux, eds, *France-Allemagne 1944–1947*, Les Cahiers de l'Institut d'Histoire du Temps Présent, December 1989–January 1990/Akten des deutsch-französisch Historikerkolloquiums, Baden-

Baden, 2–5 December 1986, 37.

30 Ibid., 15.

31 Ibid., 25.

32 Ibid., 40.

33 Ibid., 26.

34 Ibid., 28.

35 James F. Byrnes, *Speaking Frankly*, London 1947, 25.

36 Rioux, 'France 1945', 40–1.

37 Ibid., 49.

38 Ibid., 50–1.

39 Klaus-Dietmar Henke, 'Der Weg nach Potsdam – Die Alliierten und die Vertreibung', in Wolfgang Benz, ed., *Die Vertreibung der Deutschen aus dem Osten. Ursachen, Ereignisse, Folgen*, Frankfurt/Main 1985, 51–2, 55–6.

40 Andreas Lawaty, *Das Ende Preussens in polnischer Sicht. Zur kontinuität negativer Wirkungen der preussischen Geschichte auf die deutsch–polnischen Beziehungen*, Berlin and New York 1986, 56–7.

41 Ibid., 100.

42 Byrnes, *Speaking Frankly*, 29–30.

43 Detlef Brandes, 'Die Exilpolitik von Edvard Beneš 1939–1945', in Arnold Suppan and Elisabeth Vyslonzil, eds, *Edvard Beneš und die tschechoslowakische Aussenpolitik 1918–1948*, 2nd edn, Frankfurt/Main, Berlin, Bern, Brussels, New York, Oxford and Vienna 2003, 159.

44 Ibid., 160.

45 Ibid., 161.

46 Manfred Rauchensteiner, *Stalinplatz 4: Österreich unter alliieter Besatzung*, Vienna 2005, 7–8.

47 Quoted in General Béthouart, *La Bataille pour l'Autriche*, Paris 1966, 15.

48 Quoted in ibid., 16.

49 Ibid., 10.

50 Otto von Habsburg, *Ein Kampf um Österreich 1938–1945*, Aufgezeichnet von Gerhard Tötschinger, Vienna and Munich 2001, 26, 69.

51 Rauchensteiner, *Stalinplatz 4*, 14.

52 Ibid., 12.

53 Charmian Brinson, 'Ein "Sehr Ambitioniertes Projekt" – Die Anfänge des Austrian Centre', in Marietta Bearman et al., *Wien–London, hin und retour: Das Austrian Centre in London 1939 bis 1947*, Vienna 2004, 15.

54 Marietta Bearman, 'Das kommende Österreich. Die Planung für ein Nachkriegs-Österreich', in Bearman et al., *Wien–London*, 222.

55 Ibid., 207.

56 Ibid., 212

57 Ibid., 207–8.

58 See Helene Maimann, *Politik im Wartesaal*, Vienna, Cologne and Graz 1975 and F. C. West, *Zurück oder nicht zurück?*, London 1942.

59 Brinson, 'Ein "Sehr Ambitioniertes Projekt"', 22–3.

60 Anthony Grenville, 'Zeit der Prüfung, Zeit der taten, Zeit des Triumphes und der Illusionen – Die politische Tätigkeit des Austrian Centre', in Bearman et al., *Wien–London*, 29.

61 Ibid., 47.

62 Eden to Ralph Murray, 10 September 1942, kindly communicated by Johannes Popper von Podhragy; see also Peter Gosztony, *Endkampf an der Donau 1944/1945*, Vienna, Munich and Zurich 1969, 209.

63 FAM, untitled document of 15 March 1943, communicated by Johannes Popper von Podhragy.

64 Grenville, 'Zeit der Prüfung', 37.

65 Ibid., 35, 37, 38.

66 Ibid., 40.

67 Ibid., 41.

68 Ibid., 42.

69 Ibid., 43–4, 48.

70 Ibid., 49.

71 Charmian Brinson, 'Die "Robinson Crusoes" von Paddington und die Briten. Die Beziehungen zwischen Austrian Centre, Free Austrian Movement und den britischen Gastgebern', in Bearman et al., *Wien–London*, 180, 181.

72 Ibid., 184.

73 See Christiane Maasburg, 'Nikolas Maasburgs Rolle im Widerstand und bei der Wiederherstellung eines unabhängigen Österreich' (Diplomarbeit zur Erlangung des Magistergrades der Philosophie, University of Vienna 1996); Henrik Eberle and Matthias Uhl, eds, *Das Buch Hitler*, Bergisch Gladbach 2004, 335 and n.

74 Rathkolb, 'Historische Fragmente', 142–5, 156–7.

75 Grenville, 'Zeit der Prüfung', 48, 52.

CHAPTER 1: THE FALL OF VIENNA

1 Naimark, *Russians in Germany*, 77–8, 91.

2 Ibid., 73.

3 Ibid., 71; Klaus Dieter Mulley, 'Aspekte Sowjetische Besatzung in Nieder Österreich', in Ableitinger et al., eds, *Österreich unter alliierter Besatzung*, 387.

4 Giles MacDonogh, *Prussia – The Perversion of an Idea*, London 1994, 384; Naimark, *Russians in Germany*, 91.

5 Adolf Schärf, *Österreichs Wiederaufrichtung im Jahr 1945*, Vienna 1960, 29, 31.

6 Ibid., 7.

7 Ibid., 33.

8 Alois Brusatti, ed., *Zeuge der Stunde Null, das Tagebuch Eugen Margaréthas 1945–1947*, revised by Hildegard Hemetsberger-Koller, Vienna 1990, 24.

9 Ibid., 28, 39.

10 Mulley, 'Aspekte Sowjetische Besatzung', 376.

11 Rauchensteiner, *Stalinplatz 4*, 22–3; Schärf, *Wiederaufrichtung*, 18.

12 Margarétha, *Tagebuch*, 29.

13 Josef Schöner, *Wiener Tagebuch*, ed.
Eva-Marie Csáky, Franz Matscher
and Gerald Stourzh, Vienna,
Cologne and Weimar 1990, 136.

14 Margarétha, *Tagebuch*, 33.

15 Oliver Rathkolb, ed., *Gesellschaft und Politik am Beginn der zweiten Republik – vertrauliche Berichte der US-Militäradministration aus Österreich 1945 in englischer Originalfassung*, Vienna, Cologne and Graz 1985, 158; Schärf, *Wiederaufrichtung*, 24–5.

16 Margarétha, *Tagebuch*, 29.

17 Schöner, *Tagebuch*, 137–8.

18 Giles MacDonogh, *The Wine and Food of Austria*, London 1992, 19.

19 Schärf, *Wiederaufrichtung*, 25.

20 Ibid., 19–20.

21 Carl Szokoll, *Die Rettung Wiens*, Vienna 2001, 291.

22 Schöner, *Tagebuch*, 138–9.

23 Schöner, *Tagebuch*, 140.

24 Schärf, *Wiederaufrichtung*, 23.

25 Margarétha, *Tagebuch*, 52, 61.

26 Schöner, *Tagebuch*, 162.

27 Willy Prinz von Thurn und Taxis, 'Memoiren', unpublished MS in the possession of Princess Daria von Thurn und Taxis, Munich, 19–20, 24.

28 Ibid., 162–3.

29 Wolfgang Mueller, *Die sowjetische Besatzung in Österreich 1945–1955 und ihre politische Mission*, Vienna 2005, 82–4; Christiane Maasburg, 'Nikolaus Maasburg', 72–3, 75, 77.

30 Schöner, *Tagebuch*, 141–2; Margarétha, *Tagebuch*, 32.

31 Margarétha, *Tagebuch*, 31.

32 Schärf, *Wiederaufrichtung*, 25.

33 Schöner, *Tagebuch*, 144.

34 Ibid., 145.

35 Margarétha, *Tagebuch*, 33; Schärf, *Wiederaufrichtung*, 20.

36 Schöner, *Tagebuch*, 147, 172.

37 Margarétha, *Tagebuch*, 35; Schöner, *Tagebuch*, 148.

38 Schärf, *Wiederaufrichtung*, 25; Schöner, *Tagebuch*, 148–9, 169.

39 Schöner, *Tagebuch*, 150–2.

40 Margarétha, *Tagebuch*, 32.

41 Ibid., 35, 39, 50.

42 Schärf, *Wiederaufrichtung*, 37.

43 Ibid., 45–6.

44 Ibid., 58.

45 Rathkolb, ed., *Gesellschaft und Politik*, 154–8; Rathkolb, 'Historische Fragmente', 147.

46 Schöner, *Tagebuch*, 165.

47 Ibid., 153–4.

48 Margarétha, *Tagebuch*, 42.

49 Schöner, *Tagebuch*, 158–60, 171.

50 Ibid., 164.

51 Margarétha, *Tagebuch*, 42–3, 48.

52 Ibid., 44–5.

53 Schärf, *Wiederaufrichtung*, 52, 57.

54 Margarétha, *Tagebuch*, 46.

55 Schöner, *Tagebuch*, 165–6; Margarétha, *Tagebuch*, 42.

56 Schöner, *Tagebuch*, 167, 175.

57 Ibid., 181.

58 Rauchensteiner, *Stalinplatz 4*, 17.

59 Gordon Brook-Shepherd, *The Austrians – A Thousand-Year Odyssey*, London 1996, 377–8.

60 Rauchensteiner, *Stalinplatz 4*, 20.

61 Rathkolb, ed., *Gesellschaft und Politik*, 115–17.

62 Schöner, *Tagebuch*, 182–3.

63 Ibid., 184.

64 Grenville, 'Zeit der Prüfung', 60.

65 Margarétha, *Tagebuch*, 60.

66 Schöner, *Tagebuch*, 191–2.

67 Ibid., 201; Rauchensteiner, *Stalinplatz 4*, 27.

68 Rathkolb, ed., *Gesellschaft und Politik*, 114.

69 Ibid., 201–2; Schärf, *Wiederaufrichtung*, 27, 89; Rauchensteiner, *Stalinplatz 4*, 21.

70 Schöner, *Tagebuch*, 205; Schärf, *Wiederaufrichtung*, 87.

71 Siegfried Beer, 'Niederösterreich unter der Roten Armee', in Ernst Bezemek and Willibald Rossner, eds, *Niederösterreich 1945 – Südmähren 1945*, Vienna 1996, 140.

72 Béthouart, *Bataille*, 19.

73 Schöner, *Tagebuch*, 217–18.

74 Ibid., 225.
75 Margarétha, *Tagebuch*, 67–8.
76 Ibid., 233.

CHAPTER 2: WILD TIMES:
A PICTURE OF LIBERATED
CENTRAL EUROPE IN 1945

1 Ursula von Kardorff, *Berliner
Aufzeichnungen 1942–1945*, new,
unabridged edn, Munich 1994, 346.
2 Hans Graf von Lehndorff,
*Ostpreussisches Tagebuch:
Aufzeichnungen eines Arztes aus den
Jahren 1945–1947*, Munich 1961, 11.
3 Josef Henke, 'Exodus aus
Ostepreussen und Schlesien: Vier
Erlebnisberichte', in Benz, *Die
Vertreibung*, 93.
4 MacDonogh, *Prussia*, 380–1; Eberle
and Uhl, eds, *Das Buch Hitler*,
312–13.
5 Henke, 'Exodus', 95.
6 Lehndorff, *Tagebuch*, 67–8.
7 Ibid., 68.
8 Ibid., 71, 75.
9 Naimark, *Russians in Germany*, 73.
(The translation is by Robert
Conquest.)
10 Lehndorff, *Tagebuch*, 70.
11 Ibid., 71, 77.
12 Ibid., 68, 72.
13 Ibid, 79–80.
14 Ibid., 85.
15 Fritz Gause, *Die Geschichte der Stadt
Königsberg in Preussen*, 3 vols,
Cologne and Vienna 1965–71, III,
172.
16 Marianne Peyinghaus, *Stille Jahre in
Gertlauken – Erinnerungen an
Ostpreussen*, Berlin 1985, 90; Giles
MacDonogh, review of *The Amber
Room* by Catherine Scott-Clark and
Adrian Levy in *Literary Review*, June
2004.
17 Gause, *Königsberg*, III, 170n.
18 Ibid., 171.
19 Henke, 'Exodus', 97–9.

20 Ibid., 100–1.
21 Gause, *Königsberg*, III, 171.
22 Christian von Krockow, *The Hour of
the Women*, translated by Krishna
Winton, London and Boston 1991,
67, 86.
23 Käthe von Normann, *Ein Tagebuch
aus Pommern*, Munich 1987, 16.
24 Ibid., 16–17.
25 Ibid., 18–19.
26 Ibid., 21, 252.
27 Ibid., 26.
28 Carl Tighe, *Gdansk – National
Identity in the Polish–German
Borderlands*, London and Concord
1990, 194.
29 Ibid., 195; Hilberg, *Destruction*, III,
1053.
30 Hilberg, *Destruction*, III, 1052.
31 Nikolaus Wachsmann, *Hitler's Prisons:
Legal Terror in Nazi Germany*, New
Haven and London 2004, 324–5.
32 Brewster Chamberlin and Marcia
Feldman, eds, *The Liberation of the
Concentration Camps 1945: Eyewitness
Accounts of the Liberation*, with an
introduction by Robert H. Abzug,
Washinton DC 1987, 91.
33 Wachsmann, *Hitler's Prisons*, 327–8.
34 Tighe, *Gdansk*, 197–8.
35 Günter Grass, *Die Blechtrommel*,
Darmstadt and Neuwied 1988, 485.
36 Giles MacDonogh, 'Do Mention the
War', *Financial Times Magazine*, 1
November 2002.
37 Hilberg, *Destruction*, III, 1049–51.
38 Johannes Kaps, ed., *Die Tragödie
Schlesiens 1945/46 in Dokumente –
unter besonderer Berucksichtigung des
Erzbishoftums Breslau*, Munich
1952–3, 50–1.
39 Edward N. Petersen, *Russian
Commands and German Resistance: The
Soviet Occupation, 1945–1949*, New
York 1999, 224.
40 Norman Davies and Roger
Moorhouse, *Microcosm: Portrait of a
Central European City*, London 2002,
408.

41 Herbert Hupka, ed., *Letzte Tage in Schlesien: Tagebücher, Erinnerungen und Dokumente der Vertreibung*, Munich and Vienna 1982, 12.

42 Ibid., 50.

43 Ibid., 51.

44 Ibid., 53, 55.

45 Wachsmann, *Hitler's Prisons*, 332.

46 Michal Chilczuk in Chamberlain and Feldman, eds, *Liberation*, 27–8.

47 Hilberg, *Destruction*, III, 1055.

48 Margret Boveri, *Tage des Überlebens*, Frankfurt/Main 1996, 163.

49 Ibid., 167.

50 Ruth Andreas Friedrich, *Schauplatz Berlin*, Frankfurt/Main 1985, 60.

51 Saul K. Padover, *Psychologist in Germany – The Story of an American Intelligence Officer*, London 1946, 134.

52 Ibid., 218.

53 Ibid., 280–1; Kurt Buchholz, 'Die ersten Amis sagten freundlich "Hello"', *Wiesbadener Tagblatt*, 25 April 2005, kindly communicated by Frau Gertrud Loewe.

54 Missie Vassiltchikov, *Berlin Diaries*, London 1985, 290, 294.

55 Ibid., 294.

56 Elena Skrjabina, *The Allies on the Rhine 1945–1950*, translated by Norman Luxenburg, with a foreword by Harrison Salisbury, Carbondale and Edwardsville 1980, 9–13.

57 Ibid., 17.

58 Ibid., 17, 29–30, 39, 41.

59 Carl Zuckmayer, *Deutschlandbericht für das Kriegsministerium der Vereinigten Staaten von Amerika*, edited by Gunther Nickel, Johanna Schrön and Hans Wagener, Göttingen 2004, 18, 70.

60 Ibid., 69.

61 Ernst Wiechert, *Jahre und Zeiten – Erinnerungen*, Munich and Vienna 1989, 408.

62 Ibid., 410.

63 Quoted in Mary Fulbrook, *The People's State: East German Society from Hitler to Honecker*, New Haven and London 2005, 26.

64 Abraham J. Peck, 'Befreit und erneut in Lagern: jüdische DPs', in Walter H. Pehle, ed., *Der Judenpogrom 1938 – Von der 'Reichskristallnacht' zum Völkermord*, Frankfurt/ Main 1988, 204–5.

65 Kardorff, *Aufzeichnungen*, 316 n. 4, which gives the uncorrected text from the diary.

66 Ibid., 317.

67 Ibid., 329, 331.

68 Ibid., 318.

69 Ibid., 322 and n. 2.

70 Ibid., 319–20.

71 Robert H. Abzug, *Inside the Vicious Heart – Americans and the Liberation of Nazi Concentration Camps*, New York and Oxford 1985, 80.

72 Paul Berber, *Dachau 1933–1945 – The Official History*, London 1975, 183.

73 Ibid., 89–93; Michael Selzer, *Deliverance Day: The Last Hours at Dachau*, London 1980, 188–9. The latter is an unsatisfying book in that it conceals the identity of the interviewees and creates conglomerate characters. There are also large chunks of dialogue.

74 Ibid., 198, 201, 204; Abzug, *Vicious Heart*, 94–5.

75 Chamberlain and Feldman, eds, *Liberation*, 32.

76 Berber, *Dachau*, 199.

77 Ibid.

78 Wachsmann, *Hitler's Prisons*, 330.

79 Brigitte Hamann, *Winifred Wagner – A Life at the Heart of Hitler's Bayreuth*, translated by Alan Bance, London 2005, 405.

80 Walter Lüdde-Neurath, *Regierung Dönitz. Die letzten Tage des Dritten Reiches*, Göttingen 1951, 86.

81 Lutz Schwerin von Krosigk, *Memoiren*, Stuttgart 1977, 242–4.

82 Ibid., 245.

83 Lüdde-Neurath, *Regierung Dönitz*, 95.

84 Ibid., 98.

85 Karl Dönitz, *Mein Wechselvolles Leben*, Zurich, Berlin and Frankfurt 1968, 210; Reimer Hanse, *Das Ende des Dritten Reiches. Die deutsche Kapitulation, 1945*, Stuttgart 1966, 194.

86 Douglas Botting, *In the Ruins of the Reich*, London 2005, 138–40.

87 Hanse, *Kapitulation*, 196–8.

88 Boveri, *Tage*, 153.

89 Charles Whiting, *Finale at Flensburg. The Race to the Baltic – The British Army's Last Campaign*, London 1966, 152.

90 Hanse, *Kapitulation*, 186.

91 Ibid., 192.

92 Marlis Steinert, *Capitulation 1945: The Story of the Dönitz Regime*, translated by Richard Barry, London 1969, 275, 277.

93 Leonard Mosely, *Report from Germany*, London 1945, 103.

94 Whiting, *Finale at Flensburg*, 150.

95 Ibid., 153.

96 Schwerin von Krosigk, *Memoiren*, 251.

97 Lüdde-Neurath, *Regierung Dönitz*, 113–14.

98 Whiting, *Finale at Flensburg*, 160.

99 Schwerin von Krosigk, *Memoiren*, 252.

100 Boveri, *Tage*, 152.

101 Whiting, *Finale at Flensburg*, 168.

102 Schwerin von Krosigk, *Memoiren*, 252.

103 Steinert, *Capitulation 1945*, 280.

104 Whiting, *Finale at Flensburg*, 168.

105 Schwerin von Krosigk, *Memoiren*, 253.

106 Steinert, *Capitulation 1945*, 281.

107 Lüdde-Neurath, *Regierung Dönitz*, 123.

108 Botting, *Ruins*, 140–1.

109 Elisabeth Ruge, ed., *Charlotte Gräfin von der Schulenburg zur Erinnerungen*, Hamburg 1992, 70–90 passim.

110 Jünger, *Okkupation*, 11, 17.

111 Ibid., 19.

112 Ibid., 28.

113 Ibid., 32–4.

114 Ibid., 48–9.

115 Herzogin Viktoria Luise, *Ein Leben als Tochter des Kaisers*, Göttingen 1965, 320–4.

116 Friedrich Wilhelm Prinz von Preussen, *Das Haus Hohenzollern 1918–1945*, Munich and Vienna 1985, 247.

117 Ben Shepherd, *After Daybreak – The Liberation of Belsen, 1945*, London 2005, 8.

118 Eberle and Uhl, eds, *Das Buch Hitler*, 348.

119 Shepherd, *After Daybreak*, 42.

120 Ibid., 41.

121 Susanne Kirkbright: *Karl Jaspers – A Biography, Navigations in Truth*, New Haven and London 2004, 187–8.

122 Ibid., 190, 192.

123 Richard von Weizsäcker, *Vier Zeiten: Erinnerungen*, Berlin 1997, 95–6.

124 Döblin, *Schicksalsreise*, 410.

125 Jünger, *Okkupation*, 202.

126 F. Roy Willis, *The French in Germany 1945–1949*, Stanford 1962, 16–17.

127 François-George Dreyfus, 'Les Dernières Operations militaires françaises et l'avenir des relations Franco-Allemandes', in Manfrass and Rioux, eds, *France–Allemagne*, 13.

128 Hans Rommel, *Vor zehn Jahren. 16/17 April 1945: Wie es zur Zerstörung von Freudenstadt gekommen ist*, Freudenstadt 1955, 27.

129 Ibid., 26.

130 Hans Joachim Harder, 'Militärische Operationen in der Endphase des Krieges: die deutsche Sicht', in Manfrass and Rioux, eds, *France–Allemagne*, 31.

131 R. F. Keeling, *Gruesome Harvest*, Chicago 1947, 57.

132 Ibid., 56–7.

133 Harder, 'Militärishe Operationen', 32.

134 Willis, *The French in Germany*, 18.

135 Petra Weber, *Carlo Schmid,*

1896–1979. Eine Biographie, Munich 1996, 191–2.

136 Döblin, *Schicksalsreise*, 397.

137 Ibid., 397–9.

138 Hilberg, *Destruction*, III, 1050.

139 Abzug, *Vicious Heart*, 105.

140 Rathkolb, ed., *Gesellschaft und Politik*, 39.

141 Ibid., 24–5.

142 Ibid., 41–3.

143 Béthouart, *Bataille*, 51–2.

144 The full list is reproduced in Josef Müller, *Bis zur letzten Konsequenz: Ein Leben für Frieden und Freiheit*, Munich 1975, 364–7.

145 Ibid., 267; Kurt von Schuschnigg, *Austrian Requiem*, translated by Franz von Hildebrand, New York 1946, 286.

146 Ibid., 288.

147 Ibid., 270.

148 Ibid., 271.

149 Abzug, *Vicious Heart*, 3–5.

150 Peck, 'Jüdische DPs', 201.

151 Abzug, *Vicious Heart*, 31–3.

152 Ibid., 203.

153 Ibid.

154 Lewis Weinstein witnessed his vomiting: see Chamberlain and Feldman, eds, *Liberation*, 46.

155 Abzug, *Vicious Heart*, 26–30.

156 Padover, *Psychologist*, 284.

157 Volker Mauersberger, *Hitler in Weimar – Der Fall einer deutschen Kulturstadt*, Berlin 1999, 295–300; Hilberg, *Destruction*, III, 1051; Eberle and Uhl, eds, *Das Buch Hitler*, 348; Berber, *Dachau*, 182.

158 Hilberg, *Destruction*, III, 1055.

159 Abzug, *Vicious Heart*, 49, 52.

160 Schöner, *Tagebuch*, 178.

161 Quoted in Mauersberger, *Hitler*, 296.

162 Ibid., 300.

163 Padover, *Psychologist*, 293–6.

164 Ibid., 293–4.

165 Peterson, *Russian Commands*, 331.

166 Abzug, *Vicious Heart*, 72.

167 Ibid., 74, 78.

168 Ibid., 80; Marianne Günther:

Peyinghaus, *Stille Jahre in Gertlauken*, 206.

169 Peyinghaus, *Stille Jahre in Gertlauken*, 217.

170 Tisa Hess Schulenburg, *The First Days and the Last*, London 1948, 25.

171 Ibid., 26.

172 Ibid., 27.

173 Tisa von der Schulenburg, *Ich hab's gewagt – Bildhauerin und Ordensfrau – ein unkonventionelles Leben*, Freiburg im Breisgau 1981, 177.

174 Abzug, *Vicious Heart*, 62, 68.

175 Schulenburg, *Ich hab's gewagt*, 181.

176 Jenny Williams, *More Lives than One: A Biography of Hans Fallada*, London 1998, 245.

177 Kardorff, *Aufzeichnungen*, 360–2.

178 Joseph Goebbels, *Tagebücher 1945 – Die letzten Aufzeichnungen*, Hamburg 1977, 442; Padover, *Psychologist*, 200.

179 Beer, 'Niederösterreich', 136.

180 Jean Edward Smith, ed., *The Papers of Lucius D. Clay: Germany 1945–1949*, Bloomington and London 1974, I, 47.

181 Carl Zuckmayer, 'Jugend in Niemandsland', in *Deutschlandbericht*, 228–34; Krockow, *Hour of the Women*, 75.

182 Wilhelm Turnwald, ed., *Dokumente dur Austreibung der Sudetendeutschen*, Munich 1951, 152.

183 Fritz Löwenthal, *Der neue Geist von Potsdam*, Hamburg 1948, 118.

184 Ernst von Salomon, *The Answers – to the 131 Questions in the Allied Military Government 'Fragebogen'*, preface by Goronwy Rees, translated by Constantine Fitzgibbon, London 1954, 410.

185 James Stern, *Hidden Damage*, London 1990, 318.

186 Werner Schwipps, *Die Königl. Hof- und Garnisonkirche zu Potsdam*, Berlin 1991, 100–1.

187 Ibid., 104; Hilberg, *Destruction*, III, 1180.

CHAPTER 3: BERLIN

1 G. Zhukov, *Reminiscences and Reflections of the Marshal of the Soviet Union*, 2 vols, Moscow 1985, II, 383.
2 Ibid., 392, 394.
3 Friedrich, *Schauplatz Berlin*, 20.
4 Zhukov, *Reminiscences*, II, 396.
5 Quoted in Alexandra Ritchie, *Faust's Metropolis – A History of Berlin*, London 1998, 606.
6 Boveri, *Tage*, 106–8.
7 Anonymous, *A Woman in Berlin*, 86.
8 Ibid., 44.
9 Botting, *Ruins*, 87.
10 Friedrich, *Schauplatz Berlin*, 14.
11 Boveri, *Tage*, 123.
12 Anonymous, *A Woman in Berlin*, 63.
13 Nicolas Nabokov, *Old Friends and New Music*, London 1951, 211.
14 Boveri, *Tage*, 246.
15 Anonymous, *A Woman in Berlin*, 42.
16 Friedrich, *Schauplatz Berlin*, 21.
17 Boveri, *Tage*, 128.
18 Ibid., 128–9.
19 Cyril Buffet, *Berlin*, Paris 1993, 359.
20 Anonymous, *A Woman in Berlin*, 46.
21 Ibid., 53–4.
22 Boveri, *Tage*, 120.
23 Anonymous, *A Woman in Berlin*, 46–7.
24 Friedrich, *Schauplatz Berlin*, 22.
25 Ibid., 24.
26 Eberle and Uhl, eds, *Das Buch Hitler*, 411.
27 Anonymous, *A Woman in Berlin*, 50, 123, 134.
28 Boveri, *Tage*, 129.
29 Friedrich, *Schauplatz Berlin*, 70.
30 Boveri, *Tage*, 254.
31 Ibid.
32 Naimark, *Russians in Germany*, 82.
33 Anonymous, *A Woman in Berlin*, 77.
34 Ibid., 145.
35 Friedrich, *Schauplatz Berlin*, 35.
36 Anonymous, *A Woman in Berlin*, 60–1.
37 Friedrich, *Schauplatz Berlin*, 14, 16.
38 Anonymous, *A Woman in Berlin*, 144, 150, 186.
39 Friedrich, *Schauplatz Berlin*, 22.
40 Anonymous, *A Woman in Berlin*, 80, 83, 150.
41 Boveri, *Tage*, 245.
42 Naimark, *Russians in Germany*, 124.
43 Friedrich, *Schauplatz Berlin*, 94.
44 Ritchie, *Faust's Metropolis*, 617.
45 Anonymous, *A Woman in Berlin*, 131.
46 Ritchie, *Faust's Metropolis*, 616.
47 Kardorff, *Aufzeichnungen*, 358.
48 Friedrich, *Schauplatz Berlin*, 26.
49 Kay Summersby, *Eisenhower was my Boss*, Watford 1949, 230.
50 Zhukov, *Reminiscences*, II, 397–401.
51 Hedda Adlon, *Hotel Adlon – Das Berliner Hotel in dem die grosse Welt zu Gast war*, Munich 1997, 315; Peter Auer, *Adlon, Berlin*, Berlin 1997, 217.
52 Wolfgang Leonhard, *Child of the Revolution*, translated by C. M. Woodhouse, introduction by Günter Minnerup, London 1979, 287.
53 Ibid., 311–12.
54 Ibid., 299.
55 Ibid., 315.
56 Ibid.
57 Naimark, *Russians in Germany*, 253, 292.
58 Dietrich Staritz, *Geschichte der DDR*, Erweitete Ausgabe, Frankfurt/Main 1996, 273; Buffet, *Berlin*, 366.
59 Leonhard, *Revolution*, 303.
60 Ibid., 315–16; George Clare, *Berlin Days 1946–1947*, London 1989, 30–2.
61 Peterson, *Russian Commands*, 44–5.
62 Golo Mann, *The History of Germany since 1789*, Harmondsworth 1987, 817.
63 Leonhard, *Revolution*, 306.
64 Ibid., 326.
65 Ibid., 332, 337.
66 Buffet, *Berlin*, 358.
67 Boveri, *Tage*, 133.
68 Friedrich, *Schauplatz Berlin*, 36.
69 Davidson, *Death and Life*, 74–6.
70 Ritchie, *Faust's Metropolis*, 609–10.
71 Anonymous, *A Woman in Berlin*, 135.
72 Friedrich, *Schauplatz Berlin*, 106.

73 Buffet, *Berlin*, 363–4.

74 Clare, *Berlin Days*, 47.

75 Ruth Gay, *Safe among the Germans: Liberated Jews after World War II*, New Haven and London 2002, 111–12, 151.

76 Friedrich, *Schauplatz Berlin*, 12–13, 15.

77 Ibid., 27, 38, 84.

78 Boveri, *Tage*, 144–5.

79 Anonymous, *A Woman in Berlin*, 168.

80 Friedrich, *Schauplatz Berlin*, 32.

81 Boveri, *Tage*, 214.

82 Anonymous, *A Woman in Berlin*, 84, 102, 110.

83 Boveri, *Tage*, 207–8.

84 Ibid., 262, 286.

85 Ibid., 209–10.

86 Ibid., 209.

87 Smith, ed., *Clay Papers*, I, 17.

88 Frank Howley, *Berlin Command*, New York 1950, 29, 34.

89 Ibid., 41.

90 Ibid., 46.

91 Ibid., 11.

92 Ritchie, *Faust's Metropolis*, 627, 629; Friedrich, *Schauplatz Berlin*, 74.

93 Buffet, *Berlin*, 358; Friedrich, *Schauplatz Berlin*, 75.

94 Zhukov, *Reminiscences*, II, 436; Howley, *Berlin Command*, 57.

95 Howley, *Berlin Command*, 66–72.

96 Boveri, *Tage*, 234–5.

97 Howley, *Berlin Command*, 22–3.

98 Boveri, *Tage*, 237–8, 263, 267.

99 Howley, *Berlin Command*, 79, 87.

100 Ibid., 238–9.

101 Friedrich, *Schauplatz Berlin*, 36.

102 Ibid., 82.

103 Buffet, *Berlin*, 362.

104 Boveri, *Tage*, 165.

105 Friedrich, *Schauplatz Berlin*, 45.

106 Anonymous, *A Woman in Berlin*, 87.

107 Boveri, *Tage*, 269, 272.

108 Howley, *Berlin Command*, 12.

109 Ibid., 30, 41,

110 Ibid., 39.

111 Klaus Lang, *'Lieber Herr Celibidache . . .' – Wilhelm Furtwängler und sein Statthalter – Ein philharmonischer Konflict in der Berliner Nachkriegszeit*, Zurich and St Gallen 1988, 11–12.

112 Ibid., 13, Friedrich, *Schauplatz Berlin*, 97.

113 Kardorff, *Aufzeichnungen*, 356.

114 Ibid., 359.

115 Ibid., 362–3.

116 Renée Bédarida, 'Une Française à Berlin en 1945', in Manfrass and Rioux, eds, *France–Allemagne*, 149.

117 Ibid., 150.

118 Nabokov, *Old Friends*, 211; MacDonogh, *A Good German*, 73.

119 Bédarida, 'Une Française', 150–1.

120 Krockow, *Hour of the Women*, 160.

121 Friedrich, *Schauplatz Berlin*, 114.

122 Ibid., 139, 141.

123 Clare, *Berlin Days*, 59.

124 Zuckmayer, *Deutschlandbericht*, 16.

125 Albert Speer, *Spandau: The Secret Diaries*, translated by Richard and Clara Winton, London 1976, 66.

CHAPTER 4: EXPULSIONS FROM CZECHOSLOVAKIA, HUNGARY AND YUGOSLAVIA

1 Theodor Schieder, ed., *Die Vertreibung der Deutscher Bevölkerung aus Ost-Mitteleuropa*, vol. IV/1: *Tschechoslowakei*, Berlin 1957, 4.

2 Alfred M. de Zayas, *Nemesis at Potsdam: The Anglo-Americans and the Expulsion of the Germans – Background, Execution, Consequences*, with a foreword by Robert Murphy, London 1979, 27.

3 Rudolf Jaworski, 'Die Sudetendeutscher als Minderheit, in der Tschechoslowakei 1918–1938', in Benz, ed., *Die Vertreibung*, 29; for the treatment of German-speaking Jews after the war, see Melissa Müller and Reinhard Piechocki, *Alice Herz-Sommer: 'Ein Garten Eden inmitten der Hölle'*, Munich 2006, 308–9.

4 Ibid., 30.
5 Turnwald, ed., *Dokumente*, xi and n. 8, xiv.
6 Schieder, ed., *Tschechoslowakei*, 6.
7 Thurn und Taxis, 'Memoiren', 33.
8 E. Franzel, *Die Vertreibung Sudetenland 1945/1946. Nach Dokumenten des Bundesministeriums für Vertriebene, Flüchtlinge and Kriegsgeschädigte, Bonn; Nach Dokumenten aus dem Bundesarchiv in Koblenz, Fragebogen Berichten des Bundesarchivs, Erlebnis und Kreisberichten*, Bad Nauheim 1967, 108–9.
9 Henke, 'Potsdam', 56; Zbyněk Zeman with Antonin Klimek, *The Life of Edvard Beneš 1884–1948 – Czechoslovakia in Peace and War*, Oxford 1997, 225–6, 237.
10 Franzel, *Sudetenland*, 20.
11 Ibid., 240.
12 Ibid., 242.
13 Henke, 'Potsdam', 65.
14 Karl Peter Schwarz, 'Mit der Vertreibung vollendet', in Suppan and Vyslonzil, eds, *Beneš*, 180.
15 Franzel, *Sudetenland*, 23–4, 218.
16 Turnwald, ed., *Dokumente*, 527–56 – the 'Kaschauer' Statutes and Beneš Decrees are printed in full; Zeman and Klimek, *Beneš*, 245.
17 Schwarz, 'Vertreibung', 180.
18 Franzel, *Sudetenland*, 33, 104.
19 Alois Harasko, 'Die Vertreibung der Sudetendeutschen. Sechs Erlebnisberichte', in Benz, ed., *Die Vertreibung*, 107.
20 Zeman and Klimek, *Beneš*, 246.
21 Henke, 'Potsdam', 66.
22 Ibid.; Franzel, *Sudetenland*, 22.
23 Zeman and Klimek, *Beneš*, 248.
24 Alice Teichova, 'Die Tschechen in der NS-Kriegswirtschaft', in Suppan and Vyslonzil, eds, *Beneš*, 172–3; Franzel, *Sudetenland*, 19.
25 Schieder, ed., *Tschechosowakei*, 17.
26 Theodor Schieder, ed., *Die Vertreibung der Deutschen Bevölkerung aus der Tschechoslowakei*, vol. IV/2, Berlin 1957, 789.
27 Ziemer, *Deutsche Exodus*, 73.
28 Ibid., 18.
29 Franzel, *Sudetenland*, 55–6.
30 Turnwald, ed., *Dokumente*, Kurt Schmidt, 366, 375, 402–3.
31 Franzel, *Sudetenland*, 22.
32 Turnwald, ed., *Dokumente*, 18–19, Dr Hans Wagner, 38, 226–7.
33 Margarete Schell, *Ein Tagebuch aus Prag*, Beiheft II, Dokumente der Vertreibung der Deutschen aus Ost-Mitteleuropa, Kassel 1957, 9.
34 Turnwald, ed., *Dokumente*, Ludwig Breyer, 333–4; Schell, *Tagebuch*, 74.
35 Schell, *Tagebuch*, 24, 34.
36 Turnwald, ed., *Dokumente*, 15, Franz Rösch, 15–16, 28; Thurn und Taxis, 'Memoiren', 34.
37 Zhukov, II, 410.
38 Schell, *Tagebuch*, 12 n. 1.
39 Ibid., 18.
40 Turnwald, ed., *Dokumente*, 10.
41 Turnwald, ed., *Dokumente*, Hildegard Hurtinger, 14, Hans Wagner, 39, 42; Schieder, ed., *Tschechoslowakei*, 63 n. 1; Thurn und Taxis, 'Memoiren', 35.
42 Turnwald, ed., *Dokumente*, Dr Hans Wagner, 39, Sebastian Herr, 50, Kurt Schmidt, 404.
43 Schell, *Tagebuch*, 20.
44 Schieder, ed., *Tschechoslowakei*, 62; Thurn und Taxis, 'Memoiren', 33.
45 Turnwald, ed., *Dokumente*, 3–8, 21, 22, 23, 25–6.
46 Ibid., 20, 29.
47 Ibid., 9–10, 13.
48 Ibid., 26–38.
49 Quoted in Ibid., 42.
50 Ibid., 20, 24–5, 40.
51 Schell, *Tagebuch*, 89–90.
52 Schöner, *Tagebuch*, 255, 258.
53 Turnwald, ed., *Dokumente*, 45.
54 Ibid., 16–17, 41.
55 Ibid., Franz Mauder, 338–9.
56 Franzel, *Sudetenland*, 97.
57 Turnwald, ed., *Dokumente*, 64.
58 Botting, *Ruins*, 229–30.

59 Harasko, 'Sudetendeutschen', 109–10.

60 Ibid.

61 Turnwald, ed., *Dokumente*, 63–75, 76, 77, 78.

62 Franzel, *Sudetenland*, 117.

63 Turnwald, ed., *Dokumente*, Else Köchel and Franz Kaupil, 279–81.

64 Ibid., Erika Griessmann, 313–15.

65 Franzel, *Sudetenland*, 21.

66 Jünger, *Okkupation*, 193.

67 Turnwald, ed., *Dokumente*, 128–35, Edouard Fritsch, 162, 350, 353–4, Karl Oberdörfer, 389.

68 Ibid., Dr E. Siegel, 147, Hans Strobl, 161.

69 Ibid., Otto Patek and Rudolf Berthold, 290–1.

70 Ibid., Marie Weiss, 206.

71 Ibid., A.R., 200–2, Franz Wagner, 214.

72 Ibid., Gregor and Johann Partsch, 250–5.

73 Harasko, 'Sudetendeutschen', 110–11.

74 Franzel, *Sudetenland*, 72.

75 Turnwald, ed., *Dokumente*, Alfred Latzel, Karl Schneider and Karl Froning, 229–50.

76 Ibid., Anton Watzke, 184, Adolf Aust, 203.

77 Ibid., Franz Limpächer, 317–19, 429, 432.

78 Ibid., Dr Karl Grimm, 85–101, Eduard Kaltofen, 182. *Der Neue Brockhaus* encyclopaedia gives the 1939 population figure as 36,500, of whom 16,000 were Germans.

79 Ibid., 85–7.

80 Pre-war population from *Brockhaus*; Turnwald, ed., *Dokumente*, the judge Dr Franz Freyer, 105; Harasko, 'Sudetendeutschen', 116.

81 Turnwald, ed., *Dokumente*, Dr E. Siegel, 148.

82 Ibid., 105–10, passim.

83 Ibid., 121–3, 124.

84 Harasko, 'Sudetendeutschen', 113–15. SS men were identified by the blood group tattooed in their left armpit.

85 Turnwald, ed., *Dokumente*, Eduard Grimm, 217–18, 328.

86 Ibid., 124–5.

87 Ibid., 48–50, F. Fiedler, 190.

88 Hilberg, *Destruction*, III, 1056.

89 Franzel, *Sudetenland*, 222–3.

90 Turnwald, ed., *Dokumente*, Marie Weiss, Josef Zillich and Emilie Dotzauer, 206–7.

91 Ibid., Dr E. Siegel, 139–61 passim, Franz Richter, 397.

92 Ibid., Dr E. Siegel, 143.

93 Tom Lampert, *Ein einziges Leben: Geschichten aus der NS-Zeit*, Munich 2003, 168–9. I am grateful to my friend Ursula Heinzelmann in Berlin for sending me this book. See also Hans-Günther Adler, *Theresienstadt 1941–1945*, Tübingen 1955.

94 Turnwald, ed., *Dokumente*, 18, Dr E. Siegel, 153, 160, 216.

95 Ibid., 80–2, quoting *Die Brücke*, 10 June 1951.

96 Ibid., Dr E. Siegel, 146, Franz Richter, 397.

97 Ibid., Hans Freund, 17.

98 Schell, *Tagebuch*, 270–5, passim.

99 Turnwald, ed., *Dokumente*, Alfred Latzel, 235, Franz Richter, 399, Max Griehsel, 470; Wachsmann, *Hitler's Prisons*, 281–2.

100 Naimark, *Russians in Germany*, 148.

101 Ibid., 149.

102 Smith, ed., *Clay Papers*, II, 619.

103 Ibid., I, 312.

104 Zeman and Klimek, *Beneš*, 247.

105 Harasko, 'Sudetendeutschen', 107.

106 Theodor Schieder, ed., *Dokumentation der Vertreibung der Deutschen aus Ost-Mitteleuropa: Das Schicksal der Deutschen in Ungarn*, Düsseldorf 1956, 41E–45E, 50E, 60E.

107 Ibid., 62E, 65E.

108 Keeling, *Gruesome Harvest*, 14.

109 Smith, ed., *Clay Papers*, I, 313–14.

110 Theodor Schieder, ed., *Dokumentation der Vertreibung der*

Deutschen aus Ost-Mitteleuropa: Das Schicksal der Deutschen in Rumänien, Berlin 1957, 6E, 41E, 63E.

111 Theodor Schieder, ed., *Dokumentation der Vertreibung der Deutschen aus Ost-Mitteleuropa: Das Schicksal der Deutschen in Jugoslavien,* Düsseldorf 1961, 76E, 82–83E, 108–9.

112 Eva Schmidt-Hartmann, 'Menschen oder Nationen? Die Vertreibung der Deutschen aus tschechischer Sicht', in Benz, ed., *Die Vertreibung,* 143–4.

113 Franzel, *Sudetenland,* 24.

114 Eva Schmidt-Hartmann, 'Menschen oder Nationen?', 148–9.

CHAPTER 5: HOME TO THE
REICH! RECOVERED
TERRITORIES IN THE
PRUSSIAN EAST

1 Wolfgang Benz, introduction to Benz, ed., *Die Vertreibung,* 7.

2 Ibid., 8.

3 Ziemer, *Deutsche Exodus,* 63.

4 See Egbert Jahn, 'On the Phenomenology of Mass Extermination in Europe: A Comparative Perspective on the Holodomor', in Manfred Sapper and Volker Weichsel, eds, *Sketches of Europe: Old Lands, New Worlds,* Berlin 2005, a special edition of *Osteuropa,* 183–220.

5 Lehndorff, *Tagebuch,* 86–7.

6 Ibid., 88–9.

7 Ibid., 92–3.

8 Ibid., 98.

9 Ibid., 109–11

10 Ibid., 112, 115, 117.

11 Ibid., 118.

12 Ibid., 119–22, 128.

13 Ibid., 131, 133–4.

14 Ibid., 163.

15 Ibid., 136–9.

16 Ibid., 139–40.

17 Ibid., 145.

18 Ibid., 152–3.

19 Ibid, 156–7.

20 Gause, *Königsberg,* III, 174; MacDonogh, *Prussia,* 386; 'Stalin ordino: deportateli tutti, la Prussia dev'essere Sovietica', *Corriere della Sera,* 25 May 1993; 'Zum Schluss Schokolade', *Der Spiegel,* 28 June 1993.

21 Löwenthal, *Potsdam,* 187.

22 Lehndorff, *Tagebuch,* 164.

23 Ibid., 159–60.

24 Ibid., 168–70, 175.

25 Marion Gräfin Dönhoff, 'Ein Brief aus Ostpreussen in her *Weit ist der Weg nach Osten – Berichte und Betrachtungen aus fünf Jahrzehnten,* Munich 1988, 18.

26 Ibid., 19.

27 Friedrich, *Schauplatz Berlin,* 202.

28 Löwenthal, *Potsdam,* 187; Naimark, *Russians in Germany,* 74.

29 Lehndorff, *Tagebuch,* 183–5.

30 Ibid., 192.

31 Ibid., 194–6.

32 Kaps, *Tragödie,* 152–4, 156; Tighe, *Gdansk,* 205.

33 Kaps, *Tragödie,* 164–5.

34 Hupka, *Letze Tage,* 39.

35 Michael Luke, *Hansel Pless – Prisoner of History,* London 2001, 215–16.

36 Henke, 'Potsdam', 66–7.

37 Normann, *Tagebuch,* 132–5.

38 Davies and Moorhouse, *Microcosm,* 409–10.

39 Ibid., 411.

40 Tighe, *Gdansk,* 206–7.

41 Hupka, *Letzte Tage,* 12.

42 Kaps, *Tragödie,* 73.

43 Hupka, *Letzte Tage,* 23.

44 Normann, *Tagebuch,* 201.

45 Lehndorff, *Tagebuch,* 200.

46 Ibid., 34.

47 Lehndorff, *Tagebuch,* 206.

48 Ibid., 202.

49 Ibid., 45, 124.

50 Ibid., 202, 204.

51 Ibid., 254.

52 Kaps, *Tragödie,* 138, 418; Hupka,

Letzte Tage, 223.

53 Naimark, *Russians in Germany*, 75.

54 Kaps, *Tragödie*, 177.

55 Davies and Moorhouse, *Microcosm*, 413.

56 Ibid., 414.

57 Kaps, *Tragödie*, 292.

58 Naimark, *Russians in Germany*, 148.

59 Kaps, *Tragödie*, 75.

60 Hupka, *Letzte Tage*, 135, 200.

61 Tighe, *Gdansk*, 215.

62 Giles MacDonogh, *Frederick the Great*, London 1999, 269, 274; Klaus Ullmann, *Schlesien-Lexikon*, Mannheim 1985, 118; Hupka, *Letzte Tage*, 293.

63 Hupka, *Letzte Tage*, 47.

64 Kaps, *Tragödie*, 74, 139.

65 Hupka, *Letzte Tage*, 179–80.

66 Kaps, *Tragödie*, 358.

67 Hupka, *Letzte Tage*, 38.

68 Kaps, *Tragödie*, 417–20; Hupka, *Letzte Tage*, 136.

69 Kaps, *Tragödie*, 175.

70 Ibid., 252, 484.

71 Ibid., 180.

72 Ibid., 184.

73 Ibid., 178–85.

74 Ibid., 184.

75 Hupka, *Letzte Tage*, 46.

76 Kaps, *Tragödie*, 189.

77 Ibid., 157, 165.

78 Hupka, *Letzte Tage*, 23–5.

79 Ibid., 26–7.

80 Ibid., 67.

81 Ibid., 39.

82 Ibid., 63, 80.

83 Ibid., 68.

84 Ibid., 68, 78.

85 Kaps, *Tragödie*, 223–30.

86 Ibid., 497, 502.

87 Hupka, *Letzte Tage*, 85, 86.

88 Ibid., 80–1.

89 Ibid., 89–92.

90 Ibid., 92.

91 Ibid., 44–5, 105; van Pelt and Dwork, *Auschwitz*, 334.

92 Kaps, *Tragödie*, 148, 150.

93 Smith, ed., *Clay Papers*, I, 96–7.

94 Josef Foschepoth, 'Potsdam und danach: Die Westmächte, Adenauer und die Vertriebenen', in Benz, ed., *Die Vertreibung*, 82.

95 Lehndorff, *Tagebuch*, 243.

96 Kaps, *Tragödie*, 75.

97 Ibid., 359.

98 Ibid., 131–2.

99 Ibid., 132–3.

100 Ibid., 404–5.

101 Naimark, *Russians in Germany*, 149.

102 Gerhart Pohl, *Bin ich noch in meinem Haus? Die letzte Tage Gerhart Hauptmanns*, Berlin 1953, 24–5.

103 Grigori Weiss, 'Auf der Suche nach der versunkenen Glocke. Johannes R. Becher bei Gerhart Hauptmann', in *Erinnerungen an Johannes R. Becher*, Frankfurt/Main 1974, 217.

104 Pohl, *Bin ich noch*, 44–5.

105 Ibid., 50.

106 Hupka, *Letzte Tage*, 302–3.

107 Pohl, *Bin ich noch*, 72–3.

108 Ibid., 54. Pohl's *petits nègres* have a certain sameness that makes them suspicious.

109 Ibid., 66.

110 Ibid., 69.

111 Weiss, 'Auf der Suche', 227.

112 Ibid., 233.

113 Kaps, *Tragödie*, 420–1; Ullmann, *Lexikon*, 20; Hupka, *Letzte Tage*, 313–14, 316–17.

114 Lehndorff, *Tagebuch*, 302.

115 Krockow, *Hour of the Women*, 139–40; Giles MacDonogh, *The Last Kaiser: William the Impetuous*, London 2000, 123.

116 Benz, ed., *Die Vertreibung*, 8.

117 Lehndorff, *Tagebuch*, 236.

118 Krockow, *Hour of the Women*, 147.

119 Ibid., 152.

120 Ibid., 155.

121 Davies and Moorhouse, *Microcosm*, 422.

122 Keeling, *Gruesome Harvest*, 15.

123 Ibid., 16.

124 Krockow, *Hour of the Women*, 173.

125 Ibid., 188.

126 Lehndorff, *Tagebuch*, 204.
127 Normann, *Tagebuch*, 268.
128 Henke, 'Exodus', 99.
129 Löwenthal, *Potsdam*, 189.
130 Kaps, *Tragödie*, 87.
131 Krockow, *Hour of the Women*, 197.
132 Normann, *Tagebuch*, 270.

PROLOGUE TO PART II

1 Balfour and Mair, *Four Power Control*, 13.
2 Patricia Meehan, *A Strange Enemy People: Germans under the British 1945–1950*, London and Chester Springs 2001, 13.
3 Balfour and Mair, *Four Power Control*, 105.

CHAPTER 6: LIFE IN THE RUSSIAN ZONE

1 Peterson, *Russian Commands*, 7.
2 Ibid.
3 Ibid., 13.
4 Naimark, *Russians in Germany*, 24–6.
5 Ibid., 16.
6 Gregory Klimov, *The Terror Machine – The Inside Story of Soviet Administered Germany*, translated by H. C. Stevens with an introduction by Edward Crankshaw and Ernst Reuter, London n.d., 103.
7 Ibid., 26–7, 30–1.
8 Friedrich, *Schauplatz Berlin*, 69; Peterson, *Russian Commands*, 14; Hans Borgelt, *Das war der Frühling in Berlin. Die goldene Hungerjahre. Eine Berlin Chronik*, Munich 1983, 38.
9 Leonhard, *Revolution*, 302.
10 Williams, *More Lives than One*, 247–8.
11 Boveri, *Tage*, 165.
12 Leonhard, *Revolution*, 341–2.
13 Boveri, *Tage*, 217–19.
14 Quoted in Naimark, *Russians in Germany*, 142–3.

15 Friedrich, *Schauplatz Berlin*, 108.
16 Franz Prinz zu Sayn-Wittgenstein, *Streifzüge durch die Landschaften meines Lebens*, privately printed, Munich 2000, 161–4.
17 Ibid., 143.
18 Ibid., 163.
19 Harald von Koenigswald, ed., *Besuche vor der Untergang – aus Tagebuchaufzeichnungen von Udo von Alvensleben*. Frankfurt/Main 1968, 147.
20 Ibid., 162.
21 Borgelt, *Das war der Frühling in Berlin*, 45.
22 Anonymous, *A Woman in Berlin*, 116.
23 Friedrich, *Schauplatz Berlin*, 80–1.
24 Michael Cullen, *Der Reichstag – Die Geschichte eines Monumentes*, Stuttgart 1990, 399.
25 Nikolaus Bernau, 'Der Ort des Souveräns', in Fördverein Berliner Stadtschloss, *Das Schloss? Eine Ausstellung über die Mitte Berlins*, Berlin 1993, 75.
26 There have been moves to rebuild all three. The decision to put back the Berlin Schloss was approved by the German parliament, but so far the project has been stymied by lack of funds in a bankrupt city. In 2005 it was ruled that the exterior of the city palace in Potsdam would be re-erected to house the provincial parliament or Landtag. For the time being the plans to rebuild the Garrison Church remain on the drawing board.
27 Alan Balfour, *Berlin: The Politics of Order, 1737–1989*, New York 1990, 187.
28 Buffet, *Berlin*, 363.
29 Löwenthal, *Potsdam*, 10–11.
30 Naimark, *Russians in Germany*, 16; Löwenthal, *Potsdam*, 16.
31 Löwenthal, *Potsdam*, 19.
32 Ibid., 20–3.
33 Ibid., 24–5.
34 Ibid., 34, 41, 44.

35 Klimov, *Terror Machine*, 118–20; Peterson, *Russian Commands*, 104.
36 Löwenthal, *Potsdam*, 72.
37 Ibid., 97.
38 Ibid., 113–18.
39 Naimark, *Russians in Germany*, 42, 44.
40 Ibid., 85.
41 Keeling, *Gruesome Harvest*, 53.
42 Naimark, *Russians in Germany*, 105.
43 Ibid., 92, 94–6, 116.
44 Klimov, *Terror Machine*, 117.
45 Ibid., 221.
46 Ibid., 208, 219.
47 Michel Bar-Zohar, *The Hunt for German Scientists*, translated by Len Ortzen, London 1967, 9.
48 Ibid., 151–3, 161, 168.
49 Klimov, *Terror Machine*, 222–5.
50 Jana Urbancová and Claus Josef Riedel, *Riedel od roku 1756*, exhibition catalogue, Jablonec (Gablonz), 19 August–27 October 1991, 14.
51 Naimark, *Russians in Germany*, 237–40, 248–9; Petersen, *Russian Commands*, 123; Jünger, *Okkupation*, 293.
52 Naimark, *Russians in Germany*, 355–7, 360–2, 374.
53 Peterson, *Russian Commands*, 46.
54 Naimark, *Russians in Germany*, 376; Peterson, *Russian Commands*, 25.
55 Naimark, *Russians in Germany*, 378.
56 Ibid., 381–2.
57 Löwenthal, *Potsdam*, 201–2.
58 Alexander Behrens, *Johannes R. Becher, eine politische Biographie*, Cologne, Weimar and Vienna 2003, 223.
59 Wolfgang Schivelbusch, *In a Cold Crater – Cultural and Intellectual Life in Berlin 1945–1948*, Berkeley, Los Angeles and London 1998, ix.
60 Behrens, *Becher*, 223.
61 Ibid., 225.
62 Clare, *Berlin Days*, 62.
63 Ibid., 81.
64 Schivelbusch, *Cold Crater*, 31, 36–7.
65 Zuckmayer, 'Bericht über das Film- und Theaterleben', in *Deutschlandbericht*, 156–204.
66 Clare, *Berlin Days*, 64.
67 Behrens, *Becher*, 229.
68 Schivelbusch, *Cold Crater*, 40, 45.
69 Ibid., 231–3.
70 Lang, 'Lieber Herr Celibidache', 21.
71 Ibid., 28–9.
72 Clare, *Berlin Days*, 81; Lang, 'Lieber Herr Celibidache', 33.
73 Clare, *Berlin Days*, 105–7.
74 Speer, *Diaries*, 104.
75 Clare, *Berlin Days*, 182–4.
76 Speer, *Diaries*, 44.
77 Boveri, *Tage*, 159.
78 Lang, 'Lieber Herr Celibidache', 59.
79 Ibid., 71
80 Schivelbusch, *Cold Crater*, 56.
81 Friedrich, *Schauplatz Berlin*, 92; Kardorff, *Aufzeichnungen*, 364.
82 Friedrich, *Schauplatz Berlin*, 105.
83 David Pike, *The Politics and Culture in Soviet-Occupied Germany, 1945–1949*, Stanford 1992, 189–92.
84 Clare, *Berlin Days*, 128.
85 Williams, *More Lives than One*, 252.
86 Ibid., 256–7.
87 *Erinnerung an Johannes R. Becher*, 189.
88 Carsten Wurm, *Jeden Tag ein Buch – 50 Jahre Aufbau-Verlag 1945–1995*, Berlin 1995, 11–12.
89 Ibid., 10, 119.
90 Behrens, *Becher*, 234.
91 Ritchie, *Faust's Metropolis*, 624.
92 Behrens, *Becher*, 239–40.
93 Ibid., 241–2.
94 Ronald Taylor, *Berlin and its Culture*, New Haven and London, 1997, 228.
95 Ibid., 244–66.

CHAPTER 7: LIFE IN THE AMERICAN ZONE

1 John Dos Passos, *Tour of Duty*, Boston 1946, 248–50; Summersby, *Eisenhower was my Boss*, 235.
2 Kay Summersby Morgan, *Past Forgetting – My Love Affair with*

Dwight D. Eisenhower, London 1977, 198.

3 Klimov, *Terror Machine*, 136.

4 Stern, *Hidden Damages*, 350.

5 Dos Passos, *Tour of Duty*, 244, 247.

6 Ladislas Farago, *The Last Days of Patton*, New York, St Louis, San Francisco and Toronto 1981, 59–64; Carlo d'Este, *A Genius for War: A Life of George S. Patton*, London 1995, 738.

7 D'Este, *Patton*, 712.

8 Farago, *Last Days*, 68.

9 D'Este, *Patton*, 766.

10 Trevor Royle, *Patton – Old Blood and Guts*, London 2005, 194–6.

11 D'Este, *Patton*, 755.

12 Farrago, *Last Days*, 156.

13 D'Este, *Patton*, 755.

14 Davidson, *Death and Life*, 77.

15 Farago, *Last Days*, 1.

16 Smith, ed., *Clay Papers*, I, 7.

17 Ibid., 351.

18 Ibid., 459, 463.

19 Salomon, *The Answers*, 422.

20 Padover, *Psychologist*, 314–16.

21 Salomon, *The Answers*, 422; Petra Goedde, *GIs and Germans*, New Haven and London 2003, 67.

22 Marta Krauss, *Heimkehr in eines fremdes Land – Geschichte der Remigranten nach 1945*, Munich 2001, 63–5.

23 Stern, *Hidden Damage*, 71

24 Zuckmayer, *Deutschlandbericht*, 7.

25 Ibid., 71.

26 Ibid., 80.

27 Hanns Mayer, *Im guten Ratskeller zu Bremen*, 5th edn., Bremen 1985, 110–11; information from Dr Carl-Ferdinand von Schubert at Maximin-Grünhaus.

28 Dos Passos, *Tour of Duty*, 263.

29 Smith, ed., *Clay Papers*, I, 41.

30 Ibid., 69.

31 Zuckmayer, *Deutschlandbericht*, 92–3.

32 Ibid., 102–3.

33 Goedde, *GIs and Germans*, 4, 15, 46.

34 Ibid., 50–1, 57.

35 Ibid., 53–4; Salomon, *The Answers*, 415, 408.

36 Salomon, *The Answers*, 320, 321.

37 Stern, *Hidden Damage*, 216–17.

38 Boveri, *Tage*, 283–4.

39 Goedde, *GIs and Germans*, 72–6.

40 Zuckmayer, *Deutschlandbericht*, 75.

41 Ibid., 115.

42 Ibid., 95–6. 248.

43 Goedde, *GIs and Germans*, 59–60.

44 Zuckmayer, *Deutschlandbericht* 20–1.

45 Goedde, *GIs and Germans*, 94–6, 101.

46 Zuckmayer, *Deutschlandbericht*, 32 See also Saul K. Padover, *Experiment in Germany. The Story of an American Intelligence Officer*, New York 1946; also John Dos Passos, *Tour of Duty*, Boston 1946.

47 Zuckmayer, *Deutschlandbericht*, 36–8.

48 Ibid., 42.

49 Peterson, *Russian Commands*, 254.

50 Boveri, *Tage*, 320–1.

51 Stern, *Hidden Damage*, 198.

52 Ibid., 324–5.

53 Salomon, *The Answers*, 416–17; Goedde, *GIs and Germans*, 84; Naimark, *Russians in Germany*, 106 n. 172.

54 Zuckmayer, *Deutschlandbericht*, 73.

55 Goedde, *GIs and Germans*, 109, 111; Friedrich, *Schauplatz Berlin*, 163.

56 Davidson, *Death and Life*, 55.

57 Skrjabina, *Allies on the Rhine*, 86–7.

58 Keeling, *Gruesome Harvest*, 59.

59 Goedde, *GIs and Germans*, 102.

60 Friedrich, *Schauplatz Berlin*, 86.

61 Goedde, *GIs and Germans*, 102.

62 Stern, *Hidden Damage*, 313.

63 Müller, *Bis zur letzten Konsequenz*, 304–6.

64 Ibid., 307.

65 Ibid., 311.

66 Smith, ed., *Clay Papers*, I, 82, 89–90.

67 Müller, *Bis zur letzten Konsequenz*, 323.

68 Volker Hentschel, *Ludwig Erhard. Ein Politikerleben*, Munich and Landsberg am Lech 1996, 40–2.

69 Ibid., 48.

70 Ibid., 51.
71 Frederic Spotts, *Bayreuth – A History of the Wagner Festival*, New Haven and London 1994, 200.
72 Hamann, *Winifred Wagner*, 412–13.
73 Spotts, *Bayreuth*, 201.
74 Sayn-Wittgenstein, *Streifzüge*, 185.
75 Ibid., 56, 90
76 See Zuckmayer, 'Bericht über das Film- und Theaterleben'.
77 Zuckmayer, 'Allgemeiner Bericht über die Filmsituation in Deutschland', in *Deutschlandbericht*, 185–204.
78 Zuckmayer, *Deutschlandbericht*, 121–2.
79 Ibid., 57, 14.
80 Ibid., 84–5; see also Helmuth James von Moltke, *Letters to Freya 1939–1945*, edited and translated by Beate Ruhm von Oppen, London 1991, 393.
81 Reinhard Lettau, ed., *Die Gruppe 47. Bericht, Kritik, Polemik*, Neuwied 1967, 22, 35.
82 Stern, *Hidden Damage*, 280–1.

CHAPTER 8: LIFE IN THE BRITISH ZONE

1 Balfour and Mair, *Four Power Control*, 99.
2 Victor Gollancz, *In Darkest Germany*, London 1947, 17.
3 Ibid., 29.
4 Lord Longford, *Avowed Intent*, London 1994, 103–5. Longford's book is particularly unsatisfying, especially given that he was minister during currency reform and the Berlin crisis, yet mentions neither.
5 Ibid., 156.
6 Meehan, *Strange Enemy People*, 53–4.
7 See Weeks's biography in *DNB* 57. There is remarkably little written about these significant British post-war administrators.
8 Morgan, *Byrnes, Clay*, 82.
9 See his biography in *DNB* 16.

Douglas did write volumes of autobiography: *Years of Command*, London 1966, covers the period.
10 Peter Merseburger, *Der Schwieriger Deutsche – Kurt Schumacher. Eine Biographie*, Stuttgart 1995, 197–8.
11 His biography is in *DNB* 47.
12 Clare, *Berlin Days*, 146.
13 Morgan, *Byrnes, Clay*, 63.
14 Meehan, *Strange Enemy People*, 53, 60, 62, 67.
15 Ibid., 140–2; Tom Bower, *Blind Eye to Murder*, London 1981, 130.
16 Robert Birley, *The German Problem and the Responsibility of Britain*, The Burge Memorial Lecture, London 1947, 5.
17 Ibid., 7–9.
18 Meehan, *Strange Enemy People*, 163–5.
19 Ibid., 171.
20 Krauss, *Heimkehr*, 74–5.
21 Clare, *Berlin Days*, 162; See also Balfour and Mair, *Four Power Control*.
22 Meehan, *Strange Enemy People*, 173–5, 'Secret Retreat Marks 60 Years of Diplomacy', in *BBC News Online*, 12 January 2006. See Richard Mayne, *In Victory, Magnanimity, In Peace, Goodwill: A History of Wilton Park*, London 2003.
23 See A. G. Dickens, *Lübeck Diary*, London 1947.
24 Ibid., 164, 173.
25 Corine Defrance, *La Politique culturelle de la France sur la rive gauche du Rhin, 1945–1955*, Strasbourg 1994, 52.
26 Clare, *Berlin Days*, 15, 35; author's own visits to the Marlborough Club.
27 Ibid., 37, 40.
28 Ibid., 42.
29 Botting, *Ruins*, 293–5.
30 Speer, *Diaries*, 79.
31 MacDonogh, *The Last Kaiser*, 173–4.
32 George Drower, *Heligoland – The True Story of the German Bight and the Island that Britain Betrayed*, Stroud 2002, 217.
33 Ibid., 219.

34 Ibid., 226–7.
35 Ibid., 235.
36 'Der besessene Besitzer', *Frankfurter Allgemeine Zeitung*, 16 December 2005 – kindly communicated by Angela Bohrer.
37 Schulenburg, *Ich hab's gewagt*, 183–4; Ruge, ed., *Schulenburg*, 63.
38 Schulenburg, *Ich hab's gewagt*, 186–7.
39 Alan Bullock, *Ernest Bevin – Foreign Secretary 1945–1951*, London 1983, 265.
40 George F. Kennan, *Memoirs 1925–1950*, London 1968, 437.
41 Gollancz, *In Darkest Germany*, 75.
42 Ibid., 79. Gollancz fails to recognise the Emperor Fritz.
43 Herzogin Viktoria Luise, *Ein Leben*, 333. See Frieda Utley, *The High Cost of Vengeance*, Chicago 1949.
44 Meehan, *Strange Enemy People*, 191–4.
45 Ibid., 214–15, 221, 236; see also Ralf Richter, *Ivan Hirst*, 2nd edn, Wolfsburg 2004.
46 Meehan, *Strange Enemy People*, 98.
47 Ruge, ed., *Schulenburg*, 68–9.
48 Interview with Karl-Heinz Bohrer, November 2004.
49 Charles Williams, *Adenauer – The Father of the New Germany*, London 2000, 289.
50 Ibid., 295.
51 Ibid., 296.
52 Merseburger, *Schumacher*, 202.
53 Naimark, *Russians in Germany*, 60.
54 Quoted in MacDonogh, *Prussia*, 6.
55 Ibid., 297.
56 Ibid, 300–1.
57 Ibid., 302; confirmed in Heinrich Böll's short story 'Als der Krieg zu Ende war' (When the War was Over), 1962.
58 Williams, *Adenauer*, 305.
59 Merseburger, *Schumacher*, 200.
60 Gilbert Ziebura, *Die deutsch-französischen Beziehungen seit 1945: Mythen und Realitäten*, Pfullingen 1970, 57.
61 Ibid., 59.
62 Naimark, *Russians in Germany*, 387; Ziebura, *Die deutsch-französische Beziehungen*, 62.
63 Ibid., 325–6.
64 Merseburger, *Schumacher*, 7.
65 Ibid., 212.
66 Ibid., 299–300.
67 Ibid., 282.
68 Willi A. Boelcke, *Der Schwarzmarkt 1945–1948 – Vom überleben nach dem Kriege*, Brunswick 1986, 78.
69 Merseburger, *Schumacher*, 238.
70 Ibid., *Schumacher*, 224.
71 Ibid., 318.
72 Ibid., 320; Gollancz, *In Darkest Germany*, 49.
73 Clare, *Berlin Days*, 188.
74 Ibid., 169.
75 Ibid., 130.
76 Herzogin Viktoria Luise, *Ein Leben*, 330.

CHAPTER 9: LIFE IN THE FRENCH ZONE

1 Davidson, *Death and Life*, 82.
2 Defrance, *La Politique culturelle*, 29.
3 Stern, *Hidden Damage*, 161.
4 Frank Raberg, 'Landesregierungen und französisch Besatzungsmacht: Aus den Kabinettsprotokollen von Baden und Württemberg-Hohenzollern', in Kurt Hochstuhl, ed., *Deutsche und Franzosen im zusammenwachsenden Europa, 1945–2000*, Stuttgart 2003, 14.
5 Döblin, *Schicksalsreise*, 400; Balfour and Mair, *Four Power Control*, 106.
6 Balfour and Mair, *Four Power Control*, 23.
7 Young, *France*, 52, 58.
8 Edgar Wolfram, 'Die französische Politik in besetzten Deutschland: neue Forschungen, alte Klischees, vernachlässige Fragen', in Hochstuhl, ed., *Deutsche und Franzosen*, 66.
9 Ibid., 60.
10 Weber, *Schmid*, 193–4, 220.

11 Ibid., 286.
12 Willi A. Boelcke, 'Industrie und Technologie in der französische Besatzungszone', in Manfrass and Rioux, eds, *France–Allemagne*, 177–8.
13 Ibid., 178–9.
14 Ibid., 181–5.
15 Smith, ed., *Clay Papers*, I, 81.
16 Bar-Zohar, *Hunt for German Scientists*, 133–5.
17 Skrjabina, *Allies on the Rhine*, 42, 55, 58, 60.
18 Interview with Karl-Heinz Bohrer, November 2004.
19 Paul Falkenburger, 'Souvenir d'un ancient curateur adjoint de l'université de Freibourg', in Manfrass and Rioux, eds, *France–Allemagne*, 285.
20 Friedrich, *Schauplatz Berlin*, 35.
21 Young, *France*, 76.
22 Ibid., 88–9.
23 Smith, ed., *Clay Papers*, I, 88–9.
24 Young, *France*, 102–4.
25 Ibid., 106–7.
26 Ibid., 117.
27 Raymond Poidevin, *Robert Schuman*, Paris 1988, 74.
28 Ibid., 74–6.
29 Smith, ed., *Clay Papers*, I, 288.
30 Young, *France*, 145.
31 Smith, ed., *Clay Papers*, II, 1004, 1056–7.
32 Defrance, *La Politique culturelle*, 30–1.
33 Döblin, *Schicksalsreise*, 404.
34 Ibid., 429–30.
35 Ibid., 431–2.
36 Ibid., 413.

CHAPTER 10: AUSTRIA'S ZONES AND SECTORS

1 Béthouart, *Bataille*, 73.
2 Dos Passos, *Tour of Duty*, 279.
3 Margarétha, *Tagebuch*, 76.
4 Ibid., 86, 87, 89.
5 Schöner, *Tagebuch*, 242.
6 Margarétha, *Tagebuch*, 68, 71.
7 Ibid., 72.
8 Ibid., 90.
9 Rauchensteiner, *Stalinplatz 4*, 31–2.
10 Schöner, *Tagebuch*, 249.
11 Ibid., 283.
12 Private information.
13 Rauchensteiner, *Stalinplatz 4*, 49–50.
14 Beer, 'Niederösterreich', 156.
15 Franzel, *Sudetenland*, 117.
16 Schöner, *Tagebuch*, 290–1; Rathkolb, 'Historische Fragmente', 154; Margarétha, *Tagebuch*, 84.
17 Magarétha, *Tagebuch*, 89–90.
18 Michael Gehler, '"Kein Anschluss aber auch kein chinesische Mauer". Österreichs aussenpolitische Emanzipation und die deutsche Frage 1945–1955', in Ableitner et al., eds, *Österreich unter alliierter Besatzung*, 206.
19 Ibid., 207.
20 Schärf, *Wiederaufrichtung*, 122.
21 Rauchensteiner, 'Jahrzehnt', 24; Rauchsteiner, *Stalinplatz 4*, 60.
22 Rauchensteiner, *Stalinplatz 4*, 61; Gehler, '"Kein Anschluss"', 208.
23 Margarétha, *Tagebuch*, 113.
24 Balfour and Mair, *Four Power Control*, 277.
25 Papers kindly communicated by Podhragy's son, Johannes.
26 Balfour and Mair, *Four Power Control*, 292.
27 Renner, *World Review*, May 1938. Document communicated by Johannes Popper von Podhragy.
28 Rathkolb, ed., *Gesellschaft und Politik*, 110.
29 Ibid., 40.
30 General Mark Clark, *Calculated Risk*, London 1956, 411.
31 Ibid., 412; Béthouart, *Bataille*, 25–6; Dos Passos, *Tour of Duty*, 293.
32 Beer, 'Niederösterreich', 139.
33 Rathkolb, ed., *Gesellschaft und Politik*, 111.
34 Margarétha, *Tagebuch*, 106.
35 Reinhold Wagnleitner, ed., *Understanding Austria: The Political Reports and Analyses of Martin F. Herz,*

Political Officer of the US Legation in Vienna 1945–1948, Salzburg 1984, 94.

36 Ibid., 427.

37 Hermann Riepl, 'Die Neubilding der Niederösterreichisches Landesregierung und der Wiederaufbau der Niederösterreichisches Landesverwaltung im Jahre 1945', in Bezemek and Rossner, eds, *Niederösterreich – Südmähren*, 88.

38 Alfred Ableitinger, 'Grossbritannien unter der zweite Kontrollabkommen: Genese und Gehalt des britischen Regierungsentwurfes', in Ableitinger et al., eds, *Österreich unter alliieter Besatzung*, 98.

39 Rathkolb, ed., *Gesellschaft und Politik*, 122–3, 143–4.

40 Byrnes, *Speaking Frankly*, 160.

41 Rathkolb, ed., *Gesellschaft und Politik*, 185–6; Rauchensteiner, *Stalinplatz 4*, 58.

42 Siegfried Beer, 'Die Besatzungsmacht Grossbritannien und Österreich 1945–1949', in Ableitinger et al., eds, *Österreich unter alliierter Besatzung*, 59.

43 Quoted in *The Patriot*, 2 August 1945.

44 Rathkolb, 'Historische Fragmente', 151.

45 Béthouart, *Bataille*, 28.

46 Margarétha, *Tagebuch*, 105.

47 Ibid., 105, 107, 109, 112.

48 Ibid., 117; the last epithet the author learned from his Viennese godfather on a visit to Vienna in 1969.

49 Clark, *Calculated Risk*, 416–18.

50 Ibid., 434.

51 Wagnleitner, ed., *Herz*, 22.

52 Ibid., 420.

53 Ibid., 76.

54 Rauchensteiner, *Stalinplatz 4*, 55.

55 Wagnleitner, ed., *Herz*, 23, 32–3, 34, 53.

56 Ibid., 418–19.

57 Margarétha, *Tagebuch*, 125, 128; Béthouart, *Bataille*, 83.

58 Béthouart, *Bataille*, 86.

59 Ibid., 75–6.

60 Ibid., 77.

61 Clark, *Calculated Risk*, 446.

62 Ibid., 421–2.

63 Communicated by Sebastian Cody.

64 Margarétha, *Tagebuch*, 140.

65 Rathkolb, ed., *Gesellschaft und Politik*, 200; Byrnes, *Speaking Frankly*, 160.

66 Margarétha, *Tagebuch*, 149.

67 Rauchensteiner, *Stalinplatz 4*, 75.

68 Ibid., 74; Béthouart, *Bataille*, 96.

69 Rauchensteiner, *Stalinplatz 4*, 80.

70 Dos Passos, *Tour of Duty*, 281, 292.

71 Clark, *Calculated Risk*, 431.

72 Rauchensteiner, *Stalinplatz 4*, 83.

73 Ibid., 94–6.

74 Peter Leighton-Langer, *X Steht fur unbekannt – Deutsche und Österreicher in den britischen Streitkräften im zweiten Weltkrieg*, Berlin 1999, 237–8.

75 Balfour and Mair, *Four Power Control*, 325.

76 Dos Passos, *Tour of Duty*, 282, 291, 293.

77 Rauchensteiner, *Stalinplatz 4*, 47; Wagnleitner, ed., *Herz*, 130–1.

78 Rauchensteiner, *Stalinplatz 4*, 76–7.

79 Ibid., 116–17.

80 The author's maternal grandfather's family is a case in point. Before 1938 they owned a substantial corner of the Kärntnerstrasse and the Weihburggasse in the centre of Vienna. On the site was the department store Modehaus Zwieback, the restaurant Zu den drei Husaren and the Palais Pereira. After the war the family managed to regain the department store, which they resold in 1957. On the other hand they were not compensated for their lost palace and the restaurant was later sold by Göring's favourite restaurateur, Gustav Horcher, to Egon Födermayr. In the immediate post-war years it had been Renner's canteen. See Tina Walzer and Stephan Templ, *Unser Wien – Ariesierung auf Österreichisch*, Berlin 2001, 42–3, and the

Grundbücher (Land Register) for 2 and 4 Weihburggasse as well as 11, 13–15 Kärntnerstrasse.

81 Rauchensteiner, *Stalinplatz 4*, 97; Clark, *Calculated Risk*, 424.

82 Clark, *Calculated Risk*, 424 n. 1.

83 Wagnleitner, ed., *Herz*, 134, 154.

84 Rauchensteiner, *Stalinplatz 4*, 102.

85 Clark, *Calculated Risk*, 425.

86 Zuckmayer, *Deutschlandbericht*, 9.

87 Zuckmayer, 'Allgemeiner Bericht über die Filmsituation in Deutschland'.

88 Quoted in Marietta Bearman and Charmian Brinson, 'Keine einfache Sache', in Bearman et al., *Wien–London*, 238.

89 Charmian Brinson, 'Ein Stück wahrer Kultur, ein Stück Wien, ein Stück Leben', in Bearman et al., *Wien–London*, 171.

90 Walter Binnebös, *Galoppsport in Wien*, Vienna 1980, 147–8.

91 Rathkolb, 'Historische Fragmente, 148; Rauchensteiner, *Stalinplatz 4*, 36.

92 Information from Georg Stiegelmar, the late Helmut Osberger and Erich Salomon.

93 Schärf, *Wiederaufrichtung*, 125; Rauchensteiner, *Stalinplatz 4*, 48.

94 Wagnleitner, ed., *Herz*, 134.

95 Beer, 'Niederösterreich', 146, 148, 155–6, 165–6.

96 Rauchensteiner, *Stalinplatz 4*, 38; Andrew Gibson-Watt, *An Undistinguished Life*, Lewes 1990, 173.

97 Gibson-Watt, *Life*, 183.

98 Beer, 'Grossbritannien', 52–3.

99 Ibid., 63.

100 Helmut Eberhart, 'Weideraufbau in Nachkriegszeit – Das Tagebuch von Anton Pirchegger', in Siegfried Beer, ed., *Die 'Britische Steiermark' 1945–1955*, Graz 1995.

101 Stefan Karner, '"Ich bekam zehn Jahre Zwangsarbeit": zu den Verschleppungen aus der Steiermark durch sowjetische Organe in Jahre

1945', in Beer, ed., *Die 'Britische Steiermark'*, 249–50; Othmar Pickl, 'Das Kriegsende 1945 und die frühe Besatzungszeit im mittleren Mürztal', in Beer, ed., *Die 'Britische Steiermark'*. 250.

102 Beer, 'Grossbritannien', 57.

103 Alfred Ableitinger, Siegfried Beer and Eduard G. Staudinger, *Besatzungszeit in der Steiermark*, Graz, Esztergom, Paris and New York 1994, 15.

104 Ibid., 17.

105 Beer, ed., *Die 'Britische Steiermark'*, 25; Siegfried Beer, 'Die Briten und der Wiederaufbau des Justizwesens in der Steiermark 1945–1950', in ibid., 113–14.

106 Rauchensteiner, *Stalinplatz 4*, 40.

107 Gibson-Watt, *Life*, 172.

108 Rauchensteiner, *Stalinplatz 4*, 24–6.

109 Donald Cameron Watt, 'Austria as a Special Case in Cold War Europe – A Personal Note', in Ableitinger et al., eds, *Österreich unter alliierter Besatzung*, 282.

110 Rauchensteiner, *Stalinplatz 4*, 58.

111 Balfour and Mair, *Four Power Control*, 314–15.

112 Rauchensteiner, *Stalinplatz 4*, 67.

113 Arthur Radley, 'The British Military Government in Steiermark [sic] 1945–1946, Personal Reminiscences', in Beer, ed., *Die 'Britische Steiermark'*, 586–7.

114 John Corsellis and Marcus Ferrar, *Slovenia 1945: Memories of Death and Survival after World War II*, London and New York 2005, 8.

115 Gibson-Watt, *Life*, 178.

116 Corsellis and Ferrar, *Slovenia*, 19.

117 Ibid., 43.

118 Ibid., 45.

119 Gibson-Watt, *Life*, 179.

120 Corsellis and Ferrar, *Slovenia*, 47.

121 Gibson-Watt, *Life*, 173.

122 Nikolai Tolstoy, *Victims of Yalta*, London 1977, 220–1.

123 Ibid., 225–6, 229; Thurn und Taxis,

'Memoiren', 28–9.

124 Corsellis and Ferrar, *Slovenia*, 49.

125 Ibid., 50; Gibson-Watt, *Life*, 179.

126 Corsellis and Ferrar, *Slovenia*, 52, 59, 186.

127 Rauchensteiner, *Stalinplatz 4*, 44; Ralph W. Brown III, 'A Cold War Army of Occupation', in Ableitinger et al., eds, *Österreich unter alliierter Besatzung*, 349–50; Rathkolb, ed., *Gesellschaft und Politik*, 246.

128 Quoted in Rauchensteiner, *Stalinplatz 4*, 45.

129 Rathkolb, ed., *Gesellschaft und Politik*, 168–70.

130 Ibid., 303.

131 Rauchensteiner, *Stalinplatz 4*, 46.

132 Wagnleitner, ed., *Herz*, 7.

133 Brown, 'Cold War Army', 355–66.

134 Rauchensteiner, *Stalinplatz 4*, 55.

135 Clark, *Calculated Risk*, 414; for Hitler's use of the building, and the French furniture: Eberle and Uhl, *Das Buch Hitler*, 113.

136 Clark, *Calculated Risk*, 415.

137 Ibid., 415.

138 Rathkolb, ed., *Gesellschaft und Politik*, 243.

139 Ibid., 255.

140 Clark, *Calculated Risk*, 420–1.

141 Ibid., 432.

142 Günter Bischof, 'Der Nationale Sicherheitsrat und die amerikanische Österreichpolitik im frühen Kalten Krieg', in Ableitinger et al., eds, *Österreich unter alliierter Besatzung*, 112, 116.

143 Rathkolb, ed., *Gesellschaft und Politik*, 243.

144 Ibid., 49–55.

145 Ibid., 69–71.

146 Béthouart, *Bataille*, 42.

147 Ibid., 47.

148 Béthouart, *Bataille*, 54.

149 Rauchensteiner, *Stalinplatz 4*, 41–2.

150 Béthouart, *Bataille*, 55.

151 Rathkolb, ed., *Gesellschaft und Politik*, 371.

152 Béthouart, *Bataille*, 59.

153 Ibid., 67.

154 Ibid., 67–8; Rauchensteiner, *Stalinplatz 4*, 64; Otto von Habsburg, *Kampf um Österreich*, 72, 75; Balfour and Mair, *Four Power Control*, 334.

155 Habsburg, *Kampf*, 78.

156 Denys G. C. Salt, 'Reminiscences of Styria', in Beer, ed., *Die 'Britische Steiermark'*, 592.

CHAPTER 11: LIFE IN ALL FOUR ZONES

1 Clare, *Berlin Days*, 17–18.

2 Stern, *Hidden Damage*, 284.

3 Ibid., 286.

4 Zuckmayer, *Deutschlandbericht*, 97–9.

5 See Heinrich Böll, *Wanderer, kommst du nach Spa*, Munich 2004; interview with Karl-Heinz Bohrer, November 2004. Norbert Mühlen, *L'Incroyable Famille Krupp*, Paris 1961, 197.

6 Goedde, *GIs and Germans*, 132, 133–4; Zuckmayer, *Deutschlandbericht*, 149.

7 Goedde, *GIs and Germans*, 137, 144, 161–3.

8 Quoted in Zuckmayer, *Deutschlandbericht*, 272.

9 Ruge, ed., *Schulenburg*, 94.

10 Quoted in Williams, *More Lives than One*, xiii.

11 Borgelt, *Das war der Frühling in Berlin*, 69; Krauss, *Heimkehr*, 56–7, 73.

12 Ernst Jünger, *Der Friede. Ein Wort an die Jugend Europas. Ein Wort an die Jugend der Welt*, Vienna 1949, 83, 87.

13 Jünger, *Okkupation*, 147.

14 Jünger, *Der Friede*, 10.

15 Ibid., 21.

16 Ibid., 16.

17 Ibid., 76.

18 Karl O. Paetel, *Ernst Jünger. Die Wandlung eines Deutschen Dichters und Patrioten*, New York 1946, 10.

19 Salomon, *The Answers*, 524.

20 Ibid., Goronwy Rees preface, viii.

21 Ibid., 545–6.

22 Michael Kennedy, *Richard Strauss*, Oxford 1995, 107–12.
23 Leighton-Langer, *X*, 231.
24 Hans Habe, *Im Jahre Null. Ein Beitrag zur Geschichte der deutscher Presse*, Munich 1966, 50, 53, 70, 79; Kardorff, *Aufzeichnungen*, 363, 364 n. 1.
25 Zuckmayer, 'Bericht über das Film- und Theaterleben'.
26 Georg Stefan Troller, *Das fidele Grab an der Donau – Mein Wien 1918–1938*, Düsseldorf and Zurich 2004, 96.
27 Habe, *Im Jahre Null*, 119–20.
28 Smith, ed., *Clay Papers*, II, 1066.
29 Schulenburg, *Ich hab's gewagt*, 200.
30 Ibid., 206.
31 Clare, *Berlin Days*, 158–9.
32 Stern, *Hidden Damage*, 167.
33 See Inge Scholl, *Die Weisse Rose*, Frankfurt/Main 1988.
34 Stern, *Hidden Damage*, 175.
35 Kardorff, *Aufzeichnungen*, 337.
36 Ibid., 363; Ruge, ed., *Schulenburg*, 65.
37 Schulenburg, *Ich hab's gewagt*, 185.
38 Zuckmayer, *Deutschlandbericht*, 57.
39 Ibid., 104.
40 Ibid., 105–6.
41 Kardorff, *Aufzeichnungen*, 339.
42 Chamberlain and Feldman, eds, *Liberation*, 71–2; Leighton-Langer, *X*, 228.
43 Leighton-Langer, *X*, 229.
44 Ibid., 230.
45 Normann, *Tagebuch*, 207–8.
46 Stern, *Hidden Damage*, 343–4, 350.
47 Clare, *Berlin Days*, 152.
48 Rebecca West, *The Meaning of Treason*, 2nd edn, London 1982, 129.
49 Peck, 'Jüdische DPs', 205.
50 Ibid., 206.
51 Hilberg, *Destruction*, III, 1228.
52 Ruth Gay, *Safe among the Germans: Liberated Jews after World War II*, New Haven and London 2002, x–xi, 70, 72.
53 Peck, 'Jüdische DPs', 206.
54 Hilberg, *Destruction*, III, 1132.
55 Ibid., 1229; Peck, "Jüdische DPs', 206.
56 Hilberg, *Destruction*, III, 1234.
57 Ibid., 1134.
58 Ibid., 65.
59 Zuckmayer, *Deutschlandbericht*, 111–12.
60 Wagnleitner, ed., *Herz*, 131.
61 Ibid., 257.
62 Gay, *Safe*, 104–5.
63 Ibid., 59–60, 63, 103.
64 Peck, 'Jüdische DPs', 207.
65 Gay, *Safe*, 56; Peck, 'Jüdische DPs', 208.
66 Shepherd, *After Daybreak*, 44.
67 Ibid., 71.
68 Ibid., 72.
69 Ibid., 92.
70 Ibid., 116.
71 Ibid., 118, 133.
72 Ibid., 134.
73 Peck, 'Jüdische DPs', 206.
74 Gay, *Safe*, 68; Peck, 'Jüdische DPs', 209.
75 Gay, *Safe*, 81, 83.
76 Ibid., 86–7; 96–7.
77 Ibid., 89.

CHAPTER 12: GUILT

1 Kardorff, *Aufzeichnungen*, 330.
2 Ibid., 332, 334.
3 Normann, *Tagebuch*, 61.
4 Stern, *Hidden Damage*, 307.
5 Jünger, *Okkupation*, 130.
6 Zuckmayer, *Deutschlandbericht*, 72, 74.
7 Karl Jaspers, *Die Schuldfrage. Für Völkermord gibt es keine Verjährung*, Heidelberg 1946, 13.
8 Ibid., 19.
9 Ibid.
10 Quoted in Kirkbright, *Jaspers*, 141, 193.
11 Ibid., 197, 195; quoted in Zuckmayer, *Deutschlandbericht*, 245; Jaspers, *Schuldfrage*, 28–9.
12 Norbert Trippen, *Josef Cardinal Frings*

(1887–1978). *Sein Wirken für das Erzbistum Köln und für die Kirche in Deutschland*, Paderborn, Munich, Vienna and Zurich 2003, 132.

13 Ibid., 142.

14 Zuckmayer, *Deutschlandbericht*, 76; conversation with Karl-Heinz Bohrer, 12 January 2005.

15 Kirkbright, *Jaspers*, 190.

16 Stern, *Hidden Damage*, 79–81.

17 Interview with Karl-Heinz Bohrer, November 2004.

18 Abzug, *Vicious Heart*, x.

19 Ibid.

20 Ibid., 134–7.

21 Ibid., 128–32; Farago, *Last Days*, 58.

22 Shepherd, *After Daybreak*, 74–7.

23 James F. Tent, *Mission on the Rhine: Reeducation and Denazification in American Occupied Germany*, Chicago and London 1982, 11, 14.

24 Edward N. Peterson, *The American Occupation of Germany: Retreat to Victory*, Detroit 1977, 115, 59; Frank M. Buscher, *The U.S. War Crimes Trial Program in Germany, 1946–1955*, New York, Westport and London 1989, 19.

25 Keeling, *Gruesome Harvest*, 35.

26 Kardorff, *Aufzeichnungen*, 324.

27 Friedrich, *Schauplatz Berlin*, 82.

28 Stern, *Hidden Damage*, 120.

29 Justus Fürstenau, *Entnazifizierung. Ein Kapitel deutscher Nachkriegspolitik*, Neuwied and Berlin 1969, 25.

30 Kardorff, *Aufzeichnungen*, 339.

31 Jünger, *Okkupation*, 153.

32 Meehan, *Strange Enemy People*, 116.

33 Krauss, *Heimkehr*, 51.

34 Emmy Goering, *My Life with Goering*, London 1972, 142.

35 Margret Boveri, *Der Verrat im XX. Jahrhundert – für und gegen die Nation*, Hamburg 1956, 14.

36 Dos Passos, *Tour of Duty*, 253–4.

37 MacDonogh, *A Good German*, 71; see also R. G. S. Weber, *The German Student Corps in the Third Reich*, London 1986.

38 Gollancz, *In Darkest Germany*, 103.

39 MacDonogh, *Prussia*, 192–3; Hansgeorg Model, *Der deutsche Generalstabsoffizier. Seine Auswahl und Ausbildung in Reichswehr, Wehrmacht und Bundeswehr*, Frankfurt/Main 1968, 135–9.

40 Kardorff, *Aufzeichnungen*, 326 n. 1, 333.

41 Sayn-Wittgenstein, *Streifzüge*, 166.

42 Peterson, *American Occupation*, 174, 216; Tent, *Mission on the Rhine*, 51.

43 Tent, *Mission on the Rhine*, 54–5.

44 Dos Passos, *Tour of Duty*, 273.

45 Clare, *Berlin Days*, 26–8.

46 Meehan, *Strange Enemy People*, 104.

47 Smith, ed., *Clay Papers*, I, 328–9; Timothy R. Vogt, *Denazification in Soviet-Occupied Germany 1945–1948*, Cambridge, Mass. and London 2000, 7–8

48 Balfour and Mair, *Four Power Control*, 174.

49 Bower, *Blind Eye to Murder*, 182–3, 221; Wolfgang Krüger, *Entnazifiziert!: Zur Praxis der politischen Säuberung in Nordrhein-Westfalen*, Wuppertal 1982, 14–15.

50 Vogt, *Denazification*, 2–3, 71.

51 Krüger, *Entnazifiziert!*, 11.

52 Clare, *Berlin Days*, 112–13.

53 Ruge, ed., *Schulenburg*, 91.

54 Ibid., 91–2.

55 Dos Passos, *Tour of Duty*, 251–2.

56 Ibid., 309.

57 Zuckmayer, *Deutschlandbericht*, 140–1; Zuckmayer, 'Jugend im Niemandsland'.

58 Franz von Papen, M*emoirs*, translated by Brian Connell, London 1952, 577–8.

59 Schwerin von Krosigk, *Memoiren*, 261–2.

60 Goering, *My Life with Goering*, 168.

61 Nike Wagner, *The Wagners – The Dramas of a Musical Dynasty*, London 2000, 226.

62 Hamann, *Winifred Wagner*, 403; Spotts, *Bayreuth*, 199.

63 Hamann, *Winifred Wagner*, 406, 408.

64 Ibid., 410–11.

65 Franz Endler, *Herbert von Karajan: My Autobiography*, London 1989, 46.

66 Lang, *'Lieber Herr Celibidache'*, 48–50.

67 Ibid., 58.

68 Davidson, *Death and Life*, 127–8.

69 Peterson, *Russian Commands*, 84–5.

70 Smith, ed., *Clay Papers*, I, 46–7.

71 Ibid., 102.

72 Ibid., 130, 141.

73 Ibid., 433; II, 624.

74 Ibid., 224–5.

75 Peterson, *American Occupation*, 93.

76 Buscher, *War Crimes Trial Program*, 49, 60.

77 Clare, *Berlin Days*, 206–10.

78 Wagnleitner, ed., *Herz*, 98–100.

79 Rauchensteiner, *Stalinplatz 4*, 110.

80 Rathkolb, ed., *Gesellschaft und Politik*, 147–8.

81 Ibid., 209, 243.

82 Ibid., 109, 112.

83 Ibid. 153, 152 n. 1.

84 Ibid., 390.

85 Béthouart, *Bataille*, 120.

86 Richard Dove, Foreword to Bearman et al., *Wien–London*, 11.

87 Wagnleitner, ed., *Herz*, 115–17.

88 Blake Baker, 'Zur Arbeit der Field Security Service im Steirischen Grenzland', in Beer, ed., *Die 'Britische Steiermark'*, 608.

89 Beer, 'Die Briten', 130–1.

90 Ibid., 122.

91 Beer, 'Grossbritannien', 65 n. 67.

92 Beer, 'Die Briten', 122–3.

93 Ibid., 125.

94 Wolfgang Muchitsch, 'Das Volksgericht Graz', in Beer, *Die 'Britische Steiermark'*, 43.

95 Beer, 'Die Briten', 153.

96 Lorenz Jäger, *Adorno – Eine politische Biographie*, Munich 2003, 223.

97 Gollancz, *In Darkest Germany*, 18–19.

98 Victor Gollancz, *Leaving them to their Fate: The Ethics of Starvation*, London 1946, 4.

99 Ibid., 5–6, 12, 18.

100 Bullock, *Bevin*, 265.

101 Gollancz, *In Darkest Germany*, 24.

102 Ibid., 18.

103 Ibid., 14–15, 17.

104 Döblin, *Schicksalsreise*, 415.

105 Gollancz, *In Darkest Germany*, 11.

106 Ibid., 12.

107 Ibid., 23–4.

108 Ibid., 38–9.

109 Ibid., 53–7.

110 Ibid., 64.

111 Ibid., 66–7.

112 Zuckmayer, *Deutschlandbericht*, 72.

113 Gollancz, *In Darkest Germany*, 29.

114 Ibid., 13–14.

115 Jünger, *Okkupation*, 240.

116 Smith, ed., *Clay Papers*, I, 151–2, 161, 166, 179, 207.

117 Ibid., 212.

118 Gollancz, *In Darkest Germany*, 74.

119 Smith, ed., *Clay Papers*, I, 264–5.

120 Boelcke, *Schwarzmarkt*, 35–6.

121 Ibid., 164; Davidson, *Death and Life*, 137.

122 Boelcke, *Schwarzmarkt*, 48–9, 50–4, 59–60, 64.

123 Ibid., 60, 65–6, 70; Davidson, *Death and Life*, 159.

124 Zuckmayer, 'Deutschland, Sommer 1948: Jüngstes Gericht oder Stunde Null?', in *Deutschlandbericht*.

125 Trippen, *Frings*, 251.

126 Ibid., 174–5.

127 Meehan, *Strange Enemy People*, 240.

128 Paul Dahm, *Joseph Kardinal Frings, Erzbischof von Köln*, Munich 1957, 4–5.

129 Ibid., 21–2.

130 Quoted in ibid., 22.

131 Goedde, *GIs and Germans*, 43, 45.

132 Davidson, *Death and Life*, 21, 54.

133 Meehan, *Strange Enemy People*, 41–2.

134 Radley, 'British Military Government', 583.

135 Smith, ed., *Clay Papers*, I, 29.

136 Kardorff, *Aufzeichnungen*, 332; Clare, *Berlin Days*, 34, 55.

137 Goedde, *GIs and Germans*, 44;

Boveri, *Tage*, 286; Clare, *Berlin Days*, 16, 55, 60.

138 Clare, *Berlin Days*, 54.

139 Ibid., 17–18.

140 Boelcke, *Schwarzmarkt*, 82; Stern, *Hidden Damage*, 273.

141 Stern, *Hidden Damage*, 286.

CHAPTER 13: BLACK MARKET

1 Krockow, *Hour of the Women*, 167, 169; Heinrich Böll, *When the War was Over*.

2 Sayn-Wittgenstein, *Streifzüger*, 171.

3 Heinrich Böll, 'Wanderer, kommst du nach Spa . . .', in his *Erzählungen*, Munich 1997, 14–15.

4 Friedrich, *Schauplatz Berlin*, 192.

5 Smith, ed., *Clay Papers*, I, 335–6.

6 Ibid., 211–13.

7 Stern, *Hidden Damage*, 130–5.

8 Ibid., 68.

9 Goedde, *GIs and Germans*, 122.

10 Boelcke, *Schwarzmarkt*, 6.

11 Hans Habe, *In American Uniform*, quoted in ibid., 123.

12 Ibid., 12.

13 Zuckmayer, 'Jugend in Niemandsland'.

14 Zuckmayer, *Deutschlandbericht*, 142.

15 Ibid., 152.

16 Boelcke, *Schwarzmarkt*, 76–8.

17 Friedrich, *Schauplatz Berlin*, 119.

18 Jünger, *Okkupation*, 235–6.

19 Zuckmayer, *Deutschlandbericht*, 143–9.

20 Ibid., 155.

21 Cullen, *Reichstag*, 399–401.

22 Boelcke, *Schwarzmarkt*, 92, 94–5.

23 Ibid., 102.

24 Ibid., 170.

25 Mosely, *Report from Germany*, 46–7, 55, 80–1.

26 Dos Passos, *Tour of Duty*, 260; Boelcke, *Schwarzmarkt*, 164.

27 Boelcke, *Schwarzmarkt*, 206–7.

28 Skrjabina, *Allies on the Rhine*, 81.

29 Davidson, *Death and Life*, 84–5.

30 Klimov, *Terror Machine*, 178.

31 Ibid., 128, 134, 160.

32 Meehan, *Strange Enemy People*, 116, 130.

33 Gerhard Keiderling, 'Der Al Capone vom Alexanderplatz', in www.luise-berlin.de

CHAPTER 14: LIGHT FINGERS

1 Konstantin Akinscha and Grigori Koslow, *Beutekunst – Auf Schatzsuche in russischen Geheimdepots*, Munich 1995, 61, 68.

2 Smith, ed., *Clay Papers*, I, 68, 84, 268; Keeling, *Gruesome Harvest*, 40.

3 Akinscha and Koslow, *Beutekunst*, 24, 97–100.

4 Ibid., 103–5.

5 Ibid., 94–5, 113–15.

6 Ibid., 112–13, 116.

7 See Giles MacDonogh, Translator's Preface to Henrik Eberle and Matthias Uhl, eds, *The Hitler Book*, London 2005.

8 Eberle and Uhl, eds, *Das Buch Hitler*, Afterword, 462–78 passim.

9 Akinscha and Koslow, *Beutekunst*, 95, 122–3.

10 Friedrich, *Schauplatz Berlin*, 33.

11 Akinscha and Koslow, *Beutekunst*, 126–7.

12 Ibid., 129–33; A. A. Löwenthal, 'Der Hitler-Affe: Ein Zwischenfall in Schlesien', in *Gesammelte Schriften*, Tübingen 1965, VI, 636–43.

13 Giles MacDonogh, 'Parlour Games', *Guardian*, 20 December 2003. Damon de Laszlo, the artist's grandson, maintains that it is doubtful that Red Army officers carried swords, and it may well be that the damage to the painting was incurred in quite another way. On the other hand, we know that the Russians carried all sorts of weapons as trophies.

14 Akinscha and Koslow, *Beutekunst*, 106–9, and author's visits to Rheinsberg.

15 Akinscha and Koslow, *Beutekunst*, 145–8.

16 Ibid., 151. Akinscha and Koslow have Rudolf's name as Robert. See Sophie Lillie, *Was einmal war: Handbuch der enteigneten Kunstsammlungen Wiens*, Vienna 2003, 439–42, 463–5.

17 Akinscha and Koslow, *Beutekunst*, 136, 138–9, 172–5, 176.

18 Ibid., 160–1.

19 Naimark, *Russians in Germany*, 167–8.

20 Akinscha and Koslow, *Beutekunst*, 167; Giles MacDonogh, 'Vichy's last stand: a prince's story', *Financial Times*, 5 October 1996 – interview with Friedrich Wilhelm Fürst von Hohenzollern; MacDonogh, *Frederick the Great*, 8; see E. Grosetti and M. Matronola, *Il bombardimento di Monte Cassino, diario di Guerra*, Montecassino 1997.

21 Smith, ed., *Clay Papers*, I, 232.

22 Naimark, *Russians in Germany*, 173.

23 Sayn-Wittgenstein, *Streifzüge*, 156–7.

24 Dos Passos, *Tour of Duty*, 273; Keeling, *Gruesome Harvest*, 40; Botting, *Ruins*, 16.

25 Sayn-Wittgenstein, *Streifzüger*, 187–8.

26 Ibid., 182–4.

27 Zuckmayer, *Deutschlandbericht*, 107.

28 Meehan, *Strange Enemy*, 119, 121, 125.

29 Clare, *Berlin Days*, 28–9.

30 Meehan, *Strange Enemy*, 210–11.

31 Bar-Zohar, *Hunt for German Scientists*, 132.

32 Franz Kurowski, *Alliierte Jagd auf deutsche Wissenschaftler. Das Unternehmen Paperclip*, Munich 1982, 8.

33 Bar-Zohar, *Hunt for German Scientists*, 10.

34 Friedrich, *Schauplatz Berlin*, 149.

CHAPTER 15: WHERE ARE OUR MEN?

1 Arthur L. Smith, '*Die Vermisste Million*' – *Zur Schicksal deutscher Kriegsgefangener nach dem Zweiten Weltkrieg*, Munich 1992, 10.

2 Wolfgang Benz and Angelika Schardt, eds, *Kriegsgefangenschaft: Berichte über das Leben in Gefangenlagern der Alliierten von Otto Engelbert, Kurt Glaser, Hans Johnitz und Heinz Pust*, Munich 1991, 7.

3 Smith, *Die vermisste Million*, 20; Kurt W. Böhme and Helmut Wolf, *Aufzeichnungen über die Kriegsgefangenschaft im Westen*, Munich 1973, xiii.

4 Ibid., xiv.

5 Davidson, *Death and Life*, 5; Smith, *Die vermisste Million*, 18, 21.

6 Speer, *Diaries*, 41.

7 Benz and Schardt, eds, *Kriegsgefangenschaft*, 7.

8 Böhme and Wolf, *Aufzeichnungen*, xiv.

9 Jäger, *Adorno*, 224.

10 Smith, *Die Vermisste Million*, 57, 62, 63 n. 29.

11 Benz and Schardt, *Kriegsgefangenschaft*, 8.

12 De Zayas, *Nemesis at Potsdam*, xxv.

13 Ibid., 8–9.

14 Ibid., 10; Erich Maschke, ed., *Zur Geschichte des Deutschen Kriegsgefangenen des Zweiten Weltkrieges*, vol. XV: *Die deutschen Kriegsgefangenen des Zweiten Weltkrieges – Eine Zusammenfassung*, Munich 1967, 35.

15 Ibid., 11.

16 Smith, *Die vermisste Million*, 9 n. 2.

17 James Bacque, *Other Losses – An Investigation into the Mass Death of German Prisoners of War after World War II*, London 1991, 45.

18 Smith, *Die vermisste Million*, 11, 101.

19 Wagnleitner, ed., *Herz*, 252, 267.

20 Benz and Schardt, eds,

Kriegsgefangenschaft, 7–8.

21 Smith, *Die vermisste Million*, 30.

22 Maschke, *Zusammenfassung*, 225.

23 Kurt Glaser, 'Kriegsgefangener auf drei Kontinenten', in ibid., 202.

24 Böhme and Wolf, *Aufzeichnungen*, 142.

25 Ibid., 143–4.

26 Smith, *Die vermisste Million*, 24.

27 Böhme and Wolf, *Aufzeichnungen*, 225.

28 Smith, *Die vermisste Million*, 25.

29 Ibid., 40 n. 13; Böhme and Wolf, *Aufzeichnungen*, 225–6.

30 Smith, *Die vermisste Million*, 37.

31 Ibid., 43–6, 86.

32 Ibid., 26.

33 Farago, *Last Days*, 153n.

34 Rauchensteiner, *Stalinplatz 4*, 47.

35 Salomon, *The Answers*, 440.

36 Ibid., 442.

37 Ibid., 447.

38 Ibid., 453.

39 Hans Johnitz, 'In amerikanischer und französischer Kriegsgefangenschaft', in Benz and Schardt, eds, *Kriegsgefangenschaft*, 85–6.

40 Salomon, *The Answers*, 498.

41 Ibid., 505–6.

42 Schwerin von Krosigk, *Memoiren*, 258–9.

43 Salomon, *The Answers*, 536.

44 Schwerin von Krosigk, *Memoiren*, 259, 262.

45 Jan-Werner Müller, *A Dangerous Mind: Carl Schmitt in Post-War European Thought*, 3.

46 Salomon, *The Answers*, 541.

47 Papen, *Memoirs*, 578–9.

48 Salomon, *The Answers*, 542; Speer, *Diaries*, 25.

49 Salomon, *The Answers*, 543–4.

50 Webmaster Kriegsgefangener.de

51 Ian Sayer and Douglas Botting, *Hitler's Last General – The Case against Wilhelm Mohnke*, London 1989, 265.

52 Preussen, *Hohenzollern*, 191–2; information from the late Prince Kraft zu Hohenlohe-Langenburg.

53 Herzogin Viktoria Luise, *Ein Leben*, 318.

54 Sayn-Wittgenstein, *Streifzüger*, 158.

55 Paul Schmidt, *Hitler's Interpreter*, edited by R. H. C. Steed, London 1951, 280–1; Smith, ed., *Clay Papers*, II, 578.

56 Sayer and Botting, *Mohnke*, 269.

57 R. T. Paget, *Manstein – His Campaigns and his Trial*, London 1951, 109.

58 Sayer and Botting, *Mohnke*, 270–1, 282.

59 Bower, *Blind Eye to Murder*, 134.

60 Smith, ed., *Clay Papers*, II, 1054–5.

61 Gibson-Watt, *An Undistinguished Life*, 170.

62 Ruge, ed., *Schulenburg*, 62–5.

63 Ibid., 70.

64 Ibid., 66.

65 Ibid., 66–7.

66 Shepherd, *After Daybreak*, 55.

67 Maschke, *Zusammenfassung*, 210.

68 Ibid., 225.

69 David Irving, *Göring – A Biography*, London 1989, 478.

70 WW2 Memories Project – Le Marchant POW Camp; Terence Prittie in http://www.royalpioneercorps.co.uk/rpc/history_germanguns.htm

71 Leighton-Langer, *X*, 239–42.

72 Brian Bond, 'Brauchitsch', in Correlli Barnett, ed., *Hitler's Generals*, London 1990, 95.

73 Rowland Ryder, *Ravenstein – Portrait of a German General*, New York 1978, 170–1.

74 Ibid., 171.

75 Samuel W. Mitcham, Jnr, 'Arnim', in Barnett, ed., *Hitler's Generals*, 353.

76 Böhme and Wolf, *Aufzeichnungen*, xiii.

77 Keeling, *Gruesome Harvest*, 24.

78 Glaser, 'Kriegsgefangener', 208–12, 215, 218, 225.

79 Böhme and Wolf, *Aufzeichnungen*, 170.

80 Ibid., 174.

81 Ibid., 174, 178.

82 Ibid., 175, 180–1.
83 Dahm, *Frings*, 27–8, 34.
84 Sayer and Botting, *Mohnke*, 90–1.
85 Ibid., 91.
86 Ibid., 95, 190, 265; *Document*, BBC Radio 4, 9 January 2006, dedicated a programme to British torturers, and mentioned Scotland in that context.
87 Sayer and Botting, *Mohnke*, 97.
88 Keeling, *Gruesome Harvest*, 24.
89 Meehan, *Strange Enemy People*, 27–8.
90 Ibid., 38.
91 Ibid., 70, 73, 76–7.
92 Ibid., 86.
93 Ibid., 68.
94 Ian Cobain, 'The Interrogation Camp that Turned Prisoners into Living Skeletons', *Guardian*, Saturday 17 December 2005. I am grateful to Nick Jacobs for drawing my attention to this article; *Document*, BBC Radio 4, 9 January 2006; see also Meehan, *Strange Enemy People*, 82–6, who saw the papers long before the newspapers or the BBC.
95 Smith, ed., *Clay Papers*, II, 30–1.
96 Salomon, *The Answers*, 530–1; the events are substantiated by a film in the American archives that was seen by Jeremy Murray-Brown in July 1992 – untitled web document; see also Nicholas Bethell, *The Last Secret*, London 1974, and Tolstoy, *Victims of Yalta*; also Botting, *Ruins*; Keeling, *Gruesome Harvest*.
97 Salomon, *The Answers*, 534; Murray-Brown, op. cit.
98 Johnitz, 'Kriegsgefangenschaft', 102.
99 Böhme and Wolf, *Aufzeichnungen*, 285n.
100 Ibid., xiii; Smith, *Die vermisste Million*, 31.
101 Smith, *Die vermisste Million*, 32; Maschke, *Zusammenfassung*, 197.
102 Maschke, *Zusammenfassung*, 226.
103 Salomon, *The Answers*, 362.
104 Johnitz, 'Kriegsgefangenschaft', 102.

105 Böhme and Wolf, *Aufzeichnungen*, 427.
106 Ibid., 427, is another case.
107 Ibid., 391.
108 Ibid., 102, 114.
109 Ibid., 275, 279, 282.
110 Ibid., 284, 290.
111 Ibid., 290–2, 293–4; *The Progressive*, 14 January 1946, quoted in Keeling, *Gruesome Harvest*, 21.
112 Böhme and Wolf, *Aufzeichnungen*, 291.
113 Ibid., 217.
114 Ibid., 223–4.
115 Ibid., 219–22.
116 Ibid., 251–5.
117 Maschke, *Zusammenfassung*, 226.
118 Keeling, *Gruesome Harvest*, 18.
119 Maschke, *Zusammenfassung*, 224.
120 Ibid., 196–7.
121 Krockow, *Hour of the Women*, 202.
122 Herzogin Viktoria Luise, *Ein Leben*, 324–5.
123 Samuel W. Mitcham, Jnr, 'Kleist', in Barnett, ed., *Hitler's Generals*, 259.
124 Ibid., 260.
125 Sayer and Botting, *Mohnke*, 236.
126 Ibid., 317.
127 Heinz Pust, 'Als Kriegsgefangener in der Sowjetunion. Errinerungen 1945–1953', in Benz and Schardt, eds, *Kriegsgefangenschaft*, 22, 29.
128 Friedrich, *Schauplatz Berlin*, 180–1.
129 Pust, 'Sowjetunion', 32.
130 Smith, ed., *Clay Papers*, I, 331.
131 Pust, 'Sowjetunion', 33–5.
132 Ibid., 43–4.
133 Ibid., 75–6.
134 Ibid., 81–2.
135 Smith, ed., *Clay Papers*, II, 789–80.
136 Maschke, *Zusammenfassung*, 225.
137 Ibid., 196–7.
138 Ibid.
139 Ibid., 225.
140 Ibid., 224.
141 Information from my friend Janez Fajfar, general manager of the Villa Bled Hotel, who showed me the room and Tito's desk. The former

POWs frequently returned to point out to their wives and children their portraits among the figures in the battle scene.

142 Maschke, *Zusammenfassung,* 197.

143 Friedrich, *Schauplatz Berlin,* 88.

144 Wolfgang Borchert, *Das Gesamtwerk,* Hamburg 1970, 102.

145 Ibid., 172.

CHAPTER 16: THE TRIALS

1 Davidson, *Death and Life,* 100 n. 4; Bower, *Blind Eye to Murder,* 29–30.

2 MacDonogh, *The Last Kaiser,* 422, 423, 424; Hilberg, *Destruction,* III, 1142.

3 Davidson, *Death and Life,* 105; Hilberg, *Destruction,* III, 1142; papers released by the National Archive at the end of 2005 show that Churchill had always been in favour of executing the Nazi leaders. The fact that only the second tier of Nazis were captured may have altered his thinking in favour of a trial: *Sunday Times,* 1 January 2006.

4 Paget, *Manstein,* 139.

5 Ibid., 155; this was from Paget's defence submission.

6 Hilberg, *Destruction,* III, 1145.

7 Ibid.

8 Ibid., 1099.

9 Ibid., 1130–1, 1152.

10 Quoted in Paget, *Manstein,* 67, also 154.

11 Ibid., 68.

12 Smith, ed., *Clay Papers,* I, 441.

13 Paget, *Manstein,* 86–7.

14 Ibid., 69–70.

15 Ibid., 80.

16 Information from Ian Maxwell, who also informed the author that his father had told him that Trevor-Roper was called in to interrogate major war criminals.

17 Leighton-Langer, *X,* 235.

18 Ibid.

19 West, *The Meaning of Treason,* 132–3.

20 Papen, *Memoirs,* 551.

21 Peter Padfield, *Himmler – Reichsführer SS,* London, 1990, 610.

22 Ibid., 609–11; Anthony Read, *The Devil's Disciples – The Lives and Times of Hitler's Inner Circle,* London 2003, 914–15.

23 Willi Frischauer, *Goering,* London 1950, 277.

24 Irving, *Göring,* 465–70; Frischauer, *Goering,* 274–6.

25 Irving, *Göring,* 470–1, 478; Goering, *My Life with Goering,* London 1972, 136.

26 Frischauer, *Goering,* 280.

27 Read, *The Devil's Disciples,* 3.

28 Speer, *Diaries,* 65.

29 Papen, *Memoirs,* 541.

30 Speer, *Diaries,* 3.

31 Irving, *Göring,* 477, 480.

32 Papen, *Memoirs,* 563.

33 Hilberg, *Destruction,* III, 1157.

34 Speer, *Diaries,* 37.

35 Papen, *Memoirs,* 546.

36 Karl Dönitz, *Mein Wechselvolles Leben,* Zurich, Berlin and Frankfurt 1968, 212–14.

37 Dos Passos, *Tour of Duty,* 296–7.

38 Speer, *Diaries,* 3.

39 Peter Padfield, *Hess – The Führer's Disciple,* London 1995, 303–4, 312.

40 Hilberg, *Destruction,* III, 1156.

41 Irving, *Göring,* 484.

42 Ibid., 489; Papen, *Memoirs,* 574.

43 Friedrich, *Schauplatz Berlin,* 146.

44 Dos Passos, *Tour of Duty,* 298–9.

45 Papen, *Memoirs,* 559.

46 Dos Passos, *Tour of Duty,* 301, 305.

47 Hilberg, *Destruction,* III, 1149.

48 Irving, *Göring,* 487.

49 Padfield, *Hess,* 310–11; G. M. Gilbert, *Nuremberg Diary,* New York 1947, 45–6.

50 Frischauer, *Goering,* 291.

51 Ibid., 295; Gilbert, *Nuremberg Diary,* 50.

52 See Peter Maguire, *Law and War,*

New York 2001. I am grateful to Sebastian Cody for directing me to this work.

53 Hilberg, *Destruction*, III, 1149; Tom Lampert, *Ein einziges Leben – Geschichten aus der NS-Zeit*, Munich 2003, 204–29, portrays von dem Bach as a man suffering from psychosomatic illness as a result of the demands made upon him by Himmler.

54 Irving made this statement in *The Reichsmarschall's Table*, BBC Radio 4, 15 March 2005, written and presented by Giles MacDonogh, and produced by Dennis Sewell.

55 Irving, *Göring*, 492–3; Frischauer, *Goering*, 292; Walter Görlitz, 'The Desk Generals – Keitel, Jodl and Warlimont', in Barnett, ed., *Hitler's Generals*, 153–4.

56 Speer, *Diaries*, 13.

57 Papen, *Memoirs*, 551–3.

58 Frischauer, *Goering*, 296.

59 Papen, *Memoirs*, 565.

60 Irving, *Göring*, 495; Frischauer, *Goering*, 297.

61 Frischauer, *Goering*, 295; Read, *The Devil's Disciples*, 9.

62 Frischauer, *Goering*, 297.

63 Hilberg, *Destruction*, III, 1136.

64 Speer, *Diaries*, 52.

65 Ibid., 45.

66 Ibid., 499.

67 Skrjabina, *Allies on the Rhine*, 77.

68 Helmuth Auerbach, 'Que faire de l'Allemagne', in Manfrass and Rioux, eds, *France–Allemagne*, 293.

69 Speer, *Diaries*, 4.

70 Friedrich, *Schauplatz Berlin*, 147.

71 Hilberg, *Destruction*, III, 1151.

72 Ibid., 11, 14.

73 Werner Maser, *Nürnberg, Tribunal der Sieger*, Munich and Zurich 1979, 7; Read, *The Devil's Disciples*, 923.

74 Speer, *Diaries*, 11.

CHAPTER 17: THE LITTLE FISH

1 Smith, ed., *Clay Papers*, I, 247 and n. 3; Buscher, *War Crimes Trial Program*, 30.

2 Smith, ed., *Clay Papers*, I, 420.

3 Maser, *Nürnberg*, 434–42.

4 Speer, *Diaries*, 26.

5 Ibid., 32.

6 Ibid., 35.

7 Eberle and Uhl, eds, *Das Buch Hitler*, 236.

8 Mühlen, *Krupp*, 195.

9 Ibid., 200.

10 Hans Laternser, *Verteidigung deutsche Soldaten: Plädoyers vor Alliierten Gerichten*, Bonn 1950, 111, 126, 146–7, 153.

11 Ibid., 339.

12 Smith, ed., *Clay Papers*, I, 262, 310.

13 Mühlen, *Krupp*, 213.

14 Ibid., 220.

15 Ibid., 214.

16 Wachsmann, *Hitler's Prisons*, 343.

17 Carl Haensel, *Das Gericht vertagt sich. Tagebuch eines Verteidigers bei den Nürnberger Prozessen*, Wiesbaden and Munich 1980, 17.

18 Margret Boveri, *Der Diplomat vor Gericht*, Berlin and Hanover, 1948, 44.

19 Weizsäcker, *Vier Zeiten*, 119; Boveri, *Der Diplomat vor Gericht*, 18.

20 Weizsäcker, *Vier Zeiten*, 121.

21 Quoted in Boveri, *Der Diplomat vor Gericht*, 17–18.

22 Ibid., 29.

23 Weizsäcker, *Vier Zeiten*, 122.

24 Boveri, *Der Diplomat vor Gericht*, 17.

25 Weizsäcker, *Vier Zeiten*, 122; Boveri, *Der Diplomat vor Gericht*, 18.

26 Weizsäcker, *Vier Zeiten*, 125–6.

27 Paget, *Manstein*, 171.

28 Ibid., 169–72. It should be said that this sort of argument has always been very pleasing to the revisionists, and that Paget is quoted and lauded on David Irving's website for saying that the figure of six million murdered

Jews was incorrect; Hilberg, *Destruction*, III, 1158.

29 Earl F. Ziemke, 'Rundstedt', in Barnett, ed., *Hitler's Generals*, 201.

30 See Shepherd, *After Daybreak*, 166–75.

31 Tighe, *Gdansk*, 201.

32 Eberle and Uhl, eds, *Das Buch Hitler*, 238–9; MacDonogh, *Prussia*, 376.

33 Paget, *Manstein*, 77.

34 Ibid., 78, 79.

35 Shelford Bidwell, 'Kesselring', in Barnett, ed., *Hitler's Generals*, 288.

36 Berber, *Dachau*, 200.

37 Sayer and Botting, *Mohnke*, 278.

38 Smith, ed., *Clay Papers*, II, 1041–3.

39 Buscher, *War Crimes Trial Program*, 38.

40 Smith, ed., *Clay Papers*, II, 880–1, 889.

41 Ibid., 1007; Robert Wistrich, *Who's Who in Nazi Germany*, London 1995, 142–3.

42 Sayer and Botting, *Mohnke*, 283; Smith, ed., *Clay Papers*, II, 671.

43 Sayer and Botting, *Mohnke*, 91–2.

44 Ibid., 183n.

45 Ibid., 226.

46 Ibid.

47 Hamann, *Winifred Wagner*, 420–1.

48 Ibid., 423–5.

49 Ibid., 428–9.

50 Ibid., 438.

51 Ibid., 352.

52 Ibid., 345.

53 Idem, 356–8.

54 Fürstenau, *Entnazifizierung*, 231.

55 Maser, *Nürnberg*, 433; Wachsmann, *Hitler's Prisons*, 344.

CHAPTER 18: PEACEMAKING
IN POTSDAM

1 Hanna Grisebach quoted in Inge Hoeftmann and Waltraud Noack, eds, *Potsdam in alten und neuen Reisebeschreibungen*, Düsseldorf 1992, 226.

2 Hanna Grisebach, *Potsdamer Tagebuch*, with an Afterword by Hilde Domin, Heidelberg 1974, 23.

3 Ibid., 22.

4 Ibid., 48.

5 Ibid., 29, 32.

6 Quoted in Hoeftmann and Noack, eds, *Potsdam*, 235.

7 Grisebach, *Tagebuch*, 35.

8 Ibid., 38–9.

9 Ibid., 44.

10 Zhukov, *Reminiscences*, II, 438.

11 See Ingeborg Fleischhauer, *Die Chance des Sonderfriedens: Deutsch–soujetische Geheimgespräche 1941–1945*, Berlin 1986; Hugh Trevor-Roper, *The Last Days of Hitler*, 7th edn, London 1995, 29; MacDonogh, Translator's Preface to Eberle and Uhl, *The Hitler Book*, xx.

12 Eberle and Uhl, *Das Buch Hitler*. See in particular the editors' Afterword, 495–6.

13 Zhukov, *Reminiscences*, II, 429, 453.

14 Ibid., 430.

15 Ibid., 435.

16 Smith, ed., *Clay Papers*, I, 17.

17 Zhukov, *Reminiscenses*, II, 433.

18 Smith, ed., *Clay Papers*, II, 19.

19 Balfour and Mair, *Four Power Control*, 39.

20 Young, *France*, 61.

21 Smith, ed., *Clay Papers*, II, 18, 21; Bullock, *Bevin*, 17.

22 Zhukov, *Reminiscences*, II, 434, 437.

23 Kardorff, *Aufzeichnungen*, 331, 334.

24 Bullock, *Bevin*, 17.

25 Henry H. Adams, *Harry Hopkins*, New York 1977, 391.

26 Averall Harriman Foreword to ibid., 19.

27 Zhukov, *Reminiscences*, II, 440.

28 Adams, *Hopkins*, 392.

29 Ibid., 382.

30 Ibid., 377.

31 Henke, 'Potsdam', 57–9.

32 Smith, ed., *Clay Papers*, II, 22–4.

33 Henke, 'Potsdam', 52–3; Naimark, *Russians in Germany*, 146.

34 Henke, 'Potsdam', 54.
35 Akinscha and Koslow, *Beutekunst*, 99–100.
36 Goedde, *GIs and Germans*, 11–12.
37 Quoted in Boveri, *Tage*, 157, 170.
38 Smith, ed., *Clay Papers*, I, 50–1.
39 Ritchie, *Faust's Metropolis*, 629, mentions the geraniums; Harry S. Truman, *Memoirs*, 2 vols, vol. I: 1945, *Year of Decisions*, London 1955, 268, the other flora.
40 Zhukov in Hoeftmann and Noack, eds, *Potsdam*, 240.
41 Zhukov, *Reminiscences*, II, 441–3.
42 Grisebach, *Tagebuch*, 49–50.
43 Zhukov, *Reminiscences*, II, 441.
44 Truman, *Memoirs*, I, 258.
45 Ibid., 262.
46 Morgan, *Byrnes, Clay*, 94.
47 Truman, *Memoirs*, I, 266, 265.
48 Truman in Hoeftmann and Noack, eds, *Potsdam*, 245.
49 Truman, *Memoirs*, I, 265.
50 Foschepoth, 'Potsdam', 71–2.
51 Ibid., 72–4.
52 Truman in Hoeftmann and Noack, eds, *Potsdam*, 246; Truman, I, 267.
53 Friedrich, *Schauplatz Berlin*, 85.
54 Truman, *Memoirs*, I, 279.
55 Byrnes, *Speaking Frankly*, 68.
56 Truman, *Memoirs*, I, 270.
57 Ibid., 275.
58 Grisebach, *Tagebuch*, 47.
59 Kardorff, *Aufzeichnungen*, 337; Amanda Holden, *The New Penguin Opera Guide*, London, 2001, 1037.
60 Truman, *Memoirs*, 278.
61 Ibid.
62 Ibid., 281, 285.
63 Ibid., 286; Byrnes, *Speaking Frankly*, 68–9; Davidson, *Death and Life*, 64.
64 Byrnes, *Speaking Frankly*, 79–80; Truman, *Memoirs*, I, 293.
65 Truman, *Memoirs*, I, 293.
66 Ibid., 294.
67 Ibid.
68 Ibid., 295.
69 Ibid.
70 Ibid., 296.
71 Bullock, *Bevin*, 24.
72 Ibid., 22.
73 Truman, *Memoirs*, I, 297.
74 Ibid., 297–8.
75 Ibid., 300.
76 De Zayas, *Nemesis at Potsdam*, 50.
77 Truman, *Memoirs*, I, 303, 305; Byrnes, *Speaking Frankly*, 76.
78 Truman, *Memoirs*, I, 315–16.
79 Ibid., 317; Bullock, *Bevin*, 25.
80 Truman, *Memoirs*, I, 322–3.
81 Peter Weiler, *Ernest Bevin*, Manchester and New York 1993, 144–5.
82 Ibid., 145–6.
83 Bullock, *Bevin*, 25.
84 Weiler, *Bevin*, 147–8.
85 Ibid., 148–9.
86 Bullock, *Bevin*, 25.
87 Truman, *Memoirs*, I, 327.
88 Zhukov, *Reminiscences*, II, 451.
89 Truman in Hoeftmann and Noack, eds, *Potsdam*, 251.
90 Grisebach, *Tagebuch*, 70.
91 Truman, *Memoirs*, I, 329–30.
92 Kaps, *Tragödie*, 69.
93 Truman, *Memoirs*, I, 329–30.
94 Ibid., 331.
95 Bullock, *Bevin*, 28; Truman, *Memoirs*, I, 335.
96 Truman, *Memoirs*, I, 341.
97 Davies and Moorhouse, *Microcosm*, 414–15.
98 Zhukov, *Reminiscences*, II, 448.
99 Ibid., 414–16.
100 Truman, *Memoirs*, I, 337.
101 Ibid., 338.
102 Ibid., 339–40.
103 Zhukov, *Reminiscences*, II, 416–17.
104 Young, *France*, 62.
105 Ibid., 62, 64.
106 Davidson, *Death and Life*, 60.
107 Morgan, *Byrnes, Clay*, 73.
108 Kennan, *Memoirs*, 258–9.
109 Ibid., 263–6.
110 Friedrich, *Schauplatz Berlin*, 92, 103.
111 Grisebach, *Tagebuch*, 54.

CHAPTER 19: THE GREAT
FREEZE

1 Mastny, *Cold War*, 23.
2 Ibid., 4, 6.
3 Young, *France*, 70–1.
4 Ibid., 74.
5 Buffet, *Berlin*, 360; Ritchie, *Faust's Metropolis*, 638.
6 Morgan, *Byrnes, Clay*, 207.
7 Weiler, *Bevin*, 153–4.
8 Rauchensteiner, *Stalinplatz 4*, 133.
9 Harry S. Truman, *Memoirs*, vol. II: *1946 – 1953, Years of Trial and Hope*, London 1955, 100.
10 Kennan, *Memoirs*, 257.
11 Clare, *Berlin Days*, 193.
12 Weiler, *Bevin*, 154.
13 Kennan, *Memoirs*, 258.
14 Bullock, *Bevin*, 9, 11.
15 Naimark, *Russians in Germany*, 48.
16 Weiler, *Bevin*, 154.
17 Kennan, *Memoirs*, 253–4.
18 Keeling, *Gruesome Harvest*, vii–viii.
19 Ibid., 5, 8.
20 Siegfried Beer, 'Die Besatzungsmacht Grossbritannien und Österreich 1945–1949', in Ableitner et al., *Österreich unter alliierter Besatzung*, 47.
21 Byrnes, *Speaking Frankly*, 111–12, 118.
22 Graml, *Teilung Deutschlands*, 165, 182.
23 Ibid., 48–50; David Dilks, ed., *The Diaries of Sir Alexander Cadogan O.M., 1938–45*, London 1971, 778.
24 Foschepoth, 'Potsdam', 76, 79.
25 Bullock, *Bevin*, 268; Smith, ed., *Clay Papers*, I, 255.
26 Ibid., 257.
27 Weiler, *Bevin*, 159–60.
28 Bullock, *Bevin*, 309.
29 Morgan, *Byrnes, Clay*, 319; Byrnes, *Speaking Frankly*, 190–1.
30 Morgan, *Byrnes, Clay*, 319.
31 Ibid., 334–5, 338; Weiler, *Bevin*, 160–2.
32 Byrnes, *Speaking Frankly*, 192; Gulgowski, 'American Military Government', 10.
33 Keeling, *Gruesome Harvest*, 10.
34 Dos Passos, *Tour of Duty*, 321–2.
35 Graml, *Teilung Deutschlands*, 105–7, 109.
36 Rathkolb, 'Historische Fragmente', 146.
37 Alfons Gruber, *Geschichte Südtirols – Streifzüge durch das 20. Jahrhundert*, Bolzano 2002, 103.
38 Rauchensteiner, *Stalinplatz 4*, 90.
39 Rathkolb, ed., *Gesellschaft und Politik*, 192.
40 Ibid., 406.
41 Schärf, *Wiederaufrichtung*, 121.
42 Béthouart, *Bataille*, 109.
43 Rauchensteiner, *Stalinplatz 4*, 90.
44 Ibid., 107.
45 Denis Mack Smith, *Modern Italy: A Political History*, New Haven and London 1997, 421–2.
46 Buffet, *Berlin*, 366–7.
47 Naimark, *Russians in Germany*, 90.
48 Speer, *Diaries*, 62.
49 Staritz, *DDR*, 18.
50 Davidson, *Death and Life*, 129.
51 Brigadier-General Frank Howley, *Berlin Command*, New York 1950, 10.
52 Ibid., 136.
53 Sayn-Wittgenstein, *Streifzüge*, 174.
54 Zuckmayer, *Deutschlandbericht*, 83–4.
55 Anonymous, *A Woman in Berlin*, 50, 100.
56 Friedrich, *Schauplatz Berlin*, 105; Christabel Bielenberg, *The Past is Myself*, London 1985, 285.
57 Friedrich, *Schauplatz Berlin*, 151–2.
58 Zuckmayer, *Deutschlandbericht*, 86.
59 Speer, *Diaries*, 29–31.
60 Friedrich, *Schauplatz Berlin*, 158–9, 161.
61 Speer, *Diaries*, 34.
62 Friedrich, *Schauplatz Berlin*, 166.
63 Mastny, *Cold War*, 25. On Soviet Russia's long-term plans, see Wolfgang Mueller, 'Stalin and Austria: New Evidence on Soviet Policy in a Secondary Theatre of the Cold War, 1938–1953/1955', *Cold*

War History, vol. 6, no. 1, February 2006, 63–84.

64 Rauchensteiner, *Stalinplatz 4*, 113.

65 Friedrich, *Schauplatz Berlin*, 170–1.

66 Ibid., 172–3.

67 Ibid., 174–6.

68 Zuckmayer, *Deutschlandbericht*, 87.

69 Bethouart, *Bataille*, 87.

70 Obituary, Josefine Hawelka, *The Times*, Saturday 26 March 2005.

71 Smith, ed., *Clay Papers*, I, 213, 226, 230.

72 Ibid., 248.

73 Friedrich, *Schauplatz Berlin*, 182.

74 Byrnes, *Speaking Frankly*, 198.

75 Clark, *Calculated Risk*, 439–42.

76 Mastny, *Cold War*, 26–9.

77 Ibid., 40–1.

78 Balfour and Mair, *Four Power Control*, 279.

79 Rauchensteiner, *Stalinplatz 4*, 111–12.

80 Ibid., 112.

81 Ibid., 361–2.

82 Wagnleitner, ed., *Herz*, 401–3, 606–7.

83 See Staritz, *DDR*, 15.

84 Ibid., 17.

85 Friedrich, *Schauplatz Berlin*, 186, 198.

86 Staritz, *DDR*, 18.

87 Ibid., 21.

CHAPTER 20: THE BERLIN AIRLIFT AND THE BEGINNINGS OF ECONOMIC RECOVERY

1 Döblin, *Schicksalsreise*, 434, 439.

2 Ibid., 441.

3 Ibid., 444–5.

4 Ibid., 447.

5 Ibid., 452.

6 Ibid., 453–4.

7 Mastny, *Cold War*, 48.

8 Davidson, *Death and Life*, 224.

9 Smith, ed., *Clay Papers*, I, 274, 276, 302; Skrjabina, *Allies on the Rhine*, 82, 95.

10 Skrjabina, *Allies on the Rhine*, 114; Friedrich, *Schauplatz Berlin*, 230.

11 Howley, *Berlin Command*, 186.

12 Ibid., 329.

13 Staritz, *DDR*, 23.

14 Friedrich, *Schauplatz Berlin*, 249.

15 Ruge, ed., *Schulenburg*, 92.

16 Willy Brandt and Richard Lowenthal, *Ernst Reuter. Ein Leben für die Freiheit*, Munich 1957, 358–60.

17 Mastny, *Cold War*, 41.

18 Ibid., 48.

19 Howley, *Berlin Command*, 177.

20 Kennan, *Memoirs*, 420; Bullock, *Bevin*, 574.

21 Bullock, *Bevin*, 571.

22 Smith, ed., *Clay Papers*, I, 478, 483.

23 Mastny, *Cold War*, 50.

24 Ibid., 49.

25 Bullock, *Bevin*, 566, 573; Graml, *Teilung Deutschlands*, 199.

26 Smith, ed., *Clay Papers*, I, 206, 201.

27 Ibid. 567; II, 612.

28 Quoted in Ann and John Tusa, *The Berlin Blockade. Berlin in 1948. The Year the Cold War Threatened to Become Hot*, London 1989, 138.

29 Mastny, *Cold War*, 46–7.

30 Smith, ed., *Clay Papers*, II, 597, 599.

31 Friedrich, *Schauplatz Berlin*, 220–8.

32 Truman, *Memoirs*, II, 131.

33 Young, *France*, 198–9.

34 Howley, *Berlin Command*, 3–4.

35 Smith, ed., *Clay Papers*, II, 600–2.

36 Ibid., 602–5.

37 Ibid., 605.

38 Ibid., 605, 607.

39 Ibid., 618, 621 n. 2; Davidson, *Death and Life*, 211.

40 Smith, ed., *Clay Papers*, II, 649–50, 661, 677.

41 Friedrich, *Schauplatz Berlin*, 238.

42 Volker Koop, *Tagebuch der Berliner Blockade. Von Schwarzmarkt und Rollkommandos, Bergbau und Bienenzucht*, Bonn 1998, 11.

43 Friedrich, *Schauplatz Berlin*, 236.

44 Ibid., 237, 238.

45 Smith, ed., *Clay Papers*, II, 700.
46 Howley, *Berlin Command*, 196–7, 199–200.
47 Bullock, *Bevin*, 573 and n. 1.
48 Weiler, *Bevin*, 179.
49 Bullock, *Bevin*, 576.
50 Friedrich, *Schauplatz Berlin*, 238–9.
51 Goedde, *GIs and Germans*, 166–7.
52 Truman, *Memoirs*, II, 130.
53 Ibid.
54 Friedrich, *Schauplatz Berlin*, 248; Howley, *Berlin Command*, 239.
55 Friedrich, *Schauplatz Berlin*, 246.
56 Smith, ed., *Clay Papers*, II, 709, 711, 714.
57 Staritz, *DDR*, 26
58 Friedrich, *Schauplatz Berlin*, 248.
59 Staritz, *DDR*, 23.
60 Howley, *Berlin Command*, 209.
61 Lang, 'Lieber Herr Celibidache', 110.
62 Koop, *Tagebuch*, 18, 24.
63 Truman, *Memoirs*, II, 130.
64 Howley, *Berlin Command*, 202.
65 Truman, *Memoirs*, II, 132.
66 Ibid., 135.
67 Smith, ed., *Clay Papers*, II, 746.
68 Davidson, *Death and Life*, 217; Friedrich, *Schauplatz Berlin*, 242.
69 Truman, *Memoirs*, II, 132.
70 Smith, ed., *Clay Papers*, II, 763–4.
71 Koop, *Tagebuch*, 41.
72 Smith, ed., *Clay Papers*, II, 798, 820.
73 Ibid., 824.
74 Ibid., 831–2.
75 Ibid., 834, 844.
76 Mastny, *Cold War*, 52.
77 Friedrich, *Schauplatz Berlin*, 260.
78 Buffet, *Berlin*, 369.
79 Goedde, *GIs and Germans*, 185, 187; Howley, *Berlin Command*, 218.
80 Koop, *Tagebuch*, 55–6.
81 Smith, ed., *Clay Papers*, II, 856–7.
82 Ibid., 858, 860.
83 Truman, *Memoirs*, II, 136.
84 Davidson, *Death and Life*, 209.
85 Smith, ed., *Clay Papers*, II, 908.
86 Koop, *Tagebuch*, 124–5.
87 Smith, ed., *Clay Papers*, II, 928.
88 Howley, *Berlin Command*, 226.

89 Tent, *Mission*, 288.
90 Koop, *Tagebuch*, 133, pours a little cold water on this 'legend'.
91 Davidson, *Life and Death*, 216; Clare, *Berlin Days*, 185; Tusa and Tusa, *Berlin Blockade*, 330, 389–90.
92 Staritz, *DDR*, 33.
93 Koop, *Tagebuch*, 139.
94 Speer, *Diaries*, 115.
95 Ibid,, 122.
96 Smith, ed., *Clay Papers*, II, 1015.
97 Ibid., 1063.
98 Kennan, *Memoirs*, 429.
99 Ibid., 431–2.
100 Mastny, *Cold War*, 62.
101 Tusa and Tusa, *Berlin Blockade*, 395.
102 Clark, *Calculated Risk*, 429–30.
103 Smith, ed., *Clay Papers*, II, 625; Brook-Shepherd, *Austrians*, 395.
104 Béthouart, *Bataille*, 153.
105 Ibid., 157.
106 Ibid., 162.
107 Rauchensteiner, *Stalinplatz 4*, 130.
108 Wagnleitner, *Herz*, 240–2, 249–53.
109 Ibid., 523–4; Rauchensteiner, *Stalinplatz 4*, 152.
110 Béthouart, *Bataille*, 115; Rauchensteiner, *Stalinplatz 4*, 82.
111 Williams, *Adenauer*, 328.
112 Ibid., 332.
113 Ibid., 331.
114 Ibid., 332.
115 Ibid., 333.
116 Ibid., 334.
117 Young, *France*, 204–7.
118 Poidevin, *Schuman*, 77.

CONCLUSION

1 Williams, *Adenauer*, 341.
2 Dönhoff, *Weit ist der Weg nach Osten*, 305–6.
3 Staritz, *DDR*, 34.
4 Ibid., 34–5.
5 MacDonogh, *The Last Kaiser*, 196; the idea that the Kaiser was interested in European unity has been severely mocked by Volker Ulrich in

Die Zeit: see 'Der Kaiser lacht!', 16 March 2000.

6 Poidevin, *Schuman*, 84.

7 Young, *France*, 41.

8 Jünger, *Der Friede*, 56, 60, 63.

9 Young, *France*, 9–10.

10 Ibid., 10–11.

11 Poidevin, *Schuman*, 84.

12 Gollancz, *In Darkest Germany*, 16.

13 Robert Birley, *Britain in Europe: Reflections on the Development of a European Society*, Reith Lectures, London 1949, 1–2.

14 Young, France, 11, 13.

15 Ibid., 229.

16 Margret Boveri, *Der Verrat im XX. Jahrhundert – für und gegen die Nation*, Hamburg 1956, 8; Philippe Burrin, *La France à l'heure allemande*, Paris 1995, 467.

17 Clark, *Calculated Risk*, 447–8.

18 Döblin, *Schicksalsreise*, 412, 408.

Further Reading

There is no book in English that covers the whole period, the four-power military occupation of Germany and Austria between the years 1945 and 1949. Douglas Botting's *In the Ruins of the Reich* dwells on the early period, but omits Austria; while the dated but still useful *Four Power Control in Germany and Austria* by Michael Balfour and John Mair (Oxford 1956) finishes with the creation of Bizonia at the end of 1946. The former is strongest on chaos, the latter is best on administration. There are, however, some excellent monographs covering the individual German zones: Norman M. Nairmark's *The Russians in Germany* (Cambridge, Mass. and London 1995), Edward N. Peterson's *Russian Commands and German Resistance: The Soviet Occupation 1945–1949* (New York 1999) and Gregory Klimov's *Terror Machine* (London n.d.) all cover the east. On the US Zone there is Edward N. Peterson's *American Occupation of Germany* (Detroit 1977). More recently Petra Goedde has looked at occupation from a woman's angle in *GIs and Germans* (New Haven and London 2003).

The British Military Government is detailed in Patricia Meehan's excellent book *A Strange Enemy People: Germans under the British 1945–1950* (London and Chester Springs 2001). What is missing is a study of the French ZOF: John Young's *France, the Cold War and the Western Alliance* (Leicester and London 1990) is not really that, because it is more concerned with foreign policy than with administration. There is no book in French either, where the literature is largely confined to the cultural achievements of the French occupation.

Nor is there much on Austria. The standby is Gordon Brook-Shepherd's Austrocentric *The Austrians – A Thousand Year Odyssey* (London 1996), which explains the political background to the State Treaty, but does not offer much on the events of April 1945. The best source in English is probably Reinhold Wagnleitner, ed., *Understanding Austria* (Salzburg 1984), a compilation of the reports filed by the American OSS man Martin Herz. Mark Clark's account, *Calculated Risk* (London 1956), was written at the height of the Cold War, and it shows.

There is a similar lack of documentation in English on events in Czechoslovakia. The best remains Alfred M. de Zayas's *Nemesis at Potsdam* (London 1979). All the rest is in German. For a few pages of Czech perspective, see Zbynek Zeman and Antonin Klimek, *The Life of Edvard Beneš 1884–1948* (Oxford 1997).

De Zayas also provides material on the events in the Prussian east. Count Hans Lehndorf's unbelievably moving *East Prussian Diary* was published in English in 1963. It should be reissued. We also possess Christian von Krockow's *Hour of the Women* (London 1991), which charts the fortunes of his sister Libussa in Pomerania.

Two books record the fates of individual cities: Danzig is covered by Chris Tighe's *Gdansk – National Identity in the Polish–German Borderlands* (London and Concord 1990), and Breslau's fate is recounted in *Microcosm: Portrait of a Central European City* by Norman Davies and Roger Moorhouse (London 2002).

The anonymous *Woman in Berlin* (London 1965) is a graphic account of the Russian arrival in the city. There is also an abridged edition of Ursula von Kardorff's *Diary of a Nightmare* (London 1965). The most recent German edition, however, has restored the full text. Wolfgang Leonhard's *Child of the Revolution* was translated by C. M. Woodhouse (London 1979) and is the standard account of the arrival of the Moscow-based German communists.

There are a few serious American studies of denazification: James F. Tent's *Mission on the Rhine* (Chicago and London 1982) and Timothy R. Vogt's *Denazification in Soviet-Occupied Germany* (Cambridge, Mass. and London 2000). The most relaxed account of denazification is George Clare's *Berlin Days* (London 1989). On individual cases Brigitte Hamann's *Winifred Wagner – At the Heart of Hitler's Bayreuth* (London 2005) is highly recommended.

For the pursuit and conviction of Nazi war criminals there is an emotional account by Tom Bower (*Blind Eye to Murder*, London 1981). R. T. Paget's argument in *Manstein – His Campaigns and his Trial* (London 1951) is still cogent. G. M. Gilbert's *Nuremberg Diary* (New York 1947) is another old book that has its uses. There are also the translated memoirs of the Nazis who served custodial terms: Speer (1976) and Papen (1952), as well as Peter Padfield's life of Hess (1995) and lives of Göring by David Irving (1989) and Willy Frischauer (1950). Frank M. Buscher's *US War Crimes Trial Program in Germany* (New York, Westport and London 1989) presents an academic approach. On the treatment of POWs there is nothing in English, and the leading American expert – Arthur L. Smith – publishes in German. The best there is can be found in Ernst von Saloman's highly coloured account of his own imprisonment: *The Answers* (London 1954).

Robert H. Abzug gives details of the grisly discovery of the inner workings of the camps in his *Inside the Vicious Heart* (New York and Oxford 1985), as does Brewster Chamberlin and Marcia Feldman's *The Liberation of the Concentration Camps* (Washington DC 1987), to which he provides an introduction. Ben Shepherd's *After Daybreak* (London 2005) is specifically about the freeing of Belsen. On the surviving Jews there is Ruth Gay's *Safe among the Germans* (New Haven and London 2002).

Victor Gollancz's two polemics on the treatment of the Germans still make for salutary reading: *Leaving them to their Fate: The Ethics of Starvation* (London 1946) and *In Darkest Germany* (London 1947).

Marlis Steinert provides a scholarly account of the Flensburg regime in

Capitulation 1945: The Story of the Dönitz Government (London 1969). Frank Howley's account of the airlift, *Berlin Command* (New York 1950), should be read with caution. Ann and John Tusa's *Berlin Blockade* (London 1989) is a still fresh general survey.

On culture in the Soviet Zone the best sources are David Pike's *Politics and Culture in Soviet-Occupied Germany* (Stanford 1992) and Wolfgang Schivelbusch's *In a Cold Crater* (Berkeley, Los Angeles and London 1998). I have also found Jenny Williams's *More Lives than One: A Biography of Hans Fallada* (London 1998) useful. The rather muted cultural policy in the British Zone is easily gleaned from George Clare. The best source for America is Carl Zuckmayer's report – *Deutschlandbericht, für das Kriegministerium der Vereinigten Staaten von America* (Göttingen 2004).

The outstanding book on Soviet policy is Vojtech Mastny's *The Cold War and Soviet Insecurity* (New York and Oxford 1996), and more recently I have found Geoffrey Roberts's *Stalin Wars: From World War to Cold War, 1939–1953* (New Haven and London 2006) extremely useful. Something can be gleaned from Georgi Zhukov's *Reminiscences* (Moscow 1985). For the roles of other Cold Warriors, see Curtis F. Morgan Jnr's *James F. Byrnes, Lucius Clay and American Policy in Germany 1945–1947* (Lewiston, Queenston and Lampeter 2002) or Byrnes's own account in *Speaking Frankly* (London 1947). For Clay's role in Germany there is Jean Edward Smith's *The Papers of Lucius D. Clay* (Bloomington and London 1974). Truman covers his back in his two-volume *Year of Decisions* and *Years of Trial and Hope* (London 1955). They are very useful for Potsdam. George Kennan's *Memoirs* (London 1968) provide the dissenting view. Ernest Bevin's time as foreign secretary is amply covered by Alan Bullock (London 1983) and in less detail by Peter Weiler (Manchester and New York 1993). Charles Williams provides a useful, recent account of the rise of Adenauer (London 2000).

More detailed references and non-English sources will be found in the notes.

Index

Biberteich camp, Czechoslovakia, 145
Bidault, Georges, 11, 275, 503, 525
Biddle, Francis, 444
Biel, Heinz, 258
Bielenberg, Christabel, 508
Bierut, Bolesław, 485, 488
Big Lift, The (film), 537
Bildt, Paul, 99
Bimko, Dr Hadassah, 332
Birley, Sir Robert, 252–4, 545
Biscari, 465
Bismarck, Prince Otto von, xiii
Bizonia (US-British zones), 199, 202, 275, 501, 511
black market: transactions, 372–3; development and operation, 374–7, 379; and crime, 378–9
Blaha, General, 156
Blanckenburg family, 176
Blankenhorn, Herbert, 265, 539–40
Blaschtowitschka, Dr, 156
Blaskowitz, General Johannes, 443
Blomberg, Field Marshal Werner von, 443
Blum, Léon, 82, 297
Blum, Moritz, 110
Bogomolov, Alexander, 14
Bohle, Ernst, 455
Bohlen, Charles ('Chip'), 476–7
Bohlen und Halbach, Gustav von, 453
Böhler, Josef, 464
Böhm, Johann, 31, 299
Böhm, Karl, 305
Böhm-Baweerk family, 31
Bohrer, Karl-Heinz, 62, 261, 272–3, 342
Boislambert, Hettier de, 541
Böll, Heinrich: xii, 249, 427; *Die Botschaft*, 427; 'Geschäft ist Geschäft' *in Wanderer kommst du nach Spa, Erzählungen*, 381, 517; *Kreuz ohne Liebe*, 2–3; 'Kumpel mit dem langen Haar', 372; 'Lohengrins Tod', 316; 'Mein Onkel Fred', 518–19; 'When the War Was Over', 428
Bolling, General Alexander, 489
Bolzano-Bozen, 504–5
Bongers, Else, 268
Bonhoeffer, Dietrich, 355
Bonin, Colonel Bogislaw von, 83
Bonn: as West German capital, 540–1
Borchard, Leo, 99–101, 109, 118–20, 203, 216n, 219, 241

Borchert, Wolfgang: *Draussen vor der Tür* (play; filmed as *Liebe 1947*), 427
Bormann, Martin, 247n, 254, 442
Bornholm (island), Denmark, 479
Borotra, Jean, 81
Böttner, Professor Arthur, 50
Boveri, Margret: reaches Teupitz, 58–9, 204; disparages Dönitz, 69; in Charlottenburg, 95; on Red Army soldiers' behaviour, 97–102, 204, 240; on women working in Berlin, 108; meets surviving Jews, 110; on food shortage, 111–12, 117; on Americans in Germany, 115–16, 236; crosses into Franconia, 213; attends Berlin concert, 221, 268; on Bamberg, 237; on Western Allies' plundering, 240; on *Fragebogen*, 345; on shortage of German men, 370; on prisoners in Soviet Union, 421; on accused at Nuremberg, 455; on arrests in Potsdam, 473; on number of French arrests, 545; *Tage des Überlebens*, 95
Bradley, General Omar, 85, 228
Brandenburg, 58–9, 184
Brandt, Karl, 452
Brandt, Willy, 396
Brauchitsch, Field Marshal Walther von, 404, 410
Braun, Eva, 96, 220, 385
Braunschweig, Eberhard von, 51
Brech, John, 421
Brecht, Bertolt, 215, 222
Breker, Arno, 321
Bremen: ceded by British to Americans, 232–3
Brenner, 503–4
Breslau (Wrocław), 45, 56–8, 169, 176–8, 189, 492–3
Briand, Aristide, 544
Bridgend, South Wales, 410
Britain: policy on Germany, 5; advance into Germany and central Europe, 11, 42; wartime alliance with USSR, 18; refuses to recognise Renner regime in Austria, 42; dispute with Yugoslavia over Trieste and Carinthia, 44, 302–3; and Dönitz government, 68–9; and Princess Victoria Louise, 75; arrival in Berlin, 114; popularity in Berlin, 124; and development of German constitution, 162, 242; complains of Russian thefts, 204; forms Rhineland-